Developments and Future Trends in Transnational Higher Education Leadership

Gareth Richard Morris
University of Nottingham, Ningbo, China

Shayna Kozuch
University of Nottingham, Ningbo, China

A volume in the Advances in Higher Education and Professional Development (AHEPD) Book Series

Published in the United States of America by
IGI Global
Information Science Reference (an imprint of IGI Global)
701 E. Chocolate Avenue
Hershey PA, USA 17033
Tel: 717-533-8845
Fax: 717-533-8661
E-mail: cust@igi-global.com
Web site: http://www.igi-global.com

Copyright © 2024 by IGI Global. All rights reserved. No part of this publication may be reproduced, stored or distributed in any form or by any means, electronic or mechanical, including photocopying, without written permission from the publisher. Product or company names used in this set are for identification purposes only. Inclusion of the names of the products or companies does not indicate a claim of ownership by IGI Global of the trademark or registered trademark.

Library of Congress Cataloging-in-Publication Data

CIP DATA PROCESSING

2024 Information Science Reference
ISBN(hc) 9798369328576 | ISBN(sc) 9798369345733 | eISBN 9798369328583

British Cataloguing in Publication Data
A Cataloguing in Publication record for this book is available from the British Library.

The views expressed in this book are those of the authors, but not necessarily of the publisher.

For electronic access to this publication, please contact: eresources@igi-global.com.

Advances in Higher Education and Professional Development (AHEPD) Book Series

Jared Keengwe
University of North Dakota, USA

ISSN:2327-6983
EISSN:2327-6991

Mission

As world economies continue to shift and change in response to global financial situations, job markets have begun to demand a more highly-skilled workforce. In many industries a college degree is the minimum requirement and further educational development is expected to advance. With these current trends in mind, the **Advances in Higher Education & Professional Development (AHEPD) Book Series** provides an outlet for researchers and academics to publish their research in these areas and to distribute these works to practitioners and other researchers.

AHEPD encompasses all research dealing with higher education pedagogy, development, and curriculum design, as well as all areas of professional development, regardless of focus.

Coverage

- Adult Education
- Assessment in Higher Education
- Career Training
- Coaching and Mentoring
- Continuing Professional Development
- Governance in Higher Education
- Higher Education Policy
- Pedagogy of Teaching Higher Education
- Vocational Education

IGI Global is currently accepting manuscripts for publication within this series. To submit a proposal for a volume in this series, please contact our Acquisition Editors at Acquisitions@igi-global.com or visit: http://www.igi-global.com/publish/.

The Advances in Higher Education and Professional Development (AHEPD) Book Series (ISSN 2327-6983) is published by IGI Global, 701 E. Chocolate Avenue, Hershey, PA 17033-1240, USA, www.igi-global.com. This series is composed of titles available for purchase individually; each title is edited to be contextually exclusive from any other title within the series. For pricing and ordering information please visit http://www.igi-global.com/book-series/advances-higher-education-professional-development/73681. Postmaster: Send all address changes to above address. Copyright © 2024 IGI Global. All rights, including translation in other languages reserved by the publisher. No part of this series may be reproduced or used in any form or by any means – graphics, electronic, or mechanical, including photocopying, recording, taping, or information and retrieval systems – without written permission from the publisher, except for non commercial, educational use, including classroom teaching purposes. The views expressed in this series are those of the authors, but not necessarily of IGI Global.

Titles in this Series

For a list of additional titles in this series, please visit: www.igi-global.com/book-series

Global Perspectives on Decolonizing Postgraduate Education
Mishack Thiza Gumbo (University of South Africa, South Africa) Michael Gaotlhobogwe (University of Botswana, Botswana) Constantino Pedzisai (Chinhoyi University of Technology, Zimbabwe) Zingiswa Mybert Monica Jojo (Rhodes University, South Africa) and Christopher B. Knaus (University of Washington, Tacoma, USA & University of South Africa, South Africa)
Information Science Reference • copyright 2024 • 339pp • H/C (ISBN: 9798369312896) • US $230.00 (our price)

Emerging Research in Agricultural Teacher Education
R. Kirby Barrick (University of Florida, USA (Retired)) and Andrew C. Thoron (Abraham Baldwin Agricultural College, USA)
Information Science Reference • copyright 2024 • 426pp • H/C (ISBN: 9798369327661) • US $245.00 (our price)

Engaging Higher Education Teachers and Students With Transnational Leadership
Gareth Richard Morris (University of Nottingham, Ningbo, China) and Shayna Kozuch (University of Nottingham, Ningbo, China)
Information Science Reference • copyright 2024 • 306pp • H/C (ISBN: 9798369361009) • US $245.00 (our price)

Preparing Students From the Academic World to Career Paths A Comprehensive Guide
Cassandra Sligh Conway (South Carolina State University, USA) and Andy Jiahao Liu (University of Arizona, USA)
Information Science Reference • copyright 2024 • 334pp • H/C (ISBN: 9781799879992) • US $215.00 (our price)

Empowering Teams in Higher Education Strategies for Success
Tashieka Simone Burris-Melville (University of Technology, Jamaica) Shalieka Tiffia Burris (University of Technology, Jamaica) and Kristin Bledsoe (Trevecca Nazarene University, USA)
Information Science Reference • copyright 2024 • 392pp • H/C (ISBN: 9798369315200) • US $235.00 (our price)

Evaluating Global Accreditation Standards for Higher Education
Arshi Naim (King Khalid University, Saudi Arabia) Alok Saklani (Swami Rama Himalayan University, India) Shad Ahmad Khan (University of Buraimi, Oman) and Praveen Kumar Malik (Lovely Professional University, India)
Information Science Reference • copyright 2024 • 406pp • H/C (ISBN: 9798369316986) • US $230.00 (our price)

701 East Chocolate Avenue, Hershey, PA 17033, USA
Tel: 717-533-8845 x100 • Fax: 717-533-8661
E-Mail: cust@igi-global.com • www.igi-global.com

Table of Contents

Editorial Advisory Board viii

Preface ix

Chapter 1
A Capabilities Approach Towards Addressing Gender Inequality in Transnational Higher
Education Leadership 1
    Shayna Kozuch, University of Nottingham, Ningbo, China

Chapter 2
Women and Leadership in Transnational Higher Education 16
    Ying Feng, Xi'an Jiaotong-Liverpool University, China

Chapter 3
Navigating Transnational Higher Education Management: Insights From Experience 39
    Gareth Richard Morris, University of Nottingham, Ningbo, China
    Junhua Mo, Soochow University, China
    Fiseha Berhanu Tesema, University of Nottingham, Ningbo, China
    Katherine Wang, University of Nottingham, Ningbo, China
    Lei Li, Suzhou Science and Technology Town FLS, China

Chapter 4
Exploring the Influence of Leadership on Job Satisfaction in Universities and International Schools 55
    Xuan Ma, Suzhou Institute, Xi'an Jiaotong University, China
    Ji Zhang, Suzhou International Foreign Language School, China

Chapter 5
Leadership in English for Academic Purpose(EAP): A Vision for Sino-Foreign Joint University
Success 69
    Kevin Cui, University of Nottingham, Ningbo, China

Chapter 6
The Development of Professional Identity and Its Associations With Emotions: An Empirical
Study of University EAP Teachers With Diverse Ethnic Backgrounds 85
    Zhenying Shi, Dulwich International High School, Suzhou, China
    Yunyan Zhang, Xi'an Jiaotong-Liverpool University, China
    Rong Yan, Xi'an Jiaotong-Liverpool University, China

Chapter 7
Teacher Identity, Course-Based Moral Education, and the Lessons for Transnational Higher

Education Institutions 121
    Junhua Mo, Soochow University, China
    Gareth Morris, University of Nottingham, Ningbo, China
    Li Tao, Soochow University, China

Chapter 8
External Professional Development and Training: The Importance for Transnational Higher
Education Leadership.. 137
    Lei Li, Suzhou Science and Technology Town Foreign Language School, China

Chapter 9
Exploring the Importance of Practice and Leadership on Teaching and Learning in Higher
Education 149
    Zhanglin Chai, Nottingham University, Ningbo, China

Chapter 10
An Investigation Into PSE Tutors' Perception and Practice of Intonation Teaching 170
    Mahmoud Jeidani, Nottingham University, Ningbo, China

Chapter 11
Student Leaders' Motivation, Evaluation, and Suggestions in THNE Private Universities 191
    Shi Ziyang, University of Nottingham, Ningbo, China
    Yang Siyan, University of Nottingham, Ningbo, China
    Hu Chenghao, University of Nottingham, Ningbo, China

Chapter 12
Exploring the Students' Perception of Online Speaking Classes and Various Functions of Online
Learning Platforms 208
    Ying You, Suzhou Wuzhong District Yi Jian He Experimental Primary School, China
    Bin Zou, Xi'an Jiaotong-Liverpool University, China
    Chenghao Wang, Xi'an Jiaotong-Liverpool University, China

Chapter 13
Immersive Innovations: Exploring the Use of Virtual and Augmented Reality in Educational
Institutions.. 229
    Sabyasachi Pramanik, Haldia Institute of Technology, India

Chapter 14
Higher Education in the Era of AI 244
    Maihepireti Abulaiti, University of Nottingham, Ningbo, China

Chapter 15
The Future University Through the Lens of the Ecological University: A Case Study..................... 266
    Stuart Perrin, Xi'an Jiaotong-Liverpool University, China
    Ling Wang, Xi'an Jiaotong-Liverpool University, China

Chapter 16
History of Higher Education in Georgia From the Ancient Period to the Modern Times: The Main Aspects of the Involvement of the Country in the Transnational Education Process 278
    Nika Chitadze, International Black Sea University, Georgia

Chapter 17
The Transnational ICT Leadership Assessment Based on the Available Infrastructure in the Governmental Organizations: A Case Study of the Ethiopian Northern Shewa Zone 301
    Nilamadhab Mishra, VIT Bhopal University, India
    Getachew Mekuria Habtemariam, Debre Berhan University, Ethiopia
    Seblewongel Esseynew, Addis Ababa University, Ethiopia
    Rudra Kalyan Nayak, VIT Bhopal University, India
    Ramamani Tripathy, Chitkara University, India
    Basanta Kumar Padhi, Balasore College of Engineering and Technology, Balasore, India

About the Contributors 367

Index 370

Editorial Advisory Board

Saif Said Rashid Al Abri, *Ministry of Education, Oman*
Fatima Al Husseiny, *Lebanese International University, Lebanon*
Chantel Abulaiti, *University of Nottingham Ningbo, China*
Philip James Allardice, *University of Nottingham Ningbo, China*
Grzegorz Bauer, *University of Nottingham Ningbo, China*
Helen Beech, *Xi'an Jiao Tong-Liverpool University, China*
Feng Cao, *Xi'an Jiao Tong-Liverpool University, China*
Qingqing Cao, *Puyuan Physiotherapy, China*
Linda Chai, *University of Nottingham Ningbo, China*
Yuxin Chen, *Xi'an Jiao Tong-Liverpool University, China*
Luoqiang Cui, *University of Nottingham Ningbo, China*
Jonathan Culbert, *Xi'an Jiao Tong-Liverpool University, China*
Martina Dorn, *Xi'an Jiao Tong-Liverpool University, China*
Aaliyah ElAskary, *Nanjing University, China*
Shunjie Feng, *Independent Educational Consultancy*
Yin Fah Foo, *University of Nottingham Ningbo, China*
Chenghao Hu, *University of Nottingham Ningbo, China*
Andy Jiahao Liu, *University of Arizona, United States*
Xiucai Lu, *Xi'an Jiao Tong-Liverpool University, China*
Shinan Luo, *University of Nottingham Ningbo, China*
James Morris, *Independent Management Consultancy*
Sam Newbould, *University of Nottingham Ningbo, China*
Ethan Quaid, *University of Nottingham Ningbo, China*
Ziyang Shi, *University of Nottingham Ningbo, China*
Joseph Kee Ming Sia, *Curtin University Malaysia, Malaysia*
Andrea Tang, *University of Nottingham Ningbo, China*
Fiseha Berhanu Tesema, *University of Nottingham Ningbo, China*
Jonathan Tillotson, *Xi'an Jiao Tong-Liverpool University, China*
Katherine Wang, *University of Nottingham Ningbo, China*
Wendy Weng, *University of Nottingham Ningbo, China*
Jiaxin Xu, *Dublin City University, Ireland*
Ma Xuan, *Xi'an Jiao Tong University, Suzhou Institute*
Siyang Yang, *University of Nottingham Ningbo, China*
Jinting Ye, *University of Nottingham Ningbo, China*
Ji Zhang, *Shanghai Normal University TianHua College, China*
Tingting Zhao, *Xi'an Jiao Tong-Liverpool University, China*

Preface

Following the 2024 release of the *Handbook of Research on Developments and Future Trends in Transnational Higher Education*, the intention of this book, *Developments and Future Trends in Transnational Higher Education Leadership*, is to narrow the scope slightly and explore the pivotal area of leadership and, in many ways through association, management. Given how the recent past has been turbulent globally, with first the concerns of the COVID pandemic and now the unprecedented emergence of technological developments in the form of generative AI, this book arrives at a watershed moment. This is a period in which education, and especially transnational higher education, faces even more significant uncertainties as many countries have decided to revisit their educational models and designs, influences and delivery through both necessity and demand.

Around the world there are seemingly contradictory movements occurring. On a national level many countries are grappling with a reversal back to a point of greater self-reliance and independence as the open borders globalised approach of the pre-pandemic and Brexit period recedes. On a sector level, educational institutions are having to look at new ways in which to attract students in order to remain competitive after a time when student mobility was severely restricted. On an individual level, students with transnational aspirations, especially those in East Asia and China, are finding certain educational avenues harder to access, particularly in international schooling. Given this dichotomy of factors, a book considering the future of higher education from a leadership and management perspective has the potential to have a significant impact in many areas for a wide readership as the next half a decade presents a period of increased uncertainty.

Chapter 1: On that note, the book begins with the chapter *A Capabilities Approach towards Addressing Gender Inequality in Transnational Higher Education Leadership.* This chapter explores the challenges faced by women moving into leadership in the transnational higher education context. The chapter provides a detailed analysis of Amartya Sen's Capabilities Approach to understand gender inequality in leadership. Nussbaum and Robeyns' lists of central human capabilities are adapted to apply theoretically to the context of gender equality in capabilities. The chapter establishes capabilities as a framework for action in pursuit of gender equality in higher education and proposes steps that institutions can take to support women in leadership positions and reduce gender inequality.

Chapter 2: *Women and Leadership in Transnational Higher Education* considers the crucial issue of gender representation in leadership within transnational higher education institutions. It presents an analysis of theoretical perspectives and investigates the impacts that women leaders bring to the leadership roles by illustrating how these perspectives and contributions from such women foster global citizenship among students and promote inclusive leadership practices. The chapter then highlights that, despite the advantages of women's leadership and the progress achieved, women continue to face challenges as they move into leadership roles. The chapter further explores the various strategies and initiatives developed to promote gender equity and empower women in leadership roles. It emphasises the need for a supportive environment and highlights the key role various stakeholders play in driving this change, thereby empowering women in leadership roles within transnational higher education.

Chapter 3: *Navigating Transnational Higher Education Management: Insights from Experience* highlights how Transnational Higher Education (TNHE) has experienced many challenges in recent years. From the pandemic and its legacy to the emergence of generative AI, universities are now faced with the prospect of bouncing from one issue to another. Making life additionally complex is the fact that regional instability is increasingly common globally now, with issues occurring in locations that had previously experienced periods of relative long-term stability. This chapter thus considers some of the most pressing challenges that middle managers face in TNHE providers today by drawing on the insights of experienced middle managers who have worked at well-regarded TNHE providers in eastern China prior to, during and immediately after the pandemic.

Chapter 4: *Exploring the Influence of Leadership on Job Satisfaction in Universities and International Schools* examines the influence of leadership styles on the job satisfaction of teachers at a Chinese transnational higher education university and international school in the same city. Adopting qualitative research methods and in-depth interviews to investigate the job satisfaction and dissatisfaction among a group of educators the chapter highlights how, despite contentedness in some work areas, factors such as workload and wage equity provide sources of concern, along with disorganisation, punitive fines and interpersonal relationships in some cases. The study advocates the provision of employee-friendly working conditions and the enhancement of the teacher welfare to improve workplaces.

Chapter 5: *Leadership in English for Academic Purposes (EAP): A Vision for Sino-Foreign Joint University Success* considers leadership's role in English for Academic Purposes (EAP) within Sino-foreign universities, focusing on overcoming linguistic and cultural challenges through adaptable, culturally sensitive leadership. It highlights the shift from traditional to contemporary leadership theories and the importance of innovation and inclusivity in response to challenges such as online learning transitions during the COVID-19 pandemic. Additionally, it explores transformational and transactional leadership models, emphasising cultural sensitivity in merging Eastern and Western educational practices. The chapter suggests future research directions for enhancing leadership effectiveness in EAP contexts, aiming to improve student engagement and success in the complex landscape of Sino-foreign higher education.

Chapter 6: *The Development of Professional Identity and its Associations with Emotions: An Empirical Study of University EAP Teachers with Diverse Ethnical Backgrounds* notes that despite their significance, the professional identity of language teachers remains under investigated regarding the dynamic process of emotion negotiation and identity development of foreign and second teachers with different ethnical backgrounds. Through a semi-structured interview with ten EAP teachers from an EMI university in China, this study explores how professional identity changes and transforms, especially since the outbreak of the Covid-19. It also considers how it is negotiated with emotions. The results suggest that ethnical background is one of the significant factors influencing the development of teacher's professional identity and that international teachers were more susceptible to the pandemic's effects compared with their Chinese counterparts. Put simply, they experienced more negative emotions. In addition, teacher-student classroom interactions were found to be one of the significant factors triggering the emotional changes and transformation of professional identities regardless of their ethnic backgrounds.

Chapter 7: *Teacher Identity, Course-Based Moral Education and the Lessons for Transnational Higher Education Institutions* provide the focus of this chapter. The sociocultural and political context clearly plays a crucial role in influencing and shaping teacher identity, and recent developments in China's public higher education sector have seen moral education become a priority area. This has presented new challenges to Chinese university teachers in terms of their pedagogical delivery and sense of self. This chapter therefore attempts to explore the identity construction of a Chinese EFL teacher who has been incorporating course-based moral education within his teaching and research practices. Through a positioning analysis, it is found that teachers may experience a triple identity and that the identity construction process is tied to the active agency of teachers. The relevance of this chapter for transnational higher education is also highlighted, because providers are influenced by the context they are a part of, so understanding how domestic policy is changing is important for anticipating how international and transnational provision might enable proactive forward-thinking leadership practices.

Chapter 8: *External Professional Development and Training: The Importance for Transnational Higher Education Leadership* examines leadership's role in English for Academic Purposes (EAP) within Sino-foreign universities, focusing on overcoming linguistic and cultural challenges through adaptable, culturally sensitive leadership. It highlights the shift from traditional to contemporary leadership theories and the importance of innovation and inclusivity in response to challenges such as online learning transitions during the COVID-19 pandemic. Additionally, it explores transformational and transactional leadership models, emphasising cultural sensitivity in merging Eastern and Western educational practices. The chapter suggests future research directions for enhancing leadership effectiveness in EAP contexts, aiming to improve student engagement and success in the complex landscape of Sino-foreign higher education.

Chapter 9: *Exploring the importance of practice and leadership on teaching & Learning in Higher Education* discusses how, in the fast-paced world, finding time for training and reflection is essential for practice and leadership as it helps teachers develop their skills and review their effectiveness. The training that the practitioner under discussion received is investigated and its effects noted. The process of the reflection is conducted by adopting Brookfield's Four Lenses of Critical Reflection, and Gibbs Model. The training and reflection is found to have enabled the practitioner to plan and teach more effectively. Furthermore, in this evolving society, reflective practice is encouraged as an important cornerstone of leadership. It is suggested that in order to practice new skills and behaviours in appropriate contexts and to draw connections between new information and concepts and prior knowledge and experience, reflective practice is crucial for both professional and personal growth.

Chapter 10: *An investigation into PSE Tutors' Perception and Practice of Intonation Teaching*, delves into pre-sessional English (PSE) Course (PSECs) tutors' views of, and experience with, the relevance of intonation to their teaching. Motivated by the lack of a unified view among teachers in relation to its value with reference to PSECs, this study uses semi-structured interviews and teaching observations to explore these tutors' approaches to the teaching of intonation. The results show the participants' recognition of the relevance of intonation to PSE students who aim to improve their listening and speaking skills, while recognising that teaching requires significant support in terms of training and a focus on its communicative role. The significance of this study is that it rejects the view that teachers do not appreciate intonation, showing that teachers' critical reflection is a promising step towards streamlining PSECs to align with student needs.

Chapter 11: *Student Leaders' Motivation, Evaluation and Suggestions in THNE Private Universities* considers the evolving landscape of Transnational Higher Education (TNHE), understanding the perspectives and insights of student leaders. This is important for enhancing the student leadership experience. The interview study seeks to delve into the common insights of student leaders operating within the context of TNHE. More specifically, the investigation focuses on their satisfaction with leadership experiences and their motivation to gain leadership roles. Furthermore, this inquiry extends beyond mere exploration, aiming to distil practical wisdom and guidance for aspiring student leaders who are poised to navigate the complexities of TNHE.

Chapter 12: *Exploring the Students' Perception of Online Speaking Classes and Various Functions of Online Learning Platforms* examines student perceptions of synchronous online oral English classes, focusing on how the functionalities of digital platforms influence their language anxiety and the development of speaking skills. To gather both quantitative and qualitative insights, the study employs questionnaires and semi-structured interviews, involving 91 higher education students from various majors, all of whom have experienced synchronous online oral classes. Analysis reveals a notable trend, namely that students with lower levels of oral English proficiency tend to perceive greater improvement in their speaking abilities in these classes compared to their more proficient counterparts. Interestingly, the camera feature is identified as the primary source of language anxiety, while tools such as microphones, breakout rooms, text chat boxes, and individual text/voice/video chat functions are deemed most effective for fostering speaking skills.

Chapter 13: *Immersive Innovations - Exploring the use of Virtual and Augmented Reality in Educational Institutions* examines the transformative influence of immersive technology, namely Virtual Reality (VR) and Augmented Reality (AR), on higher education. The chapter illustrates the significant impact of VR and AR on education by tracing their evolutionary trajectory from their conceptual roots in the mid-20th century to their current implementations. The chapter highlights how conventional lectures and textbooks are being replaced with immersive learning environments, leading to a transformation of traditional classroom paradigms. This is because VR and AR enable students to immerse themselves in virtual environments, where they may engage with three-dimensional models, historical re-enactments, and complex simulations. The chapter also explores the challenges and consequences associated with the integration of new technology, such as the need for specialised instruction and ensuring accessibility for all students.

Chapter 14: *Higher Education in the Era of AI* considers how in the rapidly evolving landscape of higher education, the advent of Artificial Intelligence (AI) and specifically the emergence of language models like ChatGPT have sparked a transformative dialogue across academia. It notes how ChatGPT, released in November 2022, immediately became a focal point of both admiration and scepticism, illustrating the polarised perspectives on AI's role in education. This chapter explores the multi-faction of ChatGPT in higher education, seeks to navigate the intricate relationship between AI technologies and higher education, with a particular focus on teaching and learning, and consider leadership by drawing upon a wide range of academic literature to highlight the current developments, future trends, and practical advice for leaders in the field, through a critical examination of the challenges and opportunities presented by AI. This discussion aims to provide valuable insights and guidance for navigating the complexities of transnational higher education leadership in the AI era.

Chapter 15: *The Future University through the lens of the Ecological University. A Case Study* uses the lens of the Ecological University to rethink the role of education, and what this may mean for the future of university and its leadership, through a case study of innovative change at a joint venture university within China. Through this examination of a transformative approach to what an ecological university could be, and the role of the newly created position of Chief Officer of Ecology, the chapter analyses the curriculum, pedagogy and research activities of the university, and the changes that are being processed to make it 'future-ready'. It asks the university (staff and students) to adopt an ecological mindset and perspective, and to engage in a continuous process of reflection, negotiation, and innovation. The chapter concludes by arguing that the education ecology of university provides a valuable framework for rethinking the role and function of the university in the 21st century, and especially its leadership, and for promoting a more inclusive and democratic academic culture, and sustainable future for higher education going forward.

Chapter 16: The *History of Higher Education in Georgia* highlights the development of this level of education and the higher education institutions in Georgia. It also considers the role of the country within the transnational higher education process. The present-day analysis also evaluates the engagement of Georgian students in this, and the role that international students play domestically. Furthermore, attention is paid to the important influence that joining the Bologna Process has had by, amongst other developments, introducing United National Exams in the country, based on the influence of global developments.

Chapter 17: The final chapter, *The Transnational ICT Leadership Assessment Based on the Available Infrastructure in the Governmental Organisations: A Case Study of the Ethiopian Northern Shewa Zone,* considers the effectiveness, efficiency, and security of ICT-monitored systems which are assessed as part of the transnational ICT leadership assessment. This is based on the infrastructure currently in place in governmental organisations. Tailoring the assessment to each governmental entity's specific context, organisational structure and goals is one noted feature. Additionally, involving key stakeholders, including ICT professionals, leadership, and end-users, in the assessment process enhances its accuracy and relevance and is also incorporated. The study assesses the availability of ICT infrastructure and its utilisation through transnational ICT leaders in government organisations. The research finds that skill gaps, a lack of ICT infrastructure, and a lack of leadership awareness all feature within the Northern Shewa Administrative Zone. Additionally, the study identifies the challenges of aligning the infrastructure of ICT in governmental organisations to the needs of transnational ICT leaders in practice.

We hope that this book proves to be insightful and that readers are able to take away useful ideas and information that will help both them, their students and colleagues, and their institutions and communities.

Gareth Morris and **Shayna Kozuch**

Chapter 1
A Capabilities Approach Towards Addressing Gender Inequality in Transnational Higher Education Leadership

Shayna Kozuch
University of Nottingham, Ningbo, China

ABSTRACT

This chapter explores the challenges faced by women moving into leadership in the transnational higher education context. The chapter provides a detailed analysis of Amartya Sen's Capabilities Approach to understand gender inequality in leadership. Nussbaum and Robeyns' lists of central human capabilities are adapted to apply theoretically to the context of gender equality in capabilities. The chapter establishes capabilities as a framework for action in pursuit of gender equality in higher education and proposes steps that institutions can take to support women in leadership positions and reduce gender inequality.

INTRODUCTION

Equity, diversity and inclusion (EDI) agendas can be found in virtually every higher education institution (HEI) around the globe. A simple search of the web will produce countless results of policies and practices that aim to promote and support EDI in higher education. These policies focus on ensuring fairness within the institution and preventing discrimination on the basis of protected characteristics. Despite the influential role universities can have in in promoting EDI agendas, HEIs remain gendered organisations (Rosa et al., 2020). There exists a pervasive dichotomy between institutional agendas of gender equity and the actual experiences of women in HEIs. This dichotomy is compounded for women moving into leadership positions in higher education. Despite the central role of HEIs in the training, experience and career trajectory of female leaders in education, research indicates that institutions themselves perpetuate gender inequalities through their structural policies, financing, norms, frameworks, hierarchies, pedagogical practices and workplace conditions (Fennell & Arnot, 2009; Unterhalter et al., 2022). In the UK, more women pursue university education than males leading to calls that gender

DOI: 10.4018/979-8-3693-2857-6.ch001

Copyright ©2024, IGI Global. Copying or distributing in print or electronic forms without written permission of IGI Global is prohibited.

equality has been achieved and it is no longer a concern (David, 2014). This demonstrates a contradiction in HEIs that despite the increase in female undergraduate and post-graduate numbers, women's access to senior leadership positions in higher education remains limited (O'Connor et al., 2015). It is in the top leadership positions such as Dean, Provost, and President where the most significant gender gap can be seen (Park, 2020). In the EU, women represent only 25% of the proportion of professors in HEIs and less than 24% of the heads of HEIs (European Commission, 2021). Research indicates that there are significant inequalities in the ratio of women in academic employment in every country in the world (Mischau, 2001). While gender ratios are one measure used to assess levels of gender inequality in education (Unterhalter et al., 2022) it does not provide a full picture of the experiences of women in academia. A review of research into women in academia found that in addition to a persistent lack of women in leadership positions in universities across all contexts, women academics also frequently faced adverse workplace conditions that negatively impacted their work such as harassment, discrimination, work life imbalance, and slow career progression (Sang, 2018). Moreover, evidence suggests that women often need to have more education than men to get the same jobs within universities (David, 2014).

These statistics are compounded in the transnational higher education context where gender inequalities can be even more pronounced. These transnational campuses are emerging in prominence in the contemporary higher education landscape as the demand for higher education increases around the world (Sanger and Gleason, 2020). Transnational universities are defined as those in which the degree awarding institution is located in a different country to where the education is delivered (Universities UK, 2022). Despite policies and support mechanisms such as paid maternity leave, and anti-harassment policies, women still face obstacles and challenges moving into leadership positions that their male colleagues do not face as evidenced by these continued discrepancies in representation.

The transnational higher education context contributes to these challenges because compared to home campuses, transnational campuses face additional challenges such as adapting to host countries, adapting the curricula to the local contexts, and creating studying environments equivalent to those in the home institutions (Nguyen et al., 2023). These challenges mean that gender equality in institutional leadership is a low priority in these transnational institutions. An additional challenge is that EDI policies tend to be directed by home institutions and do not reflect the transnational context in which the university operates. Research conducted by Boivin et al (2022: 150) found that the patriarchal structures of higher education institutions themselves obstruct women from advancing in their career development which can be multiplied in cross-cultural contexts. Examples of these significant obstacles are related to recruitment and promotion procedures with requirements for mobility. The expectation of mobility is even further challenged in this transnational context with the requirement to move transnationally to the campus location. Academic mobility is also factored into hiring decisions and therefore impacting professional advancement opportunities. Mobility represents desirable work experience for academics and demonstrates an ability to work in another institutional context in another country (Boivin et al., 2022). Transnational higher education takes place in 228 countries and territories around the world, with the majority located in China (Universities UK, 2022). Working in this context requires moving to a different country with a different language and culture, potentially uprooting families for those with children, moving away from families and support systems in academics' home countries. This context itself contributes to further gender inequality.

Tackling gender inequalities in leadership should be a priority for HEIs, including transnational HEIs. Therefore, it is essential to consider new approaches, policies and strategies to support women leaders in HEIs, and especially those in transnational higher education leadership positions because of the unique challenges faced in this context. The aim of this chapter is to take a theoretical approach in considering Amartya Sen's (1992) Capabilities Approach with a focus on gender and answer the follow research questions:

> To what extent can the Capabilities Approach be used to address gender inequality through the development a strategic framework for transnational HEIs to support women in leadership position?
> Which capabilities can be operationalised to establish a strategy for transnational HEIs to address gender inequality?

To answer these questions, this chapter will take a theoretical approach to understanding gender inequalities in this transnational higher education context by aiming to understand why female academics have been disadvantaged in their career progression. The Capabilities Approach will be utilised to understand the reasons for gender inequalities in the transnational HEI context and focus on the process of devising a multifaceted strategy to address gender inequality in leadership. Firstly, the literature on the Capabilities Approach will be explored, identifying the main components to using the approach to measure gender inequality and devising a strategy to reduce gender inequality. After examining the Capabilities Approach, Nussbaums's (2000) central human capabilities and Robeyns' (2003) selection of relevant capabilities to approach gender inequality will be analysed. Through this analysis, central capabilities will be identified for the transnational higher education context. This chapter will then link these capabilities to useful strategies and policies that transnational higher education institutions can implement to address gender inequality and remove the barriers women face moving into leadership positions. These policy and strategy recommendations for transnational HEIs will be made as suggestions for addressing gender inequality in leadership. These policy and strategy recommendations are significant to those responsible for policy and strategy development in transnational higher education, including Human Resource departments, university leaders and managers, EDI Committees and other allies committed to reducing gender inequality. Ultimately, this chapter will provide the theoretical foundation for practical strategies to address gender inequality in transnational higher education leadership and the findings of this chapter can make an important contribution to policy development.

The Capabilities Approach in the Literature

This section will provide an overview of the Capabilities Approach with a focus on gender, highlighting the benefits of the approach in addressing gender inequality. The Capabilities Approach is beneficial in exploring gender inequality as gender inequality was especially important to Amartya Sen. Developed by Sen in the 1980s, the Capabilities Approach provided an alternative approach to measuring inequality by looking beyond economic indicators and instead focused on well-being. Sen (1992; 1999) describes these well-being indicators as capabilities. Sen (2009: 16) defines the Capabilities Approach as "an intellectual discipline that gives a central role to the evaluation of a person's achievements and freedoms in terms of his or her actual ability to do the different things a person has reason to value doing or being." This approach is especially important when measuring gender inequality as those most often disadvantaged are women (Nussbaum, 2003). The Capabilities Approach can be effective in uncovering this inequality since framing gender inequalities in terms of capabilities provides for the opportunity to explore the intricacies of how resources are distributed and converted into individual freedoms and opportunities (Unterhalter et al, 2022). Sen (1992: 81) found that in the capabilities-based assessment of justice, it is not the resources one has that are to be assessed but rather "the freedoms they actually enjoy to choose the lives that they have reason to value." It is in this way that Sen's Capabilities Approach was a divergence from other social justice theorists such as Rawls (1971) by focusing on the obstacles that exist for women in society and how those obstacles impact their ability to convert capabilities. Sen claims that the "commodities commanded are a means to the end of well-being, but can scarcely be the end itself" (Sen, 1999: 19). Accordingly, it is the measurement of how people are able to freely choose to pursue the life with which they value that is important in Sen's Approach and not just the resources available (Williams & Daniel, 2021). The Capabilities Approach is focused on the autonomy one has to participate in different activities, and the level of well-being that can be achieved through the options open to them (Robeyns, 2017). Central to this, according to Robeyns (2017: 9) is that the Capabilities Approach asks "What are people really able to do and what kind of person are they able to be?" Sen (1999) distinguishes these concepts from each other and describes them as capabilities and functionings. To understand the differences between capabilities and functionings, Walker (2006) highlights the difference between the opportunity to achieve and the actual achievement. This definition identifies that the resources themselves do not equate to achievement or a certain quality of life, but rather the agency and ability to convert the resources into achievements that are paramount (Hart, 2019). This agency to convert resources, or conversion factors, refers to one's ability to pursue goals that one values. In other words, the conversion of capabilities into functionings is directly connected to opportunities to live a full life. Therefore, it can be said that any constraint to agency would then equate to a disadvantage or barrier to choice for an individual or group (Walker, 2006).

It is not simply choice that is important for Sen. Sen (1999) argues that women often demonstrate "adaptive preferences" that have emerged over time as a result of their subordinate position. This claim of adaptive preferences is that women themselves may not be able to articulate their preferences because their history prevents the full opportunity for choice. Nussbaum (2003) claims that these adaptive preferences are the result of the unjust background conditions that women experience over time. These background conditions mean that women may lack the capability to live fully simply because they are women. It is in these unequal circumstances that lead to barriers in choice and an experience as second-class citizens (Nussbaum, 2000). Therefore, it can be understood that removing background conditions that impede women's freedom of choice can be viewed as a central goal for reducing gender inequality. This approach to understanding can be considered an improvement in understanding the challenges women face in pursuing these lives that have agency and value. As a result, the Capabilities Approach can be seen as an effective method to recognise and support the development of both capabilities and functionings to break down the barriers that exist and set the conditions for activating agency.

The Capabilities Approach as a Strategic Framework to Reduce Gender Inequalities

This section will use the Capabilities Approach within the field of higher educational leadership to consider what the approach offers in terms of establishing a strategic framework to address the areas of gender inequality in leadership positions in higher education. The Capabilities Approach has been criticised for lacking in operational explicitness and precision (Agee & Crocker, 2013). While it may not be able to answer all questions, it can be used to advocate for capabilities (Robeyns, 2003) and can be viewed as a flexible and multi-purpose framework (Robeyns, 2017; Sen, 1992). There is value in looking at the Capabilities Approach to address gender inequality as it was founded on an internal heterogeneity that allows the approach to be adapted and developed in ways that are appropriate for a particular situation (Alkire, 2002). This is the strength of the Capabilities Approach in that it can guide the focus towards evaluation, policy, and action that can have considerable impact when implemented effectively (Walker & Unterhalter (2007). Policies which advance achievements are consistent with the Capabilities Approach (Agee & Crocker, 2013). This aligns with the goal of advancing gender equality in higher education leadership.

According to Robeyns (2003: 62) the Capabilities Approach has substantial potential for addressing feminist concerns and questions. There is a long history of feminist movement support for issues that are beyond economics, and include topics that are important to women such as reproductive health, empowerment, harassment, education and social status (Robeyns, 2003). Walker (2006) also highlights the value of the Capabilities Approach in addressing issues in education as it focuses on human development and can therefore alter the way that education and the challenges within education are viewed. However, while Nussbaum (2003) supports Sen's arguments regarding women's agency and participation, she does not believe the approach goes far enough in addressing pervasive gender inequality. The Capabilities Approach, according to Nussbaum (2003), can provide the guidance towards gender equality, but the formulation of a list of the most essential capabilities is required in addressing gender inequality. If the Capabilities Approach can be used to measure gender inequality in terms of capabilities, functionings and agency, the establishment of a strategic framework to respond to gender inequality using the Capabilities Approach could provide the foundation towards gender advancement. The process of developing a framework is important, as emphasized by Sen. Establishing a strategic framework that focuses on capabilities requires understanding the complexities of the social environment and the distribution of convertible resources (Unterhalter et al., 2022). Both Sen and Nussbaum connect these capabilities with human rights and social justice.

It is important to note that feminist viewpoints have often been critical of universal normative approaches, yet Nussbaum (2000) argues that it is possible for a framework to be not only feminist in practice but also be universal in approach to cross-cultural norms of justice, equality, and rights. Considering this argument, the Capabilities Approach could be applied to a broad range of contexts, including transnational higher education.

Which Capabilities? From Sen to Nussbaum to Robeyns

In arguing for the reallocation of resources, Sen (1980) famously utilized the example of a person in a wheelchair that would require more resources connected to mobility than someone that does not require a wheelchair. Using this example, it can be argued that working towards a reduction in gender inequality would require an allocation of resources according to needs and a tailored plan. In tailoring a plan, selecting the essential capabilities to focus on is an important element of this approach. It is vital to note that essential capabilities should not only be what individuals themselves would like as this would miss the wider picture of adaptive preferences in addressing wider gender inequality (Walker & Unterhalter, 2007). Sen himself never made a list of the central capabilities, so it is essential to look at the work of others such as Nussbaum to consider which capabilities would be essential. Nussbaum (2000) argues for developing a universal theory that can address gender inequalities and make a strong, universal claim for good. Nussbaum (2003) argues that the focus on capabilities over rights is essential in avoiding a western centric view as it does not link strongly to one culture or historical tradition. Nussbaum's (2000: 35) capabilities list aims to develop "a defensible set of cross-cultural categories," which is essential for any approach that will cross cultural boundaries, such as with transnational higher education that blends different cultures in one workplace. Nussbaum's (2000) work, *Women and Human Development* produced a list of ten essential capabilities that are considered to be essential to human dignity and social justice. Her framework aims to address essential capabilities in measuring gender inequality. To do this, she distinguishes between capabilities as being basic, internal, or combined (Nussbaum, 2000). She further argues that many of the capabilities included in her list are capabilities that have been withheld from women, or not desired by women themselves as a result of adaptive preferences (Nussbaum, 2000). It is with this list that Nussbaum (2000) aims to provide a universalist approach to capabilities.

Robeyns (2003) finds that Nussbaum's attempt at establishing a universal theory too broad and instead, each application of the Capabilities Approach will require its own list of capabilities. Robeyns (2005) argues that the process of creating lists needs to be legitimate and that if those people for whom the list is intended feel the list is imposed upon them, the list will lack impact. However, Nussbaum (2003) contends that a basic conception of justice is required, and thus the list is essential in pursuing social justice. It is this epistemological position that finds it essential to construct capabilities lists in the pursuit of social justice.

Both Nussbaum's (2000) list of central human capabilities and Robeyns' (2003) list of capabilities share a number of similarities. Together they can be adapted to apply to the context of gender equality in capabilities for transnational higher education leadership. The parallels in these positions can be seen the lists below.

Nussbaum's (2003: 41-42) List of The Central Human Capabilities	Robeyns' (2003: 71-72) list of capabilities for gender equality
1. Life 2. Bodily Health 3. Bodily Integrity 4. Senses, Imagination, and Thought 5. Emotions 6. Practical Reason 7. Affiliation 8. Other Species 9. Play 10. Control over one's environment	1. Life and Physical Health 2. Mental well-being 3. Bodily integrity and safety 4. Social relations 5. Political empowerment 6. Education and knowledge 7. Domestic work and nonmarket care 8. Paid work and other projects 9. Shelter and environment 10. Mobility 11. Leisure activities 12. Time-autonomy 13. Respect 14. Religion

Establishing Capabilities as a Framework for Action in Pursuit of Gender Equality in Higher Education

Higher education institutions have a responsibility to implement strategies and policies that promote gender equality as a matter of social justice. This section will highlight the policies and strategies that HEIs can implement to impact gender inequality in the transnational context, based upon the Capabilities Approach, Nussbaum's (2000) list of capabilities and Robeyns (2003) list of capabilities for gender equality. There are a number of parallels between Nussbaum (2000) and Robeyns (2003) lists that will be incorporated in the strategy framework. It should be noted that within higher education there is a degree of skepticism about the effectiveness of policies focused on addressing gender inequality (Aiston, 2011). Robeyns (2003: 72) stresses that those drafting lists should be considerate in including information from groups with which they are less familiar. Therefore, these strategy approaches focus on removing barriers that women face in higher education so that capabilities and functionings can be experienced, well-being enhanced and space permitted to flourish. These proposed strategies place emphasis on creating spaces where women can realise their full potential which has been found to be positive in promoting gender equality (Aiston, 2011).

This list of strategies towards gender equality has been compiled by exploring Nussbaum's (2000) list of capabilities along with Robeyns (2003) list. While those lists form a useful starting point, they reflect capabilities rather than actions that can be taken to turn those capabilities into functionings. This strategic framework is meant as a subtle guide to support the direction of an EDI strategy that can reduce gender inequality. Turning those capabilities into actions within higher education institutions can be used to empower women and work to reduce obstacles that create the conditions for constrained capabilities and oppression to agency. The suggestions that will be discussed in this chapter are not easy fixes and can be expensive for institutions to implement. They do not work towards breaking down some of the more structural systems of oppression faced by women moving into leadership positions. Instead, these suggestions are subtle strategy initiatives that can work towards supporting essential human capabilities. This framework utilises the Capabilities Approach as a policy initiative designed to focus on individual freedoms within the context of higher education for women leaders to live a valued life and set conditions with which they can flourish.

1. The Capability for Life

The foremost capability recognised by both Nussbaum (2000) and Robeyns (2005) is the capability for life with a focus on the importance of health and being able to live a healthy, normal length life. Census data for the UK puts the life expectancy at birth at 79 years for males and 82.9 years for females (UK Office for National Statistics, 2021). While this discrepancy in life expectancy seems to be in favour of females, the gender gap should be viewed here as ethically irrelevant, according to Robeyns (2003). Research identifying health indicators actually points to women experiencing more ill-health than men (Robeyns, 2003). From the perspective of capabilities, Sen is not interested only in outcomes, which show women faring well, but considers the ability to live well, which according to research from Robeyns (2003), sees women as actually faring worse than their male counterparts.

In terms of how the capability for life can be viewed as part of this strategy for reducing gender inequality in higher education, it is clear that providing comprehensive medical insurance is essential as part of an EDI strategy. Nussbaum (2000) points out that even though individuals with adequate health support often fall ill, focusing on actual health capabilities are important in evaluating the health care that is available. When considering the context of transnational higher education, that medical insurance should allow for employees, both male and female, to seek medical treatment at medical centres that reflect culturally sensitive approaches to treatment. That is to say that these strategies in higher education institutions should promote the health and well-being of their employees by providing necessary medical treatment, both emergency and preventative, and allow for travel to a country that can provide that treatment. In many areas of the world this medical treatment is prohibitively expensive. Therefore, gender-specific treatment, including maternity coverage provided by HEIs can reduce barriers women face in their capabilities. In addition, paid sick leave provision can be considered as a means of supporting the *capability for life*. While medical insurance is not gender-focused, ensuring the capability for life would allow for women to have the space to live a healthy life. Providing comprehensive maternity medical coverage would reduce barriers to female academics that wish to have a child from moving into the transnational context and leadership positions.

2. Mental Health Support Provision

Robeyns' (2003) list has a focus on mental health that is also shared with Nussbaum's list (2003: 41) who, under her heading for *Emotions*, highlights that "not having one's emotional development blighted by fear and anxiety." Since women are more likely than their male counterparts to face high levels of stress in their workplace (Attell et al., 2017), an effective EDI strategy that includes mental health support provisions is essential. This approach should include both mental health support in terms of availability of counselling, but also training within the institution to address and reduce the various practices that contribute to stress. The stressors women face in higher education institutions can include a wide variety of experiences that impact their ability to flourish in their work environment. One of those stressors is in the communicative practices that are embedded within higher education institutions. Research into gender in higher education found that through their academic careers, women experience different stressors and clashes (Torino et al., 2019). One such stressor is with microaggressive communication practices such as dismissiveness and exclusion as normative practices, oftentimes unintentionally, so much so that those that are performing in this type of communication may be unaware of it (Boivin et al., 2022). This type of communication is harmful and to address these issues in communication and to reduce the stress this puts women under, training in recognizing and addressing these pervasive practices for all staff within the higher education institution is crucial. This training in inclusive communication practices would train both women and men to recognise the microaggressive communication practices and provide strategies to resist against these practices. Evidence suggests that intervention from colleagues to combat microaggressive communication practices can positively influence the experiences of women in higher education, and thus reduce stress (Kim and Meister, 2023). These communication practices can often be compounded in an international work context where a diverse range of people converge.

Counselling is also an important strategy to support mental health in the transnational context. Transnational education often straddles two cultures, in combination with a multicultural workforce. Addressing the stress this context produces supports the capability for women's mental health, reducing barriers that would prevent women from moving into leadership positions and flourishing in their careers. For this strategy to be effective, the availability of counselling should be equally available to all employees and its benefits should be promoted and encouraged so that all employees could benefit to avoid stigma for women being seen as requiring mental health support.

3. Bodily Integrity, Safety and Dignity

Both Nussbaum (2000) and Robeyns (2003) recognize bodily integrity as a central human capability. Bodily integrity refers to being free from personal violence, including sexual assault. Dignity has also been included in this strategy list as a capability, whereas Robeyns (2003) includes this separately and Nussbaum (2003) does not explicitly include. It has been argued that at the centre of all gender inequality is that women are devalued and considered not fully human (Robeyns, 2003). Therefore, it is clear that there is a strong gender dimension to this capability. Not only are women devalued but they are more likely to experience incidents of sexual violence than men (Robeyns, 2003). Women also face greater incidents of sexual harassment in the workplace (Nussbaum, 2000). Central to meeting this capability is to provide a safe workplace for women. This requires a comprehensive anti-harassment policy to be included in this framework. For this application of the capabilities approach to be successful, there should be clear rules for the protection of women from violence, harassment, including sexual harassment along with mechanisms for anonymous reporting of any harassment either experienced or witnessed. In this way, this capability can be met and women can have the opportunity to flourish, free from oppression in the workplace. To further the success of this initiative, training for all staff on anti-harassment should also be included as part of the strategy initiative. This is especially important in the transnational higher education context where those from diverse cultures and experiences converge. Similar to microaggressive communicative practices, harassment may also be unintentional and as such, recognizing and addressing harassment for those that may be unaware of it is an important element of removing barriers women face in the workplace (Boivin et al., 2022).

4. Establishing Social Network

Both Robeyns (2003) and Nussbaum (2003) highlight the importance of affiliation and building a social network as an essential capability. The capability of social networks can be realized through establishing a mentoring scheme for women that would help to establish nurturing and enjoyable social relationships. It is found that women especially valued mentoring from women (Monroe et al., 2008) and research points to participating in mentoring programmes as effective in supporting female faculty (Aiston, 2011). These social networks can be beneficial in unlocking capabilities and breaking down barriers in several ways. Firstly, female mentoring supports successful professional development by providing support and guidance in new and challenging domains (Monroe et al., 2008). This could be facilitated through a mentor relationship between women in leadership positions or between women leaders and women in subordinate positions to support their professional development and career progression. In the latter capacity, these networks could support emerging female leaders through cultural capital in the participants, whereby the leaders could act as agents to support career development. The philosophy around cultural capital was put forth by Bourdieu (1986) who added to the Capability Approach by arguing for the importance of habitus and cultural capital in capabilities. These social networks can act as a method for developing cultural capital as mentors can draw upon their cultural capital to act as agents for the transformation for their mentees (Mills, 2008: 79). The example of acting as an agent for transformation through the use of cultural capital comes from research into teachers and students, but it can be inferred that if teachers could position to work against a disadvantaged system and challenge the processes that lead to oppression for students, so too could educational leaders (Mills, 2008). Another benefit of facilitating the formation of mentor relationships is that these relationships can help to reduce stress. Social support can reduce stress and can counter many of the negative effects of workplace stressors (Attell et al., 2017). This is especially important in the transnational context where female faculty have often left their support systems in other countries and face stressors not only from the workplace but from the new, international context. Often these networks form organically out of a need for social affiliation, but institutions can further support these capabilities by formalizing the process, providing recognition for participating in this scheme, and even budget support for arranging activities for the network to participate in. It is important to note that there are challenges in establishing mentoring schemes. To be effective, mentoring schemes should not be restricted only to women, as that could foster a belief that a women-only mentoring programme would be stigmatized as being remedial

(Aiston, 2011). This challenge could be overcome through a mentoring scheme that includes all staff, but with women paired with other women.

5. Reproductive Rights and Family Support

Research identifies that HEIs normative practice, regulations and expectations are constructed for male academics and especially exclude female academics with families (Boivin et al., 2022). As a result, to move towards gender equality special provisions for women to preserve reproductive rights and support their role within families is essential. Nussbaum (2003) highlights the importance of choice in reproduction, a capability which is also reflected in Robeyns (2003) list. Robeyns (2003) furthers the capability to not just include reproductive rights, but also the capability of raising children and taking care of other dependents. The largest inequality between men and women is in domestic work (Robeyns, 2003). This results in women in higher education having more family responsibilities than their male counterparts (Nikunen, 2014). To reduce barriers faced by women and family responsibilities, paid maternity leave is essential for a higher education institution. Although many HEIs have maternity leave available, those that take this leave are often not entitled to a salary increase in the year the leave was taken. Employment priorities and salary increases do not usually allow for the interruption of work that comes from taking maternity leave (Boivin et al., 2022). This is in part what leads to salary discrepancies as women's careers are essentially put on hold during the maternity leave period, impacting access to fair wages.

Although maternity leave is often available, on-site childcare was rarely found in HEIs (Fathima et al., 2020). As much of this responsibility for childcare falls to women, they are again disadvantaged in career progression. It should be noted that raising children is not biologically linked to women but rather is a socially constructed barrier (Monroe et al., 2008). One of the biggest challenges that a woman with a family will face is how to balance all the various responsibilities. Research by Monroe et al., (2008) highlighted the bleak situation for women with families in that they are barely surviving with their attempt to balance work and family responsibilities. Senior academic women's research output can be impacted by these caring responsibilities, negatively impacting career progression (Aiston & Jung, 2015). In Nikunen's (2014) study, women faced a number of obstacles to their vertical advancement, which all referred to parenthood. Having a family is seen as creating a considerable constraint that significantly impacts an academic women's career development mother (Aiston & Jung, 2015). Not only do women struggle more than men with respect to parenting and domestic work but they must also navigate the contradictory position of successful academic and good mother (Aiston & Jung, 2015). Research indicates that women academics with children often feel as though they need to disconnect from their mothering role to be a successful academic, yet to be a good mother, a woman must place children's needs above her own (Raddon, 2002). This points to a choice that often needs to be made of whether to pursue leadership roles or choose to be a mother. In the Asian transnational context, the negative impact of this division of childcare and 'good mother' concept is even more prominent as a result of cultural expectations of women as selfless, good mothers with the bulk of the childcare responsibilities and accompanying pressures falling on the shoulders of women (Aiston & Jung, 2015).

If a higher education institution is committed to gender equality, supporting the childcaring role of women through on-site childcare and flexible work schedules could help overcome barriers created through women's domestic roles. This could provide women with more flexibility in terms of start and finish times of work, reducing the demands on their time while raising young children. Additionally, flexible opportunities with work for women, including flexible scheduling to allow for the family commitments to be met while also meeting work responsibilities would further enable this capability to be met. By supporting women in their caretaker roles, more agency in their professional roles could be experienced. This would provide a considerable benefit for women in the transnational context as they often do not have extended families nearby that could help with childcare, reducing the burden and demands on their time. On-site childcare that offered before and after school care support and periods when schools are closed such as summer and holidays would also help those women with children and allow them the time to flourish in their careers. If this capability is established, there would be fewer barriers facing women, allowing for more opportunity to move into leadership positions.

6. Empowerment and Control over one's environment

Both Robeyns (2003) and Nussbaum (2003) include empowerment as a central capability in their lists. For Nussbaum (2003), this is related to being able to participate effectively in political choices, which is also reflected in Robeyns' (2003). Since this framework is looking at gender in higher education, I have related these capabilities to the workplace in considering the empowerment for decision making within the institution. Empowerment within the workplace can come from the opportunity to weigh in on important decisions. In this way, the interview process can be adjusted to better support women's empowerment by promoting transparency and accountability. This could be further supported through women sitting on every interview panel and having the opportunity to ask questions and weigh in on important hiring decisions. This would provide the right of participation that Nussbaum (2003) advocates for.

An effective interview policy would require training to be mandatory all panel members to understand gender bias. The training would consist of consciousness-raising to expose hidden assumptions and biases regarding the skills and experiences of women in comparison to men (Aiston, 2011). One area of bias is in understanding reasons for gaps in women's CVs as women are often disadvantaged by these gaps in the criteria for hiring and promotions compared to their male colleagues (Boivin et al., 2022). Women taking maternity leave will have gaps in their work record and should not be disadvantaged by these situations because of their familial responsibilities (Jons, 2011). Working towards dismantling this bias can help to equalize opportunities and reduce gender inequality.

CONCLUSION

This chapter has argued that Sen's Capabilities Approach, together with Nussbaum and Robeyns' focus on human capabilities, can be used to unlock human capabilities and reduce gender inequalities when applied to higher education leadership. The Capabilities Approach offers a powerful tool to understand the unequal situation of women in leadership positions and the challenges that they face. By using the Capabilities Approach it is clear that there are barriers to capabilities within institutions that prevent women from converting capabilities into functionings and thriving in leadership positions. In exploring Sen, Nussbaum and Robeyns' arguments, I have suggested that their conception of capabilities can be used to construct a strategic framework to address gender inequality and support women leaders. The approach can have cross-cultural application that can support women leaders at the institutional level in transnational higher education leadership roles.

This chapter discussed six capabilities that can be understood as supportive in this strategic framework. There are other capabilities that are important for Nussbaum (2003) and Robeyns (2003) that are not included in this framework as they are related more to time away from work (such as Nussbaum's (2003) Other Species or Robeyns (2003) Leisure Activities. While these are essential capabilities in gender equality, they extend beyond the context to which this chapter explores. That is not to say that they could not be added as this list is not exhaustive. The process of converting capabilities into functionings is "continuous and iterative with the possibility of developing new capabilities and functionings as time goes on" (Hart, 2019: 554). Like Sen's Capabilities Approach providing an alternative measurement of human development, this chapter provides alternative strategies to support women's development in higher education leadership and setting the conditions for opportunity and agency.

Further exploration into the implementation of this strategic framework can provide valuable insight for leaders in constructing EDI policies and strategies that can address inequality in leadership positions and add to the richness in leadership in transnational higher education, positively impacting the future success of educational institutions. This strategy supposes that reducing the barriers would contribute to conversion factors for which further research is needed. This chapter looked at gender as binary, and therefore may perpetuate bias with regards to those leaders that do not fit into the gender binary, such as queer and trans leaders. Further look into the intersectionality of identities could further establish a bespoke framework of support.

This chapter can add to the wealth of understanding about capabilities, gender inequality and concrete methods that can be used to address issues in inequality. This framework can be used as a strategy to address gender disparities in leadership positions in higher education and work to advance equity and diversity by breaking down barriers that impact women moving into leadership positions. While there may be challenges in implementation of these strategies, addressing gender inequality and supporting female leaders is a matter of justice. Further work in exploring these strategies and working towards wider structural changes can be beneficial to furthering the work towards achieving gender equality.

REFERENCES

Agee, M., & Crocker, T. (2013) Operationalizing the capability approach to assessing well-being, *The Journal of Socio-Economics*, Volume 46, Pages 80-86, ISSN 1053-5357, 10.1016/j.socec.2013.07.003

Aiston, S. J. (2011). Equality, justice and gender: Barriers to the ethical university for women. *Ethics and Education*, 6(3), 279–291. 10.1080/17449642.2011.632721

Aiston, S. J., & Jung, J. (2015). Women academics and research productivity: An international comparison. *Gender and Education*, 27(3), 205–220. https://doi-org.ezproxy.nottingham.edu.cn/10.1080/09540253.2015.1024617. 10.1080/09540253.2015.1024617

Alkire, S. (2002). *Valuing Freedoms. Sen's Capability Approach and Poverty Reduction*. Oxford University Press. 10.1093/0199245797.001.0001

Attel, B., Brown, K., & Treiber, L. (2017). Workplace bullying, perceived job stressors and psychological distress: Gender and race differences in the stress process. *Social Science Research*, 65, 210–221. 10.1016/j.ssresearch.2017.02.00128599773

Boivin, N., Hahn, J., & Sadaf, S. (2022). Outsider Reflecting on Invisible Institutional Gender Norms. In Miller, C. (Eds.), *Leading Change in Gender and Diversity in Higher Education from Margins to Mainstream*. Taylor & Francis Group. 10.4324/9781003286943-13

Bourdieu, P. (1986). The forms of capital. In Richardson, J. (Ed.), *Handbook of Theory and Research for the Sociology of Education*. Greenwood.

David, M. E. (2014). *Feminism, gender and universities: Politics, passion and pedagogies*. Routledge.

Denker, K., & Dougherty, D. (2013). Corporate colonization of couples' work-life negotiations: Rationalization, emotion management and silencing conflict. *Journal of Family Communication*, 13(3), 242–262. 10.1080/15267431.2013.796946

European Commission. (2021) She Figures 2021. The path towards gender equality in research and innovation (R&I). Luxembourg: Publications Office of the European Union. https://op.europa.eu/en/web/eu-law-and-publications/publication-detail/-/publication/61564e1f-d55e-11eb-895a-01aa75ed71a1

Fathima, F., Awor, P., Yen, Y., Gnanaselvam, N., & Zakham, F. (2020). Challenges and coping strategies face by female scientists – A multicentric cross sectional study. *PLoS One*, 15(9), e0238635. 10.1371/journal.pone.023863532956356

Fennell, S., & Arnot, M. (2009). *Gender Education and Equality in a Global Context: Conceptual Frameworks and Policy Perspectives*. Routledge.

Hart, C. (2019). Education, inequality and social justice: A critical analysis applying the Sen-Bourdieu Analytical Framework. *Policy Futures in Education*, 17(5), 582–598. 10.1177/1478210318809758

Jöns, H. (2011). Transnational academic mobility and gender. *Globalisation, Societies and Education*, 9(2), 183–209. 10.1080/14767724.2011.577199

Kim, J. Y., & Meister, A. (2023). Microaggressions, interrupted: The experience and effects of gender microaggressions for women in STEM: JBE. *Journal of Business Ethics*, 185(3), 513–531. 10.1007/s10551-022-05203-0

Mills, C. (2008). Reproduction and transformation of inequalities in schooling: The transformative potential of the theoretical constructs of Bourdieu. *British Journal of Sociology of Education*, 29(1), 79–89. 10.1080/01425690701737481

Mischau, A. (2001). Women in higher education in Europe – a statistical overview. *The International Journal of Sociology and Social Policy*, 21(1/2), 20–31. https://doi-org.ezproxy.nottingham.edu.cn/10.1108/01443330110789529. 10.1108/01443330110789529

Monroe, K., Ozyurt, S., Wrigley, T., & Alexander, A. (2008). Gender equality in academia: Bad news from the trenches, and some possible solutions. *Perspectives on Politics*, 6(2), 215–233. 10.1017/S1537592708080572

Nguyen, T. H. N., Encarnação, C., Amado, F., & Santos, S. (2023). Challenges and success factors of transnational higher education: A systematic review. *Studies in Higher Education*, 48(1), 113–136. 10.1080/03075079.2022.2121813

Nikunen, M. (2014). The 'Entrepreneurial' university, family and gender: Changes and demands faced by fixed-term workers. *Gender and Education*, 26(2), 119–134. 10.1080/09540253.2014.888402

Nussbaum, M. (2000) Women and Human Development: The Capabilities Approach, Cambridge University Press, 2000.

Nussbaum, M. (2003). Capabilities as fundamental entitlements: Sen and social justice. *Feminist Economics*, 9(2/3), 33–59. 10.1080/1354570022000077926

O'Connor, P., Carvalho, T., Vabø, A., & Cardoso, S. (2015). Gender in Higher Education: A Critical Review. In Huisman, J., de Boer, H., Dill, D. D., & Souto-Otero, M. (Eds.), *The Palgrave International Handbook of Higher Education Policy and Governance*. Palgrave Macmillan., 10.1007/978-1-137-45617-5_30

Park, S. (2020). Seeking changes in ivory towers: The impact of gender quotas on female academics in higher education. *Women's Studies International Forum*, 79(February), 102346. https://doi-org.ezproxy.nottingham.edu.cn/10.1016/j.wsif.2020.102346. 10.1016/j.wsif.2020.102346

Raddon, A. (2002). Mothers in the Academy: Positioned and Positioning within Discourses of the 'Successful Academic' and the 'Good Mother'. *Studies in Higher Education*, 27(4), 387–403. 10.1080/0307507022000011516

Rawls, J. (1971). *A theory of justice*. Belknap Press. 10.4159/9780674042605

Robeyns, I. (2003) Sen's capability approach and gender inequality: selecting relevant capabilities, *Feminist Economics*, 9)203), 61-91.

Robeyns, I. (2005). Selecting Capabilities for Quality of Life Measurement. *Social Indicators Research*, 74(1), 191–215. 10.1007/s11205-005-6524-1

Robeyns, I. (2017). *Wellbeing, Freedom and Social Justice: The Capability Approach Re-Examined* (114th ed.). Open Book Publishers. Print 10.11647/OBP.0130

Rosa, R., Drew, E., & Canavan, S. (2020). An overview of gender inequality in EU universities. In Eileen, D., & Canavan, S. (Eds.), *The gender-sensitive university. A contradiction in terms?* (pp. 1–15). Routledge. 10.4324/9781003001348-1

Sang, K. (2018). Gender, ethnicity and feminism: An intersectional analysis of the lived experiences feminist academic women in UK higher education. *Journal of Gender Studies*, 27(2), 192–206. 10.1080/09589236.2016.1199380

Sanger, C., & Gleason, N. (2020). *Diversity and Inclusion in Global Higher Education Lessons from Across Asia* (1st ed. 2020). Springer Nature. 10.1007/978-981-15-1628-3

Sen, A. (1980) 'Equality of What?' In Tanner Lectures on Human Values. Ed. S. M. McMurrin. I. Salt Lake City: University of Utah Press. Reprinted in Sen 1982: 353-69.

Sen, A. (1992). *Inequality re-examined*. Oxford University Press.

Sen, A. (1999). *Development as freedom*. Oxford University Press.

Sen, A. (2009). Capability: Reach and Limit. In *Debating Global Society: Reach and Limits of the Capability Approach* (pp. 15–28). Fondazione Giangiacomo Feltrinelli.

Torino, G., Rivera, D., Capodilupo, C., Nadal, K., & Sue, D. W. (Eds.). (2019). *Microaggressive theory: influence and implications*. John Wiley & Sons, Inc.

UK Office for National Statistics. (2021) [Online]. Available at: https://www.ons.gov.uk/peoplepopulationandcommunity/birthsdeathsandmarriages/lifeexpectancies/bulletins/nationallifetablesunitedkingdom/2018to2020. Accessed 10 February 2024.

Universities, U. K. (2022) The scale of UK higher education transnational education 2020–21. Available: https://www.universitiesuk.ac.uk/universities-uk-international/insights-and-publications/uuki-publications/scale-uk-higher-education-transnational-3. (Accessed 16 February 2024).

University of Nottingham Ningbo China. (2024) Leadership. Available: https://www.nottingham.edu.cn/en/about/university-leadership/university-leadership.aspx [Accessed Feb 2, 2024].

Unterhalter, E., Longlands, H., & Vaughan, R. P. (2022). Gender and Intersecting Inequalities in Education: Reflections on a Framework for Measurement. *Journal of Human Development and Capabilities*, 23(4), 509–538. 10.1080/19452829.2022.2090523

Walker, M. (2006, March). Towards a capability-based theory of social justice for education policy-making. *Journal of Education Policy.Vol.*, (2), 163–185.

Walker, M., & Unterhalter, E. (2007). *Amartya Sen's capability approach and social justice in education*. Palgrave Macmillan. 10.1057/9780230604810

Williams, K. S., & Daniel, H. (2021). Applying Sen's Capabilities Approach to the Delivery of Positive Youth Justice. *Youth Justice*, 21(1), 90–106. https://doi-org.ezproxy.nottingham.edu.cn/10.1177/1473225420953208. 10.1177/1473225420953208

Chapter 2
Women and Leadership in Transnational Higher Education

Ying Feng
Xi'an Jiaotong-Liverpool University, China

ABSTRACT

This chapter investigates the crucial issue of gender representation in leadership within transnational higher education institutions. It presents an analysis of theoretical perspectives on women leaders and investigates the impacts that women leaders bring to the leadership roles by illustrating how the unique perspectives and contributions from women leaders foster global citizenship among students and promote inclusive leadership practices. The chapter then highlights that, despite the advantages of women's leadership and the progress achieved, women continue to face challenges as they move to the leadership roles. Therefore, the chapter further explores the various strategies and initiatives developed to promote gender equity and empower women in leadership roles. It emphasises the need for a supportive environment and highlights the key role various stakeholders play in driving this change, thereby empowering women in leadership roles within transnational higher education.

In recent years, gender representation in leadership positions has become an increasingly prominent issue across various sectors, including higher education. With the rise of globalisation and the growing demand for cross-border exchange, transnational higher education has emerged as a platform for expanded educational opportunities, research collaborations, and cross-cultural interactions. This expansion has presented new prospects for women to participate in leadership roles within this context. However, despite progress towards gender equality, women remain underrepresented in leadership positions in transnational higher education institutions. Extensive research consistently demonstrates a significant underrepresentation of women in top leadership roles, such as university presidents, deans, and department heads, within international educational institutions (Bothwell, 2020). This gender disparity is not limited to specific geographical regions but is a global phenomenon. For instance, a recent study conducted by UNESCO IESALC and Times Higher Education revealed that the average percentage of women in academic leadership positions worldwide, including full professors, deans, chairs, and senior university leaders, stands at a mere 36 percent (UNESCO IESALC & Times Higher Education, 2022).

Despite the persistent underrepresentation of women in transnational higher education leadership, their presence holds significant implications for the sector as a whole. Extensive research consistently highlights that gender-diverse leadership teams contribute to enhanced decision-making, improved organisational performance, and increased innovation (Herring, 2009). By excluding women from

DOI: 10.4018/979-8-3693-2857-6.ch002

leadership positions, transnational higher education institutions miss out on the unique perspectives, experiences, and talents that women bring to the table. In addition to their diverse perspectives, women leaders play a vital role in transnational higher education through their inclusive leadership styles and their ability to serve as role models for students. Their presence promotes gender equity and ensures that decision-making processes consider the needs of all students. Moreover, women leaders contribute to organisational performance by leveraging their unique skills and approaches, fostering global perspectives in the context of a globalized educational landscape, and creating inclusive and equitable environments. By actively supporting women leaders, institutions can tap into diverse talent and effectively navigate the challenges and opportunities presented by transnational higher education.

Given the importance of women's leadership in transnational higher education and the persistent gender gap, it is crucial to understand the underlying reasons for this underrepresentation. Such reasons are evident at both the institutional and systemic levels. Women face various barriers, including limited access to leadership positions, gender biases and stereotypes, cultural expectations, and challenges related to work-life balance. These barriers not only hinder women's career progression but also restrict the diversity of perspectives and experiences in decision-making processes.

Addressing this issue necessitates a comprehensive examination of the development of women in leadership roles within the context of transnational higher education. This examination involves exploring the barriers and challenges that women encounter in their career progression, such as gender biases, limited access to mentoring and networking opportunities, and considerations related to work-life balance (Gurin et al., 2002; Morley, 2013). By understanding these challenges, it becomes possible to identify strategies and interventions that support women's advancement and foster more inclusive leadership environments.

Therefore, this chapter aims to explore the specific context of women's leadership in transnational higher education. It examines the theoretical background underlying women's underrepresentation in leadership and significance of exploring women in leadership, highlights the benefits and impacts of women leadership, analyses the barriers and challenges that women leaders face, and presents recommendations for advancing gender equity within this domain. By shedding light on these issues, this chapter seeks to foster inclusive leadership environments and promote gender equity in the context of transnational higher education.

BACKGROUND AND SIGNIFICANCE OF EXPLORING WOMEN IN LEADERSHIP

Theoretical Background on Gender Diversity in Leadership Positions

Gender equality and the representation of women in leadership positions have been extensively studied and widely debated topics. The persistent underrepresentation of women in leadership roles, including within the higher education sector, has garnered significant attention in recent years (Meschitti & Marini, 2023; Searby et al., 2015). Various theoretical frameworks have been developed to provide insights into the factors contributing to this gender gap. Here, the focus is laid on some widely adopted perspectives and their relevance in exploring the underrepresentation of women in leadership roles is discussed.

Research on Glass Ceiling

One prominent framework in women leadership literature is the glass ceiling, which refers to the invisible barriers that hinder certain groups, particularly women and minorities, from advancing to higher levels of leadership and professional success within organisations (Baxter & Wright, 2000). This perspective suggests that despite possessing the necessary qualifications, skills, and abilities, individuals from underrepresented groups face systemic and societal obstacles that impede their progress and restrict their access to top positions (Alessio & Andrzejewski, 2000).

The term "glass ceiling" implies that individuals can perceive the opportunities and positions above them but are unable to break through and reach those higher levels due to discriminatory practices, biases, and structural barriers. This phenomenon is often attributed to deep-rooted gender and racial biases, stereotypes, and discriminatory practices that persist in many workplaces.

The concept of glass ceiling gained prominence in the 1980s and 1990s as research and studies highlighted the disparities in representation at top management and executive levels (Fierman, 1990; Hymowitz & Schellhardt, 1986; Jacobs, 1992; Reskin & Ross, 1992). It has since expanded to encompass broader diversity and inclusion issues, recognising that multiple factors such as gender, race, ethnicity, age, and other identities intersect to create barriers for underrepresented individuals. Scholars found that the glass ceiling not only affects individual career progression but also has broader implications for organisational diversity, innovation, and competitiveness (Kanter, 1977; Ragins et al., 1998). Organisations that fail to address these barriers may encounter challenges in attracting and retaining talent, as well as miss out on diverse perspectives and experiences necessary for effective decision-making and problem-solving (Kanter, 1977).

In the context of transnational higher education, the glass ceiling can help elucidate the challenges women face as they strive for leadership positions. The concept has been extensively applied to understand women's underrepresentation in higher education (Johnsrud, 1991; Johnsrud & Heck, 1994). A report released by UNESCO IESALC & Times Higher Education in 2021 revealed that glass ceilings persistently limit women's advancement in higher education, and these glass ceilings are often accompanied by wage gaps in many countries (UNESCO IESALC & Times Higher Education, 2021).

Research on Prejudice Against Female Leaders

Another stream of literature on the prejudice against female leaders seeks to explain the biases and discriminatory attitudes faced by women in leadership positions (Rudman et al., 2012). According to this theory, societal and cultural norms, as well as gender stereotypes, contribute to the prevalence of prejudice against women in leadership roles. The theory posits that individuals hold implicit or explicit biases that associate leadership qualities and traits with masculinity (Dodge et al., 1995; Eagly & Karau, 2002; Eagly et al., 2000). These biases often result in the perception that women are less competent, authoritative, or capable of effectively leading compared to their male counterparts. Consequently, women face additional scrutiny and scepticism in leadership positions, and their abilities may be underestimated or undervalued (Biernat & Fuegen, 2001; Foschi, 2000; Heilman et al., 1995).

Many factors contribute to the development and perpetuation of prejudice against female leaders. Socialisation processes, such as gender role expectations and cultural norms, play a significant role in shaping individuals' beliefs and attitudes towards women in leadership. For example, men are usually perceived as undertaking the role of breadwinner and higher status roles, while women are usually perceived as occupying the role of home maker and lower status roles (Eagly, 2000). Besides, other factors such as media representations, organisational practices, and social interactions also contribute to the reinforcement of gender stereotypes and biases.

Research in this area has identified various manifestations of prejudice against female leaders, including the "double bind" phenomenon (Rudman et al., 2012). The double bind refers to the dilemma faced by women in leadership, where they are expected to exhibit both stereotypically masculine qualities (e.g., assertiveness, decisiveness) and stereotypically feminine qualities (e.g., warmth, nurturance). When women display assertiveness, they may be perceived as overly aggressive, while displaying warmth may lead to perceptions of weakness or lack of competence.

Studies have also explored the role of backlash, which refers to negative reactions or punitive judgments towards women who challenge gender norms by aspiring to leadership positions (Fitzgerald, 2013; Rudman & Phelan, 2008). Backlash can manifest in various ways, such as increased scrutiny, criticism, and penalties for assertive behaviour, undermining women's leadership effectiveness and opportunities for advancement (Rudman et al., 2012). Efforts to address prejudice against female leaders involve raising awareness about gender biases and promoting diversity and inclusion in leadership roles. This includes implementing policies and practices that challenge stereotypes, providing mentorship and sponsorship opportunities, and fostering inclusive organisational cultures that value diverse leadership styles.

In conclusion, research on the prejudice against female leaders highlights the biases and discriminatory attitudes faced by women in leadership positions. By understanding and addressing these prejudices, organisations and society can work towards creating more equitable and inclusive environments that allow women to thrive as leaders.

A Short Summary

Introducing theories on women in leadership provides a solid foundation for understanding the complexities and challenges surrounding this topic. By examining these theories, we gain insights into the systemic barriers that hinder women's progress and the need for further investigation. Understanding the theories paves the way for appreciating the significance of exploring this topic in depth, as it allows us to unravel the underlying factors contributing to the gender gap in leadership positions.

Significance of Addressing Women and Leadership in Transnational Higher Education

Addressing gender diversity in transnational higher education is of crucial significance, as it plays a pivotal role in advancing research, informing policy and practice, promoting inclusive practices, and driving meaningful social change. This comprehensive exploration of the subject provides invaluable insights that shape our understanding and guide our actions. Key facets to consider within this domain include:

- **Advancing research and knowledge**

The study of gender diversity in higher education contributes to advancing research and knowledge in the field. By examining the experiences, challenges, and achievements of individuals across the gender spectrum, researchers can uncover insights and generate evidence that informs best practices. Research on gender diversity provides a foundation for understanding the impact of gender biases, stereotypes, and systemic barriers on educational outcomes. It also helps identify effective strategies and interventions to promote gender equity and create inclusive educational environments.

- **Informing policy and practice**

The topic of gender diversity in higher education is essential for informing policy and practice. Through research and evidence-based analysis, policymakers and educational institutions can make informed decisions that promote gender equity, diversity, and inclusion. Understanding the barriers, biases, and systemic factors that hinder gender diversity allows for the development of targeted policies and initiatives to address these issues. By considering the experiences and perspectives of individuals across the gender spectrum, policies and practices can be designed to be more inclusive and equitable.

- **Promoting inclusive practices**

Exploring gender diversity in higher education contributes to the promotion of inclusive practices. By studying the experiences of individuals from diverse gender backgrounds, institutions gain insights into the specific challenges they face and can develop strategies to address them. This includes creating inclusive policies, supporting diverse student populations, implementing gender-sensitive curricula, and fostering inclusive campus climates. By actively embracing gender diversity, institutions can create environments that value and empower individuals of diverse social groups, contributing to a more inclusive and supportive educational experience.

- **Driving social change**

The discussion on gender diversity in higher education plays a significant role in driving social change. By shedding light on the challenges faced by females in higher education, the conversation challenges societal norms, biases, and stereotypes. It promotes critical reflections on gender roles, expectations, and opportunities in higher education and society as a whole. By actively engaging in the discussion on gender diversity, institutions can contribute to dismantling systemic barriers, fostering social justice, and creating a more inclusive and equitable society.

After reflecting on the theoretical background exploring female leaders and the relevance of examining women leaders in transnational higher education, the next section will focus on the benefits of women's representation in transnational higher education leadership.

BENEFITS AND IMPACTS OF GENDER DIVERSITY IN TRANSNATIONAL HIGHER EDUCATION

Gender studies and theories, such as those introduced above, have provided insights into the underlying theoretical mechanisms that contribute to gender inequity, particularly regarding women in leadership positions. This section aims to examine the impacts of women representation in leadership roles. Specifically, the perspective of "the female advantage" will be discussed and incorporated into the understanding of benefits of gender diversity in transnational higher education.

The Female Advantage

"The Female Advantage" is a concept that emerged in the 1990s, highlighting the increasing presence of women in the workplace and emphasising the unique talents, skills, and ideas they bring to the table. Coined by Sally Helgesen in her book titled "The Female Advantage: Women's Ways of Leadership" (1990), this concept focuses on recognising and promoting the strengths and contributions of women in professional settings.

Helgesen's book explores how women's leadership styles, communication skills, and collaborative approaches differ from traditional male leadership styles. She argues that these differences can be advantageous and beneficial in various organisational contexts. By emphasising qualities such as empathy, relationship-building, and consensus-building, "The Female Advantage" challenges the notion that effective leadership is exclusively tied to stereotypically masculine traits. The concept gained attention as it encouraged organisations to value and leverage the diverse perspectives and leadership styles that women bring to the workplace. It aimed to shift the narrative surrounding women's involvement in leadership positions and challenge the biases and barriers that hindered their advancement.

"The Female Advantage" has sparked conversations about the importance of gender diversity in leadership, suggesting that organisations could benefit from a more balanced representation of men and women in decision-making roles. It highlighted the need to create inclusive work environments that value and support women's contributions, ultimately leading to improved organisational performance and outcomes. Since its introduction, "The Female Advantage" has contributed to ongoing discussions and efforts to promote gender equality, diversity, and inclusion in the workplace. It has provided a framework for recognising and valuing women's unique talents and skills while challenging traditional notions of leadership.

The Female Advantage in Higher Education

In the academic arena, the female advantage is manifested by the increased enrolment of women compared to men (Meza-Mejia et al., 2023). According to UNESCO (2021), female enrolment in higher education has tripled globally between 1995 and 2018. From 2000 to 2018, the gross enrolment rate of women increased from 19% to 41%, while that of men increased from 19% to 36%. As a result, the overall number of female undergraduate students has exceeded the number of male undergraduate students since 2002 worldwide. Statistics further show that not only does the number of female undergraduate students exceed that of males, but they are also more likely to complete their higher education (OECD, 2020).

The data also predicts that the gender gap in higher education has reversed in recent decades and the trend is likely to continue in the foreseeable future (UNESCO, 2021). Women have been performing exceptionally well in acquiring human capital compared to their male counterparts, which is considered one of the major social changes in recent history (Williams & Wolniak, 2021). However, studies have pointed out that the female advantage in education has received less attention than the gender gap in the general labour market.

UNESCO (2021) thoroughly investigated the underlying forces driving the female advantage in higher education. According to UNESCO (2021), the underlying forces driving the female advantage in higher education are many and complex. First and foremost, the rapid development of technology and industrialisation worldwide has created a growing demand for educated workers, both male and female (Becker et al., 2010). This increasing demand has been accompanied by institutional developments, such as political changes, which have created a more favourable legal environment for female enrolment in higher education. Additionally, cultural changes have gradually occurred. For example, surveys in Germany regarding women's retention in their jobs after marriage show a decrease in the proportion of respondents agreeing that women should leave their jobs after marriage and take full responsibility for their families, dropping from 57% in 1982 to below 30% in 2008 (Riphahn & Schwientek, 2015). The combined influence of institutional and cultural forces has provided a more favourable environment for women to receive proper education in higher education institutions and has enabled them to display their advantages in academic performance and a growing presence in the job market.

UNESCO (2021) also highlighted that, in addition to institutional and cultural changes, the reduced costs and enhanced benefits associated with the female advantage have contributed to the reversal of the educational gender gap (Becker et al., 2010). These reduced costs and increased benefits stem from gender differences in various aspects, including cognitive and non-cognitive skills. Indeed, research suggests that women usually possess better non-cognitive skills, which help reduce the total costs of education and, consequently, increase the total returns on education (Becker et al., 2010).

The Female Advantage as Reflected in Women's Leadership in Transnational Higher Education

Gender diversity and representation in leadership positions play a crucial role in shaping the academic landscape and fostering inclusive and equitable educational institutions, particularly in the context of transnational higher education. The female advantage, observed in women's leadership, brings numerous benefits to these institutions. Women leaders often contribute to more innovative and inclusive decision-making processes, enhancing organisational performance. Moreover, diverse leadership teams serve as role models for future generations of aspiring leaders. Research has consistently shown that gender-diverse leadership teams contribute to positive outcomes, fostering inclusive and globally oriented educational environments. Therefore, this part will explore the specific advantages associated with women's leadership within transnational higher education institutions.

- **Enhanced intercultural understanding**

Transnational higher education institutions cater to diverse student populations from different cultural backgrounds. Women leaders, with their diverse perspectives and experiences, can contribute to enhanced intercultural understanding and appreciation (Madsen, 2012; Longman & Madsen, 2014). Their leadership can promote inclusivity, cultural sensitivity, and cross-cultural dialogue, fostering an environment where students from various backgrounds feel valued and supported. Women leaders bring unique insights into navigating cultural differences and can serve as role models for students aspiring to develop their intercultural competence. Their leadership facilitated the formation of multicultural student groups, promoting collaborative learning and intercultural exchanges.

- **Improved decision-making in cross-cultural settings**

In the transnational higher education context, decision-making often involves navigating complex cross-cultural dynamics. Gender diversity brings a variety of perspectives, experiences, and insights to the decision-making processes within transnational higher education. By having leaders from diverse gender backgrounds, institutions can benefit from a wider range of ideas and approaches, leading to more innovative solutions and strategies. Studies have shown that gender-diverse leadership teams perform better in decision-making processes due to the diverse perspectives they bring in various contexts (Nielsen & Huse, 2010). Women leaders can offer alternative viewpoints and approaches, challenging groupthink and promoting more comprehensive and culturally sensitive decision-making. Their presence can increase the likelihood of considering multiple perspectives, resulting in more effective and inclusive strategies and policies (Ely & Padavic, 2007). Furthermore, when groups consist of individuals with diverse opinions, they are compelled to thoroughly process information pertaining to group tasks. This process can prevent the group from hastily choosing a course of action solely based on apparent consensus (Rao & Tilt, 2016; van Knippenberg et al., 2004).

As women leaders contribute to a more inclusive decision-making environment, their involvement in higher education could also lead to a broader consideration of diverse perspectives, resulting in decisions that are better aligned with the needs and aspirations of the institution's diverse stakeholders.

- **Creation of inclusive learning environments**

Moreover, gender diversity in leadership positions promotes equal representation and opportunities for individuals within transnational higher education. It helps create an inclusive environment where all voices are heard and valued, regardless of gender. This fosters a sense of belonging and supports the holistic development of students and professionals.

Transnational higher education institutions strive to create inclusive learning environments that cater to the needs of globally diverse student populations. Women leaders, through their inclusive leadership practices, can drive the creation of such environments. They can champion initiatives that address gender equity, diversity, and inclusion, ensuring that students from all backgrounds have equal opportunities to thrive (Morley, 2013). Women leaders are frequently found to engage in more democratic and participative forms of decision making and leadership (Eagly & Carli, 2007; Eagly & Johannesen-Schmidt, 2001). They also tend to emphasise and support learning among individuals they work with (Longman & Madson, 2014). Hence, in the context of higher education, as women leaders are approachable, accessible, and responsive to students' diverse needs, it will create a sense of belonging and empowerment among the student body. By fostering inclusive learning environments, women leaders could contribute to student success, well-being, and overall satisfaction.

- **Fostering global citizenship**

Women leaders in transnational higher education institutions can play a pivotal role in fostering global citizenship among students through bringing a sense of common purpose, collective good, or collective vision (Astin & Leland, 1991; Safarik, 2003). Gender-diverse leadership teams also serve as role models for aspiring leaders, particularly individuals from underrepresented genders. Visible representation of diverse leadership encourages and inspires individuals to pursue their aspirations and overcome barriers. Research on women's approach to leadership also shows that women tend to engage community when proposing initiatives for change (Longman & Madsen, 2014). Through their leadership and example, they can promote the values of global engagement, social responsibility, and cultural understanding. They can inspire students to become active participants in the global community, encouraging them to develop a sense of responsibility toward addressing global challenges and promoting positive change.

In summary, women's leadership in transnational higher education institutions brings a range of benefits. These benefits extend beyond the immediate team dynamic and have far-reaching implications for the academic sector at large. Women leaders contribute to enhanced intercultural understanding, improved decision-making in cross-cultural settings, the creation of inclusive learning environments, and fostering of global citizenship. Their unique perspectives and contributions foster global citizenship among students and promote inclusive leadership practices. Embracing gender diversity in transnational higher education leadership is not only a matter of fairness and equity but also a strategic advantage. It enhances organisational performance, fosters innovation, and contributes to the cultivation of inclusive and transformative learning environments. Therefore, recognising and supporting women's leadership in transnational higher education institutions is vital for creating inclusive and globally oriented academic communities.

CHALLENGES FACED BY WOMEN LEADERS IN TRANSNATIONAL HIGHER EDUCATION

Despite the advantages of women's leadership and the progress achieved, challenges persist. Women continue to face numerous challenges and barriers. Obstacles such as implicit biases, lack of mentorship and networking opportunities, work-life balance considerations, and cultural expectations still impede women's ability to advance into leadership roles and hinder their career progression. It is crucial to understand and address these challenges to create a more inclusive and diverse leadership landscape in transnational higher education. This section will examine the specific obstacles that impede women's access to leadership positions and hinder their career progression. It will also shed light on the impact of gender expectations, biases, and stereotypes within these institutions, as well as the unique work-life balance challenges faced by women leaders in the context of global mobility.

Glass Ceilings for Females in Academia

Based on the discussions in the previous section surrounding the female advantage in academia, driven by various forces at different levels, it is natural to consider the statistics on women's representation in academia, particularly in higher education, as rather inspiring. Indeed, there have been developments in promoting equality in women's access to higher education due to institutional, cultural, and gender-specific changes in recent history. However, the apparent female advantage in higher education does not necessarily lead to gender equality after graduation from college. For example, OECD data shows that in most OECD countries, the number of female students pursuing higher degrees after undergraduate studies, including Master's and Doctoral degrees, is lower than that of male students (OECD, 2020).

Similarly, the female advantage does not translate into encouraging changes in female representation at decision-making levels in academia (Meza-Mejia et al., 2023). The underrepresentation of women in leadership positions in academia has been a subject of investigation for a long time. As previously mentioned, UNESCO IESALC and Times Higher Education revealed that the average percentage of women in academic leadership positions worldwide, including full professors, deans, chairs, and senior university leaders, stands at a mere 36 percent (UNESCO IESALC & Times Higher Education, 2022). Furthermore, the distribution of women in leadership roles across countries and regions is not balanced (Wright et al., 1995). For instance, while some countries have made significant strides in promoting gender diversity, others lag behind. While different countries may display contrasting levels of development in women's representation in leadership roles in higher education, the median score of average representation falls between 30 to 40 across different regions (UNESCO IESALC & Times Higher Education, 2022).

The phenomenon of vertical sex segregation or gender inequality in career progression has been extensively explored in the literature. For example, researchers have used the concept of "the leaking pipeline" to describe the decreasing proportion of women at higher levels in an organisation (Camp, 1997). In a study conducted by Freeman et al. (2020), the authors demonstrate that, on average, it takes 3.5 years longer for women to be promoted to full professor than men in the US, even when holding similar qualifications (Freeman et al., 2020).

Barriers and Challenges for Women Leaders in Transnational Higher Education

The underrepresentation of women in leadership roles within transnational higher education can be attributed to various prevalent obstacles and challenges. The subsequent discussion in this section will scrutinise the common barriers hindering women's rise to leadership and the specific challenges they encounter within these roles.

- **Gender expectations, biases, and stereotypes often shape perceptions of leadership suitability.**

Gender expectations, biases, and stereotypes pose significant barriers to women leaders in transnational higher education institutions. These institutions often operate within cultural contexts where traditional gender roles and expectations persist, influencing perceptions of leadership effectiveness and appropriateness. Deeply ingrained stereotypes concerning leadership roles can lead to unconscious biases against women, affecting their opportunities for advancement. Traditional gender norms that associate leadership with masculine traits can create obstacles for women leaders, as they may face higher expectations, scepticism, and prejudice when seeking leadership positions (Ely & Padavic, 2007).

Stereotypes associating leadership with assertiveness, competitiveness, and decisiveness can create a mismatch between societal expectations and the leadership behaviour exhibited by women (Ely & Padavic, 2007). Women leaders may face pressures to conform to masculine leadership styles, while simultaneously receiving criticism for being too assertive or not conforming to traditional gender norms (Morley, 2013). They may also face discrimination associated with the specific academic "cultures", which may associate male as more suitable for a particular discipline, such as engineering and computer science (Kulis et al., 2002). These biases and stereotypes can undermine women's confidence, diminish their opportunities for advancement, and perpetuate gender inequalities within these institutions.

Moreover, the intersectionality of gender with other aspects of identity, such as race, ethnicity, and nationality, further complicates the challenges faced by women leaders. Women from marginalised or underrepresented groups may experience additional barriers due to multiple layers of discrimination and bias. Intersectional perspectives are essential for understanding the unique challenges faced by women leaders from diverse backgrounds within transnational higher education institutions.

- **Limited mentorship and sponsorship opportunities can hinder women's career progression.**

Studies have consistently demonstrated the positive impact of mentorship and sponsorship on career progression. Mentorship provides valuable guidance and advice, while sponsorship involves actively advocating for someone's advancement within an organisation and opening doors to opportunities. For instance, research has shown that employees who receive mentoring are more likely to receive promotions and salary increases (Allen et al., 2004; Eby et al., 2008).

However, despite the crucial role that mentorship and sponsorship play in career advancement, women often face challenges in accessing these opportunities due to gender dynamics and power imbalances within institutions (Morley, 2013). A recent report by McKinsey & Company further highlighted this issue, revealing that men are more likely to receive the mentorship and sponsorship they need, particularly when they work on-site. This disparity is even more pronounced for women of colour (Field et al., 2023).

The lack of female role models and mentors further compounds the problem, as it limits the guidance and support available to aspiring women leaders. This limitation makes it more challenging for women to navigate the complexities of advancing their careers. Consequently, women are often at a disadvantage when it comes to accessing the necessary mentorship and sponsorship that can facilitate their professional growth.

- **Women face challenges in receiving support and encouragement when it comes to research time.**

In the realm of academia, there exists a concerning trend that often places women at a disadvantage when it comes to career advancement. Despite sharing similar overall time commitments to their employment, female faculty members, particularly those who are mothers of young children, tend to devote less time to research compared to their male counterparts in research-intensive universities. This finding was highlighted by Misra et al. (2021), shedding light on the disparities in time allocation between male and female faculty members.

Misra et al. (2021) uncovered that male faculty members are often better able to secure dedicated research time compared to their female counterparts. One of the contributing factors to this imbalance is the differing roles that male and female faculty members often assume within the academic setting. Women are frequently encouraged to dedicate a significant amount of their time to teaching and engaging with students, which is undoubtedly an essential aspect of their professional responsibilities. However, such activities are not necessarily considered critical criteria for promotion, especially when it comes to leadership positions like that of full professors (Drake & Svenkerud, 2023).

While women tend to allocate more time to university service and student-related activities, such as teaching and mentoring, men can allocate more time to research. Consequently, male faculty members may have a more substantial research output, which is often a critical factor in promotion decisions. This disparity in the evaluation of research versus teaching and mentoring duties can inadvertently hinder the career progression of women in academia.

- **Women face lack of transparency when it comes to the qualification process and criteria.**

In the face of the challenges and barriers ahead, some researchers found that women in academia may face dilemmas when aiming for a promotional opportunity. For example, Drake & Svenkerud (2023) found that while women have the ambition in the sense that they desire the promotion and the impacts that come with the position, a number of conditions could impact whether they could realise their goals to be promoted to leadership positions, such as full professors. These conditions include more time investment into the process, more resources demanded, and transparency in the qualification process.

Therefore, another barrier that women face in their pursuit of leadership positions in academia is the lack of transparency in the qualification process and criteria. Research studies have shown that unclear promotion guidelines and subjective evaluation criteria can create ambiguity and hinder the advancement of female academics (Freeman et al, 2020). This lack of transparency may contribute to biases and inequalities in the promotion process, making it difficult for women to navigate and understand the expectations for career progression.

- **Women face work-life balance challenges and global mobility.**

Women leaders in transnational higher education institutions often encounter distinct work-life balance challenges, particularly in the context of global mobility. The nature of these institutions necessitates frequent international travel, long working hours, and demanding responsibilities, which can strain personal and family life.

The global mobility required for leadership roles can create difficulties for women who may face additional caregiving responsibilities, resulting in challenges in maintaining a healthy work-life balance (Morley, 2013). The lack of family-friendly policies, such as flexible working arrangements and adequate support for childcare, can further exacerbate these challenges. Balancing professional demands with personal responsibilities can lead to stress, burnout, and compromises in career progression for women leaders.

Reflecting on the factors underlying the challenges facing female underrepresentation in leadership positions in higher education, it can be inferred that some fundamental factors, such as cultural norms, institutional practices, and global mobility patterns significantly influence gender diversity within transnational higher education leadership. Cultural norms and expectations regarding gender roles can shape perceptions of leadership suitability, affecting women's access to leadership positions. Institutional practices related to recruitment, promotion criteria, and decision-making processes can unintentionally perpetuate gender biases, limiting women's opportunities for advancement (Morley, 2013). Moreover, patterns of global mobility in academia may contribute to gender disparities, as certain regions and cultures may be more or less accessible to women in terms of career opportunities and work-life balance.

It is also crucial to consider the intersectionality of gender with other identities in the transnational context. Factors such as nationality, language proficiency, and cultural background can intersect with gender, further shaping the experiences and opportunities available to women in transnational higher education leadership. Understanding the complex interplay of these factors provides a more holistic understanding of the development of gender diversity in transnational higher education leadership.

In conclusion, women leaders in transnational higher education institutions encounter various challenges and barriers. Addressing these challenges requires proactive measures, such as promoting gender-inclusive leadership cultures, providing mentorship and sponsorship opportunities, challenging biases and stereotypes, clarifying promotion criteria, and implementing family-friendly policies. By overcoming these obstacles, transnational higher education institutions can create more equitable and inclusive environments that harness the full potential of women leaders. This will be the focus for the next section.

STRATEGIES FOR PROMOTING GENDER DIVERSITY IN TRANSNATIONAL HIGHER EDUCATION LEADERSHIP

To address the challenges and barriers faced by women leaders in transnational higher education institutions, various strategies and initiatives have been developed to promote gender equity and empower women in leadership roles. This section will explore a range of existing programs, policies, and interventions that could play a positive role in supporting women leaders within the transnational higher education context. Specifically, it will emphasise the significance of mentorship, networking, cross-cultural leadership development opportunities, institutional commitment to diversity and inclusion, and the creation of supportive environments that address the unique challenges faced by women leaders.

- **Provide leadership development programs**

Leadership development programs, policies, and interventions play a crucial role in promoting gender equity and supporting women leaders in transnational higher education institutions. Researchers have highlighted the positive impacts of women-only opportunities, where women participate in training programs specifically designed for their leadership development (Madsen et al., 2012). These programs aim to address the unique challenges and differences that women may face in their pursuit of higher positions.

Women-only training programs are tailored to the specific needs of women leaders and have proven successful in enhancing their leadership capabilities and self-confidence. These programs offer a range of activities, such as workshops, seminars, and training sessions, which focus on key areas like self-confidence building, career planning, navigating academic politics, and addressing the specific challenges encountered by women leaders (Bonebright et al., 2012, Swan Dagen et al., 2022). An example of such a programme is the Aurora Leadership Development Programme launched by Advance HE. Targeting early-career female academics, this programme provides women with essential leadership skills, helping build their confidence and sense of leadership identity. The effectiveness of this approach is underlined by a follow-up study conducted by Barnard et al. (2022). The study surveyed 1094 participants in the programme and found that it significantly impacted participants' behaviours and attitudes. Importantly, these improvements did not diminish over time.

Moreover, cross-cultural leadership development programs play a vital role in preparing women leaders for the unique challenges of transnational higher education institutions. These programs focus on enhancing intercultural competence, understanding different cultural contexts, and developing skills necessary for effective leadership in diverse environments (Morley, 2013). By equipping women leaders with the tools to navigate cultural complexities, these programs empower them to embrace and lead in globalised educational settings.

By providing structured initiatives that address the specific needs of women leaders, these programs empower and prepare them for senior leadership roles within transnational higher education institutions. They offer valuable skills, competencies, and support systems to help women overcome barriers, excel in their careers, and contribute effectively to the advancement of gender equity in higher education.

- **Promote mentorship and networking**

Promoting mentorship and networking opportunities is crucial for facilitating the advancement of women leaders in transnational higher education institutions. By establishing formal and informal mentorship programs, women leaders can connect with experienced professionals who can provide valuable guidance, support, and access to networks and resources (Ely & Padavic, 2007). These mentorship programs create a structured framework for building relationships and fostering professional development.

Formal mentorship programs can be implemented at institutional levels or within specific departments or disciplines. They involve pairing women leaders with mentors who have relevant expertise and experience (Hill & Wheat, 2017). Clear guidelines, expectations, and goals should be established for both mentors and mentees to ensure a productive and meaningful mentoring relationship (Devos, 2008). This formal structure provides a framework for regular interactions, goal setting, and tracking progress.

In addition to formal programs, informal mentorship relationships can also play a significant role in supporting women leaders (Hill & Wheat, 2017). Informal mentorship allows women leaders to seek out mentors within their networks, professional associations, or academic conferences. These relationships can be based on shared interests, expertise, or personal connections (Searby et al., 2015). Informal mentorship offers flexibility and can supplement formal programs by providing additional perspectives and support (Barnard et al., 2022).

To enhance the effectiveness of mentorship, it is essential to provide training and resources for mentors. Mentors can benefit from workshops or seminars that focus on effective mentoring techniques, communication skills, and an understanding of the unique challenges faced by women leaders in transnational higher education. Equipping mentors with the necessary skills and knowledge ensures that they can provide valuable guidance and support tailored to the needs of women leaders.

Networking events, conferences, and workshops are also instrumental in promoting mentorship and networking opportunities. Researchers also emphasise that both professional networks within and beyond women's own institution have benefits (Baltodano et al., 2012). These gatherings bring together women leaders from different institutions, creating opportunities for networking, knowledge sharing, and building professional connections. By actively participating in these events, women leaders can expand their networks and cultivate relationships with individuals who can offer insights, support, and potential career opportunities.

In today's digital age, online platforms and communities provide additional avenues for mentorship and networking. Institutions can create online platforms where women leaders can connect virtually, facilitating networking, information sharing, and mentorship opportunities. These platforms transcend geographical boundaries and time zones, allowing women leaders to connect with professionals from diverse backgrounds and experiences. The Association for Women in Science (AWIS) represents an exemplary online platform utilised by universities. AWIS confers a comprehensive tool that universities harness to support their women in STEM, offering a rich array of resources such as webinars and a career centre, geared towards facilitating knowledge exchange and fostering professional development. Universities utilise this platform to afford their faculty a broader network and an expanded repertoire of resources. They direct their staff, particularly women engaged in STEM, towards AWIS to take advantage of networking, mentorship, and career advancement opportunities. Prominent institutions like Stanford University and Duke University, are proactive in endorsing the use of AWIS within their faculty.

By implementing strategies to promote mentorship and networking, institutions can create a supportive environment that fosters the growth and advancement of women leaders in transnational higher education. These opportunities provide women leaders with the guidance, support, and networks necessary to overcome barriers and navigate their professional journeys more effectively.

- **Enhance institutional commitment to diversity and inclusion**

Promoting gender equity within transnational higher education institutions requires a strong institutional commitment to diversity and inclusion. Institutions should prioritise creating policies and practices that foster a supportive and inclusive environment for women leaders. This includes implementing gender-sensitive recruitment and promotion processes, ensuring equitable access to leadership positions, and addressing unconscious biases and stereotypes through awareness campaigns and training programs.

Furthermore, institutional support for work-life balance is essential to enable women leaders to thrive. Implementing family-friendly policies, such as flexible working arrangements, on-site childcare facilities, and maternity leave, can help alleviate the work-life conflict faced by women leaders in transnational higher education institutions (Morley, 2013). One evidence of institutions recognising and accommodating the unique needs and responsibilities of women leaders is the implementation of "tenure clock extension" policies. These policies allow faculty members, particularly women experiencing significant life events like childbirth, to postpone their tenure reviews, thus giving them sufficient time to balance personal obligations with professional progression. Many institutions, such as the University of California system, have demonstrated commitment to this approach by extending tenure clocks in response to major life events.

It is also crucial for institutions to understand that these policies should be supplemented with continuous supportive measures to ensure their effectiveness. These could encompass comprehensive return-to-work schemes, workload redistribution, post-leave support systems, and access to mental and physical health services. By putting these supportive measures into place alongside key policies, institutions can foster an environment that facilitates the success and career advancement of women leaders.

- **Create supportive regulatory environments**

Research also shows that it is important to create regulations to ensure that institutions could take fair and systematic actions to achieve diversity and inclusion (Morais et al., 2022). Policymakers play a crucial role in shaping the regulatory frameworks and incentives that encourage transnational higher education institutions to prioritise gender equity.

Governments should advocate for policies that promote gender diversity in leadership roles. They should enact laws and policies that explicitly regulate the criteria for evaluating candidates (Drake & Svenkerud, 2023). Furthermore, these laws should strictly prohibit gender discrimination throughout the entirety of a career, including during employment processes, promotions, and, where applicable, tenure decisions. Having such measures in place is crucial. Countries like the UK and Canada exemplify the positive effects of such proactive governmental role. For instance, the UK established the Athena SWAN (Scientific Women's Academic Network) Charter in 2005. Although not law, this "soft regulation" recognises higher education institutions that support gender equality. Universities with an Athena SWAN award can benefit in research funding decisions due to the prestige and reputation associated with the award. In Canada, the government has implemented various policies and measures to promote gender diversity. Notably, the government-funded Canada Research Chairs Program (CRCP) incorporates an Equity, Diversity and Inclusion (EDI) Action Plan. This plan is intended to redress the balance of the underrepresentation of women, and other designated groups, in top-tier research positions. These initiatives and policies demonstrate their governments' commitment towards promoting gender diversity in academia.

Governments and policymakers could also support research on gender-related issues, and provide funding or incentives for initiatives aimed at advancing gender equity. For example, governments could designate funds specifically for leadership development programs targeting women in academia. Furthermore, additional financial incentives, such as extra budgetary allocations or research grants might also be offered to institutions that demonstrate a strong commitment to gender equality in leadership.

However, establishing regulations and providing funding is not enough. Governments must also ensure the rigorous enforcement of these policies and regulations. Regular audits and follow-ups should be conducted to ensure that universities are not only formulating but are also effectively implementing these gender equity policies.

To promote accountability and transparency, governments could require institutions to publicly disclose gender-related data, such as data about the gender distribution in various roles, pay gap analysis, gender-based complaints, and initiatives undertaken to address gender disparities. On that basis, systematic review and monitoring mechanisms are also essential for the successful implementation of policy measure. Government should also form independent committees or departments to regularly assess the effectiveness and impact of gender equality policies. The insights gathered could then further inform necessary amendments to existing policies or the creation of more relevant measures.

In conclusion, promoting gender equity in transnational higher education institutions requires a multifaceted approach. Programs, policies, and interventions such as mentorship, networking, cross-cultural leadership development, institutional commitment, and supportive macro environments are essential in supporting and empowering women leaders. By implementing these strategies and creating supportive environments, transnational higher education institutions can effectively address the challenges faced by women leaders and cultivate a more equitable and inclusive educational landscape.

CONCLUSION

This chapter presents a reflective analysis of the background, significance, and impacts of promoting gender diversity and equity in transnational higher education institutions. It also critically examines the challenges and barriers faced by women leaders within this context, emphasising the need for concerted strategies to address these complexities and foster a more inclusive and equitable environment for women in leadership roles. In conclusion, this section aims to summarise the key points discussed and call upon stakeholders to take actions in advancing gender equity in transnational higher education.

Summary of Key Points

Gender diversity and representation in leadership positions within transnational higher education institutions are pivotal for fostering inclusive and equitable academic environments. By ensuring that leadership roles reflect the diversity of their student populations, these institutions embrace the power of multiple perspectives and experiences, igniting a transformative impact. Extensive research consistently showcases the profound benefits of gender-diverse leadership teams, which fuel innovation, drive organisational performance, and serve as inspiring role models for aspiring leaders (Dezsö & Ross, 2012; Hoogendoorn et al., 2013; Young et al., 2013).

Moreover, gender diversity in leadership positions within transnational higher education institutions empowers these institutions to navigate complex cross-cultural dynamics and cater to culturally diverse student populations with unwavering proficiency. Women leaders, equipped with their rich tapestry of perspectives and experiences, bring forth unique insights that foster intercultural understanding and appreciation among students. They excel in cross-cultural decision-making, ensuring comprehensive outcomes that honour diverse perspectives and promote cultural sensitivity. Women leaders also spearhead the creation of inclusive learning environments, championing initiatives that cultivate an atmosphere of equity, diversity, and inclusion. Furthermore, they play an instrumental role in nurturing a sense of global citizenship, inspiring students to become engaged, responsible global citizens who embrace diverse cultures and perspectives.

The specific advantages associated with women's leadership in the transnational context serve as compelling testimonials to the transformative power of gender diversity within educational institutions. They encompass enhanced intercultural understanding, refined decision-making in cross-cultural settings, the creation of inclusive learning environments, and the cultivation of global citizenship among students. By embracing gender diversity in leadership positions, transnational higher education institutions unlock the full potential of diverse perspectives, propelling them towards a future of inclusive excellence, enlightened innovation, and global engagement.

Promoting gender equity in transnational higher education institutions is not only a matter of fairness and social justice but also a strategic imperative. Women's leadership brings unique perspectives, experiences, and skills that contribute to effective decision-making, innovation, and organisational performance. Embracing gender diversity in leadership positions enhances institutional reputation, fosters creativity, and creates a more inclusive educational environment that benefits students, staff, and the broader society.

The examination of women's representation in higher education reveals both progress and persistent challenges. Over the years, there has been a notable increase in the enrolment of women in higher education institutions, reflecting improved access and opportunities for female students. Efforts to address gender disparities have resulted in the formulation and implementation of policies and initiatives aimed at promoting gender equity and inclusivity. However, despite these advancements, significant gender gaps remain, particularly in leadership positions within higher education. Women continue to be underrepresented in senior administrative roles, department chairs, and academic leadership positions. This underrepresentation limits the diversity of perspectives and experiences in decision-making processes and affects the overall institutional culture.

The existing barriers to women's advancement in higher education are multifaceted and complex. They encompass systemic biases, cultural norms, implicit biases, and structural obstacles that hinder the progress of women in academia. Addressing these challenges requires a comprehensive approach that includes leadership development programs, mentorship and networking opportunities, fully committed higher education institutions, and supportive macro environments.

Moving forward, ongoing research, collaboration, and the implementation of evidence-based practices will be essential in driving meaningful change. By addressing the underlying systemic issues and fostering a culture of inclusivity and gender equity, higher education institutions can lead the way in empowering women and ensuring their full participation and representation in all aspects of academia.

Call to Action: Advancing Gender Equity in Leadership in Transnational Higher Education

As stated, addressing the challenges and barriers faced by women leaders in transnational higher education institutions essentially requires collective action from various stakeholders. Collaboration is key among transnational higher education institutions, policymakers, researchers, and relevant organizations in promoting gender equity and in creating supportive environments for women leaders.

Transnational higher education institutions should prioritise gender diversity and inclusion by implementing recommended strategies and initiatives tailored to the transnational context. This includes establishing formal mentoring programs, providing cross-cultural leadership development opportunities, and integrating gender-sensitive policies and practices. Institutions must also foster a culture that challenges biases and stereotypes, promotes work-life balance, and ensures equitable access to leadership positions.

It's also important to identify the areas that demand imperative attention and specify the programmatic priorities given the wide array of needs (Madsen et al., 2012).

Policymakers play a significant part in shaping regulations and creating incentives that motivate transnational higher education institutions to focus on gender equity. Their role includes promoting policies that encourage a diverse gender representation in leadership positions, backing research on issues around gender, and allocating funds for initiatives dedicated to promoting gender equity.

Researchers have a responsibility to generate evidence and knowledge that inform effective strategies and interventions for promoting gender equity in transnational higher education leadership. By conducting rigorous research, identifying best practices, and evaluating the impact of interventions, researchers can contribute to the development of evidence-based policies and practices.

In conclusion, advancing gender equity in transnational higher education leadership is a pressing and ongoing challenge that requires concerted efforts. It is essential to recognise the value and contributions that women leaders bring to the table. By providing equal opportunities for women to assume leadership positions, institutions can tap into a broader range of perspectives, experiences, and insights. This diversity of thought fosters innovation, enhances decision-making processes, and ultimately improves organisational performance.

REFERENCES:

Alessio, J. C., & Andrzejewski, J. (2000). Unveiling the hidden glass ceiling: An analysis of the cohort effect claim. *American Sociological Review*, 65(2), 311–315. 10.1177/000312240006500209

Allen, T. D., Eby, L. T., Poteet, M. L., Lentz, E., & Lima, L. (2004). Career benefits associated with mentoring for protégés: A meta-analysis. *The Journal of Applied Psychology*, 89(1), 127–136. 10.1037/0021-9010.89.1.12714769125

Astin, H. S., & Leland, C. (1991). *Women of Influence, Women of Vision: A Cross-Generational Study of Leaders and Social Change*. Jossey-Bass.

Baltodano, J. C., Carlson, S., Jackson, L. W., & Mitchell, W. (2012). Networking to leadership in higher education: National and state-based programs and networks for developing women. *Advances in Developing Human Resources*, 14(1), 62–78. 10.1177/1523422311428926

Barnard, S., Arnold, J., Bosley, S., & Munir, F. (2022). The personal and institutional impacts of a mass participation leadership programme for women working in higher education: A longitudinal analysis. *Studies in Higher Education*, 47(7), 1372–1385. 10.1080/03075079.2021.1894117

Baxter, J., & Wright, E. O. (2000). The glass ceiling hypothesis: A comparative study of the United States, Sweden, and Australia. *Gender & Society*, 14(2), 275–294. 10.1177/089124300014002004

Becker, G. S., Hubbard, W. H., & Murphy, K. M. (2010). Explaining the worldwide boom in higher education of women. *Journal of Human Capital*, 4(3), 203–241. 10.1086/657914

Biernat, M., & Fuegen, K. (2001). Shifting standards and the evaluation of competence: Complexity in gender-based judgment and decision making. *The Journal of Social Issues*, 57(4), 707–724. 10.1111/0022-4537.00237

Bonebright, D. A., Cottledge, A. D., & Lonnquist, P. (2012). Developing women leaders on campus: A human resources–women's center partnership at the University of Minnesota. *Advances in Developing Human Resources*, 14(1), 79–95. 10.1177/1523422311429733

Bothwell, E. (2020). Female leadership in top universities advances for first time since 2017. *Times Higher Education*. https://www.timeshighereducation.com/news/female-leadership-top-universities-advances-first-time-2017

Camp, T. (1997). The incredible shrinking pipeline. *Communications of the ACM*, 40(10), 103–110. 10.1145/262793.262813

Devos, A. (2008). Where enterprise and equity meet: The rise of mentoring for women in Australian universities. *Discourse (Abingdon)*, 29(2), 195–205. 10.1080/01596300801966831

Dezsö, C. L., & Ross, D. G. (2012). Does female representation in top management improve firm performance? A panel data investigation. *Strategic Management Journal*, 33(9), 1072–1089. 10.1002/smj.1955

Dodge, K. A., Gilroy, F. D., & Fenzel, L. M. (1995). Requisite management characteristics revisited: Two decades later. *Journal of Social Behavior and Personality*, 10, 253–264.

Drake, I., & Svenkerud, S. W. (2023). Career ambitions of women academics: Are women willing and able to rise to the top in higher education institutions? *Studies in Higher Education*, 1–12. Advance online publication. 10.1080/03075079.2023.2272742

Eagly, A. H., & Carli, L. L. (2007). Women and the labyrinth of leadership. *Harvard Business Review*, 85(9), 62–71.17886484

Eagly, A. H., & Johannesen-Schmidt, M. C. (2001). The leadership styles of women and men. *The Journal of Social Issues*, 57(4), 781–797. 10.1111/0022-4537.00241

Eagly, A. H., & Karau, S. J. (2002). Role congruity theory of prejudice toward female leaders. *Psychological Review*, 109(3), 573–598. 10.1037/0033-295X.109.3.57312088246

Eagly, A. H., Wood, W., & Diekman, A. B. (2000). Social role theory of sex differences and similarities: A current appraisal. In Eckes, T., & Trautner, H. M. (Eds.), *The developmental social psychology of gender* (pp. 123–174). Erlbaum.

Eby, L. T., Allen, T. D., Evans, S. C., Ng, T., & Dubois, D. (2008). Does mentoring matter? A multidisciplinary meta-analysis comparing mentored and non-mentored individuals. *Journal of Vocational Behavior*, 72(2), 254–267. 10.1016/j.jvb.2007.04.00519343074

Ely, R. J., & Padavic, I. (2007). A feminist analysis of organizational research on sex differences. *Academy of Management Review*, 32(4), 1121–1143. 10.5465/amr.2007.26585842

Field, E., Krivkovich, A., Kügele, S., Robinson, N., & Yee, L. (2023, October 5). Women in the workplace 2023, Mckinsey & Company, https://www.mckinsey.com/featured-insights/diversity-and-inclusion/women-in-the-workplace#/

Fierman, J. (1990). Why women still don't hit the top. *Fortune*, 122(3), 40.

Fitzgerald, T. (2013). *Women Leaders in Higher Education: Shattering the myths* (1st ed.). Routledge. 10.4324/9780203491515

Foschi, M. (2000). Double standards for competence: Theory and research. *Annual Review of Sociology*, 26(1), 21–42. 10.1146/annurev.soc.26.1.21

Freeman, Jr., S. T.-R., Douglas, M. O., & Goodenough, T. (2020). Toward best practices for promotion to full professor guidelines at research universities. *eJEP: eJournal of Education Policy,* 21(2), n2.

Gurin, P., Dey, E. L., Hurtado, S., & Gurin, G. (2002). Diversity and higher education: Theory and impact on educational outcomes. *Harvard Educational Review*, 72(3), 330–366. 10.17763/haer.72.3.01151786u134n051

Heilman, M. E., Block, C. J., & Martell, R. F. (1995). Sex stereotypes: Do they influence perceptions of managers? *Journal of Social Behavior and Personality*, 10, 237–252.

Helgesen, S. (1990). *The Female Advantage: Women's Ways of Leadership*. Doubleday Currency.

Herring, C. (2009). Does diversity pay?: Race, gender, and the business case for diversity. *American Sociological Review*, 74(2), 208–224. 10.1177/000312240907400203

Hill, L. H., & Wheat, C. A. (2017). The influence of mentorship and role models on university women leaders' career paths to university presidency. *The Qualitative Report*, 22(8), 2090–2111. 10.46743/2160-3715/2017.2437

Hoogendoorn, S., Oosterbeek, H., & van Praag, M. (2013). The impact of gender diversity on the performance of business teams: Evidence from a field experiment. *Management Science*, 59(7), 1514–1528. 10.1287/mnsc.1120.1674

Hymowitz, C., & Schellhardt, T. D. (1986). The glass ceiling: Why women can't break the invisible barrier that blocks them from top jobs. *The Wall Street Journal*, 1(4), 1D-24D.

Jacobs, J. A. (1992). Women's entry into management: Trends in earnings, authority, and values among salaried managers. *Administrative Science Quarterly*, 37(2), 282–301. 10.2307/2393225

Johnsrud, L. K. (1991). Administrative promotion: The power of gender. *The Journal of Higher Education*, 62(2), 119–149.

Johnsrud, L. K., & Heck, R. H. (1994). Administrative promotion within a university: The cumulative impact of gender. *The Journal of Higher Education*, 65(1), 23–44. 10.1080/00221546.1994.11778472

Kanter, R. (1977). *Men and Women of the Corporation*. Basic Books.

Kulis, S., Sicotte, D., & Collins, S. (2002). More than a pipeline problem: Labor supply constraints and gender stratification across academic science disciplines. *Research in Higher Education*, 43(6), 657–691. 10.1023/A:1020988531713

Longman, K. A., & Madsen, S. R. (Eds.). (2014). *Women and Leadership in Higher Education*. IAP.

Madsen, S. R. (2012). Women and leadership in higher education: Learning and advancement in leadership programs. *Advances in Developing Human Resources*, 14(1), 3–10. 10.1177/1523422311429668

Madsen, S. R., Longman, K. A., & Daniels, J. R. (2012). Women's leadership development in higher education: Conclusion and implications for HRD. *Advances in Developing Human Resources*, 14(1), 113–128. 10.1177/1523422311429734

Meschitti, V., & Marini, G. (2023). The balance between status quo and change when minorities try to access top ranks: A tale about women achieving professorship. *Gender in Management*, 38(1), 17–35. 10.1108/GM-04-2022-0141

Meza-Mejia, M. C., Villarreal-García, M. A., & Ortega-Barba, C. F. (2023). Women and leadership in higher education: A systematic review. *Social Sciences (Basel, Switzerland)*, 12(10), 555. 10.3390/socsci12100555

Misra, J., Kuvaeva, A., O'Meara, K., Culpepper, D. K., & Jaeger, A. (2021). Gendered and racialized perceptions of faculty workloads. *Gender & Society*, 35(3), 358–394. 10.1177/08912432211001387

Morais, R., Fernandes, C. E., & Piñeiro-Naval, V. (2022). Big girls don't cry: An Assessment of research units' leadership and gender distribution in higher education institutions. *Social Sciences (Basel, Switzerland)*, 11(8), 345–354. 10.3390/socsci11080345

Morley, L. (2013). *Women and higher education leadership: Absences and aspirations.* Leadership Foundation for Higher Education.

Nielsen, S., & Huse, M. (2010). The contribution of women on boards of directors: Going beyond the surface. *Corporate Governance*, 18(2), 136–148. 10.1111/j.1467-8683.2010.00784.x

OECD. (2020). *Education at a Glance 2020: OECD Indicators.* OECD., 10.1787/69096873-

Ragins, B. R., Townsend, B., & Mattis, M. (1998). Gender gap in the executive suite: CEOs and female executives report on breaking the glass ceiling. *The Academy of Management Perspectives*, 12(1), 28–42. 10.5465/ame.1998.254976

Rao, K., & Tilt, C. (2016). Board composition and corporate social responsibility: The role of diversity, gender, strategy and decision making. *Journal of Business Ethics*, 138(2), 327–347. 10.1007/s10551-015-2613-5

Reskin, B. F., & Ross, C. E. (1992). Jobs, authority, and earnings among managers: The continuing significance of sex. *Work and Occupations*, 19(4), 342–365. 10.1177/0730888492019004002

Riphahn, R. T., & Schwientek, C. (2015). What drives the reversal of the gender education gap? Evidence from Germany. *Applied Economics*, 47(53), 5748–5775. 10.1080/00036846.2015.1058906

Rudman, L. A., Moss-Racusin, C. A., Phelan, J. E., & Nauts, S. (2012). Status incongruity and backlash effects: Defending the gender hierarchy motivates prejudice against female leaders. *Journal of Experimental Social Psychology*, 48(1), 165–179. 10.1016/j.jesp.2011.10.008

Rudman, L. A., & Phelan, J. E. (2008). Backlash effects for disconfirming gender stereotypes in organizations. *Research in Organizational Behavior*, 28, 61–79. 10.1016/j.riob.2008.04.003

Safarik, L. (2003). Feminist transformation in higher education: Discipline, structure, and institution. *Review of Higher Education*, 26(4), 419–445. 10.1353/rhe.2003.0035

Searby, L., Ballenger, J., & Tripses, J. (2015). Climbing the ladder, holding the ladder: The mentoring experiences of higher education female leaders. *Advancing Women in Leadership*, 35, 98–107. 10.21423/awlj-v35.a141

Swan Dagen, A., DeFrank-Cole, L., Glance, C., & Lockman, J. (2022). You cannot be what you cannot see: Supporting women's leadership development in higher education. *Consulting Psychology Journal*, 74(2), 194–206. 10.1037/cpb0000207

UNESCO International Institute for Higher Education in Latin America and the Caribbean [UNESCO IESALC] & Times Higher Education. (2021). Women in higher education: Has the female advantage put an end to gender inequalities? Retrieved from https://www.iesalc.unesco.org/wp-content/uploads/2021/03/Women-Report-8032021.pdf

UNESCO International Institute for Higher Education in Latin America and the Caribbean [UNESCO IESALC] & Times Higher Education. (2022). Gender equality: How global universities are performing. Retrieved from https://www.timeshighereducation.com/sites/default/files/the_gender_equality_report_part_1.pdf van Knippenberg, D., De Dreu, C. K. W., & Homan, A. C. (2004). Work group diversity and group performance: An integrative model and research agenda. *The Journal of Applied Psychology*, 89(6), 1008–1022. 10.1037/0021-9010.89.6.100815584838

Williams, T. M., & Wolniak, G. C. (2021). Unpacking the "Female Advantage" in the Career and Economic Impacts of College. In N. S. Niemi & M. B. Weaver-Hightower (Eds.), *The Wiley Handbook of Gender Equity in Higher Education* (pp. 7-28). New York: John Wiley & Sons.

Wright, E. O., Baxter, J., & Birkelund, G. E. (1995). The gender gap in workplace authority: A cross-national study. *American Sociological Review*, 60(3), 407–435. 10.2307/2096422

Young, D. M., Rudman, L. A., Buettner, H. M., & McLean, M. C. (2013). The influence of female role models on women's implicit science cognitions. *Psychology of Women Quarterly*, 37(3), 283–292. 10.1177/0361684313482109

Chapter 3
Navigating Transnational Higher Education Management:
Insights From Experience

Gareth Richard Morris
https://orcid.org/0009-0007-4408-6511
University of Nottingham, Ningbo, China

Junhua Mo
https://orcid.org/0000-0001-6464-3628
Soochow University, China

Fiseha Berhanu Tesema
University of Nottingham, Ningbo, China

Katherine Wang
University of Nottingham, Ningbo, China

Lei Li
Suzhou Science and Technology Town FLS, China

ABSTRACT

Transnational Higher Education (TNHE) has experienced many challenges in recent years. From the pandemic, and its legacy, to the emergence of generative AI, universities are faced with the prospect of bouncing from one issue to another. Making life additionally complex is the fact that regional instability is increasingly common globally now, with issues occurring in locations that had previously experienced periods of relative long-term stability. This chapter will consider some of the most pressing challenges that middle managers face in TNHE providers today by drawing on the insights of experienced middle managers who work at well regarded TNHE providers in eastern China prior to, during and immediately after the pandemic.

DOI: 10.4018/979-8-3693-2857-6.ch003

INTRODUCTION

Transnational Higher Education (TNHE) has experienced many challenges in recent years. From the pandemic, and its legacy, to the emergence of generative AI, universities are faced with the prospect of bouncing from one issue to another. Making life additionally complex is the fact that regional instability is increasingly common globally now, with issues occurring in locations that had previously experienced periods of relative long-term stability. Policies and practices are also evolving at national levels within education, as countries seek to reassess and redress earlier teaching and learning models and the thinking which underpinned their uptake. The business mentality which was preferential for many years in a number of countries today, holds fewer compelling arguments for its continued uptake, as Collini (2012) argues, in comparison to suppositions which advocate sustainable community-enhancing designs that Morris and Berhanu Tesema (2024) advocate the importance of. Indeed, a supportive community is incredibly important for long term health and wellbeing as Gladwell (2008) stresses. Navigating all of this is challenging and many transnational providers have encountered numerous difficulties as a result. These range from recruitment to retention deliberations, to pedagogic and provisional practice difficulties, alongside challenges surrounding financing, motivation and satisfaction. This chapter will consider some of the most pressing challenges that middle managers face in TNHE providers today by drawing on the insights of experienced middle managers who work for some of the most prestigious providers in eastern China just prior to, during and immediately after the pandemic. It will employ a qualitative case study methodology, to supplement discussions arising from published literature concerning these sites. In addition, this chapter will also consider some of the most pertinent lessons learned from these workplaces and draw on cross-disciplinary insights to discuss these as Gladwell (2008) suggests that these are important as his telling of the Oppenheimer story illustrates.

Case Study Background

This study builds on the work of Morris et al. (2024), who considered the experiences and insights from three very senior figures at one of the most prestigious TNHE providers in eastern China and, arguably, Asia. In that study, three highly regarded and long-serving leaders were interviewed with the intention of helping the next generation of aspiring and emerging TNHE managers and leaders at that site. This is an emergent need identified by other middle management leadership figures at other prestigious TNHE institutions, who suggest that staff are often tasked with stepping up into roles for which they have little or no training as O'Connell et al. (2024) draw attention to. O'Connell et al. (2024) also suggest how important professional development is to staff who are stepping up into management, and through association, into perceived positions of leadership based on hierarchical roles. Indeed, this echoes the work of Morris, Morris and Li (2023), who through synthesizing a series of studies at another highly regarded TNHE provider found similar sentiments being echoed. In this instance, four experienced practitioners and middle managers reflect on their current experiences and what was learned from these. These practitioners go on to provide readers with suggestions as to what would have helped them previously, and how they have navigated the situations they have encountered.

Literature Review

TNHE: Transnational higher education is a term used to describe institutions that provide cross-border teaching and learning opportunities and mobility to their staff and student body (Francois, 2016). It can take a wide variety of forms with varying degrees of inter-dependencies and complexity as Morris et al. (2024) highlight. The appeal of TNHE is multifaceted. For the host country it provides opportunities to learn and bridge provisional gaps. For institutions, it enables them to expand their operations and outreach and generate additional income. For parents and students, it can enhance their employability and allow them to access a different educational form. In the past three decades there has been a marked increase in higher education mobility (High, 2023), and the number of programmes provided and students enrolled (Paniagua, Villó and Escrivà-Beltran, 2022). Provision is often driven by the designs of the privately-operated entities (High, 2023), at least as far as local legislation allows. Understandably, this often means that these universities adopt an English Medium of Instruction (EMI) approach, and this is certainly the case at many of the most prestigious higher education and K12 sites in eastern China. This means that the language of learning for academic subjects is often not the first language of many of the students, as Macaro et al. (2018) draw attention to. This can lead to certain groups feeling disadvantaged compared to others. It also brings challenges in the form of quality assurance between sister institutions, as Kosmützky and Putty (2016) note.

TNHE Leadership and Management: Leadership and management is a challenging endeavor. This is because it involves dealing with people who, amongst other things, have differing expectations about how this should be done and, as Robson (2022) notes, expectations are powerful forces. Additional influential forces include subconscious cultural influences such as power distance and uncertainty avoidance as Gladwell (2008) draws attention to. Morris et al. (2024) suggest that some of the skills and traits that TNHE managers need to develop are people centred, and more specifically, involve an ability to listen, critically self-reflect, and slow down, which aligns with the notions of Kahneman (2013) and his aptly titled book '*Thinking Fast and Slow*' so that intuition and emotion are tempered by deliberation and logic. Morris et al. (2024) also suggest that problem-solving, networking, support, forward-thinking and record-keeping are also important, amongst other features. Morris, Morris and Li (2023) also highlight how TNHE leadership is often situational, and of the moment as Morris et al. (2024) stress. This means that an array of leadership styles can be of value and different points in time, and based on different locations, roles, remits and demands. Clearly stipulating what encompasses good TNHE leadership and management is therefore difficult, although many generic and multidisciplinary skillsets are useful. Some of these include the ability to transition, work in teams and develop resilience.

Professional Development: Professional development, or continuous professional development, is an essential feature of almost all forms of work. Times change, roles evolve, technology moves forward and the unexpected can happen both personally and professionally. In order to meet these inevitabilities and ensure that staff are able to navigate their working realities as effortlessly as possible this chapter suggests that employees benefit from training, support and guidance that is systematic and accessible given time demands. Indeed, Kay (2018) highlights just how difficult career progression can be in a medical context even for driven professionals and burnout can lead to departures. Morris, Xu and Li (2022), and Li and Morris (2021) argue that professional development is essential in TNHE in order to bridge gaps, especially at times of fast-paced change. Morris and Xu (2024) have also recently highlighted how relevant this is today in higher education given the relatively recent emergence of programmes focusing on tomorrow's courses such as AI, IoT, robotics and intelligent manufacturing. They also note the influence of online learning platforms, such as EdX, hybrid online and onsite teaching and the rapid emergence and impact of generative AI (Morris and Xu, 2024). Adding to these temporal and global developments that necessitate adaption, there are also unique contextual and situational ones which affect all institutions and individuals through association. On that note, it is difficult to survive and thrive without adequate preparation. This is why the notions of Ericsson and Pool (2016) and the systematic targeted training they advocate are so important.

METHODOLOGY

Research Purpose: This research seeks to help new managers adjust to the new positions and roles in TNHE. It also hopes to provide useful insights to those who may become managers in the not-too-distant future. It should also provide useful and timely reminders to those already in leadership and management, and hopefully encourage reflection and empathy, both towards oneself and others. Finally, it should help staff better appreciate the challenges that some of their colleagues face, as O'Connell et al. (2024) draw attention to.

Research Questions: This study seeks to answer one research question: What leadership advice would experienced TNHE managers offer to new academic managers?

Research Participants: Four mid-level managers who worked or had worked in transnational and higher education institutions were interviewed hereafter referred to as RP1, RP2, RP3 and RP4. All held or had departmental line management and administration responsibilities. RP1 was an expatriate who had just moved into his current faculty role after serving in various academic teaching and researching capacities in a domestic institution previously. He also had experience of working and living in Africa and Asia. RP2 had been based in Asia for close to two decades and has worked in both higher education and international schooling. His experiences extended to Europe and North America. RP3 had been based in both Asia and Europe, and had worked in both Chinese and British academic and educational consultancy institutions. RP4 was a well-regarded researcher who had worked in higher education for a couple of decades and who was working towards a full professorship. All four are aged between 35-45. Their demographic backgrounds are clearly diverse, and their perspectives are based on very different experiences and perspectives as Table 1 illustrates, which should provide the reader with a more insightful understanding of some of the educational complexities, challenges and opportunities encountered. The participants were selected on a purposive and convenience-based premise.

Table 1. Participant demographic information

Participant	Gender	Age	Working Area	Regional Experience
RP1	Male	35-45	Department Faculty	Africa, Asia
RP2	Male	35-45	Centre Management	Asia, Europe, North America
RP3	Female	35-45	School Management	Asia, Europe
RP4	Male	35-45	Department Faculty	Asia

Research Methods: As an exploratory case study design this chapter has deliberately adopted an approach that will enlighten understanding. It will also consider the situational factors that impact individuals as Morris and Mo (2023) suggest is important. The benefits of this approach are that it provides the readers with a deeper appreciation and understanding of the phenomena under consideration and additionally enhances readability. These are considerations that Duff (2007) suggests are worth noting. An additional benefit of this method is that through having insider insights in terms of TNHE institutions and features, the authors can better appreciate some of the nuanced points raised and discussed.

Data Collection and Analysis: The four sets of data were collected via a series of open-ended questions administered by e-mail. Any follow up questions, queries or clarification checking was also conducted via this medium. The reason for this was the speed of information collection and the fact that it allowed the participants to offer their input in a measured and carefully worded manner that they best felt addressed the points that they wished to make. They could also do so in comfortable locations and at times that suited them. In many ways, this data collection method has many benefits associated with interviews and offsets some of the potential disadvantages such as power imbalances perceived authority-based influence as Kleinman (2012) suggests can influence decision-making, such as wishing to leave a favourable impression which is often human nature (Stephens-Davidowitz, 2017). This approach also avoided the need for transcriptions to be conducted. The data was however coded after a period of familiarization. This is an approach that Caulfield (2019) has advocated. During this approach, a dual deductive and inductive approach was adopted as Morris and Mo (2023) have previously advocated based on the work of, amongst others, Sahakyan et al. (2018).

Results

The insights from the four participants were enlightening. One of the first themes to emerge was the importance of **adaptability**. RP 1 stated:

Leadership in transnational settings must be adaptive, and able to respond to the rapid changes and diverse challenges characteristic of operating across different countries. Experienced managers stress the ability to modify leadership approaches to suit various scenarios, emphasizing the importance of promoting collaboration among teams that are geographically and culturally dispersed. [RP1]

This is an important but also a challenging consideration as the past half a decade has highlighted with educational moves towards synergy, virtual learning spaces, online-hybrid-onsite teaching and now with generative AI. RP1 stressed:

Navigating the complexities of varying regulations and being prepared for technological shifts are key challenges highlighted by experienced managers. They advise maintaining strict compliance with all local and international laws to avoid legal pitfalls. Additionally, resilience in the face of operational disruptions—such as those caused by the pandemic or geopolitical conflicts like the Ukraine-Russia war—is essential. Managers must also uphold high ethical standards to ensure decisions and actions continually reflect the institution's integrity and commitment to high-quality education, safeguarding the institution's reputation and long-term success. [RP1]

Adapting often necessitates drawing on experience which may or may not have prepared individuals for the challenges that they face. It is also important to foster the ability to continuously learn and be aware of the world around us. On this note, RP1 went on to note the importance of **cultural awareness**.

Experienced managers in transnational higher education emphasize the importance of new academic leaders deeply understanding the cultural and educational landscapes where they operate. This includes not only grasping the academic standards but also appreciating local customs and societal norms that impact education. Such awareness helps in designing curricula that resonate locally and ensures that program delivery is relevant and respectful. Building strong relationships with local stakeholders—schools, government agencies, and community leaders—further aligns the institution's goals with regional expectations and fosters mutual respect and cooperation. [RP1]

To this end RP4 felt that institutional leadership and management had an obligation to develop an **international mindset** within its leadership and community bodies as doing so would promote a host of associated benefits ranging from enhanced and more inclusive teaching materials to pedagogic delivery and assessment rigour.

Transnational higher education administrators should invest more efforts in the cultivation of international talents. To this end, transnational higher education administrators can reform the curriculum, introduce international educational resources, explore diversified teaching methods and evaluation systems, promote the teaching reform of schools, and ultimately improve the quality and level of international talent training. [RP4]

Through developing internationally minded staff, and managers, RP4 added that he felt that some of the management and leadership challenges often encountered in TNHE and international workplaces might be offset.

Transnational higher education managers are well advised to build international management teams to address cross-cultural communication and management challenges that their units and institutions may encounter. Specifically, transnational higher education managers are encouraged to introduce management talents with international vision and cross-cultural competence, who promote diversity and internationalization, and which will promote mechanisms and systems for effective problem-solving. [RP4]

The EDI, or **equity** (or equality), **diversity and inclusion** advantages of doing so were then subsequently stressed by RP4 who noted:

With greater internationalization, there is a cultural conflict and identity problem between students and teachers from different cultural backgrounds. Transnational higher education administrators need to manage the relationship between groups of different cultural backgrounds, establish an inclusive and diverse campus culture, promote the exchange and integration of various cultures, and create a harmonious and inclusive learning environment. [RP4]

Besides some of the initial skills and competencies which might help international managers in their roles, such as being adaptable, culturally aware, harbouring an international mindset and promoting diversity, within an EDI framework, a number of additional personal attributes and traits were advocated. RP2 began by mentioning the importance of **organisational skills**.

> *I would say the first thing I think managers need is organisational skills. I think they're going to have lots of things that they need to do and lots of things that compete for time. And so being organized, managing your time, being able to multitask, these are all things that loosely come under the first kind of skill or you know, piece of advice I'd offer.* [RP2]

This was also stressed by RP3 who added to this by noting the importance of being able to manage time and multitask.

> *Personally, my belief is that being able to manage time well and multitask are essential skills for managers in all school sectors. The days can be unbelievably busy, and extend into evenings, weekends and holidays so it's important to manage time well and multitask.* [RP3]

In addition to good organisational skills, RP1 emphasised the need to have **strong communication skills**, a point that RP3 echoed, in order to realised desired outcomes, while the importance of **supporting staff was also mentioned**.

> *Clear communication, fostering an inclusive culture, and encouraging idea-sharing across borders to leverage the diverse perspectives and strengths of all team members are important skills.* [RP1]
>
> *It's really important to be supportive of staff and to try and understand the situations they face and the difficulties that they encounter. It's also really important to understand senior management and what their goals and motives are and help support these.* [RP3]

RP2 added to the importance of supporting others by stressing how important it was to **lead by example**, because it encourages others to step up if your tap into both hearts and minds. **Attention to detail** was also advocated.

> *You know if you want people to work harder then you also have to do that. People are unlikely to put in a big shift if they don't see their manager doing likewise. Having an eye for detail and being meticulous, at least as much as possible also helps.* [RP2]

RP3 built on these points, stating that the importance of **determination**, or grit, alongside **resilience** were key features for managers at various times.

> *I think the next quality that I would advocate would be grit, determination, resilience. You can have tough times, busy times. You're going to have moments where people are not nice or they're difficult and sometimes it's a case of basically pushing through. I mean that's not at the expense of wellbeing, but it's just that sometimes life is tough and you've got to work through it, and sometimes work is draining and tiring, and you've got to be willing to put in some hard yards.* [RP2]

RP3 added to this feature by talking about the importance of **work life balance**, and RP2 also noted just how essential **kindness and self-care** can be as a result.

> *It's really important at times to make sure that managers take a step back and look at their work-life balance. This is not the same as managing workloads during a given day. By this the meaning is that time away from work to recharge is just as important as efficiency at it.* [RP3]
>
> *Self-care is really important. This is more than simply mindfulness. Working life is challenging and difficult, and it's only getting more difficult and challenging because of increased job competitiveness, technological developments and evolving workplace realities. So, taking breaks, relaxing, and putting technology away is really important for mental health, especially during stressful periods of time.* [RP2]

In light of this point, it is understandable that RP2 would also go on and mention the importance of also considering the staff below us, and our colleagues who work alongside us, by highlighting the value of **empathy and kindness**.

> *I think it's really important to kind of think about where the people we work with might be coming from, and the day they might be having and the challenges that they might face. And so, you know, as much as it's good to divide the personal and the professional, it's not always possible to do that meaning we bring baggage with us. Because of this empathy and kindness are important. Most people respond well to this.* [RP2]

Understandably, not all of the aforementioned skills, traits, competencies and behaviours come naturally to everyone. At various points in time, it is also helpful to be explicitly reminded. RP1 stated just how important **continuing professional development** is, albeit primarily, through a technological lens.

> *Continuing professional development is crucial in staying abreast of educational trends, technological advancements, and best practices in international education management. Seasoned managers advocate for leveraging technology not just for educational delivery but also for streamlining administrative processes and enhancing communication channels. Effective use of technology supports more efficient operations and can significantly improve the reach and quality of educational programs, particularly in adapting to shifts such as the increased need for online learning solutions.* [RP1]

RP3 noted that to realise desired and intended designs **planning** was therefore important, and perhaps pertinently, that which is strategic in orientation.

> *Planning is really important for managers. Although mid-level managers may not control ultimate decision making or direction setting, or budget allocations, they do have a say how these things work at a unit level and so therefore need to plan strategically within their working remit which supports the institutional vision, mission and goals.* [RP3]

RP4 also noted how mid-level managers have to play an important role in **reputation building** and enhancement.

> *Transnational higher education administrators need to turn more attention to university branding, because branding is the king. With the advancement of globalization and the increasingly fierce competition in the higher education market, higher education institutions in various countries and*

regions have increased their efforts to recruit foreign students, and carry out brand-building and image-building. In this context, transnational higher education administrators need to face the challenge of brand building, increase the international visibility and influence of their institutions, and attract more international students and international partners. [RP4]

Finally, regarding experience and perception-based advice from mid-level career educators, RP4 also noted how important it was to work with local government when roles required this.

Transnational higher education administrators need to win over local governments. There is a Chinese proverb that distant water cannot save the thirst of the near. Only by taking root in the local area and gaining local support can transnational higher education institutions develop better. Transnational higher education administrators not only have to conform to local customs, but also assimilate their identities, changing from outsiders to locals. As long as it has strong support from the local government, transnational higher education can survive and thrive. [RP4]

DISCUSSION

Developing Personal Competencies and Skills through Professional Development: There are many attributes, skills, competencies, traits and behaviours that the participants identified as being desirable for current and future TNHE managers and leaders. Some of the more obvious are the sort that one might expect to read about in work which discusses general leadership and management regardless of the field. For example, the need to be adaptable, culturally aware, have an international mindset to value diversity and be inclusive could be terms used by or for Wenger (2021) when he revolutionized premier league football in the mid to late nineteen nineties bringing in a period of unexpected and, for the time, unprecedented success in the process. Other features, such as having strong organizational skills, leading by example, paying attention to detail, harboring fierce determination and resilience and building a legacy and reputation could be applied to the other leading leadership figure of that period, and in that field, as outlined in a personal leadership recount by Ferguson (2016). In reality, both figures displayed both sets of features, albeit in slightly nuanced ways, and both operated in effect for transnational sporting entities. The reality however, is that the working world evolved, and so too did the competitors. In order to remain successful for exceptionally prolonged periods of time both figureheads had to continually go through processes of regeneration and, also break some of their own habits and preferential ways of working to do so. What was equally interesting was how both were also strong communicators in their working areas, supercommunicators Duhigg (2024) might term them because of the way that their teams shared the same language and frameworks, enabling success after success after success. However, here things differ. They operated in unique fields, where certain behaviors and practices were deemed acceptable. The working world of 2024 is far removed from that, and so support, empathy and kindness are all incredibly important, as it accepts that differences can be sources of strength and that everyone faces challenges periodically as Mate (2022) and Hasson and Butler (2020) draw attention to. In this respect maintaining a work-life balance is incredibly important, as too is continuing professional development as Ericsson and Pool (2016) allude to, if sustainability is an end goal. This is not always easy to manage as often managers are overworked to the point of exhaustion as Morris (2021) alludes.

Responding to the Challenges facing TNHE with Confidence, Agency and Resilience: Transnational higher education managers need to face various challenges ideally with confidence, as confidence can help to deal with uncertainty and pressure. In many instances, although it may not come naturally, it can be acquired as Fox Cabane (2013) notes, and Ericsson and Pool (2016) advocate through deliberate practice and targeted training. Firstly, confidence enables TNHE providers and leadership figures to face market competition and changes with greater assurance which makes external parties feel more settled. In the globalized education market, competition is fierce, and managers need to believe in their abilities and the strength of their teams, dare to try which often involves being prepared to see failure as a chance to learn, and innovate constantly, to maintain a leading position. This also requires much hard work, or grit as Duckworth (2018) terms it. Secondly, confidence helps them to establish and expand international cooperation. Transnational education requires collaboration with schools, institutions, and organizations from different countries and regions, and building confidence can help managers demonstrate confidence and determination in cooperation, enhancing the trust and willingness to cooperate of partners.

Transnational higher education managers also need to respond to various challenges with agency, as agency enables them to adapt flexibly to challenges and changes, establish international cooperation, effectively respond to emergencies, thereby promoting the development of education and internationalization. Indeed, Morris, Morris and Li (2023) advocate the importance of embracing and leading change in their twelve principles of TNHE management. Firstly, the agency enables leaders and managers to flexibly respond to the ever-changing international education market which has become the new norm as Morris and Xu (2024) allude to. With the development of globalization, competition in the education market is increasingly fierce, and managers need to be able to adjust strategies in a timely manner, seize opportunities, and respond to challenges because if they do not, or decision making is not appropriate, transnational educational providers can see their ventures fail as Mo and Morris (2024) draw attention to. Secondly, agency can help managers and leadership figures to establish and expand international cooperation. Transnational higher education managers need to collaborate with schools, institutions, and organizations from different countries and regions to carry out education projects and research activities together. By demonstrating a proactive attitude and flexible cooperation, they can better promote international exchange and cooperation, improve educational quality, and through association extend influence.

Transnational higher education managers additionally need to respond to various challenges with resilience, as resilience enables them to adapt to cultural differences, respond to market changes and manage uncertainty, thereby maintaining a steady development momentum and promoting the internationalization of education. According to Duckworth (2018) this can also be regarded aptly as grit, which is a common term in sporting disciplines. Firstly, resilience helps managers to cope with the challenges brought about not only by daily working life, but also global competition and market changes. As the process of globalization accelerates, the education market becomes increasingly competitive, and managers need resilience to adapt to these developments, adjust strategies in a timely manner, and maintain competitiveness. This also necessitates an awareness of the culture these figures work within as Meyer (2014) draws attention to, an ability to set realistic expectations which is important as Robson (2023) highlights, and to regulate emotions as far as possible which is challenging at times as Haidt (2021) stresses. Secondly, resilience also helps them to cope with challenges brought about by unexpected events and uncertainties. In international education, managers may face unexpected events such as natural disasters, political unrest and pandemics, and demonstrating resilience can help them remain calm, adjust plans quickly, and effectively manage crises more astutely enhancing the end outcomes or making the process smoother if nothing else.

Ushering in a Brighter Future for TNHE through Vision, Wisdom and Innovation: In addition to the points previously mentioned, transnational higher education managers also need vision to create a better future at times as Morris et al. (2024) note. Vision enables managers and staff to anticipate future trends and challenges, develop long-term development plans, seize opportunities, and promote the sustainable development and the progress of global education. To expand on this point, vision enables leaders to, at times, anticipate and respond to future trends and challenges. In many ways, this is not too dissimilar to the past when notions of a shared purpose and a commitment to the cause-built empires as Grann (2023) notes, albeit with the caveat that leadership also feature a situational, of the moment, and in the best interest of all concerned should the necessity arise element in decision making. With the continuous development of technology and globalization, the education sector also faces many changes, and managers with vision may be able to anticipate and foresee some of these changes in advance and adjust their strategies in a timely manner to meet future needs if they can ignore distractive noise as Kahneman, Sibony and Sunstein draw attention to (2022). Secondly, vision helps management to formulate long-term development plans and goals. In transnational education, managers need to consider factors such as culture, law, and economy in different countries and regions, and a clear vision can enable teams to better seize the opportunity globally, by promoting the formulation and development of blueprints for schools or institutions that conform to future educational directional movements. This is important because after business style shifts previously as Collini (2012) cautioned, the future seems to be technologically driven as Morris and Xu (2024) state.

Transnational higher education managers also have an important broader responsibility or mission in some peoples' views. In the era of globalization, these figureheads need extol wisdom to lead schools towards a better future and at the same time guide others around them as well as Morris and Xu (2024) suggest some TNHE providers are already intentionally attempting to do. Firstly, they need to deeply understand the differences between different cultures to establish cross-cultural communication and cooperation mechanisms. By promoting international exchanges and cooperation, the leaders can help reduce boundaries and provide students with a broader academic perspective and exchange platform. In many ways this aligns with the advice of leadership figures who have transcended careers and boundaries themselves who advocate the importance of being useful as they reflect on their lives (Schwarzenegger, 2023). Secondly, transnational higher education managers should strive to build an open and inclusive academic environment and promote the cultivation and exchange of international talents. They need to create an atmosphere of mutual respect and mutual learning, encourage open dialogue and cooperative research between teachers and students. By establishing an open and empathetic and caring international faculty team and academic exchange platform, these figureheads can inject new vitality and momentum into the long-term development of schools and enhance performance and loyalty in the process in all likelihood. This should help to alleviate some of the everyday struggles that we face and Hansen (2023) draws attention to, and ensures that altruism, which is so highly valued, and kindness, which is incredibly powerful as Ferrucci (2016) stresses, take a leading role in both professional and personal lives.

When facing the challenges of globalization, transnational higher education managers additionally need to explore the future with innovative thinking and methods to pave the way for a better tomorrow. Firstly, they should actively adopt new technologies and introduce informatization and intelligence into various aspects of education management to improve teaching quality and management efficiency where appropriate. By introducing advanced technologies such as virtual reality and artificial intelligence, they can create a more interactive and interesting learning environment, stimulate students' interest in learning and be at the forefront of developments. That said, the drawbacks still need to be considered and mitigated against as Morris and Xu (2024) stress. Secondly, transnational higher education managers should encourage staff to be creative, innovate and trial new practices in teaching methods and curriculum design, breaking traditional teaching models where these act more as outdated restrictive straightjackets. It is however difficult to change habits as Duhigg (2012) notes, but doing so can be highly rewarding. Thinking differently can also be highly advantageous as Gladwell (2008; 2015) advocates. Indeed, cultivating students' critical thinking skills and problem-solving abilities are facets many courses and programs aspire to achieve, and have done for decades and these are even more pertinent features in 2024. Leaders can also promote cross-disciplinary integration and the sharing of teaching resources by supporting teachers' participation in international academic exchanges and project cooperation, providing students with a richer and more diverse learning experience. Finally, transnational higher education managers need to focus on the deep integration of education and industry, and cultivate professional skills and comprehensive literacy that meet international talent needs. This is similar to the old technical college remit, albeit with an academic face and forward future thinking orientation. They should actively promote cooperation between schools and various sectors such as enterprises and research institutions, build internship opportunities, employment, and entrepreneurship platforms, and provide students with broader development space and opportunities so that graduates are having the academic career journey scaffolded as Vygotsky and Bruner advocated in education, and the input plus one message stressed which draws on elemental psychology that is nicely discussed by Kleinman (2012).

SUMMARY

This chapter has considered the skills, competencies and traits that current TNHE managers who are at the relative midpoints in their careers feel existing or future mid-level managers and leadership figures will need given the current status quo. It has mentioned how some of these key features include the need to be flexible or adaptable, culturally aware, supportive, adopt an international mindset, promote diversity and inclusion, have strong organizational and communication skills, led by example and pay attention to detail. It has also highlighted the importance of determination, resilience, a work life balance, empathy and kindness, continuing professional development and reputation building and maintenance. Many of these features overlap with the principles identified by Morris, Morris and Li (2023) reaffirming their perceived importance in this educational context. The value of this research beyond exploring a topic of importance with potentially some of the TNHE influencers and leaders of tomorrow, is also to bring greater attention to an evolving and highly lucrative educational domain. One in which the stakes are high, the pressures at time great, but the benefits, when things work out far in excess of those found in almost all other educational contexts and remits. With tomorrow emerging today this study will hopefully resonate and reassure some, inform and offer new insights to others.

Research Limitations: This research understandably has some limits. Firstly, if offers only a few insights from a small number of participants. Although it is not uncommon for acclaimed figures with rich experiences to offer case study examples, such as Ferguson (2016) and Smith (2022), it is acknowledged that some readers may suggest that this study is not a hard science-based one, and so is less valuable or rigorous than experimental science-based designs. This is a point Stephens-Davidowitz (2017) notes about his own work in the social sciences, and unlike his work this chapter does not utilize or tap into big data. That said, by considering personal narratives and experiences, it can resonate and enlighten in greater depth and with additional nuanced meaning. Another trade-off has been in terms of ensuring ethical stipulations are met, meaning some contextualization needs to be extended or expanded. This work also focuses on select areas, and future studies could expand into areas such as global policy impact; technological developments; equity, equality, diversity and inclusion practices; sustainability considerations, as well as learning impact and outcomes.

Research Ethics: This chapter adheres to, and has been informed by, the British Educational Research Association (2018) and the Data Protection Act (2018). As such, it ensures a number of ethical principles. These include, but are not limited to participant safeguarding, confidentiality and anonymity.

REFERENCES

British Educational Research Association. (2018). *Ethical Guidelines for Educational Research*. Available from: https://www.bera.ac.uk/publication/ethical-guidelines-for-educational-research-2018

Caulfield, J. (2019). *How to do Thematic Analysis*. Available at: https://www.scribbr.com/methodology/thematic-analysis/

Collini, S. (2012). *What Are Universities For?* Penguin.

Data Protection Act. (2018). *Legislation*. www.legislation.gov.uk/ukpga/2018/12/contents/enacted

Duckworth, A. (2018). *Grit: The power of passion and perseverance*. Scribner.

Duff, P. (2007). *Case study Research in applied linguistics*. Lawrence Erlbaum Associates.

Duhigg, C. (2012). *The Power of Habit: Why we do what we do in Life and Business*. Random House.

Duhigg, C. (2024). *Supercommunicators: How to Unlock the Secret Language of Communication*. Random House.

Ericsson, A., & Pool, R. (2016). *Peak: Secrets from the New Science of Expertise*. HarperOne.

Fox Cabane, O. (2013). *The charisma myth: How anyone can master the art and science of personal magnetism*. Portfolio.

Francois, E. J. (2016). What is Transnational Education? In Francois, E., Avoseh, M., & Griswold, W. (Eds.), *Perspectives in Transnational Higher Education* (pp. 3–23). Sense Publishers. 10.1007/978-94-6300-420-6_1

Gladwell, M. (2008). *Outliers*. Penguin.

Gladwell, M. (2015). *David and Goliath*. Back Bay Books.

Grann, D. (2023). *The Wager*. Simon & Schuster. Ferguson, A. (2016). *Leading*. Hachette Books. Ferruci, P. (2016). *The Power of Kindness: The Unexpected Benefits of Leading a Compassionate Life*. TarcherPerigee.

Haidt, J. (2021). *The Happiness Hypothesis*. Random House.

Hasson, G., & Buttler, D. (2020). *Mental Health and Wellbeing in the Workplace: A Practical Guide for Employers and Employees*. Capstone.

High, M. (2023). The Perils and Potential Benefits of Machine Translation in Transnational Higher Education. In Morris, G & Li. L. (Eds). *Developments and Future Trends in Transnational Higher Education* (pp. 115-135). Hershey: IGI Global. 10.4018/978-1-6684-5226-4.ch006

Kahneman, D. (2013). *Thinking Fast and Slow*. Farrar, Straus and Giroux.

Kahneman, D., Sibony, O., & Sunstein, C. (2022). *Noise: A flaw in human judgement*. William Collins.

Kay, A. (2018). *This is Going to Hurt*. Picador.

Kleinman, P. (2012). *Psych101*. Adams Media.

Kosmützky, A., & Putty, R. (2016). Transcending Borders and Traversing Boundaries: A Systematic Review of the Literature on Transnational, Offshore, Cross-border, and Borderless Higher Education. *Journal of Studies in International Education*, 20(1), 8–33. 10.1177/1028315315604719

Li, Li., & Morris, G. (2021). Thriving in the New Normal: In-Service Professional Development Needs and Experiences. In Xiang, C. H. (Ed.), *Trends and Developments for the Future of Language Education in Higher Education* (pp. 253–271). IGI Global. 10.4018/978-1-7998-7226-9.ch013

Macaro, E., Curle, S., Pun, J., An, J., & Dearden, J. (2018). A Systematic Review of English Medium Instruction in Higher Education. *Language Teaching*, 51(1), 36–76. 10.1017/S0261444817000350

Mate, G. (2022). *The Myth of Normal: Trauma, Illness and Healing in a Toxic Culture*. Avery.

Meyer, E. (2014). *The Culture map*. Public Affairs.

Mo, J., & Morris, G. (2024). Investigating the employment motivation, job satisfaction, and dissatisfaction of international high school teachers in China: The impact of the COVID-19 pandemic. *Frontiers in Psychology*, 15, 1271604. Advance online publication. 10.3389/fpsyg.2024.127160438384343

Morris, G., & Berhanu Tesema, F. (2024). *To Build a Community in Higher Education, Start from the Ground Up*. The Times Higher Education Campus. Available from: https://www.timeshighereducation.com/campus/build-community-higher-education-start-ground

Morris, G., Cao, Q., & Weng, W. Berhanu Tesema, F. & Zhao, T. (2024). Planning Ahead: Exploring the Leadership Competencies that Transnational Higher Education Managers Need. In Morris, G. & Kozuch, S. (Eds). *Engaging Higher Education Teachers and Students with Transnational Leadership* (pp.1-14). Hershey: IGI Global.

Morris, G., & Mo, J. (2023). Exploring the Employment Motivation, Job Satisfaction and Dissatisfaction of University English Instructors in Public Institutions: A Chinese Case Study Analysis. *Humanities & Social Sciences Communications*, 10(1), 717. 10.1057/s41599-023-02228-2

Morris, G., Morris, J. & Li, Lei. (2023). Enhancing Educational Leadership in Transnational Higher Education. In Morris G. & Li, L. (Eds). *Developments and Future Trends in Transnational Higher Education* (pp. 341-358). Hershey: IGI Global.

Morris, G., & Xu, J. (2024). "Journeying into the Unknown: Considering the Future of Education at the Dawn of AI." (Virtual Presentation). Teaching and Learning Conference, University of Nottingham, April 2024.

Morris, G., Xu, J., & Li, Li. (2022). Transitioning to the New Normal: Experiences from a Sino-British Institution. In Kronhke, L. (Ed.), *Cases on Teaching English for Academic Purposes (EAP) During COVID-19* (pp. 205–230). IGI Global. 10.4018/978-1-6684-4148-0.ch009

O'Connell, J., Brewer, S., Wilding, E., & Robbins, J. (2024). Management challenges and training needs in higher education institutions: A multi-case study. In Morris, G., & Kozuch, S. (Eds.), *Engaging Higher Education Teachers and Students with Transnational Leadership* (pp. 39–63). IGI Global. 10.4018/979-8-3693-6100-9.ch003

Paniagua, J., Villó, C., & Escrivà-Beltran, M. (2022). Cross-border Higher Education: The Expansion of International Branch Campuses. *Research in Higher Education*, 63(6), 1–21. 10.1007/s11162-022-09674-y35068659

Robson, D. (2023). *The expectation effect: How your mindset can change your world.* Holt.

Sahakyan, T., Lamb, M., & Chambers, G. (2018). Language Teacher Motivation: From the Ideal to the Feasible Self. In Mercer, S., & Kostoulas, A. (Eds.), *Language Teacher Psychology* (pp. 53–70). Multilingual Matters. 10.21832/9781783099467-008

Schwarzenegger, A. (2023). *Be Useful: Seven Tools for Life.* Penguin Press. Kahneman, D., Sibony, O. & Sunstein, C. (2022). *Noise: A flaw in human judgement.* William Collins.

Smith, W. (2022). *Will.* Planeta Publishing.

Stephens-Davidowitz, S. (2017). Everybody Lies: Big Data, New Data and What the Internet Can Tell Us about Who We Really Are. Dey Street Books. Robson, D. (2022). *The Expectation Effect: How Mindset Can Change Your World.* Henry Holt and Co.

Wenger, A. (2021). *My Life in Red and White.* W&N.

Chapter 4
Exploring the Influence of Leadership on Job Satisfaction in Universities and International Schools

Xuan Ma
Suzhou Institute, Xi'an Jiaotong University, China

Ji Zhang
Suzhou International Foreign Language School, China

ABSTRACT

This study aims to explore the influence of leadership styles on the job satisfaction of teachers at a Chinese transnational higher education university and at an international school. This study uses qualitative research methods and in-depth interviews to investigate the job satisfaction and dissatisfaction among four educators working at transnational higher education providers. The findings suggest that teachers working at a private university are generally satisfied with their work, especially when it comes to leadership providing guidance and trust. However, work load and wage equity are sources of concern, along with disorganization, punitive fines and interpersonal relationships in a K12 school. This study advocates the provision of employee-friendly working conditions and the enhancement of the teacher welfare to improve workplaces.

1. INTRODUCTION

Higher education has the ability to develop new knowledge and disseminate existing insights. It is important to establish and develop sustainable leadership and explore new approaches to leadership in higher education (Wilkins & Neri, 2019). Universities provide qualified human capital by leading research activities, and drawing the attention of many institutions to unsolved problems or areas of weakness in society. Universities, therefore, need educational leaders who can perform their duties with the highest efficiency, integrity, and ethical standards in order to achieve their goals. Educational leaders have many responsibilities, including research, supervision, administrative roles, job deployments,

DOI: 10.4018/979-8-3693-2857-6.ch004

events management, and extracurricular activity supervision (Bryant, 2003). The International School Consultancy estimates that as of October 2017, there were 9,200 international schools with 5 million students and 463,000 employees worldwide (Lee & Wright, 2015). There was also an increase in the number of international schools worldwide from 2000 to 2017 (Lee & Wright, 2015). This growth is primarily driven by the rise of International Baccalaureate (IB) schools in Asia Pacific and the Middle East (Lee & Wright, 2015). International schools tend to use an international education curriculum to develop international perspectives of students. The curriculum may vary depending on the school. In international schools, in addition to learning, students enhance their creativity and critical thinking by participating in a variety of extra-curricular activities, which are supported by parents, teachers and students (Walker, 2002). Recent research has examined how various leadership styles in higher education affect the quality, effectiveness, commitment, perceived organizational support, citizenship, and satisfaction of an organization (Epitropaki & Martin, 2005; Madlock, 2008; Awamleh & Al-Dmour, 2004). There are also various studies investigating the impact of leadership style on job satisfaction in schools (Madlock, 2008; Temple, 2009; Burns, 2007). Some studies have examined the impact of elementary, middle, and high school leadership styles on teacher job satisfaction (Dampson, Havor & Laryea, 2018; Harris, 2008; Oduro, 2004). However, few studies have examined the impact of leadership styles in transnational (higher) education institutions on teachers' job satisfaction. Despite the rapid growth in the number of K12 schools worldwide, there is little research literature on international school leadership. Therefore, the focus of this study is to examine the impact of leadership on teachers' job satisfaction in the unique context of transnational higher education providers and international schools in eastern China.

2. LITERATURE REVIEW

2.1 Leadership Style

Leadership is critical to the success of an organization. Leadership styles vary by industry and organization (Zahari & Shurbagi, 2012). Leadership styles also vary from situation to situation (Lok & Crawford, 2004). Most leaders adjust their leadership style according to the needs of the organization and the working environment (Zahari & Shurbagi, 2012).

2.1.1 Transactional Leadership

Transactional leaders motivate subordinates through the exchange process. For example, subordinates who fulfill job requirements are rewarded, while others can be punished. Therefore, transactional leaders focus on motivating employees through the punishment and reward mechanism. Past studies have concluded that employees tend to endure the transactional leadership style for short periods of time because of the rewards and punishments associated with them (Naidu & Van der Walt, 2005; Saleem, 2015). Rewards can be in the form of promotion and salary increments. The contingent rewards dimension implies that transactional leaders set goals for their subordinates and reward them for achieving those goals (Judge & Piccolo, 2004). Moreover, the laissez-faire leadership dimension suggests that transactional leaders delegate powers to their employees and intervene only when needed (Judge & Piccolo, 2004). On the contrary, underperforming employees will be punished. The forms of punishment may include dismissal and/or salary reduction (Jansen, Vera & Crossan, 2009). Previous studies have suggested that this leadership style may not be effective in all situations (Bryant, 2003). Under transactional leadership, employee motivation relies on transactions such as rewards and punishments. Therefore, in the long run, transactional leadership may have adverse effects on performance and satisfaction (Hartog, Muijen & Koopman, 1997; Hater & Bass, 1988).

2.1.2 Transformational Leadership

Transformational leaders are the inspiration and vision source for their subordinates in an organization (Weber, 2009). Past research has shown that this leadership style can improve organizational performance, motivation, and employee morale (Weber, 2009). Transformational leaders can increase employee motivation and satisfaction by giving employees a certain degree of autonomy (Herman & Chiu, 2014; Top, Akdere & Tarcan, 2015). Transformational leadership can improve employees' perception and dedication to the organization (Ojokuku, Odetayo & Sajuyigbe, 2012; Barling, Weber & Kelloway, 1996). Bass and Riggio (2006) believe that transformational leadership style has four dimensions, namely, "Four I's". The inspirational motivation dimension suggests that transformational leaders motivate subordinates to complete challenging tasks by sharing their vision and strategies with employees (Bass & Riggio, 2006). The idealized dimension of influence suggests that transformational leaders influence their subordinates by becoming role models (Bass & Riggio, 2006; Weber, 2009). The dimension of intellectual motivation means that transformational leaders intellectually motivate employees to solve challenging problems in creative ways. Moreover, the individual consideration dimension implies that transformational leaders act as mentors and facilitators for subordinates (Bass & Riggio, 2006).

2.1.3 Transactional Versus Transformational Leadership

Some studies have argued that neither transactional nor transformational leadership styles are capable of improving employee motivation and satisfaction levels. Transformational leadership has a greater impact on job satisfaction as compared to transactional leadership (Awamleh & Al-Dmour, 2004). Moreover, employees also favor the contingent rewards aspect of transactional leadership. On the contrary, some studies have found that both transactional and transformational leadership affect the satisfaction level of employees (Jansen, Vera, & Crossan, 2009). Some studies suggest that both transactional and transformational leadership styles can affect employee satisfaction (Jansen, Vera & Crossan, 2009). Compared to transactional leadership, transformational leadership has a greater impact on job satisfaction (Awamleh & Al Dmour, 2004). Epitropaki and Martin (2005) found that the effectiveness of transactional and transformational leadership styles varies depending on the situation and industry.

2.2 Teacher Satisfaction and Dissatisfaction

The satisfaction of higher education teachers is related to many aspects, such as pay and working conditions, but most importantly is connected with the leadership of institutions and departments. Good leaders develop strategies, take initiative, and have a vision for action (Dollard, 2018). Ambrose, Huston and Norman (2005) conducted a qualitative study and obtained results for job satisfaction and dissatisfaction. While many consider salary to be a major factor in satisfaction, it is not the most important factor (Ambrose, Huston & Norman, 2005). Areas related to the location and opportunities of family members are also important factors affecting employee satisfaction. Additionally, a working environment described as unfriendly and unsupportive was cited as a factor in the decision to leave a teaching position. Moreover, leadership in higher education is considered critical to teacher satisfaction. Poor communication, disinterest in faculty pursuits, and failure to guide their academic careers can create dissatisfaction among teachers (Ambrose, Huston & Norman, 2005). With regard to teacher dissatisfaction, Gillani et al. (2022) conducted a cross-sectional web survey to collect information on educators' experiences during the COVID-19 pandemic. The study revealed that dissatisfaction with the implementation of school policies had adverse effects on teachers' mental health, leading to a desire to leave the profession. As Morris (2021) emphasizes, teacher dissatisfaction can be attributed to the following factors, including negative personal interactions, teaching and learning elements, a dearth of recognition and progression, and issues related to the employment package, coupled with adverse external personal considerations. The research results are consistent with the research of Ambrose, Huston and Norman (2005). Negative personal interactions often stem from disengaged students, challenging relationships with colleagues, administrators, and management, as well as an unfavorable working climate. Teaching and learning factors are frequently associated with work roles and workload, and dissatisfaction linked to a perceived lack of recognition and progression often correlates with limited training and professional development opportunities, along with a deficiency in promotion and career growth prospects. Working conditions, job security concerns, and perceived or actual challenges with remuneration are commonly cited sources of dissatisfaction. External personal considerations often revolve around family issues and apprehensions about the broader social context in which teachers and their families reside and work. Similarly, Okeke and Mtyuda's (2017) study highlights specific instances where resource inadequacies, overcrowded classrooms, and student discipline problems significantly contributed to teacher unhappiness. The additional strain of administrative hurdles and the feeling of being unappreciated by school leaders and parents further exacerbated this dissatisfaction.

3. METHODOLOGY

3.1 Research Purpose

The primary aim of this research paper is to study the relationship between job satisfaction and leadership style of employees. This study intends to answer two research questions:

3.2 Research Questions

Research Question 1: From the perspective of leadership style, what makes transnational education teachers satisfied with their work?
Research Question 2: From the perspective of leadership style, what makes transnational education teachers dissatisfied with their work?

3.3 Sampling

The participants of this study work at a transnational private university and a K12 education school in a wealthy city in Eastern China. For confidentiality purposes, the transnational private university is referred to as X University and the high school K12 provider is referred to as X School. X University is one of the quickest growing university in China. It is a cutting-edge university which has a good reputation. Its transnational provision is prominent. X University aims to provide world-class education, integrate the best practices of the Chinese and British education systems, and operates under the principles of innovation, cross-cultural cooperation, and academic excellence. X School aims to teach students transnational courses and cultivate their international perspectives. X University offers undergraduate, graduate, and doctoral programs in various disciplines. It is committed to creating a multicultural learning environment, bringing together students and teachers from all over the world. X University has advanced facilities and forward-looking courses, providing opportunities for academic exploration and cross-cultural exchange for teachers and students. The purpose of this study is to understand the relationship between job satisfaction and leadership style among teachers in the unique context of X University and X School. X University and X School are selected on a convenience premise because the researchers have the access to these sites, for participants and institutions. The scope is limited because of time and workload pressures of the research team. The pseudonyms assigned to participants and the anonymous details provided aim to ensure confidentiality while providing valuable insights for broader discussions on international higher education institutions and k12 international education. This study adopted a purposive sampling strategy. Regarding purposive sampling, which is also called judgment sampling, it is a method that researchers select participants deliberately based on qualifications they possess (Etikan, Musa & Alkassim, 2016). They have the ability to provide profound insights into core issues within the context of the case study institution. This selection criterion revolves around their understandings of leadership style and job satisfaction. This study involved four main participants, two Chinese English teachers, one Chinese engineering teacher, and one foreign British English teacher. To maintain their anonymity, pseudonyms were used to identify them. Table 1 provides comprehensive and detailed information for each individual. A unique aspect of the design of this study is the intersectionality represented by the participants. Due to differences in population background, personal experience, and occupation, they have expressed different opinions. By deliberately selecting such contrasting participants, this study attempts to capture a broad and subtle perspective on the topic being studied, in order to gain more insights about the potential perspective similarities and differences. Experience in the table highlights how long each teacher worked in the same institute.

Table 1. Demographic information of the participants

Participant	Gender	Age	Location	Academic Degree	Experience
Participant 1	Male	35-45	University	Doctorate (English)	> 15 years
Participant 2	Male	30-40	University	Doctorate (Engineering)	> 1 year
Participant 3	Female	25–35	University	Master (English)	>2 years
Participant 4	Male	35-45	K12 School	Master (English)	>10 years

3.4 Data collection and analysis

The data collection for this study was completed face to face in the spring of 2024, including a separate, approximately 2-hour interview with each participant. These virtual interviews were conducted remotely and later transcribed for in-depth analysis. As suggested by Grix (2010), prior to starting the analysis, familiarity with the transcripts was conducted to ensure a comprehensive understanding of the data. The data analysis process adopts a combination of inductive reasoning and deductive reasoning, integrating the experience and method framework proposed by Morris (2021). This allows for extracting new themes from the data while also testing preconceived hypotheses or theories. The coding process has been implemented to systematically classify and interpret the answers obtained during interviews, which is consistent with the best practices of qualitative research methods. This method ensures a comprehensive review of the narratives and viewpoints of the participants.

3.5 Research Guide

In order to study these two research questions, eight questions were designed for the interview guide. The questions were designed based on the existing literature. The first four questions were designed to study whether leadership style is transformational leadership style. Question5, 6 and 7 aim to examine whether leadership style is transactional leadership style.

Table 2. Interview guide

Question 1	Do your leaders motivate and inspire you to complete challenging assignments by sharing their vision and strategies with you? Can you provide some examples?
Question 2	Do your leaders influence you by being role models? Can you provide some examples?
Question 3	Do your leaders stimulate you to solve challenging problems in a creative manner? Can you provide some examples?
Question 4	Do your leaders act as mentors and facilitators for you? Can you provide some examples?
Question 5	Do your leaders set targets for you and reward you for achieved goals? Will you be punished if you do not do what the leader wants? Can you provide some examples?
Question 6	Do your leaders evaluate you on the basis of achieved and expected goals? Can you provide some examples?
Question 7	Do your leaders delegate powers to their employees and only intervene if required? Can you provide some examples?
Question 8	Are you satisfied with your job? Would you recommend this job to your friends and family? Why?

3.6 Research Ethics

Throughout the entire research process, the researchers strictly adhered to ethical standards, followed the ethical standards of the British Educational Research Association (BERA) (2018), and complied with the Data Protection Act (2018) to protect the confidentiality and privacy rights of participants. Throughout the entire research process, institutional ethical norms were also strictly maintained, emphasizing the crucial role of ethics in research design and implementation.

4. RESULTS AND DISCUSSION

4.1 Teacher Satisfaction

4.1.1 Leadership Vision and Strategy

Participant 1, 2 and 3 all mentioned that their leaders share vision and strategy at the beginning of the new semester while the answer of participant 4 suggested otherwise. The research results reflect that leaders of participant 1, 2 and 3 are possibly more transformational leaders who are the inspiration and vision source for their subordinates (Weber, 2009). It also indicated that X University is better planned, regulated, and formal than X School. To be more specific, participant 1 said although leaders do not need to share everything with employees, sometimes being able to involve employees and gain the trust of employees can make employees feel more involved. In this way, employees can know where everything is heading and why they are doing it. If managers can also take feedback from employees into consideration, it can be a very powerful motivation source for employees. Participant 3 said "For example, my work experience is not particularly rich, and my leaders will guide me in teaching design and give me advice." This indicates that her leader provides guidance strategies based on the gaps employees feel exist.

4.1.2 Leaders as Role Models

These four participants all mentioned that some leaders have influenced them through being role models. Participant 1 and 3 said they like the way leaders work or the professional ethics they demonstrate. Participant 3 gave an example, saying "Unlike an English teacher with a doctoral degree, I hold a master's degree and have a lot of teaching hours. Sometimes, I have to give 8 classes to my students in a day, and I have a sore throat and am exhausted. However, my leader also needs to give students 8 classes a day, and her classroom is still very lively. She will guide me in designing activities in the classroom and encourage students to become the center of the classroom". This indicates that her leader can also understand employees from their perspectives and provide suggestions to them. In all, she is satisfied with this job and will recommend it to others. She mentioned although her teaching hours are long, she has a long-time vocation. Participant 4 mentioned that one of his leaders did a great job in academic pursuits and set a good example. For example, his leader actively publishes papers and participates in academic conferences, as well as guides teachers in their career development. The idealized dimension of influence suggests that transformational leaders influence their subordinates by becoming role models (Bass & Riggio, 2006; Weber, 2009). By seeing leaders setting positive examples, employees know the direction of their efforts and are more motivated.

4.1.3 Leadership and Trust

The trust of leaders motivates employees, and also increases employees' satisfaction and sense of responsibility towards the job. The dimension of intellectual motivation means that transformational leaders intellectually motivate employees to solve challenging problems in creative ways (Bass & Riggio, 2006). Participant 1 said that his leaders trust him and he has autonomy. He regularly updates leaders on the progress of completing tasks. At the same time, he pointed out that "the leaders know I can do well, so they will arrange for me to do more tasks. This is both an advantage and a disadvantage". He also mentioned that due to the limited time of the leaders, they are unable to complete all tasks alone, and many tasks are delegated according to their needs. It is important that the person assigned the task has the ability and time to complete the task. Equally important is that, if possible, the assigned tasks and personnel should be diverse to avoid being perceived as unfair and to give others the opportunity to showcase themselves. The leader first understands the strengths and interests of the teachers, and then assigns different tasks that suit their own characteristics to the teachers. Similarly, other participants provided examples. Participant 3 said "My leader encourages me to solve challenging problems and trusts me. There are many students in a class, and their English proficiency levels vary greatly. The leader encouraged me to think about incorporating targeted content in lesson preparation, so that students with different English proficiency levels can feel the effectiveness of the classroom." Participant 4 mentioned, "When I was responsible for hosting a Halloween party with two other English teachers, we received the freedom from our leaders to decide how to hold the party, rather than being told what to do". Their leaders give employees a certain degree of autonomy because of the trust. Participant 4 mentioned that leaders in academic management give teachers a certain degree of freedom to design classrooms. These leaders have clear tasks and role requirements to guide and motivate subordinates to achieve organizational goals. Leadership improves employee job satisfaction by increasing employee motivation (Kouzes & Posner, 2002).

4.1.4 Leaders as Mentors and Facilitators

These four participants all have leaders acting as mentors, although participant 4 has one leader who made him dissatisfied with his job. The individual consideration dimension implies that transformational leaders act as facilitators for subordinates (Bass & Riggio, 2006). Participant 1 said "My leader has always been very supportive of me. I have just arrived at a new work environment, so they have helped my transition and familiarized me with the job responsibilities. The leader allows me to leverage my strengths and interests, which is a win-win situation for everyone. Their trust in me motivates me to work as hard as I can." This indicates his leader's personalized care and guidance. The trust of the leader in him contributes to his sense of satisfaction and responsibility. Similar to participant 1, participant 3 answered "I have just arrived at a new work environment, so they introduced me to the situation of different students in different classes. When I first started to give classes, the leader often came to listen and gave me feedback and suggestions. Their trust and encouragement motivate me to work harder." Overall, the leadership style they encountered is transformational leadership. Participant 2 said that the leader and he jointly teach a course to students, so they need to discuss the course progress, prepare class materials and students' situation together. According to participant 4, the leader in the English department acts as a mentor and facilitator for the English teacher, such as providing guidance in lesson preparation and professional development. This indicates that the leader of his English department uses intellectual stimulation, and personalized care to make employees aware of the importance of their responsibilities and tasks, stimulate their higher-level needs, and enable them to maximize their potential to achieve the highest level of performance. Participant 3 also said "My leader evaluates me based on achieved and expected goals. In addition to attending classes in the classroom, leaders often conduct surveys on students to investigate the classroom situation, in order to establish a classroom that makes all students feel effective. I am very grateful to the leader for giving me the job opportunity and for their trust in me." She mentioned that as she is not an experienced teacher, leaders often listen to classes and ask students for feedback. This indicates the leader's attention and supervision towards her teaching.

4.1.5 Leadership and the Use of Rewards

All four participants said they set their own goals and their leaders reviewed them. They reach a consensus at the annual goal setting meeting at the beginning of the academic year. Compared to passively achieving the goals set by the leader, employees become more motivated and self-driven to achieve their own goals. This indicates that there is a high degree of freedom and autonomy in their work. They all mentioned if they achieve goals, they are likely to receive positive feedback by the end of the year. The contingent rewards dimension implies that transactional leaders reward their subordinates for achieving those goals (Judge & Piccolo, 2004). In X University and X School, leaders require students to make comments on the teachers who teach the courses and provide feedback. This also implies that these two schools attach great importance to student education and value the opinions of students. In management by exception, transaction leaders evaluate employees on the basis of achieved and expected goals (Judge & Piccolo, 2004). Participant 2 said that if the goal is achieved, the leader will give him a higher annual bonus. If the goal is not achieved, the leader will give him a lower annual bonus. The transactional leader rewards employees who achieve expected goals (Saleem, 2015). The forms of rewards can be promotions and salary increase (Jansen, Vera & Crossan, 2009). However, the leader does not give other types of punishment. The leaders of participant 1 and 2 measure their performance by their teaching, the papers they publish, and the projects they lead. On the contrary, the leadership's evaluation of participant 3 is mainly based on her teaching. She has a master's degree and focuses on teaching courses, rather than having project tasks. Participant 3 also discusses bonus, saying "In addition to work tasks, if the leader has other small tasks that require me to complete, I will be given an allowance. For example, if the leader has a legal document that requires me to translate and an article that requires me to modify, the leader will provide an allowance after I complete the task." This indicates that their leaders consider employees' well-being from employees' perspective.

4.2 Teacher Dissatisfaction

4.2.1 The Importance of Organization

Participants 1,2 and 3 mentioned that leaders share their goals and plans at the beginning of a new semester. Participant 4 is an English teacher who works for K12 education. X school is divided into Chinese management of administrative affairs and foreign management of academic affairs. His leaders from academic affairs sometimes motivates him to complete challenging assignments by sharing strategies. For example, at the beginning of the semester, his leader shared the future development trends of the school and the roles that teachers can play in it with them. For challenging tasks, leaders sometimes propose some coping methods. However, his leader working for management of administrative affairs lacks organization in her actions and often organizes meetings immediately when she comes up with any ideas.

4.2.2 Leaders not Leading by Example

Employee dissatisfaction with the leader's work style and management style often leads to employee dissatisfaction with their work. According to participant 4, although the leader in the English department acts as a mentor and facilitator for the English teacher, the leader responsible for managing administrative affairs is not a role model worth learning from. She is unwilling to delegate power to employees and hopes that they will follow her orders to complete the tasks. She has an aggressive attitude towards people, giving orders to others can hurt people's emotions. When leaders communicate their emotions and ideas to employees in a strong way, it affects employees' mood, performance, and job satisfaction (Kouzes, & Posner, 2002). The leadership relationship between academic and administrative departments in X School is also strained, and both sides are fighting for power, hoping to have more voice and decision-making power. Participant 4 mentioned that the administrative leader wants to gain more power, so she also manages academia which should not be included in her work. Participant 4 pointed out that different leaders should be responsible for different regions and divide their work accordingly

He is not satisfied with his work and will not recommend it to friends and family. He believes that this work environment is very complex, making people easily anxious and worried. In addition, the leader's unfamiliarity with the job content can lead to misunderstandings to employees, which can also lead to dissatisfaction with the work. As mentioned by participant 4, there was a time when even if there was a good feedback score on a course, that leader insisted on thoroughly checking the content of their course, because the leader misunderstood the actual content displayed in the feedback data. Participant 4 also pointed out that leaders in charge of administrative management often hold meetings, but the meetings do not have clear goals and objectives. Administrative leaders often require teachers to attend meetings without prior notice. This leadership style indicates that this leader lacks strong planning and efficiency in their work. Morris (2021) found that negative interpersonal interactions and challenging relationships with colleagues, administrators, and managers are factors that affect teachers' job satisfaction. Overall, it is not transactional leadership. Leaders do not have clear tasks and role requirements to guide and motivate subordinates to achieve organizational goals.

4.2.3 Reprimands and Punishment

Participant 4 pointed out that some teachers from other disciplines have received warning letters from their leaders, but actually this warning reason is not convincing. The school wants teachers to choose to resign themselves in order to avoid compensation for their salaries, so this action is taken. This is not a reasonable way to treat employees and save expenses. Underperforming employees will be punished. The forms of punishment may include dismissal and salary reduction (Jansen, Vera, & Crossan, 2009). Previous studies have suggested that this leadership style may not be effective in all situations (Bryant, 2003).

4.2.4 Income Expectations and Reality

Participants 1 and 4 suggested that the salary given by the leader was not high, but participants 2 and 3 were satisfied with the salary. Participants 1 and 4 are English teachers, and they mentioned that unlike engineering teachers who can earn money by collaborating with companies, the salary given to them is not high. Participant 2 is an engineering teacher from X university who is satisfied with his salary. He mentioned that his income comes from two sources. One is the salary paid by the school, and the other is his income after completing projects with the company. A contract is signed between X university and an enterprise. As an engineering teacher in X university, his subject knowledge enables him to complete projects in collaboration with the enterprise, and he can earn a substantial income. For example, he collaborates with manufacturers to design and produce products using disciplinary knowledge, establishes production lines, and updates algorithms. Although participant 3 is an English teacher and her income is not particularly high, she is not under financial pressure because she is unmarried and her family has good economic conditions. On the one hand, participant 1 and 4 face survival pressure (such as buying a house and enrolling their children in fee paying schools), with high expectations for compensation. On the other hand, they yearn to fully realize their own value and develop their teaching career. Therefore, they have relatively high motivation for achievement and opportunity.

5. CONCLUSION

This study explored the impact of leadership on job satisfaction, with a background in a transnational private university and an international school in China. This study interviewed four highly educated teachers face-to-face regarding their job satisfaction and dissatisfaction. This finding is parallel to some studies that have found that leadership improves employee job satisfaction by increasing employee motivation (Kouzes & Posner, 2002). The positive correlation between leadership ability and job satisfaction is consistent with the results of many other studies (Madlock, 2008; Temple, 2009). Specifically, this study found that sharing strategies between leaders and employees, becoming role models, trusting employees, becoming mentors, and rewarding employees can enhance job satisfaction. On the other hand, leaders who do not share strategies with employees, do not become role models, and impose unjustified punishments and give low incomes will reduce job satisfaction. The study advocates creating favorable conditions to motivate, satisfy, and gain support from staff, thereby contributing to the effectiveness and success of the institution. Considering the limitation of only interviewing four participants in this study, it may not be generalized. Further research can conduct larger and more extensive quantitative research.

REFERENCES

Afshar, H. S., & Doosti, M. (2016). Investigating the impact of job satisfaction/dissatisfaction on Iranian English teachers' job performance. *Iranian Journal of Language Teaching Research*, 4, 97–115.

Aldridge, J. M., & Fraser, B. J. (2016). 'Teachers' views of their school climate and its relationship with teacher self-efficacy and job satisfaction'. *Learning Environments Research*, 19(2), 291–307. 10.1007/s10984-015-9198-x

Ambrose, S., Huston, T., & Norman, M. (2005). A qualitative method for assessing faculty satisfaction. *Research in Higher Education*, 46(7), 803–830. 10.1007/s11162-004-6226-6

Awamleh, R., & Al-Dmour, H. (2004). The impact of transformational leadership on job satisfaction and self-perceived performance of banking employees: The case of Jordan. *The International Business & Economics Research Journal*, 3(11), 29–41.

Barling, J., Weber, T., & Kelloway, E. K. (1996). Effects of transformational leadership training on attitudinal and financial outcomes: A field experiment. *The Journal of Applied Psychology*, 81(6), 827–832. 10.1037/0021-9010.81.6.827

Bass, B. M., & Riggio, R. E. (2006). *Transformational Leadership*. Psychology Press. 10.4324/9781410617095

Bryant, S. E. (2003). The role of transformational and transactional leadership in creating, sharing and exploiting organizational knowledge. *Journal of Leadership & Organizational Studies*, 9(4), 32–44. 10.1177/107179190300900403

Burns, J. D. (2007) Analyses of transactional and transformational leadership on job satisfaction of college faculty. (Order No. 3294383, Northcentral University).

Cacioppo, S. (2022). *Wired for love: a neuroscientist's journey through romance, loss and the essence of human connection*. Robinson.

Dampson, D. G., Havor, F. M., & Laryea, P. (2018). Distributed leadership an instrument for school improvement: The study of public senior high schools in Ghana. *Journal of Education and e-learning Research*, 5(2), 79–85. 10.20448/journal.509.2018.52.79.85

Dollard, C. (2018). *Emotional intelligence is key to successful leadership*. [Online]. Retrieved April 24, 2024, from http:// www.gottman.com/blog/emotional-intelligence-key-successful-leadership/

Epitropaki, O., & Martin, R. (2005). The moderating role of individual differences in the relation between transformational/transactional leadership perceptions and organizational identification. *The Leadership Quarterly*, 16(4), 569–589. 10.1016/j.leaqua.2005.06.005

Epitropaki, O., & Martin, R. (2005a). From ideal to real: A longitudinal study of the role of implicit leadership theories on leader-member exchanges and employee outcomes. *The Journal of Applied Psychology*, 90(4), 659–676. 10.1037/0021-9010.90.4.65916060785

Etikan, I., Musa, S., & Alkassim, R. (2016). Comparison of Convenience Sampling and Purposive Sampling. *American Journal of Theoretical and Applied Statistics*, 5(1), 1–4. 10.11648/j.ajtas.20160501.11

Grix, J. (2010). *The foundations of research*. Palgrave Macmillan. 10.1007/978-0-230-36490-5

Harris, A. (2008). *Distributed school leadership: Developing tomorrow's leaders*. Routledge. https://www.routledge.com/Distributed-School-Leadership- Developing-Tomorrows-Leaders/Harris/p/book/9780415419581

Hartog, D. N., Muijen, J. J., & Koopman, P. L. (1997). Transactional versus transformational leadership: An analysis of the MLQ. *Journal of Occupational and Organizational Psychology*, 70(1), 19–34. 10.1111/j.2044-8325.1997.tb00628.x

Hater, J. J., & Bass, B. M. (1988). 'Superiors' evaluations and subordinates' perceptions of transformational and transactional leadership'. *The Journal of Applied Psychology*, 73(4), 695–715. 10.1037/0021-9010.73.4.695

Herman, H., & Chiu, W. C. (2014). Transformational leadership and job performance: A social identity perspective. *Journal of Business Research*, 67(1), 2827–2835. 10.1016/j.jbusres.2012.07.018

Jansen, J. J., Vera, D., & Crossan, M. (2009). Strategic leadership for exploration and exploitation: The moderating role of environmental dynamism. *The Leadership Quarterly*, 20(1), 5–18. 10.1016/j.leaqua.2008.11.008

Jonasson, C., Lauring, J., Selmer, J., & Trembath, J. L. (2017). Job resources and demands for expatriate academics: Linking teacher-student relations, intercultural adjustment, and job satisfaction. *Journal of Global Mobility*, 5(1), 5–21. 10.1108/JGM-05-2016-0015

Judge, T. A., & Piccolo, R. F. (2004). Transformational and transactional leadership: A meta- analytic test of their relative validity. *The Journal of Applied Psychology*, 89(5), 755–768. 10.1037/0021-9010.89.5.75515506858

Kouzes, J. M., & Posner, B. Z. (2002). *The leadership challenge*. Wiley.

Lee, M., & Wright, E. (2015). Elite schools in international education markets in Asia in a globalized era. In Hayden, M., Levy, J., & Thompson, J. (Eds.), *Handbook of research in international education* (2nd ed., pp. 583–597). Sage.

Lok, P., & Crawford, J. (2004). The effect of organisational culture and leadership style on job satisfaction and organisational commitment: A cross-national comparison. *Journal of Management Development*, 23(4), 321–338. 10.1108/02621710410529785

Luthans, F. (1989). *Organisational behaviour* (5th ed.). McGraw-Hill.

Madlock, P. E. (2008). The link between leadership style, communicator competence, and employee satisfaction. *Journal of Business Communication*, 45(1), 61–78. 10.1177/0021943607309351

Morris, G. (2021) Investigating the employment motivation and job satisfaction of expatriate language teachers (Thesis (EdD)). Exeter University, Exeter.

Naidu, J., & Van der Walt, M. (2005). An exploration of the relationship between leadership styles and the implementation of transformation interventions. *SA Journal of Human Resource Management*, 3(2), 1–10. 10.4102/sajhrm.v3i2.60

Naumann, E. (1993). Organizational predictors of expatriate job satisfaction. *Journal of International Business Studies*, 24(1), 61–80. 10.1057/palgrave.jibs.8490225

Oduro, G. K. (2004, September 16-18). *Distributed leadership in schools: What English headteachers say about the pull and push factors* [Paper presentation]. British Educational Research Association Annual Conference, University of Manchester. https://www.leeds.ac.uk/educol/documents/00003673.pdf

Ojokuku, R., Odetayo, T., & Sajuyigbe, A. (2012). Impact of leadership style on organizational performance: A case study of Nigerian banks. *American Journal of Business and Management*, 1(4), 202–207.

Saleem, H. (2015). The impact of leadership styles on job satisfaction and mediating role of perceived organizational politics. *Procedia: Social and Behavioral Sciences*, 172, 563–569. 10.1016/j.sbspro.2015.01.403

Temple, R. S. (2009) An empirical analysis of nurse manager leadership practices and staff nurse job satisfaction. (Order No. 3356436, Walden University).

Top, M., Akdere, M., & Tarcan, M. (2015). Examining transformational leadership, job satisfaction, organizational commitment and organizational trust in Turkish hospitals: Public servants versus private sector employees. *International Journal of Human Resource Management*, 26(9), 1259–1282. 10.1080/09585192.2014.939987

Walker, G. (2002). *To educate the nations: Reflections on an international education*. John Catt Educational Ltd.

Weber, M. (2009). *The Theory of Social and Economic Organization*. Simon and Schuster.

Wilkins, S., & Neri, S. (2019). Managing faculty in transnational higher education: Expatriate academics at international branch campuses. *Journal of Studies in International Education*, 23(4), 451–472. 10.1177/1028315318814200

Zahari, I. B., & Shurbagi, A. M. A. (2012). The effect of organizational culture and the relationship between transformational leadership and job satisfaction in petroleum sector of Libya. *International Business Research*, 5(9), 89–97. 10.5539/ibr.v5n9p89

Chapter 5
Leadership in English for Academic Purpose(EAP):
A Vision for Sino-Foreign Joint University Success

Kevin Cui
University of Nottingham, Ningbo, China

ABSTRACT

This chapter examines leadership's role in English for Academic Purposes (EAP) within Sino-foreign universities, focusing on overcoming linguistic and cultural challenges through adaptable, culturally sensitive leadership. It highlights the shift from traditional to contemporary leadership theories and the importance of innovation and inclusivity in response to challenges like online learning transitions during the COVID-19 pandemic. Additionally, it explores transformational and transactional leadership models, emphasizing cultural sensitivity in merging Eastern and Western educational practices. The chapter suggests future research directions for enhancing leadership effectiveness in EAP contexts, aiming to improve student engagement and success in the complex landscape of Sino-foreign higher education.

1. INTRODUCTION

The establishment of the Sino-Foreign Cooperative University Union in 2014 marked a significant milestone in the evolution of higher education within China, signifying a new era of international collaboration (Harper and Sun, 2022; Lin and Liu,2016). This initiative highlighted the critical role of Sino-foreign universities as integral platforms for bridging Eastern and Western educational philosophies and practices. Within this context, English for Academic Purposes (EAP) programs emerged as vital components, addressing the linguistic and academic challenges faced by students navigating these cross-cultural educational landscapes. As highlighted in the 2020 CSIS report (Yin,2023), the geopolitical landscape and varying educational philosophies between China and its international partners add layers of complexity to the Sino-foreign universities' mission, underscoring the intricate environment in which EAP operates.

EAP programs within Sino-foreign universities are tasked with an essential role: to bridge the linguistic divide and facilitate academic success for an increasingly diverse student body. The challenge is compounded by the need to align these programs with the academic rigor and expectations of Sino-foreign universities, which blend elements of both Eastern and Western educational traditions. In this intricate educational milieu, leadership within EAP programs becomes paramount (Kirkpatrick,2014; Han,2023). The nuanced relationship between English Medium Instruction (EMI) and EAP within Sino-foreign universities necessitates a leadership style that is innovative, forward-thinking, and capable of navigating the pedagogical challenges unique to this context. Galloway and Rose (2020)and Hang and Zhang (2022) underscore the necessity of such leadership to enable pedagogical cross-fertilization, which is essential for enhancing the accessibility and quality of EAP programs. Their insights suggest that effective leadership is not just about administrative oversight but involves deeply engaging with pedagogical strategies to ensure EAP programs meet the diverse needs of their students.

Moreover, Harper and Sun's (2022) research emphasize the importance of aligning EAP programs with the wide-ranging academic and social integration needs of students. The leadership within EAP programs must, therefore, be responsive and adaptive, capable of understanding and addressing the multifaceted demands placed on students. Adding another layer to this discussion, Chen's (2020) study highlights a challenge that extends to Sino-foreign universities: the clash between English-only policies and the diverse linguistic backgrounds of students, especially from China. It emphasizes the need for EAP leadership to champion plurilingual and inclusive education, pushing beyond challenging monolingual policies to nurture an environment that values and utilizes students' linguistic and cultural diversity. This advocacy is crucial for Sino-foreign universities, where combining different educational and linguistic traditions is essential.

This chapter attempts to explore the crucial role of leadership in overcoming the pedagogical, linguistic, and cultural challenges faced by EAP programs in Sino-foreign universities. By examining leadership theories, analyzing practical obstacles, and reviewing successful case studies, the chapter will highlight leadership's impact on EAP success and provide strategic recommendations for enhancing students' academic and intercultural competencies. This investigation is essential for understanding how leadership in EAP can evolve to meet students' immediate needs while preparing them for their future in a global academic and professional environment.

2. LEADERSHIP THEORIES RELEVANT TO EAP IN SINO-FOREIGN CONTEXTS

2.1 Brief Review of Traditional Leadership Theories

Traditional leadership theories have formed the basis for understanding dynamics in various settings, including education. Pioneered by theorists like Dinh et al. (2014) and Kezar and Lester (2009), these theories range from the Great Man theory, suggesting inherent leadership traits, to behavioral theories that advocate learned effective behaviors (Beerken and van der Hoek, 2022). Although insightful, these theories often lack the flexibility needed to tackle the unique challenges within EAP programs at Sino-foreign universities, prompting a shift towards more adaptable leadership styles that incorporate transformational and transactional elements and emphasize cultural sensitivity (Wilson, 2016).

2.2 Applicability of Transformational and Transactional Leadership Theories to EAP Contexts

Moving beyond traditional leadership theories, the relevance of transformational and transactional approaches in EAP settings, especially within Sino-foreign collaborations, highlights the necessity for adaptable and innovative leadership. Research by Bass and Riggio (2006) on collaborative leadership in international educational contexts underscores the importance of fostering synergy between EAP and EMI programs, who elaborate on transformational leadership, a model that encourages leaders to inspire followers to transcend their expectations and unite under a collective vision. It outlines the model's core components: idealized Influence, Inspirational Motivation, Intellectual Stimulation, and Individualized Consideration: as mechanisms for fostering follower development and leadership emergence. While they champion transformational leadership for its ability to improve follower satisfaction and overall performance (2006), it also cautions against its potential exploitation, underscoring the necessity for ethical leadership to ensure its positive impact. Contrasting these with Bass and Riggio's transformational leadership model, Salihu's (2019) work implies a need for educational leaders to embody transformational qualities, adapting to various situations, fostering individual growth, and moving beyond fixed attributes to shape the future of education effectively. The relationship lies in the application of the transformational model within the context of higher education leadership, where Salihu (2019) sees the potential for transformational practices to address the deficiencies of traditional theories. However, both of their findings advocate for leadership styles that are both responsive and flexible, reflecting the unique challenges faced by EAP programs in Sino-foreign universities. This shift towards models that prioritize cultural sensitivity and pedagogical innovation marks a significant departure from traditional leadership theories, focusing on the dynamic needs of a global student body.

The nuanced approach to leadership in EAP settings acknowledges the complex challenges of cross-cultural education, requiring leaders to not only uphold academic and linguistic standards but also cultivate an inclusive and dynamic learning environment (Galloway and Rose, 2022). Transformational leadership, focusing on vision, inspiration, and individualized consideration, resonates with the objectives of EAP programs to facilitate students' linguistic, cultural, and academic integration into their new educational settings. Walker's (2021) case study on transformational leadership practices in EAP demonstrates their effectiveness in boosting student engagement and learning outcomes, showcasing the potential for such leadership to navigate the intricacies of language instruction and cross-cultural adaptation within Sino-Foreign universities. Furthermore, transactional leadership's emphasis on clear objectives and performance metrics complements the transformational approach by ensuring EAP programs maintain high standards and meet educational benchmarks (Walker,2021). However, its application must be nuanced, accommodating the diverse linguistic and cultural backgrounds of students. This balance between transformational and transactional leadership styles is crucial for the success of EAP programs in Sino-foreign universities (Chen, 2020), whose research illustrates that while students recognize the pragmatic need to adhere to English-only instruction for academic success, they also see their first language as an asset, not a deficit. This research is significant in the leadership application of EAP teaching of Sino-foreign university context as it adds to the understanding of how language policies in higher education impact international students and provides evidence for the benefits of acknowledging and incorporating students' linguistic diversity into classroom practices.

Drawing from Salihu's (2019) exploration of educational leadership frameworks and Dinh et al.'s (2014) review of current leadership theories, educational leaders can address the pedagogical, linguistic, and cultural challenges unique to Sino-foreign universities. The former highlights the role of leadership in creating educational environments that enhance student competencies, aligning with the transformational aspects of leadership where vision and inspiration are crucial. However, the latter emphasize the importance of understanding leadership as a process that influences outcomes across organizational levels, underscoring the need for leadership styles that are adaptable and culturally competent. This dual approach highlights the importance of employing leadership styles that are flexible and culturally competent, able to adapt to the pedagogical, linguistic, and cultural complexities of teaching EAP in an international context. Thus, applying both transformational and transactional leadership theories within EAP contexts can significantly enhance the educational experience for students, bridging the gap between differing educational philosophies and practices.

2.3 Cultural Sensitivity in Leadership: Bridging Western and Eastern Leadership Styles

Cultural sensitivity in leadership at Sino-foreign universities is crucial, requiring more than the simple merging of Western and Eastern educational philosophies. It calls for a critical reevaluation of traditional models, such as Hofstede's cultural dimensions, which have been critiqued for oversimplifying cultural identities into static categories. This critique, notably by Livermore, advocates for a more dynamic and adaptive approach to cultural understanding that appreciates the complexities of multicultural interactions (Livermore, 2015). Similarly, Bergiel et al. (2009) argue that static cultural models fail to address the intricacies of multicultural environments, underscoring the need for leadership that is adaptable and critically aware of these challenges.

The implementation of plurilingual and culturally inclusive education also presents significant challenges, requiring leaders capable of navigating resistance and integrating diverse languages and cultures effectively (Sant'Anna, 2024). Recent scholarly discussions, such as those by Segundo (2022) and Noman and Gurr (2020), emphasize the need for leadership approaches that not only question, but actively reshape educational practices to foster genuine inclusivity. They advocate for a leadership style that is responsive to the unique cultural and situational dynamics within educational environments, moving beyond traditional models to embrace approaches like transformational, servant, or even autocratic leadership to suit specific contexts.

In addition to the models mentioned, servant leadership particularly aligns with the goals of cultural sensitivity. This approach emphasizes the leader's role as a servant first, fostering a service-oriented framework that supports and empowers team members, facilitating their personal and professional growth within culturally diverse settings (Greenleaf, 1977). This style has been effective in educational environments where leaders prioritize the well-being and development of their staff and students, thereby enhancing organizational inclusivity and effectiveness.

An example of successful culturally sensitive leadership can be found in the initiatives at Xi'an Jiaotong-Liverpool University, where leadership practices have been tailored to blend Chinese and British educational cultures. The university's leadership has implemented specialized training programs for faculty to help them understand and integrate the cultural nuances of both educational systems, thereby improving the educational experience for students from diverse backgrounds (Perrin and Wang, 2021).

In conclusion, integrating transformational and transactional leadership theories with a strong commitment to cultural sensitivity provides a robust framework for addressing the unique challenges faced by EAP programs in Sino-foreign universities. By embracing these adaptive and culturally aware leadership styles, leaders can foster an educational environment that is not only academically rigorous but also culturally inclusive, ultimately enhancing the success of EAP programs and their students.

3. CHALLENGES IN EAP EDUCATION AND LEADERSHIP RESPONSES

3.1 Identifying Key EAP Challenges in Sino-foreign Collaborations

The pandemic's onset marked a pivotal moment for educational institutions worldwide, compelling a swift transition to online learning. This shift, as Perrin and Wang (2021) highlighted, accelerated the digitalization of education, challenging EAP programs to maintain quality assurance while adapting pedagogies for online effectiveness. This critical period not only underscored the resilience and flexibility of EAP instructors and students but also emphasized the growing importance of digital literacy. Digital literacy emerged as a crucial tool for immediate response to the pandemic's challenges and as a fundamental component of contemporary education, suggesting a permanent shift in educational paradigms. Davies et al. (2020) provide further insights into the pandemic's varied impacts across different Sino-foreign institutions, shedding light on the strategies that sustained learner engagement and academic rigor during this turbulent period. These strategies, born out of necessity, underscore the importance of robust technological platforms and the adaptation of pedagogical strategies to online formats. The implications for the future design and delivery of EAP programs are significant, indicating a lasting transformation in the educational landscape.

The impact was further analyzed by Williamson, Eynon, and Potter (2020), who explored how digital technologies were employed during the coronavirus emergency and impacted pedagogical practices and policies. Their findings reveal that despite the rapid adoption of technology, the necessity for robust technological platforms and pedagogical adaptation to online formats remained critical, underscoring the need for strategic leadership in navigating these changes. However, this transition has not been without its challenges. The shift to online learning raised concerns about the efficacy of digital pedagogy in delivering the nuanced language and cultural learning objectives of EAP programs. Scholars such as Smaliakou et al. (2022) have critiqued the readiness of institutions to implement effective online pedagogical strategies that cater to the diverse needs of international students in Sino-foreign collaborations. They argue that while digital platforms offer new avenues for engagement and learning, the pedagogical approaches must be carefully tailored to ensure they uphold the rigorous academic standards and cultural sensitivity inherent to EAP education.

Moreover, the reliance on technological solutions has highlighted disparities in access and digital literacy among students and faculty, raising equity concerns within the digital learning environment (Lawrence et al., 2020). These disparities underscore the need for comprehensive support systems and targeted professional development to equip all stakeholders with the necessary skills and resources to thrive in an increasingly digital educational landscape. In response to these challenges, leadership within Sino-foreign educational collaborations has played a crucial role. Strategic leadership has been instrumental in navigating the complexities of online transition, emphasizing the need for flexibility, innovation, and a deep commitment to maintaining educational quality and inclusivity (Fu, 2023; Rasli et al. 2022). Leaders have been tasked with balancing the rapid implementation of technological solutions with the long-term vision for EAP education, ensuring that the shift to online learning enhances rather than diminishes the learning experience.

In response to these challenges, leadership within Sino-foreign educational collaborations has played a crucial role. Strategic leadership has been instrumental in navigating the complexities of online transition, emphasizing the need for flexibility, innovation, and a deep commitment to maintaining educational quality and inclusivity (Crawford et al.,2020). Leaders have been tasked with balancing the rapid implementation of technological solutions with the long-term vision for EAP education, ensuring that the shift to online learning enhances rather than diminishes the learning experience (Hodges et al.,2020).

The leadership responses to technological issues like AI and internet censorship in Sino-foreign contexts are also of great importance. Zawacki-Richter et al. (2020) discuss the use of AI in higher education. Their systematic review reveals how AI applications are shaping educational practices and the need for educators to adapt to these emerging technologies while addressing the associated challenges and opportunities. This body of work suggests that effective leadership in Sino-foreign universities involves not only technological adaptation but also strategic negotiation and advocacy to ensure access to unrestricted educational content.

3.2 Case Examples of Leadership Responses to These Challenges

The conclusion of the pandemic's acute phase presents a pivotal moment for Sino-foreign universities, which stand at the crossroads of Eastern and Western educational philosophies. Throughout the pandemic, these institutions exemplified resilience and innovation, employing adaptive and transformative leadership strategies to manage the swift transition to online learning. For instance, the experiences of universities like Xi'an Jiaotong-Liverpool University showcase the proactive enhancement of digital infrastructure and pedagogical practices, ensuring the continuity of high-quality education across diverse cultural contexts (Perrin and Wang, 2021). This period has underscored the significance of collaborative leadership in turning challenges into growth opportunities. Sino-foreign universities have demonstrated a remarkable commitment to instructional continuity, utilizing diverse online platforms and tools to support their unique student bodies. The strategic facilitation of peer interaction and strengthening of student support systems were crucial in managing the psychological and academic challenges of the transition, reflecting a nuanced understanding of the cultural and linguistic diversity within these institutions.

Moreover, Walker's (2021) case study provides an insightful example of transformational leadership in EAP, focusing on student-centered learning and motivation without the use of extrinsic rewards. In this study, instructors adopted a transformational approach by setting clear, inspiring visions and actively supporting students in achieving these goals, thereby fostering a highly engaging and interactive learning environment. They implemented specific online adaptation strategies such as synchronous and asynchronous sessions tailored to maximize interaction, the use of real-time feedback tools to keep students engaged, and group projects that leveraged collaborative online platforms to simulate a classroom experience. These methods not only elevated student engagement and learning outcomes but also exemplified the shared leadership model explored by Kezar and Holcombe (2017), where decision-making and strategic thinking were distributed across multiple stakeholders, including faculty and students, to adapt to the new teaching demands effectively.

The shift to online education in Sino-foreign universities during the COVID-19 pandemic revealed significant challenges in grading, proctoring, and ensuring equitable access, as documented by Grajek (2020). These institutions responded by adapting academic policies, introducing online proctoring tools to uphold academic integrity while addressing privacy concerns and technological disparities, and supporting faculty and students with necessary resources and digital pedagogy training. Flexible grading policies, such as pass/fail options, were implemented to accommodate diverse student needs. As the pandemic recedes, these universities are shaping a resilient and flexible educational model, integrating Eastern and Western pedagogies and leveraging digital innovations like project-based assessments to enhance the educational experience and address the evolving demands of a digitized learning landscape.

3.3 How Leadership Influences EAP Program Outcomes and Student Success

The influence of leadership on EAP program outcomes and student success in Sino-foreign universities during the COVID-19 pandemic underscores a strategic and multifaceted approach to overcoming challenges and fostering innovation. The rapid transition to online learning, driven by leaders within these educational institutions, was a pivotal response that ensured continuity and quality in education. This leadership initiative is supported by the study from Aristovnik et al. (2021), which found that proactive communication, regular updates, and the integration of flexible learning tools significantly enhanced academic student satisfaction and perceived performance across several countries during the pandemic. The study highlights the global challenge of maintaining effective e-learning environments and shows that leadership that actively engages with student feedback and adjusts strategies accordingly can greatly improve educational outcomes.

Building on the theme of effective communication, the comparative study by Kim and Shin (2022) on leadership styles in multinational corporations offers further insights into the adaptability and cultural sensitivity required in leadership. This research reveals that leaders who employ a mix of transformational and transactional leadership styles: encouraging innovation while setting clear guidelines—are better able to adapt pedagogical strategies and ensure educational continuity in the unique context of Sino-foreign collaborations. These leadership styles have been instrumental in aligning technological upgrades with pedagogical needs, thereby enhancing the overall learning experience during the shift to online education.

Continuing this trajectory of leadership effectiveness, the emphasis on professional development and support for faculty, as highlighted by Kohnke and Zou (2021), has been crucial for enabling effective online teaching practices. Recognizing the importance of continuous training and support systems, leaders have facilitated workshops and seminars that focus on improving digital pedagogy skills among faculty. This initiative is complemented by the findings of Yang, Chiu, and Yan (2021), who demonstrated that timely and constructive feedback from teachers significantly boosts student learning outcomes and satisfaction. These measures underscore the critical role of leadership in developing a supportive and responsive educational environment.

Linking professional development with broader leadership strategies, a crucial element of effective leadership within Sino-foreign universities is the implementation of robust feedback mechanisms. Bovill, Bulley, and Morss (2011) highlight the importance of involving students in curriculum design, facilitated through regular surveys, focus groups, and open forums. These platforms not only collect feedback, but also actively engage students in the educational process, enhancing their sense of agency and involvement. The utilization of this data informs continuous improvements, ensuring that programs not only meet but exceed the evolving expectations of their diverse student bodies. Trowler's (2010) review on student engagement reinforces how effective feedback mechanisms can transform student experiences, providing educational leaders with actionable insights that promote academic and interpersonal growth.

This comprehensive approach not only enhances student satisfaction and academic outcomes, but also fosters a culture of inclusivity and respect, making it a cornerstone of successful educational leadership in the context of Sino-foreign collaborations. Through these feedback mechanisms, educational leaders create a participatory culture that encourages continuous dialogue and collaboration, pivotal for the dynamic and multicultural setting of Sino-foreign universities.

In conclusion, the challenges brought about by the COVID-19 pandemic have catalyzed significant changes in EAP education within Sino-foreign collaborations. Leadership responses, particularly those focused on adapting to digital demands and enhancing teacher and student capabilities, have been crucial in addressing these challenges and influencing program outcomes and student success. The lessons learned from this period of rapid digitalization and pedagogical adaptation will undoubtedly shape the future of EAP education, making it more resilient and responsive to the evolving educational landscape. Through these strategic leadership actions, Sino-foreign universities have managed to not only maintain but also enhance student engagement and educational quality during an unprecedented global crisis.

4. IMPLICATIONS FOR FUTURE LEADERSHIP IN SINO-FOREIGN UNIVERSITIES

4.1 Strengthening Leadership Capacities in EAP Program Management in Sino-foreign Universities

Strengthening leadership capacities within EAP program management at Sino-foreign universities is a multifaceted endeavor that requires a nuanced understanding of the interplay between different cultures, educational philosophies, and strategic planning. Hollander (1978) emphasizes the importance of dynamic leadership that adapts to the evolving needs of international collaborations. Effective leaders in these contexts are not just administrators; they are visionaries capable of navigating the complexities of cross-cultural communication and collaboration, aligning the program's objectives with the overarching goals of both partnering institutions.

Building on Hollander's emphasis on dynamic leadership, the concept of cultural intelligence becomes crucial. According to Livermore (2015), cultural intelligence equips leaders with the necessary skills to bridge cultural gaps, fostering an inclusive learning environment and enhancing the educational experience for students from diverse backgrounds. This is particularly relevant in Sino-foreign universities, where leaders must integrate diverse educational methodologies and cultural values. To illustrate the effectiveness of such leadership, Ang and Van Dyne (2015) provide empirical evidence showing that leaders who exhibit high levels of cultural intelligence are better able to manage the demands of cross-cultural interactions. These leaders adapt their behavior to meet the cultural expectations and needs of their teams, leading to improved communication, reduced conflict, and enhanced team performance.

Moreover, Mintzberg (1994) critiques traditional strategic planning processes, advocating for a more flexible, responsive approach to strategy that acknowledges the unpredictable nature of international educational environments. This viewpoint is supported by Kezar and Lester (2009), who promote collaborative models of leadership that encourage partnership and shared governance between faculty, administrators, and students. By fostering a culture of collaboration and open dialogue, EAP programs can become more adaptive and responsive to the needs of their stakeholders. This enhances their effectiveness and sustainability, building on the foundational qualities of cultural intelligence and dynamic leadership to navigate the global challenges of education.

Together, these perspectives form a comprehensive framework for leadership in Sino-foreign universities. By harnessing dynamic, culturally intelligent leadership practices and fostering collaborative environments, EAP programs can effectively respond to the multifaceted challenges posed by international educational collaboration, thereby enhancing their sustainability and impact.

4.2 Encouraging Collaborative Leadership Practices Across Disciplines

In the evolving landscape of Sino-foreign universities, the implementation of collaborative leadership practices necessitates a nuanced understanding of diverse educational models and cultural dynamics. Zou et al. (2015) and Marginson and van der Wende (2007) provide foundational insights into the intricacies of international university collaborations, highlighting the need for leadership that is adaptable and culturally sensitive. Zou et al. (2015) explore diverse approaches to leadership and governance in international universities, underscoring the importance of adaptability in leadership practices to meet the educational and cultural diversities inherent in Sino-foreign collaborations. Marginson and van der Wende (2007) build upon this by examining the global landscape of higher education, pointing out the complexities and opportunities of implementing collaborative practices within such unique partnerships. Their combined perspectives emphasize the strategic role of leadership in facilitating effective cross-cultural and cross-disciplinary collaborations, which are crucial for enhancing academic quality and global competencies among students.

Moreover, the empirical evidence provided by Hue Kyung et al. (2016) on the factors influencing successful university-industry collaboration in Korea offers practical insights that can be extrapolated to the context of Sino-foreign educational collaborations. Their findings suggest that successful collaborations hinge on leadership qualities that include flexibility, cultural competence, and an ability to foster an environment of mutual respect and learning. This empirical backing enriches the discussion by providing concrete examples of how leadership influences the outcomes of collaborative efforts.

To further understand the cultural nuances of collaborative leadership, Hofstede's framework (2010) on cultural dimensions is invaluable. Hofstede identifies several key dimensions of culture that affect interpersonal and organizational behaviors: Power Distance, Individualism versus Collectivism, Masculinity versus Femininity, Uncertainty Avoidance, Long-Term Orientation, and Indulgence versus Restraint. Applying these dimensions to the leadership practices in Sino-foreign universities can help leaders recognize and navigate the cultural expectations and norms that shape decision-making and collaboration in these diverse educational settings.

In synthesizing these perspectives, it becomes evident that fostering collaborative leadership practices in Sino-foreign universities faces multifaceted challenges. These challenges include navigating cultural differences that impact team dynamics and decision-making, aligning educational objectives with diverse pedagogical approaches, and managing the logistical complexities of operating in different regulatory and operational environments. Leadership that embraces diversity, fosters mutual learning, and adapts to the evolving global educational landscape is key to unlocking the potential of Sino-foreign collaborations for enriching the educational experience and preparing students for a connected world.

4.3 Future Directions for Research on Leadership in EAP

The evolving field of EAP within Sino-foreign universities presents unique leadership challenges and opportunities, making it a rich area for future research. Drawing from the comprehensive review by Avolio et al. (2009), it suggests a move towards more inclusive, adaptive, and culturally sensitive leadership practices, recognizing the diverse needs and backgrounds of international student populations, including those from China, which lies in their mutual focus on enhancing educational outcomes within Sino-foreign university contexts, albeit from slightly different perspectives (Zou et al., 2022), who on the other hand, focus more on the curriculum aspects, specifically EMI and EAP's direct impact on academic success. Therefore, future research directions could involve investigating how leadership theories like transformational, authentic, and servant leadership can be effectively applied and possibly modified to enhance EAP teaching outcomes in Sino-foreign contexts. This might include exploring the impact of leadership on student engagement, motivation, and academic success, with a focus on cross-cultural adaptability, communication styles, and the integration of students' linguistic and cultural identities into the learning environment.

To further enhance the understanding and implementation of effective leadership in EAP teaching within Sino-foreign university contexts, incorporating the insights from Marginson and van der Wende (2010) on the dynamics of global higher education proves crucial. Their advocacy for employing comparative case studies across varied cultural and institutional backgrounds lays a robust foundation for examining how leadership models like transformational, authentic, and servant leadership can be tailored to meet the unique challenges of these educational environments. This exploration aims to adapt these leadership theories to improve student engagement, motivation, and academic success, thereby addressing the intricacies of cross-cultural adaptability, communication styles, and the integration of diverse linguistic and cultural identities.

Building on this framework, Day and Leithwood's (2007) focus on assessing leadership training programs underscores the necessity of equipping leaders with the skills and insights to navigate the specific demands of Sino-foreign educational contexts effectively. This entails a practical application of the qualitative research findings into leadership, as Hallinger and Heck (2002) recommend, to reveal the intricate relationship between leadership strategies and their educational outcomes. By delving into leadership perceptions within EAP programs through qualitative methodologies, researchers can offer a deep, nuanced understanding of how leadership influences stakeholder engagement and program morale. Such an approach not only captures the complex nature of educational leadership, but also highlights the importance of creating an inclusive environment for a diverse student body. Despite potential biases and challenges in generalizing findings, this focused exploration within Sino-foreign university settings is vital for developing leadership strategies that resonate with the cultural and linguistic diversity of the student population, thus bridging the theoretical insights with practical applications in leadership development and training programs.

Looking to the future, the integration of digital technologies in educational leadership within Sino-foreign universities is poised to play a pivotal role. As artificial intelligence (AI) and machine learning (ML) technologies become more prevalent, their impact on educational practices is undeniable. Drachsler and Kalz (2016) emphasize that AI-driven analytics can provide leaders with deeper insights into student performance and engagement patterns, enabling more informed decision-making. Predictive analytics could tailor educational content to individual needs, potentially revolutionizing the EAP landscape. However, the adoption of such technologies also demands a robust understanding of data ethics and privacy concerns. Zawacki-Richter and Marín (2018) discuss the need for transparency in AI decisions, especially in diverse cultural settings where perceptions and regulations may vary significantly.

Furthermore, the global classroom environment facilitated by virtual reality (VR) and augmented reality (AR) technologies offers new avenues for cultural exchange and interaction among students from diverse backgrounds. Radianti et al. (2020) explore how these technologies can simulate real-world interactions and provide immersive learning experiences that were previously impossible, thereby enriching the educational experience and offering new challenges and opportunities for leadership in educational settings.

5. CONCLUSION

In conclusion, the exploration of leadership in EAP programs within Sino-foreign universities illuminates a dynamic landscape shaped by the integration of Eastern and Western educational philosophies. As highlighted in the introduction, the establishment of the Sino-Foreign Cooperative University Union marked a significant milestone in higher education, emphasizing the pivotal role of Sino-foreign universities in bridging cultural and pedagogical divides.

Throughout this discourse, it becomes evident that leadership in EAP programs within Sino-foreign universities is not merely administrative, but rather visionary and transformative. The synthesis of traditional and contemporary leadership theories underscores the need for adaptable and culturally sensitive leadership approaches that resonate within the intricate educational milieu of Sino-foreign universities. Drawing from case examples, strategic leadership is indispensable in navigating challenges, such as the transition to online learning during the COVID-19 pandemic, while fostering innovation and inclusivity.

Looking forward, future research on leadership in EAP within Sino-foreign universities should delve deeper into the nuances of leadership efficacy, explore diverse leadership models through comparative case studies across varied cultural contexts, and evaluate the effectiveness of leadership training programs tailored for the unique needs of Sino-foreign universities. By embracing these avenues of inquiry, scholars can contribute to the advancement of evidence-based practices that enhance the quality and sustainability of EAP programs within Sino-foreign collaborations. Ultimately, such efforts will enrich the educational experience, preparing students for success in a globally connected academic and professional environment, echoing the vision set forth by the Sino-Foreign Universities.

REFERENCES

Aristovnik, A., Keržič, D., Ravšelj, D., Tomaževič, N., & Umek, L. (2020). Impacts of the COVID-19 Pandemic on Life of Higher Education Students: A Global Perspective. *Sustainability (Basel)*, 12(8438), 1–34. 10.3390/su12208438

Avolio, B. J., Walumbwa, F. O., & Weber, T. J. (2009). Leadership: Current Theories, Research, and Future Directions. *Annual Review of Psychology*, 60(1), 421–449. 10.1146/annurev.psych.60.110707.16362118651820

Bass, B. M., & Riggio, R. E. (2006). *Transformational Model of Leadership* (2nd ed.). Lawrence Erlbaum Associates. 10.4324/9781410617095

Beerkens, M., & van der Hoek, M. (2022). Academic leaders and leadership in the changing higher education landscape. In Research Handbook on Academic Careers and Managing Academics. Edward Elgar Publishing., Available at https://www.researchgate.net/publication/360065231, Retrieved March 15th, 2024, from. 10.4337/9781839102639.00017

Bennis, W., & Thomas, R. J. (2002). Crucibles of Leadership. *Harvard Business Review*.12227145

Bergiel, E. B., Bergiel, B. J., & Upson, J. W. (2012). Revisiting Hofstede's Dimensions: Examining the Cultural Convergence of the United States and Japan. *American Journal of Management*, 12(1), 69–79.

Bovill, C., Bulley, C. J., & Morss, K. (2011). Engaging and empowering students in higher education through curriculum design partnerships. *The International Journal for Academic Development*, 16(1), 54–68.

Chen, L. (2020). 'Problematising the English-only policy in EAP: A mixed-methods investigation of Chinese international students' perspectives of academic language policy'. *Journal of Multilingual and Multicultural Development*, 41(8), 718–735. 10.1080/01434632.2019.1643355

Crawford, J., Butler-Henderson, K., Rudolph, J., Malkawi, B., Glowatz, M., Burton, R., Magni, P., & Lam, S. (2020). COVID-19: 20 countries' higher education intra-period digital pedagogy responses. *Journal of Applied Learning & Teaching*, 3(1), 1–20.

Davies, J. A., Davies, L. J., Conlon, B., Emerson, J., Hainsworth, H., & McDonough, H. G. (2020). Responding to COVID-19 in EAP Contexts: A Comparison of Courses at Four Sino-Foreign Universities. *International Journal of TESOL Studies*, 2(2), 32–51. 10.46451/ijts.2020.09.04

Day, C., & Leithwood, K. (2007). *Successful principal leadership in times of change*. Springer. 10.1007/1-4020-5516-1

Dinh, J. E., Lord, R. G., Gardner, W. L., Meuser, J. D., Liden, R. C., & Hu, J. (2014). Leadership theory and research in the new millennium: Current theoretical trends and changing perspectives. *The Leadership Quarterly*, 25(1), 36–62. 10.1016/j.leaqua.2013.11.005

Drachsler, H., & Kalz, M. (2016). The impact of artificial intelligence and analytics on educational practices and student learning. *Journal of Educational Technology & Society*, 19(2), 34–49.

Fu, J. (2023). *Distributed Leadership in University Quality Management: An Exploration in a Sino-Foreign Cooperative University in China*. Ph.D. The University of Liverpool (United Kingdom). Available from: ProQuest Dissertations Publishing, 30713114.

Galloway, N., & Rose, H. (2022). Cross-fertilisation not bifurcation of EMI and EAP. *ELT Journal*, 76(4), 538–546. Retrieved March 16th, 2024, from https://academic.oup.com/eltj/article/76/4/538/6694743. 10.1093/elt/ccac033

Grajek, S. (2020). EDUCAUSE COVID-19 QuickPoll Results: Grading and Proctoring. *EDUCAUSE Review*. Available at: https://er.educause.edu/blogs/2020/4/educause-covid-19-quickpoll-results-grading-and-proctoring [Accessed: Feb.27th,2024].

Greenleaf, R. K. (1977). *Servant Leadership: A Journey into the Nature of Legitimate Power and Greatness*. Paulist Press.

Hallinger, P., & Heck, R. H. (2002). *What Do You Call People With Visions? The Role of Vision, Mission, and Goals in School Leadership and Improvement*. Second International Handbook of Educational Leadership and Administration., 10.1007/978-94-010-0375-9_2

Han, S. (2023). English medium instruction at Sino-foreign cooperative education institutions in China: Is internationalising teaching and learning possible? *Language, Culture and Curriculum*, 36(1), 83–99. 10.1080/07908318.2022.2032127

Hang, Y. and Zhang, X. (2022). How Chinese students manage their transition to higher education effectively: student initiative at Sino-Foreign cooperative universities. *Asia Pacific Journal of Education*, [online] 42(4), pp.517-533. Available at: https://doi.org/10.1080/02188791.2022.2047610

Harper, J., & Sun, Y. (2022). EAP Courses in Joint-Venture Institutions: A Needs Analysis Based on Learner Perceptions. *Indonesian Journal of English Language Teaching and Applied Linguistics*, 7(1), 159–179. 10.21093/ijeltal.v7i1.1282

Hodges, C., Moore, S., Lockee, B., Trust, T., & Bond, A. (2020). The difference between emergency remote teaching and online learning.

Hofstede, G., Garibaldi de Hilal, A. V., Malvezzi, S., Tanure, B., & Vinken, H. (2010). Comparing Regional Cultures Within a Country: Lessons From Brazil. *Journal of Cross-Cultural Psychology*, 41(3), 336–352. 10.1177/0022022109359696

Hollander, E. J. (1978). *Leadership dynamics: A practical guide to effective relationships*. Free Press.

Hue Kyung, L., Hyun Duk, Y., Si Jeoung, K., & Yoon Kyo, S. (2016). Factors affecting university–industry cooperation performance: Study of the mediating effects of government and enterprise support. *Journal of Science and Technology Policy Management*, 7(2), 233–254. 10.1108/JSTPM-08-2015-0029

James, M.A. (2023) "An exploratory investigation of instructors' practices and challenges in promoting students' learning transfer in EAP education," *Journal of EAPs*, 64.

Kaivanpanah, S., Alavi, S. M., Bruce, I., & Hejazi, S. Y. (2021). EAP in the expanding circle: Exploring the knowledge base, practices, and challenges of Iranian EAP practitioners. *Journal of English for Academic Purposes*, 50, 50. 10.1016/j.jeap.2021.100971

Kezar, A., & Holcombe, E. M. (2017). *Shared Leadership in Higher Education: Important Lessons from Research and Practice*. ACE Series on Higher Education. American Council on Education.

Kezar, A., & Lester, J. (2009). *Organizing higher education for collaboration: A guide for campus leaders*. Jossey-Bass.

Kim, S., & Shin, M. (2022). Effective Leadership Differs Between Organizations: A Comparative Study of US and German Multinational Corporations in South Korea. *SAGE Open*, 12(2). Advance online publication. 10.1177/21582440221097890

Kirkpatrick, A. (2014). English as a Medium of Instruction in East and Southeast Asian Universities. *The Asian Journal of Applied Linguistics*, 1(1), 3–15. 10.1007/978-94-007-7972-3_2

Kohnke, L., & Zou, D. (2021). Reflecting on Existing English for Academic Purposes Practices: Lessons for the Post-COVID Classroom. *Sustainability (Basel)*, 13(11520), 11520. Advance online publication. 10.3390/su132011520

Lawrence, G., Ahmed, F., Cole, C., & Johnston, K. P. (2020). Not More Technology but More Effective Technology: Examining the State of Technology Integration in EAP Programmes. *RELC Journal*, 51(1), 101–116. 10.1177/0033688220907199

Lin, J. H., & Liu, M. J. (2016). A Discussion on Improving the Quality of Sino-Foreign Cooperative Education. *Chinese Education & Society*, 49(4-5), 231–242. 10.1080/10611932.2016.1237845

Livermore, D. (2015). *Leading with cultural intelligence: The real secret to success*. AMACOM.

Marginson, S., & van der Wende, M. (2007). *Globalisation and Higher Education*. ECD Education Working Papers, 8. Available at: https://www.oecd.org/education/research/37552729.pdf [Accessed: Feb.10th,2024].

Mintzberg, H. (1994). *The rise and fall of strategic planning*. Free Press.

Noman, M., & Gurr, D. (2020). Contextual Leadership and Culture in Education. In G. W. Noblit (Ed.), Oxford Research Encyclopedia of Education (pp. 1–20). Oxford University Press., Retrieved February 25th, 2024, from, 10.1093/acrefore/9780190264093.013.595

Perrin, S., & Wang, L. (2021) COVID-19 and rapid digitalization of learning and teaching: quality assurance issues and solutions in a Sino-foreign higher education institution. Quality assurance issues and solutions, 29(4), pp.463-476. Available at: https://nusearch.nottingham.edu.cn/permalink/f/s8ggqh/TN_cdi_emerald_primary_10_1108_QAE-12-2020-0167 [Accessed:Dec.8th, 2023].

Radianti, J., Majchrzak, T. A., Fromm, J., & Wohlgenannt, I. (2020). A systematic review of immersive virtual reality applications for higher education: Design elements, lessons learned, and research agenda. *Computers & Education*, 147, 103778. 10.1016/j.compedu.2019.103778

Rasli, A., Tee, M., Lai, Y. L., Tiu, Z. C., & Soon, E. H. (2022). Post-COVID-19 strategies for higher education institutions in dealing with unknown and uncertainties. *Frontiers in Education*, 7, 992063. Retrieved March 15th, 2024, from https://www.frontiersin.org/articles/10.3389/feduc.2022.992063/full. 10.3389/feduc.2022.992063

Salihu, M. J. (2019). An Analysis of the Leadership Theories and Proposal of New Leadership Framework in Higher Education. *Asian Journal of Education and Social Studies*, 5(4), 1–6. Retrieved December 10th, 2023, from https://www.researchgate.net/publication/338421257. 10.9734/ajess/2019/v5i430164

Sant'Anna, A. de S. 2024. Leadership Styles Across Cultures: A Comparative Study of Western and Asian Contexts through Hofested and Deleuzian. [online] LinkedIn. Available at: https://www.linkedin.com/pulse/leadership-styles-across-cultures-comparative-study-1-anderson-2uxuf/ [Accessed 10 February 2024].

Segundo, M. G. (2022). Leadership and Culture: What Difference Does it Make? In: *2022 Regent Research Roundtables Proceedings*, pp.104-119. Regent University School of Business & Leadership.

Smaliakou, D., Wu, J., & Guo, J. (2022). *The Impact of the Pandemic on China's International Higher Education Policy*. Lingnan Normal University; Institute of Philosophy of the National Academy of Sciences of Belarus.

Spillane, J. P. (2005). Distributed Leadership. *The Educational Forum*, 69(2), 143–150. 10.1080/00131720508984678

Trowler, V. (2010). Student engagement literature review. *The Higher Education Academy*, 11, 1–15.

Walker, C. (2021). Transformational instructor leadership in English for academic purposes: A case study. Doctoral thesis, University of Calgary. Available at: http://hdl.handle.net/1880/114189 [Accessed: Mar.16th 2024].

Weber, E., Krehl, E.-H., & Büttgen, M. (2022). The Digital Transformation Leadership Framework: Conceptual and Empirical Insights into Leadership Roles in Technology-Driven Business Environments. *Journal of Leadership Studies*, 16(1), 6–22. 10.1002/jls.21810

Williamson, B., Eynon, R., & Potter, J. (2020). Pandemic politics, pedagogies and practices: Digital technologies and distance education during the coronavirus emergency. *Learning, Media and Technology*, 45(2), 107–114. 10.1080/17439884.2020.1761641

Wilson, K. (2016). Critical Reading, Critical Thinking: Delicate Scaffolding in English for Academic Purposes (EAP). *Thinking Skills and Creativity*, 22, 256–265. 10.1016/j.tsc.2016.10.002

Yang, L.,Chiu,M. M., Yan Z. (2021) The power of teacher feedback in affecting student learning and achievement: Insights from students' perspectives, *Educational Psychology*, 41:7 821-824, DOI: .10.1080/01443410.2021.1964855

Yin, Q. (2023) Even as Tensions Grow, U.S.-China Joint Venture Universities Have Room to Develop. *New Perspectives on Asia*, CSIS. Available at: Even as Tensions Grow, U.S.-China Joint Venture Universities Have Room to Develop | New Perspectives on Asia | CSIS [Accessed: Dec.9th, 2023].

Zawacki-Richter, O., Marín, V. I., Bond, M., & Gouverneur, F. (2020). Systematic review of research on artificial intelligence applications in higher education – where are the educators? *International Journal of Educational Technology in Higher Education*, 16(1), 39. 10.1186/s41239-019-0171-0

Zheng, B. B., & Warschauer, M. (2015). Participation, interaction, and academic achievement in an online discussion environment. *Computers & Education*, 84, 78–89. 10.1016/j.compedu.2015.01.008

Zou, B., Wang, X., & Yu, C. (2022). 'The impact of Sino-foreign cooperative universities in China on Chinese postgraduate students' learning performances in the United Kingdom and United States'. *Frontiers in Psychology*, 13, 1012614. Advance online publication. 10.3389/fpsyg.2022.101261436304855

Chapter 6
The Development of Professional Identity and Its Associations With Emotions:
An Empirical Study of University EAP Teachers With Diverse Ethnic Backgrounds

Zhenying Shi
Dulwich International High School, Suzhou, China

Yunyan Zhang
Xi'an Jiaotong-Liverpool University, China

Rong Yan
http://orcid.org/0000-0001-6570-4824
Xi'an Jiaotong-Liverpool University, China

ABSTRACT

Although the significance of professional identity to language teachers has been widely acknowledged, much remains unknown about the dynamic process of emotion negotiation and identity development of FL/SL teachers with different ethnical background under the Covid-19 pandemic context. Through a semi-structured interview with 10 EAP teachers from an EMI university in China, this study aimed to explore how their professional identity changed and transformed since the outbreak of the Covid-19, and how it negotiated with emotions during the pandemic. The following results were obtained: (1) Ethnical background was one of the significant factors influencing the development of teacher's professional identity; (2) international teachers were found to be more susceptible to the pandemic and compared with their Chinese counterparts, they generated more negative emotions; (3) teacher-student classroom interactions were found to be one of the significant factors triggering the emotional changes and transformation of professional identities regardless of their ethnical backgrounds.

DOI: 10.4018/979-8-3693-2857-6.ch006

1. INTRODUCTION

The importance of teacher professional identity to foreign/second language teaching and pedagogy can be attributed to the fact that what, how, and why language teachers teach is influenced explicitly and implicitly by how they view themselves as professionals. It has been widely acknowledged that new teachers' perceptions of their identities substantially impact their access to power, ownership of their languages, and professional development (Donato, 2016; Kayi-Ager & Wyatt, 2019). Among many factors relating to teacher professional identity, emotion has been identified as the most crucial variable affecting how a teacher develops their self-sense, thus increasingly attracting attention of applied linguists and language educators.

Identity, emotions, and instructional strategies interact significantly in language learning (Motha and Lin, 2014). Positive emotions have been shown to strengthen teachers' developing identities. In contrast, negative emotions might undermine those identities and even cause teachers to reevaluate and doubt their preexisting identities (Schutz & Lee, 2014). Recent research has shed a great deal of light on the solid relationship between second language teachers' emotions and the formation of their professional identities (Jeongyeon & Hye Young, 2020; Song, 2016). However, despite mounting evidence of substantial connections between emotions and the professional identity of foreign/second language teachers (Miller & Gkonou, 2018; Motha & Lin, 2014; Schutz & Lee, 2014; Song, 2016), very few have examined the issue from a cross-cultural perspective given that the majority of extant studies focused primarily on the teachers with the same ethnic background. Apart from the impact of diversity of ethnic backgrounds, it is also vital to consider the impact that Covid-19 would have on the interactions between professional identity and the emotions or feelings of FL (foreign language) and SL (second language) teachers. Unlike all the other countries, China had implemented and enforced the "Zero Case Pandemic Control Policy" since the breakout of Covid-19, which brought a tremendous challenge to many FL/SL teachers, especially the international teachers who recently relocated to China. It is apparent that many more stressors had been triggered for them to cope with under such circumstances, including the difficulties caused by online instructions, disappointments, worries and fears throughout the quarantine, a lack of support from the university and government during the lockdown, to name just a few (Gu et al., 2022; Katarzyna, 2021; MacIntyre, Gregersen, & Mercer, 2020). Consequently, when FL/SL instructors, especially international teachers, are engaged in a social and cultural context that is utterly foreign to them, such unpleasant emotional experiences, plus the threat and inconvenience caused by Covid-19, would impair their social interactions and sense of self.

Therefore, this research aims to explore the factors that influence the professional identity and emotions of language teachers with diverse ethnic backgrounds in China during the pandemic. This chapter also intends to identify the differences in the development of emotion and professional identity between Chinese and international teachers.

2. LITERATURE REVIEW

2.1 Conceptualization

2.1.1 Professional Identity

The concept of language teacher identity pertains to how language educators view both themselves and the work they do (Song, 2016); language teachers professional identity refers to the attitudes, belief systems, knowledge, and skills that are shared by all language teachers (Elsheikh & Yahia, 2020; Widodo, Fang, & Elyas, 2020). Identities are created within the immediate communities of practice according to the situated and sociocultural theory (Wenger, 1998; Lave & Wenger, 1991), and teachers' professional identity is inextricably linked to sociocultural and community-dependent professional roles. It has been recognized that teachers may work to incorporate their personal identities into their professional identity. Obviously, these incorporation behaviors are critical to the development of teacher professional identities because they are based on the teacher's relationships with students, other teachers, parents, and administrators in their positions (Haniford, 2010). Therefore, teachers' capacity to use particular methods and practices, professional training, and affiliation with a particular group all contribute to their professional identity. Moreover, it has been found that analyzing teachers' discourse narratives about classroom experiences and identities is critical to understanding the process of identity negotiation (Varghese et al., 2005), as teachers always change their identities over time in relation to discourses about themselves and their students (Haniford, 2010; Trent, 2012; Cho, 2014; Wu & Leung, 2020).

The psychological processes that make up a language teacher's professional identity could be broken down into the following five key aspects (Widodo et al., 2020). First, a feeling of gratitude should be considered as the first essential component. These kind of feelings or admirations come from either internal side, e.g. self-appreciation by the language teachers themselves, or external side, e.g. from the language teachers' colleagues, institutions, and students, and it is basically founded on the trust in the language teachers' abilities and skills. A sense of one's own competence is the second component of a language teacher's identity. Not only does one feel and look to be capable of the responsibilities that come along with being a language teacher, but one also receives acknowledgment and commendation for those responsibilities. The third component is the feeling of being linked to others. Since a great number of EFL teachers work and live in the locations other than their home countries, their identities, particularly those of expatriates are largely dependent on their sense of affiliation. Therefore, their well-being is dependent on how they feel that they can get along well with the local students, staff, and community members of the new countries. The fourth component is related to the imagination of how one's professional life might develop in the future. Language instructors, like those who work in any other profession, can keep interested and inspired to remain in their positions by the promise or prospect of future career advancement and development. This, in turn, contributes to their long-term identities. The final component is a sense of dedication, particularly to the capacity of language teachers to flawlessly carry out their professional tasks and realize their professional goals (Barkhuizen, 2016; Hanna et al., 2020; and Gkonou et al., 2018).

2.1.2 Language Teacher Emotion

The definition of emotion is a topic of ongoing discussion (Schuman & Scherer, 2014), and scholars interpret the term of emotion in ways that reflect their various theoretical stances (Oatley, 2000). Four theoretical approaches can be summarized, including psychological, social constructivist, interactionist, and integrated perspectives (Chen, 2021). According to the psychological viewpoint, emotion is a personal, unique, and physiological experience (Alpaslan & Ulubey, 2017). In comparison, the social constructionist viewpoint foregrounds connections and social situations rather than personal traits as what essentially defines how people feel (e.g. Boldt et al., 2015; Hong et al., 2016). The interactionist perspective surpasses both of the previous perspectives by attempting to reconcile their disparities and emphasizing that emotion is not only language-laden but is also physical and performative (Borrachero et al., 2014; Akbari et al., 2017). Integrated perspective defines emotion from a variety of angles (Chen, 2021). For example, Farouk (2012) characterized teacher emotions as internalized feelings that stay dormant inside their bodies but are essential to the relationships and interactions they have with their students, collaborators, and parents.

The classifications of teacher emotion could be summarized as either dichotomous or dimensional. Discrete emotions of instructors are frequently dichotomized into positive and negative states in the literature (e.g. Taxer et al., 2019). However, Sutton and Wheatley (2003) asserted that the dichotomous perspective narrows down the nature of emotion, and is too simple to adequately portray the complex and dynamic nature of emotions. Despite the criticism, the dichotomous method has still molded a foundation for research on emotion classifications (Chen, 2021). On the other hand, as humans' discrete emotions are thought to be interconnected, many researchers have attempted to assess teachers' discrete emotions by developing several dimensions in a model (Šarić, 2015). Four quantitative metrics have so far been developed, including Teacher Emotion Scales (Frenzel et al., 2016), Teacher Emotion Questionnaire (Buri et al., 2018), Achievement Emotions Questionnaire - Teachers (Frenzel et al., 2010), and Teacher Emotion Inventory (Chen, 2016). All of these measurements fall under the categories of positive and negative emotions in the models, and they all concentrate on the discrete emotions of teachers, such as joy, pride, love, fatigue, anger, anxiety (Chen, 2021).

2.2 Studies on Factors Affecting Language Teacher Professional Identity

2.2.1 Teacher Emotion

There is evidence from earlier studies (e.g., Schutz & Lee, 2014; Song, 2016; Yuan & Lee, 2016) that teacher emotions are closely related to their professional identities. The way in which teachers emotionally interact with their students in the classroom and how they identify with these emotional experiences determines how particular emotions and experiences are perceived, which in turn depends on personal identity (Zembylas, 2003). Teachers may encounter complicated emotions in a variety of situations and at various times. In order to make wise professional decisions, teachers are supposed to control and restrain their emotions (O'Connor, 2008). However, teachers frequently run across unspoken emotional guidelines that are ingrained in sociocultural conventions, expectations, and contexts (Shapiro, 2010). These guidelines suggest that teachers suppress unfavorable feelings like anxiety, concern, and vulnerability in favor of showing empathy, pride, and kindness. It's crucial to pay attention to teachers' feelings because identifying the complex practices and processes of teacher professional identity development requires a thorough understanding of teacher emotions (Alsup, 2006; Hargreaves, 2001; Kelchtermans, 2005).

Positive or negative emotions mirror teachers' professional identities (Hayik & Weiner-Levy, 2019; Nazari & Seyri, 2021). Negative emotions experienced by language teachers include anger, stress, anxiety, frustration, and resentment (Frenzel et al., 2016). Overall, negative emotions have been found to threaten language teachers' identities. For instance, Cruess et al. (2015) pointed out in their study that stress and anxiety caused language teachers to lose their sense of professional identity. Similarly, Papaja (2021) also found that stress and anxiety could lead one to lose faith in shared attitudes, beliefs, and abilities and doubt their knowledge capacity to handle the intellectual burden of being a language teacher. It has been evidenced that many language teachers, especially those teaching foreign/second languages experience stress and anxiety from different sources (Ozamiz-Etxebarria et al., 2021; Wakui et al., 2021; Shen et al., 2014). The second effect of negative emotions on language teachers is on their self-esteem. The study conducted by Schutz and Lee (2014) revealed that the emotional labor borne by language teachers always made them question their professional capabilities, thereby lowering their self-esteem. However, Yang, Shu, & Yin (2021) drew a totally different conclusion on the influence of emotions on the professional identity of language teachers. They claimed that frustration, as one of the most common negative emotions among language teachers, could drive them to accomplish a more successful job in their personal and professional endeavors.

Positive emotions, on the other hand, were found to be more welcome among language teachers due to their positive effect on the personal and professional development (Biasutti et al., 2021). Richards (2022) believed that positive emotions were an essential aspect of language teaching, which was an emotionally-charged activity since they influenced both teachers and learners. He also pointed out that some of the positive emotions experienced by language teachers include warmth, affection, and career satisfaction. Barcelos and Ruohotie-Lyhty (2018) argued that language teachers could develop warmth and affection towards their learners if their teaching and learning interactions are healthy, positive, and professional. Positive emotions among language teachers were found to be synonymous with self-confidence, high-quality professional output, academic success among learners, and healthy interactions among teachers and their colleagues. Richards (2022) also found that language teachers who exuded positive emotions always stirred up inspiration, admiration, and hope from their learners, so that language teachers may find it easier to interact and communicate effectively with their learners.

Emotional regulation among teachers is the key to their professional development (Greenier, Derakhshan, & Fathi, 2021). One of the empirical studies by Song (2016) found that Korean English teachers frequently prioritized establishing and maintaining their authority by presenting themselves as "omniscient" teachers. But as a result of feeling compassion for their students, these teachers' identities gradually changed, and they started to welcome international students with a high level of English. Additionally, those teachers worked closely with their students to plan and implement successful classes (Song, 2016). Similarly, a more recent study by Jeongyeon and Hye Young (2020) found that language instructors' professional identities were changed to resemble "friends" from authoritative teachers when emotions were transformed, such as transforming anger and annoyance into compassion for students, et.al. This negotiated teacher emotion increased classroom interactions and influenced teacher professional identity in a positive way (Jeongyeon & Hye Young, 2020).

2.2.2 Pedagogical Beliefs

Pedagogical beliefs refer to teachers' beliefs about education and learning as well as the role of technology in helping teachers translate their teaching and learning beliefs into practice within a classroom setting (Wang & Du, 2014; Muliyah & Aminatun, 2020). In the context of language teaching in China, native and non-native language teachers hold different pedagogical beliefs that influence their negotiation of identities differently. This difference is especially evident when comparing their beliefs concerning teacher-learner relationships and their various roles during teaching and learning (Vizek & Domovic, 2019). On the one hand, native language teachers view themselves as moral role models, parental authorities, and experts in their language subjects. Therefore, their interactions with learners include subtle exertions of superiority and power and attempts to form cordial interpersonal relationships with their learners. These beliefs negotiate the professional identities that dictate how native language teachers perceive their professions and interact with their colleagues and learners. On the other hand, the pedagogical beliefs of non-native language teachers in China were found to prompt them to act as learning facilitators to their learners (Li & Jin, 2020; Wang & Fang, 2020). Therefore, non-native language teachers assume a negotiated identity of strict professionalism with their learners. They often refrain from having personal relationships with their learners (Wang & Fang, 2020). Wang & Du (2014) concluded that pedagogical beliefs are primarily influenced by cultural affiliations and often effectively negotiate teacher identities within specific contexts. Consequently, pedagogical beliefs may vary from one language teacher to another, so does the negotiated identities.

2.2.3 Contextual Factors

Contextual factors are also vital when negotiating language teachers' professional identities. Pishghadam et al. (2022) and Schutz et al. (2018) posit that contextual factors are crucial to the identity formation process for any individual. In the case of language teachers in China, their negotiated identities were reported to be primarily influenced by the contextual factors such as work environment, interactions with learners, cultural context, and learners' attitudes and perceptions (Wang & Du, 2014). Teachers in a positive work environment were found to be more likely to develop a strong sense of self-identity. In contrast, the study conducted by Smagorinsky et al. (2004) on trainee teachers revealed that training in a hostile work environment created a weak sense of self-identity. Owing to the fact that language teaching is a highly-prestigious and respected profession in China, language teachers consider themselves valuable and vital to the language development of their learners. Besides the work environment, the classroom environment also contributes significantly to language teachers' negotiated identities (Pishghadam, Golzar, & Miri, 2022). It was found that language teachers with cooperative learners often showed high self-esteem that propelled their professional development. In contrast, those with uncooperative learners were found to demonstrate low self-esteem, which hindered their professional development (Schutz & Lee, 2014). Lastly, institutional environments significantly contribute to language teachers' professional identity negotiation (Pishghadam, Golzar, & Miri, 2022). For example, some institutions are positive and encourage their language teachers through constant remuneration and acknowledgment. Therefore, teaching practicums in such a supportive institution may likely facilitate more potent and reliable professional identities.

In addition, China's local language teaching context is unique compared to other countries, which may enable the language teachers to obtain exceptionally different experiences and attitudes toward themselves, their students, and the teaching professions. For instance, the research conducted by Yang (2019) showed that language teachers in China preferred to emphasize the need for their students to demonstrate professional competency by the end of their coursework. Similarly, given the fact that professional competency and capacity of language teachers are often measured and reflected by their students' linguistic skills and performance, Asif et al. (2020) maintained that language teachers in China were found to be more likely to view themselves as their students' role models. That being the case, their assumed professional responsibilities may include offering their learners personal and professional guidance when needed. Yang (2019) argued that the teaching approaches adopted by some Chinese language teachers get influenced by cultural differences. Also, language teachers in China are concerned with their respective learners' interest in the language (Wang & Fang, 2020). For instance, teachers of the Chinese language are interested in their learners' interest in Chinese characters that comprise the Chinese language. Language teachers' professional development in China is influenced by their cultural beliefs and cross-cultural interactions in various settings.

2.3 Studies on Language Teachers' Emotions During COVID-19

2.3.1 Impact of Online Teaching on Teacher Emotions During the Pandemic

For three years, the world had experienced the wrath of the Coronavirus pandemic alias Covid-19. The disruptions brought about by the Covid-19 pandemic traversed global social, political, and economic spheres. In China, the government adopted the 'Zero Case Pandemic Control Policy' measure to control the spread of the virus. The Chinese government maintained the following as part of the 'Zero Case Pandemic Control Policy' measure (Cheshmehzangi et al., 2022). First, the country would keep its borders shut against international travelers. Secondly, the government requested everyone to take frequent Covid-19 screening PCR tests. Negative results from the PCR tests were the requirements for entry into public spaces such as schools and universities. Thirdly, the government introduced automated techniques to monitor the infection status of the people. Infected people were, therefore, restricted from interacting with others (Cheshmehzangi et al., 2022). The "Zero Case Pandemic Control Policy" adopted by China has been a significant hurdle for many aspiring FL/SL teachers, particularly for foreign faculty who have recently relocated to China. It has been well established that Covid-19 has introduced several new stressors for language teachers to manage, such as challenges brought on by online instruction, disappointments, worries about isolation and fears throughout the quarantine, and a lack of support from the university and government (Gu et al., 2022).

The negative effect of the Covid-19 pandemic on language teachers' emotions has been documented in a few recent studies. The first emotional effect of Covid-19 on language teachers in China was fear (Kukreti et al., 2021). The first form of fear that the language teachers in China experienced was the job insecurity caused by the pandemic. At the onset of the pandemic, most governments, including the Chinese government, ordered the closure of schools indefinitely to curb the spread of the coronavirus. When the situation improved in 2021, schools and universities resumed but adopted online teaching methods. Many teachers lost their jobs during that time, and the lucky ones who retained their jobs constantly feared losing their jobs indefinitely (Zhang et al., 2021). This fear slowly morphed into anxiety and uncertainty over their future career trajectories (Orellana, Liu, & Angeles, 2022). The second form of fear that language teachers experienced during the coronavirus pandemic was that of getting infected (Zhang et al., 2021). Despite taking all the relevant preventive measures like wearing face masks at all times and maintaining social distance when in public spaces or interacting with others, these teachers lived in constant fear of the coronavirus. The fear of losing their jobs and getting infected with the Covid-19 pandemic is real and still present years after the onset of the virus. Therefore, language teachers in China are still subject to fear within their professions (Zhang et al., 2021).

The second emotional effect of Covid-19 on language teachers in China is the stress. Chen (2022) maintained that online learning negatively impacts teachers' emotional well-being by increasing their stress levels. The sources of stress on teachers due to online teaching and learning are as follows. First, online teaching was stressful due to inadequate digital training before the transition., the switch from face-to-face learning to online learning occurred sporadically, meaning that neither learners nor teachers had enough time to prepare themselves (Mishra et al., 2020). Teachers had to force themselves to adapt as fast as possible to using alien technology. The second source of stress from online teaching was the increased work overload that came with the online teaching and learning schedules. As schools reopened and switched from physical to online teaching and learning, teachers were under pressure to make up for the time lost when schools had been indefinitely closed (Wakui et al., 2021). This left teachers with much coursework to cover within minimal time. Lastly, the inability to balance work and family life was another major stressor for language teachers (Srimulyani & Hermanto, 2022). Working from home presented teachers with the challenge of distinguishing between work and family life. Unbalancing work and family life caused tensions between the teachers and their families.

Other emotional effects of Covid-19 on language teachers in China may also include the anxiety and depression associated with isolation (Qiu et al., 2020). The teaching profession, especially for language teachers, is highly interactive, and this profession is often interpersonal, so language teachers were used to interacting face-to-face with their learners and colleagues at the workplace (Qiu et al., 2020). However, part of China's "Zero Case Pandemic Control Policy" requirements was to avoid physical contact as much as possible to reduce the spread of the coronavirus. Qiu et al. (2020) believed that as various professionals switched to work-from-home routines, people from highly sociable professions like teachers took the biggest hit. As a result, language teachers were susceptible to mental health challenges like anxiety and depression. Silva et al. (2021) conducted a systematic review of 1372 teachers from China, the USA, India, Brazil, and Spain to determine the impact of the coronavirus pandemic on their mental wellness, which revealed that between 10% and 49.4% of teachers were prone to getting anxiety during the coronavirus pandemic. The authors also found that 15.9% of the teachers were highly likely to get depressed. On the other hand, between 12.6% and 50.6% of the teachers were at risk of getting stressed. Silva et al. (2021) concluded that stress levels were highest among teachers whose institutions adopted online teaching and learning instead of physical learning. Comparatively, teachers in other Asian countries also had similar mental health challenges during the coronavirus pandemic.

Another emotional effect of Covid-19 on language teachers in China is frustration (Qin, 2016). Teaching a second/foreign language is in itself a challenging feat. Teachers of English in China experienced frustrations from several accounts during the coronavirus pandemic. For example, Richards (2022) mentioned that learners' inability to comprehend the grammatical and phonetic requirements of the language was enough reason for frustration, and Covid-19 worsened the frustration by reducing the contact hours between language teachers and their learners. With lowered professional guidance, learners retracted in terms of their learning progress, so language teachers had more work to do when education resumed – albeit online – to get their learners to the levels of achievement they were at before the pandemic struck (Tomasik et al. 2021). Another plausible explanation for the increased frustration rates among language teachers during the pandemic was the ineffective teaching techniques afforded by the online modes of teaching according to Hasan & Khan (2020). Yang et al. (2021) also claimed that effective language teaching requires constant contact between the teacher and the learner to enhance the memorability of language concepts and perfect the use of the particular language. Language teaching is more of a hands-on practice. The coronavirus pandemic forced language teachers to switch to theoretical modes of teaching, which are comparatively less effective in this context. The frustration, in this case, came from language teachers feeling unable to achieve their teaching outcomes. Reduced contact between teachers and learners meant that the teachers witnessed reduced language proficiency among their learners, yet they had little to nothing they could do to salvage their situation (Yang et al., 2021).

2.3.2 Impact of Teacher Emotions on Teachers' Professional Development

The emotional effect caused by the pandemic (including fear, frustration, stress, anxiety, and depression) experienced by teachers can affect their professional development either negatively or positively. For example, fear may propel or inhibit teachers' professional growth depending on the circumstances and the concerned teacher's perceptions of their fears (Chong & Kong, 2012). On the one hand, fear may spark teachers' interest in widening their knowledge through learning. This can only occur when the teacher in question gets comfortable with feeling uncomfortable due to the fears brought about by different factors in their profession, especially if there are solutions to the causes of the fear. For instance, fear caused by job insecurity could be solved by increasing one's knowledge capacity to make one more indispensable. On the other hand, fear may inhibit teachers' professional development by paralyzing them. Teachers who allow themselves to get paralyzed by fear will undoubtedly start doubting themselves and their professional abilities. This feeling may magnify into a much more significant challenge called impostor syndrome. The chances of professional development become highly unlikely when teachers let their fear get them to the point of having an impostor syndrome (Chong & Kong, 2012).

Frustration could either propel or hinder a teacher from professional development as well. On the negative side, frustration could be detrimental to teachers' professional development due to the following aspects discussed by Karamchandani (2020). First, frustration might cause teachers to lose interest in their profession due to the constant feeling of career dissatisfaction. More often than not, this loss of interest in one's profession would lead to reduced productivity and reduced quality of work output. This is because a disinterested person no longer has the drive to make efforts towards efficient and effective execution of work-related tasks. Disinterest and reduced productivity often lead to disengagement (McLennan, 2008). After disengagement comes aggression. Disengaged teachers, for instance, do not want to get called out for the poor quality of their work output and are, therefore, consistently aggressive as a defense mechanism. Another effect of frustration that makes it detrimental to teachers' professional development is that it raises the turnover rates among teaching staff. Frustrated teachers are highly likely to resign from their teaching professions in favor of 'less frustrating' professional options (McLennan, 2008). On the brighter side, however, teachers could turn their frustrations into tools for professional development (McLennan, 2008). For instance, if one gets frustrated with their pay for their educational level, they can advance their education to qualify for higher income, as mentioned earlier in the paper.

Stress is often detrimental to the professional development of teachers. Stress caused by excessive workloads often causes burnout (Li et al., 2022). Teachers would be able to tell if they are burntout if they notice themselves getting less productive by the day, feeling helpless, hopeless, and resentful towards their professions (Zadok-Gurman et al., 2021). For instance, Zhang et al. pointed out that a teacher with too many lessons to teach in a week may lack enthusiasm for the classes they are to teach the following week. If they fail to recognize this symptom of burnout, they might force themselves to go to work and attend to learners only to deliver below-par lectures. In addition, another effect of stress on teachers is reduced engagement at work (Zhang, Admiraal, & Saab, 2021). Stressed teachers may slowly start dissociating from their colleagues by engaging less with them daily. This disengagement may spill into the classroom setting affecting the teacher-learner interactions negatively.

Anxiety caused by the transition from onsite to online schooling was found to have significant negative effect on teachers' professional identity (Wakui et al., 2021; Silva ey al., 2021). Tsybulsky & Muchnik-Rozanov (2019) mentioned some of the ways that anxiety could influence teachers' professional development. To begin with, anxiety reduces one's ability to concentrate on the task at hand. An anxious teacher may, for instance, be unable to focus through an entire lecture session, forcing them to end the session prematurely. Secondly, anxiety makes people very irritable, which is a trait that is frowned upon in workplaces, especially for teachers who are usually considered as moral role models. Therefore, anxious teachers create negative classroom and work experiences for their learners and colleagues. Thirdly, anxiety causes teachers to disengage themselves from others. An anxious teacher would, for instance, avoid encounters with their colleagues, whether cordial or professional. In the long run, their disengagement would keep them from acquiring skills from their colleagues that would have otherwise been pivotal to their professional development (Tsybulsky & Muchnik-Rozanov, 2019).

Depression is also detrimental to teachers' professional development (Ozamiz-Etxebarria et al., 2021; Truzoli et al., 2021). For instance, teachers who feel depressed are prone to reduced concentration tasks (Shen et al., 2014). As their depressive state worsens, it keeps getting more difficult for them to focus on the daily work-related tasks they once enjoyed. Depressed teachers are also often anxious. Another effect of depression that might be detrimental to teachers' professional development is reduced energy toward everyday activities (Shen et al., 2014). In the context of the teaching profession, depression causes teachers to make fewer efforts toward professional advancement because they are convinced that any such actions might not be worthwhile. As a result, depressed teachers often stagnate at particular stages in their professional development for longer than necessary. In their systematic review of teachers in China during the coronavirus pandemic (and online classes), Silva et al. (2021) discerned that the likelihood of depression was between 15.9% and 28.9%. The teachers involved in the study mentioned that they experienced symptoms similar to the above. It was demonstrated that they gradually watched themselves exert less pressure in their work and felt they were at risk of giving up the profession altogether. If left unattended, depression among teachers could deter them from professional advancement and development.

2.4 Research Questions

Based on the literature review and the research gaps that have been identified, this study aims to explore how the emotions of teachers from diverse ethnic backgrounds contributed to the negotiation of teacher identity in Covid-19 pandemic context. In order for a more nuanced understanding of the relationship between language teacher's emotion and identity development, the following three research questions were addressed:

RQ1: What are the factors influencing the development of a language teacher's professional identity? Is ethnic background/nationality one of the significant factors?

RQ2: What are the significant factors that influence teacher emotions in the Chinese pandemic control context? Are there differences between Chinese and international teachers?

RQ3. How does the emotional experience of foreign language teachers with different ethnic background contribute to their professional identity development in the context of Covid-19 in China?

3. METHODOLOGY

3.1 Research Design and Rationale

In order to analyze the development of teacher professional identity and its associations with emotions, a qualitative research design was employed. The researcher chose the descriptive research method because it could provide more freedom to explain the relationship between variables without having to develop hypotheses, and it only utilizes non-statistical data to generate a more nuanced and context-specific understanding than using statistical data. Also, by using the descriptive research design, the researcher can examine as many research variables as possible, unlike quantitative research designs that limit the researcher to one independent variable and two dependent variables (Aggarwal & Ranganathan, 2019). As a result, in the present study, the Teacher Emotion Questionnaire (TEQ) was administered to 10 English language teachers with different ethnic backgrounds in a Sino-UK university in China first, and then all the participants were interviewed and asked to recall their teaching and life experiences and emotions at the university.

The researcher then conducted thematic analysis to analyze the primary qualitative data collected from the interviews. This involves identifying and coding the quotes from the interview transcripts; then all the codes were collapsed into themes and subthemes in correspondence to the research questions.

3.2 Research Setting

The study was conducted in a Sino-UK joint international university (shortened as the University) in China. The University represents a typical EMI (English as Medium of Instruction) institutional context and claims a large expatriate staff. The English Language Centre of the University where the data was collected provides EAP (English for Academic Purposes) tuition for students at different levels from undergraduate to PhD.

3.3 Participants

The participants for this research are 10 undergraduate EAP teachers with diverse ethnic backgrounds selected from the English Language Centre of the University. Among them, five are international teachers (native English speakers) and five are Chinese faculty with overseas study experiences. All of them had experience in teaching English, albeit for various lengths of time and in various contexts (Table 1). Also, considering the pandemic contextual factor, all the participants had officially gotten on board and enrolled before or during the pandemic and had had working experiences both before and after the pandemic struck.

Table 1. Demographic information of the participants

Participant #	Gender	EAP teaching experience in total (by 2022)	Ethnic Background	EAP teaching at current job (by 2022)
1	F	4	Chinese	2
2	F	9	Chinese	3
3	F	4.5	Chinese	4
4	F	4.5	Chinese	4.5
5	M	8	Chinese	2
6	M	13	New Zealand	3
7	F	22	Canada	2
8	F	14	England	4
9	M	7	UK	5
10	F	11	UK	5

3.4 Research Instrument

The semi-structured interview was employed as the method to collect the data for this study. Specifically, the researcher conducted online interviews for each of the ten participants. There were 20 interview questions in total, which could be divided into three dimensions (Appendix A). Ten of the questions were designed to understand teachers' perceptions of their professional identity; three questions were developed to explore the impact of teachers' diverse ethnic backgrounds on professional identity and emotions, and the final seven questions focused on the impact of the pandemic on teachers' emotions and their identity. During the interview, the researcher also asked follow-up questions based on the participants' responses.

In this study, teachers' emotions were also measured by the Teacher Emotion Questionnaire (TEQ). The Teacher Emotion Questionnaire is a five-point Likert scale developed by Buric, Sliskovic and Macuka (2018) that measures six discrete emotions including joy, pride, love, anger, fatigue, and hopelessness. Participants indicated their level of agreement on a 5-point scale ranging from 1 (strongly disagree) to 5 (strongly agree) in response to the items on each emotion scale. The sum of each respondent's answers to each question created their total attitude score, which represented their strength of attitude on the scale. According to the researchers, each scale of the TEQ demonstrated acceptable to very good reliabilities with Cronbach's alphas ranging from 0.70 to 0.92.

3.5 Research Procedure

This study was carried out in the following steps. First of all, a prior test was conducted to optimize the interview questions. Before the formal interviews, the participants were asked to answer the Teacher Emotion Questionnaire online first. After that, the interview questions were modified and finalized according to the answers to the questionnaire. Finally, the semi-structured interviews were conducted via Tencent Meeting online. The researcher asked questions based on planned interview questions, and

The Development of Professional Identity and Its Associations With Emotions

then followed up with questions based on the interviewee's answers. Interviews were conducted in one round and each interview session lasted between thirty to sixty minutes.

4. RESULTS

4.1 The TEQ Questionnaire

The ten teachers' responses to the TEQ Questionnaire are summarized in Table 2, which details the averages of the seven scales calculated for each teacher.

Table 2. TEQ results by emotional scales

Participant #	Joy	Pride	Love	Anger	Fatigue	Hopelessness
1	4.6	3.67	3.83	2.33	3.71	3
2	4.4	4.83	3.5	2	2.43	2.33
3	4.8	4.67	4	1.4	2.5	2.33
4	5	5	3.67	3.6	3.86	3.5
5	5	4.6	4	2	3	3.2
6	4.6	3.4	3.4	1.8	1.14	3
7	4.8	4	3.2	1.6	1.6	1
8	4.2	3.2	2.6	2	4.6	1.6
9	3.8	3.8	2.2	2.6	2.4	3
10	5	4.2	3.8	1.2	1.2	1.4
Average	4.62	4.14	3.42	2.05	2.64	2.44

The averages of each item on the seven scales are listed in Table 3.

Table 3. TEQ results by items

Item #	Joy	Pride	Love	Anger	Fatigue	Hopelessness
1	4.3	4.1	3.8	3.1	3.4	2.6
2	4.7	3.8	3.3	1.9	2	2.8
3	4.8	4.3	3.3	2.3	2.9	1.9
4	4.5	4.5	3.9	1.7	2.6	2.2
5	4.8	3.9	2.7	1.3	2.5	2.6
6		4.2	4		3	2.4
7					2.1	
Average	4.62	4.14	3.42	2.05	2.64	2.44

Although the averages of the positive-emotion scales are higher than the average scores of the negative-emotion scales, it is worth highlighting the three items on the negative-emotion scales that received the highest average scores. In particular, the two items on the Anger and the Hopelessness scale seem to echo some of the findings from the qualitative data regarding the frustrated feelings that the teachers felt with online teaching where they found it more difficult to motivate their students.

Item #1 on the Anger scale: I sweat from frustration when the class is not carried in the way it is supposed to.

Item #1 of the Fatigue scale: At the end of my working day, I just want to rest.

Item 2 of the Hopelessness scale: While working with completely unmotivated students, I feel there is no way out.

4.2 The Impact of Ethnic Background on <u>Teacher's Professional Identity</u>

This research identified that teachers' nationalities and ethnic backgrounds were some of the significant factors influencing teachers' professional identity development pre and post the pandemic from teachers' discourses. Teachers from different ethnic backgrounds tended to have different perceptions of their professional identities in their teaching.

4.2.1 Chinese Teachers

Chinese participants generally perceived themselves as more of a parent to their students or between a parent and a friend. Academically, they supervised students, reminded them when to do something, and repeatedly emphasized deadlines and requirements. And not only in academics but also in life, they took care of the students. This was related to the perception of teachers in traditional Chinese culture. One Chinese teacher said,

"I am strict with assessments, when it's assessment time, when I give feedback, I tend to be quite strict. But like in classes, sometimes I feel like I am parenting my students. I go with reminding them. Sometimes you care about your students' emotions and their health status. So it's a little bit like a parent."

Another Chinese teacher also mentioned in the interview that,

"I'm open to talking to my students about their lives, anything unrelated to the course. And I also guide in areas other than the things I'm teaching."

In addition to parents, Chinese teachers generally perceived themselves as seniors in learning English for their students. They were English learners before, so they knew how to learn and how to assist their learning from their personal experience, as one of the Chinese teachers said,

"We know better about Chinese students because we are Chinese. We were language learners before, so we know how to learn and kind of know how to best assist their learning from our own personal experiences."

4.2.2 International teachers

On the other hand, the international teachers believed that they became a bridge to teach Chinese students about foreign universities. Most of the students studying at the University will go abroad for further studies in the future. As international teachers who were born and educated abroad, they had a better understanding of foreign teaching systems and were better at adopting foreign teaching styles in their classes. As a result, they saw some of their roles as preparing students for what to expect when they study abroad. As one of the international teachers said in the interview,

> "All my students will go into a master's degree, usually in the UK. I see some of my roles as preparing them for what to expect when they get there because they're not going to have Chinese teachers when they arrive in the UK; thus, the style of education will be left up to them a lot more."

International teachers also had different beliefs about student-teacher roles. Some of them believed their relationship with students was more "business-like" in teaching and it was vital to have a little bit of distance between the teacher and the student for professional reasons, so they would not compare themselves to being like a parent, and instead, they considered their role involving managing them and helping them achieve their goals:

> "I think I'm quite business-like in the classroom. I don't see myself as being like a friend or a parent because I don't think that's my role. And I think it's also important to have a little distance between the teacher and the student for professional reasons, so I wouldn't compare myself to being a sister or a parent or something like that. Still, I think my role may be a little business-like, and I think it's my role to manage them and help them achieve things."

4.3 The Impact of Teacher Emotion on the Adaption to the new Teaching Mode During the Pandemic

The analyses revealed that both Chinese teachers and international teachers were influenced by the pandemic in emotional aspect, but the international teachers were more susceptible to the pandemic and developed more negative emotions than their Chinese counterparts.

4.3.1 Chinese Teachers

The Chinese teachers generally mentioned the negative emotions of being stressed, frustrated, disappointed, and doubtful while teaching online. For example, one Chinese teacher said that she thought the pandemic had distracted people more while teaching was a very focused task. However, during the pandemic, staying concentrated in class was more challenging for both teachers and students. As a result of this distraction, she felt a lot of stress and isolation while teaching. She said,

> "I felt more distracted and sometimes more stressed because of the distractions and lack of social connections. And also helplessly, like sometimes, if you're away from your students and colleagues, and you feel like you're doing many things alone without much support. And also teaching online is,

I would say, a lonely experience for the teachers a lot of times; even though you can ask the students to turn on their microphones and cameras, it's still different. If you're like, you are the only one, that's really like engaging in the class, and so, that's a very dissatisfying teaching experience."

Some teachers also mentioned the feeling of embarrassment. When teachers asked questions in class, unlike offline classrooms, where teachers could more easily pressure students to participate in class discussions, online teaching was more silent. The fact that no one turned on the camera, and no one turned on the microphone made the teachers feel awkward and helpless.

"Normally, if it is onsite teaching, we organize the activities to be more student-centered. We encourage students to talk. While they are unwilling to talk, if you stand in front of them, they feel that kind of pressure and it kind of forces them to talk. And you can always encourage them face to face. It's easier. But if it's online, almost none of them turn on the cameras. So you don't see them or know what they're doing. And sometimes, even when you call their names, they don't answer your question. Sometimes embarrassing, especially when you have called upon someone and there's no response, it is a bit awkward."

4.3.2 International Teachers

International teachers also experienced similar negative emotions during the pandemic. For example, one international teacher mentioned that he had spent a long time preparing a perfect online lesson. However, many students still refused to participate in the class, which made him feel angry and tired, and he started to consider that the online lessons during the pandemic were often a waste of time:

"Teaching online, it's just inappropriate for language teaching. In tiny groups, individually or in small groups, I think online teaching for languages can be okay. For large group classes, it's completely useless, that combined with Chinese students, who are, in the classroom when you can see them are unwilling to speak, but you can convince them to, you can encourage them. It's just impossible online. They'll sign on, turn them off, turn off their camera or microphone, and it's impossible to get them to engage, which is very dispiriting. It feels like a waste of time for the students and me, which is not great."

On the other hand, international teachers also experienced more negative emotions than Chinese teachers. Unlike Chinese teachers, who had a variety of ways to learn and understand the pandemic control policies, international teachers often needed to know about the policies through emails sent by the University. When the University translated the policy and delivered it to international teachers, there were always misunderstandings due to language barriers that led to confusion. Also, the tone of the communication sometimes upset international teachers. As one of the international teachers mentioned,

"As a foreigner, I found the way the University communicates information to us sometimes very confusing. And the tone of the communication sometimes seems very angry or upsetting, and harsh. Because we don't always understand what's happening, it's a bit upsetting sometimes."

In addition, due to the pandemic control policy, leaving and entering the country had become particularly difficult, and this caused a great deal of trouble for foreigners working in China. Several international teachers mentioned that they had not returned to their home countries since the beginning of the pandemic, and they missed and worried about their families. Moreover, not only leaving the country but also traveling within the country was also somewhat restricted, which made them feel trapped.

Another teacher mentioned that unlike the Chinese, who were more willing to see the benefits of these policies, the Westerners felt more confused and could not understand what was happening. Significantly his friends living abroad were not affected by the pandemic very much. They were still traveling and living normally, which made him feel more anxious and frustrated. He said in the interview:

> "I think there's a bit more confusion with western people, as Chinese people are more willing to see the possible benefits of the current situation, whereas every single western person I know thinks it's insane and doesn't understand it. That makes us more anxious. I think it just seems baffling. So I don't know, like why is this happening, and when will it finish. It's frustrating looking at all my friends in basically everywhere else all around the world living normal lives."

4.3 Negotiation of Emotions and Transformation to the Professional Identity of EAP Teachers of Different Ethnic Backgrounds Under the Pandemic

The analysis also revealed that the classroom interactions between teachers and students were one of the significant factors causing the changes in emotion and professional identity negotiation regardless of their ethnic backgrounds in the pandemic control context. Although some teachers tried to transform the negative emotions like being unconfident and doubtful to develop their professional identity positively, the negative emotions caused by the pandemic generally influenced the professional identities of both international and local Chinese teachers.

4.3.1 Chinese Teachers

In the following excerpt, the teacher expressed her lack of confidence in her English proficiency because English is not their first language. Many students preferred international teachers whose native language was English in class. She explicitly identified the feeling of being doubted:

> "Your students, not just your students, but I think basically everyone has another layer of doubts about your qualifications because you are not a native speaker."

However, in the face of this challenge, she tried to transform this lack of confidence into an understanding and empathy for their students. Then she identified and built on her strengths, and she also learned English as a second language, so that she could know and understand Chinese students better:

> "I think I have gone through the experience of studying English, right? And I studied overseas and returned to my home country, which is something that many of my students are hoping to do. So, I think I can impart many of those experiences to my students. And also, I can get to empathize more with them because I have gone through a lot of the things that they are going through. And it

also helps with my teaching because I am still an English learner, so I can understand how they feel when they are learning those things, and I can hopefully use that to help them further."

At the same time, when students did not perform well, some Chinese teachers often doubted their own teaching abilities:

"Sometimes it can be a little bit annoying if we ask them to add the citations, to paraphrase the sources, and to have a good reference list. We give feedback several times, but then we see the last job, the problems persist, the problems are still there, and sometimes we may doubt whether our ways are ineffective or are saying too much, which is why they are ignored."

When this kind of doubt arose, Chinese teachers tried to turn it into a spirit of inquiry to find ways to solve the problem. Consequently, another new professional identity emerged, which was the role of the researcher. As a researcher, he did more action research in the classroom to identify and find solution to the problems, as the teacher said in the following excerpt:

"I continue to be a facilitator to help the students, but at the same time, I become more effective. And sometimes, I feel I'm like a researcher more, even though in the past, I carried out some research to investigate some teaching issues. And now, in the classroom, I do more action research because I identify problems and I would like to strategize solutions. I also try other ways, but at the same time, I collect some evidence to see whether those methods work. So I become a researcher more in this way, I think. "

In addition, during the pandemic, the teachers' emotions were affected by interaction with students in online teaching, which also affected their professional identity development.

"For the onsite teaching, it is more student-centered. However, I cannot control that when I have online teaching, I'm just like a talking machine, so I will talk most of the time. The students always have excuses like I can't turn on my microphone, my microphone is broken, is not working, my camera is not working, or something. So most of the time, I work like a teaching machine, speaking from the beginning to the end and begging them to interact with me. However, sometimes I get refused, the students will refuse me, and sometimes, I will be ignored by the students. Just no responses from the students."

In this excerpt, the negative emotions, such as frustration and helplessness, generated by the student's lack of participation and silence during online classes made them talk more. Eventually, they became "talking machines" in the classroom. Similarly, some teachers were embarrassed by the lack of students answering questions in the online class, making themselves become the "mood maker and self-entertainer" in the classroom. As the teacher mentioned,

"To make the class not that awkward, I will normally start a little bit earlier, like 10 minutes or even longer, before the class starts. I will play music and tell students that when they come to the classroom, it is a time for them to relax, a time for them to chat. And also, I normally will tell jokes before the class starts to make them feel a bit happier, and when I design class activities, I will always try to make things more fun."

4.3.2 International Teachers

Similarly, some international teachers transformed the sad and frustrated emotions towards students in online classes into the understanding of students and became more patient and forgiving to students. One of the international teachers said,

"I think I'm probably more patient now than I was at the beginning of the pandemic, simply because it's been going on for so long that I think I cannot continue to become very frustrated if something goes wrong or if the students don't participate, I think I had just to chill out basically."

Another international teacher chose to give up caring and become a "lecturer" than a facilitator due to their frustration and fatigue with the student's performance in online classes:

"I was very frustrated. I guess I've come to accept the fact, so I know what I'm going to do. I know what I'm expecting now. So I know there will be low levels of interaction, so to be honest, I've given up caring as much as I used to. I could plan a class perfectly. I've done this before, I put loads of effort into planning an online class that would work well, and it would have if students had interacted, and they just don't, and it's a complete waste of my time as well, so I've stopped doing that. I do things like meet the lowest common denominator now online."

5 DISCUSSION AND CONCLUSION

5.1 General Discussion

As mentioned earlier, this study aims to explore how the emotions of language teachers from diverse ethnic backgrounds contribute to the negotiation of teacher identity in the Covid-19 pandemic context. Consistent with our expectations, the findings revealed that ethnic backgrounds significantly influenced language teachers' professional identities. The participants' discourses confirmed that Chinese and international teachers had different professional identities, prompting them to develop different perceptions of themselves and their professions. For instance, Chinese teachers perceived themselves as more of their learners' parents and friends. In contrast, international teachers perceived their relationships with the students as more professional than friendly. Since the participants came from different ethnic backgrounds, their cultural origins had an impact on the way they engaged with the students they taught, and their perception of their roles vis-à-vis the students. Therefore, this result, to a large extent, has verified the similar findings of many previous studies (Hayik and Wiener-Levy, 2017; Donato, 2016; Chen et al., 2022; Song, 2016; Jeongyeon & Hye Young, 2020). This could be related to the traditional Chinese culture, according to which the teacher's authority is higher than that of the students, and the students need to be taken care of and supervised (Wang & Du, 2014). This cultural influence could be more or less reflected in the teachers' professional identity in that Chinese teachers were more inclined to build a close relationship with their students. For instance, they would take the role more as the parents to instruct their students about the requirements and deadlines of homework, care about whether they really understand or not, and always have high expectations for them. Not only in academic aspect, but also in life, were they willing to take care of students, including their physical and mental health. Western culture, on the other hand, places more emphasis on freedom and respect for individuality. The teacher acts simply as a guide and facilitator, not as a caregiver or an authority. Therefore, when it comes to teaching, the international teachers focus more on guiding and inspiring than building an intimate relationship with their students, and they seldom force students to do anything.

Participants' native languages (English as a native language and Chinese as a native language) also influenced the development of their professional identities. Some of the participants who had English as their native language regarded language proficiency as a fundamental aspect of their professional identities, and on the other hand, some Chinese participants indicated that they sometimes received queries from their students because their native language was not English. They usually felt unconfident about that. In China, native speakers are often more recognized and preferred than non-native speakers as EFL teachers because native speakers are perceived to have a higher level of English proficiency (Wang & Fang, 2020). This also led to differences in the professional identity development between the Chinese participants and the international participants.

The findings of the current research are comparable to those of other studies that highlight the detrimental impacts of the coronavirus pandemic and online teaching and learning on the emotions of language teachers. During the interview, the participants shared a variety of unfavorable feelings that they encountered when teaching online classes during the pandemic. For example, the feelings of anxiety, annoyance, frustration, disappointment, and uncertainty. On the other hand, the current study, unlike previous studies (MacIntyre et al., 2020; Can & Bardacki, 2022) that ignored the unique nature of international teachers working in a foreign country, found that international teachers in China experienced more negative emotions during the pandemic. They experienced more loneliness, homesickness, feelings of being trapped, and helplessness during the pandemic than their Chinese counterparts, and these are caused by language barriers, as well as the inability to return home for long periods of time, and the inability to move freely due to the strict pandemic control policies in China.

Most importantly, it was found that the interactions between teachers and students in the classroom had a major impact on the feelings and professional identities of language teachers, regardless of their ethnic backgrounds. The discourse of teachers from China and other countries indicated that the shift toward online teaching and learning dramatically lowered the amount of student involvement. In the interview, both the Chinese and the international participants expressed despondency and anger over online classes. They reported the awkwardness in online classes caused by students' lack of participation in the activities, and also complained of being forced to talk too much to compensate for their students' silence and less engagement during online classes. Without a doubt, the disruptions in the student-teacher connections caused by online teaching had a negative effect on the professional identities of foreign language teachers in China by inciting unfavorable judgments of the work that they did. Classroom interactions determine whether the processes of teaching and learning are effective, and mirror teachers' and students' perceptions of each other (Gardner, 2019; Day, 2018).

5.2 Implications

The current research has suggested that ethnic background is one of the significant factors influencing the development of teacher's professional identity pre and post the pandemic. In addition, teacher-student classroom interactions have been found to be one of the significant factors triggering the emotional changes and transformation of professional identities regardless of their ethnic backgrounds. Given these findings of the study, some implications will be discussed from the perspectives of teacher professional development, leadership approaches and management policies.

Firstly, it is important to emphasize the role of ethnic backgrounds in teachers' professional identity development. It helps Chinese and international teachers to be more aware of their own strengths and weaknesses in language teaching that involve classroom interactions with students whose native language is not English. For example, in the present study, Chinese teachers' advantages included their ability to understand students and help them from a learner's perspective, as they learn English as a second foreign language just as their Chinese students did, and the disadvantage lay in their lack of confidence in their language proficiency. The strengths of international teachers were their native language proficiency and their full knowledge of the English language and culture, and the disadvantages lay in the communication barrier caused by the cultural differences with Chinese students. Chinese and international teachers can gather knowledge from this study on how to overcome the negative and ineffective emotions and reconfigure a way to experience positive emotions, such as self-confidence and pride, that can have a positive impact on their teacher professional identity. It is worth emphasizing that by exerting a transformed and appropriate teacher professional identity, teachers can have a transformative effect on their students (Miller et al., 2017; Wu & Leung, 2020).

Secondly, this study has highlighted the negative emotions possessed by language teachers of different ethnic backgrounds. Compared with their Chinese counterparts, international teachers tend to generate more negative emotions in times of crisis as they are in a foreign context and seem to be more susceptible to challenges incurred by unexpected changes. Therefore, not only teachers themselves, but also university leadership should pay more attention to the emotional states of international teachers. Adequate care and timely psychological counseling should be provided to international language teachers in China when necessary.

Finally, the emotional changes and disrupted personal and professional identities induced by the new interaction dynamics during online classes has pointed to a need to examine these issues in the post pandemic era when technology-enhanced language learning (TELL) has become the norm. In the post pandemic new normal, the higher education is faced with the opportunities and challenges brought by the unprecedented development of digital technologies, particularly in the form of generative AI. In response, an emerging body of studies have begun to reimagine teacher identity in the new era as "a fluid concept informed by vulnerability and uncertainty" (Foreman-Browna, Fitzpatricka & Twyford, 2023, p. 9). Thus, the nexus of TELL, teacher emotions and teacher professional identities in and out of classrooms should become a fertile ground for future research in various higher education contexts in China. In response to this irreversible trend, higher education institutions should also reflect on and reshape their leadership approaches and practices that aim to enhance teacher resilience and well-being in a highly complex world full of uncertainties.

5.3 Limitations

Despite the contributions this research makes to the current literature on the development of teacher professional identity and teacher emotions, it inevitably has limitations to be improved for future studies. First, the number of research participants (ten) could have been too small to draw viable conclusions. All participants were from the same university, which may result in the inability to generalize the findings to other higher education contexts in China. Second, the dataset only included the reflections on teaching and emotional experiences publicly shared by the participants. However, the authenticity of these data may be undermined by the influence of self-report bias.

REFERENCES

Aggarwal, R., & Ranganathan, P. (2019). Study designs: Part 2–descriptive studies. *Perspectives in Clinical Research*, 10(1), 34. 10.4103/picr.PICR_154_1830834206

Akbari, R., Samar, R. G., Kiany, G. R., & Tahernia, M. (2017). A qualitative study of EFL teachers' emotion regulation behavior in the classroom. *Theory and Practice in Language Studies*, 7(4), 311–321. 10.17507/tpls.0704.10

Alpaslan, M. M., & Ulubey, O. (2017). Adaptation of the teacher emotion scale into Turkish culture. *International Periodical for the Languages. Literature and History of Turkish or Turkic*, 12(25), 119–130.

Alsup, J. (2006). *Teacher identity discourses: Negotiating personal and professional spaces*. Lawrence Erlbaum. 10.4324/9781410617286

Asif, T., Guangming, O., Haider, M. A., Colomer, J., Kayani, S., & Amin, N. U. (2020). Moral education for sustainable development: Comparison of university teachers' perceptions in China and Pakistan. *Sustainability (Basel)*, 12(7), 3014. 10.3390/su12073014

Barcelos, A. M. F., & Ruohotie-Lyhty, M. (2018). *Teachers' Emotions and Beliefs in Second Language Teaching: Implications for Teacher Education*. Springer International Publishing. https://doi-org.ez.xjtlu.edu.cn/10.1007/978-3-319-75438-3_7

Barkhuizen, G. (2016). Language teacher identity research: An introduction. In *Reflections on language teacher identity research* (pp. 9–19). Routledge. 10.4324/9781315643465-5

Beltman, S., Hascher, T., & Mansfield, C. (2022). In the Midst of a Pandemic. *Zeitschrift für Psychologie mit Zeitschrift für Angewandte Psychologie*.

Benesch, S. (2017). *Emotions in English language teaching: Exploring teachers' emotion labor*. Routledge/Taylor & Francis. 10.4324/9781315736181

Biasutti, M., Concina, E., Frate, S., & Delen, I. (2021). Teacher professional development: Experiences in an international project on intercultural education. *Sustainability (Basel)*, 13(8), 4171. 10.3390/su13084171

Boldt, G., Lewis, C., & Leander, K. M. (2015). Moving, feeling, desiring, and teaching. *Research in the Teaching of English*, 49(4), 430–441. 10.58680/rte201527351

Borrachero, A. B., Brigido, M., Costillo, E., Bermejo, L., & Mellado, V. (2014). Relationship between self-efficacy beliefs and emotions of future teachers of Physics in secondary education. *Asia-Pacific Forum on Science Learning and Teaching*, 14(2), 1–11.

Buric, I., Sliškovic, A., & Macuka, I. (2018). A Mixed-Method Approach to the Assessment of Teachers' Emotions: Development and Validation of the Teacher Emotion Questionnaire. *Educational Psychology*, 38(3), 325–349. 10.1080/01443410.2017.1382682

Can, Y., & Bardakci, S. (2022). Teachers' opinions on (urgent) distance education activities during the pandemic period. *Advances in Mobile Learning Educational Research*, 2(2), 351–374. 10.25082/AMLER.2022.02.005

Chen, H., Sun, W., Han, J., & Liu, Q. (2022). Chinese language teachers' dichotomous identities when teaching ingroup and outgroup students. *Frontiers in Psychology*, 13, 13. 10.3389/fpsyg.2022.93933335967731

Chen, J. (2016). Understanding teacher emotions: The development of a teacher emotion inventory. *Teaching and Teacher Education*, 55, 68–77. 10.1016/j.tate.2016.01.001

Chen, J. (2021). Refining the Teacher Emotion Model: Evidence from a Review of Literature Published between 1985 and 2019. *Cambridge Journal of Education*, 51(3), 327–357. 10.1080/0305764X.2020.1831440

Chen, M. (2022). Digital affordances and teacher agency in the context of teaching Chinese as a second language during COVID-19. *System*, 105, 102710. 10.1016/j.system.2021.102710

Chen, Z., Sun, Y., & Jia, Z. (2022). A Study of Student-Teachers' Emotional Experiences and Their Development of Professional Identities. *Frontiers in Psychology*, 12, 6604. 10.3389/fpsyg.2021.81014635145463

Cheshmehzangi, A., Zou, T., & Su, Z. (2022). Commentary: China's Zero-COVID Approach Depends on Shanghai's Outbreak Control. *Frontiers in Public Health*, 10, 10. 10.3389/fpubh.2022.91299235774574

Cho, H. (2014). 'It's very complicated' exploring heritage language identity with heritage language teachers in a teacher preparation program. *Language and Education*, 28(2), 181e195.

Chong, W. H., & Kong, C. A. (2012). Teacher collaborative learning and teacher self-efficacy: The case of lesson study. *Journal of Experimental Education*, 80(3), 263–283. 10.1080/00220973.2011.596854

Cruess, R. L., Cruess, S. R., Boudreau, J. D., Snell, L., & Steinert, Y. (2015). A schematic representation of the professional identity formation and socialization of medical students and residents: A guide for medical educators. *Academic Medicine*, 90(6), 718–725. 10.1097/ACM.00000000000000070025785682

Day, C. (2018). Professional identity matters: Agency, emotions, and resilience. In *Research on teacher identity* (pp. 61–70). Springer International Publishing. 10.1007/978-3-319-93836-3_6

Donato, R. (2016). Becoming a language teaching professional: What's identity got to do with it? In Barkhuizen, G. (Ed.), *Reflections on language teacher identity research (pp. 32e38)*. Routledge.

Elsheikh, A., & Yahia, E. (2020). Language Teacher Professional Identity. In *Professionalizing Your English Language Teaching* (pp. 27–38). Springer. 10.1007/978-3-030-34762-8_3

Farouk, S. (2012). What can the self-conscious emotion of guilt tell us about primary school teachers' moral purpose and the relationships they have with their pupils? *Teachers and Teaching*, 18(4), 491–507. 10.1080/13540602.2012.696049

Foreman-Brown, G., Fitzpatrick, E., & Twyford, K.Foreman-Browna. (2023). Reimagining teacher identity in the post-Covid-19 university: Becoming digitally savvy, reflective in practice, collaborative, and relational. *Educational and Developmental Psychologists*, 40(1), 18–26. 10.1080/20590776.2022.2079406

Frenzel, A. C., Pekrun, R., & Goetz, T. (2010). *Achievement emotions questionnaire for teachers (AEQ-teacher) - User's manual*. University of Munich.

Frenzel, A. C., Pekrun, R., Goetz, T., Daniels, L. M., Durksen, T. L., Becker-Kurz, B., & Klassen, R. M. (2016). Measuring Teachers' enjoyment, anger, and anxiety: The Teacher Emotions Scales (TES). *Contemporary Educational Psychology*, 46, 148–163. 10.1016/j.cedpsych.2016.05.003

Gardner, R. (2019). Classroom interaction research: The state of the art. *Research on Language and Social Interaction*, 52(3), 212–226. 10.1080/08351813.2019.1631037

Gilakjani, A. P., & Sabouri, N. B. (2017). Teachers' Beliefs in English Language Teaching and Learning: A Review of the Literature. *English Language Teaching*, 10(4), 78–86. 10.5539/elt.v10n4p78

Gkonou, C., Mercer, S., & Daubney, M. (2018). Teacher perspectives on language learning psychology. *Language Learning Journal*, 46(4), 501–513. 10.1080/09571736.2016.1172330

Golombek, P., & Doran, M. (2014). Unifying cognition, emotion, and activity in language teacher professional development. *Teaching and Teacher Education*, 39, 102–111. 10.1016/j.tate.2014.01.002

Greenier, V., Derakhshan, A., & Fathi, J. (2021). Emotion regulation and psychological well-being in teacher work engagement: A case of British and Iranian English language teachers. *System*, 97, 102446. 10.1016/j.system.2020.102446

Gu, H., Mao, Y., & Wang, Q. (2022). Exploring EFL Teachers' Emotions and the Impact on Their Sustainable Professional Development in Livestream Teaching: A Chinese Case Study. *Sustainability (Basel)*, 14(8264), 8264. 10.3390/su14148264

Gu, H., Xie, R., Adam, D. C., Tsui, J. L. H., Chu, D. K., Chang, L. D., Cheuk, S. S. Y., Gurung, S., Krishnan, P., Ng, D. Y. M., Liu, G. Y. Z., Wan, C. K. C., Cheng, S. S. M., Edwards, K. M., Leung, K. S. M., Wu, J. T., Tsang, D. N. C., Leung, G. M., Cowling, B. J., & Poon, L. L. (2022). Genomic epidemiology of SARS-CoV-2 under an elimination strategy in Hong Kong. *Nature Communications*, 13(1), 1–10. 10.1038/s41467-022-28420-735136039

Gu, M., & Benson, P. (2015). The formation of English teacher identities: A cross-cultural investigation. *Language Teaching Research*, 19(2), 187–206. 10.1177/1362168814541725

Haniford, L. C. (2010). Tracing one teacher candidate's discursive identity work. *Teaching and Teacher Education, 26*, 987e996

Hanna, F., Oostdam, R., Severiens, S. E., & Zijlstra, B. J. (2020). Assessing the professional identity of primary student teachers: Design and validation of the Teacher Identity Measurement Scale. *Studies in Educational Evaluation*, 64, 100822. 10.1016/j.stueduc.2019.100822

Haque, M. N., & Sharmin, S. (2022). Perception of Saudi Students About Non-Native English Teachers and Native English Teachers in Teaching English at Jazan University. *Journal of Language Teaching and Research*, 13(3), 503–514. 10.17507/jltr.1303.06

Hargreaves, A. (2001). Emotional geographies of teaching. *Teachers College Record*, 103(6), 1056–1080. 10.1111/0161-4681.00142

Hayik, R., & Weiner-Levy, N. (2019). Prospective Arab teachers' emotions as mirrors to their identities and culture. *Teaching and Teacher Education, 85*, 36e44.

Herman, K. C., Sebastian, J., Reinke, W. M., & Huang, F. L. (2021). Individual and school predictors of teacher stress, coping, and wellness during the COVID-19 pandemic. *School Psychology*, 36(6), 483–493. 10.1037/spq000045634766812

Hong, J., Nie, Y., Heddy, B., Monobe, G., Ruan, J., You, S., & Kambara, H. (2016). Revising and validating Achievement Emotions Questionnaire-teachers (AEQ-T). *International Journal of Educational Psychology*, 5(1), 80–107. 10.17583/ijep.2016.1395

Jeongyeon, K., & Hye Young, S. (2020). Negotiation of emotions in emerging language teacher identity of graduate instructors. *System*, 95, 102365. Advance online publication. 10.1016/j.system.2020.102365

Karamchandani, K. (2020). *Frustration at the Workplace and Employee Attitude: A Study on It Professionals*. INTERNATIONAL JOURNAL OF ADVANCE RESEARCH AND INNOVATIVE IDEAS IN EDUCATION.

Karavas, E. (2010). How satisfied are Greek EFL teachers with their work? Investigating the motivation and job satisfaction levels of Greek EFL teachers.

Kayi-Aydar, H. (2015). Teacher agency, positioning, and English language learners: Voices of pre-service classroom teachers. *Teaching and Teacher Education*, 45, 94–103. 10.1016/j.tate.2014.09.009

Keim, R., Pfitscher, G., Leitner, S., Burger, K., Giacomoni, F., & Wiedermann, C. J. (2022). Teachers' emotional well-being during the SARS-CoV-2 pandemic with long school closures: A large-scale cross-sectional survey in Northern Italy. *Public Health*, 208, 1–8. 10.1016/j.puhe.2022.04.00635659680

Kelchtermans, G. (2005). Teachers' emotions in educational reforms: Self-understanding, vulnerable commitment and micropolitical literacy. *Teaching and Teacher Education*, 21(8), 995–1006. 10.1016/j.tate.2005.06.009

Korman, K., & Mujtaba, B. G. (2020). Corporate responses to COVID-19 layoffs in North America and the role of human resources departments. *Reports on Global Health Research*, 3(2), 1–17.

Kukreti, S., Ahorsu, D. K., Strong, C., Chen, I. H., Lin, C. Y., Ko, N. Y., & Pakpour, A. H. (2021, September). Post-traumatic stress disorder in Chinese teachers during COVID-19 pandemic: Roles of fear of COVID-19, nomophobia, and psychological distress. []. MDPI.]. *Health Care*, 9(10), 1288.34682968

Lave, J., & Wenger, E. (1991). *Situated learning: Legitimate peripheral participation*. Cambridge University Press. 10.1017/CBO9780511815355

Li, S., & Jin, C. (2020, March). Analysis on whether native or non-native English-speaking teacher is better in TEFL in China. In 4th International Conference on Culture, Education and Economic Development of Modern Society (ICCESE 2020) (pp. 1098-1104). Atlantis Press. 10.2991/assehr.k.200316.240

Li, X., Xiao, W., Sun, C., Li, W., & Sun, B. (2022). Does burnout decrease with teacher professional identity among teachers in China? *Journal of Career Development*, •••, 08948453221138937.

MacIntyre, P. D., Gregersen, T., & Mercer, S. (2020). Language teachers' coping strategies during the Covid-19 conversion to online teaching: Correlations with stress, well-being and negative emotions. *System*, 94, 102352. https://doi-org.ez.xjtlu.edu.cn/10.1016/j.system.2020.102352. 10.1016/j.system.2020.102352

McLennan, G. (2008). Disinterested, disengaged, useless: Conservative or progressive idea of the university? *Globalisation, Societies and Education*, 6(2), 195–200. 10.1080/14767720802061496

Meihami, H., & Salīte, I. (2019). EFL teachers' cultural identity development through participating in cultural negotiation: Probing EFL students' perspectives. *Journal of Teacher education for Sustainability, 9*(1), 115-127.

Miller, E. R., & Gkonou, C. (2018). Language teacher agency, emotion labor and emotional rewards in tertiary-level English language programs. *System, 79,* 49e59.

Miller, E. R., Morgan, B., & Medina, A. L. (2017). Exploring language teacher identity work as ethnical self-formation. *The Modern Language Journal, 101*(s), 91e105.

Mishra, L., Gupta, T., & Shree, A. (2020). Online teaching-learning in higher education during lockdown period of COVID-19 pandemic. *International Journal of Educational Research Open*, 1, 100012. 10.1016/j.ijedro.2020.10001235059663

Mohajan, H. K. (2018). Qualitative research methodology in social sciences and related subjects. *Journal of economic development, environment and people, 7*(1), 23-48. Retrieved from:https://mpra.ub.uni-muenchen.de/105149/1/MPRA_paper_105149.pdf

Motha, S., & Lin, A. M. Y. (2014). "Non-coercive rearrangements": Theorizing desire. *Tesol Quarterly, 48,* 331e359.

Muliyah, P., & Aminatun, D. (2020). Teaching English for Specific Purposes in Vocational High School: Teachers' Beliefs and Practices. *Journal of English Teaching*, 6(2), 122–133. 10.33541/jet.v6i2.1756

, N., & Khan, N. H. (2020). Online teaching-learning during covid-19 pandemic: students' perspective. *The Online Journal of Distance Education and e-Learning, 8*(4), 202-213.

Nazari, M., & Seyri, H. (2021). Covidentity: Examining transitions in teacher identity construction from personal to online classes. European Journal of Teacher Education, 1-20. Teachers' Beliefs and Practices. *Journal of English Teaching*, 6(2), 122–133.

Nichols, S. L., Schutz, P. A., Rodgers, K., & Bilica, K. (2017). Early career teachers' emotion and emerging teacher identities. *Teachers and Teaching*, 23(4), 406–421.

O'Connor, K. (2008). "You choose to care": Teachers, emotions and professional identity. *Teaching and Teacher Education*, 24(1), 117–126. 10.1016/j.tate.2006.11.008

Oatley, K. (2000). Emotion: Theories. In Kazdin, A. E. (Ed.), *Encyclopedia of psychology* (pp. 167–171). Oxford University Press.

Orellana, M. F., Liu, L., & Ángeles, S. L. (2022). "Reinventing Ourselves" and Reimagining Education: Everyday Learning and Life Lessons from the COVID-19 Pandemic. *Harvard Educational Review*, 92(3), 413–436. 10.17763/1943-5045-92.3.413

Ozamiz-Etxebarria, N., Idoiaga Mondragon, N., Bueno-Notivol, J., Pérez-Moreno, M., & Santabárbara, J. (2021). Prevalence of anxiety, depression, and stress among teachers during the COVID-19 pandemic: A rapid systematic review with meta-analysis. *Brain Sciences*, 11(9), 1172. 10.3390/brainsci1109117234573192

Papaja, K. (2021). Negative Emotions Experienced by Polish English Teachers During COVID-19. A Qualitative Study Based on Diaries. *Lublin Studies in Modern Languages & Literature / Lubelskie Materialy Neofilologiczne, 45*(3), 3–17. https://doi-org.ez.xjtlu.edu.cn/10.17951/lsmll.2021.45.3.3-17

Pishghadam, R., Golzar, J., & Miri, M. A. (2022). A New Conceptual Framework for Teacher Identity Development. *Frontiers in Psychology*, 13, 2024. 10.3389/fpsyg.2022.87639535615191

Qin, J. (2016). Analysis of the feeling of frustration experienced by Chinese middle school ESL students—from the perspective of psychology.

Qiu, J., Shen, B., Zhao, M., Wang, Z., Xie, B., & Xu, Y. (2020). A nationwide survey of psychological distress among Chinese people in the COVID-19 epidemic: Implications and policy recommendations. *General Psychiatry*, 33(2), e100213. 10.1136/gpsych-2020-10021332215365

Redding, C. (2019). A teacher like me: A review of the effect of student–teacher racial/ethnic matching on teacher perceptions of students and student academic and behavioral outcomes. *Review of Educational Research*, 89(4), 499–535. 10.3102/0034654319853545

Richards, J. C. (2022). Exploring emotions in language teaching. *RELC Journal*, 53(1), 225–239. 10.1177/0033688220927531

Šarić, M. (2015). Teachers' emotions: A research review from a psychological perspective. *Journal of Contemporary European Studies*, 4, 10–26.

Saunders, R. (2013). The role of teacher emotions in change: Experiences, patterns and implications for professional development. *Journal of Educational Change*, 14(3), 303–333. 10.1007/s10833-012-9195-0

Schuman, V., & Scherer, K. R. (2014). Concepts and structures of emotions. In Pekrun, R., & Linnenbrink-Garcia, L. (Eds.), *International handbooks on emotions in education* (pp. 13–35). Routledge.

Schutz, P. A., Cross Francis, D., & Hong, J. (2018). Research on teacher identity: Introduction to mapping challenges and innovations. In *Research on teacher identity* (pp. 3–9). Springer. 10.1007/978-3-319-93836-3_1

Schutz, P. A., & Lee, M. (2014). Teacher emotion, emotional labor and teacher identity. In Martinez Agudo, J. P., & Richards, J. (Eds.), *English as a foreign language teacher education: Current per- spectives and challenges* (pp. 169–186). Rodopi. 10.1163/9789401210485_011

Shapiro, S. (2010). Revisiting the teachers' lounge: Reflections on emotional experience and teacher identity. *Teaching and Teacher Education, 26*(3), 616–621. https://doi.org/. 00910.1016/j.tate.2009.09

Shen, X., Yang, Y. L., Wang, Y., Liu, L., Wang, S., & Wang, L. (2014). The association between occupational stress and depressive symptoms and the mediating role of psychological capital among Chinese university teachers: A cross-sectional study. *BMC Psychiatry*, 14(1), 1–8. 10.1186/s12888-014-0329-125433676

Silva, D. F. O., Cobucci, R. N., Lima, S. C. V. C., & de Andrade, F. B. (2021). Prevalence of anxiety, depression, and stress among teachers during the COVID-19 pandemic: A PRISMA-compliant systematic review. *Medicine*, 100(44), e27684. 10.1097/MD.0000000000002768434871251

Smagorinsky, P., Cook, L. S., Moore, C., Jackson, A. Y., & Fry, P. G. (2004). Tensions in learning to teach: Accommodation and the development of a teaching identity. *Journal of Teacher Education*, 55(1), 8–24. 10.1177/0022487103260067

Song, J. (2016). Emotions and language teacher identity: Conflicts, vulnerability, and transformation. *Tesol Quarterly, 50*, 631e654.

Srimulyani, V. A., & Hermanto, Y. B. (2022). Work-Life Balance Before and During Work from Home in a Covid-19 Pandemic Situation. *Jurnal Manajemen Indonesia*, 22(1), 31–46. 10.25124/jmi.v22i1.2915

Sutton, R. E., & Wheatley, K. F. (2003). Teachers' emotions and teaching: A review of the literature and directions for future research. *Educational Psychology Review*, 15(4), 327–358. 10.1023/A:1026131715856

Taxer, J. L., Becker-Kurz, B., & Frenzel, A. C. (2019). Do quality teacher–student relationships protect teachers from emotional exhaustion? The mediating role of enjoyment and anger. *Social Psychology of Education*, 22(1), 209–226. 10.1007/s11218-018-9468-4

Tomasik, M. J., Helbling, L. A., & Moser, U. (2021). Educational gains of in-person vs. distance learning in primary and secondary schools: A natural experiment during the COVID-19 pandemic school closures in Switzerland. *International Journal of Psychology*, 56(4), 566–576. 10.1002/ijop.1272833236341

Trent, J. (2012). The discursive positioning of teachers: Native-speaking English teachers and educational discourse in Hong Kong. *Tesol Quarterly, 46*, 104e126

Truzoli, R., Pirola, V., & Conte, S. (2021). The impact of risk and protective factors on online teaching experience in high school Italian teachers during the COVID-19 pandemic. *Journal of Computer Assisted Learning*, 37(4), 940–952. 10.1111/jcal.1253333821075

Tsybulsky, D., & Muchnik-Rozanov, Y. (2019). The development of student-teachers' professional identity while team-teaching science classes using a project-based learning approach: A multi-level analysis. *Teaching and Teacher Education*, 79, 48–59. 10.1016/j.tate.2018.12.006

Varghese, M., Morgan, B., Johnston, B., & Johnson, K. A. (2005). Theorizing language teacher identity: Three perspectives and beyond. *Journal of Language, Identity, and Education*, 4(1), 21–44. 10.1207/s15327701jlie0401_2

Vizek Vidović, V., & Domović, V. (2019). Development of teachers' beliefs as a core component of their professional identity in initial teacher education: A longitudinal perspective. *Center for Educational Policy Studies Journal*, 9(2), 119–138. 10.26529/cepsj.720

Wakui, N., Abe, S., Shirozu, S., Yamamoto, Y., Yamamura, M., Abe, Y., & Kikuchi, M. (2021). Causes of anxiety among teachers giving face-to-face lessons after the reopening of schools during the COVID-19 pandemic: A cross-sectional study. *BMC Public Health*, 21(1), 1–10. 10.1186/s12889-021-11130-y34078343

Wang, L., & Du, X. (2014). Chinese teachers' professional identity and beliefs about the teacher-student relationships in an intercultural context. *Frontiers of Education in China*, 9(3), 429–455. 10.1007/BF03397030

Wang, L., & Fang, F. (2020). Native-speakerism policy in English language teaching revisited: Chinese university teachers' and students' attitudes towards native and non-native English-speaking teachers. *Cogent Education*, 7(1), 1778374. 10.1080/2331186X.2020.1778374

Wenger, E. (1998). *Communities of practice: Learning, meaning, and identity*. Cambridge University Press. 10.1017/CBO9780511803932

Widodo, H. P., Fang, F., & Elyas, T. (2020). The construction of language teacher professional identity in the Global Englishes territory: 'we are legitimate language teachers'. *Asian Englishes*, 22(3), 309–316. 10.1080/13488678.2020.1732683

Wolff, D., & De Costa, P. I. (2017). Expanding the language teacher identity land-scape: An investigation of the emotions and strategies of a NNEST. *The Modern Language Journal, 101*(S1), 76e90.

Wu, M.-H., & Leung, G. (2020). 'It's not my Chinese': A teacher and her students disrupting and dismantling conventional notions of 'Chinese' through translanguaging in a heritage language classroom. *International Journal of Bilingual Education and Bilingualism*. Advance online publication. 10.1080/13670050.2020.1804524

Yang, J. (2019). Understanding Chinese language teachers' beliefs about themselves and their students in an English context. *System*, 80, 73–82. 10.1016/j.system.2018.10.014

Yang, S., Shu, D., & Yin, H. (2021). 'Frustration drives me to grow': Unraveling EFL teachers' emotional trajectory interacting with identity development. *Teaching and Teacher Education*, 105, 103420. Advance online publication. 10.1016/j.tate.2021.103420

Yang, S., Shu, D., & Yin, H. (2022). The bright side of dark emotions: Exploring EFL teachers' emotions, emotional capital, and engagement in curriculum implementation. *Teaching and Teacher Education*, 117, 103811. 10.1016/j.tate.2022.103811

Yim, S. Y., & Hwang, K. (2019). Expatriate ELT teachers in Korea: Participation and sense of belonging. *ELT Journal*, 73(1), 72–81. 10.1093/elt/ccy036

Yin, H. (2015). The effect of teachers' emotional labour on teaching satisfaction: Moderation of emotional intelligence. *Teachers and Teaching*, 21(7), 789–810. 10.1080/13540602.2014.995482

Yip, J. W. C. (1), Huang, J. (2), & Teng, M. F. (3). (2022). Identity and emotion of university English teachers during curriculum reform in China. *Language, Culture and Curriculum, 35*(4), 421-439–439. https://doi-org.ez.xjtlu.edu.cn/10.1080/07908318.2021.2024843

Yuan, R., & Lee, I. (2016). ''I need to be strong and competent': A narrative inquiry of a student-teacher's emotions and identities in teaching practicum. *Teachers and Teaching*, 22(7), 819–841. 10.1080/13540602.2016.1185819

Zadok-Gurman, T., Jakobovich, R., Dvash, E., Zafrani, K., Rolnik, B., Ganz, A. B., & Lev-Ari, S. (2021). Effect of inquiry-based stress reduction (IBSR) intervention on well-being, resilience and burnout of teachers during the COVID-19 pandemic. *International Journal of Environmental Research and Public Health*, 18(7), 3689. 10.3390/ijerph1807368933916258

Zembylas, M. (2003). Emotions and teacher identity: A poststructural perspective. *Teachers and Teaching*, 9(3), 213–238. 10.1080/13540600309378

Zhang, C., Yan, X., & Wang, J. (2021). EFL teachers' online assessment practices during the COVID-19 pandemic: Changes and mediating factors. *The Asia-Pacific Education Researcher*, 30(6), 499–507. 10.1007/s40299-021-00589-3

Zhang, X., Admiraal, W., & Saab, N. (2021). Teachers' motivation to participate in continuous professional development: Relationship with factors at the personal and school level. *Journal of Education for Teaching*, 47(5), 714–731. 10.1080/02607476.2021.1942804

APPENDIX A

Interview Questions

Teacher Professional Identity:
1. How long have you been teaching at XJTLU?
2. Did you have teaching experience before joining XJTLU? How long?
3. What do you think are the important qualities required for an English language teacher at XJTLU?
4. What kind of teacher do you think you are? For example, a strict teacher? Or like a parent who takes care of the student? Or more like a friend?
5. Can you please recall when you first entered the school, was this what you thought at that time? Or has something changed in the last few years?
6. What do you think caused this kind of change?
7. Please recall your experiences at XJTLU before the pandemic, what are the hardships or challenges in the process of integrating into XJTLU?
8. How did you overcome it? How did your emotions change during the process?
9. Has your teaching style, and the interaction between you and your students changed during the integration process? How?
10. What do you think are the characteristics of Chinese students?
    Identity and emotions of teachers from diverse ethnic backgrounds:
11. Do you feel that the culture and environment in your country/the school you studied or worked at before are very different from XJTLU?
12. Did you meet any challenges or difficulties at XJTLU because of the cultural differences (caused by your nationality/cultural background/study experience/working experience)?

    - What impact did it have on your emotions?
    - How did you regulate your emotions and overcome those difficulties?

13. XJTLU is quite a special context because it is a Sino-foreign university, the working language and teaching language is English but most of your students and many of your colleagues are Chinese. In this case, what do you think are your advantages or disadvantages while teaching at XJTLU?
    Identity and emotions of teachers under the pandemic:
14. It has been over two years since the outbreak of COVID 19. China has been implementing a relatively strict policy of pandemic control, and the school has often switched back and forth between online and offline classes in the past two years. What were some difficulties you encountered during the pandemic?
15. What kind of impact has the pandemic had on your emotions? (e.g. stress, anxiety, loneliness, homesick…)
16. Did these emotions have an impact on your teaching? And how did you deal with this kind of emotion?
17. What kind of student's behaviors usually elicits an emotional response from you during the pandemic? (No matter happy, angry, fatigued, disappointed or hopeless)
18. Two years have passed since the outbreak of the pandemic. Now, do you feel that you have adapted to teaching in the context of the pandemic?

19. How do you think your teaching style, your role in class and you emotion while teaching has changed?
20. Do you think the interactions and relationships between you and your students have changed during the pandemic?

APPENDIX B

TEQ scales

1	2	3	4	5
Strongly disagree	disagree	undecided	agree	Strongly agree

Joy

I am glad when I achieve teaching goals that are set.
1-2-3-4-5
I am joyful when the class atmosphere is positive.
1-2-3-4-5
I am happy when I manage to motivate students to learn.
1-2-3-4-5
I am happy when students understand the material.
1-2-3-4-5
Exerting a positive influence on my students makes me happy.
1-2-3-4-5

Pride

I feel like a winner when my students succeed.
1-2-3-4-5
Due to my students' achievements, I feel as if I am 'growing'.
1-2-3-4-5
I am filled with pride when I make a student interested in my subject.
1-2-3-4-5
Meetings with successful former students of mine make me proud.
1-2-3-4-5
When I am proud of my students, I feel that my confidence is growing.
1-2-3-4-5
Pride due to my students' achievements confirms to me that I am doing a good job.
1-2-3-4-5

Love

I feel warmth when I just think about my students.
1-2-3-4-5
I love my students.
1-2-3-4-5
My students evoke feelings of love inside me.

1-2-3-4-5
I feel affection towards my students.
1-2-3-4-5
I wish to hug my students since I like them so much.
1-2-3-4-5
I honestly care about each of my student.
1-2-3-4-5

Anger

I sweat from frustration when the class is not carried in the way it is supposed to.
1-2-3-4-5
The reactions of some students frustrate me so much that I would rather just quit the job.
1-2-3-4-5
The frustration I feel while working with students undermines my job motivation.
1-2-3-4-5
Some students make me so angry that my face goes red.
1-2-3-4-5
I get an anger-caused headache from the behaviour of some students.
1-2-3-4-5

Fatigue/Exhaustion

At the end of my working day, I just want to rest.
1-2-3-4-5
When I finish classes, I feel numbed.
1-2-3-4-5
My job sometimes makes me so tired that all I want to do is 'switch off'.
1-2-3-4-5
Due to the speedy pace of work, at the end of the day I feel as if I am going to fall down.
1-2-3-4-5
Sometimes I am so exhausted at work that I only think about how to endure.
1-2-3-4-5
When I finish my work, I feel drained.
1-2-3-4-5
Sometimes working with children makes me so tired that I can barely move.
1-2-3-4-5

Hopelessness

I feel I cannot do anything more to correct the behaviour of some students.
1-2-3-4-5
While working with completely unmotivated students, I feel there is no way out.
1-2-3-4-5

Because of the behaviour of some students, I feel completely helpless.
1-2-3-4-5
I feel hopeless when I think about the achievement of some students.
1-2-3-4-5
It seems to me that I cannot do anything to get through to some students.
1-2-3-4-5
I feel defenceless because I cannot help some of my students.
1-2-3-4-5

Chapter 7
Teacher Identity, Course-Based Moral Education, and the Lessons for Transnational Higher Education Institutions

Junhua Mo
https://orcid.org/0000-0001-6464-3628
Soochow University, China

Gareth Morris
University of Nottingham, Ningbo, China

Li Tao
Soochow University, China

ABSTRACT

The sociocultural and political context plays a crucial role in influencing and shaping teacher identity, and recent developments in China's higher education have seen moral education become a priority area. This has presented new challenges to Chinese university teachers in terms of their pedagogical delivery and sense of self. This chapter therefore attempts to explore the identity construction of a Chinese EFL teacher who has been incorporating course-based moral education within his teaching and research practices. Through a positioning analysis, it is found that teachers may experience a triple identity and that the identity construction process is tied to the active agency of teachers. The relevance of this chapter for transnational higher education is also interesting, because providers are influenced by the context they are a part of, so understanding how domestic policy is changing is important for anticipating how international and transnational provision might enabling proactive forward thinking leadership.

DOI: 10.4018/979-8-3693-2857-6.ch007

1. INTRODUCTION

Teacher identity is an important construct that is concerned with "the ways teachers make sense of themselves and the images they present to others in their situated institutional and sociocultural contexts" (Yuan & Zhang, 2019, p. 3). It is a fluid construct and one that can vary depending on the role teachers are performing in a given personal or professional context, as Wang et al. (2021) allude to. As a key factor affecting the implementation of teaching (Varghese et al., 2005), teacher identity has been gaining more and more scholarly attention (Trent, 2014). The importance of teacher identity to language teaching is clearly emphasized by De Costa and Norton (2017) who contend that language teaching is in essence identity work. Sachs (2005) suggests that language teacher identity will to a large extent determine the teachers' views of "how to be", "how to act" and "how to understand" their work and place in the society (p. 15). Equally influential as far as identity creation, sustainability and development is concerned is the role that educational institutions play in shaping students' identities, as Szczurek-Boruta (2021) draws attention to.

China has a time-honored tradition of emphasizing cultivation of student morality. The emphasis on moral education gained a new momentum in 2016 when specific importance was given to all kinds of courses focusing in the same direction as ideological and political courses, forming synergies to cultivate student morality (Wu & Hu, 2016). Since then, course-based moral education has become an emerging trend in China's educational system as Yu (2018) and Ye (2023) note. A milestone came when the Chinese Ministry of Education (2020) released *The Framework of Guidelines for the Construction of Moral Education in Higher Education*, further emphasizing the importance of moral education, which is not limited to a particular course, but applicable to all.

Foreign language teaching is an indispensable part of China's higher education. Of the various foreign language courses offered to Chinese university students, English is the most conspicuous one. The necessity of integrating moral education into English teaching has been explicitly expounded by high-level official documents such as the latest version of *Guidelines for College English Teaching* (Foreign Languages Teaching Committee for Higher Education of Ministry of Education, 2020) and *Teaching Guide for Undergraduate Foreign Language and Literature Majors in General Colleges and Universities (Part 1): Teaching Guide for English Majors* (Foreign Language and Literature Major Teaching Supervising Committee, English, 2020).

Indeed, "[t]he moral landscape of the language classroom is rendered even more complex than in other contexts by the fact that the teaching of languages by definition takes place at the intersection between different national, cultural, and political boundaries, representing often radically different sets of values" (Johnston & Buzzelli, 2008, p. 95). As an on-going educational reform in China, course-based moral education has posed a new challenge to Chinese university EFL teachers (W. Zhang et al., 2022). Efforts have been made to investigate Chinese university EFL teachers' practical knowledge of course-based education and the status quo of their teaching competence (Hu & Liu, 2022; Q. Zhang, 2022a). However, how educational reforms affect the process of Chinese EFL teachers' identity construction remains under investigated (Gao et al., 2018). Therefore, the present study aims to explore the identities that a Chinese university EFL teacher constructs as a result of now having to take on added responsibility in the area of course-based moral education.

2. LITERATURE REVIEW

2.1 Teacher Identity

Teacher identity is a dynamic construct in that it is an "ongoing process of interpretation and re-interpretation of experiences" (Beijaard et al., 2004, p. 122). It is also a multidimensional or multifaceted construct that involves a series of "sub-identities" (Mishler, 2009, p. 8). Studies of teacher identity generally need to take two types of perspectives: identity in practice and identity in discourse (Trent, 2014). On the one hand, Sang (2020) suggests that "language teacher identity is formed and demonstrated in L2 teachers' participation in language teaching activities in professional communities of practice" (p. 2). For early career professionals, Kanno and Stuart (2011) find that it is through intense engagement in classroom teaching that novice L2 teachers form their professional identity. On the other hand, Peirce (1995) contends that language teacher identity is a multiple, dynamic construct that involves power relationships in social discourses. Gu and Benson (2015) find that the identity formation of ESL and EFL teachers "is enacted individually, mediated by the immediate contextual factors, shaped by their socio-economic backgrounds and constructed with reference to social discourses on teachers and teaching profession" (p. 187).

Closely related to the notion of teacher identity is the concept of teacher agency, which is defined as a teacher's "ability to act in new and creative ways, and even to resist external norms and regulations when they are understood to contrast or conflict with professionally justifiable action" (Toom et al., 2015, p. 615). Beijaard et al. (2004) maintain that teacher agency is an essential part of teacher identity construction. Agentic teachers tend to become pedagogical experts who are capable of effective new learning at both individual and community levels (Pyhältö et al., 2015). What is more, agentic teachers are more likely to strengthen confidence in their job (Priestley et al., 2016), prompting them to make more commitments to classroom teaching and more efforts in professional development.

An additional area of teacher identity that is often overlooked in discussion, but also merits acknowledgment at this point, is that which is formed and exists outside of work. This is because identity is regarded as a combination of attributes or characteristics that belong to a person, and so it is hard to truly split one's multiple personal and professional selves (Gov.UK, 2023). Clearly, identity can involve multiple varied criteria (Noonan, 2019), but the reality is also that teacher identity inevitably involves a professional-personal crossover, as Carpenter et al. (2019) highlight, and one which has blurred more in recent years with technological advancements and social media influences. This is an important acknowledgement when considering that educators are now also agents for moral education. It is also important to note the role that the imagined possible and future selves can play as Kubanyiova (2015) draws attention to, as this can influence both identity evolution and course-based moral education pedagogy and practice.

2.2 Positioning Analysis

Positioning analysis, as an alternative approach to the predominant "big story" approach to narrative analysis, represents a new narrative turn (Bamberg, 2006, p. 142). As an interactive way to understand how humans make sense of their life and themselves (Bruner, 1991), narrative analysis has been increasingly used to understand teachers' professional lives in recent years (Barkhuizen, 2008, 2010; Clandinin & Connelly, 1995). There are two general approaches to narrative analysis: narratives as cognitive structure or schema through which we understand the world" and "narratives as discursive actions" (Gergen & Gergen, 2006). While both approaches agree that human experience should be viewed as "interpretable and that such interpretations require perspective" (Bamberg, 2006, p. 242), they analyze narratives in quite different ways. The cognitive approach emphasizes the content or context (Barkhuizen, 2008), i.e., what has been said. It usually involves the identification of the participants, time and space which provide context for a story (Barkhuizen, 2008). On the other hand, the discursive approach is more interested in content arrangements, i.e., how narratives are organized and narrated reveals a lot about how a self is constructed and conveyed (Bamberg, 1997b). In this way, narratives are understood as going beyond language entities, which reflect the knowledge and power dynamics that exist in human practices.

Up till now, the cognitive approach has been predominant in narrative analysis literature (Bamberg, 2006). However, an increasing number of researchers now agree that particular descriptions and evaluations chosen by the narrator for interactive purposes contribute significantly to the interpretation of the story itself and have attempted to examine how the narrator chooses particular linguistic means for interactive purposes (Tavakol & Tavakoli, 2022). Taking up a particular position means a person sees the world from the point of that position and such experience or identity can only be expressed or understood through relevant concepts, images, metaphors and story lines available to them. Thus, the person becomes an active agent who assigns characters and is in control of the story flow. As Bamberg (2006) states, the primary purpose of positioning analysis is not on "enlightenment", but on "empathy" (p. 140). Researchers are interested in narrators who engage in the activity of giving accounts from a particular perspective for a particular discursive purpose, which represents the way the narrator wants to be understood.

Positioning analysis has been used as a compensatory analytical tool in a number of studies on teachers' professional identity in the past few years. For example, Barkhuizen (2010) used an extended positioning analytical framework to explore how a migrant, pre-service teacher attempted to lead a better life. West (2019) discussed how teachers created moral selves in response to neoliberal policies in education. Lan and Mehta (2022) investigated how a professional team in China constructed the "we-perspective". Q. Zhang (2022b) employed positioning analysis to reveal the multiple identities of a Chinese university EFL teacher, including her pedagogical identity, relational identity, institutional identity and personal identity. Although these studies deepened our understanding of teacher identity, they have received much less attention than those using the dominant cognitive approach.

Due to a lack of attention to positioning analysis in the investigation of teacher identity, this study attempts to explore how an EFL teacher constructs his identity through positioning analysis at three levels. Given that Q. Zhang (2022b) has investigated a Chinese college English teacher who is responsible for teaching non-English majors, this study will focus on an English major teacher. In addition, this study will consider the ongoing course-based moral education in China, which has not been a focal point in Q. Zhang's (2022b) study.

3. METHODOLOGY

3.1 Research Questions

This study intends to answer three research questions.

1. What identity did a Chinese EFL teacher construct through positioning of characters against the backdrop of course-based moral education?
2. What identity did a Chinese EFL teacher construct in relation to the audience against the backdrop of course-based moral education?
3. What identity did a Chinese EFL teacher construct through self-positioning against the backdrop of course-based moral education?

3.2 Research Participant

The participant who was attributed the pseudonym of Li in this case study was purposely selected. This sampling decision took into consideration important features that could affect teacher identity construction so that rich information could be derived. The participant is a male and a PhD holder in applied linguistics who is currently an associate professor of English at a Project 211 university in an affluent city in the Yangtze Delta Region. He has been teaching various courses to English majors since 2008. The participant also won first prize in his university's 2021 course-based moral education classroom teaching competition.

3.3 Data Collection

Data was collected through the administration of an online interview, which was conducted in Chinese with the participant via Tencent Meeting on January 9th, 2023. The duration of the interview was 2 hours and 8 minutes, and the transcription constituted 16,628 words. Tencent Meeting is a popular real-time online communication software tool widely used in China which is not too dissimilar to Microsoft Teams or Facetime. The purpose of the interview was to reveal how the participant, as a university English teacher, constructed his identity during a period of moral education reform within China. The interview involved the following themes: work history, an understanding of course-based moral education reform, the practice of course-based moral education, perceptions on his colleagues' views regarding course-based moral education, and suggestions on institutional course-based moral education implementation going forward.

3.4 Data Analysis

Given the fact that this study viewed teacher identity as dynamically, contextually and discursively negotiated (Tavakol & Tavakoli, 2022), it followed Bamberg (1997a, 1997b, 2006) by employing positioning analysis as it aligned with the designs of this research study. In particular, a two-step analysis which integrates the understanding of both the content and its arrangement was applied (Bamberg, 2006). In the first stage, critical events were identified that had a powerful impact on the participant's personal change and development (Woods, 1993), including the characters, time and space, so as to create a three-dimensional narrative space to understand the context for a story (Barkhuizen, 2008). In this study, the researchers were strongly interested in the incidents that led to the construction of the participant's identities against the backdrop of national moral education reform. In the second stage, the researchers examined how the story was structured and delivered to the audience through linguistic means, indicating how the speaker assembled and arranged different parts of story for interactive purposes. It was done at three levels: (1) how the characters were positioned in relation to one another within the reported events,

(2) how the speaker positioned himself to the audience and (3) how the narrator positioned himself to himself (Bamberg, 1997a). These two steps revealed how the participant constructed a sense of self and how he used stories to "actively construct social and psychological realities" (Davies & Harré, 1990, p. 45).

4. FINDINGS

4.1 Positioning of Characters: A Competent Practitioner

From the perspective of positioning of characters, it was found that the Li constructed a new identity as a competent practitioner after course-based moral education became a pedagogical reality. Before this development, although he had paid attention to moral education, he described his career as offering little satisfaction to him. However, in this part of the narrative, it was not considered as a personal failure, but rather attributed to the unfair treatment he had received from a colleague. This colleague, ascribed the pseudonym of Tang, had held an administrative position at that time. When the Li explained why it took him ten years to become an associate professor, he attributed it to Tang's wrong interpretation of the evaluation policies. He positioned himself as a passive recipient of an injustice and a victim who had to bear the unfortunate consequences of someone else's judgement.

> He had a wrong interpretation of this evaluation policy. He said we couldn't apply for teaching-oriented titles, so he cut off my path. I had three papers in top-ranking journals during my doctoral studies that year. Two were published by *Foreign Language Education* and one *Journal of PLA University of Foreign Languages*[1]. As a result, all of them were useless after I came here. If we had been allowed to apply for the teaching-oriented titles, I could have used these three articles. Then I wouldn't have had to wait for 10 years before I became an associate professor.

Li went on to express his embitterment by describing an imagined situation at the end of his complaint. The hypothetical narrative allowed him to justify his slow progress in applying for higher professional titles. In other words, he attributed his frustrations to an authoritative figure in management rather than any personal factors. He went on to list several examples of how he felt that Tang had treated him unfairly, including humiliating him at a conference. In all of these incidents, he perceived himself to have appeared as a "weak man" who had to "bear it all". Such a narrative constructed the relationship between the two characters as one of victimizer and the other as, almost helpless, victim, which was used strategically to save face ('mianzi' in Chinese) when he considered his experiences as a researcher in the past. It was also a sense of mitigating the negative influence on his professional identity that contributed to the professional narrative he expressed.

In contrast, an increasing degree of activism and confidence was expressed when Li described his experience of engaging in university-level course-based moral educational reforms. He now dominated his story arch as the major character who made conscious decisions and took definitive actions. He became familiarized with the concept of course-based moral education when he participated in a teaching competition and became interested in this area. After this, he actively began to read literature on this issue. He soon realized it "fitted" his research interests, or that he was repositioning them within this area. Then he started to seek for collaboration with other researchers to conduct studies in this field.

In June 2021, I took part in the Third Classroom Teaching Competition in Course-based Moral Education held by our university and won first prize, which was a great motivation to me. ... In the second half of 2021, I then wrote a paper on the core competences, connotation and enhancement path of foreign language teachers in universities in the context of moral education. In addition, I also wrote a paper on the five dimensions of advancing moral education in foreign language classrooms in universities. I followed this up by summarizing a teaching model based on the method I used when I participated in the teaching competition in the first half of 2021, the TLR teaching model for the moral education of English majors. ... By February 2022, after the New Year, I contacted another expert in our province, because I wanted to do a bibliometric study of course-based moral education of foreign language courses, using the software CiteSpace to produce a visual analysis.

Li also reflected on how the experiences had helped to give him clearer plans for the future. These included both short-terms goals about his further engagement in course-based moral education, and longer term professional aspirations that motivated him, noting at one point:

I'm going to apply for a project in 2023 on how English education experts see course-based moral education, what they do, how they do it, what they think, and what actions they have taken. I will use this to apply for a project from the Ministry of Education. ... I personally feel that there is a constant goal in career planning, which is to become a full professor and this might be an avenue worth exploring.

Throughout his narrative, Li emphasized his more purposeful decisions and actions, positioning himself as an active agent. His success he attributed to personal dedication and competence rather than external developments. He was positioned as the only agentive actor in the story world who had initiated a number of career building actions in his professional life, indicating his emerging identity as a competent practitioner of course-based moral education rather than a passive victim as had been the identification with his earlier research experiences.

4.2 Positioning of Narrator in Relation to the Audience: A Superior Expert

From the perspective of positioning in relation to the audience, it appeared that Li constructed an identity as an expert in course-based moral education who demonstrated a sense of superiority to the interviewer. In his interview, this teacher went to considerable lengths to demonstrate his understanding of course-based moral education in much the same way a teacher lectures in front of students. He wrapped up this part with a question which could be perceived as a challenge to the interviewer and revealed his self-positioning as a now confident trailblazer.

> Personally, I feel that since 2020 or 2021, course-based moral learning has been integrated into mainstream education. Everybody talks about cultivating talents for the Party and for the country. Everybody talks about course-based moral education. It has become a hot topic since then, so I think it is now a "catch phrase". Haven't you realized it?

He also indicated his perceived superior position by indicating his willingness to share with the interviewer his understanding of course-based moral education, presenting himself as an expert in front of a less knowledgeable subject novice. He also drew attention to the papers he had produced in this area which were used as an illustration of his newly acquired authority and accomplishment, as well as a willingness to demonstrate this:

So in the second half of 2021, I wrote several papers on course-based moral education. I can share my understanding with you.

Interestingly, unlike earlier in the discussion when recounting his past research endeavours and the perceived lack of support and acknowledgement he had received at an institutional level, he now felt greater encouragement from the university and his department in his practice of course-based moral education.

I personally feel that we have made a great effort from the school level. At the university level, whether it is postgraduate teaching or undergraduate teaching, the school has launched a lot of reform projects of course-based moral education, including the curriculum construction of course-based moral education, and the teaching competitions in course-based moral education. I remember that our department also launched a number of projects in 2021. I myself applied for a teaching reform project of English majors. So I think from the university level to the department level, the policies are very supportive and encouraging of the teaching reforms.

He also indicated his now advantageous position by comparing his efforts and achievement in this area to other teachers, claiming that they were not doing enough:

I think according to my communication with some teachers, they do not know much about course-based moral education, unlike me. I think there are not many teachers who know more about the history of moral education, its development from the beginning to the present situation and the future trend. I personally feel that most teachers are not particularly knowledgeable about this stuff, and I personally feel that their efforts in course-based moral education are not adequate.

The fact that Li presented himself now as an evaluator, rather than someone being evaluated, who was now able to judge the effort and achievement of both his workplace and his colleagues suggested an evolving sense of self-worth, and an attempt to reinforce his own mental self-positioning as an expert pioneer in course-based moral education as opposed to the interviewer, or more passive change agents.

4.3 Narrator's Self-positioning: A Conscientious Moral Agent

As for Li's self-positioning, it was interesting to note the temporal evolution and how he now positioned himself as a conscientious moral agent both in and out of his professional landscape. As a university EFL teacher who managed to integrate moral education into his courses, he now had a clear sense of purpose, area to excel in and idea of his moral responsibilities inside the classroom. He used one example to demonstrate how moral education had become an integral part of his teaching and evaluation.

I had students choose one of the 12 texts that we had covered in class to search for elements of moral education. They were required to write no less than 1500 words. I asked the students to justify the moral issues they found, to illustrate these, and preferably to provide a link to any video material. I gave them a demonstration, and the students did a good job. They were quite interested and found it reasonably rewarding. Before that, they were not aware of this (moral education), learning language as a tool. They were not aware of the humanistic nature and the nurturing function of language.

He did not only describe himself as a moral teacher who actively engaged in classroom teaching, but also a reflective observer of his own practice. Based on his teaching experience and understanding of course-based moral education, Li summarized five core competencies of university EFL teachers, these being moral, political, cultural, educational and language-based.

> The primary task of a teacher is to impart, to pass on the essence of being a human being, that is, to help students cultivate the right values and morality. ... Therefore, teachers must first of all have moral competence. I think this is the first thing. This is the foundation. ... You also need to have political competence. You must be concerned about national events, understand major policies, ideas and initiatives of the Party and the government. This is the second competence. ... The third one is foreign language competence. ... We must have target language competence. ... The fourth one is cultural competence. ... You can only strengthen your ambition, confidence, and steadfastness as a Chinese citizen if you have some understanding of the outstanding traditional culture that has continued for thousands of years. ... The last one, I think as a university EFL teacher, you must have teaching competence, that is, the ability to teach or the art of teaching.

Li also stepped out of his professional arena and reflected on his identity in a broader context as a moral agent and not simply as a teacher. He considered his role as a Chinese citizen embracing a national educational reform. As such, his moral responsibility was not about imparting knowledge and values to students but was now about linking his professional life to the development of the country and fulfilling his personal values through such a link.

> The course-based moral education, first of all, is a national strategy, an educational reform at the national level, and an educational aspiration, right? I think a person can only realize his value in the development of national education, right? ... Only when you resonate with the government and the Party can you spread the ideas of the Party and the government and speak out for the government. You will be able to convey the voice of the Party and the government.

He also used a public figure, Jack Ma, as a counterexample to suggest the importance of alignment with national values.

> Jack Ma was very popular a few years ago, but since last year there has been very little media coverage of him, right? I guess he may have some problems. He may have been excessively pursuing the growth of personal wealth, but now the country is promoting common prosperity. Maybe Jack Ma is not a good example in this respect.

By reflecting on his practice as a teacher participating in a top-down national educational reform and a citizen of a country initiating such a reform, Li was able to construct his identity as a moral agent that required him to fulfill dual societal and professional responsibilities.

4. DISCUSSION

4.1 Verifying the Facilitating Role of Teacher Agency in Identity Construction

In this study, Li actively constructs over time the triple identity of a competent practitioner, a superior expert and a conscientious moral agent which aligns his professional identity with his aspirational personal one. Indeed, self-reflection aids align these macro identities through a sense of purpose, passion and teaching ideals as Kim and Greene (2011) note. This dynamic identity construction process can be attributed to the active agency of this teacher. That is, Li has embraced the educational reform of his country and his university. He has also adopted what in business terms would be referred to as first mover advantage which has enhanced his career prospects exponentially and changed his mindset in terms of how he views himself as Hargrave (2016), Peters (2012) and Smith (2022) note as being important psychologically. This game theory first mover advantage was in evidence when considering how Li made quick responses and effective adjustments in his daily teaching and through participating in and winning teaching competitions. By aligning intrinsic values and motives with the changing external environment his sense of self and future prospects were elevated. The fact that Li also took part in the university-level classroom teaching competition in course-based moral education, despite his earlier career frustrations and disappointments, highlights that he was also willing to step out of his comfort zone to meet emerging challenges. His comments that some of his colleagues have not invested as many efforts in course-based moral education as he has also serve as evidence of his active agency, but also potentially demonstrate a desire for recognition which was not previously afforded to him. The same thing can be seen through his reflections on the core competences that a good course moral agent should have and how these now aligned with his evolving identity as an expert practitioner and moral agent.

The verified role of teacher agency in this study lends support to Li and De Costa (2017) who find that the Chinese EFL teacher in their study, who in that case was female, is able to "exercise agency within the affordances and constraints of the given work context" (p. 277). Different from Q. Zhang (2022b), which indicates that there is a dynamic relationship between the pedagogical identity, the relational identity, the institutional identity and the individual identity that a Chinese college English teacher owns, the finding of this study is more specific in that it anatomizes the pedagogical identity of the Chinese EFL teacher into three distinct identities: a competent practitioner, a superior expert and a conscientious moral agent. Like Zhang (2022b), who attributes teacher identity construction to teacher agency, this study additionally suggests that teacher identity is motivated by teacher agency.

4.2 Advocating a Discursive Perspective to Understanding Identity Construction

Through adopting positioning analysis to explore a Chinese EFL teacher's identity construction amid a national educational reform, this study heralds a discursive turn from the dominant cognitive approach that is based on the content of narrative texts. Up until now the majority of studies on teacher identity construction seek to understand teachers' professional lives from a succession of events in their life (Pappa et al., 2017; Tsui, 2007). While this approach may reveal the narrator's complicated life experiences, some scholars argue that too much emphasis is placed on content at the expense of the form and context of construction (Barkhuizen, 2010). It should be noted that narratives are not mere repertory of information. The way information is organized and conveyed provides insights into how narrators make sense of their lives.

In this study, the EFL teacher's identity construction was understood not only from the "what" he said about the changes in his professional life as a result of his engagement in the moral education reform in China, but also from "how" he talked about such changes in a way that suggested his positioning of characters, of narrator in relation to the interviewer, and of himself. This "small story" approach (Bamberg, 2006, p. 139) allowed the researchers to consider how Li constructed the aforementioned three identities through discursive practice. It attests to the value in and necessity of adopting the discursive perspective, which integrates "sociolinguistic, conversational, and ethnographic approaches" (Lan & Mehta, 2022, p. 180) to make sense of how teachers construct and position selves (inter)subjectively in complicated story lines.

4.3 Implications for Transnational Higher Education Leadership

Leadership is a complicated endeavor as it involves overseeing or influencing others actions. It is also often is derived from hierarchical positions and roles and, as such, involves managing subordinates. When these staff are also subject to their own frustrations and disappointments it can be very challenging. Leadership will not get easier when staff are having to adapt to new contextual directives and evolve their identities within these new pedagogic realities. This case study clearly highlights an important development within one highly prominent national context and the impact that this has had for some on an individual level. It also has implications for cross boarder providers who may have to tailor their delivery to align with evolving movements and developments, and potentially raise questions about how these changes differ from expectations in other localities. This example, although limited in geographic scope, does provide an interesting case about the need for transnational higher education providers to be mindful of, and proactive concerning, change. It is also important that they manage this astutely so that current and future staff are able to thrive, especially given how many of these providers are English medium of instruction institutions who recruit from domestic, as well as international, talent pools.

5. CONCLUSION

Johnston et al. (1998) suggest that "ESL teaching, like other forms of teaching, is inherently moral in nature" (p. 161). Indeed, the importance of values in English language teaching have been well documented for decades as the work of Johnston (2002) attests to. This is especially true in China where the course-based moral educational reform is being now being promoted. In this reform, moral education is not limited to any particular course, but exists in the whole curriculum. English and foreign language courses are therefore no exception, and are arguably at the forefront of developments given their popularity and widespread uptake and importance. This topic is therefore essentially important for every Chinese EFL current and future teacher and student as the expectation is that this moral dimension will be integrated into language teaching and learning. Taking a case analysis approach, this study explores how a Chinese university EFL teacher constructed his evolving professional identity against the backdrop of course-based moral education developments. Through positioning analysis, it is found that this teacher did not wait passively, but actively engaged with the change and subsequently constructed three distinct types of professional identity so as to be a good English teacher who met the requirements of his school, institution and country. This dynamic identity construction process was driven by the active professional agency of this teacher. This may have worked in his case, and it certainly presents interesting discussion points for expatriate educators. Given that this study is focused on the EFL teacher identity in discourse within a domestic institution, future studies are advised to investigate the identity in practice, or within international or transnational providers. Future studies are also advised to adopt multiple approaches in addition to positioning analysis in order to collect new types of data to shed light on the identity construction of EFL teachers in China and around world in a period of unprecedented change, challenge and opportunity.

ACKNOWLEDGEMENTS

This study was funded by the 2023 Teaching Reform Project of Soochow University *Building an Innovative Curriculum for English Majors by Emphasizing International Communication and Moral Integrity* and the Humanities and Social Sciences Interdisciplinary Research Team of Soochow University (Grant No: 5033720623).

REFERENCES

Bamberg, M. (1997a). Positioning between structure and performance. *Journal of Narrative and Life History*, 7(1–4), 335–342. 10.1075/jnlh.7.42pos

Bamberg, M. (1997b). Language, concepts and emotions: The role of language in the construction of emotions. *Language Sciences*, 19(4), 309–340. 10.1016/S0388-0001(97)00004-1

Bamberg, M. (2006). Stories: Big or small: Why do we care? *Narrative Inquiry*, 16(1), 139–147. 10.1075/ni.16.1.18bam

Barkhuizen, G. (2008). A narrative approach to exploring context in language teaching. *ELT Journal*, 62(3), 231–239. 10.1093/elt/ccm043

Barkhuizen, G. (2010). An extended positioning analysis of a pre-service teacher's better life small Story. *Applied Linguistics*, 31(2), 282–300. 10.1093/applin/amp027

Beijaard, D., Meijer, P. C., & Verloop, N. (2004). Reconsidering research on teachers' professional identity. *Teaching and Teacher Education*, 20(2), 107–128. 10.1016/j.tate.2003.07.001

Bruner, J. (1991). The narrative construction of reality. *Critical Inquiry*, 18(1), 1–21. 10.1086/448619

Carpenter, J. P., Kimmons, R., Short, C. R., Clements, K., & Staples, M. E. (2019). Teacher identity and crossing the professional-personal divide on twitter. *Teaching and Teacher Education*, 81, 1–12. 10.1016/j.tate.2019.01.011

Davies, B., & Harré, R. (1990). Positioning: The discursive production of selves. *Journal for the Theory of Social Behaviour*, 20(1), 43–63. 10.1111/j.1468-5914.1990.tb00174.x

De Costa, P. I., & Norton, B. (2017). Introduction: Identity, transdisciplinarity, and the good language teacher. *Modern Language Journal*, 101(S1), 3–14. 10.1111/modl.12368

Foreign Language and Literature Major Teaching Supervising Committee. English, M. T. S. S.-C., Ministry of Education. (2020). *Teaching Guide for Undergraduate Foreign Language and Literature Major in Ordinary Colleges and Universities (Part 1): Teaching Guide for English Majors*. Foreign Language Teaching and Research Press.

Foreign Languages Teaching Committee for Higher Education of Ministry of Education. (2020). *Guidelines for College English Teaching*. Higher Education Press.

Gao, X., Tao, J., & Gong, Y. (2018). A sociocultural inquiry on teacher agency and professional identity in curriculum reforms. *Foreign Languages and Their Teaching, 298*(1), 19-28+146. 10.13458/j.cnki.flatt.004453

Gergen, M. M., & Gergen, K. J. (2006). Narratives in action. *Narrative Inquiry*, 16(1), 112–121. 10.1075/ni.16.1.15ger

Gov.UK. (2023). *How to prove and verify someone's identity*. https://www.gov.uk/government/publications/identity-proofing-and-verification-of-an-individual/how-to-prove-and-verify-someones-identity

Gu, M., & Benson, P. (2015). The formation of English teacher identities: A cross-cultural investigation. *Language Teaching Research*, 19(2), 187–206. Advance online publication. 10.1177/1362168814541725

Hargrave, S. J. (2016). *Mind hacking: How to change your mind for good in 21 days*. Gallery Books.

Hu, P., & Liu, W. (2022). An investigation into the status quo of college English teachers' teaching competence in course-based political and virtuous awareness. *Technology Enhanced Foreign Language Education, 207*(5), 11-17+106.

Johnston, B. (2002). *Values in English language teaching*. Routledge.

Johnston, B., & Buzzelli, C. A. (2008). The moral dimensions of language education. In Hornberger, N. H. (Ed.), *Encyclopedia of Language and Education* (pp. 95–104). Springer US., 10.1007/978-0-387-30424-3_8

Johnston, B., Juhász, A., Marken, J., & Ruiz, B. R. (1998). The ESL teacher as moral agent. *Research in the Teaching of English*, 32(2), 161–181.

Kanno, Y., & Stuart, C. (2011). Learning to become a second language teacher: Identities-in-practice. *Modern Language Journal*, 95(2), 236–252. 10.1111/j.1540-4781.2011.01178.x

Kim, Y. M., & Greene, W. L. (2011). Aligning professional and personal identities: Applying core reflection in teacher education practice. *Studying Teacher Education*, 7(2), 109–119. 10.1080/17425964.2011.591132

Kubanyiova, M. (2015). The role of teachers' future self guides in creating L2 development opportunities in teacher-led classroom discourse: Reclaiming the relevance of language teacher cognition. *Modern Language Journal*, 99(3), 565–584. 10.1111/modl.12244

Lan, L., & Mehta, C. (2022). Constructing collective agency through narrative positioning in group meetings within a Chinese professional team. *Language & Communication*, 87, 179–190. 10.1016/j.langcom.2022.07.008

Li, W., & De Costa, P. I. (2017). Professional survival in a neoliberal age: A case study of an EFL teacher in China. *The Journal of Asia TEFL*, 14(2), 277–291. 10.18823/asiatefl.2017.14.2.5.277

Ministry of Education. (2020). *Publication of The Framework of Guidelines for the Construction of Ideological and Political Teaching in Higher Education*. http://www.moe.gov.cn/srcsite/A08/s7056/202006/t20200603_462437.html

Mishler, E. G. (2009). *Storylines: Craftartists' narratives of identity*. Harvard University Press.

Noonan, H. (2019). *Personal identity*. Routledge. 10.4324/9781315107240

Pappa, S., Moate, J., Ruohotie-Lyhty, M., & Eteläpelto, A. (2017). Teachers' pedagogical and relational identity negotiation in the Finnish CLIL context. *Teaching and Teacher Education*, 65, 61–70. 10.1016/j.tate.2017.03.008

Peirce, B. N. (1995). Social identity, investment, and language learning. *TESOL Quarterly*, 29(1), 9–31. 10.2307/3587803

Peters, S. (2012). *Chimp paradox*. Random House.

Priestley, M., Biesta, G., & Robinson, S. (2016). *Teacher agency: An ecological approach*. Bloomsbury Publishing.

Pyhältö, K., Pietarinen, J., & Soini, T. (2015). Teachers' professional agency and learning—From adaption to active modification in the teacher community. *Teachers and Teaching*, 21(7), 811–830. 10.1080/13540602.2014.995483

Sachs, J. (2005). Teacher education and the development of professional identity: Learning to be a teacher. In P. M. Denicolo & M. Kompf (Eds.), *Connecting Policy and Practice* (pp. 5–21). Routledge, Taylor and Francis Group. 10.4324/9780203012529

Sang, Y. (2020). Research of language teacher identity: Status quo and future directions. *RELC Journal*, 53(3), 731–738. 10.1177/0033688220961567

Smith, J. (2022). *Why has nobody told me this before?* Harper One.

Szczurek-Boruta, A. (2021). School and shaping students' identities: A report on the studies into youth in the Silesian voivodeship. *European Review (Chichester, England)*, 30(3), 408–425. 10.1017/S1062798721000120

Tavakol, M., & Tavakoli, M. (2022). The professional identity of Iranian young-learner teachers of English: A narrative inquiry. *Linguistics and Education*, 71, 101101. 10.1016/j.linged.2022.101101

Toom, A., Pyhältö, K., & Rust, F. O. (2015). Teachers' professional agency in contradictory times. *Teachers and Teaching*, 21(6), 615–623. 10.1080/13540602.2015.1044334

Trent, J. (2014). Towards a multifaceted, multidimensional framework for understanding teacher identity. In Cheung, Y. L., Said, S. B., & Park, K. (Eds.), *Advances and Current Trends in Language Teacher Identity Research* (pp. 44–58). Routledge. 10.4324/9781315775135-4

Tsui, A. B. M. (2007). Complexities of identity formation: A narrative inquiry of an EFL teacher. *TESOL Quarterly*, 41(4), 657–680. 10.1002/j.1545-7249.2007.tb00098.x

Varghese, M., Morgan, B., Johnston, B., & Johnson, K. A. (2005). Theorizing language teacher identity: Three perspectives and beyond. *Journal of Language, Identity, and Education*, 4(1), 21–44. 10.1207/s15327701jlie0401_2

Wang, F., Guo, J., Wu, B., & Lin, Z. (2021). "It is utterly out of my expectation"-A case inquiry of teacher identity of an EFL teacher in a Chinese shadow school setting. *Frontiers in Psychology*, 12, 760161. https://www.frontiersin.org/articles/10.3389/fpsyg.2021.760161. 10.3389/fpsyg.2021.760161

West, G. B. (2019). Navigating morality in neoliberal spaces of English language education. *Linguistics and Education*, 49, 31–40. 10.1016/j.linged.2018.12.004

Woods, P. (1993). Critical events in education. *British Journal of Sociology of Education*, 14(4), 355–371. 10.1080/0142569930140401

Wu, J., & Hu, H. (2016, December 9). *Xi Jinping emphasizes at the national college ideological and political work conference the importance of conducting ideological and political work throughout the whole process of education to create a new situation for the development of China's higher education*. Xinhuanet. http://www.xinhuanet.com/politics/2016-12/08/c_1120082577.htm

Ye, W. (2023). *Moral education in China*. Routledge.

Yu, Q. (2018). Inquiry into the permeation of moral education in primary. *English Teaching*, 11–15. Advance online publication. 10.2991/hssmee-18.2018.3

Yuan, R., & Zhang, L. J. (2019). Teacher metacognitions about identities: Case studies of four expert language teachers in china. *TESOL Quarterly*, 54(4), 870–899. 10.1002/tesq.561

Zhang, Q. (2022a). A qualitative analysis of university foreign language teachers' practical knowledge required by curriculum of ideological and political education. *Foreign Languages Research*, 39(3), 58–63. 10.13978/j.cnki.wyyj.2022.03.003

Zhang, Q. (2022b). Exploring a university EFL teacher's identity through positioning analysis. *Shandong Foreign Language Teaching*, 43(3), 50–59. 10.16482/j.sdwy37-1026.2022-03-006

Zhang, W., Zhao, H. M., & Hu, J. H. (2022). The status quo and needs analysis of college foreign language teachers' teaching competence in curriculum-based ideological education. *Foreign Language World*, 210(3), 28–36.

ENDNOTE

[1] Both of the two journals are core journals in the Chinese foreign language sector. Papers published by such journals are often regarded as important academic achievements and can be used as important qualifications for professional title advancement.

Chapter 8
External Professional Development and Training:
The Importance for Transnational Higher Education Leadership

Lei Li
Suzhou Science and Technology Town Foreign Language School, China

ABSTRACT

Many transnational higher education (TNHE) providers have experimented with appointing department and school leaders who either lack direct institutional insights, being externally recruited, are having to step up, or are crossing fields. In these latter cases the leaders are not being appointed for their discipline specific knowledge, but rather because they have the management skills that their superiors feel will help fulfil a role remit effectively. It is also common to see educators jump between provisional stages. School teachers become university practitioners, and TNHE managers transition into K12 to lead departments. In light of transitions such as these, and their increasing common occurrence in the Chinese educational workplace this chapter draws on experiences in a K12 setting where the writer has served in both management and teaching capacities. These experiences were reflected upon and the lessons learnt presented at a prestigious TNHE provider as part of an educational PDQ course on leadership.

1. INTRODUCTION

Educational leadership is a challenging endeavor at the best of times. Many transnational higher education (TNHE) providers have experimented with appointing department and school leaders who either lack direct institutional insights, being externally recruited, are having to step up, or are crossing fields. In these latter cases the leaders are not being appointed for their discipline specific knowledge, but rather because they have the management skills that their superiors feel will help fulfil a role remit effectively. It is also common to see educators jump between provisional stages. School teachers become university practitioners, and TNHE managers transition into mainstream, pre-university, schooling (K12) to lead departments. In light of transitions such as these, and their increasing common occurrence in the Chinese educational workplace this chapter draws on experiences in a K12 setting where the writer has

DOI: 10.4018/979-8-3693-2857-6.ch008

served in both management and teaching capacities. These experiences were reflected upon and the lessons learnt presented at a prestigious TNHE provider as part of an educational professional development qualification (PDQ) course on leadership. This knowledge and these insights are now being transferred beyond this course and shared more widely in the hope that they will help provide useful ideas to others concerning what leadership and management lessons have been acquired over the past seven years spent working at an acclaimed private K12 educational group.

2. BACKGROUND

Professional Development Journey: Professional development is an essential feature for everyone in their working lives. The places we work in and the people we work with continue to evolve just as we do and navigating the world of work and home can be challenging as Burnett (2023) highlights. My own journey into teaching really began with my own experiences of learning. I was educated through quite a traditional K12 route in eastern China before progressing on to study at a well regraded Project 211 and 985 university. The Project 211 and 985 distinction extends from 1990's educational initiatives designed to support universities reach and extend international teaching and research standards. This institution had transnational branches operating within it as some Korean institutions had small educational hubs onsite. There were also teacher exchange links with prestigious colleges in the United States. However, it was not until a few years later, having worked in management and educational consultancy that I would move overseas to study at a Russell Group institution. During all of these experiences I was constantly learning and reflecting on my own beliefs and what it was that I knew and where I felt there were still gaps. A few years later and, having been a shareholder and entrepreneur in a start up operation, and moved into mainstream quasi international K12 schooling within China, I reenrolled as a part time student at a transnational educational provider and began to learn for an educational PDQ in leadership that would bring together my working world and allow me to see it from alternative and insightful angles.

Workplace Experience Reflections: One of the most important lessons that this experience, and indeed all of my experiences up to that point, taught me was that there was a lot to still learn. Indeed, my perceptions previously had been influenced both by my own life and learning experiences, and the noise that was around me. This can be highly influential as Kahnemann, Sibony and Sunstein (2021) draw attention to, as human judgment can be adversely and powerfully affected by what is taking place around us and how much of that we are inevitably taking in. In fairness, as Kahneman, Sibony and Sunstein (2021) stress, it is not one profession only that this happens to. In fact, decision making is influenced across professions, from medical or law, economics to leadership. It is the fact that it is so prevalent, that reflections like this one are so important because many of us walk through life unaware or having forgotten just how much these forces can influence us. There is a nice theme on this topic about how much we forget in the writing of Ishiguro (2015), but Burnett (2023) also highlights how memory is hazy at best and can cast a golden glow over events that perhaps do not merit this. By taking part on this PDQ course I began to reflect on my own experiences as a middle manager and how I might do things differently going forward. I also began to reflect on my actions, the rationale behind these, and perhaps areas in which I might refine my decision making going forward. Given how helpful this all was to me in terms of reflecting on my own workplace interactions it made me wonder how much TNHE educators engaged in this process, and my interactions on the course suggested that perhaps, arguably, it could be

External Professional Development and Training

more and that this would be helpful in many cases. It also led me to think how powerful bespoke training can be when appropriately pitched as Ericsson and Pool (2016) draw attention to.

Study Rationale and TNHE Leadership Relevance: The aim of this study is to provide insights into the importance of continuing professional development opportunities for educators- both within and outside of TNHE providers. For the educators who work within these institutions it is important to continually upskill and develop key competencies as the educational landscape changes and evolves and in recent years the speed of technological development and, now, generative AI highlights why this is so important. This is a point made by Tamayo et al. (2023). It is also important for staff to learn about how their institution operates if they are moving from another HE or TNHE provider, because although there may be many similarities, there will also be slight differences as well, and it can take up to a year to really feel at ease within a new workplace. Where TNHE providers are also very adept is in providing commercial courses to external staff. These learning opportunities help to open up perspectives and challenge existing beliefs at the same time that they enable others to also build their resumes. In addition, these commercial courses also bring in revenue to the operating entity and help to build brand reputation, and it is for all of these reasons, and many more that the value of these courses is worthy of consideration and discussion. It is also important to reflect on the learning that takes place by people enrolled on them so that TNHE providers can consider ways in which to improve them. This extends beyond simple course feedback approaches that many modules adopt because these are limited by the design and the purpose to which the informative which is derived is ultimately used and disseminated. This study will therefor help to raise awareness of how Cambridge Assessment PDQs help to develop practitioners and the commercial, pedagogic and brand awareness raising value that they can have for TNHE providers. These are features that leaders and decision makers can and ought to consider.

3. METHDOLOGY

This chapter is both a case study and guided by the notions of narrative enquiry. It is a case study in the sense that it considers an individual case, which is my own. It is also a type of narrative in that my story, sense making and reflections help me, and hopefully others, better understand human experiences as Caine, Estefan and Clandinin (2019) suggest are of pivotal importance. In this instance the intention is to consider my experiences of engaging with external CPD provision. In reality this is a reflective piece of writing and not a traditional research paper in itself. It draws on literature and experience and makes suggestions based on practical experience. It is very much a discussion-based piece of writing and designed to be informed and enlightening, and hopefully useful. Because of considerations such as these it does not really draw on common qualitative or quantitative data, and does not have to be overly concerned with features such as ethics, although it is obviously mindful of such aspects.

4. DISCUSSION

The following points are all gleaned from ideas that arose while I was reflecting on my learning and experiences with educational leadership and management on the University of Nottingham Ningbo administered PDQ Cambridge Assessment programme. They have been modified and tidied up slightly but highlight the reflective practitioner and leadership stage I was then navigating.

4.1 Leadership Reflections

4.1.1 Middle Management: Being a middle manager, the expectation is often that we will be able to think and act systemically and have good communication skills and influence as we are the chain for the collaboration of the more senior leadership figures and their subordinates. Middle managers therefore play an essential role and are accountable for the team as they are the ones to put the leaders' ideas into practice. It can be very challenging and sometimes exhausting especially when their team do not share the same values as those above them or do not have the motivation to work as efficiently as they could. As a result, the middle manager can be described as "inefficient", or "lacking leadership skills". However, "Leaders can be trained" as Ericsson and Pool (2016) draw attention to. On that note, how to become a successful middle manager is something worth considering as it can help those in these positions to feel more appreciated. Some of the associated skills include the following based on experience:

Strategic Planning: Making a successful strategic plan is an important piece of the puzzle on any project, as it can give clear guidance to team members so that they can work towards the same goal. The plan needs to be well structured, clear and easy to follow.

Communication Skills: Using different strategies to communicate with the senior managers and team members is essential. Good communication skills as Baars et al. (2016) highlight is a very useful skill. Reflecting on different projects with pros and cons helps to better evaluate the situation. Learning to report to the managers appropriately and precisely is also essential, as is knowing how to appreciate and act on team feedback.

Training Facilitation: People learn from one another, and it is a great opportunity for the team members to use their strength to support each other's weakness. Workshops can help the leaders to understand the team members strengths and viewpoints better. These sessions can also make the team members better understand what their leaders can do. A healthy team environment is one in which everyone can learn something from each other to move the team forward. Being mindful of cultural differences is also important as Meyer (2015) stresses.

Mastering Empathy: Being empathetic to build and maintain good work relationships is a key attribute that enhances the perceptions of leaders in others eyes. A healthy working environment can make people feel more valued and respected which can motivate them to work better. However, standards must be met too to gain the respect and trust. It is important to know how to persuade people as well as to motivate them to enjoy being part of the team and to garner a greater sense of achievement. If necessary, principals need to be brought in for give guidance so that the teams can follow better.

4.1.2 Institutional Leadership: More broadly still, and on an institutional level, lleadership plays an important role in the success and effectiveness of any school. It can and will influence the school culture as well as teacher's work and it is important to support school improvement, as Day and Sammons (2013) allude to. On that note, leaders should ideally possess a range of skills such as an ability to influence others in a positive way, a willingness to learn, good facilitating competencies and creative problem-solving attributes. The outcome of students can reflect the effectiveness of the management team, and leaders play a significant role in this area. It is important to note however that the successful leadership in schools relies on many other factors such as creating and maintain a positive environment for the staff and supporting the teachers to become better leaders for their own career development. In the early years educational field, the learners are children under six years of age and it is difficult to judge their development and learning competencies as these are not set and forever in a state of flux. This is also true for undergraduates, but to a lesser extent.

External Professional Development and Training

Given some of these points, arguably successful school leadership should try to educate students by promoting positive values (such as integrity, compassion and fairness), and these may include a love of lifelong learning, and fostering citizenship and personal, economic and social capabilities as literature suggests (Day and Sammons, 2013; Day et al., 2009). This also applies to the kindergarten students, as for children aged under six years old, acknowledging them and recognising their endeavours has a very influential impact and and curiosity towards people and things around is especially important for the young learners' educators as the social outcomes play an important part in children's future development as they go on to become global citizens. This is also true for students at TNHE providers, but these early childhood experiences and memories have lasting effect on people as Maté and Maté (2022) and Winkler (2023) stress. Leaders in different countries may also need to follow different rules or framework, such as in England, headteachers are held accountable for school performance through a highly developed national accountability framework whereas in China, sometimes leaders have to follow a more of a top-down structure and only carry out the main principals' directions for school development. By any means, transformational and pedagogical and instructional leadership are inescapable in schools of the 21st century. The successful kindergarten leaders should thus be communicative, collaborative, good listeners, and hold their own values so that they can build the vision and chart a course that others will wish to follow.

Considering these reflections so far, there are many different factors which influence people to become who they are, and early childhood education builds the foundation for persons development and can have a lifelong impact on their future development. However, working around children can be very demanding physically and emotionally, as well as time consuming. As Lewis (2017) implies, successful leaders start by getting the staffing right and understanding these employees. This will almost certainly mean applying different methods and approaches to keep staff motivation high. For example, it may include providing staff with enough support when needed. Recruiting professional teachers with a passion for their profession and an empathy and concern for young learners is also essential. It is also important to consider their personal skills and to provide these young students with opportunities for development and show the teachers that they are valued for what they do. This ties into seminal work on zones of proximal development and learning scaffolding that training courses like to draw attention to, and the works of people such as Jerome Bruner and Lev Vygotsky. Kleinman (2012) provides a helpful summary of developments in educational psychology.

In addition to the points already considered, the next stage for the successful leaders in kindergarten should be to focus on the curriculum and to find out what is most suited for children's development under the prescribed government guidelines and criteria. Adopting project-based learning methods to support children's development can help children to develop in all domains quite quickly as it is engaging and often hands on. It also typically is communicative and brings students together so that they can learn from one another. Trust also plays an important part in successful leadership. Another important consideration is culture as Meyer (2015) discusses, and this is definitely an area which can lead to misunderstandings. Therefore, TNHE, and educational more broadly, leaders at all levels should be able to collaborate with the team by talking about things openly and solving problems in a manner that is as constructive and conciliatory as possible. Put simply, effective leaders can get things done and successful leaders can get things done in a way that encourages people to be better versions of themselves which will lead the entire team to improve.

4.2 Work Experience Reflections

Before attending the PDQ Course, my understanding of leadership and management was ensuring that each project I was a part of could be finished within the targeted timeline efficiently. However, I have always found that I was working overtime, which was leaving me very tired as Wong, Chan and Ngan (2019) raise awareness of, because I had to finish or tidy up the team's work. I did not know how to improve or solve this situation. Since I joined the course, I have learned that being an effective leader is very important for my career development as it can bring about better outcomes and enhance my professionalism. It can not only save time and energy, but also motivate myself and my team members towards common goals. However, dealing with all the little things in the K12 provider in the roles I am expected to fulfil is mentally and physically demanding. It is also time consuming and not everyone can understand or appreciate what I do. Sometimes middle managers are described as "ineffective" or "weak" (Zahira 2021), and others sometimes have seen me this way. This has made work and life challenging sometimes as others also find (Žnidaršič and Marič, 2020). Therefore, developing my leadership skills can help me to improve my personal and professional life. For teachers who have a good work ethic they will be more willing probably to support with different tasks. The difficult part is to convince teachers who do not want to put in the effort to participate. They may engage but simply do the minimum, and they only do this because I have asked them to. This requires me to draw on my communication skills and conflict resolution skills to solve the problems which arise when teachers are not willing to support, and then guide them to do the tasks as well as possible otherwise I will end up doing it all.

Self-reflection is another skill that I have learned and now better appreciate after taking this course. Writers like Gerace et al. (2017) draw attention to this. Since I joined the course, I have had many open conversations with my line managers and the principals. We have talked about leadership styles and the leadership challenges that I face. This is so they can help me to reflect on the previous tasks or projects and find out where I might improve. Reflection can also help me understand better why issues arose and the reasons behind these so that I can improve. Being a middle manager in the kindergarten as a principal's assistant also requires me to be supportive to the principals. I must lead the teachers on different projects, and be efficient and effective when managing these. This means communicating massages to both the principals and teachers appropriately so that work is as smooth as possible. Another area I need to work on is how to make strategic plans and give clear guidance to team members so that they know what is expected for each project. I also need to learn to find where the check points are for each project to ensure that the tasks are running smoothly. I think that leadership can be taught and worked on as Ryan (2016) suggests. To become an effective leader who can not only be persuasive, but also smart, needs practice. In light of these setting objectives and SMART goals are helpful. Some objectives I have set in recent years include better appreciating and considering the bigger strategic and operational picture, enhancing my interpersonal communication skills, enhancing my team leadership skills and enhancing my management skills. Associated goals I have set included enhancing rapport with team members, enhancing my line management reporting skills, enhancing my conflict resolution skills, better motivating my teams, enhancing team satisfaction, setting clear objectives for tasks, distributing task leadership responsibility and managing projects systematically.

My belief is that leaders need to produce good results and I have sought to practice all of these leadership skills as I have supported on projects that I have subsequently led. I will also continue to self-reflect in order to improve. There are many ways to be a good leader, being professional and ensuring that others

External Professional Development and Training

trust your professionalism and are willing to follow takes time. This course has not only helped me to understand my current role better, but also consider where my weaknesses are so that I can work on these.

5. TNHE LEADERSHIP IMPLICATIONS

5.1 Reflective Implications

One of the key features to come out of this reflective piece of writing is how important reflective practice is for educators. The fact that programmes like the Cambridge Assessment PDQ have a reflective element highlights this, but so to do component features of other external courses such as PGCHEs (Postgraduate Certificates in Higher Education). Indeed, Mathew, Mathew and Peechattu (2017) highlight the importance of reflective practice as a means to professional development when they stress that it is a process which facilitates learning, understanding and self-understanding. It also encourages them to consider their own behaviours and actions, alongside experiences and grow as a result (Mathew, Mathew and Peechattu, 2017). They also advocate the importance of the learning being systematic, which is something that Ericsson and Pool (2016) stress with their targeted training. What is also interesting is the impact that reflection can have on evolving professional and personal identities. Our personalities are always in a state of flux and change because of the neuroplasticity of our brains (Burnett, 2023), but it is also true for us and how we and others see ourselves. Walkington (2005) also states that reflective practice can encourage teacher identity development, and goes on to highlight the importance of the university and school setting in this. In this instance, my own experiences have taught me that on reflection, as a middle manager, and aspiring future leader, that considering the strategic planning elements and how to realise these in day to day actions and endeavours in vitally important and not always straightforward. Also, working on communication, which is challenging as different people respond well to different communication styles, depending on the person and associated inter-personal relationships, is also essential. So too is having opportunities to learn and the time to reflect, and guidance is helpful here. In addition, empathy is important, but this should be measured by considering other perspectives as well as far as possible. These are some of the salient lessons I have taken from my own reflective experiences.

5.2 CPD Importance

As the previous section alluded to, what this largely discussion paper also clearly highlights is just how important and valuable CPD is. What is also apparent is that principal's or leadership figures also need to engage with and support CPD initiatives, and the importance of management buy in is highlighted by Somantri and Iskandar (2021). Certainly, in my dual roles of teacher and manager I certainly appreciated the benefits of engaging with CPD. This is because I began to reflect more on what I was doing, and how I might improve this. I also better understood how my actions fitted within the broader working remits of others, especially those above me. Another important learning moment was when I accepted that I was constrained by my role and the expectations of those around me. Like many leaders and teachers, I genuinely wanted to make a positive impact. By this I mean I wanted to help improve practices and raise the quality of what we do and had done previously, but with an eye to the future. I now better appreciate and understand that this is not always possible. People are hard pressed for time. They also have their own agendas, motives and priorities. Some people may feel threatened. Others are happy in their comfort zones. It is very hard to bring about meaningful change in short time frames without buy in, and recruitment modifications in many cases. This is often seen in sporting teams when new managers come in, because often they are brought in when the team owners feel that performance can or should be enhanced. They also realize that to achieve this, and to keep their jobs, they need teams around them who have the expertise and drive to hopefully realize this. In education, unlike sport, change cannot happen as quickly naturally. And there are good reasons for this. One good reason is that people have commitments outside of work that they have to meet so they need a degree of stability and security as Maslow stressed (Morris, 2021). Clearly, the importance of CPD, both to myself, and others as teachers and middle managers is notable and this is something the TNHE can tap into and leadership of commercial courses at these providers aware of.

5.3 EDI Importance

Another consideration that has become increasingly apparent to me is the need for institutions to promote opportunities for staff that enable everyone to grow. This means that equality or equity, diversity and inclusion are all important considerations. Clearly, it is not always possible for all schools to provide CPD opportunities all of the time, and actually in K12 many can struggle to do so as Mo and Morris (2024) discuss. The reason for this can be varied. But for staff to reach their potential they need chances to learn, and to learn from people with different perspectives. This is where external training can be so helpful, and it is also where TNHE providers, such as the University of Nottingham Ningbo are fulfilling a useful role by providing such courses. What is also important is that teachers can learn from a diverse range of people and that opportunities reach as many as possible. What can happen is that training budgets are either spent on bringing in external speakers, or the funds diverted to other activities. This means to engage in training it may be that educators themselves have to cover the costs. This is difficult when salaries may not be that high, and other costs have to be met, often ones that are long term such as mortgage repayments. Having been in situations in which training opportunities may not have been very diverse, although they were inclusive, in that everyone had to attend, another point it is worth stressing here going back to equity and equality is about access and ensuring that a work life balance exists. Having to attend online training in the evening if the session is live can be difficult if there are commutes to consider or childcare responsibilities. Equally having to work or receive training on weekends also presents similar challenges as staff need time to recharge their batteries. These, and concerns like these, may be considered by institutions that provide courses, but making such that attendance is flexible and recorded sessions also a feature of learning provision can be advantageous. Another interesting development is the potential role that AI may have going forward as Khan (2023) discusses.

5.4 ZPD Importance

As an international master's student in the UK one of the many learning points that I took away from the course was just how important the Zone of Proximal Development (ZPD) is for learners. Names like Vygotsky and Bruner were often mentioned, and I have heard their names many times in years since, but a lot of what was discussed was incredibly relevant to me both then and now. The way that the course was scaffolded to help students adapt and learn, and dependent on their prior learning was incredibly important. Lane (2012) draws attention to just how important learning and hard work is, and Ericsson and Pool (2016) highlight why targeted training, which is systematic is essential to get the best possible

External Professional Development and Training

results. But equally important is having learning which progressively builds, and that acts as scaffolding, and which builds on prior learning, tapping into what learners know and is mindful of where it is they are trying to get to. This is also where TNHE providers have advantages because they have the capacity to understand multiple varied cultures, learning backgrounds and societal expectations, all of which effects both staff and students. By leveraging their distinct advantages, they can provide training which not only enhances their own people, but also those that enroll on their commercial courses, opening these mature students' eyes to new horizons, and potentially also supporting future recruitment initiatives.

5.5 Management Implications

The implications for management from this reflective discussion-based paper are clear. Staff benefit greatly from training and professional development, and it is also something which is highly valued. How much so is in evidence in the work of Mo and Morris (2024) and the impact that losing this provision has on employee satisfaction. Because professional development opportunities are so important, especially those provided by external institutions that challenge educators to think in different ways and to work with others by sharing experiences from different institutions, it is apparent that the washback effect is strong, and in a positive manner. The reason for this is that not only are staff reflecting on what they are doing, but they are also learning from the structure of the course, and from others who are partaking in it. The added benefit is that there are no vested interests or emotions to consider, because the learning environment is neutral and so people can share more openly without the risk of upsetting unintentionally. This all being equal it is probably fair to say that if management can provide and support staff to enroll on courses such as the Cambridge Assessment PDQ, and bring back and share with their peers their learning on these courses then a mutually beneficial cycle begins. With different PDQs on offer different staff could be enrolled on different courses and then help to promote learning with their colleagues. Over time the institution might even consider beginning its own PDQ style courses to training internally, or help train other teachers or student teachers.

5.6 Leadership Implications

Clearly there are a number of leadership implications for TNHE providers that arise from this discussion paper. The first, and most obvious, is that training and professional development is essential and highly valued. Not only does it help people to grow which is essentially important, but it enables them to see working life in new and novel ways potentially. It is also important because the staff can take these insights and experiences back to their work places and help others at the same time they are also enhancing their own performance. Beyond these points, there are also benefits to TNHE providers in offering external style courses to their staff. They enable more critical self-reflections to be realised as they are less threatening, or potentially perceived as less threatening. They also can be tailored to a specific institution's own unique needs which is very attractive as an option. Besides these benefits, TNHE providers also build collaborations with other organizations and in some cases, these might also provide validation and accreditation possibilities. The option to also generate revenue is clearly another benefit of running courses that are fee charging. On that point, schools might build strategic alliances that provide discounts to employees from affiliated institutions, and these alliances then might have other mutually beneficial working possibilities to explore. Of course, for all of these benefits to be realised, or at least viable, the provision has to be offered. One of the advantages of studying on the Cambridge

Assessment PDQs at UNNC was also the variety on offer. PDQs typically have four learning routes and in the past couple of years UNNC have offered all four. When I was studying it was on the educational leadership pathway, but being more knowledgeable in the areas of teaching and learning, bilingual learners, or technology would also enable me to take on greater responsibility roles potentially in these areas as well. Having heard how TNHE staff have benefited from enrolling on these courses, and seen other K12 providers also look into them as training opportunities it is my belief that leadership could continue to cultivate these study routes for staff, both internally and externally, and that they need to be run in a mindful and inclusive manner given the diversity of the potential learners.

6. SUMMARY

This chapter has adopted a narrative discussion based methodological approach to reflect upon my own CPD and career journey so far. It has focused primarily on my roles as an emerging middle manager in K12, although it is also relevant to me as a teacher and for those in higher education as well. It is relevant because TNHE providers that offer external training courses to external participants, such as the Cambridge Assessment PDQ not only provide a way for themselves to generate income or revenue, but to also support the developmental needs of others who may not have a wide range of opportunities otherwise. By this, the suggestion is that CPD may be limited at other workplaces, or not designed to cater to what would be of most value to the teachers and leaders. By reflecting on my own experiences undertaking a Cambridge Assessment PDQ and a TNHE institution I hope that others can learn from my experiences, musings and reflections. I also hope that the value in having a suite of provision is apparent. For example, the Cambridge Assessment PDQ offers courses in educational leadership, teaching and learning, bilingual learners and technology. Not only does completion enhance a resume, but it is a chance to network, hear other worldviews and voices and be a part of a bigger educational community, as well as to obviously learn. The implications for TNHE leadership is also apparent. These courses provide CPD opportunities for staff, they can also be offered to the educators at that institution, and act as a source of revenue generation and brand building.

Future Research Directions

This research has offered rich insights as a personal narrative with a unique lens that captures practical working and living reality. It also helps readers understand situational and contextual challenges at one educational stage and in one setting. The emphasis is clearly on the importance of reflective practice, CPD and lifelong learning. There are however numerous ways future research could extend or complement it. One way might be to consider these notions through an EDI perspective. Another option might be to look at global trends and current empirical research in much greater depth which might heighten the credibility of the work in readers eyes and support what might be deemed anecdotal views. A broader context could be achieved through drawing on insights from UNESCO and OECD statistical data potentially. More diverse case studies would provide additional enlightenment, and may or may not resonate with readers. Finally drawing on theoretical models in various areas, such as Klob's learning circle (Kleinman, 2012), adopting an educational leadership comparative analysis across countries, considering the impact of technological advancements and digital transformation, or simply discussing strategies for leadership development could all also provide additional supplementary and expansive ways forward.

REFERENCES

Baars, S., Parameshwaran, M., Menzies, L. & Chiong, C. (2016). *Firing on All Cylinders: What Makes and Effective Middle Leader.* London: Teaching Leaders and LKMCo.

Burnett, D. (2023). *Emotional Intelligence.* Faber and Faber.

Caine, A., Estefan, A. & Clandinin, J. D. (2019). *Narrative Enquiry.* Available from: https://doi.org/10.4135/9781526421036771087

Day, C., & Sammons, P. (2013). *Successful Leadership: A Review of the International Literature.* CFBT Education Trust.

Day, C., Sammons, P., Hopkins, D., Harris, A., Leithwood, K., Gu, Q., Brown, E., Atharidou, E., & Kington, A. (2009). *The Impact of School Leadership on Pupil Outcomes: Final Report.* London: DCSF.

Ericsson, A., & Pool, R. (2016). *Peak: Secrets from the New Science of Expertise.* Mariner Books.

Gerace, A., Day, A., Casey, S., & Mohr, P. (2017). *I think, You think.* Understanding the Importance of Self Refection to the Taking of Another Person's Perspective., 10.1017/jrr.2017.8

Ishiguro, K. (2015). *The Buried Giant.* Vintage.

Kahneman, D., Sibony, O., & Sunstein, C. (2021). *Noise.* William Collins.

Khan, S. (2023). *How AI Could Save (Not Destroy) Education.* Available from: https://www.ted.com/talks/sal_khan_how_ai_could_save_not_destroy_education

Kleinman, P. (2012). *Psych101.* Adams Media.

Lane, P. (2012). *10,000 Hours: You Become What You Practice.* Couture Book.

Lewis, D. (2017). The Three Stages of Leadership. Available from: https://www.london.edu/think/the-three-stages-of-leadership

Maté, G., & Maté, D. (2022). *The Myth of Normal.* Avery.

Mathew, P., Mathew, P., & Peechattu, P. (2017). Reflective Practices: A Means of Teacher Development. *Asia Pacific Journal of Contemporary Education and Communication Technology*, 3(1), 126–131.

Meyer, E. (2015). *The Culture Map.* PublicAffairs.

Mo, J., & Morris, G. (2024). Investigating the Employment Motivation, Job Satisfaction, and Dissatisfaction of International High School Teachers in China: The Impact of the COVID-19 Pandemic. *Frontiers in Psychology*, 15, 1271604. Advance online publication. 10.3389/fpsyg.2024.127160438384343

Morris, G. (2021). *Investigating the Employment Motivation and Job Satisfaction of Expatriate Language Teachers.* EdD Thesis. University of Exeter: Exeter.

Ryan, L. (2016). *Can Leadership Skills be Taught?* https://www.forbes.com/sites/lizryan/2016/04/01/can-leadership-skills-be-taught/?sh+20f3893a6579

Somantri, C., & Iskandar, H. (2021). The Impact of CPD in Teaching, and the Role of Principal in Promoting CPD: A Literature Review. *Proceedings of the 4th International Conference on Research of Educational Administration and Management (ICREAM 2020)*. Atlantis Press. 10.2991/assehr.k.210212.074

Tamayo, J., Doumi, L., Goel, S., Kovacs-Ondrejkovic, O., & Sadun, R. (2023). Reskilling in the Age of AI. Available from: https://hbr.org/2023/09/reskilling-in-the-age-of-ai

Walkington, J. (2005). Becoming a Teacher: Encouraging Development of Teacher Identity through Reflective Practice. *Asia-Pacific Journal of Teacher Education*, 33(1), 53–64. 10.1080/1359866052000341124

Winkler, H. (2023). *Being Henry*. Celadon Books.

Wong, K., Chan, A., & Ngan, S. (2019). The Effect of Long Working Hours and Overtime on Occupational Health: A Meta-Analysis of Evidence from 1998 to 2018. *International Journal of Environmental Research and Public Health*, 16(12), 2102. 10.3390/ijerph16122210231200573

Zahira, J. (2021). *The Real Value of Middle Managers*. Available from: https://hbr.org/2021/06/the-real-value-of-middle-managers

Žnidaršič, J., & Marič, M. (2020). *Understanding Work Life Conflict and its Implications*. Available from: https://www.researchgate.net/publication/350517367_Understanding_work-life_conflict_and_its_implications

Chapter 9
Exploring the Importance of Practice and Leadership on Teaching and Learning in Higher Education

Zhanglin Chai

Nottingham University, Ningbo, China

ABSTRACT

In the fast-paced world, finding time for training and reflection is essential for practice and leadership as it helps one to develop their skills and review their effectiveness. The training that I received is Postgraduate Certificate in Higher Education (PGCHE) which focus on teaching & Learning in Higher Education. The process of my reflection is conducted by using Brookfield's Four Lenses of Critical Reflection (Brookfield, 2017), and Gibbs model (Gibbs, 1988). The training and reflection enabled me to plan and teach appropriate learning activities and support students effectively. Furthermore, in this evolving society, reflection practice is the essential and cornerstone of leadership abilities. In order to practice new skills and behaviors in appropriate contexts and to draw connections between new information and concepts and prior knowledge and experience, reflective practice is crucial for both professional and personal growth.

INTRODUCTION

In this fast-paced world, finding time for training and reflection is essential for practice and leadership as it helps individuals to develop their skills and review their effectiveness. The training that this author received is therefore discussed in this chapter. The training in questions relates to the Postgraduate Certificate in Higher Education (PGCHE) which focuses on teaching and Learning in Higher Education. The process of my reflection is conducted by using Brookfield's Four Lenses of Critical Reflection (Brookfield, 2017), and Gibbs Model (Gibbs, 1988). The approach of constructive alignment was also an approach I drew on and reflected upon, and this was applied to design my teaching. The benefits of the training and reflection enabled me to plan and teach more appropriate learning activities and

DOI: 10.4018/979-8-3693-2857-6.ch009

Copyright ©2024, IGI Global. Copying or distributing in print or electronic forms without written permission of IGI Global is prohibited.

support students more effectively. Furthermore, in this evolving society, reflective practice is essential and a cornerstone of leadership. In order to practice new skills and behaviors in appropriate contexts and to draw connections between new information and concepts and prior knowledge and experience, reflective practice is crucial for both professional and personal growth. In addition, it drives teachers to reflect on their own beliefs, actions, values, and feelings while also seeking feedback from others. By using reflection, learners can pinpoint their areas of proficiency and improvement, as well as establish objectives and strategies for continued learning and growth.

BACKGROUND

I received a Master's degree in Physical Chemistry from a university in Zhejiang in 2012, and researched the preparation and electrochemical properties of conductive materials in three-dimensional ultra-thin structures. I also contributed to the national "973" pre-research project, and wrote and published papers that were included in SCI Core journals. Between 2012 and 2013, I then worked as a senior research assistant in the Full Solid-State Lithium Batteries Group in Eastern China, and the Chinese Academy of Sciences, and took charge of the research and development of silicon-based anodes for lithium-ion batteries, as well as constructed several key scientific research projects. The reason I changed career paths in 2012 was to follow my passion, and so I started working as a lecturer in chemistry and general physics, and devoted a lot of time to researching and developing new and innovative teaching methods based on STEAM (Science, Technology, Engineering, Art, and Math) and e-learning. Using these techniques, I performed a series of public classes and also taught these STEAM courses in English to visiting New Zealand students (observed by their teachers and principal). In 2022, I then moved into transnational higher education and joined CELE as a preliminary-year science and engineering tutor. I also currently work on a university-wide project named V-ROOM, which aims at developing virtual content to enhance students' learning experiences through a digitalized and immersive teaching and learning environment. My experiences so far have taught me that leadership involves the position of power and authority. It also requires a level of skill and knowledge, as well as professional and personal values. These attributes have a strong positive impact on learning inside and outside of the classroom. My research experience provided me with an opportunity to inspire students to study science and encourage their curiosity and investigative sprit. This was evidenced by the discussions initiated by the students outside of class time some of which I will now reflect upon.

Reflective Practice I

Case Study Context: This teaching reflection is based on a seminar delivered on the Foundation Physics module taught in the seventh week of the first semester of the 2023-2024 academic year. It is a 10-credit course requiring students to dedicate roughly 100 hours to their studies. It is also a required course for students planning to study at the University of Nottingham Ningbo (UNNC) Faculty of Science and Engineering (FoSE). The aim of Foundation Physics course is to equip students with foundational and prerequisite knowledge in this subject area for their further study, which requires a base understanding of physics. In addition, the aim is to provide students with a working knowledge of core subject principles and practice, approximately equivalent to A-level, and to help them to acquire an understanding of key applied physics processes. They should also be able to use the information provided. In this class there were 35 students with mixed demographic, educational, and linguistic backgrounds, along with personal motives. The class was designed to cater to mixed abilities and a diverse range of interests as Aboagye (2018) suggests is important. These students typically join the university from Chinese high schools and have just completed the college entrance 'Gaokao' university entrance examination. This means that most students enrolled in the course have some basic understanding of physics through learning in Chinese-medium settings. Because of this, they may encounter content and English challenges while studying in this new environment. In light of this, the student's understanding of the concepts and how to express their opinions in English will be the focus of the study. Since the students who come from every province have significant differences in terms of culture, education and even language (given the geographic scale of China), and there are predominantly male students enrolled on the course (approximately 70%) these factors were ones which were noted in terms of possible course delivery impact. That said, there is greater diversity in the thirty-five students attending this seminar than in many previous ones. Given these consideration it is important that lessons are designed with a mixed-ability group of students' requirements in mind. The 50-minute seminar took place in one of the institutional seminar rooms. The class aimed to foster an understanding of simple machines, fluid flow, and light, after which students should be able to differentiate the three classes of levers and implement the conditions of equilibrium, the equation of Bernoulli, the principle of Pascal, the principle of Archimedes, the law of floatation, and the law of reflection to specific objects. To achieve the aim, students need to link previous knowledge to current learning objectives using English. This is a face-to-face seminar was one of twenty parallel seminar groups taught by team of six tutors. These form the application of the key principles of physics that have been delivered in the 2×50-minute lectures during the course of a given week. These seminars provide a practical assignment and are intended to assist students in reaching their learning outcomes. In addition, this seminar also links with the previous one by achieving the same intended learning outcome (implementing the conditions of equilibrium to solve questions in simple machines). To reflect on my classroom delivery and session leadership Brookfield's Four Lenses of Critical Reflection (Brookfield, 2017) was adopted. This is because it is important to formalise the outcome of the learner's reflection, and Gibbs model (Gibbs, 1988) helps to describe the action plan from the previous section. In addition, I also referred to the approach of constructive alignment and how this applied to the design of my teaching session.

Defining the Intended Learning Outcomes (ILOs): The concept of constructive alignment is utilized in the design of the ILOs for my seminars. Constructive alignment proposes that the first step in designing a course should be determining the learning outcomes that students should acquire, and then matching the activities of teaching and the tasks of assessment to these outcomes (Wang et al., 2013). The aim of teaching is to involve students in tasks that increase their chances of attaining ILOs. The activities of learning and the tasks for assessment are designed to help students attain the ILOs and provide clear evaluation of how effectively those ILOs have been achieved (Biggs, 1996). Effective teaching requires getting the learner to engage in activities that align with the ILOs. Therefore, the teaching and learning activities are planned with the ILOs in mind. The importance of alignment is noted by Biggs and Tang (2010). Revisiting an aforementioned point, the session ILOs should be expressed as knowledge and skills learners will need to have mastery of after the course (Hailikari et al., 2022), and the activities and assessments will have facilitated the acquisition of Bloom's revised taxonomy points. This taxonomy can also be utilised to aid in the production of action verbs that express some of the session learning aims as Wilson (2016) draws attention to. An additional rationale for this is the importance of systematically targeting cognitive gains. See Table 1 below. The ILOs were created in accordance with

Bloom's taxonomy of cognitive abilities at higher levels, which supports students in exploring deeper to achieve higher-order cognitive features. The students' cognitive ability means that they can learn more fully this way, increasing the meaning of their learning and enhancing their sustained retention. These higher-order cognitive abilities not only help the students learn, but also enable them with critical thinking and problem solving (Miri et al., 2007). Moreover, the students can see how the information which they learn is useful and applicable in their lives. This ought to promoting their motivation to learn. Appendix 1 provides more details in this area.

Table 1. ILOs for foundations physics seminar 4

Intended Learning Outcome (ILO)	Revised Taxonomy Hierarchy	Cognitive Level
Identify different simple machines and their applications in engineering.	Understand (Level 2)	Lower
Implement the conditions of equilibrium to solve questions in simple machines.	Apply (Level 3)	Medium
Implement Pascal's Principle, Archimedes' Principle, Bernoulli's Equation and the Law of Floatation to solve questions in fluid mechanics.	Apply (Level 3)	Medium
Implement the Law of Reflection and plane mirrors to solve questions in the topic of light.	Apply (Level 3)	Medium
Differentiate the three classes of levers.	Analyse (Level 4)	Higher

Designing the Teaching Activities: The teaching activities can be seen in a session's plan (See Appendix 2). Considering most students have already obtained some basic understanding of physics concepts, realistically, 5-7 questions can be discussed and solved within the class during 50 minutes, while the rest will be given to the students to check the solutions on Moodle on their own or if further clarification is needed learners can attend the tutors' office hours. The time allocated for each question is typically 4-7 minutes, depending on the complexity of the question. This is to indicate that there is no uniform distribution of time in the seminar class activities, but accounting for the available time is still essential. Factors that contribute to these time fluctuations are the students' understanding of the concepts and the preparation of the seminar solutions before the seminar class. To promote student participation in this instance, the students were divided into small groups to solve the assigned seminar questions in their group. The term for this type of group activity is, 'cooperative learning'. It is defined as creating small groups in the classroom to promote collaboration among the students in order to maximize individual learning (Johnson et al., 2014). Many of these features can also be applied to teachers and staff more generally when considering CPD and project-based work. Because students can hear and be heard by their peers in small groups, these are crucial to the learning process. With UNNC being well known for its student and staff diversity, this lesson was designed to address the needs of a mixed-ability student group in the classroom and promote equality, diversity, and inclusion (EDI), which is the idea of valuing and promoting people's differences (Fuentes et al., 2021). This was partially accomplished through the lesson's pace, engaging every student through grouping design, activity engagement, collaborative activities, comprehension checks, and creating a positive learning environment. This helped to enhance their confidence in both interaction and presentation, and generate a positive learning cycle, which progressively grew each week. Another important consideration was ensuring that the material and in-class learning were scaffolded and aligned with my students' zones of proximal development as writers such as Vygotsky and Bruner (Colter et al., 2017) drew attention to in the past century. This is a prime example of constructivism, the active learning theory, since each student can expand on prior knowledge and deepen their understanding of physics in this lesson (Nakamura et al., 2016). By applying active learning in this seminar, students were more effectively engaged and motivated to learn than they might otherwise have been, as (Eison, 2010) suggests.

Designing Assessment Methods: Given that assessment tasks are made to provide precise evaluations of how well those ILOs have been reached (Biggs et al., 2010), the students were engaged in activities most appropriate to the ILOs in real-time with formative assessment, such as questioning the class at set intervals to see whether each ILO had been attained, which enables the teacher to monitor the real-time growth and changes in student understanding in the classroom. This enables the teacher gauge the learning taking place, which can be challenging. Additionally, this makes it possible to figure out whether students can effectively finish the ILOs through assessment. As a result, the concept of constructive alignment was used to design the assessment in my observed session. However, I realised that the questions were usually answered by the students who worked tirelessly, rather than those who had a tendency to arrive late for class due to other concerns. These students were less likely to engage. Therefore, this assessment method may not be a valid means of checking whether the ILOs had been achieved. In future sessions, I plan to incorporate more inclusive methods such as Mentimeter quizzes so that I can obtain answers from a wider range of students which would exhibit the ILO attainment of the general cohort. What this also highlighted was the importance of reflective practice, continual refinements and the need for various formative assessment gauges.

Student Perspective: When applying Brookfield's student lens to evaluate the class, which is incredibly important as the learners are also customers in the service industry (Kurnaz et al., 2010), I periodically 'checked in' with them during the session. Through informal discussions during group activities, direct questioning, and answering queries, I could evaluate how the students felt and were able to engage with the material. I could also identify how well the ILOs were being realised. In addition, having students write on the whiteboard and share their understanding helped me and the class to consider the learning taking place and also reflect on my teaching. These processes also enabled me to respond in real-time and bridge any learning gaps that were apparent or appearing. For the students who were quiet, or did not engage quite so actively, the relative anonymity provided can be appealing to some. One example is the potential use of interactive quizzes, which are designed to align with the session ILOs. These would aid in responding to errors and offer additional explanations for how to answer specific questions related to the session.

Colleagues Perceptions: The presence of the critical colleague was at the heart of this reflective process. Having an observer who helps you review the lesson you have just delivered and highlights things you might have missed is very insightful (Brookfield, 2017). In the Teaching Observation Form (See Appendix 3), the observer stated that the lesson had been appropriate and presented clear ILOs and learning activities, which was positive. The timings and pace of the session were also deemed appropriate. The observer also praised the methods employed, the feedback the session had provided, and, more generally, my communication. With the content also receiving a good review and the learning environment deemed to be highly conducive to learning, I was largely happy with how things had gone, but I was also mindful that there was scope for improvement. The observer suggested that dominant class voices could be mitigated, for example by encouraging quieter students to participate (Ferdinand-James and Medina-Charles, 2020), and engagement could be enhanced. Some learning issues might also be anticipated ahead of time such as the distraction of the mobile phone, and the English challenges of technical terminology. Having considered all of these points, I fully intend to take on board the advice going forward and continue to promote the positive features. I may also assign roles within groups on occasion, which will have the added benefit of being a fresh and new teaching approach. I also plan to avoid the potential distractive influence of technology by suggesting that disruptive apps be avoided (Siu et al., 2017).

Personal Reflections: My personal feelings when looking back on the class were that the session was reasonably well planned and delivered, and the students responded positively. I agreed with the observer that the class could be more conclusive by avoiding having voices that are too dominant. I also believe that interesting, well-presented and structured content that is cohesively aligned with the ILOs, and progressively builds within a class and between classes will help to enhance engagement. It is also important to be mindful of how our own learning experiences and preferences influence our preparation and delivery and this is not always what works best for those we teach. This is something leadership more broadly also needs to be conscious of. Another feature I believe it is important to note is the power of merited praise and a supportive learning environment, and to remember that different people process materials in different ways and at different speeds which is why differentiated delivery approaches are so important. Given all of the considerations so far listed, my priorities for my classes going forward are to prepare and deliver sessions that have clear aims and learning rationales so that the students understand what it is exactly that they have to do. Expectations will also be aligned as far as possible (Robinson, 2022), and learning and communication style preferences considered, as Myers et al. (2014) highlight is important in the case of the second feature. I will also ensure that the learners have enough time to complete these through careful preparations and pacing and that faster learners have extension activities or ensure their comprehension by supporting peers. It is also essential that learning does not exceed development zones and that the class is a trusting, supportive space where technology is a learning aid rather than a disruptive influence. It is also important to note that the learners bring their personal lives with them to class and to be appreciative of this.

Final Thoughts: The process of preparing a class well and then evaluating it following a clear framework has been a rewarding and enlightening experience and one formal training has supported. The advantage of working through this has also enabled me to reflect on my teaching, its rationale, and its impact. It was rewarding to see that the learners were achieving the ILOs and that these were appropriately pitched. It was also good to see that my classes were well constructed in a range of areas and now, having clear ideas on how to enhance these going forward, I feel as if I am working from a greater position of strength and have a clear action plan that will help me develop as a teacher and educator. I am also grateful for the feedback my colleague offered, which is available in Appendix 3 as a reference source to chapter readers.

Reflective Practice I Action Plan

In response to the observer's suggestions and my own reflections, the following action plan (see Table 2 below) was devised:

Table 2. Action plan for the seminar teaching

Action	Description
Adopt a flipped classroom approach	Use technology and assigned study groups to provide students with some preview physics before the class which is how some Content and Language Integrate Learning (CLIL) courses operate pre-lecture. The completed material will feed into the learning.
Regulate the usage of technology in the class	Devices that may not be conducive to learning, or which are not required at certain points during the class will be limited as far as possible. This means smartphones primarily which may be useful for scanning the QR code, but which may be less helpful when working in class will be discouraged. I will also remind students about appropriate laptop use.
Support mixed ability group forming and norming	At certain times group members will be assigned roles so that time is productively and effectively used. I will also monitor groups and provide support and feedback based on observation and output. Individual and group work reflection will be encouraged.
Diversify student participation	Providing means to encourage further output from less vocal students, and supporting overcoming shyness or engagement preferences such as visual and kinaesthetic orientations. Also, provide more differentiated learning and extension activities for more able learners.
Maintain open communication channels	To assess the engagement and participation of my students, I will ensure that student feedback is encouraged and used to adjust my teaching in a timely manner. I'll also endeavour to ensure that my student evaluation of teaching (SET) has a high completion rate (above 80%) and aggregate score of 23.00 (above the average aggregate score of the SET surveys in current year). Peer observations will also be utilised and an open class approach adopted for other staff so that collaborative learning opportunities exist.

Reflective Practice II

Case Study Context: The UK Professional Standards Framework Area 4 advocates developing effective education situations and methods to help and mentor students (Advance-He, 2011). Examples include creating an inclusive learning environment to engage and motivate the students. In this case study, I provide the background before outlining the rationale for choosing this experience to reflect on. This will be followed by a literature review surrounding the specific topics related to points that have been highlighted and forward-thinking suggestions based on a reflection of the actions taken. This case study focuses on the support provided to a former student during the autumn semester of 2022 when I was teaching on the Foundation Physics seminar. The student was not participating in the group's discussions and did not attempt to answer seminar questions which was a concern. A meeting was scheduled with the student after class to check that everything was fine, not too dissimilar to a personal tutor might, and during this discussion, the student began to cry. It transpired that the student was from a remote province in China, and had passed the Gaokao examination without any spoken English training or testing. Most of the domestic students who learnt Physics could master the subject in Chinese. However, English terminology in the content modules was more akin to learning a brand-new subject. As such, some students were struggling, especially those who had never learned how to understand questions and write solutions in English. In addition, the student felt peer pressure because every member of group she was a part of worked through the issues quickly and exchanged answers while at the same time the student was still analysing the problems. As a result, I requested other students to help the struggling student. For example, helping her to read the lecture slides and the relevant parts of the textbook in advance and asking her to create a list of the frequently used course vocabulary and terminology. My role also involved giving the student two additional 1 to 1 tutorials to review unfamiliar topics and to help fill gaps, such as regarding the topic of electric flux. To help with the peer pressure, I aided the student adjust self-expectations and gave the group extra interactions and looked at ways to manage their work pace in the seminars.

Through this series of small revisions, the student found her engagement with the materials improved, and studying with her peers certainly helped in this respect as well. What was additionally encouraging was that the student's engagement noticeably improved over a few weeks. Indeed, the student began to improve her spoken English and gain confidence. This was evidenced through the group discussions in which she started actively participating. Ultimately, the student passed the module with a satisfactory grade in the final exam which was positive from all perspectives.

Case Rationale: The UKPSF Area 4 advocates developing effective educational situations and methods to help and mentor students (Higher Education Academy, 2015). The students who were disengaged and demotivated to learn have been observable in my working context since I started working at UNNC as a Science and Engineering tutor. Personally, I have been actively involved in providing a range of modules throughout the last three academic semesters, such as Scientific Methods (CELEN038), Foundation Physics (CELEN039), and Foundation Chemistry (CELEN040), and I have tried to make my sessions as engaging and motivational as possible. The teaching experiences take the form of lectures, seminars, and laboratories, in which I have the opportunity to engage with students from a wide range of majors (for example, mathematics and engineering) and provinces in China (this means that there are differences in terms of culture, education, and even language between students). By paying attention to the classes I teach and considering the backgrounds of any struggling learners who have displayed engagement or motivation drops, I have been able to address issues more quickly with targeted interventions, such as the aforementioned example. Most students have also succeeded in progressing into Year 2. An additional reason, beyond altruism and professionalism considerations, for choosing this particular case and its relative perceived success is also because it was my first experience teaching preliminary-year students at UNNC, and looking back, I believe that I could have handled the situation even better by providing support earlier, quicker. This might have had even greater advantageous outcomes. It could have been a case of thriving rather than simply surviving for the case study student in the then immediate term. Moreover, I have sought to explore how to create an inclusive classroom to engage and motivate these students with the concerns of EDI (equality, diversity, and inclusivity) in mind.

Literature Review: Many students experience some form of exclusion instead of effective and inclusive experiences because of their learning environment (Andrews et al., 2015), and one of the challenges is that inclusivity in the classroom lacks clarity in some situations (Slee, 2001). This is most likely due to the numerous varied forms it can encompass. Most nations in Europe have recognized inclusive education as a way to provide equal access to education for each learner. Nevertheless, the ways that inclusive education is defined and applied differ greatly (Haug, 2017). Inclusion as a wide concept includes marginalized groups and all students, not just students having disabilities (Thomas, 2013). According to the 1994 Salamanca Statement which addresses every group of students at risk of experiencing difficulties in the classroom due to their diverse backgrounds (O.S.N. Education, 2004). Therefore, the right to education for every student is an essential component of inclusion. The inclusion values are related to interactionist ideology and the core values of inclusion include partnership, involvement, democratization, benefit, accessibility, quality and fairness. Partnership and involvement in school programs and culture for every student are further components of inclusion (Booth, 1996). That said, creating inclusive and effective classrooms is not always easy, though, despite the rhetoric. It means being aware of how legislation and education work in society and aligning instruction with expected standards. Practically, creating inclusive classrooms means more than this as well. It means applying the latest research on effective approaches to developing curricula, guidance, technology, evaluation, managing the classroom, collaborating, and involvement among families with the aim to promote learning for everyone. It also requires being a reflective, evidence-based teacher who routinely gathers and evaluates facts to track and improve the efficiency of an individual's work and to enhance learning and instruction differentiation through critical evaluation of values and beliefs. It includes being aware of and reactive to individual variations along with relevant emotional and mental states (Sakarneh et al., 2014). Above all, in creating inclusive and productive classrooms, educators must consider the individual talents and problems that each student experiences and implement evidence-based, broadly designed, and culturally sensitive methods and supportive technology to improve learning and address any problems arising from diversity, including race, language, gender, financial status, cultural traditions, gender identity, sexual orientation, physical ability, and life experiences.

One approach to creating an inclusive classroom is to concentrate on the individual challenges that each student must face when trying to learn. Students require special education, for instance, they require specialized instruction that is focused on the particulars of their learning difficulties and tailored to each student individually. To cater to each group of students, sufficient practitioners having the necessary set of abilities are essential for a school (Kreitz-Sandberg, 2015). In addition, teacher and school features have a positive impact on students' accomplishment in an inclusive classroom. Teacher features, such as efficiency and positivity, help to offer the environmental support that both disabled and non-disabled students need. School features could include high expectations, growth tracking, supportive leadership and learning atmospheres, and collaboration between parents and schools (Sakarneh et al., 2014). According to Shanoski and Hranitz (1992), teachers that are effective interact with their communities. They know what the students' needs are and how to cater to individual differences while maintaining high standards and promoting students' self-assurance in their abilities, which boosts their motivation (Sakarneh et al., 2014). Larrivee (1985) additionally indicated that when teachers utilized their time well, established a secure, inclusive learning environment, gave encouraging feedback, and devoted themselves to high standards, students with special needs performed better in normal classrooms. Each of these components may be utilized as the background for many different kinds of educational environments, if there is a desire. It also highlights the importance of inclusion varying in form based on the scenario and the particular requirements of the stakeholders (Florian, 2005). Furthermore, it is also critical to recognize that there are plenty of barriers to creating inclusive education and that overcoming them will require experience, patience, persistence, and time.

Personal Evaluation: Although I was happy to help the student from the case, and she did well on my module in the end, this placed a noticeable time strain on me when I was unaware of all the support services available to students as a new staff number in UNNC. Moreover, with other students like her who might have needed the same amount of support, it would not have been sustainable. It also raises equity and equality considerations and debates about fairness. In addition, she performed only moderately on other modules, and it is possible that the difficulties were also encountered in other areas. Therefore, I feel that the support should be given in a more systematic and sustainable way. In future I could alert the student's personal tutor, who is the first point of contact for students when they are facing some challenges. I could also direct her to the extra tuition offered by the institutional Writing Lab. I could strongly encourage students more to use the discussion forum on the module Moodle page and use my office hours as well as other Module tutors guidance. To help with the student's peer pressures, I paid extra attention to interacting with the group members and adjusted their pace to get the student more engaged in the group. In the future, I will better facilitate students' work in small groups and involve students' cooperation inside and outside the classroom. It should also enable the time spent with staff to be redirected and guard against questioning that is simply revisiting taught material confusion and which may not be addressed in a short time-bound lecture (Griffiths, 2008; Biggs, 2011). 24/7 communication channels where students can support one another could also be set up on the module Moodle page. Looking ahead, it will also be important to try and guard against a comparison mentality and this can add layers of unintentional peer pressure. Adjusting personal expectations and protecting the sense of self and learner confidence are other important facets to be mindful of (Kiran-Esen, 2012; Moldes et al., 2019). Because of such considerations, I will pay extra attention to how students engage in groups and interact with group members, adjust the pace, and revisit material where merited. This might involve going back over areas that learners are struggling with and explaining the ideas and concepts in a different way, and tapping into Visual-Auditory-Kinaesthetic (VAK) learning style considerations more carefully. Most importantly, I will draw more consciously on the belief that people acquire new knowledge or improved understandings by forming connections between new and previous information in order to integrate them (National Research Council, 2000). I advised the student to engage with pre-lecture resources, such as the lecture notes, relevant book sections and the vocabulary list. By doing this, the students can have a better chance to increase the amount of learning and potentially ask problem questions, especially when they found the material challenging before the class, and the cognitive load associated with new material presented in the class can be reduced. In the future, I will encourage the students to use online resources such as Google search and YouTube, and other apps, for pre-lecture preparation and for verifying their homework answers. The EDI demands would be achieved by providing each student with equitable access to online resources. More importantly, the students would get the opportunity to expand their perspectives toward the related fields and create interdisciplinary linkages based on the subjects that they intend to study in the future.

Final Thoughts: While creating an inclusive learning environment is a key consideration in my practice is to engage and motivate the students, and I think on reflection that I did well in supporting the student with her engagement challenges and through helping her to perform well on this module in this student support case. Nevertheless, I believe that I could do better in terms of improving my strategies by asking senior staff for advice. Furthermore, there could be some students like her who have engagement issues that are caused by different challenges or reasons, and those students might lack the courage to communicate with their tutors actively. Therefore, my belief is that engagement issues have to be solved systematically and should be reported to the university for acquiring the experience of creating an inclusive learning environment effectively. In future practice, since the personal tutor is the first point of contact for students when they are facing challenges, I will encourage students to communicate with the personal tutor initially and provide my support for the involvement of the personal tutor. As a result, the student could receive effective support from different perspectives, and the workload on the frontline staff member could be reduced. Of course, AI might provide an alternative in this area as well and a potential solution. It is additionally important to consult university regulations and communicate with senior workers to gain greater insight into the student's demands before providing support.

Leadership Implications: It's critical to recognize that teaching is a skill that is always changing since, similar to good students, excellent teachers never stop learning within the constraints of the available knowledge (Näykki *et al.*, 2021). Furthermore, it is commonly recognized that students who have knowledgeable teachers typically outperform their counterparts in the classroom (Bietenbeck *et al.*, 2018). Teachers' continuous professional development therefore can be a major factor in raising student satisfaction with the caliber of their instruction and in developing capable learners who possess the requisite knowledge and abilities in a variety of subject areas. Furthermore, because they are so important to the curriculum and have a significant impact on the growth and performance of the students, teacher development programs ought to be offered. Teachers who participate in training programs typically have the chance to learn new techniques, approaches, tactics, skills, and resources as part of their ongoing professional development. Teachers who upskill naturally experience increased confidence, happiness, and motivation to work harder with their students. As such, it is imperative that the leadership teams and school managers consider the continuous professional development of their staff. Schools must acknowledge the value of well-designed programs for teacher development, like the PGCHE, which align with the curriculum and standards of the educational institution (Van Geyte, and Hadjianastasis, 2022). Staff can then learn about international best practices in teaching and education by enrolling on similar courses. They can also apply this knowledge to their advantage and the benefit of their learners in whichever learning spaces. CPD courses also offer theoretical and practical foundations for teaching and learning in higher education. Furthermore, my experience enrolling on a PGCHE course led to greater motivation and managers and leadership can see the impact on teachers beliefs and practice which training provides and enables which is why providing learning opportunities to staff helps them to realize their potential (Van Geyte, and Hadjianastasis, 2022).

SUMMARY

Practice, like leadership and management, requires training and reflection since these features enable one to develop abilities and become more effective. The PGCHE training certainly enabled this practitioner to better prepare classes and reflect on pedagogic practice more. It was rewarding to see that the learners were achieving the ILOs and my classes were well constructed. The engagement and motivation of the students also improved through the creation of an even more inclusive learning environment, and effective support for the students could be supplied from different perspectives and match the demands of the students going forward. Finally, I feel that I am on the way to developing myself as a teacher and educator more because of the learning I have had the benefit of receiving. I am also grateful for the feedback my colleague offered to me and the training my school offered and hope to help others in the future.

REFERENCES

Aboagye, R. (2018). Instructional strategies for teaching students with Mixed ability in physical education in Central Region (Doctoral dissertation, University of Cape coast).

Advance-He. (2011) 'The UK Professional Standards Framework for teaching and supporting learning in higher education', Learning, p. 8. Available at: http://www.heacademy.ac.uk/ukpsf

Andrews, J. W., Drefs, M., Lupart, J., & Loreman, T. (2015). Foundations, principles, and student diversity. Diversity education: Understanding and addressing student diversity, pp.24-73.

Bietenbeck, J., Piopiunik, M., & Wiederhold, S. (2018). Africa's skill tragedy: Does teachers' lack of knowledge lead to low student performance? *The Journal of Human Resources*, 53(3), 553–578. 10.3368/jhr.53.3.0616-8002R1

Biggs, J. (1996). Enhancing teaching through constructive alignment. *Higher Education*, 32(3), 347–364. 10.1007/BF00138871

Biggs, J., & Tang, C. (2010), February. Applying constructive alignment to outcomes-based teaching and learning. In Training material for "quality teaching for learning in higher education" workshop for master trainers, Ministry of Higher Education, Kuala Lumpur (Vol. 53, No. 9, pp. 23-25).

Biggs, J., Tang, C., & Kennedy, G. (2022). Ebook: Teaching for Quality Learning at University 5e. McGraw-hill education (UK).

Booth, T. (1996). Stories of exclusion. Natural and unnatural selection. En.

Brookfield, S.D. (2017). The Four Lenses of Critical Reflection. Becoming A Critically Reflective Teacher, 2, pp.61-78.

Buckridge, M., & Guest, R. (2007). A conversation about pedagogical responses to increased diversity in university classrooms. *Higher Education Research & Development*, 26(2), 133–146. 10.1080/07294360701310771

Colter, R., & Ulatowski, J. (2017). The unexamined student is not worth teaching: Preparation, the zone of proximal development, and the Socratic Model of Scaffolded Learning. *Educational Philosophy and Theory*, 49(14), 1367–1380. 10.1080/00131857.2017.1282340

DeWitt, J., & Storksdieck, M. (2008). A short review of school field trips: Key findings from the past and implications for the future. *Visitor Studies*, 11(2), 181–197. 10.1080/10645570802355562

Dilshad, M., Hussain, B., & Batool, H. (2019). Continuous professional development of teachers: A case of public universities in Pakistan. *Bulletin of Education and Research*, 41(3), 119–130.

O.S.N. Education. (2004). The Salamanca statement and framework for action on special needs education. Special Educational Needs and Inclusive Education: Systems and contexts, 1, p.382.

Eison, J. (2010). Using active learning instructional strategies to create excitement and enhance learning. Jurnal Pendidikantentang Strategi Pembelajaran Aktif (Active Learning). *Books*, 2(1), 1–10.

Ferdinand-James, D., & Medina-Charles, C. (2020), May. Peer Review of Classroom Teaching: Addressing Student, Lecturer, and Institutional Improvement Using an Academic Literacy Approach. In The UWI Quality Education Forum (No. 24).

Florian, L. (2005). Inclusive practice: What, why and how. The Routledge Falmer reader in inclusive education, pp.29-40.

Fuentes, M. A., Zelaya, D. G., & Madsen, J. W. (2021). Rethinking the course syllabus: Considerations for promoting equity, diversity, and inclusion. *Teaching of Psychology*, 48(1), 69–79. 10.1177/0098628320959979

Gibbs, G. (1988). *Learning by doing: A guide to teaching and learning methods*. Further Education Unit.

Griffiths, S. (2008). Teaching and learning in small groups. In *A handbook for teaching and learning in higher education* (pp. 90–102). Routledge.

Hailikari, T., Virtanen, V., Vesalainen, M., & Postareff, L. (2022). Student perspectives on how different elements of constructive alignment support active learning. *Active Learning in Higher Education*, 23(3), 217–231. 10.1177/1469787421989160

Haug, P. (2017). Understanding inclusive education: Ideals and reality. *Scandinavian Journal of Disability Research*, 19(3), 206–217. 10.1080/15017419.2016.1224778

Higher Education Academy. (2015) 'UKPSF Dimensions of the Framework -demonstrate experience'. Available at: https://www.heacademy.ac.uk/system/files/downloads/ukpsf_dimensions_of_the_framework.pdf

Johnson, D. W., Johnson, R. T., & Smith, K. A. (2014). Cooperative learning: Improving university instruction by basing practice on validated theory. *Journal on Excellence in University Teaching*, 25(4), 1–26.

Kiran-Esen, B. (2012). Analyzing peer pressure and self-efficacy expectations among adolescents. *Social Behavior and Personality*, 40(8), 1301–1309. 10.2224/sbp.2012.40.8.1301

Kreitz-Sandberg, S. (2015). 'As an educator you have to fix many things on your own': A study of teachers' perspectives on organizing inclusion in various welfare contexts.

Kurnaz, M. A., & Çimer, S. O. (2010). How do students know that they have learned? An investigation of students' strategies. *Procedia: Social and Behavioral Sciences*, 2(2), 3666–3672. 10.1016/j.sbspro.2010.03.570

Larrivee, B. (1985). *Effective teaching for successful mainstreaming*. Longman Publishing Group.

Miri, B., David, B. C., & Uri, Z. (2007). Purposely teaching for the promotion of higher-order thinking skills: A case of critical thinking. *Research in Science Education*, 37(4), 353–369. 10.1007/s11165-006-9029-2

Moldes, V. M., Biton, C. L., Gonzaga, D. J., & Moneva, J. C. (2019). Students, peer pressure and their academic performance in school. *International Journal of Scientific and Research Publications*, 9(1), 300–312. 10.29322/IJSRP.9.01.2019.p8541

Myers, S.A., & Goodboy, A.K. and Members of Comm 600. (2014). College student learning, motivation, and satisfaction as a function of effective instructor communication behaviors. *The Southern Communication Journal*, 79(1), 14–26.

Nakamura, C. M., Murphy, S. K., Christel, M. G., Stevens, S. M., & Zollman, D. A. (2016). Automated analysis of short responses in an interactive synthetic tutoring system for introductory physics. *Physical Review. Physics Education Research*, 12(1), 010122. 10.1103/PhysRevPhysEducRes.12.010122

National Research Council. (2000). *How people learn: Brain, mind, experience, and school: Expanded edition* (Vol. 1). National Academies Press.

Näykki, P., Kontturi, H., Seppänen, V., Impiö, N., & Järvelä, S. (2021). Teachers as learners–a qualitative exploration of pre-service and in-service teachers' continuous learning community OpenDigi. *Journal of Education for Teaching*, 47(4), 495–512. 10.1080/02607476.2021.1904777

Robinson, C. D. (2022). A framework for motivating teacher-student relationships. *Educational Psychology Review*, 34(4), 2061–2094. 10.1007/s10648-022-09706-0

Sakarneh, M., & Nair, N. A. (2014). Effective teaching in inclusive classroom: Literature review. *Journal of Education and Practice*, 5(24), 28–35.

Shanoski, L.A. and Hranitz, J.R. (1992). Learning from America's Best Teachers: Building a Foundation for Accountability through Excellence.

Siu, K. W. M., & García, G. J. C. (2017). Disruptive Technologies and Education: Is There Any Disruption After All? In Educational leadership and administration: Concepts, methodologies, tools, and applications (pp. 757-778). IGI Global.

Slee, R. (2001). 'Inclusion in Practice': Does practice make perfect? *Educational Review*, 53(2), 113–123. 10.1080/00131910120055543

Thomas, G. (2013). A review of thinking and research about inclusive education policy, with suggestions for a new kind of inclusive thinking. *British Educational Research Journal*, 39(3), 473–490. 10.1080/01411926.2011.652070

Van Geyte, E., & Hadjianastasis, M. (2022). Quality and qualifications: The value of centralised teaching courses for postgraduates who teach. *The International Journal for Academic Development*, 27(1), 4–16. 10.1080/1360144X.2020.1863810

Wang, X., Su, Y., Cheung, S., Wong, E., & Kwong, T. (2013). An exploration of Biggs' constructive alignment in course design and its impact on students' learning approaches. *Assessment & Evaluation in Higher Education*, 38(4), 477–491. 10.1080/02602938.2012.658018

Wilson, L.O. (2016). Anderson and Krathwohl–Bloom's taxonomy revised. Understanding the new version of Bloom's taxonomy.

APPENDIX 1. SESSION AIMS AND ILOS

Session Aims:

- To enable students to define simple machines in engineering, identify different types of machine and the three classes of levers, and write down the conditions of equilibrium for the object.
- To enable students to define the density of a substance and state its applications, and to understand the use of fluid flow, which includes Pascal's principle, Archimedes' principle, Bernoulli's equation, and the law of floatation.
- Fostering an understanding of the law of reflection and plane mirrors.

Session Learning Outcomes:

At the end of this session, students will be able to:

- Identify different simple machines and their applications in engineering, including the inclined plane, the lever, the gear or screw, the wheel and axle, the block and tackle (pulley), the winch or windlass.
- Differentiate the three classes of levers.
- Implement the conditions of equilibrium to solve questions in simple machines.
- Implement Pascal's Principle, Archimedes' Principle, Bernoulli's Equation and the Law of Floatation to solve questions in fluid mechanics.
- Implement the Law of Reflection and plane mirrors to solve questions in the topic of light.

APPENDIX 2

Session Plan

Time	Outline/Teacher Activity	Student Activity	LOs	Resources
12.00-12:05 (5min) 12:05-12:10 (5min) 12:10-12:45 (35min) 12:45-12:50 (5min)	I will walk around and check the proof of the seminar solutions solved by each student and identify 6 problematic questions and divide students into 6 small groups. I will ask students about relevant previous knowledge acquired. Students will be asked interactive questions that target student's conceptual understanding and write down the most relevant equations: • Pascal's principle • Archimedes' principle • Bernoulli's equation • The law of floatation. • Focusing on the seminar topic: • Simple machines • Fluid Flow • Light Each group discuss and provide answers to the assigned problematic question. Each group will be given 3~5 minutes to present on the whiteboard to the class the answer their assigned problematic question. Then I will encourage the class to correct any errors in the student presentation in 1~2 minutes. Recall of learning objectives & reminder of seminar sheets for the next seminar & office hour	Active listening and participation Reading, analyzing, and speaking in pairs or groups about the question. The student presents a solution to their question on the whiteboard. Reading, analyzing, and speaking in pairs or groups about the question. Then compare their answer to the one provided by the teacher and discuss it with the teacher and group members. Active listening: answer questions relate to the learning objectives & seminar sheets for the next seminar & office hour		Teacher's PPT Teacher's PPT Students' seminar solutions and teacher's PPT Teacher's PPT

APPENDIX 3. TEACHING OBSERVATION FORM

Figure 1.

Teaching Observation Form

Before the session

- Complete parts A and B of this form
- Complete your session teaching plan
- Send both documents to your observer

A: Factual information

(to be completed by participants before the teaching session).

Name of Observer:	Sannia Mareta
Name of Participant:	
Name of School?	Centre for English Language Education (CELE)
Level/Year:	Year 1 (UG)- Semester 1
Topic:	The Simple machines, Fluid Flow and Reflection
Session length:	50 minutes
Observation length	50 minutes
Number of students (approx.)	35
Session date	2023-10-25
Session location	TB-119

Comments

This group consists of students who have just completed Chinese university entrance exams called Gaokao. The Gaokao is a test of basic academic knowledge in high school disciplines, including subjects like physics, chemistry, biology, mathematics, etc., for science students. So, these students have already developed integrative thinking from different knowledge and concepts and know how to apply them freely and flexibly. This means that most of the students offering the foundation physics course have already obtained some basic understanding of the physics concepts in the Chinese language. The class is all Domestic, so some students have language problems, so they have difficulty reading the questions and giving or understanding the solutions.

I am to demonstrate a student-centered teaching approach in the class. The student's understanding of the concept and how to express their opinions will be the focus of the study. Students will be asked to read questions and explain their understanding of the question to the class and how they will solve it in English. By so doing, it will build students' confidence and interest in physics, and it will help students deal with language problems easier and be more confident in their ability to communicate in English in the seminar class.

Type of session

please tick most appropriate session type					
Lecture		Problem classes		Group tutorial	
Seminar	Yes	Lab session		Workshop	
Other (please state the session type)					

Figure 2.

Session format

This is a face-to-face seminar, one of 20 parallel seminar groups taught by team of 6 tutors. These form the application of the key principles of physics which have been delivered in the lectures in previous week. These seminars, for example, give a hands-on task and are used to support students' development and learning outcome attainment. These seminars are supplemented by 2× 50-minute lectures a week, where general concepts were introduced to students. I always introduce the class by linking the previous knowledge to the seminar materials. Students are then given the chance to read the questions, explain how they understand the question by drawing out data from the questions, and then present the solution to the problem. Students' participation in seminars has been good so far.

Lessons are constructed to meet the needs of a mixed-ability group of students. This is achieved through the pacing of the lesson, involving all students in the lesson through questioning, and setting class activities appropriately. I will use PowerPoint presentations for the lesson as a tool to identify the lesson learning objectives and use visual images. Students will also have regular opportunities to discuss questions in groups to help build their confidence in both interaction and presentation.

Another peculiar problem is the time constraint. The seminar class is designed in such a way that roughly 10–15 questions need to be solved within 50 minutes. As physics questions and their solutions come along with several applications of concepts, it makes it difficult for both students and the seminar tutor to accomplish all the objectives of the seminar. This implies that, realistically, 5-7 questions can be discussed and solved in the class, while the rest will be given to the students to check the solutions on Moodle on their own. If they still find some difficulties with it, they can attend the tutors' office hours for more clarification, or wait until the end of the week (every Friday at 5:00 pm) to access the solutions to all the questions on Moodle.

The time allocated for each question is 4-7 minutes, depending on the complexity of the question. This is to indicate that there is no uniform distribution of time in the seminar class activities. Factors that contribute to these time fluctuations are the students' understanding of the concepts and the fact that some students will not solve the seminar question before the seminar class, which prolongs the discussion.

I will kindly appreciate feedback from the observer in the areas of my activity timing and my student interaction.

B: Aims and Learning Outcomes
(to be completed by participants before the teaching session).

Aim

- To enable students to define simple machines in engineering, identify different types of machine and the three classes of levers, and write down the conditions of equilibrium for the object.
- To enable students to define the density of a substance and state its applications, and to understand the use of fluid flow, which includes Pascal's principle, Archimedes' principle, Bernoulli's equation, and the law of floatation.
- Fostering an understanding of the law of reflection and plane mirrors.

Learning outcomes

At the end of this session, students will be able to:
- Identify different simple machines and their applications in engineering, including the inclined plane, the lever, the gear or screw, the wheel and axle, the block and tackle (pulley), the winch or windlass.
- Differentiate the three classes of levers.
- Implement the conditions of equilibrium to solve questions in simple machines.
- Implement Pascal's Principle, Archimedes' Principle, Bernoulli's Equation and the Law of Floatation to solve questions in fluid mechanics.
- Implement the Law of Reflection and plane mirrors to solve questions in the topic of light.

Figure 3.

Time	Outline/Teacher Activity	Student Activity	LOs	Resources
12:00-12:05 (5min)	I will walk around and check the proof of the seminar solutions solved by each student and identify 6 problematic questions and divide students into 6 small groups. I will ask students about relevant previous knowledge acquired. Students will be asked interactive questions that target student's conceptual understanding and write down the most relevant equations: • Pascal's principle • Archimedes' principle • Bernoulli's equation • The law of floatation. Focusing on the seminar topic: • Simple machines • Fluid Flow • Light	Active listening and participation		Teacher's PPT
12:05-12:10 (5min)	Each group discuss and provide answers to the assigned problematic question.	Reading, analyzing, and speaking in pairs or groups about the question.		Teacher's PPT
12:10-12:45 (35min)	Each group will be given 3~5 minutes to present on the whiteboard to the class the answer their assigned problematic question. Then I will encourage the class to correct any errors in the student presentation in 1~2 minutes.	The student presents a solution to their question on the whiteboard. Reading, analyzing, and speaking in pairs or groups about the question. Then compare their answer to the one provided by the teacher and discuss it with the teacher and group members.		Students' seminar solutions and teacher's PPT
12:45-12:50 (5min)	Recall of learning objectives & reminder of seminar sheets for the next seminar & office hour	Active listening; answer questions relate to the learning objectives & seminar sheets for the next seminar & office hour		Teacher's PPT

Figure 4.

C: Strengths and Suggestions for Improvement
Comments

	Strengths	Suggestions for development
Planning and organisation 1. "Is the session plan well designed (consideration of timings, engagement strategies and feedback strategies?" (A1)	Yes, the lesson plan provides clear details on the learning activities.	When the nature of the class was mentioned, there was a statement about the class being all Chinese and that some of them had language problems. This statement sounds like an assumption. It would be good to find statistics/research on how much struggle these students had.
2. Are the aims & learning outcomes appropriate to the session and clear to all? (V1, V2)	Yes. They are appropriate and well-presented.	
3. Is the session plan implemented effectively (If not, why not)? (A2, K1, V2)	Yes. Teacher demonstrated adaptability to the time allocation to discuss the given Physics problems in order to better facilitate students learning.	
Methods/approach 4. Are the teaching and learning methods used appropriate and learning encouraged? (A2, K2)	Teacher had positive behaviours and enthusiasm that motivated student learning.	
5. Are effective strategies used to support student engagement and inclusion (V1, V2)	Teacher was able to break down complex problems into simpler steps. Teacher walked around each students' group to monitor their work progress. All student groups were able to contribute to the seminar discussion. Teacher also used a peer learning scheme to allow students check on each other's work.	- A few students were noticed to play with their mobile phone. - During the discussion, a student in Group 2 was a dominant speaker. How to allow other students to contribute to the discussion can be explored. - Other ways of inviting students' contribution in the seminar class can be explored. So far, teacher relied only upon students' verbal participation. How about inviting them to write their answer on the board, or to include other interactivities in the class.
Evaluating learning and feedback 6. Are appropriate evaluation and feedback strategies employed? (A3, V1)	Yes. Immediate feedback was used throughout the seminar session for the work that students had done before coming to the class. Teacher also provided detailed feedback to the specific task difficulty encountered by students.	
Communication 7. Is the style of communication (tone, clarity & audibility) and pace and timing appropriate? (A2, V2)	The pace was appropriate. The timing was appropriate. The voice was sufficiently loud and clear.	English pronunciation has to be improved, especially for technical terminologies. Anticipation to students' questions could also be further improved. There was a moment where a question was not answered/responded by the teacher in the class and the students seemed lost.

Figure 5.

Content 8. Is the content appropriate to the learning outcomes and placed in context (e.g. use of current examples, inclusive, make connections between the session and prior learning)? (A5, K1, V2)	Yes. Teacher often made connections of the materials with previously learned concepts and future assignments/assessments.	How to find ways to integrate "Inclusion" of the EDI value into your teaching practice and/or materials can be explored. Even though it seems that your students share similar demography backgrounds, but EDI can be promoted from simple engagement such as by providing them with equal opportunities to talk, or to write their answers on the board.
Learning environment 9. Are the learning and teaching resources effective in enhancing the session? (A2, V1, K4)	Yes. The use of annotation on the screen was very effective. The PPT slide was clear and professional. Teacher took initiative to also make modifications to the PPT slide to cater student learning needs.	
10. To what extent is a supportive learning and effective learning environment created? (V2)	Teacher showed positive personality and has successfully created a positive learning environment.	

D: Overall Summary
Please summarise the overall quality of the session in relation to the stated learning outcomes and in line with the UKPSF dimensions of practice. Provide feedback for future development opportunities. (A2)

Session meets AdvanceHE requirements	☐ Yes	☐ No*

* If the outcome is No, please provide a detailed explanation in the feedback and contact the Module 1 convenor as soon as possible.

Participant's signature: Date:

Chapter 10
An Investigation Into PSE Tutors' Perception and Practice of Intonation Teaching

Mahmoud Jeidani
Nottingham University, Ningbo, China

ABSTRACT

This study explores Presessional English (PSE) Course (PSECs) tutors' views of, and experience with, the relevance of intonation to their teaching on these courses. Motivated by the lack of a unified view among teachers in relation to its value with reference to PSECs, this study uses semi-structured interviews and teaching observations to explore these tutors' approaches to the teaching of intonation. The results show the participants' recognition of the relevance of intonation to PSE students aiming to improve their listening and speaking skills, while recognising that teaching requires significant support in terms of training and a focus on its communicative role. The significance of this study is that it rejects the view that teachers do not appreciate intonation, showing that teachers' critical reflection is a promising step towards streamlining PSECs to align with student needs.

INTRODUCTION

With the ever evolving nature of teaching practices at Higher Education settings, teachers attempt to make sense of their unique contexts by utilizing tools such as their knowledge, skills, values, and reflections by way of streamlining their professional practices. Generally referred to as 'teacher cognition', such resources are utilized by teachers to assess their contexts and integrate theoretical knowledge with their own applied lessons and reflections in order to promote their development (Slotte and Tynjälä, 2003: 457). However, the process is not necessarily simple or even possible since teaching is a dynamic process and 'anything can happen'; this is particularly true of situations when teachers find themselves on 'unfamiliar grounds' such as teaching students who do not share with the teacher the same culture

DOI: 10.4018/979-8-3693-2857-6.ch010

Copyright ©2024, IGI Global. Copying or distributing in print or electronic forms without written permission of IGI Global is prohibited.

An Investigation Into PSE Tutors' Perception and Practice of Intonation Teaching

or language. Scenarios such as this highlight the need for teacher reflection and continuing need to understand new contexts, students, and stakeholder expectations.

Defined as 'any education or training at higher education level provided beyond national or regional borders through mobility of people, program or institution' (Sugimoto 2006: 3), transnational higher education (TNHE) has gained significant interest among many stakeholders such as students and governments to facilitate the acquisition of skills and dissemination of knowledge. In the TNHE landscape, the UK has emerged as one of the key destinations for many international students to pursue their studies. The number of international students in the UK has recently risen significantly, from 319340 in 2017-8 (HESA, 2019) to over half a million in 2022-3 (International Student Statistics in UK, 2023), with Chinese students reaching 122, 140 in 2019 (UNESCO Institute for Statistics, 2019). Among international students, some receive study offers conditional on them achieving a higher English proficiency level by attending Presessional English Courses (PSECs). Thus, the rise in international student numbers arriving in the UK is also associated with a rise in the number of those attending PSECs. Apart from their role in language support, PSECs also enable students to bridge the gap in academic literacy levels (Pearson, 2020), preparing them to cope with their prospective courses by teaching them academic skills in relation to how to e.g. complete research, read, listen, and speak effectively. Consequently, PSECs complement the roles fulfilled by HE disciplinary lecturers, who elect to focus on the subject-matter of academic courses, knowing their (international) students have developed the necessary academic skills needed to effectively demonstrate their writing and speaking skills.

Listening to lectures, delivering presentations, and engaging in seminar discussions require effective listening and speaking skills, including proficient English pronunciation. Ample research shows the significance of pronunciation for effective communication in general (e.g. Underhill, 1994; Celce-Murcia et al., 2010) and academic presentations (e.g. Pickering, 2001). Yet, pronunciation receives little attention in the EAP classroom (Foote et al. 2013). This discrepancy can be explained due to the uncertainty of teaching pronunciation in EAP programs, its time-consuming nature (Khaghainejad, 2015), teachers' lack of confidence in giving feedback, particularly in classes of different L1 backgrounds and language needs (Baker & Burri, 2016). This is compounded by pronunciation instructions having multitude of goals, ranging from a focus on intelligibility (e.g. Munro and Derwing 2015; Jenkins, 2000) all the way to native speaker accent attainment (e.g. Borg and Al-Busaidi, 2012; Jenkins, 2004).

At the heart of pronunciation lies intonation, an ill-understood language feature (Cruttenden, 1997) but crucial for both native speaker accent (Jenkins, 2004) and intelligibility when communicating with native speakers (Jenkins, 2000; Baker, 2011), with the latter scenario applying to PSEC students. Intonation, a suprasegmental feature, deals with the falls and rises of pitch to communicate important meanings (Pickering, 2001), despite disagreement among linguists regarding its meaning (Wells, 2006) and the value of teaching it (e.g. Roach, 2009; Jenkins, 2000). This explains teachers' reluctance to teach it, making intonation poorly investigated in the literature on language, including Presessional Course Tutors (PSETs). Given intonation is a source of teacher anxiety (e.g. Chapman, 2007) and that PSETs need to teach it to students to help them communicate with native speakers or for their future careers, this research aims at qualitatively investigating in-service PSETs' views and practices of intonation by way of addressing the aforementioned gap in the literature.

LITERATURE REVIEW

Intonation, a prosodic feature, is the fluctuation in the pitch of the voice to create certain meanings (Wells, 2006; Roach, 2001), though different linguists attribute different functions to it. For example, O'Conner and Arnold (1973) and Wells (2006) attribute an attitudinal function to intonation, arguing it expresses the attitude of the speaker at the moment of speaking. By contrast, Halliday (1967, 1970) argues that intonation choices correspond to grammatical ones, reflecting how sentence types determine intonation choices. However, evidence suggests these two views are not satisfactory. Linguistically, it is difficult to assign any tone a specific list of attitudes as attitudes are the result of not only intonation but also other factors present in the interaction between a speaker and listener (Cruttenden, 1997). Similarly, assigning a certain sentence type to a default tone seems difficult to support, particularly when examined against authentic speech data (Cauldwell & Hewings, 1996). A response to these two descriptions is Discourse Intonation (DI) (Brazil, 1985; Beaken, 2009), which argues that intonation is purpose-driven and that tones serve a discourse function to signal shared (a fall-rise or rising tone) or new information (a rise-fall tone or a falling tone) (Brazil, 1997; Bradford, 1988). The approach suggests that intonation is dynamic and is based on the speaker's ongoing assessment of a situation for the purpose of meaningfully engaging with it. Furthermore, DI deals with other features such as stressed syllables (prominent syllables that carry information which the listener cannot surmise from the context (McCarthy, 1991)), tone units (speech analysis units with at least one prominent syllable), and pitch levels (high, mid, and low) on prominent syllables (key and termination). Key is determined on the basis of a relational judgment against the pitch level of the previous unit and expresses notions of contrast and equativeness, while termination determines the level of the following unit, and helps seek an active response vs. passive agreement, among others (Brazil, 1997). Termination choices help in participating in a seminar discussion, while key choices can serve many functions such as signalising intonational paragraphing (paratones) (Pickering, 2004). Therefore, it can be suggested that intonation is a feature that international students completing PSECS will need to learn if they wish to develop their communication skills during their academic courses and beyond.

Studies on intonation and intelligibility highlight the need for ESL to include this feature. Pickering (2001), using DI as a theoretical framework, compared the delivery of American native lecturers with that of Chinese Teaching Assistants, demonstrating how the latter failed to make use of English tones the way the former did, negatively impacting the clarity of their message. Similarly, Hahn's (2004) research in relation to Korean teachers' placement of primary stress (i.e. the last prominent syllable in a tone unit) concluded listeners found it easier to follow speech when such stress was placed correctly. Even though Pickering's research examined tones while Hahn's examined primary stress, it is worth noting that they used different theoretical underpinnings; the signalling of *old* and *new* information in Hahn's study is attributed to primary stress while such a function is attributed to tones in DI in Pickering's study. Therefore, these two studies highlight two points:

a)- intonation is crucial for intelligibility in interacting with native speakers, and
b)- differences in terminology across linguistic descriptions of intonation can create challenges for teachers.

The complexity of intonation and its teachability/learnability serves to explain issues faced by teachers who are in the position of deciding whether or not to teach it, finding ways to explain it, sourcing and adapting appropriate examples and input materials. Collectively, teachers attempting to make sense of, and respond to, such challenges is known as teacher cognition, and intonation seems to be poorly represented in it (Couper, 2017: 821). This has naturally led to teachers being in an uncertain position; such a position is reported in Couper (2017), who found that teachers in general were far from having a unified voice on the teaching of intonation. In relation to teacher training, Chapman (2007) examined the possibility of teaching DI features to native-speaker teachers and concluded that some features such as prominence and tone units were easier to listen for, while tones proved to be difficult 'guesswork'. Chapman's findings are echoed, and further elaborated, in Jeidani (2012), who experimented with teaching DI to non-native, advanced speaker teachers of English, and concluded that learners recognising the significance of intonation is associated with doubt as to how teachable or learnable it is due to the difficulty of listening and speaking tasks, as well as the difficulty of interpreting intonation choices in relation to examples of spoken English. It seems that both native and non-native teachers and teacher-learners find intonation difficult to consciously interpret, listen to, and produce at will, a point which can be explained by Jenkins' (2000) argument that tones operate at a subconscious level, and thus are difficult to teach/learn.

Pedagogically, there is an inverse relationship between the communicative features of intonation, and its teachability (Dalton and Seidlhofer, 1994). Jenkins (2000) argues that any seeming improvement in EFL learners' tones resulting from instruction could simply be the result of a 'humming effect', a temporary and mechanical mimicking pronunciation. Similarly, Roach (2009) believes that the various functions of English tones are best acquired in immersive settings than in classroom settings. However, such reported difficulty seems to be feature-related as primary stress is one feature that many authorities agree is teachable (e.g. Baker, 2011). An example of pronunciation improvement that is based on intonation instruction is Henrikson et al., (2010), though such an improvement can be attributed to a few factors to do with immersion and learner motivation (Saito et al., 2017). Overall, most research on intonation either attempts to justify its role to intelligibility especially in ESL settings, or else it attempts to suggest ways of teaching it; however, very little research has attempted to objectively measure the role that explicit instruction plays in creating a sustained, out-of-classroom, improved learners' proficiency of intonation.

One aspect that is missing from teacher cognition in relation to intonation teaching is feedback. Salter's action research (1999) traced learners' fluctuating views in response to the meaning of tones but, given the limited scope of research, did not explore feedback strategies. Other studies (e.g. Jeidani, 2012; Jeidani, 2014) explored teachers' view on intonation teaching but did not explore the washback effect of feedback on intonation teaching planning and approach. However, feedback has received more interest in relation to pronunciation in general, an example of which is Baker and Burri (2016) exploring related difficulties in EAP settings, showing that students of L2 backgrounds create some uncertainly in respect of their needs and how to prioritize such needs in feedback. However, a key finding of this study is that pronunciation feedback enhances comprehensibility and takes a few forms such as a)- peer feedback, b)- targeted feedback, c)- use of voice recordings as feedback medium, and d)- recasting (repeating the incorrect pronunciation so that the learner would pay attention and identify their error). These findings are very interesting as they highlight the value of feedback provision but also raise some difficulty of providing feedback in the case of intonation in relation to recasting as recasting might work in the case of phonemes and word stress, but for teaching features of speech that place so much emphasis on context as DI does, reproducing e.g. a high vs. low key out of context for demonstration purposes seems counter-productive.

There are many remaining questions in need for further exploration regarding intonation. Such points are summarised in Mora and Levkina (2017), some of which have been selected in the current paper for their relevance to intonation teaching:

a) What relationship exists, if any, among the complexity of tasks, learner accuracy and fluency?
b) Is speaking output that demonstrates the desired pronunciation outcome might be unrealistic for lower-level learners, for whom a more realistic gaol would be awareness raising?
c) Do affective factors help determine the development of ESL learners?
d) What pronunciation learning differences among ESL learners can be explained in relation to their differences in e.g. attention and memory?

To explore these questions in relation to intonation learning, a researcher would have to trace the learning and performance journey of a group of learners over an extended period, both inside and outside the classroom, account for many variables that might contribute to learners' individual factors, accuracy, and fluency, to name a few. While such research falls outside the scope of this paper, it would be relevant to explore the extent to which PSETs are aware of them and/or they try to address them in their lesson design and delivery.

Intonation teaching can also be determined by contextual factors such as policymakers and stakeholders (not) viewing intonation as a priority, particularly given the complexity involved in understanding it (Hadley, 1996). This is particularly key in the case of PSECs, which tend to be relatively short, ranging from 5 weeks to 30 weeks, in the UK. To this end, this paper attempts to investigate the thinking process and practice of some in-service Presessional Tutors. Given the clear lack of research on intonation teaching cognition in relation to PSECs, this study seeks to examine the specific factors contributing to the formation of teacher cognition in this field.

METHODOLOGY

Given the limited research on teacher perception of intonation teaching on PSECs, the current research aims at PSETs' views of intonation to these courses *and* how such relevance can be translated, if at all, into classroom practice. More specifically, it has the following questions:

1- To what extent, if at all, do PSETs think of intonation as relevant to PSE students?
2- What challenges do they believe stand in the way of teaching intonation on PSECs?
3- To what extent do the PSETs' practices in relation to intonation teaching align with their views?

- Study participants:

Four PSETs (T1/T2/T3/T4) who teach at a UK university agreed to participate in the study. One participant had 3 years while the other tutors had at least 5 years' experience teaching on PSECs post their Master's Degree in ELT, and one of them had a PhD in Applied Linguistics. Prior to the interview, they were given a consent form to sign, having made it clear to them that they had the right to withdraw at any point and that they would remain anonymous. T1 is a non-native speaker. Their teaching EAP cohorts of international students slightly differed in length (10 and 15-Week PSE Courses) and language proficiency (IELTS 6 and 5.5 respectively). The listening/speaking lessons included the teaching of seminar, presentation, listening, and pronunciation skills. The syllabus includes pronunciation elements to help with listening and speaking such as phonemes, chunking, word/sentence stress, rhythm, and tones, with PSETs having the liberty to add, adapt, and prioritize. The delivery is task-based as students listen to examples, listen and mark choices, and then try to produce the feature in question at will.
- Interviews:

The interviews were semi-structured (see Appendix X for a list of interview questions) to address specific points flexibly while remaining on the topic (Dorniye, 2007). The interviews addressed the points included in Research Questions 1, 2, and 3, formulated based on various points and recommendations raised in the literature on English intonation teaching and gaps (e.g. Chapman, 2007; Baker, 2011; Jeidani, 2012) to address its relationship to the PSECs. Furthermore, to facilitate the process of engaging with the interview questions, some examples of how intonation is treated in academic manuals and PSE materials were used as a reminder, a strategy known as stimulated recall (Dorniye, 2007). In addition, after conducting both the interviews and observations, the participants were encouraged to comment on their observed lessons and offer their insights on anything that they felt needed some explanation, particularly in relation to the effort, time and approach used in teaching intonation.

The resulting data was analysed using a content analysis framework (Braun and Clarke, 2006). The analysis is data-driven to ensure taking account of any emerging themes and exercising flexibility due to the participants providing answers that did not match questions. The data was first transcribed, and then coded by the author, and an independent coder also coded some of the data, and then both sets of codes were compared before any differences were negotiated and settled. The final codes were then combined into larger categories which themselves were grouped into three themes.

- <u>Observations and fieldnotes:</u>

The participants were asked to notify the author of lessons in which they would teach intonation so that the author could observe and take notes. Further scheduling arrangements were reached to the researcher attending as many of the pronunciation sessions as possible. Having obtained consent from the tutors and students, the listening/speaking lessons containing the following intonation features and tasks were attended:

- Week 3: speech segmentation [T1, T3, T4] (Field Notes Entry 1)
- Week 4: sentence stress [T1, T2, T3] (Field Notes Entry 2)
- Week 6: falling and rising tones [T1, T2, T3, T4] (Field Notes Entry 3)
- Week 7: key (pitch step-up) [T3] (Field Notes Entry 4).

Although the course materials contain the relevant tasks, with Teacher's Notes to show how these tasks can be used in class as well as the Learning Outcomes to show their rationale, the tutors have complete freedom in adapting these and/or using their own materials. The participants showed their materials to the author in advance of the lesson. Some of these materials are taken from/based on Hewings and Thaine (2012) and Hewings (2007) (See Appendix Y for the observation sheet containing the main points being of interest to the researcher). The notes taken by the researcher included the following data:

- Learning Outcomes of observed lessons,
- Intonation tasks: how they are introduced and explained,
- Delivery method: inductive vs. deductive approach,
- Student responses: listening accuracy rates and answers,
- Student questions,
- Feedback.

The analysis of the field notes was completed on the basis of the notes relating to the interview content, e.g. clarifying, corroborating, or else contradicting the participants' views.

RESULTS

1- Relevance to PSECs:

Three tutors agree that intonation should be a key component in the listening and speaking skills taught to students. One view is that it would be more fruitful to teach intonation as embedded within academic listening and speaking by e.g. providing students with lecture transcripts with highlighted intonation features that they can read while listening to academic presentations (T4). A reason for this view is that speech carries an illocutionary force, a skill students need for academic communication and social interaction while studying in the UK in a a native-speaker fashion and to be able to recognise such force when they hear it:

"Intonation can help with listening and speaking, e.g. recognising when a speaker is serious or sarcastic…to communicate passion towards a topic or to mark off new from old information]" (T3)

Relevant to speaker intent is meaning, and the participants demonstrate awareness of the role intonation plays in it. Knowing when to stress certain words to get the listener's attention to them (T2), the choice of a tone to sound questioning versus affirmative (T4), and marking off transition across topic in order to signal an ongoing discussion (T1), all seem to be crucial speaking skills that students need to develop, as can be seen in conversational skills in and out of class. The rationale is the view that a task-based approach to teaching and learning on PSECs requires the implementation of these pronunciation features for a successful negotiation of meaning:

"Students need to learn the skill of working in pairs and groups…to argue and counter-argue in a seminar discussion…so they need to listen well, get intonation cues, and then respond appropriately" [T4]

Another reason for this view is the students aiming to sound native-like, and mastering English intonation is a key ingredient in that. T2 and T4 agree that native speakers tend to parcel up their thought groups using audible pauses which serve the listener in perceiving meaning as units, and T3 believes that this tendency plays a key role towards a native-like accent. Furthermore, PSETs have a 'duty of care' towards their students in so far as to explain such native and non-native pronunciation differences and how to gradually develop one's pronunciation. The participant also believes that many students are unable to understand this on their own, which highlights the role of PSETs. The perceived reason for this is that mere practice outside the classroom isn't going to achieve a native-like pronunciation because:

"To transform motivated students' foreign accents they need to work from within [the classroom] and from without….Many students want to carry something forward with them other than a qualification" (T1)

Promoting student effort and pronunciation is related to students' current views of employability. T1, T2 and T3 agree that sounding native-like can enable many students to go a long way in showing employability skills, particularly in ELT related professions, arguing that intonation plays a role and that teachers can enable students to 'aim high' in sounding native-like. PSETs are also tasked with discussing

An Investigation Into PSE Tutors' Perception and Practice of Intonation Teaching

issues of identity arising from teachers and students engaging with intonation teaching in a way that may have a bearing on students' perceived self-identity. T2 believes that some PSETs can face reluctance from students when they are asked to produce certain intonation features at will as they may simply feel they are batting with a pronunciation that does not feel 'natural'. The point of whether a teacher should engage with students over identity questioning debates is relevant in an EAP course as students' perceptions matter and their reluctance, if any, needs to be addressed before they can fully realise the value of any provision of intonation materials. Participants T2 and T3 believe that some students view EAP as English used for specific, narrow uses to do with the academic field while, in fact, EAP can have far-reaching uses to do with employability and even as a symbol of professionalism and giftedness. PSECs address such cognitive processes as:

"… what it means to pick up on subtle cues in a conversation …. then use them in communicating with both native and non-native speakers…[highlighting] active and critical learning that proves learners can use intonation like a native speaker, irrespective of what colleagues and peers might think" [T3].

Despite attributing different functions to intonation, the participants have in common the belief that intonation is very useful to students' language, identify, and employability. By suggesting that intonation sits naturally in PSECs as it forms a solid part of teachers' efforts to improve students' pronunciation and increase their future employability, the participants agree that an ESL context will have its own requirements for empowering students while teachers play a pivotal role in the process.

Referring to the fieldnotes (Field Notes Entry 1), it appears the participants are less consistent in their practice. For example, in dealing with speech segmentation (Hewings, 2007, p. 70), only participants T1 and T4 elected to teach it to varying levels of detail. T1 briefly introduced the idea by saying that when we speak, we do not pronounce words one by one, but rather group them together. The tutor then prompted the students to listen to examples of segmented speech, and then say these examples in pairs and give peer feedback. T4, likewise, followed the same procedure but also noted that tone units are pause-defined and that the pause would not occur between a definite / indefinite article and the following noun or between a subject and verb. However, when a student asked if a tone unit is the same as a clause, he also noted that sometimes a tone unit can be the same as a clause, but not necessarily the case. To clarify this, he wrote the following examples on the board and asked the students to visualise the two scenarios and think of the difference:

A- //let's all go //have a coffee//
B- //let's all go have a coffee//

Without an answer volunteered, the teacher suggested thinking of the difference in terms of thinking of two different actions vs. coffee as the main action of interest. With this suggestion eliciting an answer from at least have a dozen students, a question came from a student to the effect of:

Is There any Difference in Meaning Between Examples A and B?

In response, the tutor mentioned the difference may not be significant, but that in longer stretches the difference can be very noticeable in highlighting the speaker's fluency. The tutor then moved on to a new task.

In relation to prominence (Hewings, 2007, p. 72), Field Notes Entry 2 shows all the participants were enthusiastic about teaching it, though it wasn't possible to observe T4 due to a schedule clash. T2 and T3 prompted the students to listen to the recorded examples and observe how the uppercased words stood out in a tone unit, before asking them to listen to new examples and mark the prominent words. Following the materials, the students then were prompted to read out the examples on p. 73 and then compare their delivery to the recorded model answers. T2 went a step further by saying prominence has a function e.g. by highlighting //INtervierws// in the response //i've got an INterview later today// in response to the question "Why are you cleaning your shoes?".

T1, the most thorough in his approach, played a recorded stretch of speech in English, prompting the students to observe if all the words in the material received the same level of stress, having underlined some words to guide the students in their analysis. The following is a short sample:

//as i try//to make sense of the question// i notice the difficulty //of deciding which perspective to consider//it's difficult//very difficult//

Following an inductive approach, the tutor played the recording three times and asked the students to figure out why some words are said with more force and clarity, receiving such answers as 'important words' and 'helpful words'. With such answers described as 'satisfactory', the tutor asked the students to consider the examples and their explanation on p. 72 and then listen and mark prominence choices in Exercises C12. Some confusion as to the correct answers arose, evidenced by students asking to listen a third time; even then, some students couldn't agree with the answers provided (e.g. SURE, alRIGHT, problem). The same level of uncertainty arose again in the listening materials on p. 73 and the tutor had to concede that sometimes even native speakers disagree as to whether a word is prominent or not. Uncertainty also arose as to why some words were made prominent while others non-prominent, to which the tutor said that a speaker's prominence choices may be difficult to explain. Having skipped the exercises on fixed phrases and idioms, the tutor moved examples of why words can be made prominent or non-prominent (p. 78). The students read these examples and then did the listening tasks on p. 79. The students' accuracy rates ranged from 33% to 71%. Having shared the correct answers with the students, the tutor existed the intonation part.

In relation to tones (Field Notes Entry 3), three participants taught them explicitly. T2 skipped tones and opted to teach the IPA to students. By contrast, both participants T1 and T3 taught tones (Hewings, 2007, p. 84) and then prompted the students to work on Exercises 9.1 (speaking) and 9.2 (listening) (p. 85). T1 sufficed himself by briefly explaining that information can be new as in answering a question, or old because the listener already knows it. He also made the students do the exercises and then shared the correct answers without attempting to check the students' answers. By contrast, T3 introduced tones and got students to do the speaking and listening and encouraged students to voice their feelings and questions, e.g. giving feedback regarding the students' abilities to produce the tones at will, prompting them to listen twice to mark tones, and eliciting some difficulties in listening and speaking such as the difficulty of listening for tones when the tone units run into each e.g. due to a lack of a perceptible pause. Then, without explaining how or why, T3 said using rising and falling tones correctly makes the listening process easier and smoother. Finally, the tutor gave the students homework handouts (Hewings & Thaine,

2012, p. 75) to complete before Week 7 on the use of the fall-rise tone to soften disagreement, saying that this skill will facilitate successful interaction with native speakers. Conversely, T4 quickly reminded students of the intonation choices on statements vs. wh-questions vs. yes-no questions, demonstrating such tone choices with his own examples. Collectively, the participants' enthusiasm as expressed in the interviews didn't transpire to the same level when they were observed teaching intonation.

Finally, Field Notes Entry 4 describes T3 demonstrate the use of high key to express disagreement (Hewings, 2007, p. 100) by asking students to read the examples and prompting them to practice using high key on the examples on p. 101. Observing only one student not producing high key, the tutor gave feedback to that student, but otherwise was satisfied with the performance of the class. The listening accuracy for Task 7.3 was as high as 100% for some students.

The observed classes, cross-referenced with the interview data, show their views do not translate to the same level of enthusiasm. Many of the functions attributed to intonation during the interview stage (e.g. attitudinal meanings) were not mentioned in class at all, while others (e.g. grammatical meanings) were mentioned only briefly by one participant. While some of these variances could be attributed to the suggested materials (e.g. Hewings, 2007), the tutors had full control over their materials and were permitted to source such materials any way they saw fit.

2- Challenges:

The participants perceive challenges on several levels. A key challenge reported is the lack of preparedness to teach the subject, given how it requires detailed knowledge of its theory and how to communicate that theory into appropriate pedagogic practice. Relevance to meaning is seen a key consideration as PSECs are academic in nature, and PSETs will need considerable experience if they have to introduce the topic in such a way as to present it meaningfully, given the distinct lack of proper training on the subject. With certain terminology occasionally needed for an overt approach to the topic, intonation requires PSETs who can confidently introduce, discuss, produce, and evaluate examples of various intonation features to avoid any potential embarrassment should they be challenged in the classroom:

"[intonation] is hardly addressed in any teacher preparation program…how are we as tutors expected to know it well enough to teach it? ….When I looked at how a [spoken] text is annotated, I was shocked at how complex this could be…" (T1)

A clear lack of expertise also stems from the complex descriptions and debates existing around the topic (T4); and even when such knowledge is well established in teacher training, this doesn't necessarily or automatically render it teachable. For PSETs, meaning contrasts that are sometimes taught on a Master's program in ELT can be helpfully taught on PSECs overtly using terminology to students of (Applied) Linguistics, but these contrasts will need to be approached in a different way when taught to students who just want to improve their listening and speaking, otherwise the topic of intonation will be taught as a formality:

"How can you say that a statement has a falling tone when many such statements don't? [Based on my reading on the subject] there must be a meaning deeper than that but as a tutor I feel I cannot communicate it easily to students…. similar to the difference between past and present perfect tenses [in grammar teaching]… very challenging to explain to students..." [T1]

The difficulty of pedagogically simplifying the meaning of intonation and translating into student-friendly terms, as well as the lacking teacher training, may contribute to an anticipated challenge of how to effectively and confidently ensure assessing students' understanding and ability to practice intonation features. Such an evaluation challenge is seen in the observed classes (e.g. Field Notes Entries 2 and 3) where the participants either rush a task or simply give an answer to students without checking the quality of students' answers. This is discussed in the post-observation meeting with participants T1 and T3, who both agreed that in an ideal world, with ideal students and materials, it would make sense to spend much more time approaching the various features of intonation and using more helpful examples; but that, given the reality of the context, it would only be possible to introduce the features of intonation and leave it up to highlight examples in listening and speaking materials, while also giving students the opportunity to reflect on intonation on their own.

In relations to learning outcomes, students generally come to PSECs expecting to have their skills improved without realising that this is not necessarily a straightforward process, and linguistic insights may not easily translate into a perceived improved skill. This may result in students focusing on other, more learnable skills as these yield more tangible results, particularly when there is a lot at stake for teachers who will be evaluated by their students and for students who need to feel they are learning something new:

"…you can expect them to start producing a paragraph on the spot [in class]… intonation as students are not machines that can be programmed to take on board new pronunciation models….[you] can keep teaching how to stress certain syllables until you're blue in the face but they won't follow through [in speaking English] once pronunciation is not the focus of an activity or conversation" [T4]

The reality of the intangible effect of instruction on learners' pronunciation is commented on by T1 in the post-observation interview, noting that there is no need to insist on students producing the 'correct' use of a certain feature in class because real learning takes place outside the classroom when students communicate with, and listen to, native speakers, reflecting on how and when to use information to improve their pronunciation and make it native-like. This awareness-raising role of the teacher in the class, coincidentally, compensates for a negative side, which is the lack of suitable materials. Tutors do not have the time, or the resources, to select spoken materials appropriate in terms of feature contrasts to enable learning in the classroom as most listening materials will be either not graded for specific learner proficiency levels or simply too difficult to extract for analysis [T1]. While some tutors are happy to teach whatever materials are provided in the syllabus, others take issue with such materials and find them concocted and in a dire need for more natural input. T2, for example, reports to the effect that sentence stress can only be discussed in relation to given scenarios rather than simply assume it falls on the last content word in an utterance, though this would be difficult to teach in class because it would be difficult to find authentic materials that show this tendency; instead, says the participant, it would be easier for a teacher to use the existing examples which simply show content words being stressed in contrast with grammatical ones.

In response to some of the challenges outlined in the interviews and observed classes, T2 prioritises a focus on a holistic discussion and assessment of his students' work on intonation in class. In the post-observation wrap-up, Participants T1 and T2, when reminded of holistic assessment, expressed the belief that this approach to students' pronunciation evaluation *as a whole* might be more helpful than assessing their intonation alone, given the difficulty of such an assessment as well as the lacking expertise of teachers. T2 said that a student whose pronunciation is clear and intelligible, by necessity, will embody the correct use of intonation as incorrect intonation will necessarily manifest itself as unintelligible or difficult to follow.

Feedback as a challenge is also raised in T3's interview. He raised the difficulty of accurately providing an accurate assessment when it is difficult to hear a learner's intonation choices. Noting it is fairly feasible for a teacher to identify a student with 'broken' intonation, the difficulty would be to pinpoint the specific nature of an intonation problem; and even if it is possible to isolate it, there will be the added difficulty of deciding how to tackle it:

"Should I explain it using terminology I am familiar with? Should I simply repeat the error so the student can understand his/her error and correct it? Should I ignore it for the sake of fluency?..." [T3]

These questions highlight the complex nature of assessing, determining, and isolating a student's 'incorrect' use of an intonation feature and how, if at all, to respond to it. This also raises the complexity behind setting lesson aims and deciding the point at which a tutor feels compelled to react to a learner's erroneous intonation. Both T3 and T4 agree that it would be more helpful to teach intonation as a response to emerging pronunciation issues rather than to dedicate a two-hour lesson on the subject as this would be both excessive and pointless. T4 also agrees that this would also help maintain and highlight the connection between pronunciation teaching and the communicative functions of language:

"…[previously, drilling students] was time-consuming and felt like it was not part of the natural English we expect students to hear and produce…but it is better when we can discuss examples from the listening and speaking materials…. to improve a student's understanding and use of English in academic settings."

Collectively, the perceived challenges go beyond those involved in the simple procedures of listening and speaking, into expertise and time constraints. Improving students' listening and speaking skills by teaching them aspects of English intonation seems to be associated with contextual constraints that require addressing, not only at the level of individual tutors, but also at the level of PSECs. Thus, collective efforts seem crucial for a smooth introduction of various intonation features into the curriculum and teaching materials. Furthermore, as frequently highlighted *and* demonstrated by the participants, a tutor's judgement is indispensable in maintaining the balance between introducing or teaching a language feature while ensuring it is not overwhelming, evidenced by the relatively 'attenuated' enthusiasm for teaching intonation in class when compared with the tutors' strong views on the subject. This variance between beliefs and practice is the result of the tension 'thread' between perceived importance and challenges. By asking to observe the participants while teaching intonation in class, it was possible to see what happens when the two ends of the tension thread meet where the participants need to translate their ideas into a less than perfect reality.

DISCUSSION

By evaluating the place of intonation in PSECs, the participants demonstrated a critical approach in which they examined the topic from various angles such as potential contribution to students' academic skills development and anticipated challenges, thus formulating recommendations to maximise the benefit. Even when their teaching practices did not consistently or completely align with these views, their rationales can be seen as cases of active and critical teaching: by accounting for various aspects involved in teaching intonation, the participants prove that they are active agents (Borg & Liu, 2012). Such an active role is best evaluated by returning to the research questions and examining the resulting analysis against the relevant literature.

- To what extent, if at all, do PSETs think of intonation as relevant to students' needs in terms of their academic speaking and listening skills?

Recognising the role of intonation on PSECs despite attributing different specific meanings to this role represents active engagement. The various meanings (e.g. discourse, attitudes, and grammar) have been discussed in the literature, and Roach (2009) and Wells (2006) contend that intonation fulfils all these functions. Another function raised by the participants is the contribution of intonation to conversation control, e.g. useful in academic debates. The literature supports this view (e.g. Brazil 1985, Winnerstrom, 2003), pedagogically demonstrated by Salter (1999). Moreover, the participants also raised the role of intonation as vital for the attainment of native-like accent; Jenkins (2004) points out that intonation needs to be taught to motivated leaners to this end. All these views show a certain level of awareness of the importance of intonation in an EAP setting and can contribute to an active engagement with any teacher training they will sit through in the future. It can also inform their teaching in cases where intonation causes intelligibility problems for some students.

- What challenges do they believe stand in the way of teaching intonation on PSECs?

The perceived and experienced challenges echo the general views expressed in the literature to the effect that intonation is a source of anxiety to many teachers. The reported lack of expertise in the field leads them to feel unsure of what and how they can broach the subject in the classroom, and this supports the findings of Couper (2017). Baker (2011), similarly, reports a lack of pronunciation training even for teachers who have had an MA in TESOL/formal ESL training. This concern raised by the participant stems, in part, from believing proper materials and support needs to be readily available for them to utilize rather than find the suitably graded materials. In relation to the observed lessons, on more than one occasion it was clear that discussing or answering questions in detail created a difficult concept checking stage or, even, skipping intonation altogether.

Some participants mentioned they tend to teach intonation as expressing a grammatical/syntactic function. A key aspect of English intonation seems to explain the reported difficulty in reconciling intonation with sentence type. Though a syntactic view is still prevalent (e.g. Halliday & Greaves, 2008), research has shown it to be flawed when applied to natural speech data (Hewings & Cauldwell, 1996). The apparent simplicity of equating intonation with syntax offers a 'comfortable' choice for many tutors to fall back on. This was seen in one of the participants' opting to discuss the grammatical role of intonation.

A third factor identified by the participants has to do more with other skills taught on PSECs, e.g. writing and reading, 'eclipsing' the role of intonation. The relegation of intonation is well-known in the literature as it is seen as too difficult to introduce in the classroom. The study findings suggest that this view is a longstanding one: Woolard (1993: 42) noted that intonation 'receive[s] little explicit focus in the classroom.'. This underprioritizing happens even within pronunciation teaching, as Dalton and Seidlhofer (1994: 76) state *'intonation is the 'problem child' of pronunciation teaching, for materials writers and teachers alike.'*

- To what extent do the PSETs' practices in relation to intonation teaching align with their views?

Despite the participants stressing its importance, some of its aspects were treated in class either lightly, dismissed altogether (e.g. issues of identity and native-speaker accent), or else left for independent, self-study practice. Couper (2017) reports that lack of knowledge and expertise in phonology, particularly in intonation, often generates a sense of uncertainty about how pronunciation should be taught. Furthermore, echoing the participants' suggestion to focus on 'unnatural' erroneous pronunciation, Couper (2017), too, reports how pronunciation teachers in general feel compelled to teach pronunciation when feeling motivated to react to student errors.

One aspect felt to be influential was an emotive one: during the observations, a lack of confidence in teaching intonation was, not only reported, but also experienced by the author, leading to some teaching being made minimal, compounded by the presence of the author as an observer. It was even strongly felt that such emotions worked as powerful motivators in ways the participants did not even explain. Such an effect is acknowledged in the literature: *Approaches to Teaching Observations* (2023) suggests the presence of an observer may deter teachers from revealing their values and beliefs.

RESEARCH LIMITATIONS AND RECOMMENDATIONS:

- Relative to the complexity of the topic and the emphasis on having it embedded in listening and speaking teaching, the observations were too short to track any serious patterns in the way the participants introduced, explained, assessed, and gave feedback, even though only one participant said he would revisit the topic in future lessons. Lectures and seminar discussions would provide ample opportunities to put questions of intonation meaning and functions into teaching practice to see how such integration approaches, if at all, could enhance intonation teaching and learning. Such an investigation will require researchers observing a significant portion of the PSE classes to explore the effect of integration though that would necessitate tutors dedicating more time and effort to teaching intonation.

- More methodological tools need to be used to capture the participants' motives and decision-making process that can be difficult to express due to feelings of e.g. embarrassment. In this study, it was particularly felt that certain emotions served as strong motives dictating way the participants taught intonation. The use of anonymous reflective accounts could be one way of documenting such emotions.

- Effective teaching and thorough research into teaching of intonation need to ensure that resources (such as teaching materials catering to the styles and approaches of various teachers, necessary IT equipment and software for e.g. the recording and analysis of output, as well as, in particular, helpful pedagogically-oriented, watered down summaries of phonological theory) are readily available so that tutors have everything they need for them to practice their judgement: researching teaching practices while ensuring that the availability of basic knowledge and tools should contribute towards thorough research into cognition.

CONCLUSION AND IMPLICATIONS

Using primary data elicited through semi-structured interviews and class observations, this study has explored PSETs' beliefs and practices in relation to intonation teaching. It is revealed that while intonation is readily recognised as very relevant to PSE courses for its linguistic insights and aiding listening and speaking, it needs to be approached in an informed fashion as its value needs to be balanced with the challenges associated with presenting it in class. Some of the challenges include a perceived lack of expertise and confidence in relation to teaching intonation, lack of resources and time to ensure the planning and preparation of appropriate teaching materials, as well as student expectations and prioritisation of the skills they would like to acquire. Such challenges may explain, to some degree, some of the variances between their views on the one hand, and their actual teaching. The mismatch seen in the case of some participants can, furthermore, be accounted for by their own understanding of students and their reality of teaching. In such a reality, teaching backgrounds (e.g. education, experience, personal development) as well as ongoing and ad-hoc thinking shape teachers' approach to, or lack thereof, intonation teaching.

The current study can be complemented by future research examining the extent to which, if at all, intonation instruction yields any measurable results in student pronunciation in ESL settings. The various debates existing around the measurable impact of instruction in intonation will be informed by such research, which can also shed some light as to how best to introduce intonation at a broader level, benefiting from an action research methodology that experiments with various teaching approaches. A top-down approach to intonation teaching and research can, initially, also be very useful in formulating a general framework for teachers to follow, such as agreeing on the intonation features needed for EAP settings, translating theory into 'student-friendly' language, a constructive guideline for assessing and providing feedback, as well as a procedure for teacher observation and evaluation. Future research can also draw a richer picture by examining student experiences and their perceptions of what counts as useful and manageable in studying intonation and trying to use it productively. The questions of whether to teach intonation, and how best to teach it, certainly benefit from examining the views and experiences of all involved stakeholders.

The current study was carried out in the UK, with international students having the opportunity for exposure to, and interaction with, native speakers. This, however, raises questions regarding any attempt to introduce intonation in other contexts where communication with native speakers may be less available (e.g. the Expanding Circle). An example of such contexts would be TNHE partnerships where students elect to complete PSE courses prior to, or alongside, university major courses. Despite the varying needs of international students who elect to pursue their graduate or postgraduate studies in the UK when compared to those who elect to pursue their studies at one of the partnership universities, many of these students will aim to improve their spoken English, and their PSE teachers will certainly find themselves encountering the same questions and issues as those found by PSETs in UK Universities. Such issues certainly highlight the need for teachers to engage with such discussions openly and to seek any training they feel they require to plan and deliver well-informed lessons. This, too, requires communication and leadership at all levels within and across university partnerships. Indeed, communication between students and tutors, tutors and material writers/syllabus designers should help streamline intonation teaching and inform teacher cognition in relation to pronunciation teaching.

REFERENCES

Approaches to Teaching Observations. (2023). *Teaching Strategies* (https://cteresources.bc.edu/documentation/teaching-observations/approaches-to-teaching-observations/) (Accessed 02 January 2004).

Baker, A., & Burri, M. (2016). Feedback on second language pronunciation: A case study of EAP teachers' beliefs and practices. *The Australian Journal of Teacher Education*, 41(6), 1–19. 10.14221/ajte.2016v41n6.1

Baker, A. A. (2011). Discourse prosody and teachers stated beliefs and practices. *TESOL Journal*, 2(3), 263–292. 10.5054/tj.2011.259955

Beaken, M. (2009). Teaching discourse intonation with Narrative. *ELT Journal*, 63(4), 342–352. 10.1093/elt/ccp002

Borg, S. (2006). *Teacher Cognition and Language Education*. Continuum.

Borg, S., & Al-Busaidi, S. (2012). Teachers' beliefs and practices regarding learner autonomy. *ELT Journal*, 66(3), 283–292. 10.1093/elt/ccr065

Bradford, B. (1988). *Intonation in Context*. Cambridge University Press.

Borg, S, & Liu, Y. (2012). Chinese College English Teachers' Research Engagement. *TESOL Quarterly*, 47(2), 270–299.

Braun, V., & Clarke, V. (2006). Using thematic analysis in psychology. *Qualitative Research in Psychology*, 3(2), 77–101. 10.1191/1478088706qp063oa

Brazil, D., Coulthard, M, & Jones, C. (1980). *Discourse Intonation and Language Teaching*. Longman.

Brazil, D. (1985). *The Communicative Value of Intonation in English*. University of Birmingham.

Brazil, D. (1994). *Pronunciation for Advanced Learners of English*. Cambridge University Press.

Brazil, D. (1997). *The Communicative Value of Intonation*. Cambridge University Press.

Cauldwell, R., & Hewings, M. (1996). Intonation rules in ELT textbooks. *ELT Journal*, 50(4), 327–334. 10.1093/elt/50.4.327

Celce-Murcia, M., Brinton, D. M., Goodwin, J. M., & Griner, B. (2010). *Teaching pronunciation: A reference for teachers of English to speakers of other languages* (2nd ed.). Cambridge University Press.

Chapman, M. (2007). Theory and Practice of Teaching Discourse Intonation. *ELT Journal*, 61(1), 3–11. 10.1093/elt/ccl039

Chun, D. (2002). *Discourse Intonation in L2: From Theory and Research to Practice*. John Benjamins.

Clennell, C. (1997). Raising the pedagogic status of discourse intonation teaching. *ELT Journal*, 51(2), 117–125. 10.1093/elt/51.2.117

Couper, G. (2017). Teacher cognition of pronunciation teaching: Teachers' concerns and issues. *TESOL Quarterly*, 51(4), 820–843. 10.1002/tesq.354

Dalton, C, & Seidlhofer, B. (1994). *Pronunciation*. Oxford University Press.

Cruttenden, A. (1997). *Intonation* (2nd ed.). Cambridge University Press.

Dornyei, Z. (2007). *Research Methods in Applied Linguistics: Quantitative, Qualitative, and Mixed Methodologies*. Oxford University Press.

Foote, J. A., Trofimovich, P., Collins, L., & Urzúa, F. S. (2016). Pronunciation teaching practices in communicative second language classes. *Language Learning Journal*, 44(2), 181–196.

Goh, C. C. M. (1994). Exploring the teaching of Discourse Intonation. *RELC Journal*, 25(1), 77–98. 10.1177/003368829402500104

Hadley, G. (1996). A Discourse Approach to Intonation: Can it Work in Japan? Available at: http://www.cels.bham.ac.uk/resources/essays/HadleyPhon.PDF (accessed 11 August 2021).

Hahn, L. D. (2004). Primary stress and intelligibility: Research to motivate the teaching of suprasegmentals. *TESOL Quarterly*, 38(2), 201–223. 10.2307/3588378

Halliday, M.K. (1967). *Intonation and Grammar in British English*. Mouton.

Halliday, M.K. (1970). *A Course in Spoken English: Intonation*. Oxford University Press.

Halliday, M.A.K., & Greaves, W.. (2008). *Intonation in the Grammar of English*. Equinox.

Henriksen, N. C., Geeslin, K. L., & Willis, E. W. (2010). The development of L2 Spanish intonation during a study abroad immersion program in Leó n, Spain: Global contours and final boundary movements. *Studies in Hispanic and Lusophone Linguistics*, 3(1), 113–162. 10.1515/shll-2010-1067

HESA. (2019). *Where do HE students come from? Higher education statistics agency.* https://www.hesa.ac.uk/data-and-analysis/students/where-from (Accessed 25 Jan 2024)

Hewings, M. (2007). *English Pronunciation in Use Advanced with Answers* (1st ed.).

Hewings, M & Thaine, C. (2012). *Cambridge Academic English C1 Advanced Student's Book: An Integrated Skills Course for EAP* (1st edn). Cambridge

International Student Statistics in UK. (2023). *Kampus Group: Best Student Consultancy in London*. https://kampus-group.com/international-student-statistics-in-uk-2023-trends-insights-and-forecasts/#:~:text=According%20to%20the%20latest%20data,of%20the%20total%20student%20population. (Accessed 25 Jan 2024)

Jenkins, J. (2000). *The Phonology of English as an International Language*. Oxford University Press.

Jenkins, J. (2004). Research in Teaching Pronunciation and Intonation. *Annual Review of Applied Linguistics*, 24, 109–125.

Jeidani, M. (2012). *Increasing Phonological Awareness: A Discourse Intonation Approach*. PhD Thesis, University of Warwick, UK.

Jeidani, M. (2014). "Discourse Intonation and Teacher Cognition" *Sino-US English Teaching*, ISSN 1539-8072, Vol. 11, No. 10.

Khaghaninejad, M. S., & Maleki, A. (2015). The effect of explicit pronunciation instruction on listening comprehension: Evidence from Iranian English learners. *Theory and Practice in Language Studies*, 5(6), 1249–1256. 10.17507/tpls.0506.18

McCarthy, M. (1991). *Discourse Analysis for Language Teachers*. Cambridge University Press.

Mora, J. C., & Levkina, M. (2017). Task-based pronunciation teaching and research: Key issues and future directions. *Studies in Second Language Acquisition*, 39(2), 381–399. 10.1017/S0272263117000183

Munro, M. J., & Derwing, T. M. (2015). A prospectus for pronunciation research in the 21st century: A point of view. *Journal of Second Language Pronunciation*, 1(1), 11–42. 10.1075/jslp.1.1.01mun

O'Connor, J. D, & Arnold, G.F. (1973). *Intonation of Colloquial English* (2nd ed.). Longman.

Pearson, W. S. (2020). Mapping English language proficiency cut-off scores and presessional EAP programmes in UK higher education. *Journal of English for Academic Purposes*, 45, 100866. Advance online publication. 10.1016/j.jeap.2020.100866

Pickering, L. (2001). The Role of Tone Choice in Improving ITA Communication in the Classroom. *TESOL Quarterly*, 35(2), 233–255. 10.2307/3587647

Pickering, L. (2004). The structure and function of intonational paragraphs in native and nonnative speaker instructional discourse. *English for Specific Purposes*, 23(1), 19–43. 10.1016/S0889-4906(03)00020-6

Roads, J. (1999). Teaching intonation: Beliefs and practices. *Speak Out*, 25, 18–25.

Roach, P. (2000). *English Phonetics and Phonology: A Practical Course*. Cambridge University Press.

Roach, P. (2001). *Phonetics*. Oxford University Press.

Roach, P. (2009). *English Phonetics and Phonology* (4th ed.). Cambridge University Press.

Saito, K., Dewaele, J.-M., & Hanzawa, K. (2017). A longitudinal investigation of the relationship between motivation and late second language speech learning in classroom settings. *Language and Speech*, 60(4), 1–19. 10.1177/0023830916687793281193135

Salter, R (1999). *Discourse Intonation in Listening Tasks with Yes/No Questions* (accessed 5 April 2018).

Setter, J., Stojanovik, V, & Martínez-Castilla, P. (2012). Evaluating the intonation of non-native speakers of English using a computerized test battery. *International Journal of Applied Linguistics*, 20(3), 368–385.

Slotte, V., & Tynjälä, P. (2003). Industry–University collaboration for continuing professional development. *Journal of Education and Work*, 16(4), 445–464. Advance online publication. 10.1080/1363908032000093058

Underhill, A. (1994). *Sound Foundations*. Heinemann.

Sugimoto, K. (2006). Australia's Transnational Higher Education in the Asia-Pacific Region: Its Strategies and Quality Assurance. In Huang, F. (Ed.), International Publication Series: Vol. 10. *Transnational Higher Education in Asia and the Pacific Region* (pp. 1–19). Research Institute for Higher Education, Hiroshima University.

United Nations Educational, Scientific and Cultural Organization Institute for Statistics. (2019) *Global-flow of tertiary-level students*. Accessed on December 12, 2021, from http://uis.unesco.org/en/uis-student-flow#slideoutmenu

Woolard, G. (1993). Intonation matters. *Modern English Teacher*, 2(2), 23–24.

Wennerstrom, A. (2003). Students as discourse analysts in the conversation class. In Burton, J., & Clennell, C. (Eds.), *Interaction and Language Learning* (pp. 161–175). TESOL Publications.

Wells, C. (2006). *English intonation: an introduction*. Cambridge University Press.

APPENDIX A

1- Please introduce yourself in terms of your academic background, teaching experience in general, and the teaching of listening and speaking on PSE courses.
2- How do you generally approach the teaching of pronunciation in your classes in terms of content and methodology of teaching?
3- Do you teach any intonation elements to your students? If so, what and how do you teach such elements?
4- What do you usually aim to achieve in teaching intonation?
5- Are there any specific challenges you face in teaching pronunciation in general and intonation in particular? If so, how do you address these?
6- What would you like to see added/changed/removed from the pronunciation component of the teaching materials in relation to intonation?
7- Please talk me through any beliefs and practices you follow when you write your own materials or seek materials, examples, and tasks from other sources for teaching intonation to your students?
8- Do you feel you need more support in order to teach intonation effectively? If so, what is the nature of such support?

APPENDIX B

Intonational features	T1	T2	T3	T4
Speech segmentation				
Stress				
Tones				

Chapter 11
Student Leaders' Motivation, Evaluation, and Suggestions in THNE Private Universities

Shi Ziyang
https://orcid.org/0009-0009-4453-7030
University of Nottingham, Ningbo, China

Yang Siyan
University of Nottingham, Ningbo, China

Hu Chenghao
University of Nottingham, Ningbo, China

ABSTRACT

In the evolving landscape of Transnational Higher Education (THEN), understanding the perspectives and insights of student leaders becomes paramount for enhancing the student leadership experience. This interview study seeks to delve into the common insights of student leaders operating within the context of THEN. Specifically, the exploration will focus on their satisfaction with leadership experiences and their motivation to gain leadership roles. Furthermore, this inquiry extends beyond mere exploration; it aspires to distill practical wisdom and guidance for aspiring student leaders who are poised to navigate the complexities of THEN.

1. INTRODUCTION

Leadership is crucial for a team to synergize and exert more strength than accumulation as individuals. As Rape (2021) noted, collaborative effort is considered the most effective approach for delivering social services. Teamwork is fundamental to the functioning of modern human society across various domains, including economics, politics, and daily life. The significance of leadership as a core competency for team leaders cannot be overstated. Whether examining historical figures or contemporary successful

DOI: 10.4018/979-8-3693-2857-6.ch011

Copyright ©2024, IGI Global. Copying or distributing in print or electronic forms without written permission of IGI Global is prohibited.

individuals, leadership emerges as a common trait. Therefore, it is necessary to cultivate leadership skills in students, particularly in the complex realm of transnational higher education.

In the context of transnational higher education, the necessity of leadership becomes even more pronounced. Students must navigate diverse cultures, languages, and perspectives within various academic assessments, clubs, organizations, and projects. For transnational higher education students, possessing effective leadership skills is essential for leading teams across cultural boundaries and coordinating members from diverse backgrounds toward shared objectives. This demands an understanding and appreciation of cross-cultural differences, as well as an inclusive and adaptable leadership style capable of accommodating individuals from varied cultural backgrounds.

An issue appears that the selection of leadership teams and the adoption of appropriate leadership styles in the background of transnational higher education present significant challenges for students. Due to the lack of experience, there's a common phenomenon that student leaders' anticipation of becoming a leader is always much higher than the outcome they get, therefore frustrating their motivations. Hence, this research chapter aims to address this critical issue through interviews, analyzing the expectations and actual experiences of research participants in leadership roles, and exploring the discrepancy between these two aspects. By referencing and reviewing relevant literature, the chapter will seek to identify potential solutions to this discrepancy and offer insights into how students can develop and refine their leadership skills in the context of transnational higher education.

2. LITERATURE REVIEW WITH BACKGROUND

2.1 Transnational Higher Education

This era is characterized by a notable surge in educational mobility on a global scale. Interactions and collaborations among educators, students, and academic institutions have intensified and become more prevalent. Educators are no longer confined to a singular campus but are engaging in teaching activities across multiple campuses, thereby offering students a broader array of educational resources and avenues for advancement. Similarly, students are no longer tethered to a single educational institution; instead, they are traveling between community colleges and universities (Seawright and Hodges, 2016), creating a dynamic educational path that provides individuals with increased options and opportunities for personal growth.

As advancements in technology continue to progress, educational modalities are evolving in tandem. Novel courses integrate online and offline components, while innovative programs transcend traditional discipline boundaries to furnish students with a more diverse and integrated learning experience. Globally, a substantial number of students are traversing national borders in pursuit of advanced degrees, and educators are crossing nations to impart knowledge and guidance to students from diverse backgrounds. Such cross-border and cross-cultural academic exchanges establish a broader platform for the dissemination and exchange of knowledge.

The accelerating pace of globalization has generated a distinct shift towards internationalization within the realm of higher education, with an increasing number of universities embracing transnational curricula and partnerships. This trend attracts students and faculty from every corner of the globe, equipping graduates with the skills needed to excel in a globalized economy. Transnational collaborations not only facilitate the sharing of educational resources across different nations and regions but also furnish students with a wider range of employment opportunities and avenues for personal development. The trend of academic mobility has given rise to a myriad of transnational higher education institutions worldwide, fostering diversity and inclusivity that bring forth new dynamics and opportunities for the enhancement of the global educational landscape.

According to Wildavsky (2010), the substantial growth and maturation of the global education market are evidenced by statistics reflecting an 85% increase in the number of students traveling abroad for further education between 2000 and 2009. Current estimates indicate that 3.7 million international students are enrolled in universities across the globe, underscoring the significance of international higher education as a crucial trend in the global educational sphere (Wildavsky, 2010). Notably, as of 2012, the presence of over 200 operational branches of international campuses, as suggested by Lawton and Katsomitros (2012), provides students with a culturally diverse and globally oriented learning environment, presenting a wider array of opportunities and challenges for their academic and professional growth. Traditional international higher education transcends mere study experiences abroad, serving as a vital channel for fostering cultural exchange, broadening horizons, and nurturing global awareness. Transnational higher education takes this a step further by emphasizing the cross-border mobility and globalization of educational pursuits. This educational modality not only expands the choices and opportunities available to students in their home countries but also fosters increased international cooperation and exchange within educational institutions.

In conclusion, the emergence of transnational higher education is driven by a confluence of factors, including the strengthening of institutions' international competitiveness, the attraction of foreign students and investments, and the promotion of cross-cultural interactions. As globalization continues its onward pace, the trend of transnational higher education is increasingly conspicuous within the landscape of international higher education development. The mobility of students and educators across borders has generated a myriad of choices and growth opportunities within the educational domain, fostering cultural exchanges and the cultivation of global awareness. This trend not only expands students' learning and career prospects but also infuses fresh vitality and opportunities into the educational enterprise. With ongoing innovations in educational methodologies and program settings, transnational higher education is further promoting the advancement of the higher education sector, infusing it with renewed vigor and innovation within the global educational sphere.

2.2 Leadership and Teamwork

Gill (2012) noted that through a thorough examination of leadership literature, Bruce Winston and his research team developed a comprehensive definition of a leader: an individual who engages in the selection, preparation, training, and influence of one or more followers possessing a diverse range of talents, abilities, and skills. The leader's primary objective is to direct the focus of the followers toward the organization's mission and objectives in a manner that inspires them to voluntarily and enthusiastically make mental, emotional, and physical contributions toward the achievement of the organization's goals.

Nevertheless, leadership is a multidimensional concept that is interpreted differently across various leadership styles, leading to diverse perspectives among scholars regarding its conceptualization and definition. Burns (1978) proposed that leadership should be understood as a transformative process where leaders and group members mutually inspire each other to endeavor for positive changes. This transformative leadership theory gained increasing recognition during that period. The core of transformational leadership is comprised of four essential components. Firstly, idealized influence requires the leader to foster a sense of unity among group members, manifesting qualities that earn respect and trust. Secondly, fostering team dynamics involves setting high expectations for members, exhibiting confidence in achieving shared objectives, and nurturing team spirit. Inspirational motivation, the third element, focuses on stimulating group members' creativity, innovation, and problem-solving abilities. Lastly, personalized care emphasizes the leader's attentive consideration of individual needs, the cultivation of a supportive team environment, and the facilitation of open communication between leaders and members (Christine, Harold, Ana, and Susanne, 2022).

Studies have demonstrated that transformational leadership yields several positive outcomes for group members. These benefits include heightened satisfaction, strengthened alignment with common goals and values, cultivation of emotional well-being such as optimism, promotion of a sense of responsibility, increased engagement, enhanced teamwork, elevated job performance, boosted intrinsic motivation, reduced stress levels, and stimulation of creativity (Bass and Riggio, 2006; Northouse, 2021). These research findings underscore the significance of transformational leadership as an effective model for both individual and team development.

Whereas Tourish (2013) provides a cautious perspective on the concept of transformational leadership, emphasizing the necessity to avoid oversimplification. While transformational leadership is often lauded for its ability to inspire and motivate followers toward a shared prospect, Tourish (2013) warns of potential pitfalls that can arise if not implemented carefully. One probable concern is the risk of diminishing autonomy among group members, as the influence of a transformational leader may inadvertently suppress individual voices and contributions. Moreover, the concentration of authority in the hands of the leader can lead to excessive centralization, creating a power dynamic that may be prone to abuse. These challenges can be manifested in various forms, including the erosion of trust within the group, the stifling of creativity and innovation, and the emergence of internal conflicts stemming from imbalances in power. Such negative consequences can ultimately undermine the effectiveness of the leadership approach and impede the group's progress toward its goals.

To address these issues, one alternative approach is the adoption of servant leadership. In contrast to the hierarchical and directive nature of transformational leadership, servant leadership emphasizes the well-being and development of individual group members. By prioritizing the needs and interests of followers, a servant leader aims to create a supportive and empowering environment that fosters collaboration, trust, and mutual respect. Through the practice of servant leadership, leaders can cultivate a culture of empathy, humility, and inclusivity within the group, thereby promoting a sense of ownership and accountability among members. By decentralizing decision-making processes and empowering individuals to take initiative, servant leadership enables a more distributed and participatory approach to leadership that can lead to enhanced engagement, motivation, and satisfaction among group members. Ultimately, the adoption of servant leadership principles offers a potential remedy to the challenges associated with transformational leadership, promoting a more balanced and sustainable leadership model that prioritizes the well-being and growth of all individuals within the group.

Additionally, Christine et al. (2022) advocate for a novel collaborative leadership approach informed by insights from transformational leadership theory and contributions from other scholars. This model fosters mutual collaboration between leaders and team members, promotes bidirectional communication, facilitates shared leadership responsibilities, emphasizes power distribution based on expertise and individual competencies, encourages synergistic decision-making processes, and supports comprehensive team development to efficiently achieve shared objectives.

Overall, various factors including team goals, team structure, and member compositions influence the complexity of selecting appropriate leadership styles. Leaders cannot escape from the critical decision-making point in choosing a leadership approach that aligns with the specific context, promoting the team's collective strengths and ensuring sustained team effectiveness in the long term.

2.3 Leadership in Transnational Higher Education

Leadership has emerged as a fundamental quality for students engaged in transnational higher education. Within the realm of transnational higher education, students are required to possess the capacity to engage in cross-cultural communication and collaboration to effectively navigate diverse learning environments and educational modalities across various countries and regions. Leadership assumes a critical role in the domain of transnational higher education, not only in individual leadership competencies but also in the context of students' capability of adapting and evolving within multicultural environments. In such a situation, students need to exhibit excellent leadership competencies to distinguish themselves in the fiercely competitive international landscape.

Primarily, students in the sphere of transnational higher education must exhibit experienced intercultural communication skills. Interacting with peers and educators from diverse cultural backgrounds is a common occurrence for students studying in transnational higher education institutions. Proficiency in communicating and collaborating effectively with individuals from various cultures is a fundamental trait of a competent leader. Based on possessing intercultural communication skills, students can smoothly assimilate into the transnational higher education modality and effectively exhibit their leadership capabilities. Additionally, students in transnational higher education must possess robust teamwork skills. Within the context of transnational education modality, students frequently collaborate with peers from different nationalities and cultural backgrounds to accomplish diverse tasks and projects. As leaders, students must demonstrate the ability to efficiently coordinate team members, enhance individual strengths, and attain collective objectives. Beyond academic requirements, students in transnational higher education are presented with ample opportunities to cultivate their leadership abilities, including participation in student-led clubs, organizations, or university-led research projects. It is significant for students to distinguish suitable opportunities to avoid discrepancies between anticipations and acquired experience. Simultaneously, students must actively seize these opportunities, take responsibility for leadership, and overcome various challenges to ensure team sustainability.

A student's willingness to take a leadership position is also important. According to Dugan, Garland, Jacoby, and Gasiorski (2008), leadership self-efficacy, their 'internal beliefs regarding their ability to engage in the process leadership successfully' has received increasing attention as a factor in students' development as leaders. Apart from self-efficacy, motivation and anticipation are also essential areas that contribute to students' willingness to become a leader. Hannah and Avolio (2010) specified motivation to develop leadership as a primary component of one's readiness to take advantage of developmental opportunities and ultimately grow as a leader. Chan and Drasgow (2001) divided leader motivation into two parts, the 'intensity of effort at leading' and 'persistence' to which a person engages in a leadership action. There are two significant domains within the construct of leadership motivation. The first domain is "affective identity" (AI) motivation to lead, students' attractiveness to a vision of themselves occupying leadership roles in the groups to which they belong. The second, "social normative" (SN) motivation to lead, is more externally motivated and based on students' sense of duty or obligation to the group (Chan & Drasgow, 2001). According to results suggested by Rosch, Collier, and Thompson (2015), students' internal self-identity as a leader positively predicted behavior, while their 'social normative' motivation to lead (i.e. stemming from the groups to which they belong) served as a negative predictor. A strong sense of internal self-identity is capable of rendering students leaders who are more likely to exhibit proactive leadership behaviors such as taking initiative, inspiring others, and demonstrating confidence in decision-making. They may actively seek out leadership opportunities, engage in team-building activities, and demonstrate a willingness to lead by example. Conversely, students whose motivation to lead is primarily driven by external factors, such as group expectations or obligations, may exhibit reluctance or hesitation in leadership roles. They may feel pressured to conform to group norms rather than act authentically as a leader, leading to potential challenges in decision-making, team collaboration, and overall leadership effectiveness.

Nonetheless, while there exists a considerable amount of research about the international higher education realm, studies specifically focusing on the transnational higher education sphere remain relatively limited (Morris and Li, 2023). Moreover, research exploring student leadership within the context of transnational higher education is notably scarce, leaving many students to lack targeted guidance. Hence, this chapter assumes significance in helping students engaged in transnational higher education to enhance their leadership proficiencies.

3. METHODOLOGY

3.1 Research Purpose

The purpose of this research is to investigate whether college students with transnational backgrounds and the actual outcome of their leadership experience match their anticipation and motivation before they become leaders, as well as to unravel the commonalities and distinctions in their leadership roles. It is also hoped that the advice given by participants will provide useful reminders to potential student leaders as reflection is a helpful practice in improving current and future practice.

3.2 Research Questions

This study intends to answer three research questions:

RQ1. What motivates undergraduate students with a transnational background to seek a leadership opportunity?

RQ2. How do student leaders evaluate their leadership experience?

RQ3. What suggestions would you give to those college students who hesitate to become a leader?

3.3 Research Context and Participants

The research place in this paper is a transnational private university located in Southeastern China. The case study institution has enrolled hundreds of international students in the post-pandemic era, along with its high proportion of expatriate teachers, providing a transnational background for students to enhance intercultural communication abilities. It is referred to as University N for confidentiality purposes.

The participants of this study all experienced at least one year of leadership experience during their undergraduate study. The first participant referred to as RP1, is a second-year student hailing from China and possessing a Gao Kao educational background. From June 2019 to June 2020, she led the largest environmental volunteer organization in her high school. Currently, she is the founder and leader of a psychological project team, leading a team comprising 16 individuals. The second participant referred to as RP2, is a student of Chinese nationality with an A-level educational background. His prior role is as the leader of the school Debating Union. He managed a team of 30-35 individuals, directly overseeing and guiding each team member. The third participant, referred to as RP3, is a student from China with a Gao Kao background, who served as the president of the University N badminton club from May 2022 to July 2023. His leadership experience is marked by a focus on sports and club management. He led a larger team of around 40-50 members. The details of their personal information are listed in Table 1.

Table 1. Demographic information of the participants

Participant	Gender	Grade	Background	The number of people leading the team
Participant 1	Female	Year 2	Gaokao	16
Participant 2	Male	Year 3	A level	30-35
Participant 3	Male	Year 3	Gaokao	40-50

All participants were selected on a purposive premise as advocated by Creswell and Creswell (2018), with individual selection on the premise that all can provide insights that can fit with research purposes, which is to investigate the relation between motivation, anticipation, and actual outcome.

3.4 Research Methods

This research uses an exploratory method since it enlightens in discovering factors that affect an individual's degree of satisfaction about their leadership experience (Morris and Mo, 2023). The advantages of this approach are that it enables readers to gain a deeper understanding of the phenomena from a peer perspective and enhances readers' readability, as Duff (2007) highlights. One additional benefit according to Dörnyei (2007) is that all researchers can interact with insights as they are informed from an insider's perspective. This research consisted of three case studies. Semi-structured interviews have been utilized to collect the information. The advantage of this research is flexibility, as the interviewer can make necessary adjustments based on the actual responses during the interview.

3.5 Data Collection and Analysis

The data collection phase in this research was carried out face-to-face during the spring of 2024 and consisted of three separate, less-than-one-hour interview sessions with each participant. The recordings were then transcribed, and the data was coded after a period of familiarization. This is an approach advocated by Caulfield (2019). During this process, a dual inductive and deductive approach was utilized. It should be mentioned that to gain a deeper understanding of the interviewer's thoughts, the interviews were conducted in the interviewee's native Chinese, and subsequently translated into English.

3.6 Research Ethics

Throughout the study, strict adherence to ethical guidelines was complied with. The British Educational Research Association's ethical standards (2018) were followed, as well as compliance with the Data Protection Act (2018) to protect the privacy rights of the participants. Institutional ethical norms such as anonymity, confidentiality, and informed consent were also stringently upheld throughout the whole research process,

4. RESULTS

For students, transnational higher education leadership often confronts a plethora of challenges. These challenges include navigating conflicts arising from disparate cultural norms and customs. In comparison to traditional Chinese universities, they are tasked with leading a cohort of individuals who possess distinct ideas, objectives, and personalities. If we can gain a deeper understanding of leaders emerging from such challenging backgrounds, it would greatly aid our exploration of leadership.

It has been observed that students who assume leadership roles often exhibit a heightened desire for control, such as RP1 and RP3.

> I am eager for power and enjoy the freedom that comes with having decision-making authority. I am an ENTJ personality, which means I am usually happy to lead others. I enjoy the feeling of becoming a leader and want to have decisive power which determines the outcome of the club's daily affairs.

People with this kind of personality often have higher and more practical expectations for leadership experience in advance based on metrics. As RP3 said:

> I will meet many freshmen since adding my WeChat friend is the only way to join the club, besides, as the organizer of the sports events opening for whole students and teachers in school, more and more people will be familiar with my name. Besides, I will have more opportunities to apply for an award. The university sports department will hold sports awards nominations annually, and there are two categories, the president of a sports club and the sports club itself. Moreover, it is an important experience that I can add to my CV. It can be beneficial when I apply for postgraduate study or a job.

However, not all TNHE leaders fit into this mold; there are also those with more ambivalent dispositions, disinclined to assume excessive responsibility. Individuals such as RP2 with atypical leadership traits often approach leadership with a focus on self-improvement.

> I am an introvert, sensitive, and somehow fragile person. Those qualities diverge a lot from traditional masculine leadership roles; however, it does not mean I am incapable of delivering 'good' things. But there are some characteristics that 'being a leader' would bring you. Being communicable, positive, confident, cautious in making decisions, and courageous are not inherent characteristics, but the qualities we will acquire in our socializing. Meanwhile, from this experience, I have discovered the nature of society more profoundly, especially the attitude towards society and human nature.

Regardless of their disposition, these individuals often harbor idealistic goals to support themselves and their teams in progressing forward. As RP1 said:

> My experience of being sidelined from school due to bipolar and anxiety disorders in high school led me to start a psychology-related program in college in hopes of providing support and opportunities for people like me.

As for the challenges, they can be primarily categorized into four domains: incongruence with superiors' decision-making, difficulties in guiding and managing subordinates, competition among peers, and strategies for better serving target demographics.

Being a leader will inevitably lead to ideas conflicting and clinging to one's judgment in some situations, such as RP1 mentioned:

> Our personality differences have led to misunderstandings and dissatisfaction, especially when it comes to impatience with the superior's decisions and mistakes. Additionally, conflicts with the superior on the project direction have sparked discussions and debates. I feel uncomfortable, particularly when I perceive the superior's insufficient understanding of my project and excessive interference.

Compared with conflicts with superiors, conflicts with subordinates are often more common and obvious, as RP2 complained.

> Two of the executives are older than me, which means it is difficult to let them agree with my decision. If I want to make an important decision, I must discuss it with them first. Their attitudes are not so good, if they think this matter is none of their business, they just ignore my message and don't make any response. If they put any objections, then I need to make a slight revision of my decision and put the revised version back into discussion again. It makes me feel like I am working for them, as an employee instead of a leader. As I mentioned before, I adopted a tolerant policy for those retired executives or those unsuccessful in the election. They can still join my team (to be a normal secretary) without being interviewed and enjoy the privileges. However, they just want to get those privileges, forgetting all the responsibilities they took. It is not just a single phenomenon, almost 15 out of 35 people don't work well.

When it comes to the challenges brought by serving groups, both RP1 and RP3 emphasized the need to think about the users' perspectives and areas that can be improved when facing target users. As RP1 mentioned:

Faced with target users, I need to contemplate their core pain points and areas where I can make improvements. Additionally, I must consider the crucial factors influencing their decisions, such as pricing, time, location, and theme. After understanding these aspects, I need to strike a balance between their expectations and my interests, opting for a compromise. During peak user periods, I have to create allure, maintain user retention, and establish profound trust. Key to this is understanding why users trust our brand and choose us over other similar activities.

RP3 also mentioned several crises:

There are several challenges when I deal with serving groups. First are the changes in the due competition date. I have changed the due competition date three times, first because of my mistake (the lack of communication between my superior and me). I sent an email to all participants and apologized sincerely, and also told them the competition would be postponed to next week. And I promise I will compensate activity credits if they cannot join the competition next week. I passed this crisis successfully. The second time because of the pandemic, the whole school was isolated and the competition was forced to postpone. Because such an event is not my fault, and everyone just accepts it. The third time is to change the date of the semifinal competition. Because some of the participants have emergent things to do (they are members of the school Excel and they are informed that there is a competition outside the campus). Therefore, I tried to change the due semifinal competition date to make those Excel members available to take my competition. However, this changing behavior was criticized by other competitors, they thought I was not fair and had a consciousness of partiality for those excellent members. I was being condemned at that time. Under the pressure, I withdraw my decision. That means the competition date remains as the original one.

Challenges and opportunities invariably coexist. Through navigating these challenges, individuals often undergo personal growth, serving as a source of satisfaction derived from their leadership experiences. RP1 mentioned that:

As a leader, I find that the benefits compared to being an ordinary team member lie in a deeper and more involved commitment, especially in contributing more to projects, leading to increased personal growth and rewards. However, being a leader also entails greater pressure and responsibility, necessitating a focus on the overall development and atmosphere of the team. Facing challenges in this role requires enduring higher stress levels, maintaining emotional stability, and enhancing the ability to handle urgent situations.

However, they may not always be optimistic in every situation. RP3 added that experience is also discontent, particularly amidst periods of academic and employment pressure, prompting questioning of the efficacy of their leadership roles.

Coordination among teammates and other involved personnel, referring not only to administrative coordination to accomplish tasks but also inter-personal relations on a social level with other members; stress and time management, how to balance work, study, and leisure, in case of getting myself overwhelmed; creating norms and culture for the community, about how to utilize the agency of members and motivate them to be voluntarily cooperative.

In this chapter, there is a desire to encourage more students from transnational higher education backgrounds to endeavor to assume leadership roles. During interviews, respondents were asked to provide suggestions, with these highlighted as pivotal aspects. RP1 suggested that:

> To excel as a leader, I emphasize industry foresight, effective team management, skillful communication, and emotional stability. Don't worry too much about the result when dealing with people-related matters, while focusing on peace of mind, acceptance of results, and a clear conscience.

RP2 suggested that:

> The most important thing I learned is not to try to make friends with your colleagues. In teamwork, your empathy shall not be unconditional. A rational bureaucracy is crucial for a well-functioned human organization. Objective measurements under consensus must be adopted to achieve cooperation.

RP3 gave three advice:

> Firstly, do not take multiple leadership positions simultaneously if you are not a very outgoing person. I used to consider myself an outgoing person and always happy to leader, but the experience proved that I'm not so happy with social connections, especially with strangers.
>
> Secondly, don't be too strict or too kind to your subordinates. Being too strict would incur resentment towards you, and being too kind would damage your authority and the unity of a team. Try to find a balance between strict and kind, while treating everyone fairly. Remember members or normal secretaries of a student club don't have any obligations to work for you or attend your activities, the key thing is to stimulate their interests.
>
> Thirdly, Find a leadership position which suitable for you. If you are not able to lead more than 10 people, it is better to be an executive rather than a president. The supreme leader of a club usually takes as much pressure as the fame they enjoy.

5. DISCUSSION

The samples and suggestions provided by RP1, RP2, and RP3 will resonate with many student leaders across majors because they strike a chord and are underpinned by humanistic values. Their evaluation of leadership experience can be analyzed through the lenses of anticipation, motivation, challenges, and real outcomes they get. After evaluation, they all put forward useful advice to potential student leaders.

5.1 Anticipation and Motivation

Leadership motivation is diverse. Regarding the motivations that drive an undergraduate student to seek a leadership opportunity, two participants (RP1 and RP3) were motivated by their internal self-identity as a leader, while another participant (RP2) was motivated by a sense of belonging and responsibility from his group. This result followed the prediction of Rosch, Collier, and Thompson (2015), who suggested that students' internal self-identity as a leader would influence students' behavior more apparently than 'socially normative' features. RP1 mentioned her determination to support other students who have similar experiences as her, RP3 emphasized the prestige he would enjoy among his friends after he became the president of the club. Both are attracted by a vision of and for themselves occupying leadership roles in the groups to which they belong (Chan and Drasgow, 2001). RP2 stressed a sense of responsibility which drove him to undertake heavy tasks. His behavior originated from his sense of duty or obligation to the community (Chan and Drasgow, 2001).

The personal character of student leaders is also diversifying. Both RP1 and RP3 are ENTJ personalities, which means they are usually happy to lead others, while RP2 is quite introverted and not always happy to interact with peers, but they all eventually become relatively well-regarded leaders. As the research of Arvey et.al (2007) suggested, approximately 30 percent of leadership role occupancy is due to genetics, and 70 percent is developed. That means almost everyone can become a leader through preparation and practice. As the interview results showed, all the participants had put significant effort into establishing their leadership image and preparing for their leadership roles.

As for the original anticipation, all participants expressed their willingness to take advantage of developmental opportunities (Hannah and Avolio, 2010), although they did not know what they would get. RP3's expectations were relatively high, including getting to know more people, more opportunities to apply for an award, and adding something to write in his CV (curriculum vitae). Overall, since it is the first time for all participants to serve as leaders with heavy daily affairs, their anticipation is varied and views mixed. They are not able to predict what will happen before they truly become a leader.

5.2 Challenges and Evaluation

The traditional challenges that student leaders face are nothing more than conflict between academic pursuits and leadership roles and a lack of teamwork (Murage, Njoka, and Gachahi, 2019). However, three participants specified the difficulties of teamwork from novel perspectives. They divided challenges into three parts: problems with superiors, subordinates, and serving groups. Problems with superiors related to resource favoritism, misunderstanding, and lack of communication. Problems with subordinates became tricky when subordinates disagreed on the direction of the project or were unwilling to devote sufficient time. Problems with the serving group occurred when the targeted group was unsatisfied with the service or products provided by participants.

Each problem could become severe if it was not addressed properly. However, in the cases provided by RP2 and RP3, they adopted different methods to solve the problems they faced. When facing an excessive workload brought on by the resignation of the vice president of the debating Union, RP2 preferred to take on the tasks by himself, despite it making him completely lose his leisure time and unable to take care of his academic studies. When facing criticism because of the change of competition date, RP3 yielded to the perceived pressure and withdrew the decision to change of competition date. This crisis damaged RP3's external image and recognition seriously, while also weakening his enthusiasm for continuing to lead the club.

Some unexpected and instant challenges cannot be addressed without any negative consequences. Regarding long-term challenges such as incompatible ideas with superiors, loss of devotion of subordinates, and difficulties communicating with international students, these can only be solved slowly and over time with persistence. In most cases, participants simply adopted a procrastination strategy, they just neglected the negative relations with superiors or subordinates and moved on. A sense of helplessness and powerlessness is reflected in the participants' evaluation.

As for the outcome of their leadership experience, there are both gains and losses. RP2 mentioned he successfully empowered other people to participate in this activity, but his occupation of daily affairs distracted him from self-realization in other areas including academic performance, health, and intimate relationships. RP3 believed that the overall outcome was still far from his expectations and anticipation since he expected to form a cohesive group, in which the executives and members could work together to bring out the best in the club to the whole school. However, the relations between executives, members, and RP3 were indifferent and distant, they communicated with each other only when there was something to do. Besides, RP3 did not get any award which made him a bit upset.

Even though the practical gain is sometimes subtle, the psychological gain is invaluable. All participants acknowledged that they experienced psychological development during the year they served as a leader. As for RP3, he was a positivist before he became the president, believing that his colleagues would work together to make the club much better, but later he found that people do not usually share the same goal or evaluate the importance of a goal similarly. This experience gave him a more profound perspective when looking into human nature and mechanism of the society. For RP1, she learned to pay more attention to peace of mind when dealing with challenging things, accepting the results, and emphasizing a clear conscience. Overall, life and work are not always smooth sailing, and there may not be a perfect solution to the problems encountered. While recognizing the inevitability of this, all participants gained personal growth.

All participants' evaluation of their leadership experience is also quite complex. Their collective judgment is growing up in painful experience. They all mentioned that there are several tough moments, and they all admitted that experiencing hardships, challenges, or emotional distress can contribute to development and inner strength enhancement. To elaborate on the growth of problem-solving abilities and stress tolerance, RP1 stated that when confronted with difficult circumstances, whether physical, emotional, or psychological, individuals are forced to tap into their inner reserves and develop coping mechanisms.

5.3 Suggestions

Finally, each participant gave very valuable advice, which provided targeted and practical instructions to help students who may become leaders in TNHE institutions.

Thinking ahead to train your successors: training the successor in advance allows for a smoother transition of leadership which ensures that there is someone ready and capable to take over when you stand down. Besides, by training a successor, you can actively transfer this knowledge, ensuring that important information and skills are not lost when the leader departs. Moreover, training successors involves identifying and developing talented individuals within the organization. This process allows potential leaders to gain exposure to different aspects of the business, hone their skills, and be prepared for the challenges of leadership roles. As RP1 stated, the emphasis is on screening rather than cultivation.

Choose the proper type of leadership: Choosing the proper type of leadership is crucial for students as it can significantly impact their personal development, academic success, and future career prospects. As RP 3 mentioned, if you are not able to lead more than 10 people, it is better to be an executive rather than a president of university clubs. The leader of a club usually takes as much pressure as the fame they enjoy. On the other side, if you think you are capable of communication and collaboration, then joining a committee or taking a high-level leadership position is useful, as Devraj et.al. (2023) suggested, 'you will look at the bigger picture even more because you're with associates and colleagues'.

Be careful with friends as your subordinates (only in some circumstances): Leaders are responsible for making objective and unbiased decisions that are in the best interest of the organization. Establishing and maintaining professional boundaries helps ensure that these decisions are not influenced by personal relationships. RP2 also mentioned that the most important thing he learned is not to try to make friends with subordinates. In teamwork, your empathy shall not be unconditional. RP 3 said that being too kind would damage your authority and the unity of a team.

Maintain emotional calm when making decisions: RP1 mentioned that it is important to maintain emotional stability since emotional decision-making will affect the mutual trust and atmosphere within the team. Emotional stability enables clearer thinking and better judgment. When emotions are in check, individuals can more objectively assess situations, weigh pros and cons, and make decisions based on rational considerations rather than impulsive reactions.

6. CONCLUSION

In the evolving landscape of Transnational Higher Education (TNHE), understanding the perspectives and insights of student leaders becomes paramount for enhancing the student leadership experience. This research seeks to delve into the common insights of student leaders operating within the context of TNHE. Specifically, the exploration focused on satisfaction with leadership experiences and the motivation to gain leadership roles. Furthermore, this inquiry extends beyond mere exploration; it aspires to distill practical wisdom and guidance for aspiring student leaders who are poised to navigate the complexities of TNHE leadership.

For further research in the future, considerable subjects are worthy of exploration in depth regarding leadership within transnational higher education. Simultaneously, there exist various avenues of research that can be applied to optimize the research methodology. Apart from the motivations of student leaders and the discrepancy between anticipated outcomes and actual achievements as targeted in this research, a comprehensive investigation into the leadership modality and challenges faced by student leaders across diverse cultures is feasible as well, which involves categorizing these modalities based on specific circumstances, assessing their alignment with respective environments, and proposing viable optimization strategies.

Moreover, within the current globalized landscape, a thorough analysis of how diverse cultural backgrounds influence the cognitive patterns and values of student leaders and contributes to enhancing their cross-cultural leadership competency could also be explored. Further study into the developmental process of distinguished student leaders within transnational higher education institutions will facilitate a deeper understanding and synthesis of the pivotal success factors in their leadership roles. These research insights will furnish more precise guidance and recommendations for the cultivation of future student leaders.

Regarding the research methodology, the limited participant pool in this study may introduce the interference of contingency. Thus, expanding the participant base emerges as a crucial enhancement for conducting more comprehensive research in the future. By ensuring inter-individual diversity and increasing the number of participants, the research's scope can be broadened effectively through the utilization of surveys and statistical analyses to obtain a holistic comprehension of the leadership motivations and satisfaction levels of student leaders within the transnational higher education realm. Furthermore, extending the study to encompass educators within transnational higher education institutions can demonstrate their leadership in administrative realms and evaluate their impact on educational modality, contributing to further investigation of the connection between institutional leadership and student leadership.

Ultimately, it is anticipated that this research chapter can serve as an illuminating catalyst, stimulating further exploration and reflection on leadership and the domain of transnational higher education. Through sustained research endeavors and efforts and involving students in studies, future researchers are also trained. There exists a continuous opportunity to promote professional educational awareness, facilitating innovation and progression within the educational sphere. With harmonious collaboration, substantial contributions can be collectively made to nurturing the new generation of student leaders, educators, and researchers, thereby fostering the sustainable advancement of education.

REFERENCES

Arvey, R. D., Zhang, Z., Avolio, B. J., & Krueger, R. F. (2007). Developmental and genetic determinants of leadership role occupancy among women. *The Journal of Applied Psychology*, 92(3), 693–706. 10.1037/0021-9010.92.3.69317484551

Bass, B. M., & Riggio, R. E. (2006). *Transformational Leadership* (2nd ed.). Lawrence Erlbaum Associates. 10.4324/9781410617095

British Educational Research Association. (2018). Ethical Guidelines for Educational Research. Available at: https://www.bera.ac.uk/publication/ethical-guidelines-for-educational-research-2018

Burns, J. M. (1978). *Leadership*. Harper and Row.

Caulfield, J. (2019). How to Do Thematic Analysis. Available at: https://www.scribbr.com/methodology/thematic-analysis/

Chan, K. Y., & Drasgow, F. (2001). Toward a theory of individual differences and leadership: Understanding the motivation to lead. *The Journal of Applied Psychology*, 86(3), 481–498. 10.1037/0021-9010.86.3.48111419808

Christine, S., Harold, M., Ana, R., & Susanne, J. (2022). The LIFE program – University students learning leadership and teamwork through service learning in El Salvador. [online]. *Intercultural Education*, 33(4), 470–483. https://appgateway.nottingham.edu.cn/https/77726476706e69737468656265737421e7e056d133316654780787a0915b26781c4501d1e52ab258923b99e4071c6d2891bcaccb014587a0110a4decc2/doi/full/10.1080/14675986.2022.2090689. 10.1080/14675986.2022.2090689

Creswell, J. W., & Creswell, J. D. (2023). *Research design : qualitative, quantitative, and mixed methods approaches* (6th ed.). SAGE.

Devraj, R., Castleberry, A. N., Alvarez, N. A., Persky, A. M., and Poirier, T. I. (2023). Pharmacy Leaders' Advice to Students Pursuing Leadership: A Qualitative Study. *Innovations in Pharmacy*, 14(3), 10-. Available at: https://doi.org/10.24926/iip.v14i3.5528

Dörnyei, Z. (2007). *Research methods in applied linguistics*. Oxford University Press.

Duff, P. (2018). *Case study research in applied linguistics*. Routledge. 10.4324/9780203827147

Dugan, J. P., Garland, J. L., Jacoby, B., & Gasiorski, A. (2008). Understanding commuter student self-efficacy for leadership: A within-group analysis. *NASPA Journal*, 45(2), 282–310. 10.2202/1949-6605.1951

Gill, R. (2012). *Theory and Practice of Leadership* [online]. SAGE Publications., Available at https://appgateway.nottingham.edu.cn/https/77726476706e69737468656265737421f5f54e932c336d5e6a1a88a0d645313a98a42f1fdc31dea63b/lib/nottingham/reader.action?docID=7102286&query=Leadership%3A+Theory+and+Practice

Hannah, S. T., & Avolio, B. J. (2010). Ready or not: How do we accelerate the developmental readiness of leaders? *Journal of Organizational Behavior*, 31(8), 1181–1187. 10.1002/job.675

Lawton, W., & Katsomitros, A. (2012). International branch campuses: Data and developments. *The Observatory on Borderless Higher Education*, 12.

Morris, G., & Li, L. (2023). *Handbook of Research on Developments and Future Trends in Transnational Higher Education* [online]. IGI Global., Available at https://www-iresearchbook-cn.ezproxy.nottingham.edu.cn/f/cdf/read?bookId=7fbf6b3b3d394267aeb4e2d383ec890c&cdf=/202302131644093911/7fbf6b3b3d394267aeb4e2d383ec890c.cdf&range=52&type=1&TRI=110.4018/978-1-6684-5226-4

Morris, G., & Mo, J. (2023). Exploring the Employment Motivation, Job Satisfaction and Dissatisfaction of University English Instructors: A Chinese Case Study Analysis. *Humanities & Social Sciences Communications*, 2023(10), 717. 10.1057/s41599-023-02228-2

Murage, L. M., Njoka, J., & Gachahi, M. (2019). Challenges Faced by Student Leaders in Managing Student Affairs in Public Universities in Kenya. *International Journal of Education and Literacy Studies*, 7(1), 1–7. 10.7575/aiac.ijels.v.7n.1p.1

Northouse, P. G. (2021). *Leadership: Theory and Practice* (9th ed.). Sage.

Rape, T. (2021). Teamwork in social work: What are we actually talking about? [online]. *European Journal of Social Work*, 25(4), 668–680. 10.1080/13691457.2021.1995704

Rosch, D. M., Collier, D., & Thompson, S. E. (2015). An exploration of students' motivation to lead: An analysis by race, gender, and student leadership behaviors. *Journal of College Student Development*, 56(3), 286–291. 10.1353/csd.2015.0031

Seawright, L., & Hodges, A. (2016). *Learning Across Borders: Perspectives on International and Transnational Higher Education* [online]. Cambridge Scholars Publishing.

Tourish, D. (2013). *The Dark Side of Transformational Leadership: A Critical Perspective*. Routledge. 10.4324/9780203558119

Wildavsky, B. (2010). *The Great Brain Race: How Global Universities Are Reshaping the World*. Princeton University Press.

Chapter 12
Exploring the Students' Perception of Online Speaking Classes and Various Functions of Online Learning Platforms

Ying You
Suzhou Wuzhong District Yi Jian He Experimental Primary School, China

Bin Zou
 https://orcid.org/0000-0002-4863-0998
Xi'an Jiaotong-Liverpool University, China

Chenghao Wang
 https://orcid.org/0009-0009-5655-3740
Xi'an Jiaotong-Liverpool University, China

ABSTRACT

This study explores student perceptions of synchronous online oral English classes, focusing on how the functionalities of digital platforms influence their language anxiety and the development of speaking skills. To gather both quantitative and qualitative insights, the study employs questionnaires and semi-structured interviews, involving 91 higher education students from various majors, all of whom have experienced synchronous online oral classes. Analysis reveals a notable trend: students with lower levels of oral English proficiency tend to perceive greater improvement in their speaking abilities in these classes compared to their more proficient counterparts. Interestingly, the camera feature is identified as the primary source of language anxiety, while tools such as microphones, breakout rooms, text chatboxes, and individual text/voice/video chat functions are deemed most effective for fostering speaking skills. Besides presenting student perspectives on online speaking courses, this paper acknowledges its limitations and suggests avenues for future research.

DOI: 10.4018/979-8-3693-2857-6.ch012

1. INTRODUCTION

The landscape of higher education has witnessed a remarkable increase in online course enrollment in recent decades, driven by the convenience and advantages offered by distance learning (Allen & Seaman, 2016; Thomas & Thorpe, 2019). The COVID-19 pandemic, which emerged in late 2019 and early 2020, has accelerated this trend, disrupting the normal study routines of students across all levels of education, from K-12 to higher education (Adedoyin & Soykan, 2020; Cahoon et al., 2021). Consequently, the shift to online learning has become a prominent feature of modern education, often referred to as the 'new normal' (Mamolo, 2022). This transition, particularly in English language teaching, has presented both instructors and students with a unique and unprecedented experience (Zhang & Wu, 2022).

While online learning offers flexibility and accessibility, it also poses challenges, particularly in maintaining effective interaction and engagement. Synchronous online courses, which allow for real-time interaction, are favoured for their resemblance to traditional face-to-face classes (Ibatova, 2022). However, the reliance on video conferencing can impede fluid interaction and diminish attentiveness, potentially undermining the efficacy of synchronous online learning (Rapanta, 2020). Despite these challenges, online language classes have demonstrated the potential to enhance students' speaking abilities significantly. Various online platforms, such as chat rooms, verbal discussion forums, and video-conferencing tools, have played a crucial role in fostering speaking accuracy, fluency, and overall language proficiency (Ghoneim & Elghotmy, 2016; Gleason & Suvorov, 2011; Köroglu & Çakir, 2017; Namaziandost et al., 2022).

However, learning a second language is affected by certain psychological aspects, with anxiety being one of the most prevalent individual variables in foreign language learning (Teimouri et al., 2019). Anxiety may promote or hinder language learning (Aydin, 2018). Students often experience more anxiety regarding speaking than other language skills (Young, 1990). While online learning platforms can alleviate some speaking anxiety by providing a buffer from face-to-face interactions, they can also exacerbate anxiety when they become the primary mode of instruction (Fawaz & Samaha, 2021; Saadé & Kira, 2007), thereby impacting students' confidence in their ability to perform language tasks (Sun & Rueda, 2012). Given the significance of reducing learning anxiety in enhancing English-speaking ability (Zhang & Liu, 2013), it becomes crucial to investigate the effects of online speaking courses on anxiety (Kira, 2018). Additionally, research on the impact of specific e-learning platform functionalities on speaking and anxiety is currently limited. Therefore, examining the role of foreign language anxiety in speaking classes within the context of synchronous online learning is imperative and currently under research.

Research Questions:

1. What are the students' perceptions of online speaking classes?
2. How do different functionalities of platforms impact students' oral competence and language anxiety?

These questions aim to delve into the nuances of online language education, shedding light on students' experiences, expectations, and the efficacy of various platform features in facilitating language learning and alleviating anxiety.

2. LITERATURE REVIEW

This literature review aims to explore the realm of English as a Foreign Language (EFL) online learning, examining its various facets, challenges, and implications. Additionally, it delves into the complex phenomenon of anxiety in the context of EFL/ESL learning, shedding light on its triggers, manifestations, and impacts. By synthesising existing research, this review seeks to offer a comprehensive understanding of the dynamics at play in online language learning environments.

2.1 EFL online learning

2.1.1 English as a Foreign Language (EFL) Online Learning

In the realm of education, online learning has emerged as a pivotal tool, integrating the Internet and personal technology to deliver educational resources and programs, a phenomenon often termed Computer-Mediated Communication (CMC) (Fry, 2001). This learning mode offers numerous advantages, such as convenience, flexibility, and expanded access to education (Bowers & Kumar, 2015). Moreover, EFL online learning has demonstrated the potential to significantly enhance language competency by facilitating extended interactive conversations among learners (Hirotani, 2013; Levy & Stockwell, 2013). Technologies like chat rooms and verbal discussion forums serve as vital CMC tools that encourage learner participation and interaction (Gleason & Suvorov, 2011; Yanguas, 2010).

2.1.2 Asynchronous and Synchronous Online Learning

Online learning encompasses both asynchronous and synchronous modalities (Hrastinski, 2008), differing in platforms, location, and timing of learning tasks (Zhang & Wu, 2022; Ibatova, 2022). Synchronous learning, characterised by live platforms like video conferencing systems, offers real-time communication akin to traditional classrooms (Ibatova, 2022). Studies indicate that students in synchronous environments report a richer learning experience and improved fulfilment of psychological needs (Fabriz et al., 2021). Additionally, synchronous learning fosters self-discipline and resource utilisation, promoting autonomy among learners (Zhang & Wu, 2022). Furthermore, it enhances practical skills and speaking proficiency, as evidenced by numerous studies (Abrams, 2003; Ghoneim & Elghotmy, 2016; Köroglu & Çakir, 2017; Satar & Özdener, 2008; Tsang, 2018).

However, synchronous online learning also presents challenges, such as awkward silences and reduced spontaneity due to the absence of body language (Hampel & Baber, 2003). Furthermore, quieter students may be marginalised in discussions dominated by more vocal peers (Hampel & Hauck, 2004). Despite its advantages, synchronous learning may not always provide an optimal learning environment for EFL students (Zhang & Wu, 2022). Some scholars suggest that it may be more beneficial for learners with intermediate to advanced proficiency levels (Kötter, 2001; Stockwell, 2004).

2.1.3 The Functionality of Online Platforms

Online platforms offer diverse teaching functions that revolutionise traditional communication methods. Online discussion forums serve as interactive tools for critical thinking and self-awareness (Payne, 2020; Saeed & Ghazali, 2017). Similarly, video conferencing platforms like Zoom facilitate simultaneous breakout sessions, enabling discrete communication among students (Bailey et al., 2021). Functions such as microphones and chatboxes enable synchronous communication, while screen sharing enhances the classroom experience by displaying teaching materials (Bailey et al., 2021). However, challenges arise when balancing camera usage for effective communication without overloading network bandwidth (Zhang & Wu, 2022). Additionally, the simultaneous display of a teacher's face and slide content may lead to divided attention and limited expression (Katai & Iclanzan, 2022).

2.2 Anxiety in EFL/ESL

Horwitz et al. (1986) described foreign language anxiety (FLA) as a specific set of self-perceptions, beliefs, feelings, and behaviours associated with classroom language learning originating from the distinctiveness of the language learning process. The FLCAS (Foreign Language Classroom Anxiety Scale) (Horwitz et al., 1986) has been widely applied to study the relationship between language anxiety and learners' language achievements as well as other affective variables.

Anxiety is commonly observed in the context of oral communication. Anxiety, as one of the affective variables, is associated with L2 learners' language development, especially in fluency, accuracy, and complexity in L2 production (Housen et al., 2012) and with oral competence (Chen & Hwang, 2020). Although anxiety has been shown to have facilitative functions in ESL learning (Aydin, 2018), enhancing the intention of proceeding to learn for instance, the findings of research on the effects of anxiety on L2 spoken language are mostly negative. In terms of speaking fluency, breakdown (more filled pauses) and speed fluency have a strong correlation to FLA (Christenfeld & Creager, 1996; Goberman et al., 2011). Nonetheless, Sosa-López and Mora (2022) find no significant link between speaking fluency and anxiety level due to the participants' proficiency and willingness to communicate. Hewitt and Stephenson (2012) observed that learners experiencing higher anxiety tend to produce less complex grammar and make more errors. Additionally, anxiety can intrude upon attentional resources, consequently impacting the accuracy of second language (L2) speaking (Kormos, 2015).

Pertaub et al. (2001) observed that individuals recognise anxiety as an abnormal feeling, yet they struggle to resist it, leading to subsequent conditions such as depressive illnesses, irritability, and distress. Thus, it is crucial to understand what triggers anxiety and the way to deal with it. Learners' feelings of anxiety can be attributed to various factors, such as the feelings of uncertainty and low learning effectiveness of college students (Abdous, 2019), factors related to the conversation partner (Hartanto et al., 2014; Lindberg et al., 2021), the diversion of learning context (Saadé et al., 2017), and the difference between self-perception and their real skill proficiency (Chai, 2014). Regarding the collaborativeness of interlocutors, speakers may get higher anxiety levels when the interlocutor shows evidence of confusion or disinterest, such as persistent scowling or an antagonistic remark made during a conversation (Hartanto et al., 2014) due to the fact that L2 learners gauge the communicative effectiveness of their speech when completing an oral activity with the help of their interlocutor's facial expressions (Lindberg et al., 2021). Unreadiness for online courses, insufficient ability to complete the assignments, less confidence in computers and skills, separation and loneliness, and distractions trigger L2 speaking anxiety in the context of online learning (Abdous, 2019; Saadé et al., 2017). Chai (2014) also finds that college students in China are in fear of speaking because of their poor self-rated listening and speaking skill levels, while at the same time, it is generally agreed by them that the need to improve their listening and speaking skills is very high and they are eager to learn listening and speaking. In addition, the effects of two synchronous computer-mediated communication text and voice chat are comparatively investigated in terms of oral proficiency and language anxiety. The findings show that learners of the two groups improved their speaking skills while only students in the text chat group showed a significant decrease in the level of language anxiety (Mugesatar & Ozdener, 2008; Namaziandost et al., 2022).

Questionnaires with different scales are typical instruments utilised in the measurement of anxiety. Most of the research on L2 speaking anxiety has focused on testing scenarios and their immediate consequences on course grades (Horwitz et al., 1986; Teimouri et al., 2019). This study focuses on exploring the relationship between anxiety and speaking skills within the context of synchronous online speaking classes.

3. METHODOLOGY

3.1 Participants

The study included 91 participants predominantly enrolled in higher education at a Sino-foreign cooperative university in southeastern China. Given that the university conducts instruction in English, proficiency in spoken English is imperative for all students, reflected in the incorporation of specialised oral English courses. The participants, aged between 21 and 26, primarily pursue graduate degrees, constituting 75% of the sample, with undergraduate students comprising 25%. Gender distribution among participants skewed towards females, accounting for 84% of the sample, while males represented 16%. In terms of academic backgrounds, 43% of participants were from English-related majors, with the remaining 57% from non-English-related disciplines. When considering the duration of participation in synchronous online oral classes, half of the participants had engaged for less than three months, followed by 29% for three to six months, 11% for six months to one year, and another 11% for over a year. Regarding their proficiency levels, as assessed by the IELTS speaking score (on a total scale of 9 points), participants demonstrated a range of abilities, spanning from below band 5.5 points to beyond band 7.5 points. This variation implies that while some participants could produce simple speech fluently, others exhibited the ability to develop topics coherently and effectively, in accordance with IELTS speaking band descriptors.

3.2 Instruments

3.2.1 Questionnaire

The questionnaire comprised four parts: a demographic survey, the language anxiety scale, the speaking skills scale, and students' perceptions of different functions in e-learning platforms. The demographic survey included some basic background information about the participants, such as their gender, major, and spoken English proficiency. The section on students' perceptions of the various functionalities available in e-learning platforms has eight questions, five of which are multiple-choice questions and the remaining three of which are open-ended. The descriptions of the language speaking anxiety scale and speaking skills scale are explained in detail below.

Language Speaking Anxiety Scale

Öztürk and Gürbüz (2014) developed the Speaking Anxiety Scale (SAS), an 18-item questionnaire, by selecting 18 items from the 33 items of the Foreign Language Classroom Anxiety Scale (FLCAS) (Horwitz et al., 1986) and were adopted by some other studies (i.e., Pan et al., 2022). Öztürk and Gürbüz (2014) selected 18 items from FLCAS Horwitz's (1986) scale that were directly linked to foreign language speaking anxiety. The present study had nothing to do with whether the interlocutor is a native speaker or not and both L2 learners and their peers were generally Chinese. Therefore, a related item in the original scale was deleted. Ultimately, this part of the questionnaire contained 17 questions with 5-point Likert-scale items. The validity and reliability of this questionnaire were calculated by KMO (0.921), Bartlett's Test (Sig. <0.001), and Cronbach Alpha ($\alpha = 0.949$) shown in Table 1, which implied that the scale had excellent internal consistency and validity.

Table 1. Validity and reliability of the language anxiety scale and speaking skills scale

Item	KMO and Bartlett's Test		Reliability Statistics
	Kaiser-Meyer-Olkin Measure of Sampling Adequacy.	Bartlett's Test of Sphericity Sig.	Cronbach's Alpha Based on Standardised Items
Language Anxiety Scale	0.921	<0.001	0.949
Speaking Skills Scale	0.754	<0.001	0.916

Speaking Skills Scale

According to previous research, language competency and performance were multifaceted and best measured in complexity, accuracy, and fluency (CAF) (Ellis & Barkhuizen, 2005). The term "complexity" refers to language that is more developed. Ellis and Barkhuizen (2005) argued that language could be elaborated in two ways: learners' willingness to use language that was above the bounds of their interlanguage but was not fully internalised and learners' readiness to utilise a wide range of structures. Furthermore, accuracy was defined as the degree to which language learners' output was based on the target language's rule structure. It referred to language learners' ability to manage their interlanguage complexity to avoid developing incorrect structures. Finally, fluency was defined as the creation of words without excessive pauses or hesitation. It occurred when language learners prioritised meaning above form. The reliability and validity of the scale were determined using Cronbach Alpha ($\alpha = 0.916$), KMO (0.754), and Bartlett's Test (Sig. <0.001), which indicated the scale had excellent internal consistency and acceptable validity.

3.2.2 Semi-structured interview

The second instrument utilised in this research was a semi-structured interview to collect qualitative data for this study. Semi-structured interviews not only allowed participants to discuss their personal experiences and perceptions but also assisted the researcher in capturing participants' language and thoughts related to the selected themes (Rubin & Rubin, 2011). Furthermore, semi-structured interviews allowed for an in-depth study of what was important to or valued by the participants due to the adaptability, availability, and wealth of data offered by small samples (Kvale, 1996). In the current study, the semi-structured interview was to collect students' perceptions of speaking anxiety, speaking skills, function usage in synchronous online oral classes, and suggestions on improvements of online speaking classes and compared them to the asynchronous online speaking class and face-to-face classes.

3.3 Data collection and data analysis

Sampling was conducted through a 'snowball' approach, with 108 students completing an anonymous online questionnaire (relying on the Wenjuanxing survey platform) with informed consent. An item (*Have you ever taken an online synchronous speaking class?*) as a filter in the demographic information part to screen out valid questionnaires. Finally, the number of valid questionnaires was 91, of which 76 were from women and 15 from men. Further quantitative data information was analysed with the help of SPSS 27 using descriptive analysis, one-way ANOVA, independent *t*-test, and multiple response method.

In addition, the participants for the interview were selected by purposeful sampling, a form of non-probability sampling that employs samples obtained from the general population based on the criteria established by the researcher (Riazi, 2016). To represent a wide range of participant experiences and perspectives more accurately regarding synchronous online oral English learning, balanced participants were carefully selected based on demographic criteria such as gender, major, and English proficiency. Lastly, six students in non-English majors (i.e., International Business) and six students in English-related majors named TESOL (Teaching English to Speakers of Other Languages) participated in the study. The background information of the interviewees is shown in Table 2 below. Participants were coded as S1, S2, S3, etc.

Table 2. The background information of interviewees

Student	Gender	IELTS speaking	Major	E-learning Platform
S1	female	6	TESOL	Partner English
S2	female	7	TESOL	BBB Tencent Meeting
S3	female	6	TESOL	BBB Zhumu Tencent Meeting
S4	female	7	TESOL	BBB Zhumu Tencent Meeting
S5	male	6.5	TESOL	Zoom
S6	male	7	TESOL	BBB Zhumu Tencent Meeting
S7	female	6	International Business	BBB Tencent Meeting
S8	female	7	International Education	BBB
S9	female	5.5	Media and Communication	Tencent Meeting
S10	female	6.5	Social Science	HelloTalk
S11	male	6.5	International Business	Zoom
S12	male	6.5	Child Development and Family Education	BBB Zhumu

Due to the unstable situation of the epidemic, one participant conducted a face-to-face interview, and 11 participants were interviewed online through Tencent Meeting, a video-conferencing system with video and audio recording functions. Before conducting the interview, the participant's oral consent and permission to audio record the interview were obtained. To provide a more relaxed communication atmosphere for the interviewers, all interviews were done in their mother tongue, Mandarin Chinese, according to the interview guide. On average, each interview lasted between 20 and 40 minutes. A thematic analysis approach, a method for systematically detecting, categorising, and providing insight into meaning patterns (themes) throughout a data collection (Braun & Clarke, 2012), was utilised to analyse three open-ended questions in the questionnaire and interview data inductively and interpretively (Charmaz, 2014).

4. FINDINGS

4.1 RQ1: What are the students' perceptions of online speaking classes?

4.1.1 Language anxiety in online speaking classes

In general, the students who participated in the synchronous online oral English class had basically neutral feelings about language anxiety (Mean = 3.06). Learners were slightly less anxious about being overwhelmed by the number of rules they have to learn to speak English (Mean = 2.69) and fearing ridicule from others when speaking English (Mean = 2.66). On the contrary, learners were slightly more anxious about the uncertainty of speaking English in class (Mean = 3.34) and having to speak without preparation (Mean = 3.36).

To detect whether there are differences in the perception of language anxiety between different groups, independent samples t-test of gender and oneway ANOVA of age, English speaking proficiency, participants' current degrees, and duration time of synchronous online oral class were processed in SPSS 27. As shown in Table 3 and Table 4, there is no significant difference between groups under diverse variables and they hold a generally neutral attitude towards language anxiety in oral English class.

Table 3. Results of independent samples t-test of gender

Item	Gender	N	Mean	Std. Deviation	Std. Error Mean	t	Sig.
Language Anxiety Scale	Male	15	2.86	0.70	0.18	-1.114	0.268
	Female	76	3.10	0.79	0.09		
Speaking Skills Scale	Male	15	3.82	0.74	0.19	0.954	0.343
	Female	76	3.60	0.85	0.10		

continued on following page

Table 4. Continued

Table 4. Results of Oneway ANOVA of age, duration of online oral English class, current degree, English speaking proficiency

Variable	Item	F	Sig
Language Anxiety Scale	Age	1.03	0.396
	Duration	0.948	0.421
	Degree	0.329	0.804
	Speaking proficiency	0.191	0.965
Speaking Skills Scale	Age	0.465	0.761
	Duration	0.974	0.409
	Degree	2.61	0.057
	Speaking proficiency	2.319	0.050

4.1.2 Perceived speaking skills in online speaking classes

With regard to speaking skills, participants have a weak positive attitude towards all of the three dimensions. The order in perceived effectiveness of speaking skills followed the order of complexity (Mean = 3.51) to accuracy (Mean = 3.6) to fluency (Mean = 3.79) as most effective. Based on the results of the independent samples *t*-test (Table 3) and Oneway ANOVA (Table 4), only participants at different levels show a significant difference (Sig = 0.05) in perceiving their speaking skills. Participants who scored below 5.5 achieved exactly 5.5, obtained 6, and reached 6.5 points on the IELTS speaking test, respectively, and they perceived a greater improvement in their speaking skills in the online oral class compared to those who attained a score of 7 points. Through multiple comparisons to process further data analysis (Table 5), the difference is mainly reflected in speaking accuracy (Sig = 0.011). This indicates that learners who scored below seven on the IELTS speaking test believe their speaking accuracy has improved more in an online speaking session than those who scored 7.

Table 5. Results of Oneway ANOVA of English-speaking proficiency

Variable	Speaking proficiency	N	Mean	Std. Deviation	F	Sig.	Multiple comparisons
Speaking fluency	Less than Band 5.5	5	4.20	0.84	1.497	0.199	/
	Band 5.5	11	4.00	0.63			
	Band 6	25	3.88	0.73			
	Band 6.5	29	3.86	0.88			
	Band 7	17	3.35	1.00			
	More than Band 7	4	3.50	1.00			

continued on following page

Table 5. Continued

Variable	Speaking proficiency	N	Mean	Std. Deviation	F	Sig.	Multiple comparisons
Speaking accuracy	Less than Band 5.5	5	4.20	0.84	3.210	0.011	1>5, 2>5, 3>5, 4>5
	Band 5.5	11	3.82	0.60			
	Band 6	25	3.80	0.82			
	Band 6.5	29	3.69	0.93			
	Band 7	17	2.88	0.99			
	More than Band 7	4	3.50	1.00			
Speaking complexity	Less than Band 5.5	5	4.00	0.71	1.915	0.100	/
	Band 5.5	11	3.73	0.91			
	Band 6	25	3.80	0.82			
	Band 6.5	29	3.38	0.94			
	Band 7	17	3.12	1.05			
	More than Band 7	4	3.00	0.82			

* The mean difference is significant at the 0.05 level.
Note: 1 = Less than Band 5.5, 2 = Band 5.5, 3 = Band 6, 4 = Band 6.5, 5 = Band 7, 6 = More than Band 7

Concerning the factors impacting oral competence in online speaking classes, participants' reports focus on three themes: class and course, teacher, and learner. The three most frequently mentioned categories are all about external factors, involving the degrees to which teachers encourage students., the English learning environment, and the instruction level. Participants feel that if instructors can drive learners in class and effectively encourage them to make more oral output with English only in class and use different methods to teach, learners will enhance their speaking skills. In addition, course design (i.e. Whether there is a systematic logic and connection between courses), teachers' instant feedback, teacher-student interaction, learners' lexical resources and emotional or psychological factors such as social anxiety disorder or inversely being more casual and braver without face-to-face communication in online oral class are factors mentioned by many interviewees that have a great influence on oral English speaking competence.

4.1.3 Students' attitudes towards online oral class

Figure 1 shows the number of interviewees who chose their preferences and perceived more effectiveness between synchronous online oral classes and asynchronous ones, as well as between synchronous online oral classes and classroom face-to-face oral classes. Compared to asynchronous courses, synchronous courses were a landslide triumph in both preference and effect. The interviewees identified interaction as one of the keywords pertaining to synchronous courses. The interaction is more direct (S12), and therefore learners can achieve a better interaction between teachers and peers (S3), asking questions directly without wasting time (S7) and receiving immediate feedback (S9), for instance. Real-time feedback from teachers assists learners in identifying their weaknesses and enhancing their performance (S3). However, in the context of asynchronous courses, students are concerned that a lack of feedback will result in uncertainty about their own speech or chronic errors (S11). Even if there is AI feedback, it is typically pre-input, which is not necessarily consistent with the circumstances of students, which may result in incorrect feedback owing to technical constraints (S5). *"Interaction is very important in speaking. Speaking to a real person is not the same as listening and speaking to a screen."* (S5). *"Asyn-*

chronous courses are more like completing a task on your own. Everything is your own perception. I feel bad. There is no real interaction.", S6 also said. S9 expressed a similar feeling, *"It is more boring. I do it all by myself."* For synchronous speaking classes, however, the learner takes them more seriously (S4), adheres to them more readily because of limited self-discipline during asynchronous classes (S8), and does more exercises under supervision (S12).

Figure 1. Interviewees' preference and perceived effectiveness of synchronous online oral classes compared to asynchronous online oral classes and face-to-face oral classes

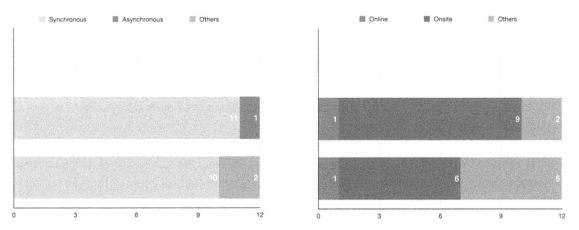

Note: The upper bar means students' preference and the lower bar means students' perceived effectiveness.
Others represent *similar* or *depending on the situation*.

Compared to synchronous online oral sessions, 75% of interviewees prefer onsite classes. Regarding the perceived effect, half of the individuals selected the onsite class, one individual selected the online class as having a better effect, and five individuals selected that the effect is similar or situation-dependent. Some interviewees believe that communication in online speaking classes cannot replace face-to-face communication, even though both parties have mics and cameras on. The explanations mostly stem from non-linguistic aspects, including teachers' facial expressions and body language and the classroom's learning atmosphere. *"When you talk to someone in real life, even if he doesn't respond to you right away, he may listen to your thoughts, and then he may have some personal thoughts, but he expresses them with his body language or with some subtle eye contact, and I think it's hard to observe all of these signals online."* (S11) On this account, S1 suggested that learners with low proficiency had better prefer F2F class while the two models of oral class are similar for learners with higher proficiency. She argues that live classrooms are able to convey knowledge more clearly because of these non-verbal elements, such as writing on the board and using objects in the classroom, which reflect a sense of low latency.

Various interviewees reported feeling more anxious or stressed in on-campus classes than in online classes. However, as compared to these negative feelings, interviewees place a higher value on improved learning outcomes. While they exhibited greater anxiety levels in F2F classes compared to online ones, they still showed a stronger preference for attending F2F classes, except for one interviewee who had the opposite option.

"Though increasing my anxiety, the classroom context makes me respect teachers and students more and more serious about the class." (S2)

"Although onsite oral English classes will give me more pressure, I think it is the best way to improve my oral English." (S3)

"(In online classes) I'm relieved, but I'm not learning." (S12)

"The students in the classroom may be strangers. I am nervous about strangers. I will not be too nervous if there is no use of the camera in online classes." (S4)

In addition, the interviewees tend to complete the class face-to-face because of the consideration of future practical communication scenarios containing atmosphere, dress, and state of mind. In the classroom, it is easier to recreate or simulate actual communication situations.

"It doesn't mimic the face-to-face interaction like when I'm talking to you right now, I'm looking around." (S2)

"Because you can't always have online communication in your daily life, you have to get over it (the anxiety from F2F)!" (S3)

S10 believes that online classes are cost-effective and eliminate the need to travel. If the interlocutor is unfamiliar, online communication will be easier. With the recording function, online classes are more appealing. S9 suggests a combination of online and offline classes, with onsite classes once a month and others online, which can not only facilitate social interaction but also reduce commuting time.

With respect to proposals about the improvements of synchronous online oral classes, the interviewees put forward their suggestions from four aspects of teachers, students, class, and platform use. 58% of interviewees think that teachers should increase their acquaintance with the functionalities of platforms to make the class more fluid, avoid wasting time, and show instructors' professionalism.

"Teachers should not only have basic training but also be combined with the teaching content to use the platform function smoothly... If not, it will result in a waste of time." (S2)

"Teachers' familiarity with platform functions has a great impact on the class. Wasting a lot of time on debugging equipment will make students feel unprofessional." (S6)

"Both teachers and students need to know more about the functions of the platform so that they can cooperate. If the course is not smooth, limited learning content will lead to students' anxiety, thus affecting the level of their oral English development." (S9)

In addition, students in oral English classes anticipate instructors to have more structured courses in class, provide more professional feedback, engage in more positive interaction, and provide emotional value to students. The content richness and controlled student numbers are other significant factors that ensure students have more opportunities to produce more and learn more. In regard to functions themselves, on the one hand, some interviewees expect to include certain motivational functions, such as bonus points, an automated display of encouraging remarks after selecting the correct answer, etc. On the other hand, it is advised that a version with only the most fundamental functionalities be created in order to preserve the course's flow.

4.2 RQ2: How can different kinds of functions of platforms impact students' oral competence and anxiety?

When it comes to functionalities that help with speaking fluency, half of the students choose the microphone and breakout room, followed by one-to-one chatbox/voice/video (27.5%). The top three choices for both improving speaking accuracy and fluency were one-to-one chatbox/voice/video, chatbox, and breakout room. With regard to language anxiety, 46.2% of participants believe chatbox reduces their anxiety, followed by one-on-one chatbox/voice/video (33%) and breakout room (27.5%). More than half of the participants think that the camera increases their language anxiety in online classes, followed by the microphone (29.7%) and the breakout room (26.4%).

The microphone is the most basic and important function in oral practice. It makes it possible for students to communicate orally in real-time, and some students think opening the mic and then practising speaking is the best way to practice the language. The quality of the microphone may lead to a change in students' learning attitudes. For example, when using the microphone function, there will be electric current sounds, which need to be adjusted several times. Some learners are worried about whether the interlocutor can hear clearly, or they deliberately pay attention to their own performance in the microphone.

The breakout room function enables students to discuss and exchange their own ideas and offers them more opportunities to output oral English, which enhances the enthusiasm of class participation. Especially, when there are fewer people in the group discussion and no use of the camera, the anxiety will be the lowest, but the language can be produced the most. It is acceptable to be corrected without worrying that performance will leave a bad impression on others in such a restricted environment. Some learners feel more comfortable without teachers' participation in the breakout room while some prefer that teachers occasionally join them to help advance their oral practice. Fluency increases as learners continue to speak. Much of the improvement in accuracy comes from correcting each other during communication. The improvement of oral complexity mainly comes from different ways of expression and various ideas adopted by different learners, which complement and stimulate each other in the process, thus producing more content. However, some interviewees also mentioned that the specific effect of practice depends on the English level or familiarity of the communication partners. Some students expect to meet speakers with higher proficiency to help them improve their oral English, while some learners worry that they will even lose confidence more in their oral English when they meet students who speak well.

The chatbox is often used to show some instant corrective feedback or hints by teachers or partners so that it helps to improve learners' speaking accuracy. Oral prompts are easy to forget, while written feedback is easy to record and read repeatedly after class. In addition, some students want to avoid speaking directly due to emotional factors such as fear of speaking in public or not using the microphone function for technical reasons. As a result, they participate in tasks through the chatbox, which can be used as a short-term buffer for the microphone function. However, since it is an oral class, participation through the chatbox in oral tasks will inhibit the development of oral English in the long term. Although the text may present colloquial content in the task, it still cannot replace the speaking practice in class. The reaction speed of a spoken conversation is faster than that of typing.

The camera function compensates for the non-verbal cues the speaker can't capture during the online class. Some students judge the accuracy of their expressions by looking at the feedback given by others. Turning on the cameras together make some of the participants a sense of community and participation in class. However, when asked to face the camera in class, more than half of the participants became more apprehensive, uneasy, distracted, and reluctant. They fear making mistakes or being unable to express themselves clearly, as well as the negative responses they receive. Some respondents mentioned eye contact or focusing excessively on one's own image restricts their ability to think and even causes them to forget what they were about to say. They feel more relaxed when they merely need to activate the microphone or type in the chatbox. If the object of communication is familiar to learners, or they have a high proficiency in spoken English, they will be more willing to turn on the camera. In addition, some participants believe that speaking class is to overcome this fear and should force themselves to communicate with others with cameras on. Given the high anxiety the camera function causes and the fact that it is not the primary element influencing spoken English development, the usage of the camera function can be regarded as optional depending on the situation of the class.

5. DISCUSSION OF FINDINGS

The goal of this study was to investigate the learners' perceptions of synchronous online oral classes and how different functions affect language anxiety and speaking skills during the class. Learners in the current study generally had English proficiency at the intermediate level or above, and they are relatively positive about the perception of improvement in speaking fluency, accuracy, and fluency in synchronous online oral classes. Learners with lower intermediate English proficiency perceived speaking skills more than learners with higher proficiency, especially in terms of speaking accuracy. Tsang (2018) also found that the low-proficient learners perceived more improvements in oral presentation skills than the high-proficient learners during the three-month program. Similarly, Kötter (2001) found that students with different levels of proficiency tend to necessitate different sorts of instructional assistance, and communication and fluency-related tasks should ideally be utilised in an online setting with at least intermediate competency in the target language. In the present study, the students with relatively low levels mentioned more about the influence of their English level while the students with relatively high levels focus more on the English level of the interlocutors. When conversing with a less proficient English speaker, learners with higher proficiency may feel increased anxiety about the dialogue's effectiveness and fluency. They worry if the other person fully comprehends them and whether they must elaborate frequently. This may lead them to perceive the interaction as less fruitful or even a waste of time. Hence, it's crucial for teachers to organise students of varying levels effectively and provide appropriate support. In oral language courses, it's beneficial for teachers to segregate classes by skill level, allowing students to choose classes that match their proficiency. Additionally, in mixed-level classes, teachers can create multiple breakout rooms for discussions. This approach enables students to engage more freely and comfortably with peers at similar proficiency levels, fostering motivation and enhancing the overall learning experience.

In terms of the level of language anxiety, participants' anxiety is moderate. A possible explanation for this might be that most of the participants in the current study are intermediate or beyond; thus, they are more confident speaking English than those with lower levels. Another possible explanation for this is that no camera use helps them decrease anxiety. Learners experienced a greater sense of ease and engagement in the audio CMC since they still stayed anonymous behind the computer's screen (Yanguas, 2010). According to the language anxiety scale, learners are more anxious that they are never completely confident about speaking English in online oral classes and fear having to speak without preparation, which corresponds to Abdous's (2019) finding that online student readiness was strongly negatively related to students' feelings of anxiety. As learners become more secure and adept in taking online courses, students' feelings of anxiety and dissatisfaction graduate away. In addition, the result of this current study also accords with Abdous's (2019) finding that age failed to predict anxiety among online users. Nevertheless, Abdous (2019) shows that female students are more prone to experience anxiety when taking online courses, which differs from the finding presented here that there is no significant anxiety difference between females and males. This could be attributed to the cultural background and the gender distribution of the participants in this study, where 84% were female and 16% male. It remains for future research to explore further whether gender difference affects anxiety levels in online oral classes.

In terms of the challenges of the synchronous online oral class, students perceived interaction differences and a sense of lack of real interaction due to non-verbal signals and the climate of learning compared to face-to-face context. This finding is consistent with that of Zhang and Wu (2022) who found audio and text communication employed in synchronous online learning failed to offer paralinguistic elements such as gaze, facial expressions, gestures, and intonation, which are thought to be of major value in English language acquisition. This also accords with Yanguas's (2010) earlier findings, which showed that Audio CMC compels learners to employ language resources, which may be replaced by visual signals in Video CMC and FTF groups. Whilst learners attempted to use linguistic approaches to non-communicative problems, leading to more detailed responses, their extensive use of language may not necessarily lead to successful negotiation outcomes. A video-conferencing environment reduces interaction fluency and attentiveness compared to the traditional classroom (Rapanta et al., 2020). This may be why learners feel the difference and are more willing to choose onsite courses. In the case of oral English training, students also need to adapt to the change of interactive mode, which may lead to more cognitive load. However, the findings of the current study do not support the previous research that students were unable to obtain timely feedback on their English learning, particularly corrective feedback in synchronous online learning due to the lack of face-to-face virtual communication (Zhang & Wu, 2022). Interviewees in the current study expressed they received instant feedback from teachers and peers through the microphone and chatbox. The factors influencing spoken language were independent of whether cameras were on or not.

The camera was identified as the most anxiety-inducing function among participants, though it came fourth in the list of functions that help students improve speaking fluency. Similar to the findings of Zhang and Wu (2022), students acknowledged the value of cameras for learning but were unwilling to activate them. In contrast to Zhang and Wu's (2022) conclusion that students' reluctance to activate cameras is a result of a network connectivity problem, interviewees ascribed it more to human-related issues. Except for their internal factors, one reason for the camera becoming the most anxiety-inducing function is interlocutor-related factors. The non-verbal expression of the speaker can not only aid learners in comprehending the topics talked about, but also heighten their anxiety to some degree. Interviewees reported that anxiety from the camera was commonly caused by teachers' and peers' negative feedback, including frowning, silence, and an anxious or hesitant tone, etc. It corresponds to Hartanto et al.'s (2014) findings that speakers may experience increased anxiety when the interlocutor displays signs of perplexity or indifference, such as a prolonged frown or an unpleasant comment made during a conversation. Positive conversation feedback resulted in decreased self-reported anxiety, a lower heart rate, and lengthier replies, whereas negative dialogue feedback had the opposite effect (Hartanto et al., 2014). Therefore, when the camera is turned on in class, the interlocutor may estimate the anxiety level of the other student based on her response and provide positive feedback accordingly. According to Lindberg et al. (2021), if a teacher or student notices that their interlocutor is blinking excessively, breaking eye contact frequently, or caressing their face or hair, they can take steps to address the possible source of this reaction by speaking more slowly, changing the topic of discussion, or providing encouragement.

Chatbox was cited as the function that contributed the most to speaking accuracy (42.9%) and the third most to speaking complexity (36.3%), as well as the function that was most helpful in reducing anxiety (46.2%). It indicates that the contribution of text communication to verbal and emotional expressions is significant. In accordance with the present results, previous studies (Mugesatar & Ozdener, 2008; Namaziandost et al., 2022) have demonstrated that synchronous text conversation had a greater impact on the speaking skills of EFL students and showed a considerable reduction in language anxiety. Namaziandost et al. (2022) stressed that the results of the speaking test for both oral and text chat groups suggested that text and voice chat are equally beneficial in increasing students' speaking skills. However, the interviewees in the current study believe that excessive use of text communication in oral English class will inhibit the development of speaking development. They hope their peers can use microphones to communicate as much as possible. In class, the chatbox can be primarily used to display corrective feedback by instructors and peers to improve their accuracy, vocabulary, and sentence structure complexity, and auxiliary to conduct text communication due to technical or personal problems. Students who find it extremely difficult to communicate with a microphone can also use the chatbox as a transition to oral practice at the beginning. After class, students can use text chat to continue practising speaking due to free time and topics.

6. CONCLUSION AND IMPLICATION

This study has uncovered significant findings regarding synchronous online oral English classes. It demonstrates that learners typically experience a moderate level of anxiety while noting an improvement in their speaking skills. Interestingly, those with lower oral English proficiency seem to gain more in terms of skill development than their higher proficiency counterparts. A notable aspect of this study is the differential impact of various technological tools on language learning: while cameras tend to increase language anxiety, tools like microphones, breakout rooms, and text/voice/video chatboxes significantly foster the development of speaking skills. According to the findings and discussion above, three pedagogical implications are presented.

Firstly, an effective teaching approach could involve a mix of online and onsite classes or synchronous and asynchronous courses tailored to the specific needs and preferences of students. The optimal frequency and balance of these methods offer a promising avenue for future research. Secondly, course design should be differentiated to cater to students with varying levels of spoken English proficiency. In situations where course content is fixed, strategic use of breakout rooms for grouping students during activities or tasks can be beneficial. Thirdly, and importantly, the study highlights the need for careful selection and use of technological functions in online classes to enhance classroom fluency and effectiveness. Educators should focus on using these functions effectively, with particular emphasis on fundamental ones. For instance, incorporating a beauty feature with the camera function, if available, could help reduce student anxiety. The choice of technological tools should align with the specific objectives of spoken English lessons. For instance, to enhance fluency, encouraging the use of microphones is advisable; for accuracy, limited use of chatboxes may be appropriate; and for fostering communication, breakout rooms could be the most effective choice.

Although this research offers valuable insights into the pedagogical implications of online oral English classes, there are certain limitations. The first limitation arises from the diversity of online oral courses experienced by the participants. Such variation in course content and structure could influence students' expectations and perceptions of their speaking classes. The inconsistency in teaching methodologies across different courses might affect students' understanding and feedback regarding these classes. Additionally, the study's findings might be influenced by the disproportionate gender representation among participants. This uneven gender ratio could potentially skew the insights, particularly in terms of how different genders experience speaking anxiety in synchronous online learning environments. Therefore, more comprehensive studies could be conducted to fully understand and address the complexities of teaching and learning in online oral English classes.

REFERENCES

Abdous, M. H. (2019). Influence of satisfaction and preparedness on online students' feelings of anxiety. *The Internet and Higher Education*, 41, 34–44. 10.1016/j.iheduc.2019.01.001

Abrams, Z. I. (2003). The effect of synchronous and asynchronous CMC on oral performance in German. *Modern Language Journal*, 87(2), 157–167. 10.1111/1540-4781.00184

Adedoyin, O. B., & Soykan, E. (2020). Covid-19 pandemic and online learning: The challenges and opportunities. *Interactive Learning Environments*, 3, 1–13. 10.1080/10494820.2020.1813180

Aydın, S. (2018). Technology and foreign language anxiety: Implications for practice and future research. *Journal of Language and Linguistic Studies*, 14(2), 193–211.

Bailey, D., Almusharraf, N., & Hatcher, R. (2021). Finding satisfaction: Intrinsic motivation for synchronous and asynchronous communication in the online language learning context. *Education and Information Technologies*, 26(3), 2563–2583. 10.1007/s10639-020-10369-z33169066

Bowers, J., & Kumar, P. (2015). Students' Perceptions of Teaching and Social Presence: A Comparative Analysis of Face-to-Face and Online Learning Environments. [IJWLTT]. *International Journal of Web-Based Learning and Teaching Technologies*, 10(1), 27–44. 10.4018/ijwltt.2015010103

Braun, V., & Clarke, V. (2012). *Thematic analysis*. American Psychological Association., 10.1037/13620-004

Cahoon, A., McGill, S., & Simms, V. (2021). Understanding home education in the context of COVID-19 lockdown. *Irish Educational Studies*, 40(2), 443–455. 10.1080/03323315.2021.1921010

Chai, Y. L. (2014). A survey of non-English major college students' English listening and speaking learning demands based on WeChat. *Technology Enhanced Foreign Language Education*, (05), 34–39.

Charmaz, K. (2014). Grounded theory in global perspective: Reviews by international researchers. *Qualitative Inquiry*, 20(9), 1074–1084. 10.1177/1077800414545235

Chen, M. R. A., & Hwang, G. J. (2020). Effects of a concept mapping-based flipped learning approach on EFL students' English speaking performance, critical thinking awareness and speaking anxiety. *British Journal of Educational Technology*, 51(3), 817–834. 10.1111/bjet.12887

Christenfeld, N., & Creager, B. (1996). Anxiety, alcohol, aphasia, and ums. *Journal of Personality and Social Psychology*, 70(3), 451–460. 10.1037/0022-3514.70.3.4518851740

Ellis, R., & Barkhuizen, G. (2005). *Analysing learner language*. Oxford University Press.

Fabriz, S., Mendzheritskaya, J., & Stehle, S. (2021). Impact of synchronous and asynchronous settings of online teaching and learning in higher education on students' learning experience during COVID-19. *Frontiers in Psychology*, 12, 733554. 10.3389/fpsyg.2021.73355434707542

Fawaz, M., & Samaha, A. (2021). E-learning: Depression, anxiety, and stress symptomatology among Lebanese university students during COVID-19 quarantine. *Nursing Forum*, 56(1), 52–57. 10.1111/nuf.1252133125744

Fry, K. (2001). E-learning markets and providers: Some issues and prospects. *Education + Training*, 43(4), 233–239. 10.1108/EUM0000000005484

Ghoneim, N. M. M., & Elghotmy, H. E. A. (2016). Using Voice Thread to Develop EFL Pre-Service Teachers' Speaking Skills. *Online Submission*, 4(6), 13–31.

Gleason, J., & Suvorov, R. (2011). *Learner perceptions of asynchronous oral computer-mediated communication tasks using Wimba Voice for developing their L2 oral proficiency. The role of CALL in hybrid and online language courses*. Iowa State University.

Goberman, A. M., Hughes, S., & Haydock, T. (2011). Acoustic characteristics of public speaking: Anxiety and practice effects. *Speech Communication*, 53(6), 867–876. Advance online publication. 10.1016/j.specom.2011.02.005

Hampel, R., & Baber, E. (2003). Using Internet-based audio-graphic and video conferencing for language teaching and learning. In Felix, U. (Ed.), *Language learning online: Towards best practice*. Swets and Zeitlinger.

Hampel, R., & Hauck, M. (2004). Towards an effective use of audio conferencing in distance language courses. *Language Learning & Technology*, 8(1), 66–82. http://llt.msu.edu/vol8num1/hampel/default.html

Hartanto, D., Kampmann, I. L., Morina, N., Emmelkamp, P. M. G., Neerincx, M. A., & Brinkman, W. P. (2014). Controlling social stress in virtual reality environments. *PLoS One*, 9(3), 1–17. 10.1371/journal.pone.009280424671006

Hewitt, E., & Stephenson, J. (2012). Foreign Language Anxiety and Oral Exam Performance: A Replication of Phillips's MLJ Study. *Modern Language Journal*, 96(2), 170–189. 10.1111/j.1540-4781.2011.01174.x

Hirotani, M. (2013). Synchronous versus asynchronous CMC and transfer to Japanese oral performance. *CALICO Journal*, 26(2), 413–438. 10.1558/cj.v26i2.413-438

Horwitz, E. K., Horwitz, M. B., & Cope, J. A. (1986). Foreign language classroom anxiety. *Modern Language Journal*, 70(2), 125–132. 10.1111/j.1540-4781.1986.tb05256.x

Housen, A., Kuiken, F., & Vedder, I. (Eds.). (2012). *Dimensions of L2 performance and proficiency: Complexity, accuracy and fluency in SLA* (Vol. 32). John Benjamins Publishing. 10.1075/lllt.32

Hrastinski, S. (2008). Asynchronous and synchronous e-learning. *EDUCAUSE Quarterly*, 31(4), 51–55.

Ibatova, A. (2022). An Investigation of EFL Learners' Speaking Anxiety and Motivation in Face-to-Face and Synchronous Text-based Chat and Voice-based Chat Environment. *Computer Assisted Language Learning*, 23(2), 278–294.

Katai, Z., & Iclanzan, D. (2022). Impact of instructor on-slide presence in synchronous e-learning. *Education and Information Technologies*, 28(3), 3089–3115. 10.1007/s10639-022-11306-y36105376

Kira, D., Nebebe, F., & Saadé, R. G. (2018). The persistence of anxiety experienced by a new generation in online learning. In *In SITE 2018: Informing Science+ IT Education Conferences: La Verne California*, 079-088. 10.28945/4040

Kormos, J. (2015). Individual differences in second language speech production. In J. W. Schwieter (Ed.) *The Cambridge handbook of bilingual processing* (Cambridge Handbooks in Language and Linguistics). Cambridge University Press. 10.1017/CBO9781107447257.017

Köroglu, Z. Ç., & Çakir, A. (2017). Implementation of flipped instruction in language classrooms: An alternative way to develop speaking skills of pre-service English language teachers. *International Journal of Education and Development Using Information and Communication Technology*, 13(2), 42–55.

Kötter, M. (2001). Developing distance language learners' interactive competence: Can synchronous audio do the trick? *International Journal of Educational Telecommunications*, 7, 327–353.

Kvale, S. (1996). InterViews: An Introduction to Qualitative Research Interviewing. *Sage (Atlanta, Ga.)*.

Levy, M., & Stockwell, G. (2013). *CALL dimensions: Options and issues in computer-assisted language learning*. Routledge. 10.4324/9780203708200

Lindberg, R., McDonough, K., & Trofimovich, P. (2021). Investigating verbal and nonverbal indicators of physiological response during second language interaction. *Applied Psycholinguistics*, 42(6), 1403–1425. 10.1017/S014271642100028X

Mamolo, L. (2022). Online Learning and Students' Mathematics Motivation, Self-Efficacy, and Anxiety in the "New Normal". *Education Research International*, 2022, 1–10. Advance online publication. 10.1155/2022/9439634

Mugesatar, H., & Ozdener, N. (2008). The effects of synchronous CMC on speaking proficiency and anxiety: Text versus voice chat. *Modern Language Journal*, 92(4), 595–613. 10.1111/j.1540-4781.2008.00789.x

Namaziandost, E., Razmi, M. H., Hernández, R. M., Ocaña-Fernández, Y., & Khabir, M. (2022). Synchronous CMC text chat versus synchronous CMC voice chat: Impacts on EFL learners' oral proficiency and anxiety. *Journal of Research on Technology in Education*, 54(4), 599–616. 10.1080/15391523.2021.1906362

Öztürk, G., & Gürbüz, N. (2014). Speaking anxiety among Turkish EFL learners: The case at a state university. *Journal of language and Linguistic Studies*, 10(1), 1-17.

Pan, H., Xia, F., Kumar, T., Li, X., & Shamsy, A. (2022). Massive Open Online Course Versus Flipped Instruction: Impacts on Foreign Language Speaking Anxiety, Foreign Language Learning Motivation, and Learning Attitude. *Frontiers in Psychology*, 13, 833616. 10.3389/fpsyg.2022.83361635197908

Payne, J. S. (2020). Developing L2 productive language skills online and the strategic use of instructional tools. *Foreign Language Annals*, 53(2), 243–249. 10.1111/flan.12457

Pertaub, D. P., Slater, M., & Barker, C. (2001). An experiment on public speaking anxiety in response to three different types of virtual audience. *Presence (Cambridge, Mass.)*, 11(1), 68–78. 10.1162/105474602317343668

Rapanta, C., Botturi, L., Goodyear, P., Guàrdia, L., & Koole, M. (2020). Online university teaching during and after the Covid-19 crisis: Refocusing teacher presence and learning activity. *Postdigital Science and Education*, 2(3), 923–945. 10.1007/s42438-020-00155-y

Riazi, A. M. (2016). *The Routledge encyclopedia of research methods in applied linguistics.* Routledge., 10.4324/9781315656762

Rubin, H. J., & Rubin, I. S. (2011). *Qualitative interviewing: The art of hearing data.* sage.

Saadé, R. G., & Kira, D. (2007). Mediating the impact of technology usage on perceived ease of use by anxiety. *Computers & Education*, 49(4), 1189–1204. 10.1016/j.compedu.2006.01.009

Saadé, R. G., Kira, D., Mak, T., & Nebebe, F. (2017). Anxiety & performance in online learning. In *In SITE 2017: Informing Science+ IT Education Conferences: Vietnam*, 147-157. 10.28945/3736

Saeed, M. A., & Ghazali, K. (2017). Asynchronous group review of EFL writing: Interactions and text revisions. *Language Learning & Technology*, 21(2), 200–226. 10125/44618

Satar, H., & Özdener, N. (2008). The effects of synchronous CMC on speaking proficiency and anxiety: Text versus voice chat. *Modern Language Journal*, 92(4), 595–613. 10.1111/j.1540-4781.2008.00789.x

Sosa-López, G., & Mora, J. C. (2022). The Role of Speaking Anxiety on L2 English Speaking Fluency, Accuracy and Complexity. *Pronunciation in Second Language Learning and Teaching Proceedings*, 12(1). Advance online publication. 10.31274/psllt.13362

Stockwell, G. R. (2004). CMC for language learning: Examining the possibilities. In *JALTCALL 2004 Conference, Tokiwa University, Mito, Japan* (Vol. 3, p. 3).

Sun, J. C. Y., & Rueda, R. (2012). Situational interest, computer self-efficacy and self-regulation: Their impact on student engagement in distance education. *British Journal of Educational Technology*, 43(2), 191–204. 10.1111/j.1467-8535.2010.01157.x

Teimouri, Y., Goetze, J., & Plonsky, L. (2019). Second language anxiety and achievement: A meta-analysis. *Studies in Second Language Acquisition*, 41(2), 363–387. Advance online publication. 10.1017/S0272263118000311

Thomas, G., & Thorpe, S. (2019). Enhancing the facilitation of online groups in higher education: A review of the literature on face-to-face and online group-facilitation. *Interactive Learning Environments*, 27(1), 62–71. 10.1080/10494820.2018.1451897

Tsang, A. (2018). Positive effects of a program on oral presentation skills: High- and low-proficient learners' self-evaluations and perspectives. *Assessment & Evaluation in Higher Education*, 43(5), 760–771. 10.1080/02602938.2017.1407917

Yanguas, Í. (2010). Oral Computer-Mediated Interaction between L2 Learners: It's about Time! *Language Learning & Technology*, 14, 72–93. 10125/44227

Young, D. J. (1990). An investigation of students' perspectives on anxiety and speaking. *Foreign Language Annals*, 23(6), 539–553. 10.1111/j.1944-9720.1990.tb00424.x

Zhang, K., & Wu, H. (2022). Synchronous Online Learning During COVID-19: Chinese University EFL Students' Perspectives. *SAGE Open*, 12(2), 1–10. 10.1177/21582440221094821

Zhang, W., & Liu, M. (2013). Evaluating the impact of oral test anxiety and speaking strategy use on oral English performance. *The Journal of Asia TEFL*, 10(2), 115–148.

Chapter 13
Immersive Innovations:
Exploring the Use of Virtual and Augmented Reality in Educational Institutions

Sabyasachi Pramanik
https://orcid.org/0000-0002-9431-8751
Haldia Institute of Technology, India

ABSTRACT

This chapter examines the transformative influence of immersive technology, namely Virtual Reality (VR) and Augmented Reality (AR), on higher education. The chapter illustrates the significant impact of VR and AR on education by tracing their evolutionary trajectory from their conceptual roots in the mid-20th century to their current implementations. Conventional lectures and textbooks are being replaced with immersive learning environments, leading to a transformation of traditional classroom paradigms. VR and AR enable students to immerse themselves in virtual environments, where they may engage with three-dimensional models, historical reenactments, and complex simulations. The chapter also explores the challenges and consequences associated with the integration of new technology, such as the need for specialized instruction and ensuring accessibility for all students.

1. INTRODUCTION

The educational domain is now experiencing a substantial and unprecedented transformation amidst relentless and swift technological progress. encountersntional constraints that previously confined the classroom encounter are now liberating themselves from the confines of physical boundaries and temporal restrictions at an astonishing speed. Within the ever-changing educational landscape, we come across the influential and transformative capabilities of immersive technologies, specifically Virtual Reality (VR) and Augmented Reality (AR). These immersive technologies are not just mere instruments; they serve as the driving force behind a pedagogical revolution that has the potential to fundamentally change the way education is delivered. The newly generated opportunities they provide are very thrilling, and they have a transformative impact on higher education. As we embark on this intellectual journey, we find ourselves in a cutting-edge environment where groundbreaking technologies, artificial intelligence, and

DOI: 10.4018/979-8-3693-2857-6.ch013

Copyright ©2024, IGI Global. Copying or distributing in print or electronic forms without written permission of IGI Global is prohibited.

teaching methods come together to provide us with a glimpse of an education future. We aim to delve into the realms of immersive technologies in esteemed higher education institutions, going beyond traditional thoughts and engaging in thorough exploration. Establishing a strong and comprehensive groundwork is the first stage of our investigation as it allows us to completely grasp the profound importance that virtual reality (VR) and augmented reality (AR) have in the realm of education. In the midst of vast possibilities, we must also address the obstacles and moral deliberations that come with incorporating immersive technology into education in a similar way we are faced with dilemmas concerning generative AI. In this discussion chapter, we will examine the complexities of privacy and ethics in immersive education and investigate the crucial role of responsible AI in guaranteeing the ethical use of these technologies and practice in educational environments.

2. THE PROGRESSION OF IMMERSIVE TECHNOLOGIES IN EDUCATION

In order to fully comprehend the substantial influence of immersive technologies on education, it is necessary to delve into their evolutionary trajectory, retracing the origins of virtual reality (VR) and augmented reality (AR) to its nascent stages in the mid-20th century. The rudimentary research and first trials conducted during this era laid the groundwork for what has now evolved into an essential component of the educational environment. The progression from the first conceptualizations to the current advanced immersive experiences demonstrates a notable technical breakthrough. The origins of virtual reality (VR) and augmented reality (AR) may be traced back to the mid-20th century, when early innovators began investigating the possibilities of constructing artificial worlds. The notion of virtual reality, albeit in its early stages, was first developed via experiments such as Morton Heilig's Sensorama in the 1950s. These studies aimed to immerse individuals in a simulated world by stimulating several senses. The development of immersive technology reached a significant milestone with the creation of the first head-mounted display (HMD) by Ivan Sutherland in the 1960s. These first endeavors established the basis for a trip that would ultimately revolutionize the field of education. The evolutionary path persisted over the years, observing incremental advancements in the capabilities of both hardware and software. The first flight simulators, created for military instruction during the 1960s, showcased the potential of virtual reality in producing authentic and engrossing encounters. However, it was not until the late 20th century, when more powerful processing technology became available, that VR and AR transitioned from experimental prototypes to practical applications. The advent of affordable and accessible technology during this time set the foundation for a more extensive incorporation of immersive technologies in various fields, such as education. The proliferation of VR and AR extended beyond research laboratories and began to permeate corporate and educational institutions. This transformation marked the beginning of a new era in which the transformative capabilities of immersive technologies became more apparent. In the realm of higher education, the adoption and incorporation of VR and AR have seen a recent surge (Hodgson, 2021). The formerly limited scope of specialized applications and experimental endeavors has now evolved into a transformative influence across several academic disciplines. Universities and educational institutions are increasingly embracing new technology as powerful tools to actively involve students in ways that conventional methods could not achieve.

The present educational environment is seeing a revival as immersive technology reevaluates instructional methodologies. VR and AR have evolved beyond being just supplementary tools and have now become catalysts for distinctive learning experiences. Educators in several domains, ranging from the sciences to humanities, are harnessing the potential of immersive technology to create interactive and captivating teaching material. New technologies are significantly impacting higher education by allowing for the replication of intricate scientific experiments, transporting students to historical locations, and facilitating practical training in healthcare. Specifically, in scientific fields, virtual laboratories equipped with simulations provide students with the opportunity to conduct experiments in a safe and regulated setting. These virtual activities enhance comprehension and foster the development of critical thinking and problem-solving abilities. VR and AR are revolutionizing medical training by facilitating lifelike surgical simulations and anatomy exploration, providing aspiring healthcare professionals with immersive experiences that were previously unattainable. In addition to the sciences, immersive technologies are reshaping the landscape of disciplines like history, literature, and the arts. Students have the ability to immerse themselves in historical locations, digitally explore ancient civilizations, or encounter the surroundings that influenced literary masterpieces. This hands-on learning goes beyond the limitations of traditional textbooks, allowing for a more profound and sophisticated understanding of historical events, literary narratives, and creative works. The use of virtual reality (VR) and augmented reality (AR) in education is leading to improved student involvement and participation.

According to Adnan (2020), educational games and interactive simulations transform the process of learning into an exciting and unforgettable experience. The shift from passive consumption to active engagement is revolutionizing students' perception and interaction with educational content, fostering a sense of inquisitiveness and exploration. The progress of immersive technologies in education has also been driven by the continuous improvement of hardware. Contemporary virtual reality (VR) headsets include high-quality screens, precise motion tracking, and lifelike haptic feedback, resulting in immersive experiences that closely mimic the real world. AR programs for smartphones and tablets have evolved to seamlessly integrate digital information into the real world. As these technologies become more widely available, educators are faced with unprecedented opportunities to create inclusive learning environments. Students with different cognitive preferences and abilities might get advantages from immersive experiences that accommodate a wide range of requirements. Visual learners excel in interactive 3D environments, whereas kinesthetic learners flourish in simulations that require physical engagement. The advancement of immersive technology in education is not a linear progression, but rather a continuous process of investigation and improvement. The interaction between technological advancements and educational creativity consistently advances the boundaries of what may be achieved. In the future, there will be even more captivating breakthroughs, such as extended reality (XR), which encompasses virtual reality (VR), augmented reality (AR), and mixed reality (MR). These technologies will continue to diminish the boundaries between the physical and digital realms. The integration of immersive technology in education is a testament to the transformative power of innovation. From the first experiments conducted in the mid-20th century to the present age of advanced virtual reality (VR) and augmented reality (AR) applications, these technologies have made significant progress. The surge in adoption and integration inside higher education signifies a paradigm shift in instructors' pedagogical approaches and students' engagement with the learning process. As the process of development progresses, the capacity of immersive technology to transform education remains extensive and captivating, providing new opportunities to foster inquisitiveness, ingenuity, and a more profound comprehension of the universe.

3. REVOLUTIONIZING TEACHING METHODS: ENGAGING AND INTERACTIVE EDUCATIONAL ENCOUNTERS

The introduction of Virtual Reality (VR) and Augmented Reality (AR) has brought about a transformative period in higher education, challenging conventional classroom practices and transforming teaching methods. Traditional teaching methods, such as lectures and textbooks, are being replaced with immersive learning environments, in which students are not only passive recipients of information but actively interact with the subject matter. The profound influence of virtual reality (VR) and augmented reality (AR) on pedagogy lies in their capacity to transport students to virtual realms, providing exceptional opportunities for interactive learning through three-dimensional models, historical reenactments, and intricate simulations (Cicek, 2021). These immersive learning experiences bring about a fundamental change in the way knowledge is imparted and absorbed. Conventional approaches have faced difficulties in capturing students' interest and generating profound comprehension. VR and AR technologies overcome this challenge by creating immersive experiences that blend the boundaries between the physical and digital realms, providing an engaging and interactive educational journey (López Belmonte, 2019). The potential of immersive learning is particularly evident in its ability to transport students to virtual environments that would otherwise be inaccessible. Imagine a biology session where students had the opportunity to explore the intricate components of a human cell in three dimensions, as if they were on a trip within it. By using virtual reality (VR), students may explore the intricacies of cellular biology, gaining a deeper understanding that surpasses the limitations of conventional diagrams and textbooks. Engaging in this practical investigation not only enhances the process of acquiring knowledge but also fosters a sense of curiosity and inquiry.

AR has the potential to animate historical events, transcending temporal and spatial limitations in the realm of history. Students get the opportunity to see historical reenactments, fully engage in the cultural ambiance of past periods, and develop a direct understanding and admiration for pivotal times in history. Instead of simply reading about the construction of the pyramids in Egypt, students can use augmented reality (AR) applications to visually witness the ancient monuments, which provides a sense of scale and historical context that surpasses traditional methods (Choi, 2020). Immersive learning experiences offer more than just engagement; they greatly enhance retention and understanding. Research repeatedly demonstrates that active engagement and hands-on learning enhance knowledge retention. VR and AR technologies allow students to engage with educational information in a meaningful manner, resulting in memorable and captivating learning experiences (Jantjies, 2018). Illustrative instances from many academic fields further highlight the profound impact of immersive learning. VR simulations are revolutionizing medical education in the field of medicine. Students have the opportunity to enhance their surgical skills in a lifelike virtual setting, allowing them to practice surgical procedures without any potential risks, prior to performing them in an actual operating room. This not only enhances their technical expertise but also cultivates a crucial feeling of self-assurance in high-stress medical environments.

Similarly, in the field of architecture and design, virtual reality (VR) enables students to explore virtual structures and settings that they have constructed. They can analyze the intricacies of their designs, scrutinize spatial connections, and make immediate modifications. By adopting a comprehensive approach to education, students are able to improve their design abilities and gain valuable practical knowledge that goes beyond conventional drafting techniques. In the field of sciences, particularly physics and chemistry, virtual reality simulations allow students to conduct experiments that may pose risks or be impractical in a traditional laboratory environment. Students have the ability to alter virtual components, observe responses, and evaluate outcomes inside a regulated and immersive environment. This not only guarantees security but also expands the possibilities for experimentation, enabling students to explore challenges that beyond the limitations of physical labs. The adaptability of virtual reality (VR) and augmented reality (AR) in accommodating diverse learning methods enhances their use in several educational settings. Visual learners may get advantages from the use of three-dimensional models and interactive visualizations, kinesthetic learners can actively participate in hands-on simulations, and auditory learners can engage in immersive experiences that include spatial sounds. The adaptability of these technologies allows instructors to meet the distinct needs and preferences of a varied student population.

As we examine these case studies, it becomes more and more clear that VR and AR are not just tools; they are agents for a transformative educational revolution. The transition from passively consuming information to actively engaging in experiential learning is reshaping the educational environment. Students are now liberated from the limitation of passively acquiring information. They actively engage in the learning process by exploring, experimenting, and internalizing knowledge in ways that were previously unimaginable. The effects of immersive learning experiences extend beyond the immediate academic setting and contribute to the development of essential skills necessary for success in today's society. Students that actively participate in virtual reality (VR) and augmented reality (AR) experiences improve their problem-solving capabilities, critical thinking aptitude, and adaptability. Engaging in virtual environments, making informed choices in simulated situations, and collaborating with peers in immersive spaces provide students with the necessary skills to tackle the demands of the digital era (Steele, 2020). While we acknowledge the profound impact that immersive learning experiences may have, it is important to recognize the constraints that arise when incorporating them. The allocation of resources towards technology and software, the need for instructors to undergo specialized training, and the imperative to address accessibility difficulties are substantial factors that require meticulous consideration. Ensuring equitable access to the advantages of immersive learning is crucial, regardless of students' socio-economic background or geographical location.

4. ENABLING EDUCATORS: CUTTING-EDGE TEACHING RESOURCES

Immersive technologies are at the forefront of a revolutionary approach to teaching, not only reshaping the educational environment for students but also fundamentally changing the role of teachers. Virtual Reality (VR) and Augmented Reality (AR) play important roles in the transformation of education, offering several aspects for the growth and empowerment of educators (Jamali, 2014). The mutualistic association between educators and immersive technology is expanding, resulting in the establishment of an educational environment that flourishes via novelty, involvement, and inclusiveness.

Teachers, acknowledging the capabilities of virtual reality (VR) and augmented reality (AR), are using these technologies to create educational experiences that go beyond conventional limitations. The key lies in their capacity to customize classes to accommodate various learning styles, addressing the distinct requirements of every learner. Through the use of virtual worlds and the integration of digital information into the actual world, educators create an interactive and captivating learning environment. The transition from traditional approaches to immersive experiences represents a significant advancement in the field of education, where learning is no longer restricted to textbooks and conventional teaching tools. As educators explore the realm of immersive technologies, the resources available to them become progressively more advanced (Muzyleva, 2021). These technologies go beyond being simple aids for visualization; they act as dynamic instruments that empower instructors to organize presentations that engage and clarify. Real-time feedback methods increase the learning process by enabling educators to promptly adjust their teaching tactics in response to students' comments (DePape, 2015). The incorporation of virtual reality (VR) and augmented reality (AR) into the educational toolset enables educators to surpass the limitations of traditional teaching methods, creating an atmosphere where learning becomes a customized and participatory experience.

In order for educators to fully harness the capabilities of immersive technologies, it is crucial to strategically include them in the curriculum. Implementing virtual reality (VR) and augmented reality (AR) into lesson plans necessitates a fundamental change in instructional design, with instructors actively integrating these technologies. The aim is not just to enhance conventional education, but to completely transform it, offering students experiences that go beyond the limitations of traditional classrooms. Lesson plans that include virtual situations and augmented aspects enhance comprehension and memory of intricate topics (Delello, 2015). In the field of assessment, educators are transforming conventional approaches by embracing the interactive features of virtual reality (VR) and augmented reality (AR). The era of static paper-and-pencil examinations has passed, giving way to dynamic and participative assessment experiences. Students engage in immersive simulated settings that require them to use their knowledge and problem-solving abilities in real-time. Assessing students' understanding and fostering their analytical and decision-making skills are the main benefits of using immersive technologies in the classroom. These technologies create a realistic environment that simulates real-world complexities. Furthermore, the transformative impact of immersive technologies is not confined to students; it also applies to the professional growth of educators. Educational institutions are adopting professional development programs that focus on immersive technology, acknowledging the need for a fundamental change in teaching approaches. The purpose of these programs is to provide educators with the essential skills and information required to effortlessly incorporate virtual reality (VR) and augmented reality (AR) into their teaching methods. Workshops, training sessions, and collaborative forums provide educators with practical experience, promoting a community of professionals where they may exchange knowledge, effective methods, and creative strategies for immersive education.

The close connection between educators and immersive technologies is strengthening, leading to the emergence of a new kind of educator who are highly skilled in digital literacy and technology. This transformation extends beyond the development of technical skills; it incorporates a change in perspective, as educators transition from being providers of knowledge to being facilitators of experiential learning. Educators' job transitions from conventional teachers to facilitators of immersive experiences, leading students through virtual environments and augmented realities that enhance their educational journey (Nesenbergs, 2020). The influence of immersive technology on special education is remarkable. These technologies provide a wide range of options for meeting the different learning requirements of students, offering tailored and adaptable learning experiences for students with differing abilities. Virtual environments provide inclusive places that enable students, irrespective of their learning methods or physical limitations, to actively participate and interact with educational information. The accessibility and flexibility of immersive technologies enhance inclusivity and equity in the educational domain. The incorporation of Virtual Reality (VR) and Augmented Reality (AR) into education signals a significant shift in teaching methods, going beyond mere technological progress to bring about a transformative change in pedagogy. Immersive technologies have the ability to greatly impact educators by allowing them to go beyond conventional limits, offering a platform for customized and interactive learning experiences. To fully use immersive technologies, it is necessary to integrate them strategically into the curriculum, prepare creative lessons, and provide ongoing professional development for instructors. As education progresses, instructors play a crucial role in leading immersive learning experiences, which are altering the future of education in ways that were previously considered inconceivable.

5. ADDRESSING DISPARITIES: PROMOTING EQUAL OPPORTUNITY AND ACCESSIBILITY IN EDUCATION

Immersive technologies are seen as powerful tools in the ongoing effort to make education more accessible to everyone. These technologies provide innovative ways to overcome obstacles and provide equal opportunities for a wide range of learners. The advanced technologies of Virtual Reality (VR) and Augmented Reality (AR) have the potential to greatly transform the field of education. They can cater to the specific needs of individuals with disabilities and overcome the geographical obstacles that have historically limited access to high-quality education.

Immersive technology has great potential to meet the requirements of those with impairments. Conventional educational institutions may have difficulties in accommodating the distinct learning needs of persons with physical, sensory, or cognitive impairments. Nevertheless, the immersive nature of virtual reality (VR) and augmented reality (AR) presents novel opportunities for fostering inclusive education. These tools enable individuals with disabilities to engage in educational experiences that go beyond the limitations of traditional learning environments. For example, a visually impaired student can explore ancient civilizations through a virtual reality tour (Nabokova, 2019). This immersive experience enables students to explore historical landscapes via detailed descriptions and spatial audio cues, fostering autonomous engagement and understanding of the topic. In the same vein, individuals with auditory impairments might get advantages from augmented reality overlays that provide instantaneous textual subtitles during educational lectures or presentations. Immersive technologies have the ability to break down barriers and create an inclusive educational environment that can accommodate a wide range of abilities (Gudoniene, 2016). In addition to addressing physical impairments, these technologies are also important in meeting different learning styles and preferences. The process of education is highly individualized, and learners differ in their methods of absorbing knowledge. Virtual Reality (VR) and Augmented Reality (AR) provide a versatile platform for educators to develop educational programs that cater to various learning preferences, thereby guaranteeing that each student has the chance to excel. For example, a kinesthetic learner might actively participate in a biology class by digitally dissecting a frog, while a visual learner may examine three-dimensional representations of complicated chemical compounds. The creation of inclusive immersive content is at the forefront of this transformation. Innovators and educators are investing time and money in creating material that goes beyond standard pedagogical limits. This extends beyond the simple incorporation of accessibility features; it requires a thorough approach to creating material that takes into account the diverse needs and preferences of learners. Creating inclusive material requires meticulous attention to detail, including compatibility with assistive devices and providing several avenues for acquiring information (Liarokapis, 2010).

Content development that is inclusive is not only a technological endeavor; rather, it represents a fundamental change in educational philosophy. The statement advocates for a departure from a standardized approach to education and advocates for a strategy that embraces diversity. Collaboration between educators, content producers, and technologists is used to create an educational experience that is immersive and acknowledges and adapts to the unique qualities of each learner. The result is a learning environment that ensures no student is excluded and provides equal opportunities for development, regardless of their abilities or preferred learning methods. The influence of immersive technology on inclusivity goes beyond the individual learner and encompasses whole communities. Historically, geographical limitations have posed significant obstacles to education, especially in distant or economically disadvantaged areas. Virtual Reality (VR) and Augmented Reality (AR) are emerging as powerful tools to democratize education by providing a virtual platform that overcomes the barriers caused by distance and limited resources. Rural students, who were previously isolated from modern educational resources, now have the ability to access the same high-quality content as their urban peers. The democratization of education through immersive technology is not just about granting access to educational material; it is about fostering a feeling of empowerment and ambition. Formerly limited by their physical surroundings, students now have the capacity to explore virtual realms, conduct simulated experiments, and interact with educational material that surpasses the constraints of their real-world environment. Engaging in this activity not only expands their intellectual perspectives but also fosters a feeling of potential and ambition that surpasses the limitations of their immediate surroundings. The progress towards complete integration via immersive technology is not without its obstacles. As the popularity of these technologies increases in educational contexts, it is essential to tackle accessibility challenges at different levels. Addressing hardware costs, technical expertise, and infrastructural constraints is crucial to enable universal accessibility to immersive technology. The promotion of inclusion necessitates a synchronized effort by legislators, educators, and technology developers to create a setting where the advantages of immersive education are accessible to all students, irrespective of their socio-economic level or geographical location.

6. UTILIZING DATA TO INFORM DECISION-MAKING IN ORDER TO IMPROVE EDUCATIONAL OUTCOMES

Artificial intelligence (AI)-powered analytics have become a revolutionary force in the field of education, reshaping both the teaching methods used by educators and the decision-making processes of institutions to enhance educational results. In the midst of this technological revolution, immersive technologies like Virtual Reality (VR) and Augmented Reality (AR) are not only tools for education, but also platforms that generate data. These technologies have the ability to uncover important information about student performance and engagement.

The integration of AI-powered analytics into education signifies a departure from conventional decision-making methods. Educators and institutions now have the opportunity to make informed choices by using data, rather than only relying on anecdotal observations and standardized assessments. The potential for transformation lies not only in the capacity to monitor student progress, but also in the ability to pinpoint specific areas that require additional support and to adjust teaching strategies accordingly. This transformation is driven by the recognition that each student is distinct, with individualized learning needs, abilities, and obstacles. AI-driven analytics empowers instructors to go beyond a generic approach, providing personalized interventions based on specific student data. Through the use of data generated by immersive technologies such as virtual reality (VR) and augmented reality (AR), educators may get a detailed understanding of how students engage with instructional material. This surpasses conventional evaluation criteria by providing insights into nuanced aspects of learning, such as attention span, engagement levels, and problem-solving approaches. For instance, imagine a virtual reality (VR) history lesson where students immerse themselves in the experience of ancient civilizations. AI algorithms have the ability to observe and analyze the students' activities and behaviors in the virtual environment. This includes not just identifying right answers, but also understanding the cognitive processes that led to those answers. This level of detail enables educators to not only assess the knowledge of students but also understand the reasoning behind their decisions. Equipped with this knowledge, educators may personalize their interventions, providing supplementary materials or individualized assistance where it is most needed.

Data-driven decision-making in education has the potential to go beyond only helping individual students and may also lead to changes at the institutional level. Academic establishments are intricate ecosystems with several components that impact results. AI-driven analytics provide a comprehensive view of these dynamics, enabling institutions to identify patterns and trends that impact overall performance. By analyzing data on student engagement in several classes, a school may identify successful teaching methods and areas that may need improvements in the curriculum. Utilizing data to make decisions is a powerful force that drives ongoing advancement. It fosters a culture that promotes adaptability and responsiveness, allowing institutions to continuously refine teaching techniques, curriculum design, and support services using up-to-date information. The traditional method of evaluating performance through end-of-semester tests has been replaced by a flexible process that allows for adjustments to be made in real-time. This ensures that educational strategies can adapt to the constantly evolving needs of students. Numerous real-life examples exist of institutions harnessing the capabilities of AI-powered analytics to improve educational results. An exemplification of this is the use of virtual reality simulations in medical education. Medical education institutions that use virtual reality (VR) technology gather substantial amounts of data on student performance during simulated operations or diagnostic situations. AI systems may analyze this data to identify patterns in decision-making, accuracy in procedural tasks, and areas of difficulty for pupils.

By using these observations, teachers may modify training modules, provide targeted feedback, and guarantee that upcoming medical professionals not only acquire theoretical information but also improve their practical skills. Utilizing data-driven methods enhances the quality of medical education and contributes to advancements in medical training techniques, resulting in positive effects on the broader healthcare industry. With this information, instructors can optimize lesson plans, customize learning experiences, and allocate resources strategically for maximum effectiveness. The result is a classroom environment in which teaching is not a fixed or unchanging activity, but rather a flexible and adaptable practice that takes into account the evolving needs of each student, based on data and information. The use of AI-driven analytics in education is not devoid of challenges. The issues of privacy, ethical implications, and the need for transparent algorithms are crucial factors that need meticulous scrutiny. Given the substantial amount of student data that schools collect and analyze, it is crucial to manage this information responsibly, prioritizing the enhancement of educational outcomes rather than infringing upon individual privacy. Educators must engage in ongoing professional development to effectively navigate the complexities of data-driven decision-making. Proficiently comprehending and effectively using data necessitates a skill set that surpasses conventional educational methods. Institutions should allocate resources towards training programs that enable teachers to proficiently use AI-powered analytics for the advancement of their pupils.

7. OBSTACLES AND MORAL DELIBERATIONS

Within the ever-evolving field of education, where advanced technologies such as Virtual Reality (VR) and Augmented Reality (AR) are rapidly advancing, their ability to bring about substantial changes is accompanied with a complex set of problems and ethical issues. As educators and institutions use these technologies to enhance learning experiences, they must confront significant concerns, especially with privacy, responsible artificial intelligence, and the ethical consequences of using immersive technology in educational environments.

The integration of VR and AR in education is a significant barrier due to emerging privacy concerns. These immersive technologies, which are intended to provide customized and interactive learning experiences, often require the gathering of sensitive data on users. The use of virtual environments and augmented reality activities allows for extensive data collection on students' interactions and responses. This immersive nature goes beyond what traditional educational tools offer. However, educators and institutions face the challenge of navigating a complex landscape of data privacy regulations, each jurisdiction having its own distinct rules and requirements. The task at hand is not just to adhere to these standards, but also to build strong measures that are beyond the bare minimum of what is legally required. Ensuring the protection of student information is of utmost importance, and institutions must take proactive steps to develop strict safeguards in order to safeguard the privacy of individuals interacting with immersive educational material (Radosavljevic, 2020). With the increasing convergence of physical and digital domains, the potential for data breaches and illegal access poses a significant and urgent threat. Institutions must allocate resources towards implementing cutting-edge security measures to protect the huge volumes of sensitive data produced by virtual reality (VR) and augmented reality (AR) apps. This encompasses encryption protocols, robust authentication procedures, and periodic security audits to detect and rectify vulnerabilities. Responsible AI, an integral aspect of the ethical considerations in immersive education, assumes a crucial function in guaranteeing equitable, transparent, and responsible algorithms. The use of artificial intelligence (AI) in educational environments gives rise to apprehensions about biases, discrimination, and the possibility of exacerbating pre-existing disparities. For example, if AI systems are taught using datasets that accurately represent social prejudices; they may unintentionally reinforce similar biases in educational decision-making processes.

In order to deal with these problems, educators and technologists need to take a proactive approach in using AI responsibly. This entails thorough examination of the algorithms used in immersive technologies, openness in the decision-making procedures of AI systems, and ways for holding algorithms accountable in case of mistakes or biases. Furthermore, it is crucial to continuously monitor and evaluate AI systems in order to detect and correct any biases that may arise over time. A fundamental element of responsible AI is ensuring that the algorithms used in immersive educational technologies can be explained and understood. The openness not only cultivates confidence among users but also enables instructors to comprehend the process of AI-driven decision-making. Educators who possess a comprehensive understanding of the reasoning behind AI-generated insights are more capable of responsibly utilizing this information. By having a clear comprehension of the underlying algorithms, they can customize interventions accordingly. The ethical dilemmas presented by immersive technologies in education extend beyond concerns of privacy and responsible AI. The inherent characteristics of modern technologies, characterized by their capacity to generate profoundly captivating and interactive encounters, give rise to inquiries on the likelihood of addiction and excessive dependence. As children increasingly engage in virtual worlds or augmented realities, there is a concern that new technologies may disrupt the equilibrium between screen time and other crucial components of a comprehensive education, such as physical exercise and in-person social connection.

Educators must confront the issue of achieving this equilibrium and advocating for responsible technology use. This entails establishing criteria for the proper use of immersive technology, as well as cultivating digital literacy among students. Developing digital literacy enables students to actively analyze and evaluate technology, comprehend its influence, and make well-informed choices about its use. It is important for educators to be aware of the possible socioeconomic inequalities in the availability of immersive technology. Although new technologies have the potential to transform education, there is a concern that students from economically disadvantaged families may face unequal access to VR headsets, AR gadgets, or high-end computer equipment. The presence of this digital gap might worsen pre-existing disparities in education, impeding the objective of establishing equal opportunities for all students. Tackling these difficulties requires a comprehensive and diverse strategy. Educational institutions should investigate novel finance mechanisms to provide equitable access to immersive technology for all students, irrespective of their financial status. Collaborations with technology firms, government programs, and community partnerships may have a crucial impact in closing the gap between those who have access to digital resources and those who do not, and in ensuring that immersive education is accessible to everyone.

Amidst these problems, it is crucial to highlight the significance of proactive ethical deliberations in the creation and use of immersive technologies in education. Creating ethical protocols and criteria that give priority to safeguarding student privacy, promoting responsible artificial intelligence, and fostering digital literacy will provide the groundwork for the conscientious use of these technologies. Effective implementation of this endeavor requires the cooperation of educators, legislators, technologists, and stakeholders in order to provide a comprehensive structure that promotes creativity and progress, while simultaneously ensuring the protection of students' welfare and rights. The use of immersive technology in education poses several problems and ethical issues that need meticulous attention. Educators and institutions must negotiate a difficult terrain that involves securing privacy, assuring responsible AI, addressing concerns of addiction, and fostering accessibility. To safely harness the transformational potential of immersive education, it is necessary to proactively address obstacles, encourage ethical standards, and prioritize inclusion. This will ensure that technology improves the educational experience for everyone, without compromising it.

8. PROSPECTS FOR THE FUTURE: INNOVATIVE OPPORTUNITIES

As we approach a future shaped by technological advancements, the combination of immersive technologies and generative Artificial Intelligence (AI) presents exciting opportunities for education. In this concluding segment, we go into unexplored domains of the future, investigating the potential impact of combining immersive technology and generative AI on learning experiences. This fusion has the potential to transform education into a dynamic, customized, and universally empowering pursuit.

Generative AI, a branch of artificial intelligence focused on machines autonomously producing material, has the potential to significantly transform the educational field. Envision an educational setting where AI algorithms not just aid but actively engage in the development of dynamic and tailored learning experiences (Martín-Gutiérrez, 2015). This signifies a shift from conventional methods, where educational content remains fixed and consistent, to a time where educational materials continuously change, adjusting to the distinct requirements and preferences of individual learners. One of the most revolutionary uses of generative AI in education is the development of customized learning paths. Artificial intelligence systems, powered by extensive datasets and sophisticated machine learning methods, have the capability to examine the learning patterns, strengths, and areas for growth of individual students. By possessing this detailed insight, the AI system is capable of producing information that closely corresponds to the specific requirements of the student, offering a customized educational experience that optimizes both involvement and understanding.

This customized approach goes beyond traditional fields to provide a comprehensive perspective on education. Generative AI has the capability to provide transdisciplinary learning experiences, enabling students to identify connections between many courses in a seamless and integrated way. An example of this is when a history lecture seamlessly incorporates elements of literature, art, and science, resulting in a comprehensive comprehension of historical events and their wider implications. The future of education is not limited to the traditional classroom setting; it encompasses lifelong learning in the larger world. Generative AI has the capacity to transform the manner in which people interact with the process of learning, by creating customized pathways for professional growth, acquisition of skills, and intellectual exploration. Envision experts use immersive technology to explore virtual environments that accurately reflect real-world problems, led by AI-generated information tailored to their specific professional objectives and learning preferences. The combination of generative artificial intelligence and immersive technology has the potential to fundamentally rethink the notion of evaluations. Conventional examinations and standardized tests might be replaced with dynamic assessments powered by artificial intelligence. These assessments would not only measure information retention but also evaluate problem-solving ability, critical thinking skills, and creativity. Utilizing generative AI, immersive simulations have the potential to expose students to authentic situations, assess their reactions, and provide immediate feedback to facilitate their educational progress.

The notion of the virtual classroom assumes a novel perspective in this utopian future. Immersive technologies, powered by generative AI, have the potential to enable worldwide collaborations and cultural exchanges, beyond geographical limitations. Students from various global locations may convene in virtual environments, participating in cooperative initiatives, cultural interactions, and collective educational encounters. The realization of establishing a worldwide community of students, united by their common quest for knowledge, is made possible. Creativity, often regarded as the fundamental element of innovation, has a prominent role in this futuristic vision. Generative artificial intelligence, with the ability to comprehend and produce imaginative material, assumes the role of a partner in the educational journey. Students have the opportunity to participate in immersive experiences where they collaborate with AI algorithms to generate material, allowing them to explore new areas of creative expression, scientific investigation, and problem-solving.

Within this future context, the function of educators experiences a profound metamorphosis. Teachers assume the role of facilitators and mentors, providing guidance to students as they navigate the ever-changing realm of AI-enhanced, immersive learning experiences. The emphasis transitions from imparting fixed knowledge to fostering students' abilities in critical thinking, creativity, and flexibility. Teachers engage with AI systems that generate material, construct learning experiences, and provide personalized assistance to individual students. As we enthusiastically explore these innovative possibilities, ethical questions become of utmost importance. Transparency, accountability, and a dedication to fairness are essential for the proper use of generative AI in the field of education. It is essential for educators and technologists to guarantee that the algorithms powering individualized learning experiences are equitable, impartial, and devoid of discriminating inclinations. Ensuring a harmonious equilibrium between the advantages of AI-powered customization and the possible hazards of perpetuating preexisting disparities emerges as a critical factor in creating this next era. The issue of privacy, which has always been a difficult problem in the field of technology, requires further focus. Given that AI algorithms are collecting and examining extensive quantities of data to customize educational experiences, it is imperative to ensure the protection of learners' privacy. In order to establish and maintain trust in this advanced educational environment, it is crucial to implement strong data security measures, clearly communicate data use regulations, and continuously monitor AI systems. The future of education, influenced by the combination of immersive technology and generative AI, has great potential. It imagines a future in which learning is not a fixed procedure, but a flexible, customized experience that adjusts to individual need. The capacity to cultivate creativity, analytical thinking, and continuous learning is limitless. As we go towards the future, it is crucial that ethical concerns play a central role in the development and deployment of new technologies. Collaboratively, educators, technologists, politicians, and learners may influence a future in which education is not limited, and where there are endless possibilities for development and exploration.

9. CONCLUSION

Our analysis of immersive technologies, namely Virtual Reality and Augmented Reality, in the context of higher education uncovers a world of remarkable change and unprecedented possibilities. As we progress through the chapters of this book, it is clear that immersive technologies have the potential to significantly change the way we learn, in ways that were not previously considered. The combination of artificial intelligence, disruptive technologies, and advanced educational methods is creating a dynamic learning environment. For effective use of these tools, collaboration between educators and technologists is essential. There are a wide range of possibilities, including revamping the educational environment, empowering educators, and promoting inclusiveness. As we embark on this groundbreaking endeavor, we must also be aware of the challenges and ethical quandaries that arise from incorporating immersive technology into the educational setting. In order to guarantee an ethical and equal future for education, it is imperative that we prioritize responsible AI and data protection. Ultimately, the purpose of this chapter is to encourage and stimulate both educators and technologists to collaborate closely, with the aim of establishing a future in which education is really empowering and available to everyone. The future has arrived, and as we explore the uncharted territories of immersive education, we invite you to accompany us on this groundbreaking journey. Collectively, we have the power to transform education and introduce a period of unimaginable opportunities.

REFERENCES

Adnan, A. H. M. (2020, September). From interactive teaching to immersive learning: Higher Education 4.0 via 360-degree videos and virtual reality in Malaysia. []. IOP Publishing.]. *IOP Conference Series. Materials Science and Engineering*, 917(1), 012023. 10.1088/1757-899X/917/1/012023

Choi, D. H., Dailey-Hebert, A., & Estes, J. S. (Eds.). (2020). *Current and prospective applications of virtual reality in higher education*. IGI Global. 10.4018/978-1-7998-4960-5

Cicek, I., Bernik, A., & Tomicic, I. (2021). Student thoughts on virtual reality in higher education—A survey questionnaire. *Information (Basel)*, 12(4), 151. 10.3390/info12040151

Delello, J. A., McWhorter, R. R., & Camp, K. M. (2015). Integrating augmented reality in higher education: A multidisciplinary study of student perceptions. *Journal of Educational Multimedia and Hypermedia*, 24(3), 209–233.

DePape, A. M., Barnes, M., & Petryschuk, J. (2019). Students' experiences in higher education with virtual and augmented reality: A qualitative systematic review. *Innovative Practice in Higher Education*, 3(3).

Gudoniene, D., & Rutkauskiene, D. (2019). Virtual and augmented reality in education. *Baltic Journal of Modern Computing*, 7(2), 293–300. 10.22364/bjmc.2019.7.2.07

Gurevych, R., Silveistr, A., Mokliuk, M., Shaposhnikova, I., Gordiichuk, G., & Saiapina, S. (2021). Using augmented reality technology in higher education institutions. *Postmodern Openings*, 12(2), 109–132. 10.18662/po/12.2/299

Hodgson, P., Lee, V. W., Chan, J. C., Fong, A., Tang, C. S., Chan, L., & Wong, C. (2019). Immersive virtual reality (IVR) in higher education: Development and implementation. Augmented reality and virtual reality: The power of AR and VR for business, 161-173.

Jamali, S., Shiratuddin, M. F., & Wong, K. (2014). An overview of mobile-augmented reality in higher education. *International Journal on Recent Trends In Engineering & Technology*, 11(1), 229–238.

Jantjies, M., Moodley, T., & Maart, R. (2018, December). Experiential learning through virtual and augmented reality in higher education. In *Proceedings of the 2018 international conference on education technology management* (pp. 42-45). 10.1145/3300942.3300956

Liarokapis, F., & Anderson, E. F. (2010). Using augmented reality as a medium to assist teaching in higher education.

López Belmonte, J., Moreno-Guerrero, A. J., López Núñez, J. A., & Pozo Sánchez, S. (2019). Analysis of the productive, structural, and dynamic development of augmented reality in higher education research on the web of science. *Applied Sciences (Basel, Switzerland)*, 9(24), 5306. 10.3390/app9245306

Martín-Gutiérrez, J., Fabiani, P., Benesova, W., Meneses, M. D., & Mora, C. E. (2015). Augmented reality to promote collaborative and autonomous learning in higher education. *Computers in Human Behavior*, 51, 752–761. 10.1016/j.chb.2014.11.093

Muzyleva, I., Yazykova, L., Gorlach, A., & Gorlach, Y. (2021, June). Augmented and Virtual Reality Technologies in Education. In 2021 1st International Conference on Technology Enhanced Learning in Higher Education (TELE) (pp. 99-103). IEEE. 10.1109/TELE52840.2021.9482568

Nabokova, L. S., & Zagidullina, F. R. (2019). Outlooks of applying augmented and virtual reality technologies in higher education. Professional education in the modern world, 9(2), 2710-2719.

Nesenbergs, K., Abolins, V., Ormanis, J., & Mednis, A. (2020). Use of augmented and virtual reality in remote higher education: A systematic umbrella review. *Education Sciences*, 11(1), 8. 10.3390/educsci11010008

Radosavljevic, S., Radosavljevic, V., & Grgurovic, B. (2020). The potential of implementing augmented reality into vocational higher education through mobile learning. *Interactive Learning Environments*, 28(4), 404–418. 10.1080/10494820.2018.1528286

Steele, P., Burleigh, C., Bailey, L., & Kroposki, M. (2020). Studio thinking framework in higher education: Exploring options for shaping immersive experiences across virtual reality/augmented reality curricula. *Journal of Educational Technology Systems*, 48(3), 416–439. 10.1177/0047239519884897

Videnov, K., Stoykova, V., & Kazlacheva, Z. (2018). Application of augmented reality in higher education. ARTTE Applied Researches in Technics. *Technologies and Education*, 6(1), 1–9.

Chapter 14
Higher Education in the Era of AI

Maihepireti Abulaiti
https://orcid.org/0009-0002-8849-123X
University of Nottingham, Ningbo, China

ABSTRACT

In the rapidly evolving landscape of higher education, the advent of Artificial Intelligence (AI) and specifically the emergence of language models like ChatGPT have sparked a transformative dialogue across academia. Released in November 2022, ChatGPT immediately became a focal point of both admiration and scepticism, illustrating the polarised perspectives on AI's role in education. This chapter will explore the multifaction of ChatGPT in higher education, seeks to navigate the intricate relationship between AI technologies and higher education, with a particular focus on teaching and learning, and leadership by drawing upon a wide range of academic literature to highlight the current developments, future trends, and practical advice for leaders in the field, through a critical examination of the challenges and opportunities presented by AI. This discussion aims to provide valuable insights and guidance for navigating the complexities of transnational higher education leadership in the AI era.

INTRODUCTION

In the rapidly evolving landscape of higher education, the advent of Artificial Intelligence (AI) and specifically the emergence of language models like ChatGPT have sparked a transformative dialogue across academia. Released in November 2022, ChatGPT immediately became a focal point of both admiration and scepticism, illustrating the polarised perspectives on AI's role in education. The integration of AI into educational practices presents a unique set of challenges and opportunities for leadership within transnational higher education institutions, leaders and administrators are tasked with steering their institutions through uncharted territories, balancing the potential benefits of AI in enhancing teaching, learning and administrative efficiencies against the risks associated with data privacy, academic integrity, and the digital divide. Furthermore, the role of AI in teaching training programs is of paramount importance, as AI tools like ChatGPT become increasingly integrated into educational settings, there is a growing need for educators to be well-versed in these technologies. This involves not only understanding how to use AI tools to enhance teaching and learning outcomes, and improve work efficiency but also being aware

DOI: 10.4018/979-8-3693-2857-6.ch014

of ethical considerations and potential biases inherent in AI-generated content. This chapter will explore the multifaction of ChatGPT in higher education, seeks to navigate the intricate relationship between AI technologies and higher education, with a particular focus on teaching and learning, and leadership by drawing upon a wide range of academic literature to highlight the current developments, future trends, and practical advice for leaders and teaching fellows in the field, through a critical examination of the challenges and opportunities presented by AI. This discussion aims to provide valuable insights and guidance for navigating the complexities of higher education leadership in the AI era.

In order to better address this topic and truly engage with the technology which has captured most imaginations I also sought to utilise this resource to evaluate what just effective it was as a tool. On that note, this chapter has in part being co-produced with ChatGPT 3.5, as effectively a co-author. Utilising this tool, or collaborating with ChatGPT depending on how the use is framed, has been pivotal in refining the language and enhancing the clarity of ideas presented herein. As a non-native writer and novice academic, on occasions, I struggled to express complicated thoughts concisely. In this scenario, I put in my ideas and instructed ChatGPT to paraphrase them and produce easy-to-read sentences. In this process, I believe, my writing has improved by actively comparing my original text and ChatGPT's improved text. The primary use involved putting in my ideas, and then ChatGPT refining the language. This is not too dissimilar to using other writing tools such as Grammarly or Marking Mate in some respects. On occasions, I also used it to brainstorm ideas, particularly when seeking advice on the usage of AI tools in leadership. This was particularly helpful given my lack of management experience, as it helped me identify possible challenges and practical considerations I may not have otherwise considered suggesting that ChatGPT could be deemed a research assistant as well as a co-author or even a tutor as Khan (2023) advocates. I, as the main author, meticulously reviewed and revised the content, assuming full responsibility for the final publication. I am grateful to OpenAI for providing free access to such a powerful tool to the public and especially the research community. Additionally, I wish to express my gratitude to my colleague, Gareth Morris, whose unwavering support and encouragement have been instrumental throughout this endeavour.

1. PERCEIVED NEGATIVE IMPACT OF AI ON ACADEMIC INTEGRITY AND ASSESSMENT

The integration of AI tools like ChatGPT into the realm of higher education brings with it a host of transformative potentials and challenges. Among the most significant concerns is the impact on traditional assessment methods, notably, essay writing which has long been a cornerstone of evaluating students' performance in higher education. This section delves into the multifaceted risks associated with ChatGPT, including the erosion of essay integrity as a reliable assessment tool, the challenges in accurately monitoring student performance, the danger of learning loss through over-reliance on AI for content generation, and the risk of template rigidity that may stifle creative and diverse academic writing styles. By exploring these challenges, this chapter aims to provide a comprehensive understanding of the precautions necessary to harness AI's benefits while mitigating its potential drawbacks in educational settings.

1.1 Ethical Concerns

The use of AI tools such as ChatGPT in higher education raises significant ethical considerations which include various aspects such as data privacy, intellectual property, and accountability. Additionally, intellectual property rights and authorship attribution become concerns as AI tools attribute to generate research paper content. Several studies have examined the originality of content generated by ChatGPT. Fitria (2021) uses Quillbot to check the ChatGPT-produced text's similarity and the similarity reached up to 87%, which is far exceeds what is expected in academia. Other tools, SmallSEOTools and Turnitin were used to detect the same, and the similarity rate was 50%. These findings suggest that while ChatGPT can produce original content to a certain extent, there are instances where the generated text indicates high similarity which raises serious concerns about plagiarism (Steponenaite and Barakat, 2023). Moreover, a study suggested that academic misconduct has tripled since the rapid development and misuse of AI tools (Natzel and Mael, 2023). Apart from this, ChatGPT can also be used for malicious purposes by spreading misinformation. To further illustrate, if false information is widely spread on the internet and becomes an open acknowledge lessening trust in published material and a regular discussion item linked to AI, it will then likely influence public opinion regarding tools such as ChatGPT and this will lead to increased social concerns as it can, in a way, control the direction of public opinion and have a widespread impact (Hua, 2023). Besides, the sophisticated language ChatGPT can generate makes creating spam easier than ever before. Therefore, as many scholars (e.g., Wach, 2023) have advocated AI tool developers must prioritise ethical concerns and emphasize the significance of privacy and security of users and data.

Apart from ethical concerns related to the usage of ChatGPT, the mistreatment of workers involved in training AI systems, as described in the example, also contributes an ethical issue. Time magazine revealed that the Kenyan workforce was underpaid while doing the content filtering job by identifying hate speech from unsavoury websites (Ray, 2023). This emphasizes the broader ethical concerns beyond its direct application and usage.

1.2 The End of the Coursework Essay as an Assessment

Assessment is widely acknowledged as a crucial component for enhancing learners' language proficiency, especially with essay writing, serving as a primary instrument to gauge learners' comprehension of knowledge, critical thinking skills and various cognitive abilities. A study has indicated that ChatGPT is used by almost 89% of American college students to complete homework assignments, with 53% using it for paper writing. In addition, 48% of students use it during exams and 22% use it to generate paper outlines (McGee, 2023). Nevertheless, the students' integration of ChatGPT into the assessment landscape has sparked considerable debate due to its potential false implications. The most noticeable, obvious challenge for now is that it threatens essay writing as an assessment. Scholars, such as Yeadon et al. (2024), have voiced concerns regarding its impact, suggesting that the use of it poses a significant threat to the integrity of essays as an assessment modality. This is supported by their research study, in which the findings show that the current natural language processing AI presents a major threat to short-from essays as an assessment method in the Physics course. Chomsky criticised it as a form of 'high-tech plagiarism' (Stewart, 2023), alluding to its transformative influence on educational practices. Students can now simply put the instructions in the Chatbox and get a passable essay as it is difficult for teachers to determine whether students are using it or not. Indeed, empirical investigations, such as those by Gill et al. (2024), have demonstrated the capacity of ChatGPT to circumvent conventional plagiarism detection mechanisms like Turnitin. This phenomenon raises profound questions regarding the academic credibility, validity, and fairness of assessments conducted with ChatGPT-generated content. Moreover, in some situations where teachers have a familiarity with students' abilities, there may indeed be instances where they suspect that a student is utilising ChatGPT or similar tools, yet lack concrete evidence or institutional support to address the issue. This can leave teachers feeling uncertain about how to proceed when universities have not yet established clear policies or procedures regarding the use of AI-assisted tools in academic settings. It also leaves the assessments as potentially pointless exercises because they do not measure what they are designed to, which is whether the student has mastered the intended learning outcomes being covered within its remit.

Additionally, students employing AI tools for assessment introduces challenges related to accurately monitoring students' performance and identifying learning difficulties. Gill et al. (2024) underscore the inherent limitations in overseeing students' engagement and progress when AI-generated assessments are used, leading to deficiencies in both evaluation and feedback mechanisms. Consequently, this compromises the effectiveness and reliability of assessment practices reliant on AI-generated content. Moreover, excessive reliance on ChatGPT may result in learning loss, particularly in developing critical thinking and creativity skills, as students may not adequately evaluate the information provided and rely on it blindly. This may undermine key objectives of writing pedagogy, such as articulating ideas with clarity and precision and greatly affect students' learning outcomes and development (Kasneci et al., 2023). Nonetheless, it can be argued that when used appropriately, ChatGPT can potentially aid non-native students and academic scholars in improving their overall academic writing skills, although this contention is subject to further discussion in section 4.4. Furthermore, ChatGPT exhibits a degree of template rigidity in writing, potentially stifling diversity in writing styles if people use it to structure or preview their writing. When prompted to write essays on various concepts, ChatGPT tends to adhere to a specific structure, beginning with a definition, followed by a historical overview, a discussion of effects, and concluding with a summary and call to action. While this structure aligns with academic conventions, it is crucial to recognize that academic writing norms evolve over time. Over-reliance on ChatGPT-generated structures could hinder progress in human writing history by homogenizing writing styles. Thus, writers should exercise caution in utilising it for assistance, recognising its limitations and preserving human intelligence and creativity. While tasks such as proofreading, idea brainstorming, and literature review are deemed accessible (Rane, 2023), it is essential not to diminish human intellect, as the writing conventions ChatGPT draws upon are products of current human intelligence. Continued reliance on it without fostering creativity and invention may impede future advancements unless AI can automatically create without relying on existing data. The above challenges might become more significant issues once Microsoft integrates ChatGPT into its products (Warren, 2023) and it becomes mainstream since it might have far more impact than possibly ruining assessment. It might perpetuate social biases as (if) the large data that the model is trained on is biased or false, which will be discussed in the following paragraph.

1.3 False, Biased, Information

Aside from posing a threat to essay writing as an assessment tool in higher education, reliability and precision issues associated with ChatGPT have also raised concerns within the educational sphere. Firstly, it has been harshly criticised for its uneven accuracy. As of its last update in 2021, ChatGPT3.5 has not been fully equipped with current information, although the new version ChatGPT 4.0 now accesses up-to-date information from the internet. This means information such as events, and scholarly articles since 2021 will be drawn up on, which has a great potential to make literature review and synthesizing information easier for scholars than it is before. A more significant concern is its propensity to generate false information, including fabricated data and citations, which could be highly misleading for users who depend on it completely (Rane, 2023). For example, a study's findings indicate that responses from ChatGPT were of low quality for scientific publication and 69% of the references cited by it were found to be fabricated (Gravel, 2023). Consequently, the full integration of ChatGPT into higher education settings without significant improvement is deemed inappropriate at this stage.

Another major concern is that ChatGPT's response is heavily influenced by the data it has been trained on (Qadir, 2023) and if the data contains potential bias or inaccuracies, the tool may reinforce such bias and may even perpetuate unfair social norms or advantage certain groups. Its implementation in higher education could inadvertently reinforce biased information in daily educational practices, potentially exacerbating- existing disparities. For example, before ChatGPT, Microsoft's Tay chatbot caused a lot of trouble in 2016 when it overflowed the internet with racist and misogynistic content. This happened because the chatbot was impacted by offensive training data that internet trolls supplied (Chomsky et al, 2023). As for now, the issue of flooding the internet with offensive content may not be a serious concern for ChatGPT as the coders have taken measures to prevent it from introducing anything novel to controversial- 'it sacrificed creativity for a kind of amorality' (Chomsky et al, 2023, p. 5). They seemed to discuss it as a limitation in terms of creativity as ChatGPT lacks taking a side. However, I contend that this characteristic is probably advantageous. By presenting multiple perspectives, and without taking a side, ChatGPT enables users to engage critically and independently, fostering informed decision-making and opinion formation. This approach mitigates the risk of imparting immoral responses or influencing users' thoughts, representing a commendable attribute of ChatGPT from an ethical standpoint.

Continuing with biased information ChatGPT may possibly reinforce, several recent studies have investigated this issue. Wen and Younes' (2024) study aimed to evaluate ChatGPT's ability to identify different types of media bias using the Media Bias Identification Benchmark (MBIB). The result indicated that ChatGPT is capable of detecting hate speech and context bias in text but, importantly, more subtle types of bias such as gender, cognitive, racial bias and fake news, are more challenging for it to identify. This again, aligns with Chomsky et al's (2023) statement on how it lacks understanding and reasoning. Similarly, Ray (2023) also emphasized how ChatGPT is prone to various biases and may potentially perpetuate stereotypes and reinforce existing biases. For example, it may exhibit bias towards language that is more predominantly presented in its training data and possibly prioritise content in the dominant language while neglecting minority language. This is shown in Jiao's (2023) study which indicated that the data used to train ChatGPT may predominantly originate from more developed countries. An example of this is its performance discrepancies between high-resource languages like English and German compared to low-resource languages like Romanian and Chinese. This in the longer term, to a certain level, disadvantages developing countries' benefits such as values and cultures. Moreover, ChatGPT's responses may reflect cultural norms prevalent in its training data, potentially favouring or disfavouring certain cultural practices or beliefs without considering their diversity and quality (Ray, 2023). This contradicts many universities' principles, which prioritise diversity, equality and inclusiveness. If such tools are to be implemented in higher education, careful adaption is essential before utilization, particularly in transnational higher education settings where students and staff hail from diverse cultural backgrounds.

Respecting each other's culture, especially those of non-dominant groups, is extremely significant and requires thoughtful consideration from leaders and management.

Another study (Urman and Makhortykh, 2023) showed Language Model models (LMMs) handle political information and false claims differently. For example, Google Bard refused to respond to questions about Russia even though the information was readily available through Google Search. Additionally, the Google Bard chatbot was more inclined to produce false claims in some cases as the media widely reports. It also avoids responding to sensitive topics in other global localities, whereas other chatbots like ChatGPT and Bing do respond. This suggests that LLMs may be influenced by censorship strategies employed by programmers. In contrast, Huang and Sun's (2023) study suggested ChatGPT demonstrate commendable performance in detecting fake news. These issues underscore the potential harm ChatGPT could cause without proper guidance and implementation strategies in higher education. Despite these challenges, there are a large number of proponents who acknowledge the potential benefits of ChatGPT when used judiciously. These will be further examined in the subsequent discussion, emphasizing its capacity to enhance the essay writing process and facilitate L2 learning outcomes.

2. ADDRESSING THE RISKS: STRATEGIES AND SOLUTIONS

The above challenges posed by ChatGPT in education demand for comprehensive responses from educational institution and educators alike. In response to them, the following solutions are suggested to mitigate the potential negative impact that it can bring to academia. The solutions involve two parts: firstly, there is a pressing need for innovation in writing assessment methodologies, which would require students to orally elucidate and defend their written ideas. Additionally, a shift towards a process-oriented assessment approach, focusing on the cognitive processes and strategies employed by students through their learning journey, and aligning assessment with class activities and including reflective components, serve to reinforce learning outcomes and diminish the likelihood of simplistic text generation. Moreover, a reconsideration of marking criteria, with a heightened emphasis on critical analysis and content quality over grammatical mechanics, is advocated. Secondly, more accurate AI detection tools need to be invented, at the same time, it is crucial to underscore the ethical imperative of transparency and responsible AI usage since detection tools may not always yield infallible results.

2.1 Beyond Plagiarism: Innovating Writing Assessment in the AI Era

To address the plagiarism challenges arising from advanced AI text generation tools in higher education, institutions must respond promptly and collaboratively. Mere prohibition or disregard of such a tool will not suffice, considering its persistent presence. Some extreme viewpoints advocating for the elimination of essays as assessments and the return of pen-and-paper exams risk regressing education. However, this might be a regression of education. Essay writing offers significant benefits (Brown, Bull & Pendlebury, 2013), especially formative essays, enabling learners to receive feedback on their plans, drafts, and interactive improvements throughout the semester, thereby enhancing their writing, analytical, and critical thinking skills. Therefore, instead of going back to pen-and-paper exams, teachers should reconsider their approach to writing assessments by incorporating interactive tools to mitigate plagiarism risks. Schools need to make appropriate adjustments to teaching methods and examinations standards to ensure that students adhere to academic integrity (Stephens, 2023). For instance, conducting viva voce examinations at the end of the semester, where students defend their written essays orally (Allen, 2022), provides an opportunity to assess the authenticity of their ideas and fosters presentation and communication skills essential for higher education and future employment. Some might argue oral exams might increase the teachers' workload. Alternatively, video submission of students reflecting on their writing process is another way to avoid cheating. This might be more manageable than having viva voce examinations as it is online and therefore offers greater flexibility, as it eliminates constraints related to time and location.

Furthermore, a process-oriented assessment can be implemented. It involves evaluating the strategies and cognitive processes employed by the learners to complete a task throughout their learning journey, instead of solely focusing on the final product or outcome (Jeltova, 2007). This can to a large extent reduce the chance of students using ChatGPT to generate a response as the thought process and demonstration of understanding are assessed and they require students' deeper level of thinking. Additionally, aligning writing assessments with classroom activities, such as reflecting on class tasks and discussions, enhances the relevance of the assessment and can very possibly reduce the likelihood of AI-driven content replication as well. Notably, it might be crucial to advise teachers to design out opportunities for plagiarism in assessments, therefore, AI-based writing identification technologies should be implemented at institutions (Gill et al., 2024) which will be discussed in the following section 3.2. While both learners and researchers may seek assistance from ChatGPT to improve language fluency Hasanein and Sobain, 2023), it is essential to recognise that this practice may be unavoidable in the modern era. Consequently, it is probably time to reassess assessment criteria, shifting the focus from language mechanics to content quality and critical analysis. This means grammar and lexis should probably be undermined or eradicated from the marking descriptor since students can easily have their work polished using AI tools. This might also provide a fairer academic environment for international students/ scholars whose first language is not English and even after taking academic courses to improve their writing proficiency, they may still struggle to convey their meaning comprehensively due to reasons such as due to L1 interference, which often put them in disadvantaged position compared to native English speakers in the context of transnational higher education.

2.2 AI Detection and Integrity Tools

Implementing AI-based writing identification technologies is imperative for ensuring fairness and academic integrity in higher education. Various tools, such as GPTZero and AICheat Check, utilise advanced technologies to detect AI involvement in written texts. The former tracks AI involvement using elements like perplexity and it can recognise longer text than shorter text (Ghani, 2023), while AICheat Check examines sentence structure and readability and, the testing algorithm of it is not transparent enough to let users know how it detects human written text and AI written text. However, they both need further accuracy improvement and such "ChatGPT detectors" appear to be rather easy to mislead (Rikab, 2023). Alternatively, "water-marking" AI-generated texts (Hern, 2022) is certainly a way to avoid plagiarism issues. However, students can always use another device to type out what is generated by themselves, instead of simply copy-pasting. While a joint effort is needed from application developers to create a reliable detector to maintain the fairness, reliability and validity of high-stakes examinations in higher education, it is worth bearing in mind that such tools may not be infallible. This is because these tools often operate based on assumptions and have inherent limitations, potentially leading to errors in analysis.

Therefore, human interpretation is also critical, as professionals must understand the tools' capabilities and contextualise their results, but most importantly, the writers should acknowledge the use of AI.

3. LEVERAGING AI FOR EDUCATIONAL ENHANCEMENT

Apart from challenges, ChatGPT has great potential to reshape the educational landscape across various domains, including Automated Essay Scoring (AES), material development, enhancing learner autonomy, and aiding non-native scholars in academic writing. These advancements herald a paradigm shift in how educational processes are approached, reducing educators' workload through streamlined grading with AES and AI-assisted material creation, enhancing learner autonomy in flipped classrooms, and democratising academic writing for scholars facing language barriers. They will be critically discussed in sequence in the following section.

3.1 Automated Essay Scoring (AES): Revolutionising Feedback and Reducing Workload

Automated essay scoring, or AES, is the process of evaluating and scoring written assessments with the use of technology. Computer programs are used to analyze and score written work according to pre-determined marking criteria (Mizumoto & Eguchi, 2023). Its origins can be seen in the Project Essay Grade (PEG) of the 1960s, which was primarily determined by comparing scores provided by human raters to measurable text qualities, such as the average sentence length and the quantity of commas (Page, 1966). It was criticized for ignoring the substance and concentrating exclusively on the surface structure, which allowed students to cheat by adding more words and commas (Attali, 2013). In the 1990s, as computers became more sophisticated, more accurate AES systems were developed that paid attention to both content and surface linguistic aspects (Hussein et al., 2019). The Educational Testing Service (ETS) created the E-rater in 1998 as an example of a novel system that enables the examination of syntax, morphology, and semantics (Burstein et al., 2013). Because of its high reliability and validity, it has been utilized in high-stakes exams including the Graduate Record Examination (GRE) and the Test of English as a Foreign Language (TOEFL) (Attali & Burstein, 2004). It offers both qualitative comments and numerical scores. In spite of its effectiveness, AES has not been widely used in higher education. However, there is growing potential for tools like ChatGPT to bridge this gap as ChatGPT has yet to be utilized in AES but has a great possible application as suggested by scholars (e.g., Essel, 2023). This is supported by various research studies. A study (Latif & Zhai, 2024) has shown the transformative potential of fine-tuned ChatGPT-3.5 in educational assessment, offering a scalable solution for enhancing accuracy and efficiency in grading students' assessments in science tests. Mayer et al (2023) also conducted a study which is comparable to AES, they used ChatGPT to classify polite and impolite business emails. It shows that without programming and by merely through a prompt-based approach, it attains a similar accuracy level as human ratings. Such a prompt-based language approach of ChatGPT enables non-experts in AES and is more user-friendly. Therefore, they further highlight that this will encourage more people to use artificial intelligence as it is easy to access, engage and use by simply putting in prompts.

In another study focusing on education, researchers compared 200 instances of human-generated feedback with 200 instances generated by ChatGPT. The findings revealed that the quality of ChatGPT's feedback closely approximated that of human-generated feedback, without necessitating any specialised training (Steiss et al., 2024). This slight variance suggests that feedback produced by ChatGPT can effectively serve as valuable instructional material, especially during the initial phases of writing, thereby stimulating students to undertake timely revision. Even though the same study observed that well-trained and remunerated evaluators, possessing ample time resources, were capable of furnishing feedback of superior quality compared to ChatGPT, it is worth bearing in mind the human evaluators were aware that their feedback was under scrutiny by the research team, potentially influencing the nature of their responses. For instance, the encouraging tone prevalent in the human-generated feedback within this study may not accurately mirror real-world scenarios where certain educators primarily emphasize error correction in feedback, leading to student disengagement (Busse, 2013). Such limitation might suggest that ChatGPT may outperform evaluators who are constrained by time limitations and an overwhelming workload, thereby hindering the ability to deliver comprehensive and supporting feedback. Human biases may inadvertently infiltrate the process of assessment, which has the potential to undermine their fairness and objectivity. I believe few educators can claim absolute certainty in their impartiality, experiencing occasional doubts regarding their grading consistency, especially in high-stakes university settings, where scores significantly influence students' future and scholarship opportunities, this becomes particularly pronounced and markers frequently content with significant levels of stress. In this light, integrating both AI and human co-marking presents a compelling solution for higher education management to address the drawbacks associated with human bias, thereby facilitating a fair and objective assessment process, this approach not only mitigates the limitations inherent in human marking but also preserves the advantages offered by experienced human markers.

Nevertheless, the implementation of such an approach requires comprehensive deliberation and collaboration between education institutions and application developers. Rather than awaiting institutional decisions, individual teachers can probably integrate this approach into their daily teaching practices. The pedagogical benefits of utilising ChatGPT in lower-stakes class practice are significant, particularly in EAP writing class. One possible way is that teachers can collect students' writings, input them into ChatGPT for language improvement, academic style checks and feedback then refine the AI-generated suggestions to align with each student's level before sharing it back to them. This method significantly benefits student writing development, as timely and personalised feedback are critical factors in improving writing skills (MacArthur, 2016) but often surpasses what teachers can feasibly provide due to their workload (Graham, 2019). By comparing the student's original work with the enhanced versions from ChatGPT, students can pinpoint areas needing improvement. Furthermore, teachers can utilise ChatGPT to identify common mistakes and improvement areas within the class and create tailored activities to address these needs by simply putting in prompts accordingly. This is not to say teachers can trust it entirely but this approach has been implemented in my classroom, yielding effective results in enhancing teaching and learning.

Interestingly, Kumar's (2023) research investigates the debate over using AI technology to grade student papers, using the case of an adjunct professor as an example. This paper discusses the convenience, pedagogical merits as well as drawbacks such as privacy, legality and ethics. The author raises several thought-provoking questions regarding the use of AI including public perception, and faculty attitude towards AI grading. Notably, inputting students' work into ChatGPT can raise ethical concerns. It is crucial to consider issues such as privacy, consent, and intellectual property rights as mentioned at the beginning of this chapter, which is one of the main issues. Moreover, students may not anticipate their work being used in such a manner and might have reservations about their ideas being analysed or potentially shared without their explicit consent. Comparable concerns arose with the widespread adoption of text-matching software tools such as Turnitin in the late 2000s (Brinkham, 2013; Vanacker, 2011). This suggests a call for reflection on potential ethical, practical and societal implications arising from the use of AI technology in education.

Apart from ethical concerns, the integration of ChatGPT into the educational framework as AES may also redefine educators' roles, steering them away from traditional evaluative tasks towards providing more tailored support and mentorship to students (Adiguzel et al., 2023). On the bright side, the advantages of AI in terms of efficiency and the simplicity with which exams can be prepared and assessed are clear, offering a stark contrast to the labour-intensive process of manual grading. This is particularly helpful considering the fact that many teachers in higher education need to balance between research and teaching (Houston, et al., 2006), potentially leading to heightened stress levels and may diminish the quality of their output. Nonetheless, these benefits are accompanied by concerns about the loss of essential human interaction and engagement in the educational journey (Latif & Zhai, 2024). The risk of overreliance and dependency on AI for evaluative feedback could undermine the development of critical thinking skills and reduce opportunities for meaningful personal exchanges, both of which are vital for holistic educational experiences (Mhlanga, 2023).

3.2 AI in Material Development: Streamlining Content Creation for Educators

Material development represents a significant aspect of educators' workload in higher education. Harnessing ChatGPT appropriately could substantially alleviate this burden, fostering greater job satisfaction among educators and affording more time for meaningful interactions with students. According to analysis by Koraishi (2023) highlights ChatGPT's utility in automating lesson planning potentially yielding standardised and high-quality materials tailored to specific themes and learning objectives. Although AI-generated lesson plans may necessitate review and customisation to align with educators' professional preferences, the collaborative potential between educators and AI holds promise for more efficient teaching practices. Additionally, ChatGPT's ability to generate academic texts can significantly reduce the time and effort required for material development, a particularly beneficial feature given the demand for up-to-date and authentic content in education settings. To further illustrate, for example, in EAP class, pedagogically, academic text (for reading and writing courses) and academic presentations (speaking and listening courses) are often used as a vehicle to carry the academic conventions or target language in an inductive way to encourage learners to figure out and identify such features or language by themselves to enhance learner autonomy, which is a commonly used pedagogical approach. With ChatGPT, teachers can put in the instructions, target language, intended learning outcome and language and grammar features to be included. It can then produce text ready to use. As for the presentation, teachers can create videos by providing the content with the newly introduced Sora, which is a video generator (OpenAI, 2024). This collaborative and innovative approach among teachers and Chatgpt has more advantages and should be encouraged by higher education to reduce teacher workload, which ultimately fosters more effective teaching practices.

3.3 Pedagogy: Promoting Learner Autonomy, Enabling Flipped Classrooms

In higher education, conventional pedagogy—such as lectures and explanations—remains prevalent despite the tremendous advancements in modern technology. Studies conducted over many years have looked at several strategies that offer personalized learning and hence increase student autonomy. In Kim's (2022) study, for example, students first complete a diagnostic evaluation. The AI tool then evaluates the data and offers lectures, explanations, and exercises according to the learners' needs and skill levels. In a similar vein, Lee et al. (2023) investigated an approach known as learner-generated context-based (LGC), which allows students to create their own learner-generated context and study within it. As learners take action and make decisions, the system adjusts to meet their needs and preferences by delivering more content. Their research indicated the need to reinforce a supportive environment for active content sharing and interaction among learners. Application developers should consider developing educational tools which implement these approaches and enable personalised learning and therefore enhance learning autonomously and independently. Universities could consider implementing such tools in their learning and teaching, which will be a game changer for higher education.

In addition to this, tools such as ChatGPT can enhance Flipped learning and promote learners' autonomy with its customised and engaging learning experience. The benefits of Flipped learning, where students are introduced to learning concepts before class and classroom time is dedicated to engaging in discussions, solving problems, and applying concepts, have been talked about for decades, however, it is still reported that pre-class learning can be challenging for the students (Sanderson, 2023). With ChatGPT, such an approach might be finally more accessible because it can act as a private tutor and extend to providing pre-class instructional materials tailored to individual learning needs, thus ensuring a more effective and personalised flipped classroom experience (Gill et al., 2024). ChatGPT's role in flipped learning can be seen in its ability to prepare students for in-class activities by offering them a platform to explore concepts at their own space. For example, through interactive dialogue, ChatGPT can guide students through complex theoretical concepts for problem-solving exercises before they attend the classroom session. This preparation enables students to engage more effectively in discussion and collaborative activities during the class, as they come equipped with a baseline understanding of the topic at hand. Its capacity to clarify concepts and facilitate independent research also enhances active learning, creating opportunities for participatory activities like group discussions and debates during class time and therefore, enables the goal of building a flipped learning classroom, particularly in language learning. Apart from this, AI also allows learners to be more active in participating in goal setting and becoming autonomous learners. For example, ChatGPT can help learners create techniques for making learning plans and semester goals (Hew et al., 2023). This is particularly applicable to students in higher education who often have plenty of free time and struggle with time management and goal setting. Notably, the success of incorporating AI tools in flipped classrooms hinges on the ability of educators and students to critically engage with technology. Educators must be adept at designing activities that leverage ChatGPT's capabilities to enhance learning outcomes, while students need to distinguish between credible and non-credible information provided by the AI.

3.4 AI-powered Writing Assistant: Empowering Non-native Scholars and Students

Beyond teaching, publishing research articles is a critical aspect of professional development for university teachers, albeit one that can be intimidating, particularly for non-native scholars. It is reported that writing academically in English presents significant challenges, including linguistic proficiency, and unfamiliarity with academic conventions, especially when comparing themselves with first-language users of English (Ferguson et al., 2011). Many studies have explored the academic writing difficulties faced by multilingual scholars publishing in internationally refereed English-medium journals such as Chinese (Flowerdew, 2000), Portuguese (Bennett, 2010) Korean (Hwang, 2023), Spanish, Hungarian and Slovakian (Lillis and Curry, 2010) researchers and academics. The difficulties are not only in terms of their limited English proficiency such as grammar, vocabulary and sentence structure. ChatGPT emerges as a promising solution, offering continuous support and language refinement, thereby reducing barriers to academic writing. Proofreading is the key drive for using ChatGPT, according to a study examining perceptions of ChatGPT in higher education. Students commented on how it aids in enhancing clarity and conveying meaning more effectively, while faculty members also emphasized its utility as an editing service when preparing research papers, thereby increasing the likelihood of scholarly publication acceptance and securing funding from agencies (Hasanein and Sobain, 2023). This shows the widespread use of ChatGPT's function as writing assistant in higher education, use not only by students but also the faculty members. Another recent study (van Inwegen et al., 2023) also shows that workers' chance of being hired is also improved by using AI-based text assistance for crafting resumes. While It cannot replace human judgment or understanding, its role as a round-the-clock reviewer can significantly assist non-native scholars to express themselves effectively. Additionally, publishing more articles often means a higher chance of being tenured professors and researchers with career promotion and salary increase, improved work package, which might then improve employee job satisfaction and retention.

The same impact AI tools possibly have on non-native scholars applies to the students too. Many studies have proved the significance of AI use in improving L2 learners' writing by improving mainly vocabulary and grammar. Dizon and Gayed (2021) found students using the AI-powered tool Grammarly made fewer grammatical errors and wrote with more lexical variation. Nazari et al. (2021) also emphasized the positive outcomes, with students improved self-efficacy in writing by using Grammarly as a feedback tool for writing. It is worth mentioning that learners need to have the right attitude and learning motivation when using these tools. Instead of simply clicking a button such as 'make it more academic' on Grammarly, students need to actively compare their original writing with the improved version to identify the difference and seek to improve their writing, or else their writing competence might stay at the same level or even get worse.

However, caution must be exercised regarding potential issues such as misinformation, and plagiarism, as mentioned previously. Additionally, some scholars might go extreme and argue the urgency of implementing ChatGPT in writing and free up time for other learning Objectives. For example, Herbold et al. (2023) systematically compared the quality of human-written versus AI-generated argumentative essays and found that ChatGPT generates higher-quality essays. They emphasize the need to re-invent homework and use AI tools in the same way as math utilises the calculator. However, writing helps to form people's thoughts logically, and it is a creative process. If it is taken away from humans and AI is writing for us, then human intelligence might be facing huge challenges. As Chomsky et al (2023) highlighted ChatGPT and similar programs are inherently in memorising vast amount of data, but they are not capable of distinguishing the possible from the impossible. In contrast, humans, who possess a universal grammar can grasp the underlying rules and meanings. For example, while humans can interpret nuances and context in a sentence to interpret it more effectively, tools like ChatGPT might make incorrect interpretations which highlights the complexity and sophistication of the human brain compared to AI, which relies heavily and solely on the pattern of data rather than true comprehension. Therefore, I believe, that when AI tools such as ChatGPT is used appropriately as a tool to, for example, polish, and brainstorm ideas, ChatGPT holds immense potential for democratising academic publication, facilitating global knowledge exchange and improve productively.

As mentioned previously, another point worth bearing in mind is that while ChatGPT adheres to a predetermined structure, its rigidity may inadvertently hinder the organic development of academic writing conventions. Although capable of emulating human intelligence in certain tasks such as proofreading, ChatGPT falls short in replicating the nuanced qualities in human expression. It lacks the emotional depth and life experiences that contribute to an individual's voice and writing distinctiveness (Ray, 2023). Moreover, ChatGPT's ability to introspect its own writing and evaluate the accuracy of self-generated content poses significant limitations, particularly in areas where consensus is lacking. Additionally, its understanding of complex concepts remains superficial, lacking the higher-order thinking skills and emotional intelligence required for deeper comprehension. Despite these constraints, ChatGPT presents unique opportunities for re-evaluating existing writing practices, especially for non-native scholars and students who encounter challenges in presenting their findings in English. Overall, the integration of LLMs like ChatGPT serves to enrich scientific discourse, enabling researchers and students in higher education to contextualise their work, enhance data analysis, and facilitate effective communication, particularly for non-native users striving to express themselves proficiently. Some journals and institutions recognise the role of LLMs in reducing language barriers, thereby fostering greater inclusivity and promoting knowledge dissemination on a global scale. Nonetheless, the feasibility of enforcing a blanket ban on LLMs remains uncertain, as these tools offer undeniable benefits despite their inherent limitations and occasional errors as discussed.

3.5 Co-Authorship in Publication

Research collaboration between AI and humans has many facets. Positively, researchers can emphasize ChatGPT's ethical and responsible use by collaborating with it. It provides scholars with a useful instrument for planning and editing research papers. Because ChatGPT can access the internet, it can help with literature reviews, recommend pertinent publications, and summarize important findings. By acting as a research assistant, it can save researchers time and effort. Nevertheless, using ChatGPT carelessly in academic research may have negative consequences. Because researchers may unintentionally include unattributed AI-generated content into their work, there is a considerable risk of unintended plagiarism. This raises ethical questions regarding the authorship of research publications in addition to endangering academic integrity (Rane, 2023). It is worth discussing how the journals perceive the usage of AI in publications. The use of Large Language Models (LLMs) such as ChatGPT in academia remains controversial, primarily concerning issues of authorship, originality, AI hallucinations and factual inaccuracies. While some publication venues have explicitly prohibited their use, such as Science, which has stated a policy whereby 'text generated from AI, machine learning, or similar algorithmic tools cannot be used in papers published in science journals, nor can the accompanying figures, images, or graphics be the product of such tools. AI cannot be an author of academic journal articles. Most other journals and organisations including the International Committee of Medical Journal Editors (ICMJE), and the Committee on Publication Ethics (COPE) do not ban the use of LLMS, instead, they emphasize the importance of transparency in indicating how such tools are used in their paper and they are advised to note down the information on it such as tool used, version number (Miller et al., 2023). However, it is imperative to underscore that papers employing LLMs must still uphold standards of originality, novelty, and clarity, with LLMs not listed as co-authors due to their inability to assume responsibility for the content they generate.

4. INSTITUTION STRATEGIES AND LEADERSHIP IN AI INTEGRATION

Studies have shown education experts/ leaders are more cautious about implementation of AI tools in education, mainly considering the possible negative consequences (Hasanein and Sobain, 2023). However, the integration of AI tools presents a transformative opportunity for higher education institutions. From enhancing leadership effectiveness through predictive modelling and financial forecasting. Nevertheless, alongside these opportunities come complex considerations, including job displacement, work motivation, and retention. By navigating these dynamics thoughtfully, institutions can harness the power of AI to augment rather than replace human expertise, fostering a learning environment that is innovative.

4.1 Enhance Leadership Effectiveness through AI Tools

Similar to how ChatGPT can support teaching and learning for both teachers and students, it can also play a vital role in leadership and management within higher education institutions. Many of the capabilities mentioned, such as material development, automated assessment marking, innovative pedagogy, and writing assistance, are closely related to management in the context of teaching and learning. AI tools can play a huge role in Student Support Services as they can offer comprehensive support by fielding inquiries, providing guidance on academic pursuits and career trajectories as well as directing students to the relevant sources. This virtual assistant can be 24/7. Leaders can leverage these approaches to enhance their effectiveness. This section specifically discuss how AI tools such as ChatGPT can improve leadership and help overcome challenges.

First of all, predictive modelling for risk management can be established. This can help leaders to manage potential risks. This is done by using AI algorithms to assess risk factors and predict potential challenges, enabling management to address issues before they occur and therefore maintain institutional stability. This can be used in several cases. For example, by analysing all students' attendance, performance, and background, AI tool can predict which students are at risk of dropping out. This could be also used to foresee the failing rate and better manage the student failure rates and ensure a sufficient number of students progress to the next year or graduate.

Financial forecasting could also help to manage potential risks. This can be done based on AI tool analysis the trend of the historical data, current market conditions, and other relevant factors and therefore, make decisions such as declining enrolment or changes in funding sources. This allows institutions to make informed decisions about resource allocation and financial planning. There are countless ways it can be implemented but the gist is that with this logic, institution management can be creative in using AI tools to analyse patterns and make predictions based on them to do better risk management.

4.2 Preparing Educators for the AI Revolution: Effective Training and Awareness Programs

Educational institutions must adopt a holistic approach to prepare educators for the integration of AI because AI tools as productivity-boosting tools will undoubtedly be contingent on users' proficiency in using them. Teachers who are already struggling with basic IT might not benefit from these tools and this may result in wandering of the productivity gap. Teacher training then becomes significant which involves cultivating skills for effectively utilising AI instructional tools, fostering AI literacy, and integrating critical examinations of AI technology within the curriculum (Klein, 2023). A key aspect of this preparation is the development of hands-on, exploratory learning experiences that enable educators and students alike to understand and apply AI knowledge in real-world scenarios (Klein, 2023). Moreover, infusing AI literacy across existing curricula and promoting a critical understanding of AI's ethical implications are paramount (Klein, 2023), especially for the material development and assessment team in the institution, such tools should be utilised to enhance teaching and learning. Therefore, as many scholars (e.g., Gill et al., 2024) have emphasized the management in the institution should arrange sharing and training sessions where information is passed on and teachers are informed and equipped.

4.3 Improve AI Literacy of the Students

The imperative to enhance students' awareness and ethical knowledge of using AI tools is increasingly recognised and significant in the higher education context, which aligns with the recommendations of many scholars (Tlili et al., 2023). Teachers should publicly address the use of AI in their classes and it should be included in the curriculum (Kasneci et al., 2023). Some educators (e.g., Villasenor, 2023) allow students to use ChatGPT in assignments while ensuring that it is used correctly and effectively, to ensure that their learning process is meaningful and efficient. As AI technology becomes more embedded in educational processes, from personalised learning to assessment methodologies, understanding the ethical dimensions associated with their use is crucial for students. This understanding not only prepares students to navigate potential biases and privacy concerns but also fosters responsible usage and critical thinking regarding the implications of AI on society. The European Framework for Digital Competence of Educators underscores the necessity for educators to develop their digital competence, thereby facilitating an environment where ethical considerations regarding the AI era are prominently addressed in curricula (European Commission, 2022). Furthermore, UNESCO emphasizes the development of global standards to ensure the ethical deployment of AI, protecting human rights and dignity while maximizing educational benefits. By integrating ethical considerations into the curriculum, educators can stimulate critical discussions among students about the responsible use of AI, encouraging a reflective approach to its implications on equity, privacy, and academic integrity. This holistic educational strategy ensures that students are not only technically proficient in using AI tools but are also equipped with the ethical discernment necessary to navigate the complex digital landscape of the 21st century.

4.4 Job Displacement, Work Motivation and Retention in Higher Education

The integration of ChatGPT and similar AI tools into higher education brings to the forefront the complex dynamics of job displacement, alongside the potential for enhancing work motivation and retention through the redistribution of tasks. While AI's capacity to automate tasks such as lesson planning, material development, and assessment can lead to concerns about the reduction in the need for human teachers, it is crucial to recognize the irreplaceable value of human teachers in providing emotional and personal support, an area where AI currently falls short (Brookings, 2019; McKinsey, 2023). However, the advancement of language models and their application in educational settings does not unequivocally translate to job losses. Rather, it necessitates a re-evaluation of the roles within educational institutions. The scenario is not merely about job displacement but also about job transformation and creation. New roles, such as AI-focused research positions, underscore the emergence of opportunities that leverage the unique capabilities of AI to complement the expertise of human educators (Brookings, 2020). For example, there are roles such as Head of Research of AI in learning (Cambridge, 2023). Moreover, the application of AI in higher education can lead to a reallocation of human resources towards more impactful and nuanced tasks, thereby potentially increasing job satisfaction and retention. Educators can redirect their focus towards more personalized student engagement, critical thinking facilitation, and the development of emotional intelligence among students—areas where human interaction remains paramount (McKinsey, 2023). Thus, the narrative around AI in higher education should pivot from a simplistic view of job losses to a more nuanced understanding of job evolution. Institutions must navigate these changes thoughtfully, ensuring that the integration of AI into educational processes enhances rather than diminishes the quality and accessibility of learning.

5. CONCLUSION

The integration of AI into the domain of higher education, particularly through innovations like ChatGPT, has instigated a comprehensive dialogue across academic spheres, highlighting both the transformative potential and the challenges inherent in adopting such technologies. This article has been divided into five sections. In section one, several challenges are highlighted, including possible damage to the essay as an assessment as students can ask AI tools to generate a passable essay easily, students' over-reliance on it in writing that might stop the development of different writing styles and generating misleading or incorrect content, jeopardizing academic integrity, as well as significant ethical worry that it might produce biased or flawed information. In section two, possible methods to cope with challenges are discussed, including innovation of assessment by adding more reflective and oral examinations and marking descriptors by focusing less on grammar and lexis and more on content and criticality as well as the use of AI detectors in higher education. Section 3 discussed how ChatGPT has great potential to reshape the educational landscape across various domains including assessment, material development, and teaching pedagogy. The final section mainly focused on the institution and leadership perspective. The capacity of AI to enhance educational methodologies and administrative processes must be balanced against concerns regarding academic integrity, the digital divide, and the implications for traditional academic roles. As educators and administrators navigate these complexities, the development of AI literacy and ethical guidelines emerges as a paramount consideration. Institutions are encouraged to explore innovative assessment methods that transcend traditional formats, thereby mitigating the risks associated with AI-generated content. Moreover, the evolving landscape of educational roles, prompted by AI integration, necessitates a proactive approach towards retraining and role adaptation, ensuring that educators remain at the forefront of pedagogical innovation. Collaborative research efforts focused on AI's impact on education will further enrich the discourse, providing evidence-based strategies for effective integration. Ensuring equitable access to AI-enhanced educational tools underscores the commitment to inclusivity, addressing the digital divide to ensure all students benefit from technological advancements. As AI continues to evolve, the future of higher education will be characterized by an enhanced capacity for personalized learning and increased administrative efficiency, contingent upon the ethical and thoughtful integration of AI technologies. This forward-looking approach will enable institutions to leverage AI's benefits while preparing students for a future in which AI plays a pivotal role, ensuring that the educational experience is enriched rather than diminished by technological advancements. Finally, scholars and students should advocate for transparency regarding AI involvement in proofreading language or content to ensure academic fairness and honesty.

REFERENCES:

Adiguzel, T., Kaya, M. H., & Cansu, F. K. (2023). Revolutionizing education with AI: Exploring the transformative potential of ChatGPT. *Contemporary Educational Technology*, 15(3), 429. 10.30935/cedtech/13152

Allen, M. (2022). Professor warns about chatbot cheating: "Expect a flood". *Axios*. Available at: https://www.axios.com/2022/12/26/chatbot-cheating-university-warningchatgpt [Accessed 29 February 2024].

Attali, Y. (2013). Validity and reliability of automated essay scoring. In Shermis, M. D., & Burstein, J. (Eds.), *Handbook on automated essay evaluation: Current applications and new directions* (pp. 181–198). Routledge.

Bennett, K. (2010). Academic writing practices in Portugal: survey of humanities and social science researchers. *diacrítica*, 24(1), 193-209.

Brown, G. A., Bull, J., & Pendlebury, M. (2013). *Assessing student learning in higher education*. Routledge. 10.4324/9781315004914

Burstein, J., Tetreault, J., & Madnani, N. (2013). The e-rater® automated essay scoring system. In Shermis, M. D., & Burstein, J. (Eds.), *Handbook of Automated Essay Evaluation* (pp. 55–67). Routledge.

Busse, V. (2013). How do students of German perceive feedback practices at university? A motivational exploration. *Journal of Second Language Writing*, 22(4), 406–424. 10.1016/j.jslw.2013.09.005

Cambridge (2023) available at: Head of Research in AI for Learning | Cambridge University Press & Assessment [Accessed 1 January 2024]

Chomsky, N., Roberts, I., & Watumull, J. (2023). Noam chomsky: The false promise of chatgpt. *The New York Times*, 8.

Dizon, G., & Gayed, J. M. (2021). Examining the impact of Grammarly on the quality of mobile L2 writing. *The JALT CALL Journal*, 17(2), 74–92. 10.29140/jaltcall.v17n2.336

Essel, H. (2023). 7 things you should know about ChatGPT. Available at OSF | 7 THINGS YOU SHOULD KNOW ABOUT CHATGPT [Accessed 27 April 27, 2024]

European Commission Eu Science Hub (2022) Available at: DigCompEdu - European Commission (europa.eu) [Accessed 22 February 2024]

Ferguson, G., Pérez-Llantada, C., & Plo, R. (2011). English as an international language of scientific publication: A study of attitudes. *World Englishes*, 30(1), 41–59. 10.1111/j.1467-971X.2010.01656.x

Fitria, T. N. (2021). QuillBot as an online tool: Students' alternative in paraphrasing and rewriting of English writing. *Englisia: Journal of Language, Education, and Humanities*, 9(1), 183–196. 10.22373/ej.v9i1.10233

Flowerdew, J. (2000). Discourse community, legitimate peripheral participation, and the nonnative-English-speaking scholar. *TESOL Quarterly*, 34(1), 127–150. 10.2307/3588099

Ghani, A., (2023). GPT Zero Is Designed To Recognize Texts Written By AI. GPT Zero Is Designed To Recognize Texts Written By AI | by Abdul Ghani | *DataDrivenInvestor*. [Accessed 26 April 2024].

Gill, S. S., Xu, M., Patros, P., Wu, H., Kaur, R., Kaur, K., Fuller, S., Singh, M., Arora, P., Parlikad, A. K., Stankovski, V., Abraham, A., Ghosh, S. K., Lutfiyya, H., Kanhere, S. S., Bahsoon, R., Rana, O., Dustdar, S., Sakellariou, R., & Buyya, R. (2024). Transformative effects of ChatGPT on modern education: Emerging Era of AI Chatbots. *Internet of Things and Cyber-Physical Systems*, 4, 19–23. 10.1016/j.iotcps.2023.06.002

Graham, S. (2019). Changing how writing is taught. *Review of Research in Education*, 43(1), 277–303. 10.3102/0091732X18821125

Gravel, J., D'Amours-Gravel, M., & Osmanlliu, E. (2023). Learning to fake it: Limited responses and fabricated references provided by ChatGPT for medical questions. *Mayo Clinic Proceedings. Digital Health*, 1(3), 226–234. 10.1016/j.mcpdig.2023.05.004

Hasanein, A. M., & Sobaih, A. E. E. (2023). Drivers and Consequences of ChatGPT Use in Higher Education: Key Stakeholder Perspectives. *European Journal of Investigation in Health, Psychology and Education*, 13(11), 2599–2614. 10.3390/ejihpe1311018137998071

Herbold, S., Hautli-Janisz, A., Heuer, U., Kikteva, Z., & Trautsch, A. (2023). A large-scale comparison of human-written versus ChatGPT-generated essays. *Scientific Reports*, 13(1), 18617. 10.1038/s41598-023-45644-937903836

Hern, A. (2022) 'AI-assisted plagiarism? ChatGPT bot says it has an answer for that', The Guardian. Available at: https://www.theguardian.com/technology/2022/dec/31/ai-assisted-plagiarism-chatgpt-bot-says-it-has-an-answer-for-that [Accessed: 2 February 2023].

Hew, K. F., Huang, W., Du, J., & Jia, C. (2023). Using chatbots to support pupil goal setting and social presence in fully online activities: Learner engagement and perceptions. *Journal of Computing in Higher Education*, 5(1), 40–68. 10.1007/s12528-022-09338-x36101883

Houston, D., Meyer, L. H., & Paewai, S. (2006). Academic staff workloads and job satisfaction: Expectations and values in academe. *Journal of Higher Education Policy and Management*, 28(1), 17–30. 10.1080/13600800500283734

Huang, Y., & Sun, L. (2023). Harnessing the power of chatgpt in fake news: An in-depth exploration in generation, detection and explanation. *arXiv preprint arXiv:2310.05046*.

Hussein, M. A., Hassan, H., & Nassef, M. (2019). Automated language essay scoring systems: A literature review. *PeerJ. Computer Science*, 5, e208. 10.7717/peerj-cs.20833816861

Hwang, S. I., Lim, J. S., Lee, R. W., Matsui, Y., Iguchi, T., Hiraki, T., & Ahn, H. (2023). Is ChatGPT a "fire of prometheus" for non-native English-speaking researchers in academic writing? *Korean Journal of Radiology*, 24(10), 952. 10.3348/kjr.2023.077337793668

Jeltova, I., Birney, D., Fredine, N., Jarvin, L., Sternberg, R. J., & Grigorenko, E. L. (2007). Dynamic assessment as a process-oriented assessment in educational settings. *Advances in Speech Language Pathology*, 9(4), 273–285. 10.1080/14417040701460390

Jiao, W., Wang, W., Huang, J. T., Wang, X., Shi, S., & Tu, Z. (2023). Is ChatGPT a good translator? Yes with GPT-4 as the engine. *arXiv preprint arXiv:2301.08745.*

Kasneci, E., Seßler, K., Küchemann, S., Bannert, M., Dementieva, D., Fischer, F., Gasser, U., Groh, G., Günnemann, S., Hüllermeier, E., Krusche, S., Kutyniok, G., Michaeli, T., Nerdel, C., Pfeffer, J., Poquet, O., Sailer, M., Schmidt, A., Seidel, T., & Kasneci, G. (2023). ChatGPT for good? On opportunities and challenges of large language models for education. *Learning and Individual Differences*, 103, 102274. 10.1016/j.lindif.2023.102274

Khan, S. (2023). How AI could save (not destroy) education. Available at: Sal Khan: How AI could save (not destroy) education | TED Talk [Accessed 3 May 2024]

Kim, N.-Y. (2022). AI-integrated mobile-assisted language learning: Is it an effective way of preparing for the TOEIC test in classroom environments? *English Teaching*, 77(3), 79–102. 10.15858/engtea.77.3.202209.79

Klein, A. (2023). Strategies to Prepare Educators to Teach With AI. Education Week. Available at: https://www.edweek.org/technology/7-strategies-to-prepare-educators-to-teach-with-ai [Accessed 29 February 2024].

Koraishi, O. (2023) 'Teaching English in the age of AI: Embracing ChatGPT to optimize EFL materials and assessment', *Language Education and Technology*, 3(1).

Kumar, R. (2023). Faculty members' use of artificial intelligence to grade student papers: A case of implications. *International Journal for Educational Integrity*, 19(1), 9. 10.1007/s40979-023-00130-7

Latif, E., & Zhai, X. (2024). Fine-tuning ChatGPT for automatic scoring. Computers and Education. *Artificial Intelligence*, •••, 100210.

Lee, D., Kim, H.-H., & Sung, S.-H. (2023). Development research on an AI English learning support system to facilitate learner-generated-context-based learning. *Educational Technology Research and Development*, 71(2), 629–666. 10.1007/s11423-022-10172-236533222

Levesque, E. M. (2018). The role of AI in education and the changing US workforce. Brookings. https://www.brookings.edu

Lillis, T. M., & Curry, M. J. (2010). *Academic writing in global context*. Routledge.

MacArthur, C. A. (2016). *Instruction in evaluation and revision, handbook of writing research* (2nd ed.). Guilfordpp.

Mayer, C. W. F., Ludwig, S., & Brandt, S. (2023). Prompt text classifications with transformer models! An exemplary introduction to prompt-based learning with large language models. *Journal of Research on Technology in Education*, 55(1), 125–141. 10.1080/15391523.2022.2142872

McKinsey & Company. (2023). Generative AI and the future of work in America. Available at: https://www.mckinsey.com [Accessed 29 February 2024]

Mhlanga, D. (2023). Open AI in education, the responsible and ethical use of ChatGPT towards lifelong learning. In *FinTech and Artificial Intelligence for Sustainable Development: The Role of Smart Technologies in Achieving Development Goals* (pp. 387–409). Springer Nature Switzerland. 10.1007/978-3-031-37776-1_17

Miller, D. (2023). 'Exploring the impact of artificial intelligence language model ChatGPT on the user experience', International Journal of Technology *[IJTIM]*. *Innovation and Management*, 3(1), 1–8.

Mizumoto, A., & Eguchi, M. (2023). Exploring the potential of using an AI language model for automated essay scoring. *Research Methods in Applied Linguistics*, 2(2), 100050. 10.1016/j.rmal.2023.100050

Muro, M., Whiton, J., & Maxim, R. (2019). What jobs are affected by AI? Better-paid, better-educated workers face the most exposure. Metropolitan Policy Program Report.

Nazari, N., Shabbir, M. S., & Setiawan, R. (2021). Application of artificial intelligence powered digital writing assistance in higher education: Randomized controlled trial. *Heliyon*, 7(5), e07014. 10.1016/j.heliyon.2021.e0701434027198

Open, A. I. (2024) Home. Available at: https://www.openai.com [Accessed: 22 March 2024].

Page, E. B. (1966). The imminence of... grading essays by computer. *Phi Delta Kappan*, 47(5), 238–243.

Rane, N. L., Choudhary, S. P., Tawde, A., & Rane, J. (2023). ChatGPT is not capable of serving as an author: Ethical concerns and challenges of large language models in education. *International Research Journal of Modernization in Engineering Technology and Science*, 5(10), 851–874.

Ray, P. P. (2023). ChatGPT: A comprehensive review on background, applications, key challenges, bias, ethics, limitations and future scope. *Internet of Things and Cyber-Physical Systems*.

Rikab, W. (2023) 'Detectors of AI-generated text often fail. Here is what to do', Better Programming. Available at https://betterprogramming.pub/ai-generated-text-detectors-are-useless-here-is-what-to-do-e7a640815087 [Accessed: 25 January 2024].

Rudolph, J., Tan, S., & Tan, S. (2023). ChatGPT: Bullshit spewer or the end of traditional assessments in higher education?. *Journal of applied learning and teaching*, 6(1), 342-363.

Sanderson, K. (2023). GPT-4 is here: What scientists think. *Nature*, 615(7954), 773. 10.1038/d41586-023-00816-536928404

Steiss, J., Tate, T., Graham, S., Cruz, J., Hebert, M., Wang, J., Moon, Y., Tseng, W., Warschauer, M., & Olson, C. B. (2024). Comparing the quality of human and ChatGPT feedback of students' writing. *Learning and Instruction*, 91, 101894. 10.1016/j.learninstruc.2024.101894

Stephens, M. (2023). The University of Cambridge will allow students to use ChatGPT. [EB/OL] [2023-05-14]. Available online at: https://www.telegraph.co.uk/news/2023/03/02/university-cambridge-will-allow-students-use-chatgpt/ [accessed March 02, 2024].

Steponenaite, A., & Barakat, B. (2023). Plagiarism in AI empowered world. In *International Conference on Human-Computer Interaction* (pp. 434-442). Cham: Springer Nature Switzerland.

Stewart, J. (2023). *Noam Chomsky says ChatGPT is a form of "high-tech plagiarism"*. My Modern Met.

Tatzel, A., & Mael, D. (2023). Write a paper on AI plagiarism": An analysis on ChatGPT and its impact on academic dishonesty in higher education.

Tlili, A., Shehata, B., Adarkwah, M. A., Bozkurt, A., Hickey, D. T., Huang, R., & Agyemang, B. (2023). What if the devil is my guardian angel: ChatGPT as a case study of using chatbots in education. *Smart Learning Environments*, 10(1), 15. 10.1186/s40561-023-00237-x

Urman, A., & Makhortykh, M. (2023). *The Silence of the LLMs: Cross-Lingual Analysis of Political Bias and False Information Prevalence in ChatGPT*. Google Bard, and Bing Chat.

van Inwegen, E., Munyikwa, Z., & Horton, J. (2023) Algorithmic writing assistance on jobseekers' resumes increases hires. *Working paper*. https://arxiv.org/abs/2301.08083

Villasenor, J. (2023). How ChatGPT Can Improve Education, Not Threaten it. [EB/OL] [2023-05-14]. Available online at: https://www.scientficamerican.com/article/how-chatgpt-can~improve-education-not-threaten-it/. [Accessed 27 April 2024]

Wach, K., Duong, C. D., Ejdys, J., Kazlauskaitė, R., Korzynski, P., Mazurek, G., Paliszkiewicz, J., & Ziemba, E. (2023). The dark side of generative artificial intelligence: A critical analysis of controversies and risks of ChatGPT. *Entrepreneurial Business and Economics Review*, 11(2), 7–30. 10.15678/EBER.2023.110201

Warren, T. (2023). Microsoft is looking at OpenAI's GPT for word, outlook, and PowerPoint. The Verge., Retrieved April 26, 2024, from.

Wen, Z., & Younes, R. (2024). ChatGPT vs Media Bias: A Comparative Study of GPT-3.5 and Fine-tuned Language Models. *arXiv preprint arXiv:2403.20158*.

Yeadon, W., Agra, E., Inyang, O. O., Mackay, P., & Mizouri, A. (2024). Evaluating AI and human authorship quality in academic writing through physics essays. *arXiv preprint*. Available at: https://arxiv.org/abs/2403.05458

Chapter 15
The Future University Through the Lens of the Ecological University:
A Case Study

Stuart Perrin
https://orcid.org/0000-0001-6473-4255
Xi'an Jiaotong-Liverpool University, China

Ling Wang
Xi'an Jiaotong-Liverpool University, China

ABSTRACT

This chapter uses the lens of the Ecological University to rethink the role of education (Barnett, 2013), and what this may mean for the future of university and its leadership, through a case study of innovative change at a joint venture university within China. Through a case study of a transformative approach to what an ecological university could be, and the role of the newly created position of Chief Officer of Ecology, the chapter analyses the curriculum, pedagogy and research activities of the university, and the changes that are being processed to make it 'future-ready'. It asks the university (staff and students) to adopt an ecological mindset and perspective, and to engage in a continuous process of reflection, negotiation, and innovation. The chapter concludes by arguing that the education ecology of university provides a valuable framework for rethinking the role and function of the university in the 21st century, and especially its leadership, and for promoting a more inclusive and democratic academic culture, and sustainable future for higher education going forward.

INTRODUCTION

Education is a complex and multifaceted phenomenon that involves not only the transmission of knowledge, skills, and values, but also the cultivation of human potential, the development of critical thinking, and the promotion of social justice. Education is not a neutral or static process, but a dynamic and contested one that reflects the historical, cultural, political, and economic contexts in which it takes place. Education is also not a one-way or linear process, but a reciprocal and dialogical one that involves the interaction of teachers, students, parents, communities, and other stakeholders. Education is not only a means to an end, but an end in itself, as it enables individuals and societies to achieve their goals and aspirations, as well as to contribute to the common good.

In 2011, the British education philosopher Dr Ronald Barnett suggested that society's ideas about the university are "hopelessly impoverished" (2011, 261). He used a critical realist approach to evaluate and imagine different conceptualizations of the university, such as the 'liquid university' and the 'authentic university', before settling on the idea of the ecological university. From this, it is possible to establish that an ecological university is a concept that envisions a transformative approach to higher education, one that integrates ecological, social, and ethical considerations. While this idea or concept may seem utopian and unachievable in many respects, the idea holds significant potential for reshaping university policy and practice beyond traditional approaches, especially with regard to the student experience.

To fully understand this position, we need to have an understanding of what the current state of higher education, is, and how higher education has attempted to mitigate these.

The Current State of Higher Education

Higher Education generally is grappling with funding issues, changing student preferences, rising costs, and a number of external pressures. These issues are compounded in many ways by the rapid development of disruptive technologies, which have been exacerbated by the global pandemic at the beginning of the 2020's.

For most institutions, tuition fees are one of the primary sources of income, especially within the UK. However, student fees for local students have not increased for a number of years, which combined with declining enrollments as fewer people are opting for traditional higher education, signaling changing student preferences, has meant increased pressure on these income streams. Additionally, demographic changes, common as countries become more prosperous, mean that this pressure on income is unlikely to change any time soon. Universities therefore are forced to look for alternative income streams, but the traditional fallback option of increasing higher fee-paying international student numbers is not necessarily a realistic option currently as geopolitical tensions globally seem to be on the increase. Following on from the pandemic, the desire by students and their families to study for long periods overseas seems to less positive than it once was.

There are increasing discourses about the value added of a university education, with alternatives emerging to the traditional study routes. The increased attractiveness of micro-credentials for example mean that in an age of rapidly changing technologies and availability of knowledge online, students can build their education from multiple sources. As a result, many degree programmes and universities are coming under increasing financial pressure, with closures and mergers on the horizon. Political interference is on the increase within the education systems, both directly and indirectly, with for example limitations on post study work limiting the attractiveness of traditional English speaking destinations such as the UK Australia and USA, as politicians use limiting students as a way of tackling bigger political issues such as immigration.

As a result, universities are having to make changes, either voluntarily or forced, to adapt to the challenges that they face. These include looking at alternative delivery models, taking into account lessons learnt from the pandemic, with increases in the use of hybridity, which has the bonus of adding flexibility to the learning journey, opening up doors for non-traditional students. Universities are starting to invest in/update robust digital infrastructure, creating high-quality online courses and enhancing the virtual learning environment; building on a post-pandemic world. There is a greater alignment of degrees with industry needs, and the potential for industry education collaboration being explored, which has the added benefit of new potential revenue streams, and research directions. Issues such as sustainability and eco-friendly practices, creating global citizens, engaging with the local and non-academic communities to address societal challenges are all taking place, helping to counter the growing skepticism of the value of higher education (Alexander, 2020; Blumenstyk, 2014).

The big question then is what should universities do about all of these threats. Whilst this is easy to ask, what institutions should do is not easy to answer. Different universities will of course require different strategies, but the worst way to begin making change is by implementing new innovations without asking these questions in the first place (Derby-Talbot & Coburn, 2023). Innovation is not a solution in itself, and needs to come from within, from a desire to do so. But, as Derby-Talbot & Coburn (2023) argue, higher education benefits from innovative institutions, which provide lived examples of institutional change, and ensure a wider range of educational offerings. It is therefore a time to rethink and re-evaluate what the role of the university will be in the future, and what it will look like.

The rest of this chapter provides insights into some of the decisions and directions that an innovative university with China has taken from the perspectives of the ecological university. In doing so it also introduces the concept of ecology of knowledge, to which the chapter now moves.

Ecology of Knowledge

Knowledge and learning can be thought of as social activities (Por, 2020), by which we evolve ourselves as individuals and communities. Knowledge exists in ecosystems, in which information, ideas, and inspiration cross-fertilize and feed one another.

Ecology of Knowledge (EoK) refers to (the study of) how different forms of knowledge interact, coexist and transform each other in complex and dynamic systems (Damsa & Ludvigsen, 2016). It recognizes and valorizes diverse forms of knowledge beyond the usual western dominant forms that can marginalize other ways of knowing. EoK is not a fixed or static concept, rather it is dynamic and negotiated, and therefore continually evolving, thus it can be seen as complex and challenging. It is circular and recursive, requiring reflection and flexibility to change.

Looking at the university through the lens of EoK allows higher education to question the structures and processes that are in place, asking if they are fit for (todays) purpose. The Education Ecology of Universities (Ellis & Goodyear, 2019) is a concept that proposes such a new way of understanding and improving the learning environments of higher education institutions. It recognizes that universities are complex and dynamic systems that are multi-transactional in nature involving complex elements such as people, spaces, technologies, activities, and outcomes, which form the EoK and related interactions and coexistences. Ellis & Goodyear (2019) suggest that by applying the principles and methods of ecology, such as diversity, balance, adaptation, and integration, to the design and evaluation of university learning environments, their quality, effectiveness, and relevance for todays and tomorrows world can be enhanced.

The Ecological University

The idea of the Ecological university was developed by Barnett (2010, 2017), who described it as a 'feasible utopia for higher education' (2010, p. 12). Barnett continues by describing the ecological university as a university for 'the other' (Barnett, 2010, p. 151), which would be expected to have an impact across cultural, political environmental and social dimensions. He contrasts this with for example the neoliberal or entrepreneurial university which he describes as a university for-itself. In other words, Barnett (2010) sees the ecological university as the epitome of the idea of the university.

In developing his ideas, Barnett is influenced by the work of Guattari (2000). Guattari highlights that 'the ecological is understood in terms of the ontological, epistemological and ethical interconnections that exist between our mental, social and natural ecologies (Stratford, 2024, p.3). Barnett (2020) expands this to eight domains, dynamic complexity and interconnection ranging over social institutions, persons, culture, learning, knowledge, the economy, the natural environment and the polity. Further drawing on the work of Maxwell (2011), who suggests that knowledge is part of a contextualized focus on wisdom inquiry, which impacts how universities think about 'reason'. Maxwell highlights how this comes about through challenges in the concept of academic units and their relationship to problem-solving, which Barnett (2013) also outlines in the ability of the ecological university to contribute to multiple domains (Stratford, 2015) and the need for knowledge and action (Stratford, 2024).

Barnett (2011) highlights five criteria that are needed for the development of the university, namely; range (how deep is the imagining, how good are the concepts and ideas, does it lead to a range of practices, and implications for policy); depth (what is the epistemological depth of the concept or idea, how does it connect with lived experiences, what is the complexity of the depth); feasibility (how feasible is the idea in the structures that it operates in); ethics (can the vision be considered worthy of accomplishing); and emergence (can the vision be continually developed, in ways that are new and interesting).

Stratford (2015) highlights that the idea of the ecological university presents quite a challenge to higher education policy and practice. Two specific challenges are highlighted; the need for policy structures in being more flexible in understanding the value of education, and secondly the need to find new ways to teach and learn. Stratford (2015) argues that the universities would need to change their focus away from common concepts of economic growth, employment, and international competitiveness, the types of matrices that are commonplace for example in annual submissions to the university ranking agencies to try to sustain ranking growth. Instead the ecological university would change its focus to the ecologies highlighted by Guattari (2000), which by their nature are less quantifiable; with a focus more on quality of world impact, and less on the number of publications (Stratford, 2015). This in effect would signal a move away from technocratically dominated institutions, where numbers matter. The second challenges are around changes to how teaching and learning takes place as a result of change in the way that knowledge is seen. Stratford (2015) summarizes this as a move away from universities as knowledge producers to one of being communities of human flourishing and development, arguing that universities need to develop new ways to help students respond to the world. This means that universities need to move away from the traditional ideas of silo/boundary based knowledge and assessment measured concepts of academic excellence to helping students become compassionate, empathetic system thinkers.

The Case Study

The concept of an ecological university represents a radical departure from traditional higher education institutions. It transcends the boundaries of disciplines, emphasizing not only academic knowledge but also ethical consciousness, sustainability, and holistic well-being. The chapter goes on now to look at an extended case study within a joint venture university (JVU) within China. The case study looks at an attempt to create an ecological education system within a more traditional university through the development of an educational philosophy named Syntegrative Education. It continues by describing the development of a new position within the university, named the Chief Officer of Ecology, whose role is to analyze the university's curriculum, pedagogy, and research activities and propose changes to make the university move towards one of being a "future-ready" ecology.

Curry (2023) proposes a new transdisciplinary learning system in higher education, which he identified as ethical-maker-learning. In doing so he suggested that the well-established modern literacies such as information, digital media, IT and AI need a holistic ethical-systems-based approach which incorporates the material, ecological and social aspects of these literacies, as without it there would be a danger of ignoring key modern day concerns for the welfare of the population and the planet. He highlighted pedagogical opportunities enabled by a pedagogy of daring (Stetsenko, 2017) in the STEAM areas of Science, Technology, Engineering, Arts and Mathematics, as well as the humanities. Curry based this argument on his research into critical-maker-learning (2017, 2022) as a way to teach students without advanced scientific knowledge an awareness of the importance of material matters in our surface-level consumer-led society (Curry, 2023).

Curry (2023) argues therefore that at the heart of the ecological university lies the principle of ethical-maker-learning. As highlighted, unlike conventional education, which often compartmentalizes knowledge, this approach integrates material, ecological, and social aspects. The Executive President of the university has taken this principle and developed a visionary approach to learning and what education should look like and started the journey of making it a reality for students who study at the university. Part of this vision has been the development of the concept and philosophy of Syntegrative Education (SE). SE has been developed from a business concept of syntegration (Malik, 2019), the joining together of synergy and integration, to describe the importance and process of bringing together a large number of people to join in a highly harmonious symphony in order to interconnect a range and variety of knowledge, creating something as a rule that is totally new and important. The university has taken this concept and applied it to education with a focus on effective communication, especially between universities, industry, and government. Leydesdorff (2012) suggests that the overlay of communications between industrial, academic, and government discourses can develop new options and synergies that can strengthen knowledge integration, and overcome barriers to innovation (Perrin & Sun, 2023). The approach can be described as teaching and learning that forefronts industry-oriented education, combining it with professional education to meet the demands and needs of future industry elites, where elites would be a typical way of describing those students who are destined for managerial or leadership roles within private industry or state-run business (Perrin & Sun, 2023). However, the future is already here as a result of disruptive technologies and the digital age compounded by the (recent growth in) things such as generative AI and Robotics, which are making traditional education redundant. SE therefore, has taken up this challenge with the aim to cultivate future industry leaders who possess a strong integration of skills and entrepreneurial abilities through their education and training, with a key focus on foundational literacy skills. Perhaps the best example is the (development of the) an Entrepreneur College, an additional campus within the wider university concept. The Entrepreneur offers industry-focused academic programmes through partnership with domestic and international companies to develop though skills and entrepreneurial abilities combined with subject knowledge. The case study goes on to use the Entrepreneur College to highlight some student stories within two aspects of ethical-maker-learning.

Transdisciplinary Exploration: Students engage in cross-disciplinary learning, breaking down silos between fields. They collaborate with peers from diverse backgrounds, fostering creativity and critical thinking.

The best example of this is the entrepreneurial education delivered to undergraduate students in the new campus, using a major and minor model. The Executive President correctly predicted the need for all students to study for an entrepreneurial minor in their industry and technology focused degree programmes, working with students from different disciplines to solve industry problems. He insisted that all students would be business students by studying at the college, without the need for a business school; the campus and the learning experience was the business school. The first cohort of students was very keen to take up the challenge of the university's entrepreneurial education. The annual program choice events, where students choose their future degree of study, raised intrigue and also highlighted opportunities. In meetings that followed, students saw themselves as pioneers of the new education model, pushing forward boundaries as they dared to do something different. They enthused about the possibilities from the projects that they would work on, and the joy of working with students from other disciplines, who would see things in a different way. Their parents were equally supportive, demonstrating an equal pioneering spirit. But traditional education has a way of drawing you back in, the tradition is often embedded in people's minds and thinking, and needs something tumultuous to overcome it. This also happened to the pioneering students in the Entrepreneur College, who, as year 2 turned to year 3, started to worry about their future. They wondered if they were studying enough specialist subject knowledge to have a good future, they struggled to adapt to entrepreneurial classes which asked them to develop the new literacy skills, and they worried about a possible lack of opportunities compared to students with traditional degrees. The student voice changed from one of pioneers to one of being guinea pigs. They became blinkered with their fears and felt anxious about what the future would hold. Using those literacy skills that they had developed, but seemed unaware of, they argued and they questioned the value of their entrepreneurial education. Then the tumultuous events started to happen as they moved into their final year, and the smiles returned to the students' faces as they started to bring everything together. The tumultuous event that changed the students was in reality quite simple, they discovered that those students (at the college) who were applying for masters' degrees were getting better offers than those studying in traditional undergraduate degree programmes. Those applying for jobs were getting better offers than the 'traditional student', and others were taking the first steps to starting their own businesses as entrepreneurs. Finally, the penny dropped after their academic and personal voyage of discovery during their studies; the SE model that they had been following had prepared them for the future before time, the transdisciplinary nature of their degree was the key to their future, not the chain holding them back. At the first graduation ceremony in July 2024, as students were awarded their degrees, a significant number came to the college leadership team, including the Executive President and thanked him for creating the opportunity to experience how education should be, for giving the students the opportunity to follow their dream, and the space to grow and develop whilst doing so.

Experiential Learning: SE prioritizes hands-on experiences. Students participate in project and problem-based learning with and through industry partners, and community engagement.

When students come to the university, they are still dominated by their traditional, more passive learning styles from high school. Throughout their educational and life journey within the university, students are taught and experience becoming active in what they do. Active in program decision-making, active in choosing clubs and societies, active inclusivity in how programmes and modules are developed. Slowly but surely, students move slowly away from being passive recipients of information to active seekers of knowledge. This is in the DNA of how the university has developed. A Summer Undergraduate Research Fellowship (or SURF) for example not only gives students an opportunity to be involved in cutting-edge research projects from year 1, but gives the students the opportunity to experience project-based learning through the research project. This is an option available for all students, but those who choose to study at the new campus embark on a problem and project-based learning and teaching journey as a normal part of their education experience. Education should equip students with the skills needed to be successful, and should allow students to experience these skills rather than just read about them in a book. The problem and project-based learning approach that the entrepreneur college uses allow just this, in the main academic discipline and embedded into the entrepreneurial minors. Lecture based lessons are out and project-based lessons are in. The industry partners that the schools in the college work with provide many of the projects that students work on, which ideally will go across semesters and also years. To be successful, the approach needs to be agile and flexible, and the university needs to have similarly agile and flexible systems in place to administer the projects. Observations would suggest that students take a while to get used to this style of learning, as do academic staff. Therefore, a holistic approach is needed over the lifetime of the studies, releasing the students' creativity and inquisitiveness stage by stage. Year two has been summarized by students as one of fear, fear of the new system and fear of the responsibilities that project-based learning and teaching need and unleash. Year three is resentment when compared to their peers who are on a more traditional route and who seem to have a nice easy life. And year four is where students 'get it', understand what all the 'pain' was about, and this is where their potential truly gets unleashed.

Faced with pressure from students and parents to return to the traditional would also be the easy route for the university, but tradition would mean having a philosophy of what 'education has been' not what education should be in these disruptive times. The leadership teams vision and bravery in steering an innovative course through a sea of blandness has meant that an innovative education philosophy delivered through innovative approaches has produced innovative students who are ready for the challenges that society throws at them daily.

As well as the development of the entrepreneur college, the university this case study also highlights the efforts of the university to implement changes through the newly created position of Chief Officer of Ecology. The key aspects of balance, integration, alignment and capability are briefly highlighted.

One of the key principles guiding the Chief Officer of Ecology's work is balance. This refers to the need to ensure that the demands of various stakeholders, such as students, faculty, employers, society, and government, are met. As new industry-focused degrees with 21st-century technology skills are developed, striking a balance between these diverse interests becomes crucial. The curriculum is being reviewed to ensure that it meets industry's demand for skilled professionals while also incorporating academic rigor and theoretical foundations. Additionally, it needs to address societal concerns about the ethical implications of AI and data-driven technologies.

Integration refers to managing academic responsibilities alongside social and economic responsibilities, including meeting the United Nations Sustainable Development Goals (SDGs) and incorporating them into the curriculum. The Chief Officer of Ecology has spearheaded efforts to integrate sustainability principles and practices across the university's operations and academic programs. One such initiative is the development of a new interdisciplinary course on sustainable urban development, which brings together perspectives from architecture, urban planning, environmental science, and public policy. The course not only equips students with theoretical knowledge but also includes hands-on projects and community engagement components, allowing them to apply their learning to real-world challenges.

Alignment highlights how the university aligns its vision, mission, values, and goals with global, national, regional, and local challenges and opportunities, without compromising quality. The Chief Officer of Ecology has played a pivotal role in ensuring that the university's strategic plans and initiatives are aligned with the needs and priorities of its various stakeholders. For instance, the university has established research collaborations with local industries and government agencies to address pressing issues such as aging population, environmental pollution and sustainable energy solutions. These collaborations not only contribute to the region's economic and social development but also provide valuable learning opportunities for students and faculty, aligning academic pursuits with real-world challenges.

Capability highlights the need for universities to innovate, adapt, and respond to the changing needs and expectations of their learners and partners. The Chief Officer of Ecology has championed initiatives to enhance the university's capabilities in areas such as online and blended learning, experiential education, and industry partnerships. One example is the development of a virtual reality (VR) laboratory, which allows students to conduct simulated experiments and explore complex concepts in an immersive and interactive environment. This initiative not only enhances the learning experience but also prepares students for the technological advancements they will encounter in their future careers. Additionally, the university has established a dedicated center for entrepreneurship and innovation, which provides support and resources for students and faculty to develop and commercialize their ideas. This center fosters collaboration with industry partners, facilitating knowledge transfer and ensuring that the university's research and education remain relevant and impactful.

The five criteria revisited

The case study highlights that the university is a strong advocate for the ecological university as it meets well the five criteria set out by Barnett (2011). In terms of range, the educational approach of syntegrative education is visionary as it links educational institutions, industry and government to develop an educational model to build knowledge integration for a future of disruption due to the digital age. A range of practices have been developed, especially in entrepreneurial education, but also in the ideas of providing lifelong learning to ensure talents remain up to date and therefore relevant. The development of this new educational model has implications for policy at all levels, which has led to the development of the position of Chief Officer of Ecology to overcome blocks in traditional thinking, and implement the new approach through a network of connections rather than siloed thinking. The approach has depth at a conceptual level, resulting in the development of a new education approach, which requires proponents and practitioners to utilize new explorations of learning and teaching in their daily practices, and depth at a policy level, requiring the institution to rethink its strategies and processes. The approach is feasible in that it has already been enacted, and continues to facilitate new explorations within the institution. Its ethical approach has started with a concern for the future and relevance of education, and that the concept of syntegration through education is a possible solution to this concern. Finally, the university highlights emergent qualities that encourage reflection and the need to continue to reimagine (Barnet,

2011), which has led to the idea of taking the university concept away from its traditional borders and into society and wider community, through the creation of a new virtual college of entrepreneurs.

Challenges and Opportunities

The case study has highlighted the importance of Barnett's five criteria in guiding what steps institutions need to take if they wish to try similar approaches in transforming the university. It highlights the importance of multiple networks, and the need for flexibility. However, as the case study shows, this is not all smooth sailing.

While the efforts of the Chief Officer of Ecology and the adoption of an education ecology of Universities framework represent a significant step towards transforming the university, several challenges and opportunities remain. One of the primary challenges is the resistance to change that is often inherent in academic institutions. Academia can be slow to adapt, with resistance or a lack of understanding of the broader world being common concerns. Disruptive technologies, such as generative AI, have given the wider world unprecedented access to knowledge, exacerbating this disconnect. Higher education institutions are accustomed to communicating within their own confines, typified by writing for scholarly journals read primarily by other academics or developing degree programmes reviewed by fellow academics rather than the industries that graduates will eventually work in. To address this challenge, the Chief Officer of Ecology has initiated a series of workshops and seminars aimed at fostering an ecological mindset and promoting continuous reflection, negotiation, and innovation among faculty, staff, and students. These sessions encourage open dialogue, collaboration, and a willingness to embrace change and adapt to the evolving needs of society.

Another challenge lies in balancing the diverse and sometimes conflicting demands of various stakeholders. While the university strives to meet the needs of students, employers, and society, there may be instances where these interests diverge. The ecological university plays a crucial role in facilitating open communication and finding common ground, ensuring that the university's decisions and actions are aligned with its core values and principles. Despite these challenges, the adoption of the education ecology of Universities framework presents numerous opportunities for the university to position itself as a leader in innovative and transformative education. By embracing an ecological mindset and fostering a culture of collaboration, the university can become a hub for interdisciplinary research, experiential learning, and community engagement. Furthermore, the university's commitment to sustainability and social responsibility aligns with the growing global emphasis on addressing pressing environmental and societal challenges. By integrating these principles into its curriculum and operations, the university can attract socially conscious students and partners, contributing to the development of responsible and ethical leaders for the future.

CONCLUSION

Higher education is therefore now at an important crossroads, do we go back to all that is comfortable with all the problems and issues that existed before the recent disruptions, or do we go forward into a relative unknown where all that was clear becomes murky. Higher education may not fully understand it, but it is entering an era of reform. For higher education institutions globally, disruption means that we have begun to question the role of the university, of existing pedagogies, the role of new technologies (which are often seen as a threat not an opportunity), the changing needs of students and what we understand to be a student, the role and need for the physical campus, the leadership models, and the validity of the traditional degree, amongst others.

The concept of The Education Ecology of Universities and the role of the Chief Officer of Ecology, as highlighted within the chapter, is not a fixed or prescriptive model, but rather a flexible and generative one. It asks the university leaders at all levels, as well as those engaged in the university learning and teaching, and research activities (both staff and students) to adopt an ecological mindset and perspective, and to engage in a continuous process of reflection, negotiation, and innovation. It also encourages collaboration and dialogue among different stakeholders and knowledge holders, both within and without the university.

Al-Mahmood (2013) suggested that we need radical paradigms to adequately address the complexity of today's world, the idea of the university and its role in knowledge-making. However, if universities are willing to re-imagine their future through a more ecological approach then it becomes ever more feasible, embraces the values of what higher education should be, rather than is, so that the university always remains ever imagining (Barnett, 2013).

REFERENCES

Al-Mahmood, R. 2013. Re-imagining the university: Vibrant matters and radical research paradigms for the 21st century. *30th Ascilite Conference Proceedings*, 23-36.

Alexander, B. (2020). *Academia next: The futures of higher education*. John Hopkins University Press.

Barnett, R. (2010). *Being a University*. Routledge. 10.4324/9780203842485

Barnett, R. 2011. The Idea of the University in the Twenty-First Century: Where's the Imagination? *International Higher Education Congress: New Trends and Issues*, Istanbul, May 27-29: 261–68.

Barnett, R. (2013). *Imagining the University*. Routledge. 10.4324/9780203072103

Barnett, R. (2017). *The Ecological University: A Feasible Utopia*. Routledge. 10.4324/9781315194899

Barnett, R. (2020). Realizing the world-class university: an ecological approach. In Rider, S., Peters, M. A., & Hyvonen, M. (Eds.), *World Class Universities: A Contested Concept* (pp. 269–283). Springer Nature. 10.1007/978-981-15-7598-3_16

Blumenstyk, G. (2014). *American higher education in crisis? What everyone needs to know*. Oxford University Press. 10.1093/wentk/9780199374090.001.0001

Curry, R. (2017). Makerspaces: A beneficial new service for academic libraries? *Library Review*, 66(4/5), 201–212. 10.1108/LR-09-2016-0081

Curry, R. (2022). Insights from a cultural-historical HE library makerspace case study on the potential for academic libraries to lead on supporting ethical-making underpinned by 'critical material literacy'. *Journal of Librarianship and Information Science*.

Curry, R. 2023. Enabling the Ecological University – An Argument for Developing Transdisciplinary Ethical-Maker-Learning in Higher Education. In Radenkovic, M. (Ed). *Ethics - Scientific Research, Ethical Issues, Artificial Intelligence and Education*. InTechOpen.

Damsa, C. L., & Ludvigsen, S. (2016). Learning through interaction and co-construction of knowledge objects in teacher education. *Learning, Culture and Social Interaction*, 11, 1–18. 10.1016/j.lcsi.2016.03.001

Ellis, R., & Goodyear, P. (2019). *The Education Ecology of Universities: Integrating Learning, Strategy and the Academy*. Routledge. 10.4324/9781351135863

Guattari, F. (2000). *The Three Ecologies*. Athlone Press.

Leydesdorff, L. 2012. The triple helix of university-industry-government relations. SSRN *Electronic Journal*. 10.2139/ssrn.1996760

Malik, F. 2019. www.malik-management.com [Online]. (Accessed 18 April 2024).

Maxwell, N. (2007). From knowledge to wisdom: The need for an academic revolution. *London Review of Education*, 5(2), 97–115. 10.1080/14748460701440350

Perrin, S. & Sun, H. 2022. Graduate Employability through Industry-Oriented, Problem-Based Learning: A Case Study. *African Journal of Inter/Multidisciplinary Studies,* 4: 43-56

Por, G. 2000. The Ecology of Knowledge: A Field of Theory and Practice, Key to Research & Technology Development. *Position paper presented to The European Commission's Directorate-General Information Society Technologies.*

Ryan Derby-Talbot, R., & Coburn, N. (2023). Beyond "Innovation": Lessons for Making Change in Higher Educational Institutions. In Coburn, N., & Derby-Talbot, R. (Eds.), *The Impacts of Innovative Institutions in Higher Education* (pp. 277–292). Palgrave Macmillan. 10.1007/978-3-031-38785-2_12

Stetsenko, A. (2017). *The Transformative Mind: Expanding Vygotsky's Approach to Development and Education.* Cambridge University Press.

Stratford, R. (2015). What is the ecological university and why is it a significant challenge for higher education policy and practice? In *PESA - Philosophy of Education Society of Australasia.* ANCU.

Stratford, R. J. (2024). Towards ecological everything – The ecological university, ecological subjectivity and the ecological curriculum. *Policy Futures in Education*, 0(0), 1–9. 10.1177/14782103241227005

Chapter 16
History of Higher Education in Georgia From the Ancient Period to the Modern Times:
The Main Aspects of the Involvement of the Country in the Transnational Education Process

Nika Chitadze
International Black Sea University, Georgia

ABSTRACT

This research paper there are analyses different periods of the functioning of the High Educational Institutions in Georgia starting from the ancient period to the modern period and the role of the country within the transnational education process from the ancient period till the modern times. Particularly, parallelly with the educational institutions functioning, there are observed the preconditions of the involvement of Georgia in transnational education, by the engagement of Georgian students in the study process abroad and promotion of the arrival of foreign students for the getting education in the different high institutions of Georgia. Furthermore, attention is paid to the current situation in the framework of the high educational system of Georgia, by discussing the importance of joining the Bologna Process as a clear example of Transnational education and introducing the United National Exams in the country, based on the experience of leading countries of the world etc.

1. INTRODUCTION

Higher education in Georgia has a long history. Despite soverignity challenges and change higher educational centers, including the institutions of foreign countries have functioned within the country for a prolonged period of time. Thus, it should be noted that within its history, Georgia has actively been engaged with transnational higher education. Today there are various branches of foreign educational institutions, and the development of these can be traced back to the Greek-style gymnasiums up to the present day and the branches of foreign Universities in Georgia. Furthermore, many Georgian students have studied abroad and Georgia itself was and is an attractive place for foreign students (Encyclopedia, 2011). Based on those factors, the purpose of the chapter is to discuss the history of higher education in a case study geographic location, namely Georgia, and analyze the importance of the integration of the country into the international educational and scientific systems, which are reflected in the country signing up to the Bologna process (European common High Educational space), the opening and functioning of educational branches of foreign Universities in Georgia, the increased frequency of Georgian students gaining high education abroad and the attraction of foreign students to Georgian Universities.

2. STUDY METHODS

2.1 Research Questions

1) What are the higher educational system origins in Georgia?
2) Which historic events promoted the foundation of higher educational institutions in Georgia?
3) Which historic events hampered the development of higher educational institutions in Georgia?
4) What is Georgia's current status quo with regards to transnational higher education?

2.2 Research Methods

1) **Quantitative Research Methods** were used in the research paper, particularly in order to investigate the different educational institutions in Georgia, including the branches of foreign Universities. This approach was also employed for the nearest historical period, and for presenting the number of Georgian students who are involved in the education process in the branches of foreign Universities in the country and abroad, as well as for foreign students.
2) **Comparative Analysis** was employed to for the analysis of the different methods that were introduced in the high educational system of Georgia during the communist and post-communist periods and during the preconditions of the foundation of the branches of foreign universities in Georgia.
3) **Content Aalysis** was adopted in this study when researching leading specialists in the field of Higher education.
4) **Narrative Analysis** was utilised for a more indepth analysis of all those processes, which were and are going on in the sphere of transnational higher education regionally.

2.3 Methodological Framework

The **functional approach of sociology** has been utilised. This theory considers the positive function that education plays in society. Sociologist Emile Durkheim highlighted that the main function of education represents the transmission of the values of the dominant culture. Taking this into account, and noting the different societies which exist, cultural goals and values are clearly different from one another. It can also be noted that the study systems in the different educational institutions of Georgia during the different national historical periods have varied, which requires the analysis of the educational system during the differing periods in order to better understand the present. This means that this paper has considered the middle century, new history and modern history of Georgia (Society for a Better Society, 2023).

2.4 Study Findings

There is a detailed analysis of the different periods in the history of higher education in Georgia presented within this paper. The precondition for the involvement of the country in the transnational education process, has also been considered in light of the more recent past.

3. CONTEXTUAL DISCUSSION

3.1 Early Developments

There are different authentic Georgian sources about the initial stage of the history of Georgian education and, accordingly, the early characteristics of the education system. It is also possible to discuss them based on Greek sources. Records of Greek historians testify that "gymnasiums" were widespread in ancient Georgia. Presumably, these "Georgian gymnasiums" should have been a kind of analogy to the three gymnasiums in Athens - Lyceon, Academy, and Kinosargos (Lominashvili, 2020). Therefore, it can be considered, that the higher school of rhetoric in Kolkheti, near Fazis, of the III-IV Century AD, is an institution similar to its Greek counterparts existed. The only direct reference to it is found in one of the letters of the Greek philosopher Themistos (317). There is some information about the program and language of the teaching or who taught the different subjects. It can be seen from Themistos's report that the Colchis Academy with its content dating back to BC was functional. It should not differ much from the Greek and Roman schools of rhetoric. The mentioned school was located in the city of Fazisi (Mkurnalidze, Khamkhadze, 2000). According to historical documents, Ioanne Lazi received his education there, and later, together with his famous disciple Petre Iberi, worked in Constantinople and Palestine. Taken as a hostage to Byzantium, Prince Murvanos, later known as Peter the Iberian and Dionysius Areopagel, received a thorough education abroad (Chitadze, 2016).

In the later period, monasteries played an educational role. However, until the 10th and 11th centuries, the existence of a specific educational institution is not observed. At that time, education considered the Holy Scriptures and church rituals in the monastic schools. In the higher theological schools, no information can be found in the sources. In general, this type of teaching had a rather organized and systematic character, which was based on the approach of scholastic teaching. Examining the hagiographical works allows us to say that in the pre-feudal age, homeschooling - an institution of upbringing, which had a kind of elitist character and was only a luxury of the population standing higher on the social ladder. It should be noted that teaching in this period started from the age of 6-7 years. Information about this is provided by the documentation depicting the life of Grigol Khandzeteli, in which the ages of the children given for education are specifically named. The educational process was led by specially invited teachers (tutors). Grigol Khandzeteli is connected with the organization and arrangement of educational processes in the monastic complexes created in Tao-Klarjeti (Southern part of Georgia). A special literary school of Tao-Klarjeti was formed here, which developed its grammar, language, and direction. This is the first time the state was the direct customer and participant of the educational space. School education was advanced when Georgians started receiving Byzantine education. It is worth noting that Georgian scholars founded a new educational center far from their homeland, which played the greatest cultural and educational role in the Middle East. During the period of early feudalism, Georgians had their educational centers in several monastic centers abroad, as well as in Georgia itself, where educational institutions existed in such religious centers as Khandza and Shatberdi, Bana and Parkhali, Ishkhani and Opiza, Oshki and Karastavi. During the period of feudalism, aeas such as Mount Athos and Mount Sinai, in Constantinople, and the Petritsoni monastery, were acclaimed and the Georgian education system flourished (LOminashvili, 2020).

At the end of the 12th century, under the leadership of Davit the Builder (Agmashenebeli), the Gelati Academy was founded, which contemporaries refer to as "the other Athens, the second Jerusalem of the East" (Shubitidze, 2002). In the Gelati Academy, youth education, not only from Georgia but from the various kingdoms and principalities of the wide Black Sea area grew. Just like the universities of Europe in the following centuries, the Gelati Academy was headed by a Modzgvari "main teacher". Famous scholars taught here: mathematics, rhetoric, astronomy, theology, and philosophy. Within the framework of the study of philosophy, for example, when discussing the works of Plato and Aristotle, or Cicero, the doctrines of the presented philosophers about the forms of state organization and governance and the development of the country and the implementation of its policy in the international arena were also the subject and object of the study of the educational system of that time. The academies of Ikalto and Gelati, where foreign students also were receiving their education, have been the distant ancestors of our present universities. They stopped functioning in the 14th century however. For four centuries, Georgians had to fight against manyexternal forces. In the difficult part of this history, the issue of cultural and heritage protection was faced, along with the physical survival of the nation. The invasion of the Mongols within the XIII-XIV Centuries hurt educational processes. During this difficult period, many representatives of the younger generation of Georgia were involved in the education process outside the state, particularly in Europe and the Middle East.

From the 17th century onwards, the teaching and learning system included both religious and secular education. It can be said that people's interest was more toward secular education. Teimuraz the First (King of Kartli and Kakheti) mentions in his work: "No one wants the Gospel, nor the book of the apostles" (Mkurnalizde, Khamkhadze, 2000). Studying the teaching process was still carried out in the feudal families during this period, and the members of the royal court received education through special teachers or via self-education. Researchers believe that the first progressive views on education were given by King-Poet Archill, who believed that education should be available to the wider population because education is one of the main foundations of a nation's well-being. Archil understood the need for the principle of universality of education, which in turn represented one of the most important principles of building the education system. Archile's view on teaching methodology is as follows: The teacher should be guided by the method of gradual transition from easy to difficult in the teaching-learning process. This is the scaffolding of today's educational systems. Archile's views were quite progressive at that time. With regard to the second important innovation that promoted transnational education, this was the establishment of schools by Catholic missionaries. The first Capuchins (Catholic monks), who founded a school in Georgia, arrived in Tbilisi in 1662-1663. In the school, they taught reading, writing, Italian, Latin, chanting, and arithmetic. The most talented of the children prepared at the school, at the age of 15-20, were sent to Rome to continue their studies at the Propaganda College.

3.2 King Vakhtang VI and Sulkhan-Saba Orbeliani.

The dictionary compiled by Sulkhan-Saba Orbeliani was a study guide at the beginning of the 18th Century. It is also known as a work of a didactic-moralistic nature - "Sibzne Sisruisa" (The Wisdom of Lies), which put forward original ideas in pedagogical thinking. In 1711, the first Georgian methodical manual was printed in the Tbilisi printing house - "Learning if the teacher should teach the disciple". At that time, 14 books were printed in the Tbilisi printing house - although 11 were religious, 2 were educational manuals. In 1712 Shota Rustaveli's "Vefxistkaosani" (The Knight in the Tiger`s Skin) was published. Vakhushti Bagration translated the world geography textbook from Russian, to which 21 color maps were attached. Vakhtang VI compiled a short course on astronomy-cosmography. It should be mentioned in the book "On Blending and Chemistry of Oils" was a notable work. Vakhtang VI`s view was that education should be a declared priority for the people in the different regions of the world. In 1800's. The political image of Georgia during that period is presented in Vakhushti Bagration's excellent work (Description of the Kingdom of Georgia) and his geographical atlas. The prominent political figure and scientist describes with the same tenderness both the lands that were part of the Georgian kingdoms and principalities of that time, as well as the lands captured by other nation states, which the author perceives as an inseparable part of his homeland. In the same work, the researcher notes with great heartache about such an important problem as the difficult political situation, which in turn was reflected in the level of education in the country was a discussion point (Vakhushti, 1745).

Later, the desire to revive the centers of higher education arose more than once. This was served by the theological seminaries established in 1755 in Tbilisi and 1782 in Telavi (Liluashvili, 2006 2002). A large staff of Georgian scientists and figures was created. In such a situation, the idea of establishing a higher education institution gradually matured in Georgian society. Ioane Batonishvili, a prominent Georgian figure at the end of the 18th century, worked on the project of the state transformation of Georgia. It was later approved by Kartl-Kakheti King George XII. Ioane Batonishvili in his work called "Sjulisdeba"(Legal Sciences) meant the establishment of high schools in Tbilisi, Telavi, and Gori. In the higher educational institutions, in which the children of the nobles themselves and the "first citizens" had to be "entrusted", the matter should have been set up in such a way "to show them knowledgeable men to teach scientific and military studies, as well as languages. At the educational institution, they studied Georgian, Armenian, Turkish, Russian, and, if most probably, Greek and Latin" (Chitadze, 2016). This initiative was one of the serious, progressive projects for that time, which was, in fact, a thorough study of the languages of the people who lived in Georgia. The implementation of this idea was prevented by the manifesto issued by the Russian emperor in 1801, which resulted in the loss of Georgia's independence and the exile of the royal family to St. Petersburg.

3.3 The 1800's

The annexation of the Kartli-Kakheti Kingdom (Eastern Part of Georgia) by Russia in 1801 put Georgia in front of various challenges. From the beginning of the nineteenth century, the formation of the education system was dictated by Russian policy. Subsequently, for 117 years there were no higher educational institutions in the country, and hence no preconditions for the transnational education development existed, and the language of learning was Russian. As far as educational developments went in 1802, a two-class primary school was established for the children of the Georgian nobility. In these schools, the "beginnings of morality" were taught as a special subject. In 1804, three main types of secondary and primary schools were established. In 1804, Tbilisi Noble School was founded. This school was for children of high rank. Later, Tbilisi Theological Seminary was founded in 1817 and this existed for 100 years. This school was responsible for retraining and theprofessional training of teachers. This was the first attempt at professional training of teachers. It also had a dormitory for all students. Later, in 1818, theological and parochial schools began to be opened in Georgia. Gori, Telavi, Sighnaghi,

Kutaisi. All these seminaries were subject to the Holy Synod of St. Petersburg. In 1828, a new "charter" of schools was approved. The nomenclature of schools remained the same, namely, parish, marketplace and gymnasiums. In 1830, the intensive establishment of private schools began. The private school was already intended for all classes and aimed at widespread primary education. Furthermore, there were also the so-called "Home schools". The forms of individual teaching were also expanding. It was the direction of non-formal education. In 1840, the "Transcaucasian Women's Institute" opened. It was a closed school with strict regulations. It should be pointed out that at this point in time the principle of compulsory education did not apply.

The situation partly changed in the second half of the nineteenth Century. Particularly, in 1879 and the second half of the nineteenth century: "Writing among Georgians - a Society spreading Reading" was established by Chavchavadze, Kipiani, Gogebashvili, and others to open a Georgian school. Jacob Gogebashvili wrote: "Moreover, a highly important society has not yet been born in our country, its purpose is to educate the nation"(Mkurnalidze and Khamkhadze, 2000). In the first stage, this society founded schools in Tbilisi, Batumi, Tianeti, Kheltubani, and Gomareti. The society had the right to establish reading rooms, and libraries, to invite experienced teachers to schools, and to publish children's books and textbooks in the Georgian language. The Society for Promoting Literacy opened the first school in 1880 in Tbilisi, where there were 2 sections, each with 16 students, 10 girls and 6 boys. Since this community was often unable to maintain a school due to lack of funds, the idea arose to hire an itinerant teacher who would travel from place to place and teach reading and writing. The first chairman of the community was Dimitri Kipiani. Four years later, in 1883, a new type of school was also created under the leadership of Ilia Tsinamdashvili, on his initiative and at his expense. It was the so-called Author's school, which was the only educational institution of this profile in Transcaucasia. Within of this school, the special importance was attached to the textbooks compiled by Jacob Gogebashvili: "Mother Language" and "Door of Nature", which was published in 1876. Chubinashvili's "Georgian Chrestomathy", his grammar of the Georgian language, was also created, as was Bakradze's works in the history and ethnography of Georgia.

The nineteenth century also saw the political orientation of Georgia become more closely connected to Russia. Georgian people had moved to a new path of socio-political and cultural development. However, despite the efforts of tsarist Russia to prevent it, there was almost no field of science where Georgian scholars did not showcase their own ideas and perspectives. Along with the longing of the Georgian nation towards Europe, the efforts of the progressive-minded society were directed toward the fact that the development of culture in Georgia would be guided mainly based on national traditions. In this respect, the Georgian nation faced several contradictions. The authority of Russia considered the communion of the nations they oversaw as essential, with the European civilization on the periphery. It was not in its interests, and that's why it sought to establish a colonial cultural orientation, permissible only for the policy of tsarism. The Georgian people however were looking towards Europe. Against such a backdrop, naturally, a part of the advanced Georgian society fought to protect the national self-consciousness and culture and allow the nation to absorb European achievements as far as possible. Thus, the connection with European civilization was one of the most convenient and acceptable for Georgian culture at the time. The starting point of this was receiving a European orientated education. After the establishment of relations with Russia, Georgian youth began to receive both a European and Russian education and study scientific and artistic literature within this framework. Getting an education abroad by the Georgian intellectual elite contributed to the spread of European ideas in Georgia, while the time-consuming autocratic Russian educational system was geared towards other areas. Therefore, within this context Georgian traditions and ambitions were promoted through both public and private educational structures.

There were many additional challenges within the nineteenth century. The development of scientific thinking and the preparation of conditions for the creation of a local higher education institution became a core goal of the Georgian society during this period. At first, the negative influence of tsarist policy on the development of national education and scientific thinking seemed apparent to many as the existing education system was overhauled. This limited the Georgian language in primary Georgian schools and saw it removed in certain social spheres. Social upheaval was also experienced, such as the relocation of members of the Georgian royal family and other nobles to St. Petersburg and Moscow, which, naturally, represented a loss for the country. However, creative work continued unabated and centers of Georgian culture were established in Russia. In the circles of Georgian emigrants in St. Petersburg and Moscow, debates continued on various issues that had originated within Georgia. One discussion and action point was the idea of opening a local high school, in particular, a university in Tbilisi. Due to the lack of a center of higher education in Georgia at that time, Georgian youth traveled to Russia and abroad to study, which was naturally associated with great economic and linguistic difficulties. The Tsar's Russian government was also aware of the need for specialists in various fields in Georgia. This necessitated a large body of qualified officials which was lacking at the time. This made the existing situation even more difficult. Furthering the desire to expand educational provision, Prince Golovin (1838-1842) petitioned the Russian Emperor to open a higher education institution in Tbilisi that would be similar to a university. This proved to be unsuccessful as educational designs now had more centralized and broader orientations during the period between 1801 to 1917 as Liluashvili (2006) highlights.

In the middle of the 19th century, during the reign of Prince Vorontsov, the idea of opening a University arose, which was based on the existence of a language barrier for Georgian youth studying in Russia which was seeing them disadvantaged. Yanovsky, the Russian official in charge of the Caucasus educational district, was also interested in the opening of Tbilisi University. According to his project, the higher educational institute should be a technological institute, where the faculty of oriental languages could be based. That said, even though Russia considered the precedent of opening an institute in Georgia, for many decades, many officials opposed the idea of establishing a University in Tbilisi. One reason was that the establishment of this institution might create issues in other social areas. During the middle of the century an increase in the number of Georgian gymnasiums, private boarding schools, and monastic and family schools was apparent. The idea of opening a Georgian university was also more firmly set, but it was challenging to realise. In the work of Ilia Chavchavadze, the issue of education occupies an important place in our concious.

Some practical steps were taken under the leadership by Giorgi Tsereteli to open the university. They considered philosophy to be the basis of the foundations of all sciences. The mentioned plan meant the organization of the University on a European scale. The struggle for the University was also spread on the pages of the local Russian and Georgian press. Newspapers "Kavkazi", "Droeba", "Tifliski Vestnik", and "Obzor" were active (Shota Rustaveli National Fund, 2017). Newspapers raised questions about the possibility of creating a university, its purpose, staff of teachers, and students, which were directly or indirectly related to the problems of higher education. Many of these same discussion points exist around higher education today. The Tbilisi city administration determined to allocate 100 thousand manats for this case at the same time and to contribute 40 thousand manats to the University funds (Liluashvili, 2006). At that time, representatives of the Russian Emperor in the Caucasus, the brother of the Emperor was the great Duke Mikheil, and his first assistant was the poet Grigol Orbeliani. In the speeches of the officials of the ruling circles, a certain fear could be seen. They considered it dangerous to spread higher education opportunities because it might galvanise the youth to seek change. All those factors forced the government of the Russian Tsar to think that the future University would become a source of problems. Therefore, development was opposed by emphasizing the low levels of education among the local population in Georgia, and the lack of a developed network of primary and secondary education. Still, this was an important discussion point as numerous interested parties were involved and had strong motives. This period also saw the introduction of the national traditional experience in the education system. The work carried out by the Georgian society in this field was the first step in the later Europeanization of educational institutions.

During this period, in particular, in the 1860s and 1870s, important processes took place both in the Russian Empire and in its provinces. Russia's defeat in the Crimean War (1853-1856) was one, and this, in part, led to reforms although these were not always successful and, in fact, worsened the situation at times (Muskhelishvili, 2012). In 1871, the some of the Georgian nobility appealed to Emperor Alexander II for the opening of a University in Tbilisi, but their request was declined. However, it should be noted that the Georgian nobility were not unanimouson the point. A significant part of the people asked the emperor to establish a cadet corps, and this coincided with the wishes of the then government. The "Kavkaz" newspaper went as far as to question the idea of establishing a University as "helpless and pointless" because, according to it, in such a higher education institution "there will be more professors than young people who want to acquire education" (Liluashvili, 2006). Towards the end of the 19th century, the question of establishing a higher center was raised more intensely in front of Georgian society, and the search for the ways and means necessary for the realization of this goal again began to attract interest. The establishment of a higher school of learning became even more evident after the establishment of the People`s Bank. It was the only one among the banks in the Russian Empire, which did not use its income for official purposes, but used its financial resources for the cultural, educational, and economic interests of the nation. If we look at the various business operations carried out by the Georgian National Bank, it will become clear that it allocated the most financial resources for the construction of the Georgian gymnasium and the future university building (Javakhishvili, 1906).

3.4 The Early 1900's

From the beginning of the twentieth century, Ivane Javakhishvili, a graduate of St. Petersburg University and its private docent (Associate Professor), became the organizer of the foundation of the Georgian University. He drew up a concrete plan for the opening of the National University in Tbilisi, "which was fundamentally different from the idea of establishing the Caucasus University in Tbilisi" (Chitadze, 2016). It should be noted here that the idea of the Caucasus University in a way prepared the public opinion about the need to establish a higher school of learning in Tbilisi. During the First World War, in 1917, the Russian University was also established in Tbilisi. The city council endorsed the establishment of a Russian university. Later, the Education Commissariat of the Provisional Government of Russia handed over the project of Tbilisi University, which was developed under the leadership of Ivane Javakhishvili and submitted to the authorities for approval, to Niko Mari. Niko Mari was a Scottish origin scientist raised in Georgia. After the upheaval in Russia in 1917 the situation changed dramatically. In the following years external influence was curbed and the Tbilisi-based Caucasus University lost backing sway, both financially and scientifically. During this period, the newly founded Tbilisi State University gradually strengthened and provided significant competition to the Caucasus University, as a result, the latter ceased to exist in 1920 (Liluashvili, 2006).

3.5 Tbilisi State University

One of the first steps taken at the beginning of the twentieth century, before Georgia's national independence was the establishment of the National University in Tbilisi. During this period, Tbilisi State University (TSU) was able to establish well-known scientific schools in mathematics, psychology, philosophy, linguistics, history and oriental studies. Amongst others laying the foundation for the creation of many higher educational institutions and the Georgian Academy of Sciences. After 1917 it was also possible to establish a non-Russian language university in the Russian Empire, and the beginning of 1918 is widely considered the approximate date of the establishment of more formalized educational institutions. The founding society of the university established two commissions: academic and financial. The financial department was tasked with raising funds for the establishment of the University, and the academic department was tasked with implementing relevant policies in the direction of the scientific organization. The commission would ultimately hold 9 sessions at different times (Encyclopedia, 2011). At the meeting of November 26, 1917, it was decided to establish one faculty of philosophy, to which other faculties and departments would be added later (Liluashvili, 2006). On January 13, 1918, the first session of the university was held, where they wanted to elect Ivane Javakhishvili as rector, but the latter refused and Petre Melikishvili (an internationally recognized scientist) was elected instead. On January 26, 1918, the University was offivially opened. On September 3 of the same year, the University was declared to be a State University (Liluashvili, 2006). Accordingly, the oldest and largest higher education institution in Georgia was founded in Tbilisi, in the building of the old gymnasium, on the day of the commemoration of Davit Agmashenebeli (The Builder). This was the first and the only University in the entire Caucasus at that time. Thus, it served as a higher education center for the different nations of the Caucasus Region. In 1918-1919, the University was represented by the following structure: "1. Faculty of Wisdom and Philosophy; 2. Faculty of Mathematics and Science; 3. Medical Faculty; 4. From September 1919, the Faculty of Agronomy was added to TSU; 5. Faculty of Law; 6. Scientific-educational division; 7. Sanitary Institute, which was founded in 1919. This was part of the Ministry of Education and subordinated to Tbilisi State University, although it was not a structural part of it" (Liluashvili, 2006). In 1918-1921, the structure of Tbilisi State University was established by the Scientific Council of the University. It was developed under the leadership of Javakhishvili. The structure would go on to gradually change along with the growth of the scientific staff.

3.6 Post World War I

In February 1921, new education conditions arose with the establishment of the Soviet school system which began in 1924. The implementation of communist ideology and politics was connected with substantial changes in the system of education and science. Emphasis was placed on the quantitative growth of educated personnel and the special training of pupils and students in specific spheres and to foster a clear lifestyle mindset. At the same time, a decision was made to strengthen Russian language teaching in Georgia and other national republics. In the years after the war, significant changes took place in the education and science system of Georgia, which led to the rise of education and science. Georgian mathematical, geological, physiological, psychological, and other schools were thus formed. The

Soviet era served the Bolshevik principles of a collective identity formation. Both secondary and higher education, formal and informal, served to create common markers of identity. This led to the formation of the Soviet people and the upbringing of the next generation with a socialist ideology determined by a tiered system of secondary education. It also led to create a system of socialist staff. School textbooks were centrally screened. This is confirmed by the 1954 collection of the Scientific-Research Institute of Pedagogical Sciences of the Ministry of Education of the USSR "Issues of Teaching History in School", which includes the works of Georgian Soviet scientists and the main idea is related to the teaching of history. An important level of education was represented by the higher education institutions, the staff trained by them joined the ranks of the Soviet intelligentsia. By 1936, there were 20 higher education institutions in the country, where 21,584 students from Georgia and other Soviet socialist republics studied, and 21,752 students in 113 vocational-technical institutions (Cultural Studies, 2017). The Soviet empire was based on the principle of internationalism. At the same time, Soviet nationalities should have stories that, on the one hand, would strengthen their national pride and, on the other hand, adhere to communism. This goal was served by the creation of icons of public or cultural heroes. The works of Pushkin, Rustaveli, Shevchenko, and other poets were translated and distributed throughout the Soviet Union. In 1937, Georgia celebrated the 100th anniversary of Ilia Chavchavadze; In the same year, Georgia and the entire Soviet Union celebrated the 750th anniversary of Shota Rustaveli's "The Knight in the Tigers Skin" (this poem is translated into 38 languages of the world), and in 1940 the 100th anniversary of Jacob Gogebashvili; In 1976, the 100th anniversary of "Mother Language" was held, and in 1983, 14 events dedicated to the 200th anniversary of the "Georgievsky Treatise" were held as a "manifesto of friendship and brotherhood between the Russian and Georgian peoples". Anniversaries, congresses, and other activities were framed in a single Soviet narrative. Print media also supported developments (Shervashidze, 2022). It is worth noting the fact that at the end of the 1980s, 17 higher education institutions were functioning in Georgia, 10 of which were located in Tbilisi. At those institutions, students from 20 countries (especially communist and pro-soviet countries of Central and Eastern Europe, Asia, and Africa) and 10 Soviet socialist republics were gaining their education here. At the same time, there were no foreign University branches in Georgia during this period (Chitadze, 2016).

3.7 New Directions

In October 1990, Soviet rule ended in Georgia. As a result, changing the system of education and science was on the agenda. The new socio-political reality required the creation of a new system of education and science, but between December-January 1991-1992 internal developments shifted the emphasis. Thus, in this part of the chapter, the way of educational, scientific, and health care reforming of post-Soviet Georgia and the theoretical and practical measures implemented by the authorities and ruling political parties: namely the Georgian Citizens' Union", "National Movement" and "Georgian Dream" are specially discussed. It is emphasized that the reforms or any type of changes introduced in the Georgian educational system were related to the pursuit of Western values, and the entry and establishment of the European-American educational and scientific spaces. The new reform paved the way for informational knowledge flows, advancing the cause of knowledge acquisition, its use, and development. Emphasis was placed on management education, and the growth prospects of the knowledge-based economy, the introduction of the electronic education system, and the formation of a new, harmonious person. The education and science system of Georgia joining the Bologna process meant joining the unified system of education and the promotion of the transnational high education system. The Bologna process was supposed to accelerate the global marketing of higher education. Moreover, the educational market, in which tried-and-tested training programs, methods, and piloted textbooks appeared, did not have a national mark and was part of the educational and educational business. As for the situation in the field of education in the 1990's the concept and programs of educational and scientific development were advanced. The changes carried out by the authorities in the education system were experimental, characterized by subjective tendencies, and paved the way for issues to arise. It is also worth noting that some of the educational pedagogical community did not agree with the idea of the rapid internationalization set in place by the Ministry of Education and the direct transfer of new programs, curricula, and teaching methods from other countries.

3.8 The Bologna Process and TNHE Integration

After May 2005, Georgia became a part of the Bologna process, and this significantly changed the country's higher education system, bringing it closer to European standards. Georgia joined the Bologna process in the Norwegian city of Bergen. The Bologna process is a process of convergence and harmonization of the education systems of European countries, which aims to create a single European space for higher education. The latter aims to strengthen the employment and mobility of European citizens and to increase the international competitiveness of European higher education. The Bologna process began with the Great Charter of Universities (lat. Magna Charta Universitatum). It was the program document of the process adopted in the city of Bologna, on the 900th anniversary of the oldest university in the world, in 1988 by 382 universities (Chitadze, 2016). The Bologna Declaration was signed by ministers responsible for higher education in 29 European countries in 1999. However, its foundation was laid earlier, in 1998 by the declaration of the Sorbonne conference, which was accepted by 4 countries (France, Germany, Great Britain, and Italy). In Bologna, education ministers agreed on a common vision for the European Higher Education Area (EHEA). They decided that this vision was highly relevant for their countries and reflected it in the operational objectives of the Bologna Declaration. At that time, the main elements of the European higher education space were as follows: European countries, with different political, cultural, and academic traditions, would engage in cooperation to achieve common goals, and it would give the opportunity to European students and graduates the ability to move easily from one country to another with full recognition of qualifications and periods of study and access to the European employment market. Furthermore, the European Higher Education Institutions (HEIs) will have the opportunity to cooperate and exchange students/staff based on mutual trust and confidence, as well as transparency and quality. For this purpose, the European governments would align national higher education reforms with the wider European context; The initiators of the signing the Bologna Declaration had the view, that Higher education in the European region would increase its international competitiveness, as well as enter into dialogue and improve cooperation with higher education in other regions of the world. As a result, over the past 20 years, the Bologna Process, through voluntary integration and an intergovernmental approach, has been able to bring out the main pillars of the European Higher Education Area, and these are:

- A common framework, including the EHEA Comprehensive Qualifications Framework, the Common Credit System (ECTS), common principles for the development of student-centered learning, European standards and guidelines for quality assurance, a common register for quality

assurance agencies, and common methodologies developed by European higher education institutions and sustainable achievements.
• Several common tools, namely ECTS User Guide, Diploma Supplement, and Lisbon Recognition Convention.

Simply put, the goal of the Bologna Process is designed to create a European Higher Education Area (EHEA) by harmonizing academic quality standards and quality assurance standards for each faculty across Europe. The Bologna process is one of the most important voluntary processes at the European level and is currently implemented in 48 countries that make up the European Higher Education Area (EHEA). The Bologna Process is a series of ministerial meetings and agreements between European countries to ensure the comparability of standards and quality of higher education qualifications. Every 2-3 years, a ministerial conference is held in the European Higher Education Area (EHEA) to assess the progress made and to set new steps. As it was mentioned, Georgia has been a member of the European Higher Education Area since 2005. Currently, 49 European countries are involved in the Bologna process. Countries participating in the Bologna process are represented at the level of government, higher education institutions, students, academic staff, and employers. The main participants of the process are: Ministers responsible for the higher education of the countries that have signed the Bologna Declaration; Council of Europe; European University Association (EUA), Institutions of Higher Professional Education (EURASHE), European University Student Union (ESU), European Higher Education Quality Assurance Agency (ENQA), United Nations Organization (UNESCO); Pan-European international structure of education; Business Europe (National Center of the Education Development, 2023). Together with the joining the Bologna Process, The system of unified national examinations was introduced in Georgia in 2005, although since 2002 there was already a national center for assessment and examinations, which represented an organization separate from the state administration bodies. Since 2005, administration of national exams has been added to these duties. The reform of the unified national exams has meant that students are selected for any higher education institution based on the scores obtained in the exam. Results obtained in exams remain the only criteria for student selection and funding. Unified national exams in Georgia do not have a long history, although they have been actively changing since 2005.

According to the original model, three mandatory exams were held in 2005: Georgian language and literature, foreign language, and a general skills exam. The entrant received funding based on the results of the compulsory exams. The mathematics exam was the only optional subject and the applicant took it according to the faculty's requirements. In the case of passing all four exams, the highest score obtained between the foreign language and mathematics exams was used in the calculation of state funding. This system was completely foreign to local society, and like all innovations, a large part met it with fear and distrust. Indeed, some applicants refused to take the exam due to anxiety, but those students of the graduating class who accepted the challenge and successfully passed the exams were admitted to the desired faculties based more transparent selection processes. In 2006, four more subjects were added to the list of optional exams: natural sciences, history of Georgia, public sciences, and literature. The state funding system was also changed, and instead of three tests, grants were awarded based on a general skills test. The format of the exams did not change in 2007-2009. In 2010, state funding was awarded according to four tests. Accordingly, an applicant who wanted to receive state funding, regardless of the requirements of the desired faculty, had to pass the optional exam along with the mandatory exams. In 2012, instead of seven, applicants could choose twenty desired faculties from the beginning. In 2013, this restriction was completely abolished. Entrants were allowed to indicate in the application all the educational programs for which the examinations of their choice were applied. In some faculties, the minimum competence limit has been increased. In 2014-2015, several more optional subject exams were added, and it became possible to take the general skills exam in English. In 2016, the practice of switching to the electronic format of the exam began. So far, only part of the test is provided in electronic format, and the entrants fill in the answer sheet in writing. In the long term, it is planned to introduce exams in a fully electronic format. The biggest change in the model of unified national exams took place in 2020. The new model includes three mandatory exams: Georgian language and literature, foreign language, and, depending on the specific program, history or mathematics. For admission to natural science and technical courses, entrants take mathematics, and for humanitarian programs, history. The fourth exam remains optional, and educational institutions have the right to require an additional exam for individual programs. General aptitude tests are also included in the list of optional subject tests. There is a separate healthcare education program for which four subjects must be passed. The entrant passes the Georgian language and literature, foreign language, and biology and together with them chooses to pass the math, chemistry, or physics exam. In 2021, the format and duration of some exams changed further. As for state financing, today its amount is 2,250 GEL (about 800 USD). Applicants can receive 100%, 70%, or 50% funding depending on the scores obtained in the exams. It should be noted that the maximum amount of the state educational grant has not changed since 2004. The state grant is not granted to citizens of foreign countries, persons with dual citizenship, and persons who will receive the right to continue their studies in non-accredited programs (Tabula, 2023). The reform of the national exams has successfully achieved its main goal and solved various issues related to fund mismanagement, however, new challenges are currently on the agenda both in terms of administration and format. Considering this, the assumption is that models will continue to form and reform. What form these will take in the future remains to be seen. However, there is no doubt that it needs to be updated and refined (Tabula, 2023).

4 TRANSNATIONAL HIGHER EDUCATION IN GEORGIA

Some examples of current transnational providers and how thecurrently operate within this case study context includes the former institutions:

4.1 The International Black Sea University (IBSU)

One of the first International Universities in Georgia with foreign shareholders was the International Black Sea University, which was founded in 1995 and up to 2023 has represented a network of Turkish higher educational institutions abroad. The university is the first English-language educational institution in Georgia, offering programs in both English and Georgian languages at all three levels of education. Currently, the university operates close to 40 bachelor's, master's, and doctoral accredited educational programs, where citizens of more than 20 countries get their education. Six refereed scientific journals are published annually (IBSU, 2024). Within this institution there are a number of well regarded schools. The School of Computer Science and Architecture offers students education at the undergraduate, graduate, and doctoral levels. There are six educational programs within the school: bachelor's program in computer science (Georgian and English sectors), bachelor's program of architecture (English sector), master's and doctoral programs in computer science (English sector), internationally accredited double diploma master's program "Management and Computer Science" (IBSU, 2024). The goal of the School of Computer Science and Architecture is to offer students an education that meets modern standards and to train internationally competitive specialists. The Business School is one of the largest and most sought-after schools not only in the local but also in the international market. The graduates have all the necessary skills and relevant education that increase their competitiveness in the global employment market.The School of Business offers students bachelor's, master's, and doctoral programs in Georgian and English according to modern standards. The school is staffed by both local and foreign highly qualified professors, as well as practicing specialists. The most demanded specialties in the labor market are taught here. The goal of the school is to train competitive specialists with student-oriented education who will be able to participate in the activities of various sectors of business according to modern standards at the local and international level, which provides employment opportunities in the state, private, and non-governmental sectors; Educational programs provide students with fundamental knowledge and practical skills of theoretical and practical issues of business; The programs allow students to respond to the challenges of the modern business environment and help them plan and develop their careers (IBSU, 2024). The School of Education, Humanities, and Social Sciences has equally high academic standards and a combination of practical skills, ensures the competitiveness of graduates in the employment market, and visiting scholars ensures that a wide range of ideas are heard from Europe and North America. Most of the programs of the School of Education, Humanities, and Social Sciences are in English, which allows graduates to master the English language professionally, and to continue their studies in English speaking contexts. In addition to the courses provided by the specialty, students will also learn a second foreign language (Spanish, French, German, Russian, Turkish) (IBSU, 2024). The School of Law and Public Administration offers education in law at the undergraduate and graduate levels and public administration at the undergraduate level. The goal of the school is to offer students an education that meets modern and affordable standards and to create an environment that promotes the development of state and legal thinking, theoretical and practical aspects of law, and scientific research (IBSU, 2024). Finally, the School of Medicine was founded in 2023. The school operates a graduate medical program, the purpose of which is to prepare qualified, highly ethical, deep, and systematic knowledge, appropriate skills, necessary competencies, and professional values for local and international labor markets, and to meet the demands of the society, which ensures the promotion of the mission of the Black Sea International University (IBSU, 2024).

4.2 The Institute of European Studies of the Tbilisi State University

The Institute of European Studies of Tbilisi State University was established in 2007 within the framework of the TACIS program of the European Union with the financial support of the European Union and with the cooperation of the European Union Representation in Georgia. Students at the Institute of European Studies study EU economics, EU financial and monetary policy, EU law, competition policy, Europeanization and European integration theories, EU energy policy, free trade, and foreign direct investment. Students also have the opportunity to get acquainted with the aspects of the Georgia-EU relationship, and acquire knowledge about the history of Europe and the European Union, and certain aspects of the European cultural mosaic (Lomouri, 2020). Ivane Javakhishvili Tbilisi State University (TSU) Institute of European Studies (ESI) is an interdisciplinary and English-language master's program in European studies, which has been operating since 2006. In this master's program, EC includes four TSU faculties to provide students with knowledge about Europe: Business and Economics, Humanities, Law, and Social and Political Sciences. The vision of the institute promotes the introduction and spread of shared European values, as well as the promotion of Georgian values in EU countries by supporting modern European studies in Georgia and promoting studies about Georgia in EU countries. EU professors from HEA providers such as the University Pierre Mendés France of Grenoble (France), the Center for Public Reforms at the University of Innsbruck (Austria) da Panteion University of Social and Political Sciences in Athens (Greece) often help with delivery. High standards of staffing and academic mobility enable European standards of teaching quality, as outlined by the Bologna process to be met. The program is two years long and involves the accumulation of at least 120 ECTS credits by the master's student (Lomouri, 2020). Along with the constant efforts to strengthen the pedagogical, research, and consulting potential, the institute systematically takes care of establishing institutional cooperation with higher education institutions of the European Union through the implementation of academic and student mobility, research, and joint/dual scientific degree programs.

4.3 Georgian-American University

The Georgian-American University (GAU) was formed as an MBA project of one of the Georgian scientists, Elene Jamarjashvili, in 2001 during her studies at Atlantic State University (Georgia). Initially, the university was called the American University of the Caucasus and was thought of as a law school, after graduating from which students received the degrees of Doctor of Laws (JD) and Bachelor of Laws (LLB). While in Atlanta, Elene Jamarjashvili met with others interested in transnational higher education and set about the task of establishing a university based on the MBA project in partnership with one of the leading American law schools, namely the American University's Washington College of Law (GAU, 2024). At the beginning of 2002, Elene Jamarjashvili returned to Tbilisi and started looking for a suitable investor. It was at this time that he met a US-funded consultant who assisted Georgia with the Baku-Tbilisi-Ceyhan (BTC) and South Caucasus (SCP) pipeline projects. Mr. Cowgil agreed to act as an advisor to Elene Jamarjashvili at the initial stage of the university's formation and then became the president of the university (GAU, 2024). Even though there were two international business schools in Tbilisi, there was still a need in Georgia for the creation of a more international orientated university, which would offer students additional courses necessary for the business sector, for example, a combined course in business and law. Accordingly, a decision was made to open a business school at the university. As a result, a joint LLC of American and Georgian investors was established in February 2005 (GAU, 2024). It was agreed by LLC and its Board of Directors that the financial and operational management of the University should be conducted according to the strictest international legal, ethical, and educational standards. It was also agreed that the name of the institution woul be the Georgian-American University (GAU) rather than the Caucasus American University. Since the institutions opening in 2005, GAU now supports approximately 2,000 students and about 250 lecturers in 5 different faculties, where teaching is conducted in Georgian and English languages (GAU, 2024). These faculties include the School of Business, the School of Law, Social Sciences, and Diplomacy, the School of Informatics and Engineering, the School of Humanities and School of Liberal Education and the School of Medicine. GAU is distinguished by innovations, including the Quantitative Finance (QUANTS) program and a powerful component of business analytics in the direction of marketing, finance, and management, and is the first legal clinic in Georgia with an ultra-modern IT laboratory. It also features Geolab, professional English language teaching at all faculties, various startup programs and hosts competitions.The location of GAU, modern infrastructure, green spaces help to ensure a comfortable environment for university life and the intention is to keep improving it appears.

4.4 San Diego State University

San Diego State University Georgia, funded by the Millennium Challenge Corporation, an agency of the United States, offers students a unique opportunity to receive an American-quality education in Tbilisi. Students have the opportunity to earn an internationally recognized American bachelor's degree in the heart of the Caucasus. San Diego State University, along with three leading Georgian universities, namely Tbilisi State University, Ilia State University, and Georgia Technical University, offer applicants internationally accredited bachelor's degrees in science, technology, engineering, and mathematics (STEM) fields. By offering the mentioned programs, the university supports the development of the fields of construction, science, and technology, as well as the improvement of Georgia's human capital and, in this way, the country's economic growth. More specifically, San Diego State University Georgia offers six undergraduate programs: chemistry/biochemistry, computer science, computer engineering, electrical engineering, civil engineering and construction engineering. These programs include a full course of liberal education offerings. They are accredited by organizations such as the Western Association of Schools and Colleges, the Accreditation Board for Engineering and Technology (ABET), and the American Chemical Society (ACS). San Diego State University Georgia graduates will have the multifaceted knowledge and critical thinking skills needed to succeed in the exact and natural sciences at a local, regional, and international level the institution notes. Additionally, San Diego State University Georgia students are said to enjoy the same academic benefits as their peers at San Diego State University's main campus in California, which includes access to state-of-the-art technology and laboratories. The San Diego State Aztec alumni family includes 400,000 local and international leaders (SDSU, 2024).

4.5 Webster University (Georgia Campus)

The leading American university locally, Webster University, opened the first campus in the region in Georgia, in what is termed the "Silicon Valley of Tbilisi", where the fastest growing and innovative higher educational institution of the country, such as the University of Business and Technology (BTU) are located. Webster campuses are located in different countries around the world, including Holland, Austria, Switzerland, and Greece, or in trems of continents, North America, Europe, Asia, and Africa (BTU, 2024). Entering the Webster University region has provided students with the opportunity to receive an American styled education and diploma in Georgia from 2021 without having to leave the country which was important during the pandemic.The innovative programs of the University of Business and Technology and the training program corresponding to international standards, its recognized high quality and important partners, a strong technological base, high-tech laboratories and educational ecosystem are all some of the reasons why the American institution chose the University of Business and Technology and Silicon Valley of Tbilisi to set up operations. Indeed, Webster University is located on an area of 2000 square meters in the territory of Silicon Valley Tbilisi, where laboratories, auditoriums, a library, and work spaces have been established (BTU, 2024). Webster Uiversity ranked among the top 2019 Forbes universities, and has been a leader since its founding in 1915. In 2018, with its programs abroad, Webster became the fourth ranked US institution in the ranking of "America's best universities", where only 44 out of 1500 US institutions were ranked (BTU, 2024). Webster's reputation is driven by several influential rating systems, presenting it as one of the best universities in the US. These rating systems include the Washington Monthly, College NET, National Council for Accreditation of Teacher Education (NCATE), the College Choice, and Accredited Schools Online Organisation.

5 GEORGIAN STUDENTS AND TRANSNATIONAL HIGHER EDUCATION ENGAGEMENT

5.1 Georgian Students Abroad

Georgian universities send about 500 students to study abroad every year. Germany, Poland, and Lithuania are the leading destinations. Recently, China has also become attractive to students. According to the data of the National Statistics Service, both private and public universities send inceasing numbers of students abroad every year. For example In the 2015-2016 academic year, 403 students were sent abroad, including 207 from state universities, and 196 from private universities, one year later, 565 students were sent, 400 from state universities, and 165 from private ones. With regard to the 2017-2018 academic year, 582 students were sent, 390 from state universities, and 192 from private ones. It should be noted that the number of students who went to study in China has almost doubled. Only in the academic year 2017-2018, 32 students were sent to China, while the number of students sent to China in the academic year 2016-2017 did not exceed 16. It is also worth noting that according to the countries in 2015-2018, the most Georgian students studied in the following countries as Table 1 illustrates:

Table 1. Georgian students enrolled overseas

Germany	370 Students
Poland	227
Lithuania	78
Italy	66
China	65
Turkey	64
France	59
Spain	57
Estonia	52

Source: National Statistic Office of Georgia (2023)

As for the 2022/2023 academic year, the number of students sent to study abroad from Georgia increased by 239 compared to the same period last year and equaled 723 (National Statistical Office of Georgia, 2023). In addition, during the given period, the number of students sent to study abroad from state higher educational institutions is 2.6 times higher than from private educational institutions (National Statistical Office of Georgia, 2023).

5.2 Georgian Students in North America

According to a report published by the United States Department of State, the US accepted a total of 1,095,299 international students during the 2018-2019 academic year. For 57% of these students, their primary source of tuition funding was not US government or university grants, but their own personal finances or that of their families. In total, international students make up 5.5% of American higher education enrollments (Tkeshelashvili, 2020). By country, the largest number of foreign students in the US come from the People's Republic of China, accounting for 34% of all international students. India ranks second with 18.4% of the number of students, and South Korea is in third place with 5% (Tkeshelashvili, 2020). Foreign students face several major difficulties in the process of obtaining an education in the USA, and the main barriers of which are the tuition fee and the level of English language proficiency. According to the number of international students, New York University is the most popular institution. The top 10 universities by the number of foreign students is highlighted in Table 2:

Table 2. International students in US universities

Institution	Student Numbers
1. New York University	19,605
2. University of Southern California	16340
3. Northeastern University - Boston	16075
4. Columbia University	15897
5. University of Illinois, Urbana	11497
6. Arizona State University	13324
7. University of California, Los Angeles	11942
8. Purdue University - West Lafayette	10943
9. University of California, San Diego	10652
10. Boston University	10598

Source: Tkeshelashvili (2020)

According to academic directions, 33% of students study at the faculties of exact and natural sciences, 17% in the engineering direction, 14.6% in the healthcare direction, and 7.1% in the social sciences direction. Only 3.2% of international students study business (Tkeshelashvili, 2020). According to the State Department, in 2018, the total contribution of international students to the country's gross domestic product was equal to $44.7 billion (Tkeshelashvili, 2020). Finally, the State Department report in the 2019-2020 academic year noted that 574 Georgian students studied in the USA, according to their educational levels, they were distributed as Table 3 displays:

Table 3. Georgian students in the US

Bachelor program	322 Students
Upper-level programs	157
Non-degree	29
OPT work-academic program for students	66

Source: Tkeshelashvili (2020)

According to neighboring countries of Georgia, the number of foreign students in the US is distributed as Table 4 mentions:

Table 4. Regional students in the US

Armenia	328 Students
Azerbaijan	489
Turkey	10 159
Russia	5 292

Source: Tkeshelashvili (2020)

5.3 International Students in Georgia

The number of foreign students in higher education institutions between 2010-2022 has increased by 20 times. According to the data, up to 25,100 overseas students are studying in higher education institutions in Georgia. International students accounted for 15.2% of total enrollments in 2022/23. The majority of students are from India (52.1% in 2022/23), Jordan (8.7%), and Israel (5.5%) (Business Press News, 2023). It should be added, that the majority of foreign students (74.6%) are studying in private universities as of 2022/23 and health degree programs remain the most popular courses among international students in 2022/23 (88.1% of enrolments) (Business Press News, 2023). Furthermore, according to the study, the increase in private sector income is due to increased demand from international students. The income of the private sector increased from 82.9 million GEL to 312.1 million GEL in 2011-22. Higher education in Georgia is mainly financed by out-of-pocket payments, while state funding is still low (Business Press News, 2023). As to the annual tuition fee, in the private sector it varies between 2,250 and 30,000 GEL. In the majority of surveyed universities (52.4%), the annual fee is 2,500-5,000 GEL (Business Press News, 2023).

CONCLUSION

Georgia has a long history of high education within its national boarders.Currently, there are more than 50 state and private higher education institutions in Georgia, or equivalent ones, that have passed accreditation by the Ministry of Education and Science. Most of the state universities are gathered in Tbilisi. In particular, Tbilisi is home to Ivane Javakhishvili University, Georgian Technical University, Agricultural University, Medical University, Medical Academy, Ilia State University, Art Academy, University of Theater and Cinema, Conservatory, as well as religious and military academies (National Statistics Office of Georgia, 2023). There are also close to four dozen accredited higher education institutions in Tbilisi. After this Kutaisi (4), Batumi, Gori, Zugdidi (2), Telavi, Rustavi, Akhaltsikhe, Sighnaghi, and Akhalkalaki (one educational institution in each city) are all areas in which higher education institutions operate. In terms of the number of students and the level of higher education per 1000 people, Georgia is still one of the first globally (National Statistics Office of Georgia, 2023). Given these features it is also important to note that the main goals of higher education in Georgia are facilitating the formation of Georgian and world cultural values, orientation to the ideals of democracy and humanism, meeting the needs of obtaining higher education, raising qualifications and retraining, matching the interests and abilities of the person. In addition, the intention is to enhance the realization of development of students' creative skills, developing competencies whichalign with modern requirements, ensuring the competitiveness of learners within the domestic and foreign labor market they will have to be a part of, and providing a high-quality higher education corresponding to the demands of students. Finally, the intention is to ensure the development of the country and the viability of the higher education system itself, training and retraining of new scientific personnel, creation, provision, and development of conditions for scientific research, encouraging the mobility of students and academic staff from higher educational institutions, and ultimately, to play a constructive role in the transnational education world.

REFERENCES

BTU. (2024). The leading American university - Webster University enters Georgia. Retrieved from: https://btu.edu.ge/tsamqhvani-amerikuli-universiteti-vebsteri-webster-university-saqarthveloshi-shemodis/

Business Press News. (2023). The number of foreign students in higher education institutions has increased 20 times - how many citizens of foreign countries study in Georgia? Retrieved from: https://www.bpn.ge/article/111513-umaglesi-ganatlebis-sascavleblebshi-ucxoeli-studentebis-raodenoba-20-jer-gaizarda-ucxo-kveqnis-ramdeni-mokalake-scavlobs-sakartveloshi/

Chitadze, N. (2016). *Political Science*. International Black Sea University.

Chitadze, N. (2017). *World Geography*. Scholars Press.

Civil. Ge. (2023). Geostat Report on General Education Institution. Retrieved from: https://civil.ge/ka/archives/517342

Davitashvili, Z. Elizbarashvili, & N. Beruchashvili, N. (2014). *Geography of Georgia*. Meridiani.

Encyclopedy, G. (2011). *Tbilisi State University*. TSU.

GAU. (2024). Academic Information. Retrieved from: https://www.gau.edu.ge/ka

Geostat, (2023). Number of Schools in Georgia. Retrieved from: https://www.geostat.ge/ka/modules/categories/59/zogadi-ganatleba

Gurgenidze, M. (2016). Education, Science, and Health in Georgia in the Post-Soviet Period. Retrieved from: https://gtu.ge/bef/pdf/Doqtorantura/avtoreferatebi_2016/Soc-mecn_05.07.16/m.gurgeniZe.pdf

IBSU. (2024). Schools. Retrieved from: https://ibsu.edu.ge/ge/schools/

IBSU. (2024). Main function of the University. Retrieved from: https://ibsu.edu.ge/ge/about-ibsu/

Javakhishvili, I. (2016). *Political and Social Movement in the 19th Century of Georgia*. Institute of History of Ethnology.

Liluashvili, M. (2006). *Georgian Culture and Tbilisi State University in 1918-1921 years*. Tbilisi State University.

Lominashvili, D. (2020). International standards of the right to education and the challenges of modern Georgian legislation. Retrieved from: chrome-extension://efaidnbmnnnibpcajpcglclefindmkaj/https://www.tsu.ge/assets/media/files/48/disertaciebi4/Davit_Lominashvili.pdf

Lomouri, G. (2020). Historic Bases of the Georgian Education System. Retrieved from: https://giorgilomouri.wordpress.com

Mkurnalizde, G., & Khamkhadze, G. (2000). *Political Science*. Tsodna.

Muskhelishvili, D., Samsonadze, M., & Daushvili, A. (2010). *History of Georgia from ancient times to 2009*. Institute of History and Ethnology.

National Center for Education Quality Development. (2023). Bologna Process. Retrieved from: https://eqe.ge/en/page/static/71/boloniis-protsesi

National Center for Educational Quality Enhancement. (2023). Higher Education. Retrieved from: https://eqe.ge/en/page/static/69/umaghlesi-ganatleba

National Parliamentary Library of Georgia. (2023). Chronicle of Ilia Chavchavadze's life and work. Retrieved from: https://dspace.nplg.gov.ge/bitstream/1234/204739/1/Ilia_Chavchavazis-Cxovrebis_da_Shemoqmedebis_Matiane.pdf

National Statistical Office of Georgia. (2023). High Education. Retrieved from: https://www.geostat.ge/en/modules/categories/61/higher-education

Plus, E. (2020). 15 Years of Bologna Process in Georgia. Retrieved from: http://erasmusplus.org.ge/files/publications/Research

San Diego State University. (2024). Academic Information. Retrieved from: https://sdsu.edu.ge/ka/spages/chven-shesakheb/17

Shota Rustaveli Batumi State Univerisity. (2016). Repressions of the 20s-30s of the 20th century in the context of political and cultural memory Retrieved from: https://bsu.edu.ge/text_files/ge_file_16146_2.pdf

Shubitidze, V. (2002). *Political Science*. Georgian Technical University.

Smelzer, N. (2023). Education. Functional Approach Retrieved from: http://www.socium.ge/downloads/socshesavali/ganatleba_smelzeri.pdf

Tabula, (2023). History of United National exams Retrieved from https://tabula.ge/ge/news/703749-ertiani-erovnuli-gamotsdebis-istoria

The Centre For Contemporary History, (2023). Number of mass media in Georgia. Retrieved from:https//:permalink.php?story_fbid=4892837370831636&id=2171706859611381&paipv=0&eav=AfbdieWquEnpppiaFswM9bhyMjVrntPaa4KfH7l7UHMSDrJpvWitxkvJaclNlcEXQok&_rdr

Tkeshelashvili, S. (2020). How many Georgian students study in the USA? Retrieved from: https://bm.ge/news/ramdeni-qartveli-studenti-swavlobs-ashsh-shi/63064

KEY TERMS AND DEFINITIONS

Student Exchange Program: is a program in which students from a secondary school (high school) or higher education study abroad at one of their institution's partner institutions. A student exchange program may involve international travel but does not necessarily require the student to study outside their home country.

Higher Education: is tertiary level education leading to the award of an academic degree. Higher education, which makes up a component of post-secondary or third-level education, is an optional final stage of formal learning that occurs after the completion of secondary education. It represents levels 5, 6, 7, and 8 of the 2011 version of the International Standard Classification of Education structure. Tertiary education at a non-degree level is sometimes referred to as further education or continuing education as distinct from higher education.

International Education: is a dynamic concept that involves a journey or the movement of people, minds, or ideas across frontiers. It is facilitated by the globalization phenomenon, which increasingly erases the constraints of geography on economic, social, and cultural arrangements.

Transnational Education: All types of higher education study programs, sets of courses of study, or educational services (including those of distance education) in which the learners are located in a country different from the one where the awarding institution is based. Such programs may belong to the educational system of a State or be distinct from the State in which it operates or may operate independently of any national system.

Chapter 17
The Transnational ICT Leadership Assessment Based on the Available Infrastructure in the Governmental Organizations:
A Case Study of the Ethiopian Northern Shewa Zone

Nilamadhab Mishra
http://orcid.org/0000-0002-1330-4869
VIT Bhopal University, India

Getachew Mekuria Habtemariam
http://orcid.org/0009-0006-7841-5662
Debre Berhan University, Ethiopia

Seblewongel Esseynew
Addis Ababa University, Ethiopia

Rudra Kalyan Nayak
VIT Bhopal University, India

Ramamani Tripathy
Chitkara University, India

Basanta Kumar Padhi
Balasore College of Engineering and Technology, Balasore, India

ABSTRACT

The effectiveness, efficiency, and security of ICT-monitored systems are assessed as part of the Transnational ICT Leadership Assessment, which is based on the infrastructure currently in place in governmental organizations. Tailoring the assessment to each governmental entity's specific context, organizational structure, and goals is essential. Additionally, involving key stakeholders, including ICT professionals, leadership, and end-users, in the assessment process enhances its accuracy and relevance. This study aims to assess the availability of ICT infrastructure and its utilization through transnational ICT leaders in government organizations. The researchers investigated that there is a skill gap (68.89%), a lack of ICT infrastructure (50.925%), and a lack of leadership awareness (71.6%) regarding new trends towards the transnational ICT leaders of the Northern Shewa Administrative Zone. Therefore, this study identifies the challenges of aligning the infrastructure of ICT in governmental organizations for the transnational

ICT leaders.

1. INTRODUCTION

A Transnational ICT (Information and Communication Technology) Leadership Assessment involves evaluating the effectiveness of leadership in overseeing ICT initiatives across borders, particularly in governmental or transnational organizations. Information and Communication Technology (ICT) refers to all forms of technology applied to processing, storing, and transmitting information electronically. The physical equipment used for this purpose includes computers, communications equipment and networks, fax machines, and even electronic pocket organizers (Kebede, 2020). ICT is a major national competitive advantage, providing increased efficiency, knowledge, and human development capacity (Ndou, 2004). Nowadays, the world economy is experiencing the effects of rapid globalization and liberalization as the impact of the emerging information age characterized by Information and Communication Technology (ICT). This will create a new global economic order dominated by information and information age knowledge economies (Rahman, 2007). The vital role that ICT can play in facilitating and accelerating socio-economic development has been recognized worldwide. For instance, developed countries like Canada have benefited greatly from the opportunities ICT brings (Mammo, 2016). The goal is for information technology investments and the portfolio to be heading in the right direction to maximize the value of those investments to the business (Lyons, 2007).

ICT seems well understood as a tool and an infrastructure for delivering information and services to society and for allowing communications through interactions among the service users - mostly, the digital society. Using ICT to ensure a better life requires far more than good infrastructure, ICT know-how, and the various techniques and tools. Suppose ICT has to address the real problems of society. In that case, it should be environment-friendly at a rescue, with real and tangible impact, sustainable, seamless, down to the grassroots, and reproducible experiences. A digital society should benefit from ICT in various aspects of life, from getting ordinary public services to supporting daily routine work via e-services and e-practices. So far, ICT has been used in addressing society's problems in a biased way, such that those lucky to be on the far front have high penetration of ICT more quickly. At the same time, those with low infrastructure and finance were deprived for significantly longer (Darshan, 2011).

Computer-based communication services such as E-mail, online discussion groups, and teleconferencing technologies have revolutionized how people and organizations communicate and interact. Information technologies like the Internet and related services like the World Wide Web provide society with new avenues for distributing and accessing information. Moreover, these technologies make communication and information retrieval easier. These and similar assumptions and actual utilization of the technology align information technology with BPR [Bogale, Amoroso, & Negash, 2009).

National governments are increasingly aware of the potential of ICT to improve the performance of their organizations and offer potential benefits to their citizens and business partners. However, using ICT is not straightforward and cannot be done in a limited period; rather, it requires a good framework approach. This is one of the reasons why many government organizations are still in the immature stage of ICT usage. Another important reason for this hold is that ICT requires significant changes in organizational infrastructure, which, in turn, can create resistance. This study aims to help IT practitioners in the public sector learn how to use and manage information technologies to renew business processes, improve decision-making, and gain a competitive advantage from the appropriate use of ICT (Mulugeta

& Pandian, 2020; Daniels, 2002). This is also an important issue for transnational higher education providers who operate in multiple national geographic locations and often provide cutting edge educational provision in these countries.

This study for ICT utilization will reduce confusion surrounding ICT infrastructure in the public sector through understanding the implementation processes, identifying requirements of ICT tools, and highlighting the importance of organizational management resources and the impact of barriers. The study can also help the decision makers to set an idea statement and strategic action plan for future direction in the information technology age by identifying key elements and stages for action. The study's main objective is to "Improve the Utilization and Infrastructures of ICT in Government Organization: In the case of Northern Shewa" by reducing the challenges of integrating ICT in their day-to-day activities and strategic activities for Northern Shewa Administrative Staff. That said, the cross over and applicability to transnational higher education is also obvious.

Specifically, this research is expected to:

Identify the skill gap of the transnational ICT leaders related to ICT in Northern Shewa Government sectors.
Assess the availability of ICT infrastructure in Northern Shewa Government sectors.
Identify the transnational ICT leaders' experience using ICT in Northern Shewa Government sectors.
Assessing the transnational ICT leaders' interest in meeting the emerging ICT technology in Northern Shewa Government sectors.

Almost all governmental organizations use Information and Communication Technology (ICT) for their day-to-day activities. Still, we have observed a problem aligning the ICT infrastructure with their routine tasks. Also, there is a skill gap between emerging technology and transnational ICT leaders. Therefore, we raise the following research questions:
1. Are transnational ICT leaders interested in using ICT at their workplace?
2. Do ICT infrastructures support their routine tasks as well as desired?
3. What factors contribute to the gap between emerging technology and their transnational ICT leaders?
4. Are there enough up-to-date ICT infrastructures in the study areas?

1.1 Study Significance

It enables transnational ICT leaders to integrate ICT technology better to accomplish their tasks.
Transnational ICT leaders can perform tasks and activities more efficiently and effectively.
It will improve the organization's performance and customer satisfaction rate.
It enables the university to engage in outward activities grounded in governmental sectors in the community.

The study is bounded to the skill gap in ICT use, the availability of ICT infrastructure, the leadership awareness of transnational ICT leaders in using ICT, transnational ICT leaders' interest in using the emerging ICT technology, and transnational ICT leaders' performance in using ICT. Due to time constraints and the teaching-learning process, the study is limited in scope. 243 questionnaires were collected to gather the information. However, the best practices for ICT application, the application gap, and the available infrastructures in NGOs are beyond the scope of this study.

1.2 Ethical Considerations

Debre Berhan University has approved this research. When questionnaires were distributed, the researchers informed the respondents about the title and objectives of the study in the introduction part of the paper. Moreover, to develop respondent's confidence, they have been informed that their response will be confidential and anonymity preserved. To avoid misunderstanding and related problems with the quality of data, the questionnaires for the customers have been translated from English to the Amharic language for respected bodies.

2. LITERATURE REVIEW

Information and Communications Technology (ICT) is the technology that chains activities involving the creation, storage, handling, and communication of information, together with the related methods, management, and application. In other words, ICT enables us to record, store, process, retrieve and transmit information. It encompasses modern technology technologies such as computers, telecommunication, facsimile, and microelectronics. Older technologies such as document-filling systems, mechanical accenting machines, printing, and care drawings are also included in the term information technology. Information and communication technology in this real-world refers to those technologies that determine the efficiency and effectiveness with which we communicate and the devices that allow us to handle information. Information and Communication Technology (ICT) has become a key device in acquiring, processing, and freeing knowledge. It has become an essential tool for investing in the development of a nation in this century for the revolutionary impact of ICT on all aspects of society.

ICT (Information and Communications Technology - or technologies) is an umbrella term that includes any communication tool or application about radio, television, cellular phones, computer and networking, and satellite systems, amongst others, as well as the various services and applications associated with them, such as videoconferencing and distance learning. ICTs have become one of the basic building blocks of modern society within a very short time. Many countries now regard understanding ICT and mastering the basic skills and concepts of ICT as part of the core of education, alongside reading, writing, and numeracy. However, there appears to be a misconception that ICTs generally refer to 'computers and computing-related activities.' This is fortunately not the case; although computers and their application play a significant role in modern information management, other technologies and systems also comprise the phenomenon commonly regarded as ICTs (Daniels, 2002).

The term 'computers' was replaced by 'IT' (information technology), signifying a focus shift from computing technology to the capacity to store and retrieve information. This was followed by introducing the term 'ICT' (information and communication technology) in 1992 when e-mail became available to the general public (Duressa and Asfaw, 2014). According to UNESCO (2002), information and communication technology (ICT) may be regarded as the combination of 'Informatics technology' with other related technology, specifically communication technology. Various kinds of ICT products are available, which have obvious relevance to education, such as teleconferencing, email, audio conferencing, television lessons, radio broadcasts, interactive radio counseling, interactive voice response systems, audiocassettes, and CD ROMs. They have been used in education for different purposes (UNESCO, 2002). These 'new functions of higher education and ICT (help) to achieve education for all' (Sharma, 2003).

Economic needs and human development concerns have driven the demand for ICT in Africa. The globalized world is a knowledge-based economy in which goods and services are developed and sold over electronic networks. Information is considered a currency, and connectivity provides access to the market. ICT technologies are considered market drivers. From the foreign investor's perspective, a country with reliable ICT has laid the foundation for efficient management and information-sharing. Better governance and transparency ensue because there are no longer lags in communication, and data is traceable. From a businessperson, farmer, and trader point of view, these platforms provide accurate, up-to-date market information for more informed decision-making (Mekonnen and Bayissa, 2023; Besha, Amoroso, and Negash, 2009).

ICT platforms allow foreign and private investors to access Africa's commercial market and resources. Africa is an untapped market for consumers. As William Roedy, Vice Chairman for MTV networks, noted, "(Africa) is the last remaining void." The commercial benefits are lucrative if competition and profit margins for mobile telephony are any indication. Private firms like MTV, Microsoft, and Intel are entering the market through large-scale education and health initiatives. Foreign investors like China also need resources and trading partners to boost their growing economy (Belayneh, 2022; Kebede and Demeke, 2017).

Beyond the economic benefits, ICT is considered crucial for African nations to meet the Millennium Development Goals (MDGs). Given the high correlation between ICT and human development, equitable access to ICT is another major step towards the MDGs: eradicate poverty, provide universal education, promote gender equality, reduce child mortality, and improve mental health. Some experts speculate that as the reach of ICT expands, urban migration could slow due to the decentralization of information and opportunities. At the Africa Connect Conference in October 2007, the World Bank, the African Union, and their multilateral, bilateral, and private sector partners discussed how to best leverage ICT for the social welfare of individual countries and the continent as a whole (Gemeda and Lee, 2020).

3. METHODOLOGY

3.1 Research Site

The study was conducted in Semen Shewa, one of the Central Regions of Ethiopia, which lies between 38.5oE and 40.5oE, and it is 9. oN and 11.^{oN} Latitude. It has a total area of about 18,000 sq. km and is organized under 24 Woredas and 5 urban centers. The total population of the area is estimated at 2 million. The density of the settlement is 100 inhabitants per square kilometer, much higher than the national average of 60 persons per square kilometer. The Zone is bordered on the south and the west by the Oromia Region, on the north by Debub Wollo, on the northeast by the Oromia Zone, and the east by the Afar Region. It comprises the traditional administrative areas of Berehet, Bulga, Tera, Angolela, Merehabete, Ensaro, Jirru, Ankober, Tegulet, Menz and Yifat. The region comprises highlands, plateaus, deeply cut gorges, and steeply sloped valleys. The physiographic characteristics of the area are highlands (Dega), plateau (Woyna Dega), and lowland plains (Kola). The people of the Region are regarded as hard-working and have been exerting tremendous efforts to survive and sustain their existence. Semen Shewa, which is well-watered, cool, and healthy, has been conducive for breeding cattle and sheep and cultivating varied grain crops and vegetables (Demissie and Gajendran, 2016; Abadama, 2020; Reta, 2021). For this study, six woredas (Medaoromo, Berhet, D/Sina, Deneba, Hagremariam, and Basso) are selected purposely from Northern Shewa of the Amhara region; data has been collected for each word. The following **Figure 1** shows the study area of the region.

Figure 1. ICT study area as represented in the map

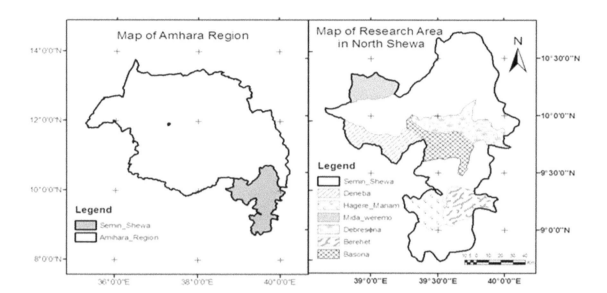

3.2 Data Collection Tools

In this study, both primary and secondary data sources are used. The data from primary sources is collected by using questionnaires and interviews. Additionally, secondary sources have been elicited from literature on the subject area. Further, site observation is used to validate questionnaire and interview data. In this study, the researchers apply purposive techniques to select six woredas from the Northern Shewa zone and ten sectors from each woreda. Among these six woredas, three are far, and three are near the zone city. Sectors such as ICT centers, finance, courts, and the civil service were selected mainly because ICT operations are used for day-to-day activities. Five respondents were selected randomly from each sector, and questionnaires were distributed to them. Those interviewees were selected purposely from the organizations' top, middle, and bottom levels to get precise, detailed, and well-rounded information.

3.3 Data Analysis

Quantitative data collected through questionnaires are coded, analyzed, and interpreted through SPSS (Statistical Package for Social Science). The Qualitative data are also analyzed and interpreted using statistical approaches such as data tabulation, frequency distribution, and percentages for viewing ease. After organizing and presenting the data, it is analyzed to form meaning about the research questions and draw appropriate conclusions and recommendations (Mishra et al., 2023; Mishra, Habtemariam and De, 2023).

Figure 2. ICT in the case of Africa (why ICT Is important to Africa)

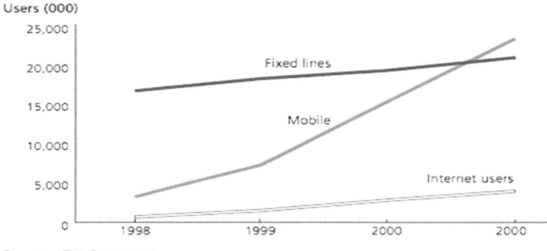

Figure 3. ICT trends across Africa

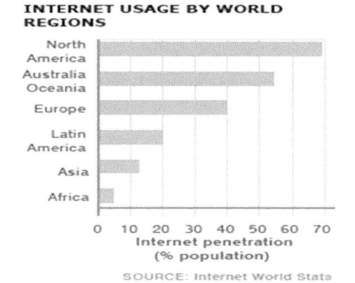

At this point, it is important to note:

Cost: The cost of broadband access in Africa is the highest globally, on average, three times higher than in Asia. The cost barrier has limited Internet penetration to around 1%. Mobile telephony, which is more affordable, has more users [United Nations. Economic Commission for Africa; United Nations. Economic Commission for Africa (2023-12)].

Access: There is a digital divide between Africa and the rest of the world. While only 2.6% of Africans have access to the Internet, 10% of Asians, 36% of Europeans, and 69% of North Americans have Internet access. Furthermore, there is a severe gap in access between urban centers and rural areas. While cities benefit from increasing access to mobile telephones and Internet services, many smaller towns and rural communities remain without ICT access [United Nations. Economic Commission for Africa; United Nations. Economic Commission for Africa (2023-12)].

Quality: Few internet users have the patience for a slow internet connection. Africa needs faster connections due to a lack of IXPs and reliance on satellite technology. These satellite connections have inherent delays and do not offer competitive pricing conditions.

Governance and Policy: Many African nations, like Ghana and Nigeria, use a liberalized free-market approach to ICT expansion to overcome cost and access issues. However, policy coordination across the government (federal/state/local levels) and regulatory arena is often fragmented. Furthermore, keeping up with "leap-frogging" technological advances compounds the challenges of implementation and decision-making.

4. RESULTS AND DISCUSSION

4.1 Participant Characteristics

In any research, the personal characteristics of respondents have a very significant role to play in expressing and giving responses about the problem; keeping this in mind, in this study, a set of personal characteristics, namely age, sex and education, for example, of the 238 respondents have been examined and presented in this section.

Age: The age of the respondents is one of the most important characteristics in understanding their views about particular problems; by and large, age indicates individuals' maturity level. In that sense, age becomes more important to examine the response. The detail of this analysis is given in Table 1.

Table 1. Age of the respondents

Age in years	Frequency	Percentages
15 – 25	61	25.2
26 – 35	119	49.2
36 – 45	38	15.7
46 – 55	16	6.6
56 and Above	4	1.7
Total	238	

It is evident from Table 1 the quartile value that nearly 25.2 percent are 15 -25 years of age, whereas almost half (49.2%) of respondents are 26- 35. To be more specific large number of respondents are from 26 to 35 years of age in the sample. An interesting feature of this data is that very young respondents are responsible for utilizing ICT in this study.

Gender: Gender is an important variable in a given problem; hence, it is inquired for this study. Data related to the respondents' gender is presented in Table 2 below.

Table 2. Gender of the respondents

Gender	Frequency	Percentages
Male	164	69.2
Female	73	30.8
Total	237	100%

It is clear that out of the total respondents included in this study, the majority (69.2 percent) are male, whereas about 30.8 percent are female.

Education: Education is one of the most important characteristics that might affect a person's attitudes and the way of looking at and understanding any particular phenomenon. In a way, an individual's response is likely to be determined by his educational status. Therefore, it becomes imperative to know the academic background of the respondents and studies such as Morris, Morris and Li (2023) along with Rodríguez-Feria, et al. (2024) have done likewise. Hence, the researchers investigate the variable 'Educational level,' and the data about education is presented in Table 3.

Table 3. Respondents educational background

Level of Education	Frequency	Percentages
High school	7	2.9
Diploma	116	48.5
Degree	108	45.2
Masters	3	1.3
Other	5	2.1
Total	239	100%

This table shows that about 2.9 percent of the respondents are educated up to high school, and a much larger number, 48.5 percent, are educated up to the diploma level. The number of respondents attaining a degree is also more (45.2%). Only 1.3 percent of the respondents are educated at the postgraduate (master's) level. A considerable number of respondents are just functionally literate. It can be concluded from Table 3 above that, by and large, the respondents were progressive in education, but they are still far away from higher education, which is so important today to create a knowledge-based society.

4.2 Skill Gaps

In this research, the skill gap of transnational ICT leaders shows the ability of the transnational ICT leaders to operate the most commonly used ICT software and hardware. To assess the skill gap of transnational ICT leaders, the researchers used open-ended and closed-ended questions on the questionnaires and during the interviews (Tiika et al., 2024). The following table shows the ICT skill gaps among the transnational ICT leaders of the targeted samples in the six woredas.

Table 4. Employee's skill level

S. No	Items in Questionnaire	Options with assigned variable names	Response N%	Mean	Std. Deviation
4.1	The woreda Transnational ICT leaders are using Computer in their daily routines	Never (1)	24 (9.9)	2.71	0.862
		Sometimes (2)	63 (25.9)		
		Every day (3)	115 (47.3)		
		Rarely (4)	41 (16.9)		
4.2	Transnational ICT leader's Computer Skill	Excellent (1)	18 (7.6)	2.97	0.909
		Very good (2)	47 (19.8)		
		Good (3)	96 (40.5)		
		Not good enough (4)	76 (32.1)		
4.3	Whether the transnational ICT leaders are familiar with Computer Applications	Microsoft Word (1)	175 (78.5)	1.42	0.931
		Microsoft Excel (2)	22 (9.9)		
		Database (3)	9 (4.0)		
		Internet (4)	14 (6.3)		
		E-mail (5)	3 (1.3)		
4.4	Transnational ICT Leaders' Skills at the Database Management Level	None (1)	96 (51.6)	1.83	1.004
		Low (2)	42 (22.6)		
		Moderate (3)	32 (17.2)		
		High (4)	16 (8.6)		
4.5	Transnational ICT Leaders' Skills at the Microsoft Word Level	None (1)	14 (6.3)	3.01	0.897
		Low (2)	45 (20.4)		
		Moderate (3)	86 (38.9)		
		High (4)	76 (31.3)		
4.6	Transnational ICT leaders Skills in Microsoft Excel Level	None (1)	44 (22.1)	1.83	1.004
		Low (2)	55 (27.6)		
		Moderate (3)	67 (33.7)		
		High (4)	33 (16.6)		
4.7	Transnational ICT Leaders' Skills in Using the Internet	None (1)	109 (59.6)	1.77	1.056
		Low (2)	27 (14.8)		
		Moderate (3)	28 (15.3)		
		High (4)	19 (10.4)		
4.8	Transnational ICT leader's Skills in using email	None (1)	112 (63.6)	1.67	1.022
		Low (2)	28 (15.9)		
		Moderate (3)	18 (10.2)		
		High (4)	18 (10.2)		

continued on following page

Table 4. Continued

S. No	Items in Questionnaire	Options with assigned variable names	Response N%	Mean	Std. Deviation
4.9	Whether the transnational ICT leaders are using ICT-related tasks in their day-to-day lives, such as preparing letters or documents	Yes (1)	152 (63.3)	1.37	0.483
		No (2)	88 (36.7)		
4.10	Whether the transnational ICT leaders are sending emails related to their jobs within their offices	Yes (1)	28 (11.6)	8.3154	70.46471
		No (2)	211 (87.6)		
4.11	Whether the transnational ICT leaders are sending any mail outside the office (Personal use)	Yes (1)	23 (9.5)	8.3099	70.31753
		No (2)	217 (89.7)		
4.12	Whether the transnational ICT leaders are using any tasks related to ICT for Database Management Systems in their Organizations	Yes (1)	103 (42.7)	7.8672	70.50679
		No (2)	136 (56.4)		
4.13	Whether the transnational ICT leaders are doing any data analysis tasks related to their job	Yes (1)	57 (23.7)	8.1950	70.47629
		No (2)	182 (75.5)		
4.14	Whether the transnational ICT leaders are using ICT to share resources	Yes (1)	74 (30.6)	8.0992	70.33770
		No (2)	166 (68.6)		

As indicated in Table 4 (4.1), responses showed that 47.3% of the transnational ICT leaders use computers for their daily routine; 25.9% responded that they use computers sometimes; 16.9% of the respondents stated that they use computers very rarely in their daily routine tasks; whereas 9.9% of respondents are not using the computers for their tasks. It is indicated that 52.7% of transnational ICT leaders in local industry are rarely using computers for daily routine tasks compared to other global locations where they are daily necessities. From Table 4 (4.2), out of 237 respondents, only 18(7.6%) of transnational ICT leaders believe that they have excellent skills in computers; 47 (19.8%) responded that they have very good skills in using computers; 96 (40.5%) said that they were good; 76 (32.1%) answered that they are not good enough to perform anything by using computers. Many (72.6%) transnational ICT leaders lack high confidence in this area, one which is not a source of competitive advantage anymore, but more of a core norm in many locations.

As can be seen in Table 4 (4.3), among 223 respondents, 175 (78.5%) are familiar with Microsoft Word; 22 (9.9%) of transnational ICT leaders responded that they have an idea with Microsoft Excel; 9 (4.0%) responded they are familiar with the internet; whereas only 3 (1.3%) of transnational ICT leaders are comfortable with email. So, it is a concern that most transnational ICT leaders do not use ICT applications. From Table 4 (4.4), it can be noted that from the 186 respondents, 96 (51.6%) of transnational ICT leaders are not aware of database management systems; 42 (22.6%) responded that they are low in handling this system; 32(17.2%) responded they are moderately managing the database tasks; 16 (8.6%) respondent's states that they are good in database skills. Hence, it is apparent that 74.2% of transnational ICT leaders are not good at handling database management systems. This is another, albeit perhaps, less concerning trend.

From Table 4 (4.5), out of 221 respondents, 14 (6.3%) of them confirmed that they are not familiae with Microsoft Word applications; 45 (20.4%) of transnational ICT leaders responded that they feel they have limited skill towards Microsoft Word application; 86 (38.9%) responded suggesting that they are moderate in ability using the Microsoft Word application; 76 (31.3%) of respondents suggested that they felt that they had strong skills in Microsoft Word application. Hence, the study found that 26.7% of respondents have a gap in Microsoft Word applications. This indicates that more than a quarter of transnational ICT leaders are unfamiliar with Microsoft Word applications which presents an opportunity and a concern in an increasingly technological world.

From Table 4 (4.6), out of 199 respondents, 44 (22.1%) of the transnational ICT leaders confirmed that they have no idea about Microsoft Excel applications; 55 (27.6%) answered they have low-level skills in Microsoft Excel applications; 67 (33.7%) confirmed that they fairly manage Microsoft Excel applications; whereas only 33 (16.6%) of transnational ICT leaders felt that they were able using Microsoft Excel applications. It is therefore suggested that 49.7% of respondents, nearly 50% stated they face problems using Microsoft Excel applications. Another opportunity and concern depending on your standpoint.

From Table 4 (4.7), out of 183 respondents, only 19 (10.4%) transnational ICT leaders are confident using internet applications; 28 (15.3%) respondents said that they are fair in using the internet; 27 (14.8%) of transnational ICT leaders rarely use the internet in their tasks; 109 (59.6%) of the transnational ICT leaders are not at all using the internet in their routine tasks. The table proves that 74.3% of transnational ICT leaders lack the skills, or do not have the opportunity, to use the Internet in their daily work.

From Table 4 (4.8), out of 176 respondents, it is apparent that 112(63.6%) are not aware of email applications; 28 (15.9%) of respondents stated that they rarely use email; 18 (10.2%) of transnational ICT leaders are moderate users of email; 18 (10.2%) confirmed they are regular email users in their ICT related tasks. Hence, it is evident that 83.6% are not regular email users in their organisation. Therefore, there is a gap between transnational ICT leaders and ICT-related tasks potentially in this area given the routine business nature e-mailing provides in many countries and indsutries.

From Table 4 (4.9), 153 (63.3%) of respondents are using ICT for their day-to-day tasks; 88 (36.7%) of transnational ICT leaders respond they are not using any ICT-related tasks, such as preparing letters or documents. Moreover, more than a quarter of the transnational ICT leaders are unaware of recent technologies. Therefore, there is a lack of resources and awareness and uptake in their organizations.

From Table 4 (4.10), out of 239 respondents, 211 (87.6%) are not using email facilities; only 28 (11.6%) are using email in their organization. Echoing Table 4 (4.8) findngs t is apparent that there is an enormous usage gap in using email in their organisations.

From Table 4 (4.11), out of 240 respondents, 23(9.5%) of transnational ICT leaders are exchanging information via email, whereas 217(89.7%) of transnational ICT leaders stated they are not using email to exchange information with other organizations. It is confirmed therefore that the vast majority of transnational ICT leaders are not exchanging information through email with those outside their organizations which is surprisingly in 2024 in many ways if seen from the perspective of those in many locations.

Table 4 (4.12) highlights out of 239 respondents, 103 (42.7%) noted that their use of database management applications was in place. Moreover, 136 (56.4%) are unfamiliar with database management applications to perform their tasks. Therefore, there is a skill gap in the area of database management applications.

From Table 4 (4.13), out of 239 respondents, only 57(23.7%) of the transnational ICT leaders responded that they are doing some data analysis task in their organizations; 182 (75.5%) stated they are not performing any data analysis work. This implies that over three-quarters of transnational ICT leaders are not performing work-related ICT tasks which is again an interesting finding when considered from other national and geographic locations based on working norms there.

From Table 4 (4.14), out of 240 respondents, only 74 (30.6%) of transnational ICT leaders are sharing their information through ICT resources; 166 (68.6%) responded they are not aware of the latest trends about sharing resources. This highlights how less than three-quarters of transnational ICT leaders in this study are not performing document-sharing resource operations in their organizations.

It could be concluded that more than 52.7% of transnational ICT leaders do not have computer skills. However, most of them are only familiar with Microsoft Word applications. In addition, more than half (56.4%) are unaware of database management systems. Nearly half (49.7%) have very little appreciation of Microsoft Excel application or low-level skills and usually face problems using it. However, a quarter of the respondents believed that they were competent with Microsoft Excel Applications. Most transnational ICT leaders are not skilled enough to use the Internet and do not use it at their offices however in this locality. Regarding email, most of those taking part in this study are not familiar with it, though a quarter of them showed moderate status in using emails. Hence, there is a serious skill gap in using email in their organisations. Generally, most transnational ICT leaders (68.89%) have skill gap problems using computers.

Through the interview, the researchers observed from the top, middle to bottom level management, in each woreda sector suggested that they do not have strong ICT skills. The administration's transnational ICT leaders face tremendous problems while sending documents, maintaining viruses attacks, and upskilling and gradig facilities, For instance, for a little defect, they are asked to pay a huge amount of money to ensure that work does not simply stop (Rodríguez-Feria et al., 2024).

Overall Transnational ICT Leaders Skills by Woreda

To illustrate the transnational ICT leaders' ICT skills in each woreda, cross-tabulation is used as follows.

Table 5. ICT skill gap by Woreda

Woreda	N %	Mean (x)	Standard Deviation (SD)
Meda Oromo	46	2.11	0.82
Berehet	33	2.58	0.87
Debre Sina	41	2.31	0.69
Hagre Mariam	30	1.84	0.71
Denebe	49	2.18	0.83
Bassona Woreda (Debre Berhan)	29	2.52	0.81
Total	228	2.26	0.79

From Table 5, the mean value for computer skills is found to be 2.26, which means transnational ICT leaders' skill level in Microsoft Word, Microsoft Excel, databases, the internet, and email is low. Looking at by woreda, only Berehet (2.58, SD = 0.87) and Bassona Worena (2.52, SD=0.81) revealed moderate levels of transnational ICT leaders' skills. The other Woredas show below-moderate skills.

4.3 ICT Infrastructure Availability in North Showa Zone

This assessment measured whether the basic ICT equipment, machines, telecommunication devices, and application software were sufficiently present. To know the availability of ICT Infrastructures of the sample woredas' of government sector offices, the researchers are focusing on those infrastructures which are the most commonly used equipment and machines.

Table 6. Availability of ICT infrastructures

Availability of Office Automation Equipment			
Types of Hardware ICT infrastructure	Response	No of respondents	Responses in Percentages
Desktop	Yes	208	86.0
	No	34	14.0
Laptop	Yes	55	22.7
	No	187	77.3
Printer	Yes	159	65.7
	No	83	34.3
Scanner	Yes	53	21.9
	No	189	78.1

As a result, ICT facilities such as the Internet, computers, printers, and scanners are considered to investigate the availability of ICT infrastructure and its uptake and usage. Several questions were presented to the respondents for answering to verify the availability of ICT types of equipment. Table 6 above shows that 86% of respondents have desktop computers in their offices, and only 14% do not. This confirmed that most of staff access desktop computers from their offices 77.3% of respondents have no laptop computer, and only 22.7% have laptop computers. 65.7% of respondents have printers in their offices, and only 34.3% did not. 78.1% have no scanners, and only 21.9% have scanners in their office. These results imply the availability of desktop and printer infrastructures in the sector. However, regarding laptop computers and scanners, there is a big scarcity. Through the interview, it was found out that some members of the transnational ICT leaders could not access some ICT facilities like laptop computers. Most sectors in woredas seem to acquire standalone Desktop computers and printers in some form. Computers are not new in most offices. However, computer utilization becomes scarce as we go further to remote locations. Fluctuation of electricity and lack of funding are the main causes.

4.4 The Availability of Internet Connectivity and Utilization

The following table shows the distribution of Internet connections in the zone amongst the 6 woredas government administration surveyed offices. From the total number of respondents, the number of LAN installations identified is very low at 7.5%. Most respondents (81.4%) also revealed that their computers are not connected to the Internet, and most confirmed that they really do need the Internet to do their work.

Table 7. Availability of internet connectivity and utilization

Internet Connectivity			
Internet connection	Yes	44	18.6
	No	193	81.4
LAN connection	Yes	18	7.5
	No	223	92.5
Types of Internet connection	Responses	No of respondents	Responses in percentages
Broad Band	Yes	28	63.6

continued on following page

Table 7. Continued

Internet Connectivity			
Dial-Up	Yes	15	34.09
Wi-Fi	Yes	1	2.27
Total		44	

Moreover, as indicated above, 63.6% of the respondents' whose offices are connected to the Internet via broadband, 34.09% via dial-up, and only a very few 2.27% have access to Wi-Fi. The researchers observed no internet connection in most woreda sectors through the interview. The overall computed ICT Infrastructure is stated in Table 8.

Table 8. Overall computing ICT infrastructure

Woreda	N %	Mean (x)	Standard Deviation SD
Medaoromo	48	1.73	0.16
Berehet	33	1.70	0.16
Debre Sina	45	1.77	0.13
Hagre Mariam	34	1.80	0.14
Denebe	50	1.74	0.16
Bassona Worena (Debre Berhan)	33	1.61	0.28
Total	243	1.72	0.171

From Table 8, the overall ICT Infrastructure in each woreda was aggregated and found to be 1.72, indicating that the availability of Desktop, Printers, Laptops, internet connection, fax machines, and photocopy machines is inadequate. Yet the percentage calculation shows that Desktops and Printers are better made available than others in all woredas. This study concludes that the availability of ICT infrastructure, by and large, is not adequate to run sectoral functions efficiently. Employee's challenges and obstacles are stated in Table 9. Here greater resources and education would be advantageous.

Table 9. ICT leaders's challenges and obstacles

S. No	Items in Questionnaire	Options with assigned variable names	Response N%	Mean	Std. Deviation
9.1	Obstacles to using ICT	Yes (1)	182	1.21	0.410
		No (2)	49		
9.2	Woreda's Attention in ICT Aspects	Very High Weight(1)	71	2.25	1.175
		High Weight (2)	57		
		Little (3)	58		
		Nothing (4)	34		
9.3	Budget Allocation	Yes (1)	28	1.87	0.338
		No (2)	186		
9.4	Your organization gives training	Yes (1)	53	1.75	0.435
		No (2)	158		

From Table 9 (9.1), out of 231 respondents, 182 (78.7%) confirmed they faced several obstacles in using ICT, whereas 21.2% responded that they did not. This implies a serious challenge in using ICT technology by transnational ICT leaders of government organizations in all sectors. Table 9 (9.2) illustrates that, in the subject of woreda government attention concerning ICT infrastructure provision and proper utilization, more than half (51.4%) noted that there is little or no attention by woreda and sectorial officials. This implies that less attention is given to ICT infrastructure provision and utilization. From Table 9 (9.3), out of 214 respondents, the overwhelming majority of the respondents (86.9%) evaluated that there is no budget allocation for ICT resources. While only (13.1%) of them showed their agreement with their budget. From Table 9 (9.4), out of 211 respondents, the majority of respondents (74.9%) disclosed that there is no training schedule planned and implemented for transnational ICT leaders. However, a quarter of them (25.1%) witnessed that their organization on ICT gives a training program. To conclude provision of ICT infrastructure is not given due attention in budget allocation, training planning, and implementation for staff and experts. Through the interview, the transnational ICT leaders stated that there was no proper finance allocation to purchase ICT resources. Even with the existing status quo, they don't have the appropriate skills to utilize these. The employee's Attitude towards ICT is stated below in Table 10.

Table 10. ICT leaders's attitude towards ICT

S. No	Items in Questionnaire	Options with assigned variable names	Response N%	Mean	Std. Deviation
10.1	Are the transnational ICT leaders ready to improve their skills	Yes	235 (97.5)	0.02	0.156
		No	6(2.5)		
10.2	Are the transnational ICT leaders ready for adaption	Yes	131(56)	1.56	0.497
		No	103(44)		
10.3	Readiness less to Adapt ICT	Yes	225 (96.6)	1.03	0.182
		No	8 (3.4)		
10.4	Relevance of ICT is necessary	Very Important	211(88.7)	1.18	0.588
		Important	16(67)		
		Not Important	5(2.1)		
		Not sure	6(2.5)		

As Table 10 shows, most (97.5%) of the sample transnational ICT leaders agreed that they are interested in further improving their ICT skills in their work settings. In contrast, only 2.5% disagreed on enhancing their ICT skills. This indicates that government transnational ICT leaders working with ICT applications appeared interested in continuously upgrading their skills. On related items, respondents identified technical pieces of training maintenance, new software applications, and internet applications, among others, to improve. The other item presented to the respondent on their interest was an adaptation of capability, and less than half (44%) noted this. They believe that adaptation of ICT is difficult, whereas the majority (56%) of them accepted that adaptation of ICT is not too difficult. This implies that things there might be challenging in adapting to ICT upgrades.

Besides, respondent were asked to report on their readiness to adapt to ICT developments, and interestingly, the overwhelming majority (96.6%) confirmed that they are ready enough to adapt Information communication technology in their work. In addition, only (3.4%) of them suggested that they lacked the courage to do so. This implies that transnational ICT leaders are ready to adapt to ICT. Additionally, the respondents detained continuous training on computer skills maintenance, internet, and LAN connection on the open-ended scale items.

The other feature worth mentioning hereis that the topic presented to the respondent was the relevance of ICT in their working area. Accordingly, 227 (95.45%) of the interviewees replied it is very important, whereas 4.6% did not believe in the relevance of ICT. It is possible to conclude therefore that government transnational ICT leaders working with ICT are interested in improving their skills in technical training, maintenance, and new software applications and believe that they can adapt ICT to most transnational ICT devevelopments in their day-to-day institutional work. Through the interview, the transnational ICT leaders stated they are ready for change and using new technologies. An investigated Employee Leadership awareness in ICT Applications is indicated in Table 11.

Table 11. ICT leaders's leadership awareness in ICT applications

Woreda	Leadership Awareness		Total (100%)
	Yes (%)	No (%)	
Medaoromo	16 (34.8)	30 (65.2)	46
Berehet	10(31.3)	22(68.8)	32
Debre sina	15(35.7)	27(64.3)	42
Hagre Mariam	7(20.6)	27(79.4)	34
Denebe	13(26.0)	37(74)	50
Bassona Worena (Debre Berhan)	7(21.9)	25(78.1)	32
Total	68(28.8)	168(71.2)	236(100%)

Splitting by woreda, the leadership awareness gap appears to be a problem. To put in order of priority Hagre Mariam (79.4%) and Bassona Worena (78.1%) are the most pressing areas of concern, followed by Denebe (74%), Berehet (68.8%), Debre sina (64.3%), and Medaoroma (65.2%). Hence, leadership awareness of ICT applications like government websites, the internet, and video conferencing by transnational ICT leaders is a real gap. According to follow up interviews, the administration's transnational ICT leaders are unaware of recent trends / technological aspects. It might be there is a lack of internet connection or a lack of new exposure, and a lack of a genuine need to change either from the entities or individual's perspective.

This review aims to provide a holistic assessment of transnational ICT leadership, considering the unique challenges and opportunities associated with managing ICT initiatives across borders by considering one geographic location and some of its businesses. It is crucial to tailor the evaluation to the specific context and objectives of the transnational organization while involving key stakeholders from different regions in the evaluation process. Regular reviews and updates to the assessment framework will help ensure its relevance in a dynamic and evolving ICT landscape.

ICT leaders must create a strategic vision, engage stakeholders effectively, set up governance structures, exercise leadership, invest in capacity building, adopt agile project management methodologies, prioritize user-centric design, proactively manage risks, and embrace continuous evaluation and improvement for digital transformation and change management in government organizations to be successful. Government agencies are starting to realize how intertwined the world's digital potential and challenges are. To address shared issues, including cybersecurity risks, data privacy concerns, and the growth of digital infrastructure, transnational leadership awareness highlights the significance of comprehending and interacting with international stakeholders, networks, and trends.

4.5 Implications for Transnational Higher Education Universities

Clearly the findings from this study suggest a number of important points. The first is that in some global contexts today's leaders, and those who do and will operate across boarders are under prepared and under resourced. This is far from ideal if a region aspires to be competitive today, or indeed the local population. The second notable finding is that beyond training and resource budgeting and allocation, a degree of future proofing is important because technology is becoming so commonplace in so many areas. This suggests that transnational higher education providers might wish to consider providing training for these enterprises or their employees. It can be achieved through outreach initiatives, and perhaps corporate discounts can be provided. If business and government entities prefer to hire local trainers, then staff could still look for international external courses at esteemed providers and bring their learning back into the organization for the benefit of their colleagues. In simple terms, transnational institutions can work with local enterprises and in different locations so that outreach is global and local simultaneously.

5. CONCLUSION AND RECOMMENDATIONS

The following conclusions have been drawn based on the data collected, the analysis made, and the findings obtained.

Skills Gap

Many transnational ICT leaders are not good at basic ICT applications, although they are familiar with various applications.

A large number of transnational ICT leaders are not adequately aware of database management systems and do not fully exploit the potential of other applications.

Transnational ICT leaders are not as able as expected in making good use of online resources in their workplaces to better facilitate their work.

Communication practice can be enhanced when using ICT.

ICT leaders themselves are typically unable to maintain the ICT equipment and need support.

Mnay transnational ICT leaders are unaware of the latest trends in document-sharing and device-sharing operations in their organizations.

Availability of ICT Infrastructure

In most sectors, limited resources are available, whereas many machines are scarce in organizations. In addition, usage is often not optimal.

Some sectors in each woreda have an internet connection, but preferable utilization is an apparent issue.

ICT infrastructure is not adequate to run sectorial functions efficiently.

The Status of using ICT

Provision and innovation of ICT, and utilization of ICT are not given due attention as reflected in budget allocation, training planning, and the allocation of staff and experts.

The interest and intention of transnational ICT leaders in improving their skills and continuously upgrading appears to be encouraging. Many leadership figures demonstrated a positive ICT adaptability in their work. They appeared willing to integrate to the ever-changing and dynamic hardware and software products available in order to support the designs of their organization.

Government transnational ICT leaders illustrated a positive desire to improve their skills in technical training, maintenance, and new software applications.

Recommendations

As indicated in the conclusion, a skill gap exists in utilizing ICT for day-to-day activities. So, training should be provided to all Northern Shewa government sectors.

The Northern Shewa Administration zone should regularly assist and follow up to ensure the effective and efficient utilization of the technology for all staff in the zone.

Well, ICT-trained transnational ICT leaders should be assigned to the ICT sector. Additionally, they should be given continuous training to upgrade their knowledge/skills.

The zonal ICT sector has to create leadership awareness about the benefits of ICT to facilitate the day-to-day routine tasks of the Northern Shewa for their current and aspiring transnational ICT leaders.

NGOs and other well-ICT-equipped federal organizations should help by donating ICT infrastructure and funds to the zone.

Regional as well as the zonal state of Amhara region should help to bridge ICT infrastructure gaps in zonal woredas, especially those woredas which are far away from the zone, like Berhet, Mida Oromo, Gishie Rabel.

REFERENCES:

Abadama, D. S. (2020). A comparative study of perceived transformational, transactional and passive avoidant leadership styles effectiveness within the Ethiopian Public Universities. *International Journal of Higher Education Management*, 7(1). Advance online publication. 10.24052/IJHEM/V07N01/ART-3

Belayneh, B. (2022). The Effects of Leadership Styles on Organizational Performance: A Survey of Selected Federal Civil Service Institutions in Ethiopia. *African Journal of Leadership and Development*, 7(1), 1–27.

Besha, T., Amoroso, D. L. & Negash, S. (2009). *The Impact of Transactional and Transformational Leadership on Organizational Performance - The Case of Selected Ethiopian Companies.*

Bogale, M., Amoroso, D. L., & Negash, S. (2009). *The Impact of Transactional and Transformational Leader on Organizational Performance-The Case of Selected Ethiopian Companies.* AMCIS 2009 Proceedings, 264.

Daniels, J. S. (2002). *"Foreword" in Information and Communication Technology in Education–A Curriculum for Schools and Programme for Teacher Development.* UNESCO.

Darshan, G. (2011). Effects of transformational leadership on subordinate job satisfaction in leather companies in Ethiopia. *International Journal of Business Management and Economic Research*, 2(5), 284–296.

Demissie, A., & Gajendran, A. (2016). *The Influence of Various Leadership Styles on Acceleration of Organizational Performance in Government Bureaus of Benishangul Gumuz Region.*

Duressa, Z., & Asfaw, M. (2014). Transformational leadership and its applications in the public service organizations of Ethiopia. *International Affairs and Global Strategy*, 23. Available:www.worldcatlibraries.org/wcpa/ow/02d077080fcf3210a19afeb4da09e526.html

Gemeda, H. K., & Lee, J. (2020). Leadership styles, work engagement and outcomes among information and communications technology professionals: A cross-national study. *Heliyon*, 6(4), e03699. 10.1016/j.heliyon.2020.e0369932280799

Kebede, A. M., & Demeke, G. W. (2017). The influence of leadership styles on employees' job satisfaction in Ethiopian public universities. *Contemporary Management Research*, 13(3). Advance online publication. 10.7903/cmr.17668

Kebede, M. S. (2020). *Transnational Educational Leadership of International Organizations Working in Ethiopia: Walking the Local-Global Development Tightrope* (Doctoral dissertation, The Pennsylvania State University).

Lyons, T. (2007). Conflict-generated diasporas and transnational politics in Ethiopia: Analysis. *Conflict Security and Development*, 7(4), 529–549. 10.1080/14678800701692951

Mammo, Y. (2016). Analysis of Ethiopia's national ICT policy and strategy: Insights into policy issues and policy goals. *Ethiopian Journal of Education and Sciences*, 11(2), 75–89.

Mekonnen, M., & Bayissa, Z. (2023). The Effect of Transformational and Transactional Leadership Styles on Organizational Readiness for Change Among Health Professionals. *SAGE Open Nursing*, 9, 23779608231185923. 10.1177/23779608231185923374448973

Mishra, N., Desai, N. P., Wadhwani, A., & Baluch, M. F. (2023). Visual Analysis of Cardiac Arrest Prediction Using Machine Learning Algorithms: A Health Education Awareness Initiative. In *Handbook of Research on Instructional Technologies in Health Education and Allied Disciplines* (pp. 331-363). IGI Global. 10.4018/978-1-6684-7164-7.ch015

Mishra, N., Habtemariam, G. M., & De, A. (2023). Investigation of High-Performance Computing Tools for Higher Education Institutions Using the IoE Grid Computing Framework. In *Internet of Behaviors Implementation in Organizational Contexts* (pp. 217–241). IGI Global. 10.4018/978-1-6684-9039-6.ch011

Morris, G. R., Morris, J., & Li, L. (2023). Enhancing educational leadership in transnational higher education. In Morris, G., & Li, L. (Eds.), *Handbook of Research on Developments and Future Trends in Transnational Higher Education* (pp. 341–358). IGI Global. 10.4018/978-1-6684-5226-4.ch018

Mulugeta, A., & Pandian, A. V. R. (2020). The relationship between leadership styles and employee commitment in public organizations of Dire Dawa administration, Ethiopia. *International Journal of Advanced Science and Technology*, 29(8), 2018–2025.

Ndou, V. (2004). E-government for developing countries: Opportunities and challenges. *The Electronic Journal on Information Systems in Developing Countries*, 18(1), 1–24. 10.1002/j.1681-4835.2004.tb00117.x

Rahman, H. (2007). *Developing successful ICT strategies: Competitive advantages in a global knowledge-driven society*. IGI.

Reta, M. A. (2021). The Influence of Leadership Styles on the Effectiveness of the Public Policy Implementation Process in Ethiopia: The Case of Addis Ababa City Government. *American Journal of Management Science and Engineering*, 6(5), 142–160. 10.11648/j.ajmse.20210605.12

Rodríguez-Feria, P., Paric, M., Flórez, L. J. H., Babich, S. & Czabanowska, K. (2024). Critical route for development of medical student leadership competencies in 35 Pan American Health Organization member states: A scoping review and thematic analysis. *The International Journal of Health Planning and Management*.

Sharma, R. (2003). Barriers in Using Technology for Education in Developing Countries. *Computers & Education*, 41(1), 49–63.

Tiika, B. J., Tang, Z., Azaare, J., Dagadu, J. C., & Otoo, S. N. A. (2024). Evaluating E-Government Development among Africa Union Member States: An Analysis of the Impact of E-Government on Public Administration and Governance in Ghana. *Sustainability (Basel)*, 16(3), 1333. 10.3390/su16031333

UNESCO. (2002). *'Open and Distance Learning Trends, Policy and Strategy Considerations'*, 14 UNESCO. "United Nations. Economic Commission for Africa; United Nations. Economic Commission for Africa (2023-12). Digital Infrastructure in Africa. Addis Ababa. © UN. ECA, https://hdl.handle.net/10855/50027"

KEY TERMS AND DEFINITIONS

Computing Technology and Change Management for ICT Leaders: ICT leaders must create a strategic vision, effectively engage stakeholders, set up governance structures, exercise leadership, invest in capacity building, adopt agile project management methodologies, prioritize user-centric design, proactively manage risks and embrace continuous evaluation and improvement if they are to implement digital transformation and change management in government organizations successfully. ICT leaders may promote positive change, enhance organizational performance, and improve the provision of public services to citizens by utilizing these ideas and practices.

Digital Transformation and Innovation Ecosystems: To modernize public services, promote innovation, and propel socioeconomic development, government entities must embrace digital transformation and innovation ecosystems. Through technology, government institutions undergo a digital transformation that increases citizen participation, improves service delivery, and streamlines operations. Additionally, government agencies foster innovation ecosystems that aid in creating and using cutting-edge technology and approaches to social problems.

ICT Skill Gap and Trends for Leaders: Government leaders must have a broad skill set that includes technical proficiency, strategic vision, data literacy, cybersecurity awareness, agile leadership, collaboration skills, inclusivity, and ethical leadership to close the ICT skill gap and remain ahead of emerging trends. Government organizations can provide their leaders with the right tools to drive digital transformation and effectively address the changing requirements of citizens in the digital age by investing in ongoing learning and cultivating a culture of creativity and cooperation. The speed at which technology develops has resulted in an increasing ICT skills gap for government entities. Leaders must constantly refresh their skills to stay updated with emerging technologies like blockchain, the Internet of Things (IoT), and artificial intelligence (AI). This is necessary to take advantage of innovation and service delivery opportunities effectively.

ICT-Implemented Government Organizations: Governmental entities that have successfully incorporated information and communication technology (ICT) into their operations, services, and procedures are called ICT-implemented government organizations.

Leadership Performance Assessment: The process of assessing a leader's effectiveness in managing a team, accomplishing organizational objectives, and exhibiting critical leadership characteristics is known as leadership performance evaluation. Typically, the evaluation process includes obtaining input from several sources, examining leadership practices, and providing helpful guidance and actionable suggestions to improve leadership qualities.

Transnational ICT Leaders: Global connectivity, cross-border innovation, digital diplomacy, coordinating multilateral policies, exhibiting cross-cultural leadership, advancing ethical innovation, and navigating geopolitical complexities are all made possible by transnational ICT leaders in governmental organizations. Their work is crucial to creating a global digital future that is robust, inclusive, and sustainable.

Transnational Leadership Awareness: Navigating the complexity of the global digital ecosystem in government entities requires a transnational leadership understanding. Government agencies are becoming increasingly aware of how global issues and digital opportunities are interconnected. Transnational leadership awareness highlights the significance of comprehending and interacting with international networks, stakeholders, and trends to tackle shared problems, including data privacy, cybersecurity risks, and the growth of digital infrastructure.

Compilation of References

, N., & Khan, N. H. (2020). Online teaching-learning during covid-19 pandemic: students' perspective. *The Online Journal of Distance Education and e-Learning, 8*(4), 202-213.

Abadama, D. S. (2020). A comparative study of perceived transformational, transactional and passive avoidant leadership styles effectiveness within the Ethiopian Public Universities. *International Journal of Higher Education Management, 7*(1). Advance online publication. 10.24052/IJHEM/V07N01/ART-3

Abdous, M. H. (2019). Influence of satisfaction and preparedness on online students' feelings of anxiety. *The Internet and Higher Education*, 41, 34–44. 10.1016/j.iheduc.2019.01.001

Aboagye, R. (2018). Instructional strategies for teaching students with Mixed ability in physical education in Central Region (Doctoral dissertation, University of Cape coast).

Abrams, Z. I. (2003). The effect of synchronous and asynchronous CMC on oral performance in German. *Modern Language Journal, 87*(2), 157–167. 10.1111/1540-4781.00184

Adedoyin, O. B., & Soykan, E. (2020). Covid-19 pandemic and online learning: The challenges and opportunities. *Interactive Learning Environments*, 3, 1–13. 10.1080/10494820.2020.1813180

Adiguzel, T., Kaya, M. H., & Cansu, F. K. (2023). Revolutionizing education with AI: Exploring the transformative potential of ChatGPT. *Contemporary Educational Technology, 15*(3), 429. 10.30935/cedtech/13152

Adnan, A. H. M. (2020, September). From interactive teaching to immersive learning: Higher Education 4.0 via 360-degree videos and virtual reality in Malaysia. []. IOP Publishing.]. *IOP Conference Series. Materials Science and Engineering, 917*(1), 012023. 10.1088/1757-899X/917/1/012023

Advance-He. (2011) 'The UK Professional Standards Framework for teaching and supporting learning in higher education', Learning, p. 8. Available at: http://www.heacademy.ac.uk/ukpsf

Afshar, H. S., & Doosti, M. (2016). Investigating the impact of job satisfaction/dissatisfaction on Iranian English teachers' job performance. *Iranian Journal of Language Teaching Research*, 4, 97–115.

Agee, M., & Crocker, T. (2013) Operationalizing the capability approach to assessing well-being, *The Journal of Socio-Economics*, Volume 46, Pages 80-86, ISSN 1053-5357, 10.1016/j.socec.2013.07.003

Aggarwal, R., & Ranganathan, P. (2019). Study designs: Part 2–descriptive studies. *Perspectives in Clinical Research, 10*(1), 34. 10.4103/picr.PICR_154_1830834206

Aiston, S. J. (2011). Equality, justice and gender: Barriers to the ethical university for women. *Ethics and Education, 6*(3), 279–291. 10.1080/17449642.2011.632721

Aiston, S. J., & Jung, J. (2015). Women academics and research productivity: An international comparison. *Gender and Education, 27*(3), 205–220. https://doi-org.ezproxy.nottingham.edu.cn/10.1080/09540253.2015.1024617. 10.1080/09540253.2015.1024617

Akbari, R., Samar, R. G., Kiany, G. R., & Tahernia, M. (2017). A qualitative study of EFL teachers' emotion regulation behavior in the classroom. *Theory and Practice in Language Studies*, 7(4), 311–321. 10.17507/tpls.0704.10

Aldridge, J. M., & Fraser, B. J. (2016). 'Teachers' views of their school climate and its relationship with teacher self-efficacy and job satisfaction'. *Learning Environments Research*, 19(2), 291–307. 10.1007/s10984-015-9198-x

Alessio, J. C., & Andrzejewski, J. (2000). Unveiling the hidden glass ceiling: An analysis of the cohort effect claim. *American Sociological Review*, 65(2), 311–315. 10.1177/000312240006500209

Alexander, B. (2020). *Academia next: The futures of higher education*. John Hopkins University Press.

Alkire, S. (2002). *Valuing Freedoms. Sen's Capability Approach and Poverty Reduction*. Oxford University Press. 10.1093/0199245797.001.0001

Allen, M. (2022). Professor warns about chatbot cheating: "Expect a flood". *Axios*. Available at: https://www.axios.com/2022/12/26/chatbot-cheating-university-warningchatgpt [Accessed 29 February 2024].

Allen, T. D., Eby, L. T., Poteet, M. L., Lentz, E., & Lima, L. (2004). Career benefits associated with mentoring for protégés: A meta-analysis. *The Journal of Applied Psychology*, 89(1), 127–136. 10.1037/0021-9010.89.1.12714769125

Al-Mahmood, R. 2013. Re-imagining the university: Vibrant matters and radical research paradigms for the 21st century. *30th Ascilite Conference Proceedings*, 23-36.

Alpaslan, M. M., & Ulubey, O. (2017). Adaptation of the teacher emotion scale into Turkish culture. *International Periodical for the Languages. Literature and History of Turkish or Turkic*, 12(25), 119–130.

Alsup, J. (2006). *Teacher identity discourses: Negotiating personal and professional spaces*. Lawrence Erlbaum. 10.4324/9781410617286

Ambrose, S., Huston, T., & Norman, M. (2005). A qualitative method for assessing faculty satisfaction. *Research in Higher Education*, 46(7), 803–830. 10.1007/s11162-004-6226-6

Andrews, J. W., Drefs, M., Lupart, J., & Loreman, T. (2015). Foundations, principles, and student diversity. Diversity education: Understanding and addressing student diversity, pp.24-73.

Approaches to Teaching Observations. (2023). *Teaching Strategies* (https://cteresources.bc.edu/documentation/teaching-observations/approaches-to-teaching-observations/) (Accessed 02 January 2004).

Aristovnik, A., Keržič, D., Ravšelj, D., Tomaževič, N., & Umek, L. (2020). Impacts of the COVID-19 Pandemic on Life of Higher Education Students: A Global Perspective. *Sustainability (Basel)*, 12(8438), 1–34. 10.3390/su12208438

Arvey, R. D., Zhang, Z., Avolio, B. J., & Krueger, R. F. (2007). Developmental and genetic determinants of leadership role occupancy among women. *The Journal of Applied Psychology*, 92(3), 693–706. 10.1037/0021-9010.92.3.69317484551

Asif, T., Guangming, O., Haider, M. A., Colomer, J., Kayani, S., & Amin, N. U. (2020). Moral education for sustainable development: Comparison of university teachers' perceptions in China and Pakistan. *Sustainability (Basel)*, 12(7), 3014. 10.3390/su12073014

Astin, H. S., & Leland, C. (1991). *Women of Influence, Women of Vision: A Cross-Generational Study of Leaders and Social Change*. Jossey-Bass.

Attali, Y. (2013). Validity and reliability of automated essay scoring. In Shermis, M. D., & Burstein, J. (Eds.), *Handbook on automated essay evaluation: Current applications and new directions* (pp. 181–198). Routledge.

Attel, B., Brown, K., & Treiber, L. (2017). Workplace bullying, perceived job stressors and psychological distress: Gender and race differences in the stress process. *Social Science Research*, 65, 210–221. 10.1016/j.ssresearch.2017.02.00128599773

Avolio, B. J., Walumbwa, F. O., & Weber, T. J. (2009). Leadership: Current Theories, Research, and Future Directions. *Annual Review of Psychology*, 60(1), 421–449. 10.1146/annurev.psych.60.110707.16362118651820

Awamleh, R., & Al-Dmour, H. (2004). The impact of transformational leadership on job satisfaction and self-perceived performance of banking employees: The case of Jordan. *The International Business & Economics Research Journal*, 3(11), 29–41.

Aydın, S. (2018). Technology and foreign language anxiety: Implications for practice and future research. *Journal of Language and Linguistic Studies*, 14(2), 193–211.

Baars, S., Parameshwaran, M., Menzies, L. & Chiong, C. (2016). *Firing on All Cylinders: What Makes and Effective Middle Leader.* London: Teaching Leaders and LKMCo.

Bailey, D., Almusharraf, N., & Hatcher, R. (2021). Finding satisfaction: Intrinsic motivation for synchronous and asynchronous communication in the online language learning context. *Education and Information Technologies*, 26(3), 2563–2583. 10.1007/s10639-020-10369-z33169066

Baker, A. A. (2011). Discourse prosody and teachers stated beliefs and practices. *TESOL Journal*, 2(3), 263–292. 10.5054/tj.2011.259955

Baker, A., & Burri, M. (2016). Feedback on second language pronunciation: A case study of EAP teachers' beliefs and practices. *The Australian Journal of Teacher Education*, 41(6), 1–19. 10.14221/ajte.2016v41n6.1

Baltodano, J. C., Carlson, S., Jackson, L. W., & Mitchell, W. (2012). Networking to leadership in higher education: National and state-based programs and networks for developing women. *Advances in Developing Human Resources*, 14(1), 62–78. 10.1177/1523422311428926

Bamberg, M. (1997a). Positioning between structure and performance. *Journal of Narrative and Life History*, 7(1–4), 335–342. 10.1075/jnlh.7.42pos

Bamberg, M. (1997b). Language, concepts and emotions: The role of language in the construction of emotions. *Language Sciences*, 19(4), 309–340. 10.1016/S0388-0001(97)00004-1

Bamberg, M. (2006). Stories: Big or small: Why do we care? *Narrative Inquiry*, 16(1), 139–147. 10.1075/ni.16.1.18bam

Barcelos, A. M. F., & Ruohotie-Lyhty, M. (2018). *Teachers' Emotions and Beliefs in Second Language Teaching: Implications for Teacher Education*. Springer International Publishing. https://doi-org.ez.xjtlu.edu.cn/10.1007/978-3-319-75438-3_7

Barkhuizen, G. (2008). A narrative approach to exploring context in language teaching. *ELT Journal*, 62(3), 231–239. 10.1093/elt/ccm043

Barkhuizen, G. (2010). An extended positioning analysis of a pre-service teacher's better life small Story. *Applied Linguistics*, 31(2), 282–300. 10.1093/applin/amp027

Barkhuizen, G. (2016). Language teacher identity research: An introduction. In *Reflections on language teacher identity research* (pp. 9–19). Routledge. 10.4324/9781315643465-5

Barling, J., Weber, T., & Kelloway, E. K. (1996). Effects of transformational leadership training on attitudinal and financial outcomes: A field experiment. *The Journal of Applied Psychology*, 81(6), 827–832. 10.1037/0021-9010.81.6.827

Barnard, S., Arnold, J., Bosley, S., & Munir, F. (2022). The personal and institutional impacts of a mass participation leadership programme for women working in higher education: A longitudinal analysis. *Studies in Higher Education*, 47(7), 1372–1385. 10.1080/03075079.2021.1894117

Barnett, R. (2010). *Being a University*. Routledge. 10.4324/9780203842485

Barnett, R. (2013). *Imagining the University*. Routledge. 10.4324/9780203072103

Barnett, R. (2017). *The Ecological University: A Feasible Utopia*. Routledge. 10.4324/9781315194899

Barnett, R. (2020). Realizing the world-class university: an ecological approach. In Rider, S., Peters, M. A., & Hyvonen, M. (Eds.), *World Class Universities: A Contested Concept* (pp. 269–283). Springer Nature. 10.1007/978-981-15-7598-3_16

Barnett, R. 2011. The Idea of the University in the Twenty-First Century: Where's the Imagination?*International Higher Education Congress: New Trends and Issues*, Istanbul, May 27-29: 261–68.

Bass, B. M., & Riggio, R. E. (2006). *Transformational Leadership*. Psychology Press. 10.4324/9781410617095

Baxter, J., & Wright, E. O. (2000). The glass ceiling hypothesis: A comparative study of the United States, Sweden, and Australia. *Gender & Society*, 14(2), 275–294. 10.1177/089124300014002004

Beaken, M. (2009). Teaching discourse intonation with Narrative. *ELT Journal*, 63(4), 342–352. 10.1093/elt/ccp002

Becker, G. S., Hubbard, W. H., & Murphy, K. M. (2010). Explaining the worldwide boom in higher education of women. *Journal of Human Capital*, 4(3), 203–241. 10.1086/657914

Beerkens, M., & van der Hoek, M. (2022). Academic leaders and leadership in the changing higher education landscape. In Research Handbook on Academic Careers and Managing Academics. Edward Elgar Publishing., Available at https://www.researchgate.net/publication/360065231, Retrieved March 15th, 2024, from. 10.4337/9781839102639.00017

Beijaard, D., Meijer, P. C., & Verloop, N. (2004). Reconsidering research on teachers' professional identity. *Teaching and Teacher Education*, 20(2), 107–128. 10.1016/j.tate.2003.07.001

Belayneh, B. (2022). The Effects of Leadership Styles on Organizational Performance: A Survey of Selected Federal Civil Service Institutions in Ethiopia. *African Journal of Leadership and Development*, 7(1), 1–27.

Beltman, S., Hascher, T., & Mansfield, C. (2022). In the Midst of a Pandemic. *Zeitschrift für Psychologie mit Zeitschrift für Angewandte Psychologie*.

Benesch, S. (2017). *Emotions in English language teaching: Exploring teachers' emotion labor*. Routledge/Taylor & Francis. 10.4324/9781315736181

Bennett, K. (2010). Academic writing practices in Portugal: survey of humanities and social science researchers. *diacrítica*, 24(1), 193-209.

Bennis, W., & Thomas, R. J. (2002). Crucibles of Leadership. *Harvard Business Review*.12227145

Bergiel, E. B., Bergiel, B. J., & Upson, J. W. (2012). Revisiting Hofstede's Dimensions: Examining the Cultural Convergence of the United States and Japan. *American Journal of Management*, 12(1), 69–79.

Besha, T., Amoroso, D. L. & Negash, S. (2009). *The Impact of Transactional and Transformational Leadership on Organizational Performance - The Case of Selected Ethiopian Companies*.

Biasutti, M., Concina, E., Frate, S., & Delen, I. (2021). Teacher professional development: Experiences in an international project on intercultural education. *Sustainability (Basel)*, 13(8), 4171. 10.3390/su13084171

Biernat, M., & Fuegen, K. (2001). Shifting standards and the evaluation of competence: Complexity in gender-based judgment and decision making. *The Journal of Social Issues*, 57(4), 707–724. 10.1111/0022-4537.00237

Bietenbeck, J., Piopiunik, M., & Wiederhold, S. (2018). Africa's skill tragedy: Does teachers' lack of knowledge lead to low student performance? *The Journal of Human Resources*, 53(3), 553–578. 10.3368/jhr.53.3.0616-8002R1

Biggs, J., & Tang, C. (2010), February. Applying constructive alignment to outcomes-based teaching and learning. In Training material for "quality teaching for learning in higher education" workshop for master trainers, Ministry of Higher Education, Kuala Lumpur (Vol. 53, No. 9, pp. 23-25).

Biggs, J., Tang, C., & Kennedy, G. (2022). Ebook: Teaching for Quality Learning at University 5e. McGraw-hill education (UK).

Biggs, J. (1996). Enhancing teaching through constructive alignment. *Higher Education*, 32(3), 347–364. 10.1007/BF00138871

Blumenstyk, G. (2014). *American higher education in crisis? What everyone needs to know*. Oxford University Press. 10.1093/wentk/9780199374090.001.0001

Bogale, M., Amoroso, D. L., & Negash, S. (2009). *The Impact of Transactional and Transformational Leader on Organizational Performance-The Case of Selected Ethiopian Companies*. AMCIS 2009 Proceedings, 264.

Boivin, N., Hahn, J., & Sadaf, S. (2022). Outsider Reflecting on Invisible Institutional Gender Norms. In Miller, C. (Eds.), *Leading Change in Gender and Diversity in Higher Education from Margins to Mainstream*. Taylor & Francis Group. 10.4324/9781003286943-13

Boldt, G., Lewis, C., & Leander, K. M. (2015). Moving, feeling, desiring, and teaching. *Research in the Teaching of English*, 49(4), 430–441. 10.58680/rte201527351

Bonebright, D. A., Cottledge, A. D., & Lonnquist, P. (2012). Developing women leaders on campus: A human resources–women's center partnership at the University of Minnesota. *Advances in Developing Human Resources*, 14(1), 79–95. 10.1177/1523422311429733

Booth, T. (1996). Stories of exclusion. Natural and unnatural selection. En.

Borg, S. (2006). *Teacher Cognition and Language Education*. Continuum.

Borg, S., & Al-Busaidi, S. (2012). Teachers' beliefs and practices regarding learner autonomy. *ELT Journal*, 66(3), 283–292. 10.1093/elt/ccr065

Borg, S, & Liu, Y. (2012). Chinese College English Teachers' Research Engagement. *TESOL Quarterly*, 47(2), 270–299.

Borrachero, A. B., Brigido, M., Costillo, E., Bermejo, L., & Mellado, V. (2014). Relationship between self-efficacy beliefs and emotions of future teachers of Physics in secondary education. *Asia-Pacific Forum on Science Learning and Teaching*, 14(2), 1–11.

Bothwell, E. (2020). Female leadership in top universities advances for first time since 2017. *Times Higher Education*. https://www.timeshighereducation.com/news/female-leadership-top-universities-advances-first-time-2017

Bourdieu, P. (1986). The forms of capital. In Richardson, J. (Ed.), *Handbook of Theory and Research for the Sociology of Education*. Greenwood.

Bovill, C., Bulley, C. J., & Morss, K. (2011). Engaging and empowering students in higher education through curriculum design partnerships. *The International Journal for Academic Development*, 16(1), 54–68.

Bowers, J., & Kumar, P. (2015). Students' Perceptions of Teaching and Social Presence: A Comparative Analysis of Face-to-Face and Online Learning Environments. [IJWLTT]. *International Journal of Web-Based Learning and Teaching Technologies*, 10(1), 27–44. 10.4018/ijwltt.2015010103

Bradford, B. (1988). *Intonation in Context*. Cambridge University Press.

Braun, V., & Clarke, V. (2006). Using thematic analysis in psychology. *Qualitative Research in Psychology*, 3(2), 77–101. 10.1191/1478088706qp063oa

Braun, V., & Clarke, V. (2012). *Thematic analysis*. American Psychological Association., 10.1037/13620-004

Brazil, D. (1985). *The Communicative Value of Intonation in English*. University of Birmingham.

Brazil, D. (1994). *Pronunciation for Advanced Learners of English*. Cambridge University Press.

Brazil, D. (1997). *The Communicative Value of Intonation*. Cambridge University Press.

Brazil, D., Coulthard, M, & Jones, C. (1980). *Discourse Intonation and Language Teaching*. Longman.

British Educational Research Association. (2018). Ethical Guidelines for Educational Research. Available at: https://www.bera.ac.uk/publication/ethical-guidelines-for-educational-research-2018

British Educational Research Association. (2018). *Ethical Guidelines for Educational Research*. Available from: https://www.bera.ac.uk/publication/ethical-guidelines-for-educational-research-2018

Brookfield, S.D. (2017). The Four Lenses of Critical Reflection. Becoming A Critically Reflective Teacher, 2, pp.61-78.

Brown, G. A., Bull, J., & Pendlebury, M. (2013). *Assessing student learning in higher education*. Routledge. 10.4324/9781315004914

Bruner, J. (1991). The narrative construction of reality. *Critical Inquiry*, 18(1), 1–21. 10.1086/448619

Bryant, S. E. (2003). The role of transformational and transactional leadership in creating, sharing and exploiting organizational knowledge. *Journal of Leadership & Organizational Studies*, 9(4), 32–44. 10.1177/107179190300900403

BTU. (2024). The leading American university - Webster University enters Georgia. Retrieved from: https://btu.edu.ge/tsamqhvani-amerikuli-universiteti-vebsteri-webster-university-saqarthveloshi-shemodis/

Buckridge, M., & Guest, R. (2007). A conversation about pedagogical responses to increased diversity in university classrooms. *Higher Education Research & Development*, 26(2), 133–146. 10.1080/07294360701310771

Buric, I., Sliškovic, A., & Macuka, I. (2018). A Mixed-Method Approach to the Assessment of Teachers' Emotions: Development and Validation of the Teacher Emotion Questionnaire. *Educational Psychology*, 38(3), 325–349. 10.1080/01443410.2017.1382682

Burnett, D. (2023). *Emotional Intelligence*. Faber and Faber.

Burns, J. D. (2007) Analyses of transactional and transformational leadership on job satisfaction of college faculty. (Order No. 3294383, Northcentral University).

Burns, J. M. (1978). *Leadership*. Harper and Row.

Burstein, J., Tetreault, J., & Madnani, N. (2013). The e-rater® automated essay scoring system. In Shermis, M. D., & Burstein, J. (Eds.), *Handbook of Automated Essay Evaluation* (pp. 55–67). Routledge.

Business Press News. (2023). The number of foreign students in higher education institutions has increased 20 times - how many citizens of foreign countries study in Georgia? Retrieved from: https://www.bpn.ge/article/111513-umaglesi-ganatlebis-sascavleblebshi-ucxoeli-studentebis-raodenoba-20-jer-gaizarda-ucxo-kveqnis-ramdeni-mokalake-scavlobs-sakartveloshi/

Busse, V. (2013). How do students of German perceive feedback practices at university? A motivational exploration. *Journal of Second Language Writing*, 22(4), 406–424. 10.1016/j.jslw.2013.09.005

Cacioppo, S. (2022). *Wired for love: a neuroscientist's journey through romance, loss and the essence of human connection*. Robinson.

Cahoon, A., McGill, S., & Simms, V. (2021). Understanding home education in the context of COVID-19 lockdown. *Irish Educational Studies*, 40(2), 443–455. 10.1080/03323315.2021.1921010

Caine, A., Estefan, A. & Clandinin, J. D. (2019). *Narrative Enquiry*. Available from: https://doi.org/10.4135/9781526421036771087

Cambridge (2023) available at: Head of Research in AI for Learning | Cambridge University Press & Assessment [Accessed 1 January 2024]

Camp, T. (1997). The incredible shrinking pipeline. *Communications of the ACM*, 40(10), 103–110. 10.1145/262793.262813

Can, Y., & Bardakci, S. (2022). Teachers' opinions on (urgent) distance education activities during the pandemic period. *Advances in Mobile Learning Educational Research*, 2(2), 351–374. 10.25082/AMLER.2022.02.005

Carpenter, J. P., Kimmons, R., Short, C. R., Clements, K., & Staples, M. E. (2019). Teacher identity and crossing the professional-personal divide on twitter. *Teaching and Teacher Education*, 81, 1–12. 10.1016/j.tate.2019.01.011

Cauldwell, R., & Hewings, M. (1996). Intonation rules in ELT textbooks. *ELT Journal*, 50(4), 327–334. 10.1093/elt/50.4.327

Caulfield, J. (2019). *How to do Thematic Analysis*. Available at: https://www.scribbr.com/methodology/thematic-analysis/

Caulfield, J. (2019). How to Do Thematic Analysis. Available at: https://www.scribbr.com/methodology/thematic-analysis/

Celce-Murcia, M., Brinton, D. M., Goodwin, J. M., & Griner, B. (2010). *Teaching pronunciation: A reference for teachers of English to speakers of other languages* (2nd ed.). Cambridge University Press.

Chai, Y. L. (2014). A survey of non-English major college students' English listening and speaking learning demands based on WeChat. *Technology Enhanced Foreign Language Education*, (05), 34–39.

Chan, K. Y., & Drasgow, F. (2001). Toward a theory of individual differences and leadership: Understanding the motivation to lead. *The Journal of Applied Psychology*, 86(3), 481–498. 10.1037/0021-9010.86.3.48111419808

Chapman, M. (2007). Theory and Practice of Teaching Discourse Intonation. *ELT Journal*, 61(1), 3–11. 10.1093/elt/ccl039

Charmaz, K. (2014). Grounded theory in global perspective: Reviews by international researchers. *Qualitative Inquiry*, 20(9), 1074–1084. 10.1177/1077800414545235

Chen, H., Sun, W., Han, J., & Liu, Q. (2022). Chinese language teachers' dichotomous identities when teaching ingroup and outgroup students. *Frontiers in Psychology*, 13, 13. 10.3389/fpsyg.2022.93933335967731

Chen, J. (2016). Understanding teacher emotions: The development of a teacher emotion inventory. *Teaching and Teacher Education*, 55, 68–77. 10.1016/j.tate.2016.01.001

Chen, J. (2021). Refining the Teacher Emotion Model: Evidence from a Review of Literature Published between 1985 and 2019. *Cambridge Journal of Education*, 51(3), 327–357. 10.1080/0305764X.2020.1831440

Chen, L. (2020). 'Problematising the English-only policy in EAP: A mixed-methods investigation of Chinese international students' perspectives of academic language policy'. *Journal of Multilingual and Multicultural Development*, 41(8), 718–735. 10.1080/01434632.2019.1643355

Chen, M. (2022). Digital affordances and teacher agency in the context of teaching Chinese as a second language during COVID-19. *System*, 105, 102710. 10.1016/j.system.2021.102710

Chen, M. R. A., & Hwang, G. J. (2020). Effects of a concept mapping-based flipped learning approach on EFL students' English speaking performance, critical thinking awareness and speaking anxiety. *British Journal of Educational Technology*, 51(3), 817–834. 10.1111/bjet.12887

Chen, Z., Sun, Y., & Jia, Z. (2022). A Study of Student-Teachers' Emotional Experiences and Their Development of Professional Identities. *Frontiers in Psychology*, 12, 6604. 10.3389/fpsyg.2021.81014635145463

Cheshmehzangi, A., Zou, T., & Su, Z. (2022). Commentary: China's Zero-COVID Approach Depends on Shanghai's Outbreak Control. *Frontiers in Public Health*, 10, 10. 10.3389/fpubh.2022.91299235774574

Chitadze, N. (2016). *Political Science*. International Black Sea University.

Chitadze, N. (2017). *World Geography*. Scholars Press.

Cho, H. (2014). 'It's very complicated' exploring heritage language identity with heritage language teachers in a teacher preparation program. *Language and Education, 28*(2), 181e195.

Choi, D. H., Dailey-Hebert, A., & Estes, J. S. (Eds.). (2020). *Current and prospective applications of virtual reality in higher education*. IGI Global. 10.4018/978-1-7998-4960-5

Chomsky, N., Roberts, I., & Watumull, J. (2023). Noam chomsky: The false promise of chatgpt. *The New York Times, 8*.

Chong, W. H., & Kong, C. A. (2012). Teacher collaborative learning and teacher self-efficacy: The case of lesson study. *Journal of Experimental Education*, 80(3), 263–283. 10.1080/00220973.2011.596854

Christenfeld, N., & Creager, B. (1996). Anxiety, alcohol, aphasia, and ums. *Journal of Personality and Social Psychology*, 70(3), 451–460. 10.1037/0022-3514.70.3.4518851740

Christine, S., Harold, M., Ana, R., & Susanne, J. (2022). The LIFE program – University students learning leadership and teamwork through service learning in El Salvador. [online]. *Intercultural Education*, 33(4), 470–483. https://appgateway.nottingham.edu.cn/https/77726476706e69737468656265737421e7e056d133316654780787a0915b26781c4501d1e52ab258923b99e4071c6d2891bcaccb014587a0110a4decc2/doi/full/10.1080/14675986.2022.2090689. 10.1080/14675986.2022.2090689

Chun, D. (2002). *Discourse Intonation in L2: From Theory and Research to Practice*. John Benjamins.

Cicek, I., Bernik, A., & Tomicic, I. (2021). Student thoughts on virtual reality in higher education—A survey questionnaire. *Information (Basel)*, 12(4), 151. 10.3390/info12040151

Civil. Ge. (2023). Geostat Report on General Education Institution. Retrieved from: https://civil.ge/ka/archives/517342

Clennell, C. (1997). Raising the pedagogic status of discourse intonation teaching. *ELT Journal*, 51(2), 117–125. 10.1093/elt/51.2.117

Collini, S. (2012). *What Are Universities For?* Penguin.

Colter, R., & Ulatowski, J. (2017). The unexamined student is not worth teaching: Preparation, the zone of proximal development, and the Socratic Model of Scaffolded Learning. *Educational Philosophy and Theory*, 49(14), 1367–1380. 10.1080/00131857.2017.1282340

Couper, G. (2017). Teacher cognition of pronunciation teaching: Teachers' concerns and issues. *TESOL Quarterly*, 51(4), 820–843. 10.1002/tesq.354

Crawford, J., Butler-Henderson, K., Rudolph, J., Malkawi, B., Glowatz, M., Burton, R., Magni, P., & Lam, S. (2020). COVID-19: 20 countries' higher education intra-period digital pedagogy responses. *Journal of Applied Learning & Teaching*, 3(1), 1–20.

Creswell, J. W., & Creswell, J. D. (2023). *Research design : qualitative, quantitative, and mixed methods approaches* (6th ed.). SAGE.

Cruess, R. L., Cruess, S. R., Boudreau, J. D., Snell, L., & Steinert, Y. (2015). A schematic representation of the professional identity formation and socialization of medical students and residents: A guide for medical educators. *Academic Medicine*, 90(6), 718–725. 10.1097/ACM.0000000000000070025785682

Cruttenden, A. (1997). *Intonation* (2nd ed.). Cambridge University Press.

Curry, R. 2023. Enabling the Ecological University – An Argument for Developing Transdisciplinary Ethical-Maker-Learning in Higher Education. In Radenkovic, M. (Ed) *Ethics - Scientific Research, Ethical Issues, Artificial Intelligence and Education.* InTechOpen.

Curry, R. (2017). Makerspaces: A beneficial new service for academic libraries? *Library Review*, 66(4/5), 201–212. 10.1108/LR-09-2016-0081

Curry, R. (2022). Insights from a cultural-historical HE library makerspace case study on the potential for academic libraries to lead on supporting ethical-making underpinned by 'critical material literacy'. *Journal of Librarianship and Information Science*.

Dalton, C, & Seidlhofer, B. (1994). *Pronunciation*. Oxford University Press.

Dampson, D. G., Havor, F. M., & Laryea, P. (2018). Distributed leadership an instrument for school improvement: The study of public senior high schools in Ghana. *Journal of Education and e-learning Research*, 5(2), 79–85. 10.20448/journal.509.2018.52.79.85

Damsa, C. L., & Ludvigsen, S. (2016). Learning through interaction and co-construction of knowledge objects in teacher education. *Learning, Culture and Social Interaction*, 11, 1–18. 10.1016/j.lcsi.2016.03.001

Daniels, J. S. (2002). *"Foreword" in Information and Communication Technology in Education–A Curriculum for Schools and Programme for Teacher Development*. UNESCO.

Darshan, G. (2011). Effects of transformational leadership on subordinate job satisfaction in leather companies in Ethiopia. *International Journal of Business Management and Economic Research*, 2(5), 284–296.

Data Protection Act. (2018). *Legislation*. www.legislation.gov.uk/ukpga/2018/12/contents/enacted

David, M. E. (2014). *Feminism, gender and universities: Politics, passion and pedagogies*. Routledge.

Davies, B., & Harré, R. (1990). Positioning: The discursive production of selves. *Journal for the Theory of Social Behaviour*, 20(1), 43–63. 10.1111/j.1468-5914.1990.tb00174.x

Davies, J. A., Davies, L. J., Conlon, B., Emerson, J., Hainsworth, H., & McDonough, H. G. (2020). Responding to COVID-19 in EAP Contexts: A Comparison of Courses at Four Sino-Foreign Universities. *International Journal of TESOL Studies*, 2(2), 32–51. 10.46451/ijts.2020.09.04

Davitashvili, Z. Elizbarashvili, & N. Beruchashvili, N. (2014). *Geography of Georgia*. Meridiani.

Day, C., Sammons, P., Hopkins, D., Harris, A., Leithwood, K., Gu, Q., Brown, E., Atharidou, E., & Kington, A. (2009). *The Impact of School Leadership on Pupil Outcomes: Final Report*. London: DCSF.

Day, C. (2018). Professional identity matters: Agency, emotions, and resilience. In *Research on teacher identity* (pp. 61–70). Springer International Publishing. 10.1007/978-3-319-93836-3_6

Day, C., & Leithwood, K. (2007). *Successful principal leadership in times of change*. Springer. 10.1007/1-4020-5516-1

Day, C., & Sammons, P. (2013). *Successful Leadership: A Review of the International Literature*. CFBT Education Trust.

De Costa, P. I., & Norton, B. (2017). Introduction: Identity, transdisciplinarity, and the good language teacher. *Modern Language Journal*, 101(S1), 3–14. 10.1111/modl.12368

Delello, J. A., McWhorter, R. R., & Camp, K. M. (2015). Integrating augmented reality in higher education: A multidisciplinary study of student perceptions. *Journal of Educational Multimedia and Hypermedia*, 24(3), 209–233.

Demissie, A., & Gajendran, A. (2016). *The Influence of Various Leadership Styles on Acceleration of Organizational Performance in Government Bureaus of Benishangul Gumuz Region*.

Denker, K., & Dougherty, D. (2013). Corporate colonization of couples' work-life negotiations: Rationalization, emotion management and silencing conflict. *Journal of Family Communication*, 13(3), 242–262. 10.1080/15267431.2013.796946

DePape, A. M., Barnes, M., & Petryschuk, J. (2019). Students' experiences in higher education with virtual and augmented reality: A qualitative systematic review. *Innovative Practice in Higher Education*, 3(3).

Devos, A. (2008). Where enterprise and equity meet: The rise of mentoring for women in Australian universities. *Discourse (Abingdon)*, 29(2), 195–205. 10.1080/01596300801966831

Devraj, R., Castleberry, A. N., Alvarez, N. A., Persky, A. M., and Poirier, T. I. (2023). Pharmacy Leaders' Advice to Students Pursuing Leadership: A Qualitative Study. *Innovations in Pharmacy*, 14(3), 10-. Available at: https://doi.org/10.24926/iip.v14i3.5528

DeWitt, J., & Storksdieck, M. (2008). A short review of school field trips: Key findings from the past and implications for the future. *Visitor Studies*, 11(2), 181–197. 10.1080/10645570802355562

Dezsö, C. L., & Ross, D. G. (2012). Does female representation in top management improve firm performance? A panel data investigation. *Strategic Management Journal*, 33(9), 1072–1089. 10.1002/smj.1955

Dilshad, M., Hussain, B., & Batool, H. (2019). Continuous professional development of teachers: A case of public universities in Pakistan. *Bulletin of Education and Research*, 41(3), 119–130.

Dinh, J. E., Lord, R. G., Gardner, W. L., Meuser, J. D., Liden, R. C., & Hu, J. (2014). Leadership theory and research in the new millennium: Current theoretical trends and changing perspectives. *The Leadership Quarterly*, 25(1), 36–62. 10.1016/j.leaqua.2013.11.005

Dizon, G., & Gayed, J. M. (2021). Examining the impact of Grammarly on the quality of mobile L2 writing. *The JALT CALL Journal*, 17(2), 74–92. 10.29140/jaltcall.v17n2.336

Compilation of References

Dodge, K. A., Gilroy, F. D., & Fenzel, L. M. (1995). Requisite management characteristics revisited: Two decades later. *Journal of Social Behavior and Personality*, 10, 253–264.

Dollard, C. (2018). *Emotional intelligence is key to successful leadership.* [Online]. Retrieved April 24, 2024, from http://www.gottman.com/blog/emotional-intelligence-key-successful-leadership/

Donato, R. (2016). Becoming a language teaching professional: What's identity got to do with it? In Barkhuizen, G. (Ed.), *Reflections on language teacher identity research (pp. 32e38).* Routledge.

Dörnyei, Z. (2007). *Research methods in applied linguistics.* Oxford University Press.

Dornyei, Z. (2007). *Research Methods in Applied Linguistics: Quantitative, Qualitative, and Mixed Methodologies.* Oxford University Press.

Drachsler, H., & Kalz, M. (2016). The impact of artificial intelligence and analytics on educational practices and student learning. *Journal of Educational Technology & Society*, 19(2), 34–49.

Drake, I., & Svenkerud, S. W. (2023). Career ambitions of women academics: Are women willing and able to rise to the top in higher education institutions? *Studies in Higher Education*, 1–12. Advance online publication. 10.1080/03075079.2023.2272742

Duckworth, A. (2018). *Grit: The power of passion and perseverance.* Scribner.

Duff, P. (2007). *Case study Research in applied linguistics.* Lawrence Erlbaum Associates.

Duff, P. (2018). *Case study research in applied linguistics.* Routledge. 10.4324/9780203827147

Dugan, J. P., Garland, J. L., Jacoby, B., & Gasiorski, A. (2008). Understanding commuter student self-efficacy for leadership: A within-group analysis. *NASPA Journal*, 45(2), 282–310. 10.2202/1949-6605.1951

Duhigg, C. (2012). *The Power of Habit: Why we do what we do in Life and Business.* Random House.

Duhigg, C. (2024). *Supercommunicators: How to Unlock the Secret Language of Communication.* Random House.

Duressa, Z., & Asfaw, M. (2014). Transformational leadership and its applications in the public service organizations of Ethiopia. *International Affairs and Global Strategy*, 23. Available:www.worldcatlibraries.org/wcpa/ow/02d077080fcf3210a19afeb4da09e526.html

Eagly, A. H., & Carli, L. L. (2007). Women and the labyrinth of leadership. *Harvard Business Review*, 85(9), 62–71.17886484

Eagly, A. H., & Johannesen-Schmidt, M. C. (2001). The leadership styles of women and men. *The Journal of Social Issues*, 57(4), 781–797. 10.1111/0022-4537.00241

Eagly, A. H., & Karau, S. J. (2002). Role congruity theory of prejudice toward female leaders. *Psychological Review*, 109(3), 573–598. 10.1037/0033-295X.109.3.57312088246

Eagly, A. H., Wood, W., & Diekman, A. B. (2000). Social role theory of sex differences and similarities: A current appraisal. In Eckes, T., & Trautner, H. M. (Eds.), *The developmental social psychology of gender* (pp. 123–174). Erlbaum.

Eby, L. T., Allen, T. D., Evans, S. C., Ng, T., & Dubois, D. (2008). Does mentoring matter? A multidisciplinary meta-analysis comparing mentored and non-mentored individuals. *Journal of Vocational Behavior*, 72(2), 254–267. 10.1016/j.jvb.2007.04.00519343074

Eison, J. (2010). Using active learning instructional strategies to create excitement and enhance learning. Jurnal Pendidikantentang Strategi Pembelajaran Aktif (Active Learning). *Books*, 2(1), 1–10.

Ellis, R., & Barkhuizen, G. (2005). *Analysing learner language*. Oxford University Press.

Ellis, R., & Goodyear, P. (2019). *The Education Ecology of Universities: Integrating Learning, Strategy and the Academy*. Routledge. 10.4324/9781351135863

Elsheikh, A., & Yahia, E. (2020). Language Teacher Professional Identity. In *Professionalizing Your English Language Teaching* (pp. 27–38). Springer. 10.1007/978-3-030-34762-8_3

Ely, R. J., & Padavic, I. (2007). A feminist analysis of organizational research on sex differences. *Academy of Management Review*, 32(4), 1121–1143. 10.5465/amr.2007.26585842

Encyclopedy, G. (2011). *Tbilisi State University*. TSU.

Epitropaki, O., & Martin, R. (2005). The moderating role of individual differences in the relation between transformational/transactional leadership perceptions and organizational identification. *The Leadership Quarterly*, 16(4), 569–589. 10.1016/j.leaqua.2005.06.005

Epitropaki, O., & Martin, R. (2005a). From ideal to real: A longitudinal study of the role of implicit leadership theories on leader-member exchanges and employee outcomes. *The Journal of Applied Psychology*, 90(4), 659–676. 10.1037/0021-9010.90.4.65916060785

Ericsson, A., & Pool, R. (2016). *Peak: Secrets from the New Science of Expertise*. HarperOne.

Essel, H. (2023). 7 things you should know about ChatGPT. Available at OSF | 7 THINGS YOU SHOULD KNOW ABOUT CHATGPT [Accessed 27 April 27, 2024]

Etikan, I., Musa, S., & Alkassim, R. (2016). Comparison of Convenience Sampling and Purposive Sampling. *American Journal of Theoretical and Applied Statistics*, 5(1), 1–4. 10.11648/j.ajtas.20160501.11

European Commission Eu Science Hub (2022) Available at: DigCompEdu - European Commission (europa.eu) [Accessed 22 February 2024]

European Commission. (2021) She Figures 2021. The path towards gender equality in research and innovation (R&I). Luxembourg: Publications Office of the European Union. https://op.europa.eu/en/web/eu-law-and-publications/publication-detail/-/publication/61564e1f-d55e-11eb-895a-01aa75ed71a1

Fabriz, S., Mendzheritskaya, J., & Stehle, S. (2021). Impact of synchronous and asynchronous settings of online teaching and learning in higher education on students' learning experience during COVID-19. *Frontiers in Psychology*, 12, 733554. 10.3389/fpsyg.2021.73355434707542

Farouk, S. (2012). What can the self-conscious emotion of guilt tell us about primary school teachers' moral purpose and the relationships they have with their pupils? *Teachers and Teaching*, 18(4), 491–507. 10.1080/13540602.2012.696049

Fathima, F., Awor, P., Yen, Y., Gnanaselvam, N., & Zakham, F. (2020). Challenges and coping strategies face by female scientists – A multicentric cross sectional study. *PLoS One*, 15(9), e0238635. 10.1371/journal.pone.023863532956356

Fawaz, M., & Samaha, A. (2021). E-learning: Depression, anxiety, and stress symptomatology among Lebanese university students during COVID-19 quarantine. *Nursing Forum*, 56(1), 52–57. 10.1111/nuf.1252133125744

Fennell, S., & Arnot, M. (2009). *Gender Education and Equality in a Global Context: Conceptual Frameworks and Policy Perspectives*. Routledge.

Ferdinand-James, D., & Medina-Charles, C. (2020), May. Peer Review of Classroom Teaching: Addressing Student, Lecturer, and Institutional Improvement Using an Academic Literacy Approach. In The UWI Quality Education Forum (No. 24).

Ferguson, G., Pérez-Llantada, C., & Plo, R. (2011). English as an international language of scientific publication: A study of attitudes. *World Englishes*, 30(1), 41–59. 10.1111/j.1467-971X.2010.01656.x

Field, E., Krivkovich, A., Kügele, S., Robinson, N., & Yee, L. (2023, October 5). Women in the workplace 2023, Mckinsey & Company, https://www.mckinsey.com/featured-insights/diversity-and-inclusion/women-in-the-workplace#/

Fierman, J. (1990). Why women still don't hit the top. *Fortune*, 122(3), 40.

Fitria, T. N. (2021). QuillBot as an online tool: Students' alternative in paraphrasing and rewriting of English writing. *Englisia: Journal of Language, Education, and Humanities*, 9(1), 183–196. 10.22373/ej.v9i1.10233

Fitzgerald, T. (2013). *Women Leaders in Higher Education: Shattering the myths* (1st ed.). Routledge. 10.4324/9780203491515

Florian, L. (2005). Inclusive practice: What, why and how. The Routledge Falmer reader in inclusive education, pp.29-40.

Flowerdew, J. (2000). Discourse community, legitimate peripheral participation, and the nonnative-English-speaking scholar. *TESOL Quarterly*, 34(1), 127–150. 10.2307/3588099

Foote, J. A., Trofimovich, P., Collins, L., & Urzúa, F. S. (2016). Pronunciation teaching practices in communicative second language classes. *Language Learning Journal*, 44(2), 181–196.

Foreign Language and Literature Major Teaching Supervising Committee. English, M. T. S. S.-C., Ministry of Education. (2020). *Teaching Guide for Undergraduate Foreign Language and Literature Major in Ordinary Colleges and Universities (Part 1): Teaching Guide for English Majors*. Foreign Language Teaching and Research Press.

Foreign Languages Teaching Committee for Higher Education of Ministry of Education. (2020). *Guidelines for College English Teaching*. Higher Education Press.

Foreman-Brown, G., Fitzpatrick, E., & Twyford, K.Foreman-Browna. (2023). Reimagining teacher identity in the post-Covid-19 university: Becoming digitally savvy, reflective in practice, collaborative, and relational. *Educational and Developmental Psychologists*, 40(1), 18–26. 10.1080/20590776.2022.2079406

Foschi, M. (2000). Double standards for competence: Theory and research. *Annual Review of Sociology*, 26(1), 21–42. 10.1146/annurev.soc.26.1.21

Fox Cabane, O. (2013). *The charisma myth: How anyone can master the art and science of personal magnetism*. Portfolio.

Francois, E. J. (2016). What is Transnational Education? In Francois, E., Avoseh, M., & Griswold, W. (Eds.), *Perspectives in Transnational Higher Education* (pp. 3–23). Sense Publishers. 10.1007/978-94-6300-420-6_1

Freeman, Jr., S. T.-R., Douglas, M. O., & Goodenough, T. (2020). Toward best practices for promotion to full professor guidelines at research universities. *eJEP: eJournal of Education Policy,* 21(2), n2.

Frenzel, A. C., Pekrun, R., & Goetz, T. (2010). *Achievement emotions questionnaire for teachers (AEQ-teacher) - User's manual*. University of Munich.

Frenzel, A. C., Pekrun, R., Goetz, T., Daniels, L. M., Durksen, T. L., Becker-Kurz, B., & Klassen, R. M. (2016). Measuring Teachers' enjoyment, anger, and anxiety: The Teacher Emotions Scales (TES). *Contemporary Educational Psychology*, 46, 148–163. 10.1016/j.cedpsych.2016.05.003

Fry, K. (2001). E-learning markets and providers: Some issues and prospects. *Education + Training*, 43(4), 233–239. 10.1108/EUM0000000005484

Fu, J. (2023). *Distributed Leadership in University Quality Management: An Exploration in a Sino-Foreign Cooperative University in China*. Ph.D. The University of Liverpool (United Kingdom). Available from: ProQuest Dissertations Publishing, 30713114.

Fuentes, M. A., Zelaya, D. G., & Madsen, J. W. (2021). Rethinking the course syllabus: Considerations for promoting equity, diversity, and inclusion. *Teaching of Psychology*, 48(1), 69–79. 10.1177/0098628320959979

Galloway, N., & Rose, H. (2022). Cross-fertilisation not bifurcation of EMI and EAP. *ELT Journal*, 76(4), 538–546. Retrieved March 16th, 2024, from https://academic.oup.com/eltj/article/76/4/538/6694743. 10.1093/elt/ccac033

Gao, X., Tao, J., & Gong, Y. (2018). A sociocultural inquiry on teacher agency and professional identity in curriculum reforms. *Foreign Languages and Their Teaching, 298*(1), 19-28+146. 10.13458/j.cnki.flatt.004453

Gardner, R. (2019). Classroom interaction research: The state of the art. *Research on Language and Social Interaction*, 52(3), 212–226. 10.1080/08351813.2019.1631037

GAU. (2024). Academic Information. Retrieved from: https://www.gau.edu.ge/ka

Gemeda, H. K., & Lee, J. (2020). Leadership styles, work engagement and outcomes among information and communications technology professionals: A cross-national study. *Heliyon*, 6(4), e03699. 10.1016/j.heliyon.2020.e0369932280799

Geostat, (2023). Number of Schools in Georgia. Retrieved from: https://www.geostat.ge/ka/modules/categories/59/zogadi-ganatleba

Gerace, A., Day, A., Casey, S., & Mohr, P. (2017). *I think, You think*. Understanding the Importance of Self Refection to the Taking of Another Person's Perspective., 10.1017/jrr.2017.8

Gergen, M. M., & Gergen, K. J. (2006). Narratives in action. *Narrative Inquiry*, 16(1), 112–121. 10.1075/ni.16.1.15ger

Ghani, A., (2023). GPT Zero Is Designed To Recognize Texts Written By AI. GPT Zero Is Designed To Recognize Texts Written By AI | by Abdul Ghani | *DataDrivenInvestor*. [Accessed 26 April 2024].

Ghoneim, N. M. M., & Elghotmy, H. E. A. (2016). Using Voice Thread to Develop EFL Pre-Service Teachers' Speaking Skills. *Online Submission*, 4(6), 13–31.

Gibbs, G. (1988). *Learning by doing: A guide to teaching and learning methods*. Further Education Unit.

Gilakjani, A. P., & Sabouri, N. B. (2017). Teachers' Beliefs in English Language Teaching and Learning: A Review of the Literature. *English Language Teaching*, 10(4), 78–86. 10.5539/elt.v10n4p78

Gill, R. (2012). *Theory and Practice of Leadership* [online]. SAGE Publications., Available at https://appgateway.nottingham.edu.cn/https/77726476706e69737468656265737421f5f54e932c336d5e6a1a88a0d645313a98a42f1fdc31dea63b/lib/nottingham/reader.action?docID=7102286&query=Leadership%3A+Theory+and+Practice

Gill, S. S., Xu, M., Patros, P., Wu, H., Kaur, R., Kaur, K., Fuller, S., Singh, M., Arora, P., Parlikad, A. K., Stankovski, V., Abraham, A., Ghosh, S. K., Lutfiyya, H., Kanhere, S. S., Bahsoon, R., Rana, O., Dustdar, S., Sakellariou, R., & Buyya, R. (2024). Transformative effects of ChatGPT on modern education: Emerging Era of AI Chatbots. *Internet of Things and Cyber-Physical Systems*, 4, 19–23. 10.1016/j.iotcps.2023.06.002

Gkonou, C., Mercer, S., & Daubney, M. (2018). Teacher perspectives on language learning psychology. *Language Learning Journal*, 46(4), 501–513. 10.1080/09571736.2016.1172330

Gladwell, M. (2008). *Outliers*. Penguin.

Gladwell, M. (2015). *David and Goliath*. Back Bay Books.

Gleason, J., & Suvorov, R. (2011). *Learner perceptions of asynchronous oral computer-mediated communication tasks using Wimba Voice for developing their L2 oral proficiency. The role of CALL in hybrid and online language courses.* Iowa State University.

Goberman, A. M., Hughes, S., & Haydock, T. (2011). Acoustic characteristics of public speaking: Anxiety and practice effects. *Speech Communication*, 53(6), 867–876. Advance online publication. 10.1016/j.specom.2011.02.005

Goh, C. C. M. (1994). Exploring the teaching of Discourse Intonation. *RELC Journal*, 25(1), 77–98. 10.1177/003368829402500104

Golombek, P., & Doran, M. (2014). Unifying cognition, emotion, and activity in language teacher professional development. *Teaching and Teacher Education*, 39, 102–111. 10.1016/j.tate.2014.01.002

Gov.UK. (2023). *How to prove and verify someone's identity.* https://www.gov.uk/government/publications/identity-proofing-and-verification-of-an-individual/how-to-prove-and-verify-someones-identity

Graham, S. (2019). Changing how writing is taught. *Review of Research in Education*, 43(1), 277–303. 10.3102/0091732X18821125

Grajek, S. (2020). EDUCAUSE COVID-19 QuickPoll Results: Grading and Proctoring. *EDUCAUSE Review*. Available at: https://er.educause.edu/blogs/2020/4/educause-covid-19-quickpoll-results-grading-and-proctoring [Accessed: Feb.27th,2024].

Grann, D. (2023). *The Wager.* Simon & Schuster. Ferguson, A. (2016). *Leading.* Hachette Books. Ferruci, P. (2016). *The Power of Kindness: The Unexpected Benefits of Leading a Compassionate Life.* TarcherPerigee.

Gravel, J., D'Amours-Gravel, M., & Osmanlliu, E. (2023). Learning to fake it: Limited responses and fabricated references provided by ChatGPT for medical questions. *Mayo Clinic Proceedings. Digital Health*, 1(3), 226–234. 10.1016/j.mcpdig.2023.05.004

Greenier, V., Derakhshan, A., & Fathi, J. (2021). Emotion regulation and psychological well-being in teacher work engagement: A case of British and Iranian English language teachers. *System*, 97, 102446. 10.1016/j.system.2020.102446

Greenleaf, R. K. (1977). *Servant Leadership: A Journey into the Nature of Legitimate Power and Greatness.* Paulist Press.

Griffiths, S. (2008). Teaching and learning in small groups. In *A handbook for teaching and learning in higher education* (pp. 90–102). Routledge.

Grix, J. (2010). *The foundations of research.* Palgrave Macmillan. 10.1007/978-0-230-36490-5

Guattari, F. (2000). *The Three Ecologies.* Athlone Press.

Gudoniene, D., & Rutkauskiene, D. (2019). Virtual and augmented reality in education. *Baltic Journal of Modern Computing*, 7(2), 293–300. 10.22364/bjmc.2019.7.2.07

Gu, H., Mao, Y., & Wang, Q. (2022). Exploring EFL Teachers' Emotions and the Impact on Their Sustainable Professional Development in Livestream Teaching: A Chinese Case Study. *Sustainability (Basel)*, 14(8264), 8264. 10.3390/su14148264

Gu, H., Xie, R., Adam, D. C., Tsui, J. L. H., Chu, D. K., Chang, L. D., Cheuk, S. S. Y., Gurung, S., Krishnan, P., Ng, D. Y. M., Liu, G. Y. Z., Wan, C. K. C., Cheng, S. S. M., Edwards, K. M., Leung, K. S. M., Wu, J. T., Tsang, D. N. C., Leung, G. M., Cowling, B. J., & Poon, L. L. (2022). Genomic epidemiology of SARS-CoV-2 under an elimination strategy in Hong Kong. *Nature Communications*, 13(1), 1–10. 10.1038/s41467-022-28420-735136039

Gu, M., & Benson, P. (2015). The formation of English teacher identities: A cross-cultural investigation. *Language Teaching Research*, 19(2), 187–206. 10.1177/1362168814541725

Gurevych, R., Silveistr, A., Mokliuk, M., Shaposhnikova, I., Gordiichuk, G., & Saiapina, S. (2021). Using augmented reality technology in higher education institutions. *Postmodern Openings*, 12(2), 109–132. 10.18662/po/12.2/299

Gurgenidze, M. (2016). Education, Science, and Health in Georgia in the Post-Soviet Period. Retrieved from: https://gtu.ge/bef/pdf/Doqtorantura/avtoreferatebi_2016/Soc-mecn_05.07.16/m.gurgeniZe.pdf

Gurin, P., Dey, E. L., Hurtado, S., & Gurin, G. (2002). Diversity and higher education: Theory and impact on educational outcomes. *Harvard Educational Review*, 72(3), 330–366. 10.17763/haer.72.3.01151786u134n051

Hadley, G. (1996). A Discourse Approach to Intonation: Can it Work in Japan? Available at: http://www.cels.bham.ac.uk/resources/essays/HadleyPhon.PDF (accessed 11 August 2021).

Hahn, L. D. (2004). Primary stress and intelligibility: Research to motivate the teaching of suprasegmentals. *TESOL Quarterly*, 38(2), 201–223. 10.2307/3588378

Haidt, J. (2021). *The Happiness Hypothesis*. Random House.

Hailikari, T., Virtanen, V., Vesalainen, M., & Postareff, L. (2022). Student perspectives on how different elements of constructive alignment support active learning. *Active Learning in Higher Education*, 23(3), 217–231. 10.1177/1469787421989160

Halliday, M.A.K., & Greaves, W.. (2008). *Intonation in the Grammar of English*. Equinox.

Halliday, M.K. (1967). *Intonation and Grammar in British English*. Mouton.

Halliday, M.K. (1970). *A Course in Spoken English: Intonation*. Oxford University Press.

Hallinger, P., & Heck, R. H. (2002). *What Do You Call People With Visions? The Role of Vision, Mission, and Goals in School Leadership and Improvement*. Second International Handbook of Educational Leadership and Administration., 10.1007/978-94-010-0375-9_2

Hampel, R., & Baber, E. (2003). Using Internet-based audio-graphic and video conferencing for language teaching and learning. In Felix, U. (Ed.), *Language learning online: Towards best practice*. Swets and Zeitlinger.

Hampel, R., & Hauck, M. (2004). Towards an effective use of audio conferencing in distance language courses. *Language Learning & Technology*, 8(1), 66–82. http://llt.msu.edu/vol8num1/hampel/default.html

Hang, Y. and Zhang, X. (2022). How Chinese students manage their transition to higher education effectively: student initiative at Sino-Foreign cooperative universities. *Asia Pacific Journal of Education*, [online] 42(4), pp.517-533. Available at: https://doi.org/10.1080/02188791.2022.2047610

Haniford, L. C. (2010). Tracing one teacher candidate's discursive identity work. *Teaching and Teacher Education, 26*, 987e996

Hanna, F., Oostdam, R., Severiens, S. E., & Zijlstra, B. J. (2020). Assessing the professional identity of primary student teachers: Design and validation of the Teacher Identity Measurement Scale. *Studies in Educational Evaluation*, 64, 100822. 10.1016/j.stueduc.2019.100822

Hannah, S. T., & Avolio, B. J. (2010). Ready or not: How do we accelerate the developmental readiness of leaders? *Journal of Organizational Behavior*, 31(8), 1181–1187. 10.1002/job.675

Han, S. (2023). English medium instruction at Sino-foreign cooperative education institutions in China: Is internationalising teaching and learning possible? *Language, Culture and Curriculum*, 36(1), 83–99. 10.1080/07908318.2022.2032127

Haque, M. N., & Sharmin, S. (2022). Perception of Saudi Students About Non-Native English Teachers and Native English Teachers in Teaching English at Jazan University. *Journal of Language Teaching and Research*, 13(3), 503–514. 10.17507/jltr.1303.06

Hargrave, S. J. (2016). *Mind hacking: How to change your mind for good in 21 days*. Gallery Books.

Hargreaves, A. (2001). Emotional geographies of teaching. *Teachers College Record*, 103(6), 1056–1080. 10.1111/0161-4681.00142

Harper, J., & Sun, Y. (2022). EAP Courses in Joint-Venture Institutions: A Needs Analysis Based on Learner Perceptions. *Indonesian Journal of English Language Teaching and Applied Linguistics*, 7(1), 159–179. 10.21093/ijeltal.v7i1.1282

Harris, A. (2008). *Distributed school leadership: Developing tomorrow's leaders*. Routledge. https://www.routledge.com/Distributed-School-Leadership- Developing-Tomorrows-Leaders/Harris/p/book/9780415419581

Hartanto, D., Kampmann, I. L., Morina, N., Emmelkamp, P. M. G., Neerincx, M. A., & Brinkman, W. P. (2014). Controlling social stress in virtual reality environments. *PLoS One*, 9(3), 1–17. 10.1371/journal.pone.009280424671006

Hart, C. (2019). Education, inequality and social justice: A critical analysis applying the Sen-Bourdieu Analytical Framework. *Policy Futures in Education*, 17(5), 582–598. 10.1177/1478210318809758

Hartog, D. N., Muijen, J. J., & Koopman, P. L. (1997). Transactional versus transformational leadership: An analysis of the MLQ. *Journal of Occupational and Organizational Psychology*, 70(1), 19–34. 10.1111/j.2044-8325.1997.tb00628.x

Hasanein, A. M., & Sobaih, A. E. E. (2023). Drivers and Consequences of ChatGPT Use in Higher Education: Key Stakeholder Perspectives. *European Journal of Investigation in Health, Psychology and Education*, 13(11), 2599–2614. 10.3390/ejihpe1311018137998071

Hasson, G., & Buttler, D. (2020). *Mental Health and Wellbeing in the Workplace: A Practical Guide for Employers and Employees*. Capstone.

Hater, J. J., & Bass, B. M. (1988). 'Superiors' evaluations and subordinates' perceptions of transformational and transactional leadership'. *The Journal of Applied Psychology*, 73(4), 695–715. 10.1037/0021-9010.73.4.695

Haug, P. (2017). Understanding inclusive education: Ideals and reality. *Scandinavian Journal of Disability Research*, 19(3), 206–217. 10.1080/15017419.2016.1224778

Hayik, R., & Weiner-Levy, N. (2019). Prospective Arab teachers' emotions as mirrors to their identities and culture. *Teaching and Teacher Education, 85*, 36e44.

Heilman, M. E., Block, C. J., & Martell, R. F. (1995). Sex stereotypes: Do they influence perceptions of managers? *Journal of Social Behavior and Personality*, 10, 237–252.

Helgesen, S. (1990). *The Female Advantage: Women's Ways of Leadership*. Doubleday Currency.

Henriksen, N. C., Geeslin, K. L., & Willis, E. W. (2010). The development of L2 Spanish intonation during a study abroad immersion program in Leó n, Spain: Global contours and final boundary movements. *Studies in Hispanic and Lusophone Linguistics*, 3(1), 113–162. 10.1515/shll-2010-1067

Herbold, S., Hautli-Janisz, A., Heuer, U., Kikteva, Z., & Trautsch, A. (2023). A large-scale comparison of human-written versus ChatGPT-generated essays. *Scientific Reports*, 13(1), 18617. 10.1038/s41598-023-45644-937903836

Herman, H., & Chiu, W. C. (2014). Transformational leadership and job performance: A social identity perspective. *Journal of Business Research*, 67(1), 2827–2835. 10.1016/j.jbusres.2012.07.018

Herman, K. C., Sebastian, J., Reinke, W. M., & Huang, F. L. (2021). Individual and school predictors of teacher stress, coping, and wellness during the COVID-19 pandemic. *School Psychology*, 36(6), 483–493. 10.1037/spq000045634766812

Hern, A. (2022) 'AI-assisted plagiarism? ChatGPT bot says it has an answer for that', The Guardian. Available at: https://www.theguardian.com/technology/2022/dec/31/ai-assisted-plagiarism-chatgpt-bot-says-it-has-an-answer-for-that [Accessed: 2 February 2023].

Herring, C. (2009). Does diversity pay?: Race, gender, and the business case for diversity. *American Sociological Review*, 74(2), 208–224. 10.1177/000312240907400203

HESA. (2019). *Where do HE students come from? Higher education statistics agency.* https://www.hesa.ac.uk/data-and-analysis/students/where-from (Accessed 25 Jan 2024)

Hewings, M & Thaine, C. (2012). *Cambridge Academic English C1 Advanced Student's Book: An Integrated Skills Course for EAP* (1st edn). Cambridge

Hewings, M. (2007). *English Pronunciation in Use Advanced with Answers* (1st ed.).

Hewitt, E., & Stephenson, J. (2012). Foreign Language Anxiety and Oral Exam Performance: A Replication of Phillips's MLJ Study. *Modern Language Journal*, 96(2), 170–189. 10.1111/j.1540-4781.2011.01174.x

Hew, K. F., Huang, W., Du, J., & Jia, C. (2023). Using chatbots to support pupil goal setting and social presence in fully online activities: Learner engagement and perceptions. *Journal of Computing in Higher Education*, 5(1), 40–68. 10.1007/s12528-022-09338-x36101883

High, M. (2023). The Perils and Potential Benefits of Machine Translation in Transnational Higher Education. In Morris, G & Li. L. (Eds). *Developments and Future Trends in Transnational Higher Education* (pp. 115-135). Hershey: IGI Global. 10.4018/978-1-6684-5226-4.ch006

Higher Education Academy. (2015) 'UKPSF Dimensions of the Framework -demonstrate experience'. Available at: https://www.heacademy.ac.uk/system/files/downloads/ukpsf_dimensions_of_the_framework.pdf

Hill, L. H., & Wheat, C. A. (2017). The influence of mentorship and role models on university women leaders' career paths to university presidency. *The Qualitative Report*, 22(8), 2090–2111. 10.46743/2160-3715/2017.2437

Hirotani, M. (2013). Synchronous versus asynchronous CMC and transfer to Japanese oral performance. *CALICO Journal*, 26(2), 413–438. 10.1558/cj.v26i2.413-438

Hodges, C., Moore, S., Lockee, B., Trust, T., & Bond, A. (2020). The difference between emergency remote teaching and online learning.

Hodgson, P., Lee, V. W., Chan, J. C., Fong, A., Tang, C. S., Chan, L., & Wong, C. (2019). Immersive virtual reality (IVR) in higher education: Development and implementation. Augmented reality and virtual reality: The power of AR and VR for business, 161-173.

Hofstede, G., Garibaldi de Hilal, A. V., Malvezzi, S., Tanure, B., & Vinken, H. (2010). Comparing Regional Cultures Within a Country: Lessons From Brazil. *Journal of Cross-Cultural Psychology*, 41(3), 336–352. 10.1177/0022022109359696

Hollander, E. J. (1978). *Leadership dynamics: A practical guide to effective relationships*. Free Press.

Hong, J., Nie, Y., Heddy, B., Monobe, G., Ruan, J., You, S., & Kambara, H. (2016). Revising and validating Achievement Emotions Questionnaire-teachers (AEQ-T). *International Journal of Educational Psychology*, 5(1), 80–107. 10.17583/ijep.2016.1395

Hoogendoorn, S., Oosterbeek, H., & van Praag, M. (2013). The impact of gender diversity on the performance of business teams: Evidence from a field experiment. *Management Science*, 59(7), 1514–1528. 10.1287/mnsc.1120.1674

Horwitz, E. K., Horwitz, M. B., & Cope, J. A. (1986). Foreign language classroom anxiety. *Modern Language Journal*, 70(2), 125–132. 10.1111/j.1540-4781.1986.tb05256.x

Housen, A., Kuiken, F., & Vedder, I. (Eds.). (2012). *Dimensions of L2 performance and proficiency: Complexity, accuracy and fluency in SLA* (Vol. 32). John Benjamins Publishing. 10.1075/lllt.32

Houston, D., Meyer, L. H., & Paewai, S. (2006). Academic staff workloads and job satisfaction: Expectations and values in academe. *Journal of Higher Education Policy and Management*, 28(1), 17–30. 10.1080/13600800500283734

Hrastinski, S. (2008). Asynchronous and synchronous e-learning. *EDUCAUSE Quarterly*, 31(4), 51–55.

Hu, P., & Liu, W. (2022). An investigation into the status quo of college English teachers' teaching competence in course-based political and virtuous awareness. *Technology Enhanced Foreign Language Education, 207*(5), 11-17+106.

Huang, Y., & Sun, L. (2023). Harnessing the power of chatgpt in fake news: An in-depth exploration in generation, detection and explanation. *arXiv preprint arXiv:2310.05046*.

Hue Kyung, L., Hyun Duk, Y., Si Jeoung, K., & Yoon Kyo, S. (2016). Factors affecting university–industry cooperation performance: Study of the mediating effects of government and enterprise support. *Journal of Science and Technology Policy Management*, 7(2), 233–254. 10.1108/JSTPM-08-2015-0029

Hussein, M. A., Hassan, H., & Nassef, M. (2019). Automated language essay scoring systems: A literature review. *PeerJ. Computer Science*, 5, e208. 10.7717/peerj-cs.20833816861

Hwang, S. I., Lim, J. S., Lee, R. W., Matsui, Y., Iguchi, T., Hiraki, T., & Ahn, H. (2023). Is ChatGPT a "fire of prometheus" for non-native English-speaking researchers in academic writing? *Korean Journal of Radiology*, 24(10), 952. 10.3348/kjr.2023.077337793668

Hymowitz, C., & Schellhardt, T. D. (1986). The glass ceiling: Why women can't break the invisible barrier that blocks them from top jobs. *The Wall Street Journal*, 1(4), 1D-24D.

Ibatova, A. (2022). An Investigation of EFL Learners' Speaking Anxiety and Motivation in Face-to-Face and Synchronous Text-based Chat and Voice-based Chat Environment. *Computer Assisted Language Learning*, 23(2), 278–294.

IBSU. (2024). Main function of the University. Retrieved from: https://ibsu.edu.ge/ge/about-ibsu/

IBSU. (2024). Schools. Retrieved from: https://ibsu.edu.ge/ge/schools/

International Student Statistics in UK. (2023). *Kampus Group: Best Student Consultancy in London.* https://kampus-group.com/international-student-statistics-in-uk-2023-trends-insights-and-forecasts/#:~:text=According%20to%20the%20latest%20data,of%20the%20total%20student%20population. (Accessed 25 Jan 2024)

Ishiguro, K. (2015). *The Buried Giant*. Vintage.

Jacobs, J. A. (1992). Women's entry into management: Trends in earnings, authority, and values among salaried managers. *Administrative Science Quarterly*, 37(2), 282–301. 10.2307/2393225

Jamali, S., Shiratuddin, M. F., & Wong, K. (2014). An overview of mobile-augmented reality in higher education. *International Journal on Recent Trends In Engineering & Technology*, 11(1), 229–238.

James, M.A. (2023) "An exploratory investigation of instructors' practices and challenges in promoting students' learning transfer in EAP education," *Journal of EAPs*, 64.

Jansen, J. J., Vera, D., & Crossan, M. (2009). Strategic leadership for exploration and exploitation: The moderating role of environmental dynamism. *The Leadership Quarterly*, 20(1), 5–18. 10.1016/j.leaqua.2008.11.008

Jantjies, M., Moodley, T., & Maart, R. (2018, December). Experiential learning through virtual and augmented reality in higher education. In *Proceedings of the 2018 international conference on education technology management* (pp. 42-45). 10.1145/3300942.3300956

Javakhishvili, I. (2016). *Political and Social Movement in the 19th Century of Georgia*. Institute of History of Ethnology.

Jeidani, M. (2012). *Increasing Phonological Awareness: A Discourse Intonation Approach*. PhD Thesis, University of Warwick, UK.

Jeidani, M. (2014). "Discourse Intonation and Teacher Cognition" *Sino-US English Teaching*, ISSN 1539-8072, Vol. 11, No. 10.

Jeltova, I., Birney, D., Fredine, N., Jarvin, L., Sternberg, R. J., & Grigorenko, E. L. (2007). Dynamic assessment as a process-oriented assessment in educational settings. *Advances in Speech Language Pathology*, 9(4), 273–285. 10.1080/14417040701460390

Jenkins, J. (2000). *The Phonology of English as an International Language*. Oxford University Press.

Jenkins, J. (2004). Research in Teaching Pronunciation and Intonation. *Annual Review of Applied Linguistics*, 24, 109–125.

Jeongyeon, K., & Hye Young, S. (2020). Negotiation of emotions in emerging language teacher identity of graduate instructors. *System*, 95, 102365. Advance online publication. 10.1016/j.system.2020.102365

Jiao, W., Wang, W., Huang, J. T., Wang, X., Shi, S., & Tu, Z. (2023). Is ChatGPT a good translator? Yes with GPT-4 as the engine. *arXiv preprint arXiv:2301.08745*.

Johnson, D. W., Johnson, R. T., & Smith, K. A. (2014). Cooperative learning: Improving university instruction by basing practice on validated theory. *Journal on Excellence in University Teaching*, 25(4), 1–26.

Johnsrud, L. K. (1991). Administrative promotion: The power of gender. *The Journal of Higher Education*, 62(2), 119–149.

Johnsrud, L. K., & Heck, R. H. (1994). Administrative promotion within a university: The cumulative impact of gender. *The Journal of Higher Education*, 65(1), 23–44. 10.1080/00221546.1994.11778472

Johnston, B. (2002). *Values in English language teaching*. Routledge.

Johnston, B., & Buzzelli, C. A. (2008). The moral dimensions of language education. In Hornberger, N. H. (Ed.), *Encyclopedia of Language and Education* (pp. 95–104). Springer US., 10.1007/978-0-387-30424-3_8

Johnston, B., Juhász, A., Marken, J., & Ruiz, B. R. (1998). The ESL teacher as moral agent. *Research in the Teaching of English*, 32(2), 161–181.

Jonasson, C., Lauring, J., Selmer, J., & Trembath, J. L. (2017). Job resources and demands for expatriate academics: Linking teacher-student relations, intercultural adjustment, and job satisfaction. *Journal of Global Mobility*, 5(1), 5–21. 10.1108/JGM-05-2016-0015

Jöns, H. (2011). Transnational academic mobility and gender. *Globalisation, Societies and Education*, 9(2), 183–209. 10.1080/14767724.2011.577199

Judge, T. A., & Piccolo, R. F. (2004). Transformational and transactional leadership: A meta-analytic test of their relative validity. *The Journal of Applied Psychology*, 89(5), 755–768. 10.1037/0021-9010.89.5.75515506858

Kahneman, D. (2013). *Thinking Fast and Slow*. Farrar, Straus and Giroux.

Kahneman, D., Sibony, O., & Sunstein, C. (2021). *Noise*. William Collins.

Kahneman, D., Sibony, O., & Sunstein, C. (2022). *Noise: A flaw in human judgement*. William Collins.

Kaivanpanah, S., Alavi, S. M., Bruce, I., & Hejazi, S. Y. (2021). EAP in the expanding circle: Exploring the knowledge base, practices, and challenges of Iranian EAP practitioners. *Journal of English for Academic Purposes*, 50, 50. 10.1016/j.jeap.2021.100971

Kanno, Y., & Stuart, C. (2011). Learning to become a second language teacher: Identities-in-practice. *Modern Language Journal*, 95(2), 236–252. 10.1111/j.1540-4781.2011.01178.x

Kanter, R. (1977). *Men and Women of the Corporation*. Basic Books.

Karamchandani, K. (2020). *Frustration at the Workplace and Employee Attitude: A Study on It Professionals*. INTERNATIONAL JOURNAL OF ADVANCE RESEARCH AND INNOVATIVE IDEAS IN EDUCATION.

Karavas, E. (2010). How satisfied are Greek EFL teachers with their work? Investigating the motivation and job satisfaction levels of Greek EFL teachers.

Kasneci, E., Seßler, K., Küchemann, S., Bannert, M., Dementieva, D., Fischer, F., Gasser, U., Groh, G., Günnemann, S., Hüllermeier, E., Krusche, S., Kutyniok, G., Michaeli, T., Nerdel, C., Pfeffer, J., Poquet, O., Sailer, M., Schmidt, A., Seidel, T., & Kasneci, G. (2023). ChatGPT for good? On opportunities and challenges of large language models for education. *Learning and Individual Differences*, 103, 102274. 10.1016/j.lindif.2023.102274

Katai, Z., & Iclanzan, D. (2022). Impact of instructor on-slide presence in synchronous e-learning. *Education and Information Technologies*, 28(3), 3089–3115. 10.1007/s10639-022-11306-y36105376

Kay, A. (2018). *This is Going to Hurt*. Picador.

Kayi-Aydar, H. (2015). Teacher agency, positioning, and English language learners: Voices of pre-service classroom teachers. *Teaching and Teacher Education*, 45, 94–103. 10.1016/j.tate.2014.09.009

Kebede, M. S. (2020). *Transnational Educational Leadership of International Organizations Working in Ethiopia: Walking the Local-Global Development Tightrope* (Doctoral dissertation, The Pennsylvania State University).

Kebede, A. M., & Demeke, G. W. (2017). The influence of leadership styles on employees' job satisfaction in Ethiopian public universities. *Contemporary Management Research*, 13(3). Advance online publication. 10.7903/cmr.17668

Keim, R., Pfitscher, G., Leitner, S., Burger, K., Giacomoni, F., & Wiedermann, C. J. (2022). Teachers' emotional well-being during the SARS-CoV-2 pandemic with long school closures: A large-scale cross-sectional survey in Northern Italy. *Public Health*, 208, 1–8. 10.1016/j.puhe.2022.04.00635659680

Kelchtermans, G. (2005). Teachers' emotions in educational reforms: Self-understanding, vulnerable commitment and micropolitical literacy. *Teaching and Teacher Education*, 21(8), 995–1006. 10.1016/j.tate.2005.06.009

Kezar, A., & Holcombe, E. M. (2017). *Shared Leadership in Higher Education: Important Lessons from Research and Practice*. ACE Series on Higher Education. American Council on Education.

Kezar, A., & Lester, J. (2009). *Organizing higher education for collaboration: A guide for campus leaders*. Jossey-Bass.

Khaghaninejad, M. S., & Maleki, A. (2015). The effect of explicit pronunciation instruction on listening comprehension: Evidence from Iranian English learners. *Theory and Practice in Language Studies*, 5(6), 1249–1256. 10.17507/tpls.0506.18

Khan, S. (2023). How AI could save (not destroy) education. Available at: Sal Khan: How AI could save (not destroy) education | TED Talk [Accessed 3 May 2024]

Khan, S. (2023). *How AI Could Save (Not Destroy) Education*. Available from: https://www.ted.com/talks/sal_khan_how_ai_could_save_not_destroy_education

Kim, J. Y., & Meister, A. (2023). Microaggressions, interrupted: The experience and effects of gender microaggressions for women in STEM: JBE. *Journal of Business Ethics*, 185(3), 513–531. 10.1007/s10551-022-05203-0

Kim, N.-Y. (2022). AI-integrated mobile-assisted language learning: Is it an effective way of preparing for the TOEIC test in classroom environments? *English Teaching*, 77(3), 79–102. 10.15858/engtea.77.3.202209.79

Kim, S., & Shin, M. (2022). Effective Leadership Differs Between Organizations: A Comparative Study of US and German Multinational Corporations in South Korea. *SAGE Open*, 12(2). Advance online publication. 10.1177/21582440221097890

Kim, Y. M., & Greene, W. L. (2011). Aligning professional and personal identities: Applying core reflection in teacher education practice. *Studying Teacher Education*, 7(2), 109–119. 10.1080/17425964.2011.591132

Kira, D., Nebebe, F., & Saadé, R. G. (2018). The persistence of anxiety experienced by a new generation in online learning. In *In SITE 2018: Informing Science+ IT Education Conferences: La Verne California*, 079-088. 10.28945/4040

Kiran-Esen, B. (2012). Analyzing peer pressure and self-efficacy expectations among adolescents. *Social Behavior and Personality*, 40(8), 1301–1309. 10.2224/sbp.2012.40.8.1301

Kirkpatrick, A. (2014). English as a Medium of Instruction in East and Southeast Asian Universities. *The Asian Journal of Applied Linguistics*, 1(1), 3–15. 10.1007/978-94-007-7972-3_2

Klein, A. (2023). Strategies to Prepare Educators to Teach With AI. Education Week. Available at: https://www.edweek.org/technology/7-strategies-to-prepare-educators-to-teach-with-ai [Accessed 29 February 2024].

Kleinman, P. (2012). *Psych101*. Adams Media.

Kohnke, L., & Zou, D. (2021). Reflecting on Existing English for Academic Purposes Practices: Lessons for the Post-COVID Classroom. *Sustainability (Basel)*, 13(11520), 11520. Advance online publication. 10.3390/su132011520

Koraishi, O. (2023) 'Teaching English in the age of AI: Embracing ChatGPT to optimize EFL materials and assessment', *Language Education and Technology*, 3(1).

Korman, K., & Mujtaba, B. G. (2020). Corporate responses to COVID-19 layoffs in North America and the role of human resources departments. *Reports on Global Health Research*, 3(2), 1–17.

Kormos, J. (2015). Individual differences in second language speech production. In J. W. Schwieter (Ed.) *The Cambridge handbook of bilingual processing* (Cambridge Handbooks in Language and Linguistics). Cambridge University Press. 10.1017/CBO9781107447257.017

Köroglu, Z. Ç., & Çakir, A. (2017). Implementation of flipped instruction in language classrooms: An alternative way to develop speaking skills of pre-service English language teachers. *International Journal of Education and Development Using Information and Communication Technology*, 13(2), 42–55.

Kosmützky, A., & Putty, R. (2016). Transcending Borders and Traversing Boundaries: A Systematic Review of the Literature on Transnational, Offshore, Cross-border, and Borderless Higher Education. *Journal of Studies in International Education*, 20(1), 8–33. 10.1177/1028315315604719

Kötter, M. (2001). Developing distance language learners' interactive competence: Can synchronous audio do the trick? *International Journal of Educational Telecommunications*, 7, 327–353.

Kouzes, J. M., & Posner, B. Z. (2002). *The leadership challenge*. Wiley.

Kreitz-Sandberg, S. (2015). 'As an educator you have to fix many things on your own': A study of teachers' perspectives on organizing inclusion in various welfare contexts.

Kubanyiova, M. (2015). The role of teachers' future self guides in creating L2 development opportunities in teacher-led classroom discourse: Reclaiming the relevance of language teacher cognition. *Modern Language Journal*, 99(3), 565–584. 10.1111/modl.12244

Kukreti, S., Ahorsu, D. K., Strong, C., Chen, I. H., Lin, C. Y., Ko, N. Y., & Pakpour, A. H. (2021, September). Post-traumatic stress disorder in Chinese teachers during COVID-19 pandemic: Roles of fear of COVID-19, nomophobia, and psychological distress. []. MDPI.]. *Health Care*, 9(10), 1288.34682968

Kulis, S., Sicotte, D., & Collins, S. (2002). More than a pipeline problem: Labor supply constraints and gender stratification across academic science disciplines. *Research in Higher Education*, 43(6), 657–691. 10.1023/A:1020988531713

Kumar, R. (2023). Faculty members' use of artificial intelligence to grade student papers: A case of implications. *International Journal for Educational Integrity*, 19(1), 9. 10.1007/s40979-023-00130-7

Kurnaz, M. A., & Çimer, S. O. (2010). How do students know that they have learned? An investigation of students' strategies. *Procedia: Social and Behavioral Sciences*, 2(2), 3666–3672. 10.1016/j.sbspro.2010.03.570

Kvale, S. (1996). InterViews: An Introduction to Qualitative Research Interviewing. *Sage (Atlanta, Ga.)*.

Lane, P. (2012). *10,000 Hours: You Become What You Practice*. Couture Book.

Lan, L., & Mehta, C. (2022). Constructing collective agency through narrative positioning in group meetings within a Chinese professional team. *Language & Communication*, 87, 179–190. 10.1016/j.langcom.2022.07.008

Larrivee, B. (1985). *Effective teaching for successful mainstreaming*. Longman Publishing Group.

Latif, E., & Zhai, X. (2024). Fine-tuning ChatGPT for automatic scoring. Computers and Education. *Artificial Intelligence*, •••, 100210.

Lave, J., & Wenger, E. (1991). *Situated learning: Legitimate peripheral participation*. Cambridge University Press. 10.1017/CBO9780511815355

Lawrence, G., Ahmed, F., Cole, C., & Johnston, K. P. (2020). Not More Technology but More Effective Technology: Examining the State of Technology Integration in EAP Programmes. *RELC Journal*, 51(1), 101–116. 10.1177/0033688220907199

Lawton, W., & Katsomitros, A. (2012). International branch campuses: Data and developments. *The Observatory on Borderless Higher Education*, 12.

Lee, D., Kim, H.-H., & Sung, S.-H. (2023). Development research on an AI English learning support system to facilitate learner-generated-context-based learning. *Educational Technology Research and Development*, 71(2), 629–666. 10.1007/s11423-022-10172-236533222

Lee, M., & Wright, E. (2015). Elite schools in international education markets in Asia in a globalized era. In Hayden, M., Levy, J., & Thompson, J. (Eds.), *Handbook of research in international education* (2nd ed., pp. 583–597). Sage.

Levesque, E. M. (2018). The role of AI in education and the changing US workforce. Brookings. https://www.brookings.edu

Levy, M., & Stockwell, G. (2013). *CALL dimensions: Options and issues in computer-assisted language learning*. Routledge. 10.4324/9780203708200

Lewis, D. (2017). The Three Stages of Leadership. Available from: https://www.london.edu/think/the-three-stages-of-leadership

Leydesdorff, L. 2012. The triple helix of university-industry-government relations. SSRN *Electronic Journal*. 10.2139/ssrn.1996760

Li, S., & Jin, C. (2020, March). Analysis on whether native or non-native English-speaking teacher is better in TEFL in China. In 4th International Conference on Culture, Education and Economic Development of Modern Society (ICCESE 2020) (pp. 1098-1104). Atlantis Press. 10.2991/assehr.k.200316.240

Liarokapis, F., & Anderson, E. F. (2010). Using augmented reality as a medium to assist teaching in higher education.

Li, Li., & Morris, G. (2021). Thriving in the New Normal: In-Service Professional Development Needs and Experiences. In Xiang, C. H. (Ed.), *Trends and Developments for the Future of Language Education in Higher Education* (pp. 253–271). IGI Global. 10.4018/978-1-7998-7226-9.ch013

Lillis, T. M., & Curry, M. J. (2010). *Academic writing in global context*. Routledge.

Liluashvili, M. (2006). *Georgian Culture and Tbilisi State University in 1918-1921 years*. Tbilisi State University.

Lindberg, R., McDonough, K., & Trofimovich, P. (2021). Investigating verbal and nonverbal indicators of physiological response during second language interaction. *Applied Psycholinguistics*, 42(6), 1403–1425. 10.1017/S014271642100028X

Lin, J. H., & Liu, M. J. (2016). A Discussion on Improving the Quality of Sino-Foreign Cooperative Education. *Chinese Education & Society*, 49(4-5), 231–242. 10.1080/10611932.2016.1237845

Livermore, D. (2015). *Leading with cultural intelligence: The real secret to success*. AMACOM.

Li, W., & De Costa, P. I. (2017). Professional survival in a neoliberal age: A case study of an EFL teacher in China. *The Journal of Asia TEFL*, 14(2), 277–291. 10.18823/asiatefl.2017.14.2.5.277

Li, X., Xiao, W., Sun, C., Li, W., & Sun, B. (2022). Does burnout decrease with teacher professional identity among teachers in China? *Journal of Career Development*, •••, 08948453221138937.

Lok, P., & Crawford, J. (2004). The effect of organisational culture and leadership style on job satisfaction and organisational commitment: A cross-national comparison. *Journal of Management Development*, 23(4), 321–338. 10.1108/02621710410529785

Lominashvili, D. (2020). International standards of the right to education and the challenges of modern Georgian legislation. Retrieved from: chrome-extension://efaidnbmnnnibpcajpcglclefindmkaj/https://www.tsu.ge/assets/media/files/48/disertaciebi4/Davit_Lominashvili.pdf

Lomouri, G. (2020). Historic Bases of the Georgian Education System. Retrieved from: https://giorgilomouri.wordpress.com

Longman, K. A., & Madsen, S. R. (Eds.). (2014). *Women and Leadership in Higher Education*. IAP.

López Belmonte, J., Moreno-Guerrero, A. J., López Núñez, J. A., & Pozo Sánchez, S. (2019). Analysis of the productive, structural, and dynamic development of augmented reality in higher education research on the web of science. *Applied Sciences (Basel, Switzerland)*, 9(24), 5306. 10.3390/app9245306

Luthans, F. (1989). *Organisational behaviour* (5th ed.). McGraw-Hill.

Lyons, T. (2007). Conflict-generated diasporas and transnational politics in Ethiopia: Analysis. *Conflict Security and Development*, 7(4), 529–549. 10.1080/14678800701692951

Macaro, E., Curle, S., Pun, J., An, J., & Dearden, J. (2018). A Systematic Review of English Medium Instruction in Higher Education. *Language Teaching*, 51(1), 36–76. 10.1017/S0261444817000350

MacArthur, C. A. (2016). *Instruction in evaluation and revision, handbook of writing research* (2nd ed.). Guilfordpp.

Compilation of References

MacIntyre, P. D., Gregersen, T., & Mercer, S. (2020). Language teachers' coping strategies during the Covid-19 conversion to online teaching: Correlations with stress, well-being and negative emotions. *System*, 94, 102352. https://doi-org.ez.xjtlu.edu.cn/10.1016/j.system.2020.102352. 10.1016/j.system.2020.102352

Madlock, P. E. (2008). The link between leadership style, communicator competence, and employee satisfaction. *Journal of Business Communication*, 45(1), 61–78. 10.1177/0021943607309351

Madsen, S. R. (2012). Women and leadership in higher education: Learning and advancement in leadership programs. *Advances in Developing Human Resources*, 14(1), 3–10. 10.1177/1523422311429668

Madsen, S. R., Longman, K. A., & Daniels, J. R. (2012). Women's leadership development in higher education: Conclusion and implications for HRD. *Advances in Developing Human Resources*, 14(1), 113–128. 10.1177/1523422311429734

Malik, F. 2019. www.malik-management.com [Online]. (Accessed 18 April 2024).

Mammo, Y. (2016). Analysis of Ethiopia's national ICT policy and strategy: Insights into policy issues and policy goals. *Ethiopian Journal of Education and Sciences*, 11(2), 75–89.

Mamolo, L. (2022). Online Learning and Students' Mathematics Motivation, Self-Efficacy, and Anxiety in the "New Normal". *Education Research International*, 2022, 1–10. Advance online publication. 10.1155/2022/9439634

Marginson, S., & van der Wende, M. (2007). *Globalisation and Higher Education*. ECD Education Working Papers, 8. Available at: https://www.oecd.org/education/research/37552729.pdf [Accessed: Feb.10th,2024].

Martín-Gutiérrez, J., Fabiani, P., Benesova, W., Meneses, M. D., & Mora, C. E. (2015). Augmented reality to promote collaborative and autonomous learning in higher education. *Computers in Human Behavior*, 51, 752–761. 10.1016/j.chb.2014.11.093

Mate, G. (2022). *The Myth of Normal: Trauma, Illness and Healing in a Toxic Culture*. Avery.

Maté, G., & Maté, D. (2022). *The Myth of Normal*. Avery.

Mathew, P., Mathew, P., & Peechattu, P. (2017). Reflective Practices: A Means of Teacher Development. *Asia Pacific Journal of Contemporary Education and Communication Technology*, 3(1), 126–131.

Maxwell, N. (2007). From knowledge to wisdom: The need for an academic revolution. *London Review of Education*, 5(2), 97–115. 10.1080/14748460701440350

Mayer, C. W. F., Ludwig, S., & Brandt, S. (2023). Prompt text classifications with transformer models! An exemplary introduction to prompt-based learning with large language models. *Journal of Research on Technology in Education*, 55(1), 125–141. 10.1080/15391523.2022.2142872

McCarthy, M. (1991). *Discourse Analysis for Language Teachers*. Cambridge University Press.

McKinsey & Company. (2023). Generative AI and the future of work in America. Available at: https://www.mckinsey.com [Accessed 29 February 2024]

McLennan, G. (2008). Disinterested, disengaged, useless: Conservative or progressive idea of the university? *Globalisation, Societies and Education*, 6(2), 195–200. 10.1080/14767720802061496

Meihami, H., & Salīte, I. (2019). EFL teachers' cultural identity development through participating in cultural negotiation: Probing EFL students' perspectives. *Journal of Teacher education for Sustainability*, 9(1), 115-127.

Mekonnen, M., & Bayissa, Z. (2023). The Effect of Transformational and Transactional Leadership Styles on Organizational Readiness for Change Among Health Professionals. *SAGE Open Nursing*, 9, 23779608231185923. 10.1177/2 3779608231185923 37448973

Meschitti, V., & Marini, G. (2023). The balance between status quo and change when minorities try to access top ranks: A tale about women achieving professorship. *Gender in Management*, 38(1), 17–35. 10.1108/GM-04-2022-0141

Meyer, E. (2014). *The Culture map*. Public Affairs.

Meyer, E. (2015). *The Culture Map*. PublicAffairs.

Meza-Mejia, M. C., Villarreal-García, M. A., & Ortega-Barba, C. F. (2023). Women and leadership in higher education: A systematic review. *Social Sciences (Basel, Switzerland)*, 12(10), 555. 10.3390/socsci12100555

Mhlanga, D. (2023). Open AI in education, the responsible and ethical use of ChatGPT towards lifelong learning. In *FinTech and Artificial Intelligence for Sustainable Development: The Role of Smart Technologies in Achieving Development Goals* (pp. 387–409). Springer Nature Switzerland. 10.1007/978-3-031-37776-1_17

Miller, E. R., & Gkonou, C. (2018). Language teacher agency, emotion labor and emotional rewards in tertiary-level English language programs. *System, 79*, 49e59.

Miller, E. R., Morgan, B., & Medina, A. L. (2017). Exploring language teacher identity work as ethnical self-formation. *The Modern Language Journal, 101*(s), 91e105.

Miller, D. (2023). 'Exploring the impact of artificial intelligence language model ChatGPT on the user experience', International Journal of Technology *[IJTIM]. Innovation and Management*, 3(1), 1–8.

Mills, C. (2008). Reproduction and transformation of inequalities in schooling: The transformative potential of the theoretical constructs of Bourdieu. *British Journal of Sociology of Education*, 29(1), 79–89. 10.1080/01425690701737481

Ministry of Education. (2020). *Publication of The Framework of Guidelines for the Construction of Ideological and Political Teaching in Higher Education*. http://www.moe.gov.cn/srcsite/A08/s7056/202006/t20200603_462437.html

Mintzberg, H. (1994). *The rise and fall of strategic planning*. Free Press.

Miri, B., David, B. C., & Uri, Z. (2007). Purposely teaching for the promotion of higher-order thinking skills: A case of critical thinking. *Research in Science Education*, 37(4), 353–369. 10.1007/s11165-006-9029-2

Mischau, A. (2001). Women in higher education in Europe – a statistical overview. *The International Journal of Sociology and Social Policy*, 21(1/2), 20–31. https://doi-org.ezproxy.nottingham.edu.cn/10.1108/01443330110789529. 10.1108/01443330110789529

Mishler, E. G. (2009). *Storylines: Craftartists' narratives of identity*. Harvard University Press.

Mishra, N., Desai, N. P., Wadhwani, A., & Baluch, M. F. (2023). Visual Analysis of Cardiac Arrest Prediction Using Machine Learning Algorithms: A Health Education Awareness Initiative. In *Handbook of Research on Instructional Technologies in Health Education and Allied Disciplines* (pp. 331-363). IGI Global. 10.4018/978-1-6684-7164-7.ch015

Mishra, L., Gupta, T., & Shree, A. (2020). Online teaching-learning in higher education during lockdown period of COVID-19 pandemic. *International Journal of Educational Research Open*, 1, 100012. 10.1016/j.ijedro.2020.10001235059663

Mishra, N., Habtemariam, G. M., & De, A. (2023). Investigation of High-Performance Computing Tools for Higher Education Institutions Using the IoE Grid Computing Framework. In *Internet of Behaviors Implementation in Organizational Contexts* (pp. 217–241). IGI Global. 10.4018/978-1-6684-9039-6.ch011

Compilation of References

Misra, J., Kuvaeva, A., O'Meara, K., Culpepper, D. K., & Jaeger, A. (2021). Gendered and racialized perceptions of faculty workloads. *Gender & Society*, 35(3), 358–394. 10.1177/08912432211001387

Mizumoto, A., & Eguchi, M. (2023). Exploring the potential of using an AI language model for automated essay scoring. *Research Methods in Applied Linguistics*, 2(2), 100050. 10.1016/j.rmal.2023.100050

Mohajan, H. K. (2018). Qualitative research methodology in social sciences and related subjects. *Journal of economic development, environment and people*, 7(1), 23-48. Retrieved from:https://mpra.ub.uni-muenchen.de/105149/1/MPRA_paper_105149.pdf

Mo, J., & Morris, G. (2024). Investigating the employment motivation, job satisfaction, and dissatisfaction of international high school teachers in China: The impact of the COVID-19 pandemic. *Frontiers in Psychology*, 15, 1271604. Advance online publication. 10.3389/fpsyg.2024.127160438384343

Moldes, V. M., Biton, C. L., Gonzaga, D. J., & Moneva, J. C. (2019). Students, peer pressure and their academic performance in school. *International Journal of Scientific and Research Publications*, 9(1), 300–312. 10.29322/IJSRP.9.01.2019.p8541

Monroe, K., Ozyurt, S., Wrigley, T., & Alexander, A. (2008). Gender equality in academia: Bad news from the trenches, and some possible solutions. *Perspectives on Politics*, 6(2), 215–233. 10.1017/S1537592708080572

Morais, R., Fernandes, C. E., & Piñeiro-Naval, V. (2022). Big girls don't cry: An Assessment of research units' leadership and gender distribution in higher education institutions. *Social Sciences (Basel, Switzerland)*, 11(8), 345–354. 10.3390/socsci11080345

Mora, J. C., & Levkina, M. (2017). Task-based pronunciation teaching and research: Key issues and future directions. *Studies in Second Language Acquisition*, 39(2), 381–399. 10.1017/S0272263117000183

Morley, L. (2013). *Women and higher education leadership: Absences and aspirations*. Leadership Foundation for Higher Education.

Morris, G. (2021) Investigating the employment motivation and job satisfaction of expatriate language teachers (Thesis (EdD)). Exeter University, Exeter.

Morris, G. (2021). *Investigating the Employment Motivation and Job Satisfaction of Expatriate Language Teachers*. EdD Thesis. University of Exeter: Exeter.

Morris, G., & Berhanu Tesema, F. (2024). *To Build a Community in Higher Education, Start from the Ground Up*. The Times Higher Education Campus. Available from: https://www.timeshighereducation.com/campus/build-community-higher-education-start-ground

Morris, G., & Xu, J. (2024). "Journeying into the Unknown: Considering the Future of Education at the Dawn of AI." (Virtual Presentation). Teaching and Learning Conference, University of Nottingham, April 2024.

Morris, G., Cao, Q., & Weng, W. Berhanu Tesema, F. & Zhao, T. (2024). Planning Ahead: Exploring the Leadership Competencies that Transnational Higher Education Managers Need. In Morris, G. & Kozuch, S. (Eds). *Engaging Higher Education Teachers and Students with Transnational Leadership* (pp.1-14). Hershey: IGI Global.

Morris, G., Morris, J. & Li, Lei. (2023). Enhancing Educational Leadership in Transnational Higher Education. In Morris G. & Li, L. (Eds). *Developments and Future Trends in Transnational Higher Education* (pp. 341-358). Hershey: IGI Global.

Morris, G., & Li, L. (2023). *Handbook of Research on Developments and Future Trends in Transnational Higher Education* [online]. IGI Global., Available at https://www-iresearchbook-cn.ezproxy.nottingham.edu.cn/f/cdf/read?bookId=7fbf6b3b3d394267aeb4e2d383ec890c&cdf=/202302131644093911/7fbf6b3b3d394267aeb4e2d383ec890c.cdf&range=52&type=1&TRI=110.4018/978-1-6684-5226-4

Morris, G., & Mo, J. (2023). Exploring the Employment Motivation, Job Satisfaction and Dissatisfaction of University English Instructors in Public Institutions: A Chinese Case Study Analysis. *Humanities & Social Sciences Communications*, 10(1), 717. 10.1057/s41599-023-02228-2

Morris, G., Xu, J., & Li, Li. (2022). Transitioning to the New Normal: Experiences from a Sino-British Institution. In Kronhke, L. (Ed.), *Cases on Teaching English for Academic Purposes (EAP) During COVID-19* (pp. 205–230). IGI Global. 10.4018/978-1-6684-4148-0.ch009

Motha, S., & Lin, A. M. Y. (2014). "Non-coercive rearrangements": Theorizing desire. *Tesol Quarterly, 48*, 331e359.

Mugesatar, H., & Ozdener, N. (2008). The effects of synchronous CMC on speaking proficiency and anxiety: Text versus voice chat. *Modern Language Journal*, 92(4), 595–613. 10.1111/j.1540-4781.2008.00789.x

Muliyah, P., & Aminatun, D. (2020). Teaching English for Specific Purposes in Vocational High School: Teachers' Beliefs and Practices. *Journal of English Teaching*, 6(2), 122–133. 10.33541/jet.v6i2.1756

Mulugeta, A., & Pandian, A. V. R. (2020). The relationship between leadership styles and employee commitment in public organizations of Dire Dawa administration, Ethiopia. *International Journal of Advanced Science and Technology*, 29(8), 2018–2025.

Munro, M. J., & Derwing, T. M. (2015). A prospectus for pronunciation research in the 21st century: A point of view. *Journal of Second Language Pronunciation*, 1(1), 11–42. 10.1075/jslp.1.1.01mun

Murage, L. M., Njoka, J., & Gachahi, M. (2019). Challenges Faced by Student Leaders in Managing Student Affairs in Public Universities in Kenya. *International Journal of Education and Literacy Studies*, 7(1), 1–7. 10.7575/aiac.ijels.v.7n.1p.1

Muro, M., Whiton, J., & Maxim, R. (2019). What jobs are affected by AI? Better-paid, better-educated workers face the most exposure. Metropolitan Policy Program Report.

Muskhelishvili, D., Samsonadze, M., & Daushvili, A. (2010). *History of Georgia from ancient times to 2009*. Institute of History and Ethnology.

Muzyleva, I., Yazykova, L., Gorlach, A., & Gorlach, Y. (2021, June). Augmented and Virtual Reality Technologies in Education. In 2021 1st International Conference on Technology Enhanced Learning in Higher Education (TELE) (pp. 99-103). IEEE. 10.1109/TELE52840.2021.9482568

Myers, S.A., & Goodboy, A.K. and Members of Comm 600. (2014). College student learning, motivation, and satisfaction as a function of effective instructor communication behaviors. *The Southern Communication Journal*, 79(1), 14–26.

Nabokova, L. S., & Zagidullina, F. R. (2019). Outlooks of applying augmented and virtual reality technologies in higher education. Professional education in the modern world, 9(2), 2710-2719.

Naidu, J., & Van der Walt, M. (2005). An exploration of the relationship between leadership styles and the implementation of transformation interventions. *SA Journal of Human Resource Management*, 3(2), 1–10. 10.4102/sajhrm.v3i2.60

Nakamura, C. M., Murphy, S. K., Christel, M. G., Stevens, S. M., & Zollman, D. A. (2016). Automated analysis of short responses in an interactive synthetic tutoring system for introductory physics. *Physical Review. Physics Education Research*, 12(1), 010122. 10.1103/PhysRevPhysEducRes.12.010122

Namaziandost, E., Razmi, M. H., Hernández, R. M., Ocaña-Fernández, Y., & Khabir, M. (2022). Synchronous CMC text chat versus synchronous CMC voice chat: Impacts on EFL learners' oral proficiency and anxiety. *Journal of Research on Technology in Education*, 54(4), 599–616. 10.1080/15391523.2021.1906362

National Center for Education Quality Development. (2023). Bologna Process. Retrieved from: https://eqe.ge/en/page/static/71/boloniis-protsesi

National Center for Educational Quality Enhancement. (2023). Higher Education. Retrieved from: https://eqe.ge/en/page/static/69/umaghlesi-ganatleba

National Parliamentary Library of Georgia. (2023). Chronicle of Ilia Chavchavadze's life and work. Retrieved from: https://dspace.nplg.gov.ge/bitstream/1234/204739/1/Ilia_Chavchavazis-Cxovrebis_da_Shemoqmedebis_Matiane.pdf

National Research Council. (2000). *How people learn: Brain, mind, experience, and school: Expanded edition* (Vol. 1). National Academies Press.

National Statistical Office of Georgia. (2023). High Education. Retrieved from: https://www.geostat.ge/en/modules/categories/61/higher-education

Naumann, E. (1993). Organizational predictors of expatriate job satisfaction. *Journal of International Business Studies*, 24(1), 61–80. 10.1057/palgrave.jibs.8490225

Näykki, P., Kontturi, H., Seppänen, V., Impiö, N., & Järvelä, S. (2021). Teachers as learners–a qualitative exploration of pre-service and in-service teachers' continuous learning community OpenDigi. *Journal of Education for Teaching*, 47(4), 495–512. 10.1080/02607476.2021.1904777

Nazari, M., & Seyri, H. (2021). Covidentity: Examining transitions in teacher identity construction from personal to online classes. European Journal of Teacher Education, 1-20. Teachers' Beliefs and Practices. *Journal of English Teaching*, 6(2), 122–133.

Nazari, N., Shabbir, M. S., & Setiawan, R. (2021). Application of artificial intelligence powered digital writing assistance in higher education: Randomized controlled trial. *Heliyon*, 7(5), e07014. 10.1016/j.heliyon.2021.e0701434027198

Ndou, V. (2004). E-government for developing countries: Opportunities and challenges. *The Electronic Journal on Information Systems in Developing Countries*, 18(1), 1–24. 10.1002/j.1681-4835.2004.tb00117.x

Nesenbergs, K., Abolins, V., Ormanis, J., & Mednis, A. (2020). Use of augmented and virtual reality in remote higher education: A systematic umbrella review. *Education Sciences*, 11(1), 8. 10.3390/educsci11010008

Nguyen, T. H. N., Encarnação, C., Amado, F., & Santos, S. (2023). Challenges and success factors of transnational higher education: A systematic review. *Studies in Higher Education*, 48(1), 113–136. 10.1080/03075079.2022.2121813

Nichols, S. L., Schutz, P. A., Rodgers, K., & Bilica, K. (2017). Early career teachers' emotion and emerging teacher identities. *Teachers and Teaching*, 23(4), 406–421.

Nielsen, S., & Huse, M. (2010). The contribution of women on boards of directors: Going beyond the surface. *Corporate Governance*, 18(2), 136–148. 10.1111/j.1467-8683.2010.00784.x

Nikunen, M. (2014). The 'Entrepreneurial' university, family and gender: Changes and demands faced by fixed-term workers. *Gender and Education*, 26(2), 119–134. 10.1080/09540253.2014.888402

Noman, M., & Gurr, D. (2020). Contextual Leadership and Culture in Education. In G. W. Noblit (Ed.), Oxford Research Encyclopedia of Education (pp. 1–20). Oxford University Press., Retrieved February 25th, 2024, from, 10.1093/acrefore/9780190264093.013.595

Noonan, H. (2019). *Personal identity*. Routledge. 10.4324/9781315107240

Northouse, P. G. (2021). *Leadership: Theory and Practice* (9th ed.). Sage.

Nussbaum, M. (2000) Women and Human Development: The Capabilities Approach, Cambridge University Press, 2000.

Nussbaum, M. (2003). Capabilities as fundamental entitlements: Sen and social justice. *Feminist Economics*, 9(2/3), 33–59. 10.1080/1354570022000077926

O.S.N. Education. (2004). The Salamanca statement and framework for action on special needs education. Special Educational Needs and Inclusive Education: Systems and contexts, 1, p.382.

O'Connell, J., Brewer, S., Wilding, E., & Robbins, J. (2024). Management challenges and training needs in higher education institutions: A multi-case study. In Morris, G., & Kozuch, S. (Eds.), *Engaging Higher Education Teachers and Students with Transnational Leadership* (pp. 39–63). IGI Global. 10.4018/979-8-3693-6100-9.ch003

O'Connor, J. D, & Arnold, G.F. (1973). *Intonation of Colloquial English* (2nd ed.). Longman.

O'Connor, K. (2008). "You choose to care": Teachers, emotions and professional identity. *Teaching and Teacher Education*, 24(1), 117–126. 10.1016/j.tate.2006.11.008

O'Connor, P., Carvalho, T., Vabø, A., & Cardoso, S. (2015). Gender in Higher Education: A Critical Review. In Huisman, J., de Boer, H., Dill, D. D., & Souto-Otero, M. (Eds.), *The Palgrave International Handbook of Higher Education Policy and Governance*. Palgrave Macmillan., 10.1007/978-1-137-45617-5_30

Oatley, K. (2000). Emotion: Theories. In Kazdin, A. E. (Ed.), *Encyclopedia of psychology* (pp. 167–171). Oxford University Press.

Oduro, G. K. (2004, September 16-18). *Distributed leadership in schools: What English headteachers say about the pull and push factors* [Paper presentation]. British Educational Research Association Annual Conference, University of Manchester. https://www.leeds.ac.uk/educol/documents/00003673.pdf

OECD. (2020). *Education at a Glance 2020: OECD Indicators*. OECD., 10.1787/69096873-

Ojokuku, R., Odetayo, T., & Sajuyigbe, A. (2012). Impact of leadership style on organizational performance: A case study of Nigerian banks. *American Journal of Business and Management*, 1(4), 202–207.

Open, A. I. (2024) Home. Available at: https://www.openai.com [Accessed: 22 March 2024].

Orellana, M. F., Liu, L., & Ángeles, S. L. (2022). "Reinventing Ourselves" and Reimagining Education: Everyday Learning and Life Lessons from the COVID-19 Pandemic. *Harvard Educational Review*, 92(3), 413–436. 10.17763/1943-5045-92.3.413

Ozamiz-Etxebarria, N., Idoiaga Mondragon, N., Bueno-Notivol, J., Pérez-Moreno, M., & Santabárbara, J. (2021). Prevalence of anxiety, depression, and stress among teachers during the COVID-19 pandemic: A rapid systematic review with meta-analysis. *Brain Sciences*, 11(9), 1172. 10.3390/brainsci1109117234573192

Öztürk, G., & Gürbüz, N. (2014). Speaking anxiety among Turkish EFL learners: The case at a state university. *Journal of language and Linguistic Studies, 10*(1), 1-17.

Page, E. B. (1966). The imminence of... grading essays by computer. *Phi Delta Kappan*, 47(5), 238–243.

Pan, H., Xia, F., Kumar, T., Li, X., & Shamsy, A. (2022). Massive Open Online Course Versus Flipped Instruction: Impacts on Foreign Language Speaking Anxiety, Foreign Language Learning Motivation, and Learning Attitude. *Frontiers in Psychology*, 13, 833616. 10.3389/fpsyg.2022.83361635197908

Paniagua, J., Villó, C., & Escrivà-Beltran, M. (2022). Cross-border Higher Education: The Expansion of International Branch Campuses. *Research in Higher Education*, 63(6), 1–21. 10.1007/s11162-022-09674-y35068659

Papaja, K. (2021). Negative Emotions Experienced by Polish English Teachers During COVID-19. A Qualitative Study Based on Diaries. *Lublin Studies in Modern Languages & Literature / Lubelskie Materialy Neofilologiczne, 45*(3), 3–17. https://doi-org.ez.xjtlu.edu.cn/10.17951/lsmll.2021.45.3.3-17

Pappa, S., Moate, J., Ruohotie-Lyhty, M., & Eteläpelto, A. (2017). Teachers' pedagogical and relational identity negotiation in the Finnish CLIL context. *Teaching and Teacher Education, 65*, 61–70. 10.1016/j.tate.2017.03.008

Park, S. (2020). Seeking changes in ivory towers: The impact of gender quotas on female academics in higher education. *Women's Studies International Forum, 79*(February), 102346. https://doi-org.ezproxy.nottingham.edu.cn/10.1016/j.wsif.2020.102346. 10.1016/j.wsif.2020.102346

Payne, J. S. (2020). Developing L2 productive language skills online and the strategic use of instructional tools. *Foreign Language Annals, 53*(2), 243–249. 10.1111/flan.12457

Pearson, W. S. (2020). Mapping English language proficiency cut-off scores and presessional EAP programmes in UK higher education. *Journal of English for Academic Purposes, 45*, 100866. Advance online publication. 10.1016/j.jeap.2020.100866

Peirce, B. N. (1995). Social identity, investment, and language learning. *TESOL Quarterly, 29*(1), 9–31. 10.2307/3587803

Perrin, S. & Sun, H. 2022. Graduate Employability through Industry-Oriented, Problem-Based Learning: A Case Study. *African Journal of Inter/Multidisciplinary Studies,* 4: 43-56

Perrin, S., & Wang, L. (2021) COVID-19 and rapid digitalization of learning and teaching: quality assurance issues and solutions in a Sino-foreign higher education institution. Quality assurance issues and solutions, 29(4), pp.463-476. Available at: https://nusearch.nottingham.edu.cn/permalink/f/s8ggqh/TN_cdi_emerald_primary_10_1108_QAE-12-2020-0167 [Accessed:Dec.8th, 2023].

Pertaub, D. P., Slater, M., & Barker, C. (2001). An experiment on public speaking anxiety in response to three different types of virtual audience. *Presence (Cambridge, Mass.), 11*(1), 68–78. 10.1162/105474602317343668

Peters, S. (2012). *Chimp paradox*. Random House.

Pickering, L. (2001). The Role of Tone Choice in Improving ITA Communication in the Classroom. *TESOL Quarterly, 35*(2), 233–255. 10.2307/3587647

Pickering, L. (2004). The structure and function of intonational paragraphs in native and nonnative speaker instructional discourse. *English for Specific Purposes, 23*(1), 19–43. 10.1016/S0889-4906(03)00020-6

Pishghadam, R., Golzar, J., & Miri, M. A. (2022). A New Conceptual Framework for Teacher Identity Development. *Frontiers in Psychology, 13*, 2024. 10.3389/fpsyg.2022.87639535615191

Plus, E. (2020). 15 Years of Bologna Process in Georgia. Retrieved from: http://erasmusplus.org.ge/files/publications/Research

Por, G. 2000. The Ecology of Knowledge: A Field of Theory and Practice, Key to Research & Technology Development. *Position paper presented to The European Commission's Directorate-General Information Society Technologies.*

Priestley, M., Biesta, G., & Robinson, S. (2016). *Teacher agency: An ecological approach*. Bloomsbury Publishing.

Pyhältö, K., Pietarinen, J., & Soini, T. (2015). Teachers' professional agency and learning—From adaption to active modification in the teacher community. *Teachers and Teaching, 21*(7), 811–830. 10.1080/13540602.2014.995483

Qin, J. (2016). Analysis of the feeling of frustration experienced by Chinese middle school ESL students—from the perspective of psychology.

Qiu, J., Shen, B., Zhao, M., Wang, Z., Xie, B., & Xu, Y. (2020). A nationwide survey of psychological distress among Chinese people in the COVID-19 epidemic: Implications and policy recommendations. *General Psychiatry*, 33(2), e100213. 10.1136/gpsych-2020-10021332215365

Raddon, A. (2002). Mothers in the Academy: Positioned and Positioning within Discourses of the 'Successful Academic' and the 'Good Mother'. *Studies in Higher Education*, 27(4), 387–403. 10.1080/0307507022000011516

Radianti, J., Majchrzak, T. A., Fromm, J., & Wohlgenannt, I. (2020). A systematic review of immersive virtual reality applications for higher education: Design elements, lessons learned, and research agenda. *Computers & Education*, 147, 103778. 10.1016/j.compedu.2019.103778

Radosavljevic, S., Radosavljevic, V., & Grgurovic, B. (2020). The potential of implementing augmented reality into vocational higher education through mobile learning. *Interactive Learning Environments*, 28(4), 404–418. 10.1080/10494820.2018.1528286

Ragins, B. R., Townsend, B., & Mattis, M. (1998). Gender gap in the executive suite: CEOs and female executives report on breaking the glass ceiling. *The Academy of Management Perspectives*, 12(1), 28–42. 10.5465/ame.1998.254976

Rahman, H. (2007). *Developing successful ICT strategies: Competitive advantages in a global knowledge-driven society*. IGI.

Rane, N. L., Choudhary, S. P., Tawde, A., & Rane, J. (2023). ChatGPT is not capable of serving as an author: Ethical concerns and challenges of large language models in education. *International Research Journal of Modernization in Engineering Technology and Science*, 5(10), 851–874.

Rao, K., & Tilt, C. (2016). Board composition and corporate social responsibility: The role of diversity, gender, strategy and decision making. *Journal of Business Ethics*, 138(2), 327–347. 10.1007/s10551-015-2613-5

Rapanta, C., Botturi, L., Goodyear, P., Guàrdia, L., & Koole, M. (2020). Online university teaching during and after the Covid-19 crisis: Refocusing teacher presence and learning activity. *Postdigital Science and Education*, 2(3), 923–945. 10.1007/s42438-020-00155-y

Rape, T. (2021). Teamwork in social work: What are we actually talking about? [online]. *European Journal of Social Work*, 25(4), 668–680. 10.1080/13691457.2021.1995704

Rasli, A., Tee, M., Lai, Y. L., Tiu, Z. C., & Soon, E. H. (2022). Post-COVID-19 strategies for higher education institutions in dealing with unknown and uncertainties. *Frontiers in Education*, 7, 992063. Retrieved March 15th, 2024, from https://www.frontiersin.org/articles/10.3389/feduc.2022.992063/full. 10.3389/feduc.2022.992063

Rawls, J. (1971). *A theory of justice*. Belknap Press. 10.4159/9780674042605

Ray, P. P. (2023). ChatGPT: A comprehensive review on background, applications, key challenges, bias, ethics, limitations and future scope. *Internet of Things and Cyber-Physical Systems*.

Redding, C. (2019). A teacher like me: A review of the effect of student–teacher racial/ethnic matching on teacher perceptions of students and student academic and behavioral outcomes. *Review of Educational Research*, 89(4), 499–535. 10.3102/0034654319853545

Reskin, B. F., & Ross, C. E. (1992). Jobs, authority, and earnings among managers: The continuing significance of sex. *Work and Occupations*, 19(4), 342–365. 10.1177/0730888492019004002

Reta, M. A. (2021). The Influence of Leadership Styles on the Effectiveness of the Public Policy Implementation Process in Ethiopia: The Case of Addis Ababa City Government. *American Journal of Management Science and Engineering*, 6(5), 142–160. 10.11648/j.ajmse.20210605.12

Riazi, A. M. (2016). *The Routledge encyclopedia of research methods in applied linguistics*. Routledge., 10.4324/9781315656762

Richards, J. C. (2022). Exploring emotions in language teaching. *RELC Journal*, 53(1), 225–239. 10.1177/0033688220927531

Rikab, W. (2023) 'Detectors of AI-generated text often fail. Here is what to do', Better Programming. Available at https://betterprogramming.pub/ai-generated-text-detectors-are-useless-here-is-what-to-do-e7a640815087 [Accessed: 25 January 2024].

Riphahn, R. T., & Schwientek, C. (2015). What drives the reversal of the gender education gap? Evidence from Germany. *Applied Economics*, 47(53), 5748–5775. 10.1080/00036846.2015.1058906

Roach, P. (2000). *English Phonetics and Phonology: A Practical Course*. Cambridge University Press.

Roach, P. (2001). *Phonetics*. Oxford University Press.

Roach, P. (2009). *English Phonetics and Phonology* (4th ed.). Cambridge University Press.

Roads, J. (1999). Teaching intonation: Beliefs and practices. *Speak Out*, 25, 18–25.

Robeyns, I. (2003) Sen's capability approach and gender inequality: selecting relevant capabilities, *Feminist Economics*, 9)203), 61-91.

Robeyns, I. (2005). Selecting Capabilities for Quality of Life Measurement. *Social Indicators Research*, 74(1), 191–215. 10.1007/s11205-005-6524-1

Robeyns, I. (2017). *Wellbeing, Freedom and Social Justice: The Capability Approach Re-Examined* (114th ed.). Open Book Publishers. Print 10.11647/OBP.0130

Robinson, C. D. (2022). A framework for motivating teacher-student relationships. *Educational Psychology Review*, 34(4), 2061–2094. 10.1007/s10648-022-09706-0

Robson, D. (2023). *The expectation effect: How your mindset can change your world*. Holt.

Rodríguez-Feria, P., Paric, M., Flórez, L. J. H., Babich, S. & Czabanowska, K. (2024). Critical route for development of medical student leadership competencies in 35 Pan American Health Organization member states: A scoping review and thematic analysis. *The International Journal of Health Planning and Management*.

Rosa, R., Drew, E., & Canavan, S. (2020). An overview of gender inequality in EU universities. In Eileen, D., & Canavan, S. (Eds.), *The gender-sensitive university. A contradiction in terms?* (pp. 1–15). Routledge. 10.4324/9781003001348-1

Rosch, D. M., Collier, D., & Thompson, S. E. (2015). An exploration of students' motivation to lead: An analysis by race, gender, and student leadership behaviors. *Journal of College Student Development*, 56(3), 286–291. 10.1353/csd.2015.0031

Rubin, H. J., & Rubin, I. S. (2011). *Qualitative interviewing: The art of hearing data*. sage.

Rudman, L. A., Moss-Racusin, C. A., Phelan, J. E., & Nauts, S. (2012). Status incongruity and backlash effects: Defending the gender hierarchy motivates prejudice against female leaders. *Journal of Experimental Social Psychology*, 48(1), 165–179. 10.1016/j.jesp.2011.10.008

Rudman, L. A., & Phelan, J. E. (2008). Backlash effects for disconfirming gender stereotypes in organizations. *Research in Organizational Behavior*, 28, 61–79. 10.1016/j.riob.2008.04.003

Rudolph, J., Tan, S., & Tan, S. (2023). ChatGPT: Bullshit spewer or the end of traditional assessments in higher education?. *Journal of applied learning and teaching*, 6(1), 342-363.

Ryan Derby-Talbot, R., & Coburn, N. (2023). Beyond "Innovation": Lessons for Making Change in Higher Educational Institutions. In Coburn, N., & Derby-Talbot, R. (Eds.), *The Impacts of Innovative Institutions in Higher Education* (pp. 277–292). Palgrave Macmillan. 10.1007/978-3-031-38785-2_12

Ryan, L. (2016). *Can Leadership Skills be Taught?* https://www.forbes.com/sites/lizryan/2016/04/01/can-leadership-skills-be-taught/?sh+20f3893a6579

Saadé, R. G., Kira, D., Mak, T., & Nebebe, F. (2017). Anxiety & performance in online learning. In *In SITE 2017: Informing Science+ IT Education Conferences: Vietnam*, 147-157. 10.28945/3736

Saadé, R. G., & Kira, D. (2007). Mediating the impact of technology usage on perceived ease of use by anxiety. *Computers & Education*, 49(4), 1189–1204. 10.1016/j.compedu.2006.01.009

Sachs, J. (2005). Teacher education and the development of professional identity: Learning to be a teacher. In P. M. Denicolo & M. Kompf (Eds.), *Connecting Policy and Practice* (pp. 5–21). Routledge, Taylor and Francis Group. 10.4324/9780203012529

Saeed, M. A., & Ghazali, K. (2017). Asynchronous group review of EFL writing: Interactions and text revisions. *Language Learning & Technology*, 21(2), 200–226. 10125/44618

Safarik, L. (2003). Feminist transformation in higher education: Discipline, structure, and institution. *Review of Higher Education*, 26(4), 419–445. 10.1353/rhe.2003.0035

Sahakyan, T., Lamb, M., & Chambers, G. (2018). Language Teacher Motivation: From the Ideal to the Feasible Self. In Mercer, S., & Kostoulas, A. (Eds.), *Language Teacher Psychology* (pp. 53–70). Multilingual Matters. 10.21832/9781783099467-008

Saito, K., Dewaele, J.-M., & Hanzawa, K. (2017). A longitudinal investigation of the relationship between motivation and late second language speech learning in classroom settings. *Language and Speech*, 60(4), 1–19. 10.1177/0023830916687793 28193135

Sakarneh, M., & Nair, N. A. (2014). Effective teaching in inclusive classroom: Literature review. *Journal of Education and Practice*, 5(24), 28–35.

Saleem, H. (2015). The impact of leadership styles on job satisfaction and mediating role of perceived organizational politics. *Procedia: Social and Behavioral Sciences*, 172, 563–569. 10.1016/j.sbspro.2015.01.403

Salihu, M. J. (2019). An Analysis of the Leadership Theories and Proposal of New Leadership Framework in Higher Education. *Asian Journal of Education and Social Studies*, 5(4), 1–6. Retrieved December 10th, 2023, from https://www.researchgate.net/publication/338421257. 10.9734/ajess/2019/v5i430164

Salter, R (1999). *Discourse Intonation in Listening Tasks with Yes/No Questions* (accessed 5 April 2018).

San Diego State University. (2024). Academic Information. Retrieved from: https://sdsu.edu.ge/ka/spages/chven-shesakheb/17

Sanderson, K. (2023). GPT-4 is here: What scientists think. *Nature*, 615(7954), 773. 10.1038/d41586-023-00816-536928404

Sanger, C., & Gleason, N. (2020). *Diversity and Inclusion in Global Higher Education Lessons from Across Asia* (1st ed. 2020). Springer Nature. 10.1007/978-981-15-1628-3

Sang, K. (2018). Gender, ethnicity and feminism: An intersectional analysis of the lived experiences feminist academic women in UK higher education. *Journal of Gender Studies*, 27(2), 192–206. 10.1080/09589236.2016.1199380

Sang, Y. (2020). Research of language teacher identity: Status quo and future directions. *RELC Journal*, 53(3), 731–738. 10.1177/0033688220961567

Sant'Anna, A. de S. 2024. Leadership Styles Across Cultures: A Comparative Study of Western and Asian Contexts through Hofested and Deleuzian. [online] LinkedIn. Available at: https://www.linkedin.com/pulse/leadership-styles-across-cultures-comparative-study-1-anderson-2uxuf/ [Accessed 10 February 2024].

Šarić, M. (2015). Teachers' emotions: A research review from a psychological perspective. *Journal of Contemporary European Studies*, 4, 10–26.

Saunders, R. (2013). The role of teacher emotions in change: Experiences, patterns and implications for professional development. *Journal of Educational Change*, 14(3), 303–333. 10.1007/s10833-012-9195-0

Schuman, V., & Scherer, K. R. (2014). Concepts and structures of emotions. In Pekrun, R., & Linnenbrink-Garcia, L. (Eds.), *International handbooks on emotions in education* (pp. 13–35). Routledge.

Schutz, P. A., & Lee, M. (2014). Teacher emotion, emotional labor and teacher identity. In Martinez Agudo, J. P., & Richards, J. (Eds.), *English as a foreign language teacher education: Current per- spectives and challenges* (pp. 169–186). Rodopi. 10.1163/9789401210485_011

Schwarzenegger, A. (2023). *Be Useful: Seven Tools for Life*. Penguin Press. Kahneman, D., Sibony, O. & Sunstein, C. (2022). *Noise: A flaw in human judgement*. William Collins.

Searby, L., Ballenger, J., & Tripses, J. (2015). Climbing the ladder, holding the ladder: The mentoring experiences of higher education female leaders. *Advancing Women in Leadership*, 35, 98–107. 10.21423/awlj-v35.a141

Seawright, L., & Hodges, A. (2016). *Learning Across Borders: Perspectives on International and Transnational Higher Education* [online]. Cambridge Scholars Publishing.

Segundo, M. G. (2022). Leadership and Culture: What Difference Does it Make? In: *2022 Regent Research Roundtables Proceedings*, pp.104-119. Regent University School of Business & Leadership.

Sen, A. (1980) 'Equality of What?' In Tanner Lectures on Human Values. Ed. S. M. McMurrin. I. Salt Lake City: University of Utah Press. Reprinted in Sen 1982: 353-69.

Sen, A. (1992). *Inequality re-examined*. Oxford University Press.

Sen, A. (1999). *Development as freedom*. Oxford University Press.

Sen, A. (2009). Capability: Reach and Limit. In *Debating Global Society: Reach and Limits of the Capability Approach* (pp. 15–28). Fondazione Giangiacomo Feltrinelli.

Setter, J., Stojanovik, V, & Martínez-Castilla, P. (2012). Evaluating the intonation of non-native speakers of English using a computerized test battery. *International Journal of Applied Linguistics*, 20(3), 368–385.

Shanoski, L.A. and Hranitz, J.R. (1992). Learning from America's Best Teachers: Building a Foundation for Accountability through Excellence.

Shapiro, S. (2010). Revisiting the teachers' lounge: Reflections on emotional experience and teacher identity. *Teaching and Teacher Education, 26*(3), 616–621. https://doi.org/. 00910.1016/j.tate.2009.09

Sharma, R. (2003). Barriers in Using Technology for Education in Developing Countries. *Computers & Education*, 41(1), 49–63.

Shen, X., Yang, Y. L., Wang, Y., Liu, L., Wang, S., & Wang, L. (2014). The association between occupational stress and depressive symptoms and the mediating role of psychological capital among Chinese university teachers: A cross-sectional study. *BMC Psychiatry*, 14(1), 1–8. 10.1186/s12888-014-0329-125433676

Shota Rustaveli Batumi State Univerisity. (2016). *Repressions of the 20s-30s of the 20th century in the context of political and cultural memory* Retrieved from: https://bsu.edu.ge/text_files/ge_file_16146_2.pdf

Silva, D. F. O., Cobucci, R. N., Lima, S. C. V. C., & de Andrade, F. B. (2021). Prevalence of anxiety, depression, and stress among teachers during the COVID-19 pandemic: A PRISMA-compliant systematic review. *Medicine*, 100(44), e27684. 10.1097/MD.0000000000002768434871251

Siu, K. W. M., & García, G. J. C. (2017). Disruptive Technologies and Education: Is There Any Disruption After All? In Educational leadership and administration: Concepts, methodologies, tools, and applications (pp. 757-778). IGI Global.

Slee, R. (2001). 'Inclusion in Practice': Does practice make perfect? *Educational Review*, 53(2), 113–123. 10.1080/00131910120055543

Slotte, V., & Tynjälä, P. (2003). Industry–University collaboration for continuing professional development. *Journal of Education and Work*, 16(4), 445–464. Advance online publication. 10.1080/1363908032000093058

Smagorinsky, P., Cook, L. S., Moore, C., Jackson, A. Y., & Fry, P. G. (2004). Tensions in learning to teach: Accommodation and the development of a teaching identity. *Journal of Teacher Education*, 55(1), 8–24. 10.1177/0022487103260067

Smaliakou, D., Wu, J., & Guo, J. (2022). *The Impact of the Pandemic on China's International Higher Education Policy*. Lingnan Normal University; Institute of Philosophy of the National Academy of Sciences of Belarus.

Smelzer, N. (2023). *Education. Functional Approach* Retrieved from: http://www.socium.ge/downloads/socshesavali/ganatleba_smelzeri.pdf

Smith, J. (2022). *Why has nobody told me this before?* Harper One.

Smith, W. (2022). *Will*. Planeta Publishing.

Somantri, C., & Iskandar, H. (2021). The Impact of CPD in Teaching, and the Role of Principal in Promoting CPD: A Literature Review. *Proceedings of the 4th International Conference on Research of Educational Administration and Management (ICREAM 2020)*. Atlantis Press. 10.2991/assehr.k.210212.074

Song, J. (2016). Emotions and language teacher identity: Conflicts, vulnerability, and transformation. *Tesol Quarterly*, 50, 631e654.

Sosa-López, G., & Mora, J. C. (2022). The Role of Speaking Anxiety on L2 English Speaking Fluency, Accuracy and Complexity. *Pronunciation in Second Language Learning and Teaching Proceedings*, 12(1). Advance online publication. 10.31274/psllt.13362

Spillane, J. P. (2005). Distributed Leadership. *The Educational Forum*, 69(2), 143–150. 10.1080/00131720508984678

Srimulyani, V. A., & Hermanto, Y. B. (2022). Work-Life Balance Before and During Work from Home in a Covid-19 Pandemic Situation. *Jurnal Manajemen Indonesia*, 22(1), 31–46. 10.25124/jmi.v22i1.2915

Steele, P., Burleigh, C., Bailey, L., & Kroposki, M. (2020). Studio thinking framework in higher education: Exploring options for shaping immersive experiences across virtual reality/augmented reality curricula. *Journal of Educational Technology Systems*, 48(3), 416–439. 10.1177/0047239519884897

Steiss, J., Tate, T., Graham, S., Cruz, J., Hebert, M., Wang, J., Moon, Y., Tseng, W., Warschauer, M., & Olson, C. B. (2024). Comparing the quality of human and ChatGPT feedback of students' writing. *Learning and Instruction*, 91, 101894. 10.1016/j.learninstruc.2024.101894

Stephens, M. (2023). The University of Cambridge will allow students to use ChatGPT. [EB/OL][2023-05-14]. Available online at: https://www.telegraph.co.uk/news/2023/03/02/university-cambridge-will-allow-students-use-chatgpt/ [accessed March 02, 2024].

Stephens-Davidowitz, S. (2017). Everybody Lies: Big Data, New Data and What the Internet Can Tell Us about Who We Really Are. Dey Street Books. Robson, D. (2022). *The Expectation Effect: How Mindset Can Change Your World*. Henry Holt and Co.

Steponenaite, A., & Barakat, B. (2023). Plagiarism in AI empowered world. In *International Conference on Human-Computer Interaction* (pp. 434-442). Cham: Springer Nature Switzerland.

Stetsenko, A. (2017). *The Transformative Mind: Expanding Vygotsky's Approach to Development and Education*. Cambridge University Press.

Stewart, J. (2023). *Noam Chomsky says ChatGPT is a form of "high-tech plagiarism"*. My Modern Met.

Stockwell, G. R. (2004). CMC for language learning: Examining the possibilities. In *JALTCALL 2004 Conference, Tokiwa University, Mito, Japan* (Vol. 3, p. 3).

Stratford, R. (2015). What is the ecological university and why is it a significant challenge for higher education policy and practice? In *PESA - Philosophy of Education Society of Australasia*. ANCU.

Stratford, R. J. (2024). Towards ecological everything – The ecological university, ecological subjectivity and the ecological curriculum. *Policy Futures in Education*, 0(0), 1–9. 10.1177/14782103241227005

Sugimoto, K. (2006). Australia's Transnational Higher Education in the Asia-Pacific Region: Its Strategies and Quality Assurance. In Huang, F. (Ed.), International Publication Series: Vol. 10. *Transnational Higher Education in Asia and the Pacific Region* (pp. 1–19). Research Institute for Higher Education, Hiroshima University.

Sun, J. C. Y., & Rueda, R. (2012). Situational interest, computer self-efficacy and self-regulation: Their impact on student engagement in distance education. *British Journal of Educational Technology*, 43(2), 191–204. 10.1111/j.1467-8535.2010.01157.x

Sutton, R. E., & Wheatley, K. F. (2003). Teachers' emotions and teaching: A review of the literature and directions for future research. *Educational Psychology Review*, 15(4), 327–358. 10.1023/A:1026131715856

Swan Dagen, A., DeFrank-Cole, L., Glance, C., & Lockman, J. (2022). You cannot be what you cannot see: Supporting women's leadership development in higher education. *Consulting Psychology Journal*, 74(2), 194–206. 10.1037/cpb0000207

Szczurek-Boruta, A. (2021). School and shaping students' identities: A report on the studies into youth in the Silesian voivodeship. *European Review (Chichester, England)*, 30(3), 408–425. 10.1017/S1062798721000120

Tabula, (2023). History of United National exams Retrieved from https://tabula.ge/ge/news/703749-ertiani-erovnuli-gamotsdebis-istoria

Tamayo, J., Doumi, L., Goel, S., Kovacs-Ondrejkovic, O., & Sadun, R. (2023). Reskilling in the Age of AI. Available from: https://hbr.org/2023/09/reskilling-in-the-age-of-ai

Tatzel, A., & Mael, D. (2023). Write a paper on AI plagiarism": An analysis on ChatGPT and its impact on academic dishonesty in higher education.

Tavakol, M., & Tavakoli, M. (2022). The professional identity of Iranian young-learner teachers of English: A narrative inquiry. *Linguistics and Education*, 71, 101101. 10.1016/j.linged.2022.101101

Taxer, J. L., Becker-Kurz, B., & Frenzel, A. C. (2019). Do quality teacher–student relationships protect teachers from emotional exhaustion? The mediating role of enjoyment and anger. *Social Psychology of Education*, 22(1), 209–226. 10.1007/s11218-018-9468-4

Teimouri, Y., Goetze, J., & Plonsky, L. (2019). Second language anxiety and achievement: A meta-analysis. *Studies in Second Language Acquisition*, 41(2), 363–387. Advance online publication. 10.1017/S0272263118000311

Temple, R. S. (2009) An empirical analysis of nurse manager leadership practices and staff nurse job satisfaction. (Order No. 3356436, Walden University).

The Centre For Contemporary History, (2023). Number of mass media in Georgia. Retrieved from:https//:permalink. php?story_fbid=4892837370831636&id=2171706859611381&paipv=0&eav=AfbdieWquEnpppiaFswM9bhyMjVrn tPaa4KfH7l7UHMSDrJpvWitxkvJaclNlcEXQok&_rdr

Thomas, G. (2013). A review of thinking and research about inclusive education policy, with suggestions for a new kind of inclusive thinking. *British Educational Research Journal*, 39(3), 473–490. 10.1080/01411926.2011.652070

Thomas, G., & Thorpe, S. (2019). Enhancing the facilitation of online groups in higher education: A review of the literature on face-to-face and online group-facilitation. *Interactive Learning Environments*, 27(1), 62–71. 10.1080/10494820.2018.1451897

Tiika, B. J., Tang, Z., Azaare, J., Dagadu, J. C., & Otoo, S. N. A. (2024). Evaluating E-Government Development among Africa Union Member States: An Analysis of the Impact of E-Government on Public Administration and Governance in Ghana. *Sustainability (Basel)*, 16(3), 1333. 10.3390/su16031333

Tkeshelashvili, S. (2020). How many Georgian students study in the USA? Retrieved from: https://bm.ge/news/ramdeni -qartveli-studenti-swavlobs-ashsh-shi/63064

Tlili, A., Shehata, B., Adarkwah, M. A., Bozkurt, A., Hickey, D. T., Huang, R., & Agyemang, B. (2023). What if the devil is my guardian angel: ChatGPT as a case study of using chatbots in education. *Smart Learning Environments*, 10(1), 15. 10.1186/s40561-023-00237-x

Tomasik, M. J., Helbling, L. A., & Moser, U. (2021). Educational gains of in-person vs. distance learning in primary and secondary schools: A natural experiment during the COVID-19 pandemic school closures in Switzerland. *International Journal of Psychology*, 56(4), 566–576. 10.1002/ijop.1272833236341

Toom, A., Pyhältö, K., & Rust, F. O. (2015). Teachers' professional agency in contradictory times. *Teachers and Teaching*, 21(6), 615–623. 10.1080/13540602.2015.1044334

Top, M., Akdere, M., & Tarcan, M. (2015). Examining transformational leadership, job satisfaction, organizational commitment and organizational trust in Turkish hospitals: Public servants versus private sector employees. *International Journal of Human Resource Management*, 26(9), 1259–1282. 10.1080/09585192.2014.939987

Torino, G., Rivera, D., Capodilupo, C., Nadal, K., & Sue, D. W. (Eds.). (2019). *Microaggressive theory: influence and implications*. John Wiley & Sons, Inc.

Tourish, D. (2013). *The Dark Side of Transformational Leadership: A Critical Perspective*. Routledge. 10.4324/9780203558119

Trent, J. (2012). The discursive positioning of teachers: Native-speaking English teachers and educational discourse in Hong Kong. *Tesol Quarterly, 46*, 104e126

Compilation of References

Trent, J. (2014). Towards a multifaceted, multidimensional framework for understanding teacher identity. In Cheung, Y. L., Said, S. B., & Park, K. (Eds.), *Advances and Current Trends in Language Teacher Identity Research* (pp. 44–58). Routledge. 10.4324/9781315775135-4

Trowler, V. (2010). Student engagement literature review. *The Higher Education Academy*, 11, 1–15.

Truzoli, R., Pirola, V., & Conte, S. (2021). The impact of risk and protective factors on online teaching experience in high school Italian teachers during the COVID-19 pandemic. *Journal of Computer Assisted Learning*, 37(4), 940–952. 10.1111/jcal.1253333821075

Tsang, A. (2018). Positive effects of a program on oral presentation skills: High- and low-proficient learners' self-evaluations and perspectives. *Assessment & Evaluation in Higher Education*, 43(5), 760–771. 10.1080/02602938.2017.1407917

Tsui, A. B. M. (2007). Complexities of identity formation: A narrative inquiry of an EFL teacher. *TESOL Quarterly*, 41(4), 657–680. 10.1002/j.1545-7249.2007.tb00098.x

Tsybulsky, D., & Muchnik-Rozanov, Y. (2019). The development of student-teachers' professional identity while team-teaching science classes using a project-based learning approach: A multi-level analysis. *Teaching and Teacher Education*, 79, 48–59. 10.1016/j.tate.2018.12.006

UK Office for National Statistics. (2021) [Online]. Available at: https://www.ons.gov.uk/peoplepopulationandcommunity/birthsdeathsandmarriages/lifeexpectancies/bulletins/nationallifetablesunitedkingdom/2018to2020. Accessed 10 February 2024.

Underhill, A. (1994). *Sound Foundations*. Heinemann.

UNESCO International Institute for Higher Education in Latin America and the Caribbean [UNESCO IESALC] & Times Higher Education. (2021). Women in higher education: Has the female advantage put an end to gender inequalities? Retrieved from https://www.iesalc.unesco.org/wp-content/uploads/2021/03/Women-Report-8032021.pdf

UNESCO International Institute for Higher Education in Latin America and the Caribbean [UNESCO IESALC] & Times Higher Education. (2022). Gender equality: How global universities are performing. Retrieved from https://www.timeshighereducation.com/sites/default/files/the_gender_equality_report_part_1.pdf

UNESCO. (2002). *'Open and Distance Learning Trends, Policy and Strategy Considerations'*, 14 UNESCO. "United Nations. Economic Commission for Africa; United Nations. Economic Commission for Africa (2023-12). Digital Infrastructure in Africa. Addis Ababa. © UN. ECA, https://hdl.handle.net/10855/50027"

United Nations Educational, Scientific and Cultural Organization Institute for Statistics. (2019) *Global flow of tertiary-level students*. Accessed on December 12, 2021, from http://uis.unesco.org/en/uis-student-flow#slideoutmenu

Universities, U. K. (2022) The scale of UK higher education transnational education 2020–21. Available: https://www.universitiesuk.ac.uk/universities-uk-international/insights-and-publications/uuki-publications/scale-uk-higher-education-transnational-3. (Accessed 16 February 2024).

University of Nottingham Ningbo China. (2024) Leadership. Available: https://www.nottingham.edu.cn/en/about/university-leadership/university-leadership.aspx [Accessed Feb 2, 2024].

Unterhalter, E., Longlands, H., & Vaughan, R. P. (2022). Gender and Intersecting Inequalities in Education: Reflections on a Framework for Measurement. *Journal of Human Development and Capabilities*, 23(4), 509–538. 10.1080/19452829.2022.2090523

Urman, A., & Makhortykh, M. (2023). *The Silence of the LLMs: Cross-Lingual Analysis of Political Bias and False Information Prevalence in ChatGPT*. Google Bard, and Bing Chat.

Van Geyte, E., & Hadjianastasis, M. (2022). Quality and qualifications: The value of centralised teaching courses for postgraduates who teach. *The International Journal for Academic Development*, 27(1), 4–16. 10.1080/1360144X.2020.1863810

van Inwegen, E., Munyikwa, Z., & Horton, J. (2023) Algorithmic writing assistance on jobseekers' resumes increases hires. *Working paper.* https://arxiv.org/abs/2301.08083

van Knippenberg, D., De Dreu, C. K. W., & Homan, A. C. (2004). Work group diversity and group performance: An integrative model and research agenda. *The Journal of Applied Psychology*, 89(6), 1008–1022. 10.1037/0021-9010.89.6.100815584838

Varghese, M., Morgan, B., Johnston, B., & Johnson, K. A. (2005). Theorizing language teacher identity: Three perspectives and beyond. *Journal of Language, Identity, and Education*, 4(1), 21–44. 10.1207/s15327701jlie0401_2

Videnov, K., Stoykova, V., & Kazlacheva, Z. (2018). Application of augmented reality in higher education. ARTTE Applied Researches in Technics. *Technologies and Education*, 6(1), 1–9.

Villasenor, J. (2023). How ChatGPT Can Improve Education, Not Threaten it. [EB/OL] [2023-05-14]. Available online at: https://www.scientficamerican.com/article/how-chatgpt-can~improve-education-not-threaten-it/. [Accessed 27 April 2024]

Vizek Vidović, V., & Domović, V. (2019). Development of teachers' beliefs as a core component of their professional identity in initial teacher education: A longitudinal perspective. *Center for Educational Policy Studies Journal*, 9(2), 119–138. 10.26529/cepsj.720

Wach, K., Duong, C. D., Ejdys, J., Kazlauskaitė, R., Korzynski, P., Mazurek, G., Paliszkiewicz, J., & Ziemba, E. (2023). The dark side of generative artificial intelligence: A critical analysis of controversies and risks of ChatGPT. *Entrepreneurial Business and Economics Review*, 11(2), 7–30. 10.15678/EBER.2023.110201

Wakui, N., Abe, S., Shirozu, S., Yamamoto, Y., Yamamura, M., Abe, Y., & Kikuchi, M. (2021). Causes of anxiety among teachers giving face-to-face lessons after the reopening of schools during the COVID-19 pandemic: A cross-sectional study. *BMC Public Health*, 21(1), 1–10. 10.1186/s12889-021-11130-y34078343

Walker, C. (2021). Transformational instructor leadership in English for academic purposes: A case study. Doctoral thesis, University of Calgary. Available at: http://hdl.handle.net/1880/114189 [Accessed: Mar.16th 2024].

Walker, G. (2002). *To educate the nations: Reflections on an international education.* John Catt Educational Ltd.

Walker, M. (2006, March). Towards a capability-based theory of social justice for education policy-making. *Journal of Education Policy. Vol*, (2), 163–185.

Walker, M., & Unterhalter, E. (2007). *Amartya Sen's capability approach and social justice in education.* Palgrave Macmillan. 10.1057/9780230604810

Walkington, J. (2005). Becoming a Teacher: Encouraging Development of Teacher Identity through Reflective Practice. *Asia-Pacific Journal of Teacher Education*, 33(1), 53–64. 10.1080/1359866052000341124

Wang, F., Guo, J., Wu, B., & Lin, Z. (2021). "It is utterly out of my expectation"-A case inquiry of teacher identity of an EFL teacher in a Chinese shadow school setting. *Frontiers in Psychology*, 12, 760161. https://www.frontiersin.org/articles/10.3389/fpsyg.2021.760161. 10.3389/fpsyg.2021.760161

Wang, L., & Du, X. (2014). Chinese teachers' professional identity and beliefs about the teacher-student relationships in an intercultural context. *Frontiers of Education in China*, 9(3), 429–455. 10.1007/BF03397030

Wang, L., & Fang, F. (2020). Native-speakerism policy in English language teaching revisited: Chinese university teachers' and students' attitudes towards native and non-native English-speaking teachers. *Cogent Education*, 7(1), 1778374. 10.1080/2331186X.2020.1778374

Wang, X., Su, Y., Cheung, S., Wong, E., & Kwong, T. (2013). An exploration of Biggs' constructive alignment in course design and its impact on students' learning approaches. *Assessment & Evaluation in Higher Education*, 38(4), 477–491. 10.1080/02602938.2012.658018

Warren, T. (2023). Microsoft is looking at OpenAI's GPT for word, outlook, and PowerPoint. The Verge., Retrieved April 26, 2024, from.

Weber, E., Krehl, E.-H., & Büttgen, M. (2022). The Digital Transformation Leadership Framework: Conceptual and Empirical Insights into Leadership Roles in Technology-Driven Business Environments. *Journal of Leadership Studies*, 16(1), 6–22. 10.1002/jls.21810

Weber, M. (2009). *The Theory of Social and Economic Organization*. Simon and Schuster.

Wells, C. (2006). *English intonation: an introduction*. Cambridge University Press.

Wen, Z., & Younes, R. (2024). ChatGPT vs Media Bias: A Comparative Study of GPT-3.5 and Fine-tuned Language Models. *arXiv preprint arXiv:2403.20158*.

Wenger, A. (2021). *My Life in Red and White*. W&N.

Wenger, E. (1998). *Communities of practice: Learning, meaning, and identity*. Cambridge University Press. 10.1017/CBO9780511803932

Wennerstrom, A. (2003). Students as discourse analysts in the conversation class. In Burton, J., & Clennell, C. (Eds.), *Interaction and Language Learning* (pp. 161–175). TESOL Publications.

West, G. B. (2019). Navigating morality in neoliberal spaces of English language education. *Linguistics and Education*, 49, 31–40. 10.1016/j.linged.2018.12.004

Widodo, H. P., Fang, F., & Elyas, T. (2020). The construction of language teacher professional identity in the Global Englishes territory: 'we are legitimate language teachers'. *Asian Englishes*, 22(3), 309–316. 10.1080/13488678.2020.1732683

Wildavsky, B. (2010). *The Great Brain Race: How Global Universities Are Reshaping the World*. Princeton University Press.

Wilkins, S., & Neri, S. (2019). Managing faculty in transnational higher education: Expatriate academics at international branch campuses. *Journal of Studies in International Education*, 23(4), 451–472. 10.1177/1028315318814200

Williams, T. M., & Wolniak, G. C. (2021). Unpacking the "Female Advantage" in the Career and Economic Impacts of College. In N. S. Niemi & M. B. Weaver-Hightower (Eds.), *The Wiley Handbook of Gender Equity in Higher Education* (pp. 7-28). New York: John Wiley & Sons.

Williams, K. S., & Daniel, H. (2021). Applying Sen's Capabilities Approach to the Delivery of Positive Youth Justice. *Youth Justice*, 21(1), 90–106. https://doi-org.ezproxy.nottingham.edu.cn/10.1177/1473225420953208. 10.1177/1473225420953208

Williamson, B., Eynon, R., & Potter, J. (2020). Pandemic politics, pedagogies and practices: Digital technologies and distance education during the coronavirus emergency. *Learning, Media and Technology*, 45(2), 107–114. 10.1080/17439884.2020.1761641

Wilson, L.O. (2016). Anderson and Krathwohl–Bloom's taxonomy revised. Understanding the new version of Bloom's taxonomy.

Wilson, K. (2016). Critical Reading, Critical Thinking: Delicate Scaffolding in English for Academic Purposes (EAP). *Thinking Skills and Creativity*, 22, 256–265. 10.1016/j.tsc.2016.10.002

Winkler, H. (2023). *Being Henry*. Celadon Books.

Wolff, D., & De Costa, P. I. (2017). Expanding the language teacher identity land-scape: An investigation of the emotions and strategies of a NNEST. *The Modern Language Journal, 101*(S1), 76e90.

Wong, K., Chan, A., & Ngan, S. (2019). The Effect of Long Working Hours and Overtime on Occupational Health: A Meta-Analysis of Evidence from 1998 to 2018. *International Journal of Environmental Research and Public Health*, 16(12), 2102. 10.3390/ijerph1612210231200573

Woods, P. (1993). Critical events in education. *British Journal of Sociology of Education*, 14(4), 355–371. 10.1080/0142569930140401

Woolard, G. (1993). Intonation matters. *Modern English Teacher*, 2(2), 23–24.

Wright, E. O., Baxter, J., & Birkelund, G. E. (1995). The gender gap in workplace authority: A cross-national study. *American Sociological Review*, 60(3), 407–435. 10.2307/2096422

Wu, J., & Hu, H. (2016, December 9). *Xi Jinping emphasizes at the national college ideological and political work conference the importance of conducting ideological and political work throughout the whole process of education to create a new situation for the development of China's higher education*. Xinhuanet. http://www.xinhuanet.com/politics/2016-12/08/c_1120082577.htm

Wu, M.-H., & Leung, G. (2020). 'It's not my Chinese': A teacher and her students disrupting and dismantling conventional notions of 'Chinese' through translanguaging in a heritage language classroom. *International Journal of Bilingual Education and Bilingualism*. Advance online publication. 10.1080/13670050.2020.1804524

Yang, L., Chiu, M. M., Yan Z. (2021) The power of teacher feedback in affecting student learning and achievement: Insights from students' perspectives, *Educational Psychology*, 41:7 821-824, DOI: .10.1080/01443410.2021.1964855

Yang, J. (2019). Understanding Chinese language teachers' beliefs about themselves and their students in an English context. *System*, 80, 73–82. 10.1016/j.system.2018.10.014

Yang, S., Shu, D., & Yin, H. (2021). 'Frustration drives me to grow': Unraveling EFL teachers' emotional trajectory interacting with identity development. *Teaching and Teacher Education*, 105, 103420. Advance online publication. 10.1016/j.tate.2021.103420

Yang, S., Shu, D., & Yin, H. (2022). The bright side of dark emotions: Exploring EFL teachers' emotions, emotional capital, and engagement in curriculum implementation. *Teaching and Teacher Education*, 117, 103811. 10.1016/j.tate.2022.103811

Yanguas, Í. (2010). Oral Computer-Mediated Interaction between L2 Learners: It's about Time! *Language Learning & Technology*, 14, 72–93. 10125/44227

Yeadon, W., Agra, E., Inyang, O. O., Mackay, P., & Mizouri, A. (2024). Evaluating AI and human authorship quality in academic writing through physics essays. *arXiv preprint.* Available at: https://arxiv.org/abs/2403.05458

Ye, W. (2023). *Moral education in China*. Routledge.

Yim, S. Y., & Hwang, K. (2019). Expatriate ELT teachers in Korea: Participation and sense of belonging. *ELT Journal*, 73(1), 72–81. 10.1093/elt/ccy036

Compilation of References

Yin, Q. (2023) Even as Tensions Grow, U.S.-China Joint Venture Universities Have Room to Develop. *New Perspectives on Asia*, CSIS. Available at: Even as Tensions Grow, U.S.-China Joint Venture Universities Have Room to Develop | New Perspectives on Asia | CSIS [Accessed: Dec.9th, 2023].

Yin, H. (2015). The effect of teachers' emotional labour on teaching satisfaction: Moderation of emotional intelligence. *Teachers and Teaching*, 21(7), 789–810. 10.1080/13540602.2014.995482

Yip, J. W. C. (1), Huang, J. (2), & Teng, M. F. (3). (2022). Identity and emotion of university English teachers during curriculum reform in China. *Language, Culture and Curriculum, 35*(4), 421-439–439. https://doi-org.ez.xjtlu.edu.cn/10.1080/07908318.2021.2024843

Young, D. J. (1990). An investigation of students' perspectives on anxiety and speaking. *Foreign Language Annals*, 23(6), 539–553. 10.1111/j.1944-9720.1990.tb00424.x

Young, D. M., Rudman, L. A., Buettner, H. M., & McLean, M. C. (2013). The influence of female role models on women's implicit science cognitions. *Psychology of Women Quarterly*, 37(3), 283–292. 10.1177/0361684313482109

Yuan, R., & Lee, I. (2016). ''I need to be strong and competent': A narrative inquiry of a student-teacher's emotions and identities in teaching practicum. *Teachers and Teaching*, 22(7), 819–841. 10.1080/13540602.2016.1185819

Yuan, R., & Zhang, L. J. (2019). Teacher metacognitions about identities: Case studies of four expert language teachers in china. *TESOL Quarterly*, 54(4), 870–899. 10.1002/tesq.561

Yu, Q. (2018). Inquiry into the permeation of moral education in primary. *English Teaching*, 11–15. Advance online publication. 10.2991/hssmee-18.2018.3

Zadok-Gurman, T., Jakobovich, R., Dvash, E., Zafrani, K., Rolnik, B., Ganz, A. B., & Lev-Ari, S. (2021). Effect of inquiry-based stress reduction (IBSR) intervention on well-being, resilience and burnout of teachers during the COVID-19 pandemic. *International Journal of Environmental Research and Public Health*, 18(7), 3689. 10.3390/ijerph1807368933916258

Zahari, I. B., & Shurbagi, A. M. A. (2012). The effect of organizational culture and the relationship between transformational leadership and job satisfaction in petroleum sector of Libya. *International Business Research*, 5(9), 89–97. 10.5539/ibr.v5n9p89

Zahira, J. (2021). *The Real Value of Middle Managers*. Available from: https://hbr.org/2021/06/the-real-value-of-middle-managers

Zawacki-Richter, O., Marín, V. I., Bond, M., & Gouverneur, F. (2020). Systematic review of research on artificial intelligence applications in higher education – where are the educators? *International Journal of Educational Technology in Higher Education*, 16(1), 39. 10.1186/s41239-019-0171-0

Zembylas, M. (2003). Emotions and teacher identity: A poststructural perspective. *Teachers and Teaching*, 9(3), 213–238. 10.1080/13540600309378

Zhang, C., Yan, X., & Wang, J. (2021). EFL teachers' online assessment practices during the COVID-19 pandemic: Changes and mediating factors. *The Asia-Pacific Education Researcher*, 30(6), 499–507. 10.1007/s40299-021-00589-3

Zhang, K., & Wu, H. (2022). Synchronous Online Learning During COVID-19: Chinese University EFL Students' Perspectives. *SAGE Open*, 12(2), 1–10. 10.1177/21582440221094821

Zhang, Q. (2022a). A qualitative analysis of university foreign language teachers' practical knowledge required by curriculum of ideological and political education. *Foreign Languages Research*, 39(3), 58–63. 10.13978/j.cnki.wyyj.2022.03.003

Zhang, Q. (2022b). Exploring a university EFL teacher's identity through positioning analysis. *Shandong Foreign Language Teaching*, 43(3), 50–59. 10.16482/j.sdwy37-1026.2022-03-006

Zhang, W., & Liu, M. (2013). Evaluating the impact of oral test anxiety and speaking strategy use on oral English performance. *The Journal of Asia TEFL*, 10(2), 115–148.

Zhang, W., Zhao, H. M., & Hu, J. H. (2022). The status quo and needs analysis of college foreign language teachers' teaching competence in curriculum-based ideological education. *Foreign Language World*, 210(3), 28–36.

Zhang, X., Admiraal, W., & Saab, N. (2021). Teachers' motivation to participate in continuous professional development: Relationship with factors at the personal and school level. *Journal of Education for Teaching*, 47(5), 714–731. 10.1080/02607476.2021.1942804

Zheng, B. B., & Warschauer, M. (2015). Participation, interaction, and academic achievement in an online discussion environment. *Computers & Education*, 84, 78–89. 10.1016/j.compedu.2015.01.008

Žnidaršič, J., & Marič, M. (2020). *Understanding Work Life Conflict and its Implications*. Available from: https://www.researchgate.net/publication/350517367_Understanding_work-life_conflict_and_its_implications

Zou, B., Wang, X., & Yu, C. (2022). 'The impact of Sino-foreign cooperative universities in China on Chinese postgraduate students' learning performances in the United Kingdom and United States'. *Frontiers in Psychology*, 13, 1012614. Advance online publication. 10.3389/fpsyg.2022.101261436304855

About the Contributors

Gareth Morris *(SFHEA) works at University of Nottingham Ningbo (UNNC) as a Senior Tutor in CELE. Prior to joining UNNC Gareth worked for two years at the Perse School (Suzhou) and for a decade at Xi'an Jiao Tong-Liverpool University (XJTLU). During his time at XJTLU Gareth also completed his doctorate at the University of Exeter. His current research interests are in the areas of leadership and management, motivation and satisfaction, recruitment and retention, professional development, organisational and educational psychology, and health and wellbeing.*

***

Seblewongel Esseynew *Research Scholar, Addis Ababa University Addis Ababa, Ethiopia. sebess2000@yahoo.com*

Ying Feng *is Assistant Professor in Strategic Management. Prior to her position in IBSS, Ying worked as Assistant Professor in Strategic Management in Rennes School of Business, France. Ying's research covers a wide range of topics in business, including technology innovation and entrepreneurship, strategic decision-making, resource allocation and corporate governance in both large and small businesses. Her work appears in top-tier journals such as Organization Studies. She uses quantitative and qualitative methods in her research.*

Chenghao Hu *currently bases on the University of Nottingham Ningbo China, Faculty of Science and Engineering, Department of Electrical and Electronic Engineering. He has been researching and studying in UNNC for approximately two years, assuming responsibility of leadership in diverse teams regarding both academic and sports fields. Chenghao is recently leading a student group in several Electrical and Electronic Engineering Projects and a Squash Engage Course in the Sports Department of UNNC. He has experienced various leadership roles and is interested in student leadership within the realm of transnational higher education.*

Mahmoud Jeidani *is an EAP Tutor at the University of Nottingham, China. He has previously taught at the Universities of Warwick, Coventry, and The Chinese University of Hong Kong. His primary interests include the research and teaching of English Intonation.*

Vanessa Ma *has a master's degree from University College London. I am currently working as an academic English teacher in Suzhou Institute of Xi'an Jiaotong University. I attended an academic conference at Zhejiang University to present the impact of science and technology on education. My research interests include English education, student learning motivation, teacher job motivation and satisfaction.*

Getachew Mekuria Habtemariam *is in the department of Software Engineering Debre Berhan University, Ethiopia. getachewmekuria19@gmail.com*

Nilamadhab Mishra *is an Associate Professor in the School of Computer Science and Engineering, AI-ML Division, at VIT Bhopal University, India. He received his Doctor of Philosophy (Ph.D.) in Computer Science & Information Engineering with a specialization in Data Science & Machine Learning from Chang Gung University, Taiwan. He has more than 22 years of national and international involvement in academic teaching and research at recognized Indian, Taiwanese, and African universities. He has over 50 publications in SCI/SCIE and SCOPUS-indexed journals, ISBN books and chapters, Indian and Australian patents, IEEE conference proceedings, and others. He has served as a reviewer, associate editor, and editorial board member for SCI/SCIE-indexed journals and conferences. Dr. Mishra worked on multiple funded research projects from the MOST, NSC, and CGU Memorial Hospital, Taiwan, during his Ph.D. and has been involved with several professional bodies. He is currently an Associate Editor for two SCOPUS-indexed journals, and his research interests span the areas of AI, Data Science, Machine Learning, and Cognitive Analytics & Applications.*

Junhua Mo *is associate professor of English in the School of Foreign Languages, Soochow University, Suzhou, China. He obtained his PhD in applied linguistics from Nanjing University, China. His major interests include teacher development, second language acquisition, and discourse analysis.*

About the Contributors

Rudra Kalyan Nayak *is in the School of Computing Science and Engineering, VIT Bhopal University, Sehore, Madhya Pradesh – 466114, India rudrakalyannayak@gmail.com*

Basanta Kumar Padhi *is an Associate Professor at Balasore College Of Engineering and Technology, Sergarh, Balasore-756060, Odisha.*

Stuart Perrin *is currently the Chief Officer of Ecology at XJTLU. Prior to this, he was the founding Associate Principal of the XJTLU Entrepreneur College, a new education venture built around technology-based education through concepts of AI and industry 4.0. Other positions that he has held in the university include Dean for Internationalisation (2017-2019), Dean for Learning and Teaching (2013-2017), and Director of the Language Centre (2012-2016). In this role he was responsible for the introduction of modern foreign languages into the curriculum. He has previously worked in management positions in language centres at Queen Mary, University of London, and Brunel University, as well as within the private sector.*

Sabyasachi Pramanik *is a professional IEEE member. He obtained a PhD in Computer Science and Engineering from Sri Satya Sai University of Technology and Medical Sciences, Bhopal, India. Presently, he is an Associate Professor, Department of Computer Science and Engineering, Haldia Institute of Technology, India. He has many publications in various reputed international conferences, journals, and book chapters (Indexed by SCIE, Scopus, ESCI, etc). He is doing research in the fields of Artificial Intelligence, Data Privacy, Cybersecurity, Network Security, and Machine Learning. He also serves on the editorial boards of several international journals. He is a reviewer of journal articles from IEEE, Springer, Elsevier, Inderscience, IET and IGI Global. He has reviewed many conference papers, has been a keynote speaker, session chair, and technical program committee member at many international conferences. He has authored a book on Wireless Sensor Network. He has edited 8 books from IGI Global, CRC Press, Springer and Wiley Publications.*

Li Tao *is associate professor of English in the School of Foreign Languages, Soochow University, Suzhou, China. She obtained her PhD in applied linguistics from Soochow University, China. Her major interests include teacher development and materials development.*

Ramamani Tripathy *Chitkara University School of Engineering & Technology, Chitkara University, Himachal Pradesh, India. ramamani.tripathy@chitkarauniversity.edu.in*

Chenghao Wang *is a PhD student in the Department of Applied Linguistics, Xi'an Jiaotong-Liverpool University, Suzhou, China. His research interests include Computer-Assisted Language Learning (CALL), AI-assisted language learning and teaching, EAP and WTC.*

Katherine Wang *is an English for Academic Purposes (EAP) tutor within the Centre for English Language Education at the University of Nottingham, Ningbo, China. She has been actively engaging in higher education to teach general and specific academic English to university students. Her academic interests focus on EAP teaching methodology in higher education contexts.*

Ling Wang *is currently an Educational Developer at Xi'an Jiaotong-Liverpool University (XJTLU), delivering the Postgraduate Certificate in Teaching and Supporting Learning in Higher Education (PGCert) programme, Continuing Professional Development (CPD) programme, working with academics by providing assistance and guidance on peer review, curriculum and assessment design, and other learning and teaching projects. Previously, Ling worked as the English Language Lecturer and the inaugural head of Programme Management and Quality Assurance Office at XJTLU. She holds MSc in Education in the University of Groningen, the Netherlands. Her research interests include assessment, feedback, quality assurance and quality enhancement, teacher training and development.*

Rong Yan *is the Deputy Director of the M.A. Programme in Child Development & Family Education and a Senior Associate Professor of Psychology at the Department of Educational Studies, Academy of Future Education, Xi'an Jiaotong-Liverpool University. His research interests include language acquisition, early childhood & bilingual education and developmental & educational Psychology.*

Claudia Yang *joined UNNC in September of 2022 and majored in Finance, Accounting, and Management. As a year 2 student, she has had diverse leadership experiences that shaped her character and passion for entrepreneurship. Her current research interest is in firm innovation, leaders' well-being, and Alone Together among students at Chinese universities.*

Ziyang Shi *currently based in University of Nottingham, Ningbo, and he has exchanged to University of Copenhagen in the spring semester of his year 3 study. His major is international relations and international affairs, and he has served as a research assistant in the Centre for global studies, School of Social Science, Tsinghua University for more than one year. Besides, he also once served as president of UNNC badminton club, captain of UNNC squash excel, vice president of UNNC poetry club. His current interest field is East Asia regional politics and China study from a comparative perspective.*

About the Contributors

Ying You, *graduating from Xi'an Jiaotong-Liverpool University, is currently employed at Yijianhe Experimental Primary School in Wuzhong District, Suzhou. Her research interests encompass CALL (Computer-Assisted Language Learning), AI applications in English education, oral English teaching techniques, and integrated teaching of primary school English textbooks and picture books.*

Bin Zou *received his PhD degree in TESOL and Computer Technology from the University of Bristol, UK. He is a Senior Associate Professor and PhD supervisor at the Department of Applied Linguistics, Xi'an Jiaotong-Liverpool University. His research interests include Computer-Assisted Language Learning (CALL), AI, EAP and ELT. He is the Founding Editor and Co-Editor-in-Chief of two international journals: the International Journal of Computer-Assisted Language Learning and Teaching and the International Journal of EAP: Research and Practice.*

Index

A

Academic listening and speaking 176
Academy 14, 35, 37, 83, 150, 156, 161, 276, 280, 281, 286, 296
Augmented Reality 79, 229, 230, 231, 232, 233, 234, 235, 236, 238, 241, 242, 243

C

Case Studies 70, 78, 79, 136, 146, 197, 233
Computing Technology 304, 322
COVID-19 pandemic 53, 58, 69, 75, 76, 79, 80, 85, 91, 92, 94, 103, 109, 110, 111, 112, 113, 114, 115, 147, 209, 225

E

EAP 53, 69, 70, 71, 72, 73, 74, 75, 76, 77, 78, 79, 80, 81, 82, 83, 85, 95, 96, 101, 171, 173, 174, 177, 182, 184, 185, 186, 187, 252, 253
Ecology of Knowledge 268, 277
Education 1, 2, 3, 4, 5, 6, 7, 8, 9, 10, 11, 12, 13, 14, 15, 16, 17, 18, 19, 20, 21, 22, 23, 24, 25, 27, 28, 29, 30, 31, 32, 33, 34, 35, 36, 37, 38, 39, 40, 41, 42, 43, 44, 46, 47, 48, 49, 50, 52, 53, 54, 55, 56, 57, 58, 59, 63, 66, 67, 68, 69, 70, 71, 72, 73, 74, 75, 76, 77, 78, 79, 80, 81, 82, 83, 90, 93, 99, 105, 106, 107, 108, 109, 110, 111, 112, 113, 114, 115, 121, 122, 123, 124, 125, 126, 127, 128, 129, 130, 131, 133, 134, 135, 136, 137, 141, 143, 144, 146, 147, 148, 149, 150, 151, 155, 156, 157, 159, 160, 161, 162, 170, 171, 184, 185, 186, 187, 191, 192, 193, 195, 196, 198, 201, 204, 205, 206, 207, 208, 209, 210, 212, 214, 225, 226, 227, 228, 229, 230, 231, 232, 233, 234, 235, 236, 237, 238, 239, 240, 241, 242, 243, 244, 245, 246, 247, 248, 249, 250, 251, 252, 253, 254, 255, 256, 257, 258, 259, 260, 261, 262, 263, 264, 265, 266, 267, 268, 269, 270, 271, 272, 273, 274, 275, 276, 277, 278, 279, 280, 281, 282, 283, 284, 285, 286, 287, 288, 289, 290, 291, 292, 293, 294, 295, 296, 297, 298, 299, 300, 303, 304, 305, 308, 309, 315, 318, 320, 321
Educational Technology 80, 83, 225, 228, 243, 261, 263
Experience 1, 2, 4, 8, 14, 20, 25, 28, 39, 42, 43, 47, 50, 59, 60, 61, 72, 74, 75, 76, 77, 79, 88, 89, 95, 96, 98, 100, 101, 105, 112, 113, 116, 121, 124, 126, 129, 138, 139, 140, 142, 149, 150, 154, 155, 156, 157, 158, 159, 161, 162, 170, 174, 179, 184, 189, 191, 192, 195, 196, 197, 198, 199, 200, 201, 203, 204, 209, 210, 211, 221, 222, 223, 224, 225, 231, 234, 235, 236, 239, 240, 241, 245, 254, 260, 264, 267, 271, 272, 273, 278, 285, 303
Experiential 233, 234, 242, 271, 273, 274
Experiential Learning 233, 234, 242, 271, 274

G

Gender Diversity 17, 19, 20, 21, 22, 23, 24, 27, 30, 31, 32, 36
Gender equality 1, 2, 5, 6, 7, 10, 12, 13, 14, 16, 17, 21, 24, 30, 31, 37, 305
Gender Equity 1, 16, 17, 20, 23, 27, 28, 29, 30, 31, 32, 33, 38
Glass Ceiling 18, 34, 36, 37
Global Citizenship 16, 23, 24, 31, 32
Government Organizations 301, 302, 316, 317, 322

H

Higher Education 1, 2, 3, 4, 5, 6, 7, 8, 9, 10, 11, 12, 13, 14, 15, 16, 17, 18, 19, 20, 21, 22, 23, 24, 25, 27, 28, 29, 30, 31, 32, 33, 34, 35, 36, 37, 38, 39, 40, 41, 42, 44, 46, 47, 48, 49, 50, 52, 53, 54, 55, 56, 57, 58, 59, 66, 68, 69, 71, 74, 77, 78, 79, 80, 81, 82, 83, 105, 106, 111, 121, 122, 131, 133, 134, 136, 137, 143, 146, 149, 150, 156, 159, 160, 161, 162, 170, 171, 186, 187, 191, 192, 193, 195, 196, 198, 201, 204, 205, 206, 207, 208, 209, 212, 225, 228, 229, 230, 231, 232, 241, 242, 243, 244, 245, 246, 247, 248, 249, 250, 251, 252, 253, 254, 255, 256, 257, 258, 259, 260, 261, 262, 264, 265, 266, 267, 268, 269, 270, 274, 275, 276, 277, 278, 279, 280, 282, 284, 285, 286, 287, 288, 289, 290, 292, 294, 296, 297, 298, 299, 300, 303, 304, 309, 318, 320, 321
History 4, 5, 21, 24, 107, 125, 128, 133, 231, 232, 236, 240, 247, 278, 279, 280, 281, 283, 286, 287, 289, 290, 291, 296, 298, 299

I

Immersive Technologies 229, 230, 231, 233, 234, 235, 236, 238, 239, 240, 241
Inclusive Leadership 16, 17, 23, 24, 27
Innovative 22, 49, 70, 71, 110, 133, 150, 192, 235, 239, 240, 242, 253, 257, 259, 266, 268, 272, 274, 277, 293

Insights 15, 17, 19, 20, 22, 29, 31, 33, 35, 39, 40, 42, 43, 50, 55, 59, 70, 73, 75, 76, 77, 78, 83, 131, 137, 138, 139, 145, 146, 175, 180, 183, 186, 191, 192, 194, 197, 204, 208, 224, 236, 238, 244, 245, 268, 276, 320

Institution 1, 2, 8, 10, 11, 23, 29, 37, 42, 43, 44, 53, 59, 65, 82, 91, 132, 138, 139, 145, 146, 159, 171, 192, 197, 249, 257, 258, 259, 273, 280, 282, 283, 284, 285, 286, 289, 290, 292, 293, 295, 296, 298, 299, 300

International School 55, 56, 65

Intonation 170, 171, 172, 173, 174, 175, 176, 177, 178, 179, 180, 181, 182, 183, 184, 185, 186, 187, 188, 189, 222

J

Job Satisfaction 53, 55, 56, 57, 58, 59, 62, 63, 64, 65, 66, 67, 68, 110, 147, 207, 253, 255, 259, 262, 320

K

K12 Education 58, 63

L

language anxiety 208, 209, 211, 212, 213, 215, 216, 220, 221, 223, 225, 226, 228

Leadership 1, 2, 3, 4, 5, 6, 7, 8, 9, 10, 11, 12, 15, 16, 17, 18, 19, 20, 21, 22, 23, 24, 25, 26, 27, 28, 29, 30, 31, 32, 33, 34, 35, 36, 37, 40, 41, 42, 43, 44, 47, 48, 49, 50, 53, 55, 56, 57, 58, 59, 60, 61, 62, 63, 64, 65, 66, 67, 68, 69, 70, 71, 72, 73, 74, 75, 76, 77, 78, 79, 80, 81, 82, 83, 105, 121, 131, 137, 138, 139, 140, 141, 142, 143, 144, 145, 146, 147, 149, 150, 151, 154, 157, 158, 159, 162, 184, 191, 192, 193, 194, 195, 196, 197, 198, 199, 200, 201, 202, 203, 204, 205, 206, 207, 244, 245, 257, 259, 266, 270, 271, 272, 275, 281, 283, 284, 285, 286, 301, 302, 303, 317, 318, 319, 320, 321, 322

Leadership awareness 301, 303, 317, 318, 319, 322

M

Management 13, 18, 34, 35, 36, 37, 39, 40, 41, 42, 44, 45, 46, 47, 48, 49, 53, 56, 58, 62, 63, 64, 67, 68, 76, 80, 81, 105, 126, 137, 138, 139, 140, 142, 143, 145, 148, 159, 197, 200, 201, 242, 245, 249, 252, 254, 257, 258, 262, 264, 276, 287, 290, 292, 303, 304, 305, 310, 311, 312, 313, 317, 318, 320, 321, 322

Mentorship 19, 24, 25, 26, 27, 28, 29, 31, 32, 36, 253

Motivation 40, 53, 54, 57, 61, 62, 64, 65, 67, 71, 74, 78, 110, 115, 119, 127, 140, 141, 147, 152, 156, 157, 159, 162, 173, 187, 191, 194, 195, 196, 197, 201, 204, 206, 207, 221, 225, 226, 227, 255, 257, 258

N

Natural Ecologies 269

O

online learning 42, 46, 69, 73, 74, 75, 79, 81, 92, 208, 209, 210, 211, 222, 224, 225, 226, 227, 228

P

Professional Development 9, 28, 29, 40, 41, 46, 47, 50, 53, 58, 62, 73, 75, 86, 89, 90, 91, 93, 94, 105, 107, 109, 112, 115, 123, 137, 138, 139, 143, 145, 158, 159, 160, 187, 234, 235, 237, 255

Pronunciation teaching 181, 182, 184, 185, 186, 187

R

Role Congruity 35

S

Science 13, 25, 29, 36, 38, 39, 50, 52, 81, 107, 113, 137, 147, 150, 156, 161, 214, 226, 227, 228, 240, 242, 251, 256, 261, 262, 264, 270, 273, 276, 283, 286, 287, 290, 291, 293, 296, 298, 299, 306, 321

Sino-foreign joint university 69

Skill Gap and trends 322

speaking skills 170, 171, 176, 181, 208, 211, 212, 213, 214, 215, 216, 217, 221, 223, 226, 227

Student 20, 22, 23, 26, 31, 41, 58, 63, 67, 69, 70, 71, 72, 74, 75, 76, 78, 80, 81, 83, 85, 99, 100, 102, 103, 104, 105, 108, 109, 112, 113, 114, 116, 118, 119, 122, 131, 138, 144, 145, 151, 152, 153, 155, 156, 157, 158, 160, 161, 162, 164, 170, 171, 175, 176, 177, 179, 180, 181, 182, 183, 184, 186, 188, 191, 192, 195, 196, 197, 201, 202, 204, 205, 206, 207, 208, 214, 217, 219, 221, 222, 223, 228, 231, 233, 235, 236, 237, 238, 239, 240, 242, 245, 247, 252, 254, 257, 259, 261, 263, 267, 271, 275, 288, 289, 291, 292, 295, 299, 321

Suggestion 146, 177, 182

Syntegrative Education 270, 273

T

Teacher cognition 134, 170, 173, 174, 184, 185, 186
Teacher emotion 88, 89, 95, 96, 99, 107, 108, 112
Teacher identity, Course-based moral education 121
Teacher professional identity 86, 88, 89, 95, 105, 106, 108, 110, 114, 116
Teacher Training 173, 179, 180, 182, 258
Teaching and learning 40, 41, 53, 58, 81, 89, 90, 92, 104, 109, 131, 146, 149, 150, 151, 159, 160, 161, 176, 183, 224, 225, 226, 244, 245, 252, 257, 258, 269, 270, 281
The Ecological University 266, 267, 268, 269, 270, 273, 274, 276, 277
The Female Advantage 20, 21, 22, 24, 35, 37
Transdisciplinary 240, 270, 271, 276
Transformative Learning 24
Transnational 1, 2, 3, 5, 6, 7, 8, 9, 10, 11, 12, 13, 14, 15, 16, 17, 18, 19, 20, 22, 23, 24, 25, 27, 28, 29, 30, 31, 32, 33, 39, 40, 41, 42, 43, 44, 46, 47, 48, 49, 50, 52, 53, 55, 56, 58, 59, 65, 68, 121, 131, 132, 137, 138, 150, 171, 187, 191, 192, 193, 195, 196, 197, 198, 201, 204, 205, 207, 244, 248, 250, 278, 279, 280, 281, 282, 287, 290, 292, 294, 297, 300, 301, 302, 303, 309, 310, 311, 312, 313, 314, 316, 317, 318, 319, 320, 321, 322
Transnational education 8, 15, 48, 49, 52, 58, 195, 278, 280, 281, 282, 297, 300
Transnational Higher Education 1, 2, 3, 5, 6, 7, 9, 12, 14, 16, 17, 18, 19, 20, 22, 23, 24, 25, 27, 28, 29, 30, 31, 32, 33, 39, 40, 41, 44, 46, 47, 48, 49, 50, 52, 53, 55, 56, 68, 121, 131, 137, 150, 171, 187, 191, 192, 193, 195, 196, 198, 201, 204, 205, 207, 244, 248, 250, 278, 279, 290, 292, 294, 303, 318, 321
Transnational ICT leaders 301, 303, 309, 310, 311, 312, 313, 314, 316, 317, 318, 319, 322

U

University 1, 2, 3, 13, 14, 15, 16, 24, 26, 29, 30, 34, 36, 39, 46, 53, 55, 58, 59, 61, 63, 64, 65, 66, 67, 68, 69, 71, 72, 74, 77, 78, 79, 81, 82, 83, 85, 86, 91, 95, 99, 100, 105, 106, 107, 108, 109, 110, 111, 112, 113, 114, 116, 121, 122, 124, 125, 126, 127, 128, 129, 130, 131, 133, 134, 136, 137, 138, 139, 143, 144, 147, 149, 150, 151, 158, 160, 161, 170, 174, 184, 185, 186, 187, 188, 191, 195, 197, 198, 203, 206, 207, 208, 212, 225, 226, 227, 228, 244, 252, 255, 261, 264, 266, 267, 268, 269, 270, 271, 272, 273, 274, 275, 276, 277, 278, 284, 285, 286, 287, 288, 289, 290, 291, 292, 293, 294, 295, 296, 298, 299, 301, 303, 304, 320

V

Virtual Reality 49, 79, 82, 226, 229, 230, 231, 232, 233, 234, 235, 236, 237, 238, 241, 242, 243, 273

Publishing Tomorrow's Research Today

Uncover Current Insights and Future Trends in Education
with IGI Global's Cutting-Edge Recommended Books

Print Only, E-Book Only, or Print + E-Book.
Order direct through IGI Global's Online Bookstore at www.igi-global.com or through your preferred provider.

ISBN: 9781668493007
© 2023; 234 pp.
List Price: US$ 215

ISBN: 9798369300749
© 2024; 383 pp.
List Price: US$ 230

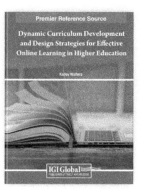

ISBN: 9781668486467
© 2023; 471 pp.
List Price: US$ 215

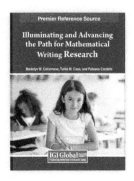

ISBN: 9781668465387
© 2024; 389 pp.
List Price: US$ 215

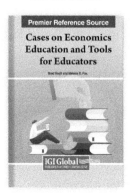

ISBN: 9781668475836
© 2024; 359 pp.
List Price: US$ 215

ISBN: 9781668444238
© 2023; 334 pp.
List Price: US$ 240

Do you want to stay current on the latest research trends, product announcements, news, and special offers?
Join IGI Global's mailing list to receive customized recommendations, exclusive discounts, and more.
Sign up at: www.igi-global.com/newsletters.

Scan the QR Code here to view more related titles in Education.

www.igi-global.com | Sign up at www.igi-global.com/newsletters | facebook.com/igiglobal | twitter.com/igiglobal | linkedin.com/igiglobal

Ensure Quality Research is Introduced to the Academic Community

Become a Reviewer for IGI Global Authored Book Projects

  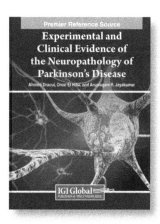 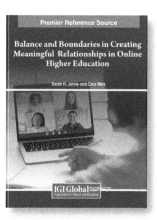

The overall success of an authored book project is dependent on quality and timely manuscript evaluations.

Applications and Inquiries may be sent to:
development@igi-global.com

Applicants must have a doctorate (or equivalent degree) as well as publishing, research, and reviewing experience. Authored Book Evaluators are appointed for one-year terms and are expected to complete at least three evaluations per term. Upon successful completion of this term, evaluators can be considered for an additional term.

If you have a colleague that may be interested in this opportunity, we encourage you to share this information with them.

Are You Ready to Publish Your Research

IGI Global offers book authorship and editorship opportunities across three major subject areas, including Business, STM, and Education.

Benefits of Publishing with IGI Global:

- Free one-on-one editorial and promotional support.
- Expedited publishing timelines that can take your book from start to finish in less than one (1) year.
- Choose from a variety of formats, including Edited and Authored References, Handbooks of Research, Encyclopedias, and Research Insights.
- Utilize IGI Global's eEditorial Discovery® submission system in support of conducting the submission and double-blind peer review process.
- IGI Global maintains a strict adherence to ethical practices due in part to our full membership with the Committee on Publication Ethics (COPE).
- Indexing potential in prestigious indices such as Scopus®, Web of Science™, PsycINFO®, and ERIC – Education Resources Information Center.
- Ability to connect your ORCID iD to your IGI Global publications.
- Earn honorariums and royalties on your full book publications as well as complimentary content and exclusive discounts.

Learn More at: www.igi-global.com/publish
or Contact IGI Global's Aquisitions Team at: acquisition@igi-global.com

Individual Article & Chapter Downloads
US$ 37.50/each

 Easily Identify, Acquire, and Utilize Published Peer-Reviewed Findings in Support of Your Current Research

- Browse Over **170,000+ Articles & Chapters**
- **Accurate & Advanced** Search
- Affordably Acquire **International Research**
- **Instantly Access** Your Content
- Benefit from the **InfoSci® Platform Features**

It really provides an excellent entry into the research literature of the field. It presents a manageable number of highly relevant sources on topics of interest to a wide range of researchers. The sources are scholarly, but also accessible to 'practitioners'.

- Ms. Lisa Stimatz, MLS, University of North Carolina at Chapel Hill, USA

Milton Keynes UK
Ingram Content Group UK Ltd.
UKHW010228300724
446304UK00005B/110

To Carle who started me on my purpose for this life. Thank you for traveling with me and giving me grace. To Imani who continues to give me faith in being the best version of myself I love you. To my husband I am honored by your love and kindness. To my Mom please continue to watch over your children. To my BFF Love and my craft sisters thank you for always supporting me.
With Love, Tiffany

Inside these pages is an interactive tale with thought-provoking questions that engage children to voice their thoughts. While acknowledging it is okay to be upset. Children are provided an opportunity to share positive outlets they can explore to control their emotions.

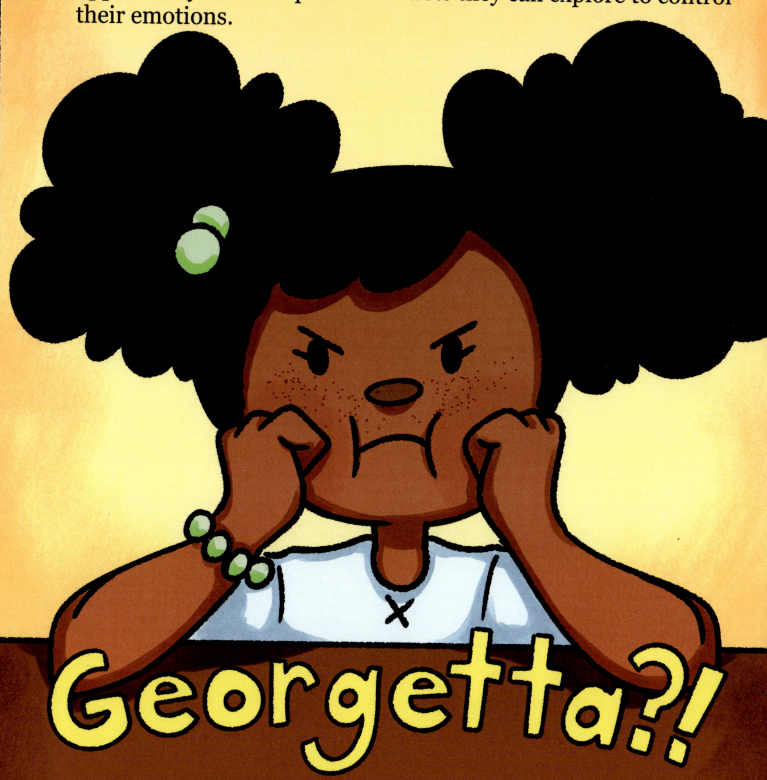

Georgetta?!

Looking at this picture, how do you think this child feels?

Class 22 got a new student this week with the sweetest teacher named Mrs.Wheat. While sound asleep, she dreamed of all the wonderful friends she would soon greet.
Her room was covered in mermaids, glitter, slime, and unicorns.

Until one day, her classmate took her favorite seat!
Oh boy was she mad...
Her nose turned up and her smiled turned down.

Her best friend Jordan tried to give her his seat, as good friends do.

But, Georgetta just yelled
"I don't want to!"
and with his kind gesture
her anger grew.
She huffed and puffed.
She stomped and she roamed.

How do you think the child in this picture feels? Have you ever cried in class or saw someone crying? What did you do?

Georgetta began to make Jordan sad.
All that hollering made him wet his pants!
Embarrassed and scared Jordan ran home!
He knew his dads would help him feel better and maybe explain what's wrong with Georgetta?!

The Teacher, Mrs. Wheat said, "This stinks!" "You made Jordan cry, that's not how you treat a good friend, don't you think?"

So, today class Mark will do a lesson with me on self management to help Georgetta.
He pretended to be grumpy because someone called him stumpy.
Class what are some ideas of what he can do to calm himself?

Self Management Ideas
1. Butterfly Breathing
2.
3.

"Georgetta what are some of our class rules that we can use as tools?"

Georgetta grumbled and told the teacher her troubles.
"I can't see and it smells like feet!"
She complained and shouted pointing at her new rotten seat.

All of the other students began to stare.
Her teacher cried, "you're hurting your friends, don't you care?"
But Georgetta snorted and her face grew redder.
Mrs Wheat hopelessly sighed, "Can we help you Georgetta?"

"Oh no Georgetta! That's not how we treat our friends. In class 22 we use our words, not our hands".
It was then Mrs Wheat hatched a plan to get out of this jam to give Georgetta the perfect seat, changing her tune from sour to sweet by writing a behavior management plan that everyone could meet.

Mrs. Wheat read the letter from Georgetta asking for a second chance. She apologized to the class for being a bully and especially to Jordan for treating him so rudely. Embarrassed, she realized her behavior was unruly. She sat out of circle time for treating them so cruelly.

Each student in class had new expectations and pitched in to create class 22's rules and regulations. Mrs. Wheat asked for their participation and they all gave ideas to promote kindness and patience.
With all their voices heard and released frustrations the students danced in celebration!

Georgetta learned a great deal and was more respectful of others. Her grades improved just by moving seats, but mostly because she told her teacher, about her learning needs.

Now, if you ever come by and visit Class 22, you will see students engaged, not enraged; learning scientific facts, testing with high scores, and munching on yummy s'mores! Because in Class 22, we love everyone to their core and we help one another soar!

I don't have control of my feelings yet!